"AMERICA'S MOST FAMOUS COOKBOOK"

BOSTON GLOBE

This is America's most valued and trusted cookbook. Its easily followed recipes and cooking instructions will make you an accomplished cook. In these pages you will find the correct ingredients and the simplest methods for preparing delicious, appetizing food, from basic "meat and potatoes" to a fancy party masterpiece.

This book includes complete information about modern kitchen equipment, new mixing and cooking techniques; sections on planning meals and menus; useful suggestions for beginners; a special supplement giving measurements, substitutions, temperatures for meat, game and fish; a timetable for pressure cooking.

No American home can afford to be without this indispensable household reference book.

THE ALL NEW FANNIE FARMER BOSTON COOKING SCHOOL COOKBOOK

THE ALL NEW FANNIE FARMER BOSTON COOKING SCHOOL COOKBOOK

TENTH EDITION

COMPLETELY REVISED BY WILMA LORD PERKINS

DRAWINGS BY ALISON MASON KINGSBURY

BANTAM BOOKS
TORONTO · NEW YORK · LONDON

This low-priced Bantam Book has been completely reset in a type face designed for easy reading, and was printed from new plates. It contains the complete text of the original hard-cover edition.
NOT ONE WORD HAS BEEN OMITTED.

THE ALL NEW FANNIE FARMER
BOSTON COOKING SCHOOL COOKBOOK
A Bantam Book / published by arrangement with Little, Brown & Company, Inc.

PRINTING HISTORY

Original Little, Brown edition published 1896
TEN PRINTINGS
Revised edition published 1906
TWELVE PRINTINGS
Revised edition published 1918
TEN PRINTINGS
Revised edition published 1923
TWELVE PRINTINGS
New completely revised edition published 1930
SIX PRINTINGS
New completely revised edition published 1936
SIX PRINTINGS
New completely revised edition published 1941
ELEVEN PRINTINGS
New completely revised edition published 1946
FIVE PRINTINGS
New completely revised edition published 1951
SIX PRINTINGS
Tenth and completely revised edition published 1959

Bantam edition published March 1957
TWO PRINTINGS
New Bantam edition published March 1961
2nd printing ....April 1961
3rd printing ..... February 1963
4th printing ....March 1964
Bantam Cookbook Shelf edition published May 1965
6th printing
7th printing

Published simultaneously in the United States and Canada.

Bantam Books are published by Bantam Books, Inc., a subsidiary of Grosset & Dunlap, Inc. Its trade-mark, consisting of the words "Bantam Books" and the portrayal of a bantam, is registered in the United States Patent Office and in other countries. Marca Registrada. Bantam Books, Inc., 271 Madison Avenue, New York, N. Y. 10016.

PRINTED IN THE UNITED STATES OF AMERICA

Preface

Thirty years ago I made my first revision of Aunt Fannie's famous cookbook. Since then there have been others and this one—sobering thought—is my sixth. Each time I have thought I would never do it again—recipes had been adapted to new ways, modern ingredients used, the mode of the day considered. But as soon as each revision was completed and the presses began to grind, new ideas began pouring in and I found myself starting off again.

However, no other revision has been as fundamental as this one. Aunt Fannie "invented" the use of level measurements, a method which has been almost universally accepted by recipe writers ever since. In this revision there is a complete change in recipe presentation which I hope will be equally helpful.

New recipes, new ingredients, a new approach to menu-making for both everyday and party fare—all these are here. In spite of the wealth of new recipes, very few old ones have been removed and some from earlier editions have been brought back because there has been a demand for them.

As in preparing the previous revisions, I have been fortunate in the many good friends who have helped me. Some are unknown to me—kind readers who have sent me suggestions and treasured recipes. Some are close to me—my daughter-in-law, Nancy Tucker Perkins, Mrs. Stanley S. Kent, Mrs. John B. Christopher and Mrs. Clive MacCay, to name the ones who have done the most. All of these have helped me, too, with the preparation of the text, as did Margaret Anagnost. One of the delights of working on this edition was having Alison Mason Kingsbury do the illustrations, which are the work not only of an artist but of one who knows and practices *la haute cuisine*.

Everyone at Little, Brown and Company has taken a family interest in the progress of the book, especially Mrs. Mary Rackliffe, whose meticulous care as an editor has led to countless improvements in the text.

To all my old friends and to the new ones I hope to make with this latest revision, my warmest gratitude. *Bon appétit!*

Wilma Lord Perkins

Harvard, Massachusetts

Preface to the First Edition

"But for life the universe were nothing; and all that has life requires nourishment."

With the progress of knowledge the needs of the human body have not been forgotten. During the last decade much time has been given by scientists to the study of foods and their dietetic value, and it is a subject which rightfully should demand much consideration from all. I certainly feel that the time is not far distant when a knowledge of the principles of diet will be an essential part of one's education. Then mankind will eat to live, will be able to do better mental and physical work, and disease will be less frequent.

At the earnest solicitation of educators, pupils, and friends, I have been urged to prepare this book, and I trust it may be a help to many who need its aid. It is my wish that it may not only be looked upon as a compilation of tried and tested recipes, but that it may awaken an interest through its condensed scientific knowledge which will lead to deeper thought and broader study of what to eat.

F. M. F.

Contents

THE ALL NEW

Fannie Farmer

BOSTON COOKING SCHOOL

Cookbook

Success with Recipes

Cooking is much more appealing in our day than in our grandmothers' era. The range of recipes is so wide that meals need never be routine. Our markets offer a far wider variety, especially of fruits and vegetables. Countless "convenience foods" free us of some of the duller tasks so that we have time to concoct a culinary work of art.

USING A COOKBOOK

Read a recipe all the way through before you start. Check on the necessary ingredients and equipment. If any of the directions are not clear to you, read the general information at the beginning of the section or the introductory material in this chapter.

MEASURING INGREDIENTS

Level measurements are the rule in modern recipes. Use standard measuring cups and spoons. To save washing an extra cup, measure the dry ingredients first, put them on wax paper, then use the same cup for liquids or fats.

Dry ingredients. Fill the cup or spoon. Do not shake or pack down (except brown sugar). Level with a straight-edged knife. Sift flour before measuring. Stir or sift sugar, baking soda, baking powder and dry mustard if they are lumpy.

Liquids. When you are measuring cooking oils, syrups, honey or molasses, scrape out the measure with a rubber scraper to get the full amount.

Fats. For easy measuring, have solid fats at room temperature, not icy-hard. Pack firmly into the measure and level off with a knife. Measuring cups with sloping sides are easily scraped out with a rubber scraper.

Butter, margarine and lard in quarter pound sticks are easy to measure. One stick (¼ pound) equals ½ cup or 8 tablespoons.

WEIGHTS AND MEASURES

In most modern American recipes the amount of each ingredient is given in measures rather than in weight. Old-fashioned recipes, many English recipes and most other foreign recipes use weights. In adapting a foreign recipe it may be necessary to experiment a little, since the ingredients may be slightly different from American ones.

A few grains, pinch, dash, etc. (dry)	= less than ⅛ teaspoon
A dash (liquid)	= a few drops
3 teaspoons	= 1 tablespoon
4 tablespoons	= ¼ cup
2 cups	= 1 pint

2 pints	= 1 quart
4 quarts (liquid)	= 1 gallon
8 quarts (dry)	= 1 peck
4 pecks (dry)	= 1 bushel
1 ounce	= 28 grams (about)
1 pound	= 454 grams (about)
1 kilo	= $2\frac{1}{10}$ pounds (about)
1 liter	= 1 quart (about)

EQUIVALENTS

Bread crumbs
- 4 ounces = ¾ cup less 1 tablespoon
- 100 grams = ½ cup

Butter, lard, other fats and cheese
- 1 pound = 2 cups
- 1 ounce = 2 tablespoons
- 100 grams = 7 tablespoons (½ cup less 1 tablespoon)

Currants and raisins
- 1 pound = 2⅜ cups
- 100 grams = ⅝ cup less 1 tablespoon

Flour
- 1 pound = 3½ to 4 cups
- 1 ounce = 3 tablespoons
- 100 grams = ¾ cup less 2 tablespoons

Nut meats
- 4 ounces (¼ pound) = ⅔ cup (chopped)
- 100 grams = ⅝ cup (chopped)

Rice (uncooked)
- 1 pound = 2 cups

Brown sugar
- 1 pound = 2¾ cups (about)
- 100 grams = ¾ cup, less 2 tablespoons

Confectioners' sugar
- 1 pound = 3¾ cups (about)
- 100 grams = ¾ cup

Granulated sugar
- 1 pound = 2 cups
- 100 grams = ½ cup, less 1 tablespoon

SUBSTITUTIONS

1 square chocolate = 3 tablespoons cocoa plus 1 teaspoon to 1 tablespoon shortening (less for Dutch-type cocoa)

1 cup pastry flour = 1 cup all-purpose or bread flour less 2 tablespoons

1 tablespoon potato flour = 2 tablespoons flour (as thickening)

1 tablespoon cornstarch = 2 tablespoons flour (as thickening)

1 teaspoon baking powder = ¼ teaspoon baking soda plus ½ teaspoon cream of tartar

1 cup fresh milk = ½ cup evaporated milk plus ½ cup water *or* ½ cup condensed milk plus ½ cup water (reduce sugar in recipe) *or* 4 teaspoons powdered whole milk plus 1 cup water *or* 4 tablespoons powdered skim milk plus 2 tablespoons butter plus 1 cup water

MIXING INGREDIENTS

The recipe will suggest the method to be used to blend the ingredients.

To stir. Hold the spoon upright and move it in wider and wider circles until all is blended.

To beat. The purpose of beating is to make a mixture light by enclosing air. Briskly turn the ingredients over and over, using a large mixing spoon or a wire whisk. Once the mixture is light, be careful not to overbeat, especially with an electric mixer. Otherwise the air bubbles are broken down into smaller ones and the mixture will not rise as it should.

To cut and fold. When a mixture has been beaten until light, other ingredients must be added very gently so that the air will not be lost. Add new ingredients little by little and blend in by two motions with a mixing spoon—cut down with the edge of the mixing spoon, then move the bowl of the spoon along the bottom and up to the surface again in order to turn the mixture very gently. Continue only until the ingredients are evenly blended.

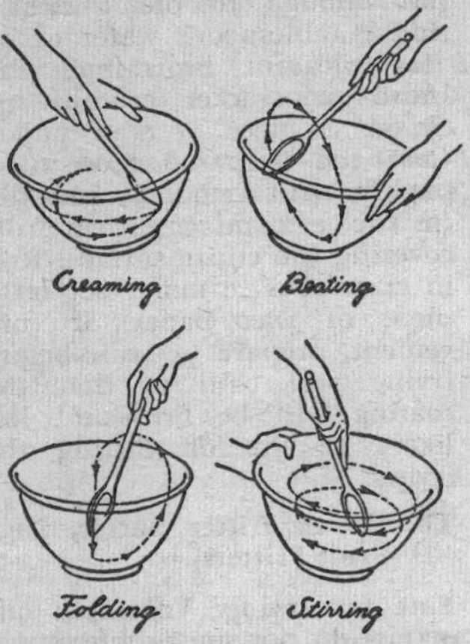

To cream. Put the butter or other shortening in a bowl and let stand at room temperature until soft but not melted. Beat with an electric beater or rub against the side of the bowl with the back of a wooden spoon or a blending fork until smooth and fluffy. Gradually beat or rub in sugar or flour according to the recipe. The more thorough the creaming, the finer will be the grain of butter cakes and cookies. *You cannot overcream.*

To cut in shortening (for pastry), page 438 (Plain Pastry).

COOKING METHODS

The various methods of cooking sound more complicated than they really are. All are variations of two basic methods—cooking by dry heat and cooking by moist heat.

BAKING AND ROASTING

Preheat the oven unless it heats so rapidly that it is not necessary. Do not crowd the oven—free circulation is essential for even baking. Directions for roasting meats are on page 161, for baking bread on page 336, for baking cookies on page 460 and for baking cakes on page 484. Have the oven control checked occasionally by the utility company.

250°	very slow
300°	slow
325°	moderately slow
350°	moderate
375°	moderately hot
400°	hot
450–500°	very hot

BRAISING

Cook, tightly covered, in a small quantity of liquid at a low temperature, either in the oven or over direct heat. When braising meat, brown it in the fat before adding the liquid to give the gravy rich color and flavor. Braising is an excellent method for cooking the less tender cuts of meat.

BROILING (GRILLING)

Preheat the broiler or prepare the charcoal fire. Grease the broiling rack and arrange the food on it. Unless the recipe suggests a special method, cook the food briefly on one side, turn and cook about half the total time required, then turn again to complete the cooking. Thin pieces of fish need not be turned at all; cook until they flake when tested with a fork.

BARBECUING

Broil, basting during the cooking with a savory sause (p. 93). Usually, extra sauce is served with the food.

PAN-BROILING

Cook in a shallow, heavy pan over direct heat. Unless the food to be cooked is very lean such as minute steaks and liver, you will not need to grease the pan. A sprinkling of salt will be all that is necessary. Otherwise, grease the pan very lightly, just enough to keep the food from sticking.

PAN-FRYING (SAUTÉING)

Heat cooking oil or fat in a frying pan large enough to hold the food in a single layer. If necessary, use two pans. Have the fat about ¼ inch deep for most foods. For such foods as Southern Fried Chicken, have the fat 1 inch deep but never deep enough to cover the food completely. When the fat is hot but not smoking, put in the food and cook until it is nicely browned and tender. Adjust the heat as necessary to cook without burning.

FRENCH (DEEP-FAT) FRYING

This quick method of cooking is excellent and, contrary to old-fashioned ideas, is as healthful as any other, if the fat is kept at the proper temperature during the frying. An electric frying kettle with controlled heat is the best equipment, but any straight-sided heavy pan will do if it is at least 5 inches deep. Unless you are using an electric fryer, put a frying thermometer in the kettle so that you will be certain to have the correct temperature.

To egg and crumb. Beat an egg just enough to blend evenly. Add 2 tablespoons water or oil (for pleasant browning). Put bread or cracker crumbs (p. 6) on a piece of wax paper. Coat the prepared food thoroughly with crumbs, then dip in the egg mixture, carefully covering the entire surface. Roll in crumbs once more. Set on a piece of wax paper. If convenient, prepare ½ hour before frying and chill so that the coating will be firm and less likely to slip off during the frying.

To dip in fritter batter, page 409 (Fruit Fritters).

Fats for frying. Vegetable oils or fats do not smoke and break down as easily as lard and may be stored for reuse without spoiling. If you have used fat for fritters or potatoes, pour it back into its container through a strainer lined with a double thickness of cheesecloth. Discard the scraps. If you have cooked onions, fish or other foods with a strong flavor, cut a potato in ¼-inch slices, add to the fat, and set over low heat until the fat stops bubbling and the potato slices are brown, then strain as above. Store in a cold place. It is important to good nutrition to discard fat that has been overheated or that has become rancid.

To heat the fat. Put enough oil or fat in the kettle to cover the food to be cooked, but keep it at least 3 inches below the top of the kettle. Put the thermometer in place if you are not using an automatic fryer with controlled heat. Heat to the required temperature and regulate the heat to keep the temperature even during frying. Do not overheat the fat or food will brown on the outside—or even burn—before it is cooked in the center. Follow instructions as to temperature as given in individual recipes. As a general guide, use the following:

370°—doughtnuts, fritters, fish fillets, breaded chops, oysters and other uncooked foods
380°—potatoes, onion rings and other watery foods
390°—croquettes and other precooked foods

To fry. If you are using a frying basket, dip it in and out of the fat so that the food will not stick to it. Fry a small quantity at a time so that the fat will not be cooled. If the fat is too cool, it will not cook the surface quickly enough to keep the fat from soaking into the food. Cook the length of time required by the recipe.

To drain. Lift the cooked food from the fat and put on crumpled paper towels to absorb any excess fat. Keep warm until all the food is fried.

POACHING

Cook in liquid kept just below the boiling point. Except for poached eggs, the liquid is not deep enough to cover the food completely and is often used to make a sauce.

STEAMING

Cook on a rack over boiling water or in a double boiler over boiling water. Do not have the water deep enough to touch the bottom of the upper pan. Consult the index for steamed puddings and fruit cakes.

STEWING

Cook in a liquid deep enough to cover. Use the liquid to make sauce or gravy. See the various recipes for stews, fricassees and ragouts.

PRESSURE-COOKING

Cook in steam under pressure in a special pan. Follow the instructions which come with the pan. Excellent for dishes which would otherwise require long cooking and for vegetables which can be cooked this way in very little water so that soluble vitamins are not lost.

OTHER COOKING TERMS

Baste. Moisten by spooning a liquid over a roast or other food as it cooks.
Batter. A mixture of flour or meal and a liquid which is thin enough to pour.
Blanch. Dip in and out of boiling water to loosen the skins of fruit or nuts or to prepare food for freezing.
Dough. A mixture of flour or meal and a liquid which is stiff enough to handle.
Dredge. Coat with flour or sugar.
Dust. Sprinkle lightly with flour or sugar.
Glaze. Cover with a transparent coating of jelly, meat juices or caramel.

Lard. Very lean meats need added fat to roast without drying out. Have the butcher thread strips of fat salt pork through the meat or lay strips of fat or bacon on top of the roast.

Marinate. Cover with a liquid (usually wine or a highly seasoned sauce) and let stand to season or become tender. See Marinades (pp. 93–94).

Parboil. Partially cook (usually in boiling water) in preparation for further cooking.

Reduce. Cook a liquid until some has been carried off as steam.

Scallop. Bake in a sauce with crumbs on top. Often with grated cheese as well.

Score. Make a series of shallow cuts on the surface of a food.

Sear. Cook at high temperature over direct heat or in the oven until the surface is browned.

Sponge. A batter to which yeast has been added. Also a light fluffy dessert made with beaten egg whites and gelatine.

PREPARING INGREDIENTS

Many basic ingredients are prepared the same way for use in different recipes. Instead of repeating the directions with each recipe, reference is made to the information which follows.

CRUMBS

Packaged crumbs are a convenience—plain or seasoned, ready to use in stuffing or meat loaf.

Dry bread crumbs. Use bread which is several days old. Dry it thoroughly in a very slow oven (250°) until it is crisp but not brown. Put through a food chopper or a blender or put in a paper bag and crush with a rolling pin. Sift. Store in a closed jar ready to use for topping scalloped dishes, for coating croquettes or as required in other recipes.

Soft bread crumbs. Crumble the soft part (no crusts) of day-old bread with your fingers until it is in even bits. Soft crumbs are used for stuffings, fondues and puddings.

Cracker crumbs, potato chips, corn flakes. Roll like dry bread crumbs. Potato chips, corn flakes and wheat germ make delicious topping, buttered or not.

Buttered crumbs. Melt 1 tablespoon butter for each ½ cup of crumbs. Add the crumbs and stir lightly with a fork until the crumbs are well coated.

EGGS

Strictly fresh eggs are best for poaching, boiling and frying and for dishes in which the eggs and yolks are separated. Storage eggs from a reliable dealer are satisfactory for general cooking. Dried eggs are seldom an economy but may be a convenience for camping trips. For the equivalent of 1 fresh egg, mix 2 tablespoons egg powder with 2½ tablespoons water.

The color of the shell does not affect the flavor of the egg.

To test for freshness. Place in deep cold water. A fresh egg sinks to the bottom.

To store. Place in the refrigerator, unwashed, because the shells have a protective film which helps to keep the eggs fresh.

To measure eggs. Recipes in this book are based on 2-ounce eggs, usually described as "large." In many recipes it is unimportant if a little more or a little less egg is used. For example, if you wish to make half a cake recipe that calls for 3 eggs, use 2 eggs with no fear of trouble.

4 to 6 egg whites	=	½ cup
6 or 7 egg yolks	=	½ cup
1 egg white	=	1½ tablespoons
1 egg yolk	=	1 tablespoon
1 egg	=	2½ tablespoons
½ egg	=	4 teaspoons

To separate eggs. Eggs separate most easily if they are very cold. Tap the center of the egg against the sharp edge of a bowl or pan to crack it slightly. Hold it over a bowl and lift off the top half, letting some of the egg white flow into the bowl but keeping the yolk in the shell. Pour from one half of the shell to the other until all the egg white has flowed out and only the egg yolk remains in the shell.

To beat egg whites. Use a wire whisk, rotary beater or electric beater. Thin wires or blades produce fine foam and good volume. Use a deep bowl with a rounded bottom and sides that flare only slightly. Have it small enough so that the whites are at least 1 inch deep but large enough so that the beater does not scrape against the side.

Separate the whites from the yolks. If even a tiny particle of yolk drops into the bowl with the whites, remove it carefully with a piece of eggshell. Otherwise the whites will not beat well. Add a few grains of salt. If the eggs are very cold, let the whites stand for a few minutes before beating.

Beat until "stiff but not dry" if the egg whites are to be used to make a mixture light and fluffy. If the whites are overbeaten, some of the elasticity of the albumen is broken down. When at the proper stage, egg whites will stand in soft peaks when you lift out the beater but the tops will droop over a bit and the surface will still look somewhat moist.

Beat until "stiff and dry" for meringues and meringue-type cookies. When you lift out the beater, the peaks will stand up straight and the surface will look dry.

To beat egg yolks. Beat with a rotary beater until the yolks are thick and lemon-colored.

To add beaten whites to a mixture. If there is sugar in the recipe, beat some of it (1 tablespoon for each egg white) into the beaten whites. This keeps the egg whites fluffy until you are ready to add them. Cut and fold (p. 2) only long enough to blend. Do not beat the mixture after folding in the whites.

To add beaten yolks to a hot mixture. Add a little of the hot mixture to the yolks, stirring thoroughly, then add this to the rest of the hot mixture and continue stirring until it thickens. Be careful not to overcook.

If you have leftover egg whites, use them in:

- Frostings (p. 509)
- Chocolate Meringue Cookies (p. 479)
- Divinity Fudge (p. 527)
- Angel Food Cake (p.492) or other white cakes (pp. 492, 501)
- Meringues (p. 478)

If you have leftover egg yolks, use them in:

- Sauces (pp. 92–105 and pp. 429–436)
- Custards (pp. 384–386)
- French Vanilla Ice Cream (p. 416)
- Butterscotch Parfait (p. 426)
- Orange Cookies (p. 463)
- Gold Cake (p. 500) and Golden Layer Cake (p. 500)
- Orange Portsmouth (p. 512) and Butter Frostings (p. 516)
- Soup garnishes such as Egg Balls (p. 60) or Royal Custard (p. 59)
- Mayonnaise (p. 302)
- Scrambled Eggs (p. 110)
- Cream Soups (stir in just before serving)

FATS AND SHORTENINGS

Vegetable and animal fats add both food value and flavor to many dishes. As "shortening" fat is used to make a flour mixture tender and flaky ("short") by separating the flour into thin layers between layers of fat.

BUTTER

Butter has a special place in fine cooking. Other fats may be used successfully in gingerbread or molasses cookies, but the best cooks prefer not to economize on butter in recipes where its incomparable flavor is important, such as hard sauce, butter cakes and butter cookies.

To cream butter. See page 3.

To wash butter. For special recipes such as Puff Paste (p. 453), washing butter is recommended by perfectionists because it makes the butter more pliable. Put the butter in a large bowl of ice water and squeeze it gently between your fingers until it feels smooth and waxy. Shape it in a flat cake and pat it briskly to remove all extra water.

Butter pats. Cut neat squares from a bar of butter. To add a bit of decoration, dip a fork in hot water and draw it diagonally across each square. Or put a tiny sprig of parsley on each square.

Butter balls. Scald and chill a pair of wooden butter paddles. Measure the butter by teaspoonfuls to have the balls the same size. Roll lightly between the paddles to shape into balls or cylinders. Place on a chilled plate and store in the refrigerator or drop into a bowl of ice water.

Butter curls. Beginning at the far side of a pound block of butter, draw a butter curler lightly and quickly toward you, making a thin shaving of butter which curls into a cylinder. Dip the curler into hot water each time.

MARGARINE

Margarine is enriched to have the same nutritional value as butter and may be substituted for it.

COOKING OILS

Olive oil is used principally in salad dressings. Combined with an equal amount of butter, it is excellent for sautéing.

Other cooking oils (corn, peanut, soy and cottonseed) are used for frying and sautéing and in salad dressings. There are special recipes for cakes made with oil as the shortening (p. 493, Chiffon Cakes). Many nutritionists consider vegetable oils superior to solid fats.

OTHER FATS

In substituting lard or a vegetable fat for butter in a recipe, use 1/8 less, since butter is not solid fat but contains some liquid. Add salt to taste.

Lard. Pastry made with lard is especially flaky. Store old-fashioned lard in the refrigerator. Some lard may be stored on the pantry shelf—read the label.

Vegetable shortenings. Use as an ingredient and for sautéing and deep-fat frying.

Bacon fat. Strain into a jar, cover and store in the refrigerator. Use within 3 or 4 days for pan-frying potatoes, eggs, lamb patties, liver, etc.

Salt pork. Recommended in special recipes such as fish chowder for its excellent flavor.

Chicken fat. Try out (below). Excellent for gingerbread, cookies and steamed puddings. In substituting for butter, use 2/3 as much and increase the liquid slightly.

Fats from roasts are used chiefly in making gravy to serve with the roast or as the basis for second-day dishes.

Suet is excellent for oven-fried potatoes (p. 269) and is the traditional pastry shortening in English cooking. Render (below). Store in the refrigerator.

To render (try out) fats. Cut solid uncooked fat in small pieces or put through a food chopper. Melt in a double boiler over hot but not boiling water or in a shallow pan in a 250° oven. Melt a small amount in a heavy pan over very very low heat. Pour off the melted fat. If bits of meat or gristle still cling to the fat, add boiling water and let stand until cool. Lift off the cake of fat and scrape the under side with a knife. Store in the refrigerator.

WHEAT FLOURS

Store in a cool dry place in a tightly closed container. Buy in small amounts, especially if you use unbleached flour, which has an attractive creamy color and excellent flavor. Freshly ground whole-wheat flour has the highest food value and is sometimes to be found in a small local mill. Some nutrition-conscious homemakers grind their own flour in a small electric mill. Enriched flour is a great improvement over the earlier bleached flour. The most nutritious flour contains at least 2 per cent of the wheat germ.

Flours vary in starch content or thickening property. Experienced cooks reserve a fraction of the amount of flour called for in a recipe for cakes or cookies and add it at the last if the "feel" of the batter requires it. In substituting all-purpose or bread flour for pastry or cake flour, reduce the amount by one-eighth (2 tablespoons per cup).

All-purpose flour is widely used and is made of a mixture of hard and soft wheats. It is satisfactory for most recipes except the most delicate cakes and pastries.

Bread flour is made of hard wheat, rich in gluten. Gluten makes a mixture elastic so that it can expand without bursting. It is used for bread and popovers and certain cakes.

Pastry flour (white or whole-wheat) is more delicate than bread or all-purpose flour. It is perfect for pastry and fine cakes.

Cake flour makes a very fine-textured cake but it may be somewhat dry.

Whole-wheat (graham) flour contains the bran and germ of the wheat. It is rich in protein and other food values and has a pleasant nutty flavor.

OTHER FLOURS AND MEALS

Buckwheat is usually mixed with wheat flour. Its distinctive flavor makes it popular for pancakes.

Potato flour is especially successful as a thickening. It cooks quickly and smoothly in a liquid and leaves no "raw" taste. Use one third the amount of flour called for in the recipe.

Rye flour is used for bread, but is usually mixed with wheat flour, since it makes a heavy bread if used alone. Pumpernickel is made from rye flour with no added wheat flour.

Soybean flour (ground soybeans) has high protein content and may be added in small amounts to enrich white flours.

Arrowroot is made from the ground rootstock of certain Central American plants. It is an excellent thickener and is clear and almost tasteless.

Cornstarch is refined starch made from corn. As a thickening agent, it cooks smoothly and is particularly useful for clear sauces, gravies and puddings.

Corn meal may be yellow or white. "Water-ground" meal (usually white) retains much of the skin and germ and should be refrigerated.

Oatmeal, flaked, coarse, or fine, is used as a cereal or as an ingredient in breads and cookies.

LEAVENING AGENTS

Flour mixtures would bake in heavy flat masses unless a leavening agent were used to lighten the mixture by distributing through it carbon dioxide gas, air or steam, which expand in the hot oven during baking. Yeast, baking powder and baking soda develop carbon dioxide gas. Beaten eggs enclose air in the mixture and liquid turns to steam during the baking.

Compressed yeast is sold in cakes and **dry (granular) yeast** in packages or envelopes. Compressed yeast is more perishable because of higher moisture content and must be kept refrigerated. Dry yeast will keep without refrigeration for weeks, but must be stored in a cool dry place. Use interchangeably.

Baking powder is of several types, each plainly marked on the package. Use interchangeably in recipes in this book unless otherwise indicated. "Double action" baking powder is so called because expansion of the gas does not begin until heat is present. It is therefore useful when the baking is to be done a considerable time after mixing.

Baking soda (bicarbonate of soda) reacts with an acid (such as sour milk) to release carbon dioxide gas which makes a batter or dough rise. The usual amount is ½ teaspoon soda to each cup of molasses, buttermilk or sour cream.

Cream of tartar may be combined with baking soda to make baking powder. To substitute for 1 teaspoon baking powder, use ¼ teaspoon baking soda and ½ teaspoon cream of tartar.

Eggs, when beaten, enclose air in tiny cells. See page 7 for details.

MILK

Use milk generously, since it has an important role in good nutrition.

To scald milk, heat, preferably in a double boiler, until a row of tiny bubbles appears around the edge.

Whole milk. For a small family, you may have enough cream for coffee and desserts by skimming it from the whole milk with a small dipper after the cream rises to the top.

Whole milk, homogenized, is milk which has been mechanically treated so that the globules of cream will not separate from the rest of the milk.

Skim milk is higher in protein and calcium than whole milk because the cream has been replaced by milk.

Buttermilk is excellent in many recipes such as pancakes, doughnuts and spice cake. Many cooks like the distinctive flavor and substitute it for sweet milk in a recipe without changing the flavor by adding baking soda.

Sour milk provides the acid which combines with baking soda to produce leavening action in some biscuits, pancakes and other dishes. **To sour sweet milk,** stir in lemon juice or vinegar (1 tablespoon to 1 cup) and let stand a few minutes.

Condensed milk is sweetened, so use less sugar when substituting it for regular milk. Follow package directions.

Evaporated milk is not sweetened. Whip it as a low-calorie substitute for whipped cream. Chill thoroughly before whipping. It has a different flavor and is best used when a dish has highly flavored ingredients such as coffee, lemon or spices.

Dry milk solids or powdered milk. To make 1 cup of milk, sprinkle 4 tablespoons over a cup of water and shake or stir to blend. Add extra calcium and protein to a cream soup or casserole by stirring in a tablespoon or two of powdered milk in addition to the liquid milk. If you are substituting powdered milk for liquid milk in a recipe, mix the dry milk with the dry ingredients and use water as the liquid.

Yogurt is prepared from milk partly evaporated and fermented. Since it is thick, it is an excellent lower-calorie substitute for sour cream.

CREAM

Powdered cream is a good item for the emergency shelf and is also excellent in such dishes as creamed spinach.

Sour cream is a useful ingredient, very rich and distinctive. Commercial "soured" cream is treated to make an even product. If you are using cream which has soured naturally, use it before it is so thick that it is like cheese. When you use sour cream as an ingredient, add it slowly so that the acid in it will not cause the mixture to curdle.

Light cream is too low in butterfat to whip without adding a commercial whipping aid. Follow instructions on the package.

Heavy cream whips best if at least 24 hours old. Chill the cream, bowl and beater. Use a straight-sided bowl, small enough so that the cream is at least 1½ inches deep. Use a beater (rotary or other type) small enough to fit in the bowl without knocking against the sides. As the cream begins to thicken, whip slowly, particularly with an electric beater, so that you can stop before the cream begins to turn to butter. Cream doubles in bulk when whipped. **To whip a small amount of cream,** use a cup or a jar and beat with a tiny rotary beater. A small electric beater of the turbine type is very useful for this. If the cream is very heavy, add a little top milk as you beat.

Prepared whipped cream, ready to use, is whipped by forcing carbon dioxide into it. The volume is much greater than in cream whipped by beating in air, but it does not hold up as well as heavy cream whipped with a beater.

CHOCOLATE AND COCOA

Cakes of cooking chocolate are usually marked in 1-ounce blocks so that it is simple to measure out the required amount. Unless otherwise indicated in the recipe, use unsweetened baking chocolate. Some recipes call for sweetened or sweetened and flavored chocolate or for chocolate in small bits or pieces. Dipping chocolate is especially prepared for dipping candies.

To melt. Melt over hot water in a small double boiler or in a small bowl set in hot water. One or two ounces may be melted on aluminum foil or wax paper set in a warm (not hot) place on the stove.

Cocoa usually has most of the fat removed. Dutch-process type cocoa is richer in fat than the regular type.

To use cocoa in place of chocolate. For each ounce of chocolate use 3 tablespoons cocoa. To make the mixture as rich as if made with chocolate, add 1 tablespoon shortening.

GELATINE

Plain unflavored gelatine is sold in small packages of 4 envelopes, each containing 1 tablespoon. However, it is both economical and convenient to buy gelatine in a 1-pound package. A recipe sometimes requires more or less than 1 tablespoon. Gelatine keeps almost indefinitely in a tightly covered box.

One tablespoon of gelatine stiffens 1 pint of liquid, as a general rule. However, a jelly requires more (see recipes) if fruit or an acid is added or if it is molded in a large mold. Measure gelatine with care, remembering that it is better to use too little than too much. Stiff, rubbery jelly is unappetizing, but you can serve soft jelly in dessert glasses if it is not firm enough to hold its shape.

Mold jelly in large or small metal molds or chill in dessert glasses or a bowl ready for the table. Dip molds in cold water before filling and shake out the loose drops of water. Brush molds for salad with olive or other cooking oil. A **ring mold** makes a most attractive jelly with the center filled with a sauce or other accompaniment. A 1-quart ring mold is very practical—whether the amount prepared fills it completely or not. If more than enough is prepared, chill the extra amount in cups or small timbale molds.

Set filled molds in the refrigerator. Allow 2 hours for plain jellies to stiffen or as much as 4 hours for jellies containing fruit or vegetables. If jelly is very stiff, set in a warm room to soften slightly before serving.

To unmold jelly, dip the mold in warm water almost deep enough to cover it. Let stand 30 seconds and lift out. Loosen around the edges with a thin sharp knife, invert on the serving dish, and tap the mold. If the jelly does not drop out easily, cover the outside of the mold with a cloth wrung out of hot water; let stand for 2 minutes and try again. Ease the jelly out so that it will not break apart.

Serve jelly plain or garnished appropriately. (See suggestions with individual recipes.) One pint yields 3 or 4 servings.

NUTS

Nuts are high in food value and also add delicious flavor to many foods. Consult the index for recipes for cakes, cookies, candies, desserts and hors d'oeuvres which feature some special nut. Salted Nuts (p. 520). Glacéed Nuts (p. 523).

To crack nuts. One pound in the shell yields about ½ pound of nut meats. Crack **soft-shell nuts** (almonds, peanuts and lichi nuts) with the fingers and remove the kernels. Use a nutcracker for **hard-shell nuts** (filberts, walnuts, pecans, butternuts and Brazil nuts). To shell **butternuts** easily, pour boiling water over the nuts, let stand 15 minutes, and drain. Cover **Brazil nuts** with boiling water, boil 3 minutes, drain, and cool.

To blanch nuts. Shell **almonds** and **pistachios** and cover with boiling water. Let stand 2 minutes. Drain, put in cold water, rub off the skins with the fingers, and dry on a paper towel. To blanch **chestnuts,** cut a ½-inch criss-cross gash on the flat side with a sharp vegetable knife. Cover with water and bring slowly to the boiling point. Take out the nuts one by one and remove the shell and inner skin with a sharp pointed knife. Shell **filberts.** Cover with boiling water. Let stand 6 minutes, drain, and remove the skins with a sharp knife.

To chop nuts. Use a special nut grinder, not a meat grinder, which makes nuts pasty. To chop a few, cut on a board with a long straight knife; to chop a larger amount, chop in a bowl or in a special nut grinder. Another way is to put walnuts, pecans or thoroughly dried blanched nuts in a small cloth bag or a clean dish towel and roll with a rolling pin.

COCONUT

A fresh coconut should sound full of liquid when you shake it. Grated coconut is sold dry or moist. Moist coconut tastes more like fresh coconut.

To grate fresh coconut. Pierce the "eyes" with a screwdriver. Set the coconut upside down on a jar to let the milk drain off. Set the coconut in a 400° oven for 20 minutes. Tap all over with a hammer to loosen the shell. Split with a heavy knife or crack with a mallet or hammer. Pry out the white meat with a strong sharp knife. Pare off the dark skin. Grate the white meat on a rotary grater or in a blender. *A medium-sized coconut yields 3 to 4 cups of grated coconut.*

To toast grated or shredded coconut (fresh or canned). Spread in a shallow pan. Set in a 350° oven until delicately brown (about 20 minutes).

To tint coconut. Put a few drops of food coloring in a jar. Add a few drops of water. Put in shredded coconut and shake until evenly tinted.

SUGAR

Granulated sugar is called for in most recipes.

Powdered (fine or superfine) sugar is used in some recipes and to sprinkle over fruit.

Confectioners' sugar is used for uncooked frostings and for some sauces.

Loaf sugar is pressed in cubes or dominoes. One pound contains 100 dominoes or 110 half-inch cubes.

Brown sugar contains some molasses. It is packaged according to color. To prevent caking, store it in the refrigerator. If it gets lumpy, set it in the oven until it softens enough to crumble. Or whirl it in an electric blender. Pack brown sugar firmly when you measure it.

Maple sugar has a distinctive flavor. Use it in special recipes (see index), as a confection or, crushed, on breakfast cereal or pancakes.

To sprinkle (dredge) with sugar. Sift sugar out of a shaker-top container. To sugar fresh hot doughnuts or lady fingers, put a few at a time in a paper bag with ½ cup sugar and shake gently until they are lightly coated. Repeat until all are sugared, adding more sugar as you need it.

To caramelize sugar. Rub a heavy frying pan lightly with butter. Put in the sugar (not more than ½ cup) and set the pan over moderate heat. Stir constantly until the sugar melts. Add more sugar by half-cupfuls and stir as before until you have as much clear brown syrup as you need.

Caramel syrup. Caramelize 1 cup sugar and add ½ cup boiling water very slowly so that the mixture will not boil over. Simmer 10 minutes.

Caramel (for coloring gravies). Caramelize sugar and continue cooking it until it is almost black. Then add boiling water very slowly and simmer until all the sugar dissolves. Store in a covered jar and use as needed to color gravy. No sweet flavor remains.

Brittle (for flavoring). Caramelize sugar and pour it into a slightly buttered pan. Cool, roll with a rolling pin and sift.

Nut Brittle or **Praline Powder.** Add a few grains of salt and an equal amount of chopped blanched almonds or pecans to caramelized sugar. Proceed as for Brittle.

SYRUPS

Molasses is the product remaining after granulated sugar has been removed from sugar cane. It may be light or dark. Molasses ferments easily unless it has a preservative in it, but natural molasses has the better flavor.

Store it in a tightly closed jar in a cool place.

Corn syrups. Use light or dark corn syrup in sauces, frostings and other recipes. Corn syrup helps prevent sugaring or crystallization.

Honey. Honey varies according to the flowers the bees have fed on. Strained honey is sometimes mixed with glucose syrup. Serve hone either in the comb (the comb is edible) or else heat it in a double boiler until the liquid separates so that you can strain it off.

Maple syrup is boiled-down maple sap. If you buy syrup by the gallon, heat it to the boiling point, pour into sterilized pint jars, and seal. Otherwise it will sugar or ferment unless used promptly.

CHOPPING FRUITS AND VEGETABLES

Prepare for chopping by washing, peeling, removing pits, tough stems and wilted or discolored parts.

Chopping a large quantity

On a board. Place on a chopping board, preferably fairly large so that you can work without spilling. Hold a long, flexible French-type knife by the handle and the tip of the blade. Chop straight up and down, turning the knife to chop evenly. If you are chopping a small amount (nuts or parsley, for example) pivot the blade on its tip and chop in a semicircle.

In a glass. Discard heavy stems and bruised leaves of mint, watercress, parsley or other herbs. Wash. Dry thoroughly on a towel. Put in a glass and snip with scissors until finely cut.

Chopping a small quantity

To mince or dice onions, beets, potatoes, etc. Cut off a slice. Cut the flat surface in squares, as deep as required. Slice off with a long sharp knife.

To cut dates, marshmallows or other sticky foods. Cut with scissors or a sharp knife, dipping it frequently in cold water.

To cut in julienne strips. Cut in pieces about the size and shape of kitchen matches.

SEASONINGS

Seasonings add sparkle and zest to your cooking. Many foreign recipes owe much of their special quality to unusual seasonings. Use unfamiliar seasonings with discretion. Seasoning should enhance the natural flavor of a dish, not overwhelm it. No recipe can do more than suggest the right amount, since seasonings and individual tastes vary.

To keep seasonings at their best, store them in tightly closed containers.

Salt. Table salt is mixed with another ingredient to keep it from caking. Common salt has no added ingredient and so is stronger. Iodized salt should be used in the many parts of the country where the soil is low in iodine and foods grown there lack this important element for good nutrition. Sea salt (available at health food stores) is rich in many valuable minerals but may not be as "salty" as you like. Rock salt, freshly ground in a tiny wooden mill, has perfect flavor. Seasoned salts have other seasonings blended with them, such as powdered garlic, onion and herbs.

Pepper. Whole peppercorns or ground. **Black pepper** is made from the whole berry, **white pepper** from the inner kernel. For sparkling flavor, grind whole peppercorns in a pepper mill. **Cayenne pepper** is red pepper. It is very strong. Use it sparingly.

Paprika. The dried and ground shell of large red peppers. The best quality is Spanish or Hungarian or a blend of the two. Never use pepper in a dish seasoned with paprika. The pepper overwhelms the flavor of paprika.

Chili peppers. Tiny red peppers with very pungent flavor, used in meat stews.

Pimiento. Sweet red peppers preserved in oil. Use whole, stuffed (see index) or cut small in salads and sauces.

Pimiento purée. Press canned pimientos through a sieve.

Monosodium glutamate. A powder which is not actually a seasoning but which is used to emphasize flavor. It is packaged under various trade names. It has been used for many years in oriental cooking.

Meat concentrates and bouillon cubes. Use to intensify color and to add flavor to sauces, soups, stews, gravy, hash, meat loaf, casseroles, etc.

Mustard. Dry mustard is made of mustard seeds ground fine. **Prepared** mustard is dry mustard mixed with vinegar or water. **French (Dijon)** and **Louisiana** mustards are mild-flavored prepared mustards sometimes seasoned with added herbs. **English** mustard is very sharp. **Herb** mustard is flavored with herbs.

Sugar, as a condiment. Use very sparingly in sauces and gravies. It helps brown meats. See also Caramel (p. 14).

Vinegar. Be cautious in using vinegar. Old-fashioned cider vinegar is often mild, but white vinegars may be very sharp. **To make wine vinegar,** let opened red or white wine stand in a warm dark place for several months. If you add "mother" from cider vinegar, the vinegar will be ready to use in 4 or 5 weeks. **Tarragon vinegar, mint vinegar, herb vinegar** (p. 20–21) are vinegars flavored by having various herbs steeped in them. They add a delicious zest to salad dressings.

Garlic adds particularly appetizing seasoning to many dishes. A garlic bulb is composed of several smaller bulbs, called "cloves," "beads" or "buds." Put a split clove in the French dressing bottle or rub the salad bowl with a cut clove. For convenience use garlic powder (garlic cloves, dried and ground) or garlic-flavored salt. To make garlic salt, split a clove of garlic and crush it with 1 teaspoon salt in a small mortar or on a board with the tip of a knife.

Onion juice. Cut a slice from the root end of the onion; scrape out the juice with the edge of a teaspoon.

Shallots. Milder and more delicate than onions.

Tomato paste. Use this highly concentrated product not only to add tomato flavor but, in smaller amounts, to add color to soups and other dishes, especially ones made with lobster.

Lemon juice. One medium-sized lemon yields 3 tablespoons juice and 1 tablespoon grated rind. However, some lemons have thick skins and are so pulpy that they yield much less juice.

Grated orange and lemon peel. Wash the fruit, wipe dry, and grate without peeling. Do not grate beyond the color margin. Clean the grater with the point of a knife.

WHOLE SPICES

Whole spices keep their pungency longer than ground spices. Grate **nutmeg** in a special grater. Grind whole **peppercorns** in a pepper mill. Put pieces of **stick cinnamon** or **dried gingerroot** into the dish to be flavored and remove them before serving. Put a few **cassia buds** in each jar of grape juice to add a pleasant flavor. To flavor with a **spice bag,** put whole spices (according to the recipe) in a small cloth bag, tie firmly and cook with the dish to be flavored, removing the bag before serving. **Pickling spices** are mixed whole spices in a suitable combination for pickling.

GROUND SPICES

P v ground spices (such as allspice, cinnamon, cloves, ginger, mace and nutmeg) in the smallest packages available because spices begin to lose their strength after grinding. You may find you need to use more as you get to the bottom of the box.

Use spices in cakes, cookies and desserts according to the recipes. **Mace** is particularly good in pound cake or cherry pie and adds a pleasant flavor to fish. Use **nutmeg** with chicken, mushrooms, spinach and stewed or baked fruits. **Saffron** is used principally for its brilliant yellow color and is distinctive in Bouillabaisse. Imported saffron is very expensive but domestic saffron is almost as good. Buy it at a drugstore.

Pepper is a spice by definition but is listed with the basic seasonings for convenience.

Curry is a blend of turmeric, garlic, pepper, ginger and other strong spices. See index for special dishes but try a little in soups, sauces and salad dressing.

SEEDS

For cookies, breads and coffee cakes. Benne, caraway, cardamon, poppy seed and sesame seed.

For pickles, sauces and stews. Caraway, coriander, dill, mustard, celery, onion and fennel seeds. Add in small amounts.

For fish, fish salads and sauces. Pickled capers and nasturtium seeds.

For cottage and cream cheese. Caraway seeds.

For vegetables. Mustard seed for beets, cabbage and sauerkraut; anise seeds for buttered carrots.

HERBS

Long neglected in American cooking, herbs are being used more and more. Added discreetly—overdoing can ruin a dish—herbs can turn a familiar simple dish into a memorable culinary experience. Consult the index for special recipes such as Herb Butter, Herb Vinegar, Herbed Roast Chicken, Mint Sauce, etc. See also the general suggestions below.

Fresh herbs (free of woody stems and wilted leaves) may be used as sprigs or chopped fine. **Dried herbs** are at least three times as strong as fresh herbs, so measure accordingly. To bring out the flavor of dried herbs, soak them in lemon juice or wine before adding them to a dish.

HERBS AND THEIR USES

Experiment on your own as well as following the suggestions below. Add a few tender sprigs to a green salad or flavor a salad dressing with a pinch of dried herbs. Add herbs to a stew for the last hour of cooking so that the seasoning will be delicate.

BASIL

With eggs, fish and cheese, meat loaf, hash, meat pie and stews. Especially good with venison and duck and with tomatoes, tomato soup and spaghetti sauces.

BAY LEAF

For meat pie, stews and soups, pea soup and tomato juice.

BORAGE *and* BURNET

Cucumber-like in flavor. Add to iced tea, lemonade or claret cup. Add young leaves to salad.

CHERVIL

Fresh sprigs in green salad; chopped as a garnish on soup.

CHIVES

Snip fine with scissors. Add to cottage or cream cheese, to egg or fish dishes or any dish in which a very delicate onion flavor is needed. Delicious on new potatoes, peas or carrots.

DILL

For pickles and in fish sauces and cheese dishes. Fresh sprigs in salads.

MARJORAM

With pork or lamb, meat loaf, hash, meat pie and stews.

MINT

For any lamb dish or with new peas or tiny boiled potatoes. Sprigs in iced tea or lemonade. Mint Sauce (p. 105).

OREGANO (WILD MARJORAM)

The most familiar herb in Italian cookery. Add to spaghetti sauce, tomato sauce and minestrone. A "must" on a pizza. Good in a green salad.

PARSLEY

The perfect garnish for eggs, meat, fish or salad. Chopped fine, add it to cottage or cream cheese and sprinkle it on soup and creamed or boiled potatoes.

A Few Aromatic Herbs
Garlic
Nasturtium Seeds
Basil
Chives
Borage
Sage
Burnet
Sweet Bay Leaf
Rosemary
Thyme
Peppermint and Apple Mint
Marjoram, related to Oregano
Celery Leaves
Caraway Seeds
Dill, related to Caraway, Anise, Cummin, and Fennel

ROSEMARY

With chicken, fish, lamb, pork, hash or meat pie. A few sprigs in green salad.

SAGE

With sausage or pork dishes, and in stuffings (pp. 82–85).

SAVORY

Similar to sage but more delicate. For omelets and salads and with green beans.

TARRAGON

With eggs, fish, chicken and veal. Fresh sprigs in salad. Tarragon Vinegar (p. 21).

THYME

For fish, chowder, oyster or clam bisque, meat loaf, hash, meat pie and stews. Especially good with chicken and turkey and in salads.

Gathering and storing herbs. Herbs take up little space in the garden and it is interesting to store them for future use or for gifts for gourmet friends. **To store herbs in the freezer,** select perfect young sprigs. Dip quickly in and out of boiling water. Pat dry on paper towels. Put small amounts in cellophane bags or envelopes, seal, label, and store in the freezer. **To store herbs in the refrigerator,** wash perfect sprigs, gently shake dry, and put in a jar. Close tightly. Store in the refrigerator. Parsley and watercress stay fresh and crisp for days this way.

To dry herbs. Use only the young tender leaves that appear before the plant flowers. Then there will be a second growth as tender as the first. Pick the leaves in the morning after the dew has disappeared. Pick from the stems and spread in shallow pans. Dry in a 150° oven until they crumble between the fingers (1 to 2 hours). Discard any stiff stems that remain. Pack in airtight jars and label.

To prepare herb seeds. Gather the entire stalk when the seed pods are just ready to burst. Spread in a thin layer on a cloth stretched over a wooden rack. Dry in the sun, bringing in at night and turning daily until thoroughly dried. Fennel leaves and seeds are both used, so keep the flower stalks picked off early in the season while you are gathering the young leaves and then let the flower heads develop so that you can gather the seeds.

Aux fines herbes means that a dish is flavored with a mixture of finely chopped fresh herbs, usually including both parsley and chives. Vary the amount of each to suit your taste. Some successful combinations are:

- Parsley, chives, watercress and tarragon
- Parsley, chives and chervil
- Parsley, chives and basil
- Parsley, burnet and thyme

Herb butter (for sandwiches, to spread on Italian bread or to serve in pats with hamburgers or fish). Soften butter and cream into it finely chopped chives or watercress or a combination of several fresh herbs. Taste and add a few drops of lemon juice if needed.

Mint vinegar. Pick young mint leaves before the blossoms appear. Pack into a pint jar. Fill the jar with wine vinegar. Close and let stand at least 2 weeks before using. Strain through cheesecloth. Bottle. For a delicious fruit salad dressing, add 2 tablespoons mint vinegar and 2 tablespoons cream to 1 cup mayonnaise.

Herb vinegar. In place of mint, use a combination of herbs, such as tarragon and rosemary, thyme and marjoram or chervil and basil.

Tarragon vinegar. Crush 2 cups fresh tarragon leaves, add 1 pint wine vinegar, 2 cloves and 1 clove garlic (cut in half). Cover. Let stand 24 hours. Take out the garlic. Cover and let stand 2 weeks. Strain and bottle.

Kitchen bouquet (bouquet garni). Tie in a small cheesecloth bag ½ carrot, cut lengthwise, 1 leek, a few sprigs of parsley, 1 sprig of celery top, a bit of thyme, 2 cloves and ¼ bay leaf. Cook in a stew or soup. Remove before serving. Vary the combination as you like, adding other herbs, such as marjoram, and omitting the leek.

WINE AS SEASONING

Wine in cookery adds an elusive flavor which makes many a dish memorable. Use it with discretion so that the wine emphasizes and improves the flavor of the other ingredients but does not dominate them. Certain recipes list wine as an ingredient, but it is simple to experiment with wine in others. Inexpensive wines are useful in cooking, but the better the wine, the better the flavor of the finished dish. Save any leftover wine to use in cooking.

Sherry. Add to soups and sauces. Particularly delicious with sea food and chicken dishes and in many desserts. See special recipes such as Oysters in Sherry Cream (p. 154) and English Trifle (p. 385).

White wines. Add to fish or chicken dishes.

Red wines. Marinate meats in wine to improve both texture and flavor. Use the marinade in making gravy or sauce. Add red wine to meat stews.

Dessert wines improve hot or cold fruit compotes and season sweet sauces pleasantly. Marsala is the traditional flavoring for Zabaglione (p. 386).

Brandy adds fine flavor to many dishes.

To flame, warm a small amount of brandy, pour it over the food and light it with a match. Spoon over the food until the flame dies down.

Rum is delicious over any fruit cup, especially one which includes pineapple. Use rum as the flavoring in any chocolate dessert.

Vodka flames very successfully. See directions for flaming brandy (above).

WINE-SEASONED DISHES

Beef Bourguignonne (p. 174)
Kidney Stew (p. 208)
Scallopini of Veal (p. 191)
Chicken à la Contadine (p. 224)
Chicken à la King (p. 233)
Braised Duck à l'Orange (p. 230
Poached Fillets of Fish (p. 126)
Lobster Newburg (p. 151)
Oysters in Sherry Cream (p. 154)
Scallops à la Newburg (p. 157)

Shrimp à la Newburg (p. 159)
Creamed Shrimp with Curaçao (p. 159)

WINE-FLAVORED DESSERTS

Cherries Jubilee (p. 369)
Fresh Fruit Cup (p. 363)
Strawberries Flambé (p. 377)
English Trifle (p. 385)
Rum Cake (p. 490)
French Chocolate Mousse (p. 395)
Wine Jelly (p. 397)
Zabaglione (p. 386)
Pudding Sauces (pp. 429–436)

BARBECUES AND COOKOUTS

Cooking out of doors is increasingly popular. The food tastes superb and work is simplified. Out-of-door appetites are apt to be huge, so plan on at least ½ pound of boned meat or 1 pound with the bone for each person.

Broiling on the grill. There are many suggestions in the chapters on meat, fish and poultry. Among the best are steaks, broilers (split in half), and lamb chops (marinated in French dressing). Fish, hamburg or chopped lamb patties, sausages and frankfurters are easier to turn in a greased folding grill or a well-salted pan. As a variation, sandwich two thin hamburg patties with a slice of tomato or dill pickle or with a bit of cheese, relish or chopped onion. Press firmly around the edges. Split frankfurters and stuff with relish or a slice of cheese or wrap in bacon. Shish Kebabs (p. 186). Barbecuing (p. 4).

Rotisserie cooking is excellent for a large piece of meat—a boned roast of lamb or beef or an unsliced strip of Canadian bacon. Marinate at least 2 hours and baste frequently with the marinade (p. 93) during the cooking.

Foil cooking is successful for many foods. Wrap in aluminum foil and cook on the grill. Potatoes take about 1 hour, corn 15 minutes, frozen vegetables (with a dab of butter and a sprinkling of salt) about 30 minutes. Dip small whole fish in salad oil, sprinkle with salt and pepper and roll in corn meal. Sprinkle fish fillets and sliced fish with salt and pepper and dot with butter. Cook 10 minutes on each side. Serve wrapped in the foil.

Grilled fruits and vegetables. Brush vegetables with salad oil seasoned with salt and pepper. Good vegetables for broiling are halved tomatoes, sliced eggplant and potatoes and wedges of zucchini and carrot. Fresh or canned pineapple wedges, halved peaches and apricots and quartered apples are tasty as relishes with broiled meats and are delicious as dessert. Sprinkle with sugar or not as you prefer. Turn to brown evenly and serve hot.

Planning Meals

Menu making should put zest into housekeeping. If you are bored with planning meals, look for variations to use with dishes already familiar—new garnishes or accompaniments, a new sauce or salad dressing or new shapes or seasonings for bread.

PLANNING THE AMOUNT TO SERVE

Recipes suggest *serves 4* or *serves 6* to indicate the number of average-sized servings. But appetites vary according to many factors—the weather or the way a dish is presented, whether at a meal of many courses or just one or two. A pudding or ice cream served in dessert glasses "goes farther" than one served from a bowl.

NUTRITION

A balanced diet provides all the necessary vitamins without the necessity of adding vitamin concentrates. To achieve such a diet for your family, include the following each day in planning meals. Then add other foods as you like. The amount listed for each type of food is the approximate amount a person should have each day.

Milk provides high quality protein, plenty of calcium and several important vitamins. Some may be in the form of cheese. *1 quart.*

Cereals (preferably whole-grain or enriched) as breakfast foods, puddings and breads. *Three or 4 servings.*

Fruits. Citrus fruit, *one serving;* and *one serving* of another fruit.

Vegetables are rich in vitamins and minerals. Tomatoes, parsley and peppers are high in vitamin C. *Three servings, including one raw vegetable.*

Meat (especially liver), fish and poultry are the best sources of "complete" protein and the B vitamins. *One or 2 servings.*

Eggs for many important food values. *One a day.*

Fats and oils are valuable for their vitamin and mineral content. Both animal and vegetable fats are important. *Butter and a salad oil daily.*

PROTEIN

Most diets are surprisingly low in protein. Sixty grams a day is the recommended minimum for adults, 75 to 100 for teen-agers. Check the following list of the richest sources to be sure you are providing enough for your family.

Source	*Grams*
¼ pound meat, fish or fowl (without bones)	10 to 20
1 egg	6
1 quart milk	32
½ cup cottage cheese	20

½ cup walnuts or pecans	6
½ cup peanuts	20
1 tablespoon peanut butter	4
¼ cup powdered skim milk	10
¼ cup brewer's yeast	25
¼ cup wheat germ	12
Bread, cereals and vegetables	Small amounts

To increase protein content, add toasted wheat germ and brewer's yeast to breads, cookies, waffles, pancakes, fritters and meat loaf. Sprinkle wheat germ on puddings, ice cream, salads and soups. Use only a little at first until your family learns to like the unfamiliar flavor.

CALORIE TABLES

The number of calories given is approximate. For more detailed information consult government bulletins.

	Approximate Calories
Beverages	
Coffee, tea, any amount	0
Cocoa made with milk, 1 cup	200
Cider, 1 cup	125
Ginger ale, lemonade, 1 cup	100
Grape juice, 1 cup	170
Tomato juice, 1 cup	50
Beer, 12 ounces	170
Breads and Cereals	
Bread, whole-wheat or enriched, 1 slice	65
Muffins, sweet rolls, 1	100 to 165
Pancakes, 1 (4-inch)	60
Waffles, 1	215
Dry cereal, 1 cup	120 to 140
Rice, cooked, ½ cup	50
Wheat germ, 1 tablespoon	15
Oatmeal, cooked, ½ cup	75
Crackers, 2	15
Macaroni, cooked, 1 cup	200

	Approximate Calories
Dairy Foods	
Milk, whole, 1 cup	165
skimmed, buttermilk, 1 cup	85
dry skimmed, 1 tablespoon	30
evaporated, unsweetened, 1 tablespoon	25
condensed, sweetened, 1 tablespoon	75
Cream, light, 1 tablespoon	30
heavy, 1 tablespoon	50
Yogurt, 1 tablespoon	50
Cheese, cottage, 1 cup	170
other, 1 ounce	100 to 200
Meats, Poultry, Fish and Eggs	
Beef, lamb, veal, lean to medium fat, no bones, cooked, 3 ounces	250
Pork, no bones, cooked, 3 ounces	300
Bacon, 1 slice	50
Frankfurters, 1	125
Meat stew with vegetables, 1 cup	200
Poultry, no bones, cooked, 3 ounces	150
Creamed chicken, ½ cup	200
Fish, lean, cooked, 3 ounces	100
fat, cooked, 3 ounces	175
Shellfish, cooked, shelled, 4 ounces	100
Eggs, 1	75
Fruits	
Canned fruits in syrup—double the calorie count.	
Apples, 1	60
Apricots, 3	50
Avocados, ¼	140
Bananas, 1	90
Berries (except strawberries), 1 cup	80
Cherries, pitted, 1 cup	65
Dates, pitted, ½ cup	250
Figs, dried, 1	50
Grapefruit, ½	75
Oranges, 1	70
Peaches, 1	50

	Approximate Calories
Pears, 1	100
Pineapple, diced, 1 cup	75
canned, with juice, 2 slices	100
Prunes, unsweetened, 4	75
Raisins, dry, 1 tablespoon	25
Strawberries, 1 cup	50
Tomatoes, 1 medium (½ cup)	20

Vegetables

Beans and peas, dried, cooked, ½ cup	150
Celery, ½ cup diced	10
Corn, 1 ear (½ cup)	80
Lettuce, 2 large leaves	5
Lima beans, fresh, cooked, ½ cup	90
Mushrooms, cooked, ½ cup	15
Peas, fresh, ½ cup	50
Peppers, green, 1	15
Potatoes, sweet, 1 medium	165
Potatoes, white, 1 medium	110
Radishes, 1	1
Others, cooked, ½ cup	30 to 50

Desserts

Cake, angel, 2-inch wedge	110
cupcake, iced, 1	160
fruit cake, 1 ounce	105
plain cake, 3 by 2½ inches	180
pound cake, 1 ounce	130
sponge cake, 2-inch wedge	120
Gingerbread, 2-inch cube	180
Cookies, plain, 1 (3-inch)	110
Doughnuts,1	135
Custard, ½ cup	150
Gelatin dessert (plain), ½ cup	75
Ice cream, ½ cup	150
Sherbet, ½ cup	120
Pie, 2-crust, 4-inch wedge (9-inch pie)	325
1 crust, 4-inch wedge (9-inch pie)	270

Salad Dressings, Gravies and Sauces

	Approximate Calories
French dressing, 1 tablespoon	100
Mayonnaise, 1 tablespoon	100
Thin gravy, 1 tablespoon	15
Thickened gravy, 1 tablespoon	25
Cream sauce, 1 tablespoon	25
Cheese sauce, 1 tablespoon	35
Catsup, tomato sauce, 1 tablespoon	25
Hollandaise, 1 tablespoon	90
Butterscotch sauce, 1 tablespoon	100
Chocolate sauce, 1 tablespoon	45
Hard sauce, 1 tablespoon	50

Nuts

Brazil nuts, 1	50
Filberts (hazelnuts), hickory nuts, shelled, ¼ cup	250
Peanuts, almonds, shelled, ¼ cup	200
Pecans, walnuts, shelled, ¼ cup	160

Candies

Caramels, 1	100
Chocolate creams, 1	40
Fudge, plain, 1-inch cube	100
Marshmallow, 1 large	25
Nut brittle, 3-inch square	130

Soups

Consommé, 1 cup	10
Cream soup, 1 cup	200

Miscellaneous

Brewer's yeast, 1 tablespoon	20
Butter, margarine, 1 tablespoon	100
Cooking fats and salad oils, 1 tablespoon	115
Chocolate, unsweetened, 1 ounce	140
Olives, 1	7
Peanut butter, 1 tablespoon	90
Sugar, syrups, jam, 1 tablespoon	90

BREAKFAST

Nutritionists advise starting the day with a sturdy breakfast to provide plenty of energy-building foods for the day's activities. The pattern is standardized in most families—fruit or fruit juice, cereal and/or eggs and bacon, a beverage and toast or a hot bread. For an occasional change, serve waffles with sausage patties, chicken hash, French toast, pancakes, sautéed tomatoes with strips of bacon, fish cakes, or, in the old New England fashion, warm apple pie.

LUNCH

Lunch is usually simple, but it should be rich enough in protein to supply energy for the afternoon's activities. Salad with crackers and plenty of cheese, or a sandwich with a bowl of soup or a glass of milk, will often be satisfying. Top off with fruit or a sweet, if you like. Even in summer, lunch is more refreshing if it includes one hot thing—a beverage, a cup of soup or a hot bread.

DINNER

As the principal meal of the day, dinner deserves careful planning, but long, elaborate meals are outmoded except for state occasions.

The first course (omit it altogether if you like) may be fruit or tomato juice, a fruit or seafood cocktail or a simple soup. To simplify service at the table, pass fruit juice or a clear broth in the living room beforehand.

The main course is usually a satisfyingly hearty one. With it serve one or two vegetables and a simple salad or fresh relishes such as celery or carrot sticks. Many families serve either potatoes or bread, not both at the same meal.

Salad may be served as a separate course either following the main course or—in the West Coast fashion—as the first course. Dinner salads should be simple, especially if they are served with the main course. A mixed green salad is always right, or a salad of grapefruit or avocado pear with lettuce and watercress.

Dessert possibilities are many. If the main course is very rich and hearty, serve fruit or a simple fruit dessert, or let the salad course be the final one, served, if you like, with cheese or cheese wafers.

Coffee in small cups (demitasse) is the proper finale to dinner, but many enjoy coffee throughout the meal. If you have omitted the dessert course, you may like to serve candy or salted nuts or both with the coffee.

MEALS TO PREPARE QUICKLY

Be ready for at least one emergency meal by keeping on hand a supply of canned foods and/or frozen foods sufficient for a complete menu. Even if you do not have a freezer, keep a few packages of frozen foods in the storage compartment of your refrigerator. Among the most satisfactory are minute steaks, ground beef, broilers and prepared dishes such as Lobster Newburg. Suggestions for using a freezer (p. 556). With a pressure cooker, many other dishes are also suitable for quick meals.

Concentrate on the main dish and with it serve canned or frozen vegetables, or fresh ones that cook quickly, or whole peeled tomatoes or tossed green salad. For dessert, serve fruit or crackers and cheese.

Quick main dishes

- American Minestrone made with frozen vegetables (p. 74)
- Eggs (p. 106)
- Broiled Fillets of Fish (p. 125)
- Broiled Ham (p. 201), Chops (p. 184) or Steak (p. 169)
- Cold Sliced Meats (p. 213)
- Meats reheated in gravy or sauce (p. 213)
- Fashion Park Salad (p. 282)
- Hamburg Patties in various ways (pp. 176–178)
- Hash (pp. 137, 176, 189, 213)
- Hearty Soups and Chowders (p. 58)
- Cream Soups (pp. 64–70) with Cheese Sandwiches (p. 359)
- Liver and Bacon (p. 209)
- Oyster, Lobster or Scallop Stew (pp. 79–80)
- Sautéed Oysters (p. 153) or Scallops (p. 157)
- Scrambled Eggs New York Style (p. 110)
- Shrimp (p. 297), Lobster (p. 297), or Chicken Salad (p. 296)
- Stuffed Mushrooms (p. 259)
- Spanish Rice (p. 310)
- Waffles (p. 321) or Pancakes (p. 318) with sausage cakes or bacon
- Welsh Rabbit (p. 119)

CASSEROLE DISHES

In addition to the suggestions listed below, prepare any braised, creamed or scalloped dish or stew. Keep it hot in a covered casserole and serve directly from the casserole.

- Casserole of Meat (p. 214)
- Cheese and Olive Casserole (p. 122)
- Deviled Crabs (p. 146)
- Eggs Florentine (p. 109)
- Epicurean Finnan Haddie (p. 141)
- Fish Soufflé (p. 137)
- Jo Mazzotti (p. 198)
- Macaroni and Cheese (p. 312)
- Baked Rice with Cheese (p. 311)
- Scalloped Eggs, Fish or Ham (p. 107)
- Scalloped Lobster (p. 151)
- Savoy Scallops (p. 157)
- Shapleigh Luncheon Cheese (p. 122)
- Spanish Rice (p. 310)
- Beef and Corn Casserole (p. 179)

USING LEFTOVERS

If there is only a little meat or vegetable to use, chop it, season well, heat in a sauce, and serve in a Rice, Parsley, or Noodle ring (pp. 309, 310, 315).

Breads. Toast (p. 354). Crumbs (p. 6). Bread Puddings (p. 391). Stuffings (p. 82).

Cake. Cottage Pudding (p. 394). Trifle (p. 385). Icebox Pudding (394).

Cheese. Special recipes (p. 116). Sandwiches (p. 359). Canapés (pp. 44, 47). Top casseroles or soups with grated cheese.

Chicken. Special recipes (p. 232). See suggestions for Meats.

Egg yolks and whites (p. 8).

Fish. Special recipes (p. 136). Canapés (p. 44). Salads (pp. 292, 295–297).

Meats. Special recipes (p. 213). Stuffed Peppers (p. 264); Tomatoes (p. 276); Zucchini (p. 279). Sandwiches (p. 358). Canapés (p. 44). Fashion Park Salad (p. 282).

Vegetables. Cream of Vegetable Soup (p. 64), American Minestrone (p. 74). Stuffed Peppers (p. 264); Tomatoes (p. 277); Zucchini (p. 279).

ENTERTAINING

Serve to guests only those dishes which you are sure of preparing well, no matter how simple they are. Practice new recipes on the family first. There are no rigid rules in planning a party menu. Dishes once considered appropriate for only the plainest family meals now appear at parties—corned beef hash, kidney stew or finnan haddie, for example. Serve them with a flair! Most important of all, plan ahead so that there will be no last-minute rush. Nobody enjoys a party given by a harried hostess.

Luncheon parties. Even for a party, the menu should be light. First (but omit this course if you like) a clear or delicate cream soup, a fruit cocktail or other appetizer; then an interesting but not too hearty main dish such as Crêpes Nicholas (p. 320), Curried Shrimp (p. 159), Cheese Soufflé (p. 121), Chicken Almond Suprême (p. 233), Huntington Scalloped Fish (p. 137) or Fashion Park Salad (p. 282). Afterward either fruit or a light but delicious dessert such as a fruit sherbet, Coffee Soufflé (p. 399) or Pears with Zabaglione (p. 386).

Bridge luncheons are often one-course affairs. A suitable menu might be Crab Bisque (p. 77) with salad and hot biscuits, or Fruit Salad (p. 289) with toasted cheese sandwiches.

Sunday lunch ("brunch") is a combination of breakfast and lunch served at table or buffet-style. Serve hearty breakfast dishes such as Chicken Hash (p. 235), Eggs (p. 106), Waffles (p. 321) or Pancakes (p. 318) with sausages, bacon or ham. Complete the menu with fruit or fruit juices, plenty of coffee and a hot bread such as Blueberry Muffins (p. 328). Popovers (p. 329) or Corn Bread (p. 329).

Dinner parties. Follow the pattern for dinner (p. 26). Add an extra course if you like—a shrimp cocktail before the soup or a delicate fish course after it. Some of the best **soups for a dinner party** are homemade or canned consommé or chicken broth with a simple garnish or green turtle soup. Others are Cream of Almond (p. 65), Lobster Bisque (p. 77), or Shrimp Bisque (p. 77). Nothing is better for **the main dish** than a fine roast of beef or lamb, turkey or guinea hen or herbed roast chicken, but unless you are following a strict old-fashioned pattern, you will serve whatever you like, such as broiled chops, steak, veal cutlets or baked ham.

Dessert may be festive for a special occasion. A few popular ones are Baked Alaska (p. 427), Coupes (p. 423), Gâteau Riche (p. 428), Crème Brûlée (p. 386), and Meringues Glacé (p. 425), but fruit desserts are definitely in vogue and most refreshing after a rich dinner.

Buffet meals make for easy entertaining. The food should be easy to serve and easy to eat, especially if the guests must balance a plate and cup at the same time. Replenish hot foods frequently if you are not using a chafing dish or a hot plate. For suggestions, see the list of Casserole Dishes (p. 27) and the recipes for hearty salads (pp. 295 ff.).

Chafing dish entertaining. Many a man enjoys preparing a chafing dish specialty for guests. All the preliminaries, even to measuring the ingredients, should be accomplished well in advance, so that preparation may seem miraculously simple.

Chafing dish main dishes

Beef Stroganoff (p. 172)
Sautéed Liver (p. 209)
Broiled Ham (p. 201)
Buttered Lobster (p. 149)
Chop Suey (p. 179)
Corn Fritters (p. 253)
Hamburg Patties heated in red wine (p. 177)
Kidney Stew (p. 208)
Lobster Newburg (p. 151)
Lobster Stew (p. 79)
Omelets (pp. 111–114)
Oyster Stew (p. 79)
Oysters in Sherry Cream (p. 154)
Pancakes (pp. 318–321)
Scallop Stew (p. 80)
Scrambled Eggs (p. 110)
Welsh Rabbit (p. 119)

Chafing dish desserts

Sautéed Bananas (p. 368)
Bananas au Rhum (p. 368)
Cherries Jubilee (p. 369)
Crêpes Suzette (p. 320)
Hot Fruit Compote (p. 364)
Soufflé au Rhum (p. 400)
Stewed Pears (p. 374)
Strawberries Flambé (p. 377)

CHILDREN'S PARTIES

Ice cream and cake are a "must." The cake should be a simple one but the decoration may be as elaborate as you like (p. 510)

For very young children, serve sliced chicken, scrambled eggs or thin broiled meat patties. Peas and baked potatoes are invariably popular. So are Carrot Curls (p. 280) and Bunny Salads (p. 288). For a very simple party, serve a variety of sandwiches (peanut butter, chopped chicken, jelly) with tomato juice, milk or a cream soup.

For older children serve any plain dish, easy to cut or serve.

Lamb Chops (boned) (p. 184)
Hamburg Patties (p. 176)
Pea Soup (p. 71) with assorted sandwiches
Roast Chicken (p. 217)
Spaghetti with meat balls (pp. 313–314)
Swiss Steak (p. 169)
Beef and Corn Casserole (p. 179)

LARGE TEAS AND RECEPTIONS

Set a large table in the dining room or living room with plenty of space for tea or coffee service at one end and an ice or punch at the other. Along the sides, arrange plates of small sandwiches or canapés and small cakes. Do not crowd the table or the plates. Replenish the plates from time to time so that the table will always look attractive.

Cocktail party suggestions (p. 43).

Wedding receptions. Serve sandwiches and small cakes or cookies with coffee and champagne or punch. Let the wedding cake be the chief decoration of the table and do not cut it until all the guests have arrived.

Wedding breakfasts *or* luncheons. Toast the bride and groom in champagne, Sauterne Cup (p. 42), Champagne Punch (p. 41) or a fruit punch (p. 38). Serve any canapés or hors d'oeuvres. For a **luncheon served at tables,** the first course may be something very light, such as clear Chicken Broth (p. 62) or a Fruit Cocktail (p. 364). For a buffet luncheon, omit this course. **For the main course,** Creamed Lobster (p. 151), Chicken à la King (p. 233), Chicken Tetrazzini (p. 234),

Chicken (p. 296) or Lobster Salad (p. 297), Chicken Mousse with Mushroom Sauce (p. 231), Fish Mousse with Lobster Sauce or Brown Almond Sauce (p. 137). Relishes, hot rolls and coffee with this course.

For dessert, the wedding cake alone or with ice cream.

QUANTITY COOKING

In a family-size kitchen, preparing food for a large number means very careful planning. Simplify by serving food which can be prepared in advance and kept warm in casseroles. Serve individual molded salads, tossed salad in your largest bowl or a variety of crisp relishes. Hot buttered rolls, coffee (Coffee for Fifty, p. 33) and an assortment of pickles and jellies complete the main course. Some of the best vegetables are Potatoes Hashed in Cream (p. 271), Candied Sweet Potatoes (p. 273) and any of the frozen vegetables.

Main course. Casserole Dishes (p. 27), Chicken Almond (p. 233), Individual Chicken or Meat Pies (pp. 214, 227), Scalloped Scallops (p. 158), Spaghetti (p. 313), Jo Mazzotti (p. 198) or Spanish Rice (p. 310) are suitable, as well as such old stand-bys as Meat Loaf (pp. 180, 202–203), Baked Beans (p. 245) or Baked Ham (p. 199).

Dessert. Ice cream must be taken out at just the right moment, so consider other desserts as well.

Baked Lemon Pudding (p. 393)
Tortes (p. 404)
Denver Chocolate Pudding (p. 406)
English Trifle (p. 385)
Fruit Cup (p. 363)
Fruit Tarts (p. 455)
Fudge Pie (p. 406)
Gingerbread (p. 497)
Coconut Macaroon Pie (p. 407)
Washington Pie (p. 495)

Buying to serve 100. The amounts suggested are approximate.

Coffee, 2½ pounds.
Tea, ½ pound.
Cream. For coffee, 6 pints. For whipped cream, 2 quarts.
Butter (to cut in squares), 2 pounds.
Ice cream, 3 gallons.
Meat loaf, 18 pounds.
Roast pork, 36 pounds.
Roast beef or veal, 40 pounds.
Roast chicken or turkey, 60 pounds.
Baked ham, 30 pounds.
Potatoes, 35 pounds.
Salad dressing, 2 quarts.
Peas. Frozen, 10 packages (40-ounce size). Canned, 3 #10 cans.
Apples for applesauce, 2 pecks.
Canned applesauce, 3 #10 cans.

WINE WITH MEALS

Wine adds a festive, but not necessarily extravagant, touch to a meal. There are excellent moderately priced wines, both imported and domestic. The best American wines are not imitations of European ones but have a character of their own. Eastern wines are generally made from native grapes, such as Delaware and Catawba. The best California wines are made from European-type grapes in the valleys near San Francisco Bay, and are labeled with the name of the valley (Napa, Sonoma, Livermore, Santa Clara, Santa Cruz, etc.) and with the variety of the grape used (Semillon, Cabernet, Pinot Noir, Pinot Blanc, Riesling, etc.) to show that they are "varietal," i.e., not made of an indiscriminate blend of grape juices. The vintage year is not important for American wines, since the climate is almost uniform in the wine-producing areas.

Buying wine. Follow the advice of a dependable dealer or the recommendation of a wine expert as indicated on the label. A bottle contains 28 ounces, which is a modest amount for 4 persons, if you are serving wine throughout a meal—2 or 3 small glassfuls each.

Storing wine. Keep in a cool dry place. Place bottles of unfortified wines on their sides so that the cork will stay damp. If the cork dries out, air gets into the bottle and the flavor of the wine begins to change. Fortified wines (sherry, Madeira and port) keep well upright, since the added alcohol helps to preserve the flavor. Move bottles gently so that any sediment in the bottom is undisturbed.

Serving wine. Serve red wines at cool room temperatures (about 65°). Chill white or rosé wines in the refrigerator several hours before serving. Chill champagne in an ice bucket so that it is icy-cold. Remove the cork very carefully so that bits of cork will not drop into the bottle. Serve in simple uncolored glasses, half to three-quarters full. Chill the glasses for champagne.

It is not necessary to follow a strict pattern in serving wine. Try various types and serve what you enjoy. In general, delicate white wines (such as sauterne or Rhine wine) or rosé wines seem to go best with chicken and fish, while the stronger-flavored red wines (such as Burgundy or claret) maintain their character with sturdier foods like beef, pork, game, and cheese. To serve throughout a meal, select a wine that is not too sweet (called "dry" or "sec"). Serve a sweet wine with dessert or between meals. Before a meal, serve dry sherry or chilled vermouth with a thin twist of lemon peel. Sherry and Madeira go well with clear soup. Port is excellent at the close of a hearty meal, with cheese, walnuts or fruit. Serve champagne for any festive occasion, at a reception, throughout a meal or with dessert.

Beverages

Selecting the appropriate beverage is important. Coffee goes with every meal and every occasion. Tea is welcome at breakfast or at afternoon functions. Cocoa and chocolate with whipped cream are popular with the young. Cold drinks are especially good for summer meals and functions. Fruit punches—with or without liquor—are party refreshment.

COFFEE

Try different blends to learn which type you like best. Change once in a while, too. French-type coffee is mixed with chicory, which gives it a distinctive sharp flavor.

Buy fresh-roasted coffee in small quantities for the finest flavor. Buy it in the bean or ground according to the way you make it. Some shops sell excellent coffee at a very low price as a special feature, but inexpensive coffee is not always an economy since you may need to use more of it to make coffee as strong as you like it.

Instant coffee is convenient, not only for making a single cup of coffee in a hurry but in milk shakes and as a flavoring.

Store coffee in a can or a glass jar with a tight lid. Store it in the refrigerator, upside down, to retain the pungent flavor.

MAKING COFFEE

Buy the grind recommended for the type of coffee maker you are using. Two level tablespoons of coffee for each cup is the standard amount to use, but experiment—you may prefer stronger or weaker coffee, or you may need to vary the amount according to the quality of the coffee.

Use a coffee maker the right size for the amount you are making. Keep it scrupulously clean. Wash it with baking soda or, if you wash it with soap, be extra careful to rinse it thoroughly so that there will be no trace of soap to spoil the fine coffee flavor.

If the water in your area has a definite taste due to minerals in it, you may prefer to use bottled spring water (not carbonated, of course).

Automatic coffee makers simplify coffee making and keep the coffee at the correct temperature. Follow the manufacturer's directions.

Drip. Measure the coffee into the proper section. Set the pot in hot water or on an asbestos mat over low heat. Add fresh boiling water. For the finest flavor, add the water a little at a time, so that it will drip through slowly.

Filtered. Measure the coffee into the upper section. Add the measured amount of boiling water all at once. Keep the pot warm as for drip coffee above.

Vacuum. Measure the water into the lower bowl. Adjust the filter in the upper bowl and fit it in place. Measure the coffee into the upper bowl. Set over moderate heat. When most of the water has risen into the upper bowl and is bubbling hard, reduce the heat. After 4 minutes, turn off the heat and let the coffee drain into the lower bowl.

Percolator. Measure the coffee into the strainer section. Measure either cold or boiling water into the pot. Set over moderate heat or turn on the current. Bring to the boiling point, reduce the heat and percolate gently until the coffee looks dark enough (about 10 minutes). If your electric percolator is not automatic, pull out the plug three times to slow the percolating.

BOILED COFFEE

Old-timers think that boiled coffee, made with an egg, has the finest flavor of all. Make it strong and boil it long enough (or it will be cloudy) but not too long (or it will be bitter).

Heat the coffeepot (or a saucepan with a tight cover) by rinsing with boiling water. Mix in the pot

1 egg, slightly beaten
1 eggshell, crushed
½ cup cold water
½ cup coffee (regular grind)
Few grains salt

Add and stir thoroughly

6 cups freshly boiling water

Stuff the spout of the pot with soft paper to prevent escape of fragrant aroma. Set the pot over moderate heat, bring slowly to the boiling point, and simmer 3 minutes. Add, to aid clearing,

½ cup cold water

Set the coffeepot in a pan of hot water and place over very low heat to steep and keep hot without boiling.

Pour carefully into cups without straining (it will be crystal-clear, since the egg and the coffee grounds stay in the bottom of the pot).

COFFEE FOR FIFTY

In a clean cotton bag or cloth, large enough to allow for expansion, put

1 pound coffee (regular grind)

Tie loosely. Place in a big kettle. Add

8 quarts cold water

Let stand several hours or overnight. Bring to the boiling point three times, removing from the heat each time the boiling point is reached so that the coffee will steep slowly, which improves the flavor.

PICNIC COFFEE

For each cup of water, measure 2 level tablespoons coffee (regular grind) into a cotton bag or cloth and tie loosely to allow for expansion. Add the water, bring to the boiling point three times, removing from the fire each time the boiling point is reached.

CAFÉ AU LAIT

Serve strong hot coffee with hot milk. Pour the milk and the coffee into the cup simultaneously—a pot in each hand.

AFTER-DINNER COFFEE (CAFÉ NOIR)

Make strong coffee, using 3 tablespoons to each cup of water. Serve in demitasse cups.

Vienna Coffee. Serve with whipped cream.

CAFE BRÛLOT (CAFÉ AU DIABLE)

In New Orleans, café brûlot is made in a special silver bowl kept hot over an alcohol flame.

In a chafing dish or brûlot bowl, mix

½ stick cinnamon
6 whole cloves
1 curl orange peel
6 lumps sugar
6 ounces brandy *or* 2 ounces rum and 4 ounces brandy

Heat and set afire with a lighted match. Stir with a ladle. Add slowly

3 cups strong hot coffee

Stir. Ladle into demitasse cups. *Serves 6.*

ICED COFFEE

Strain very strong hot coffee over ice in glasses or in a pitcher. Or use 1 teaspoon instant coffee for each cup of cold water, shake thoroughly and pour over crushed ice.

Serve with cream and powdered sugar. Or serve clear and unsweetened as a particularly refreshing drink on a warm summer day.

Iced Coffee with Ice Cream. Serve in tall glasses, with a small scoop of vanilla ice cream in each glass.

TEA

Keep a variety of teas on hand. Orange pekoe and English breakfast are the most popular blends to serve with a meal. Delicate oolong, smoky Souchong and the spicy blends are appropriate for afternoon tea.

One-fourth pound of tea will make 50 or more cups, according to the strength you like. With loose tea you can use as little or as much as you need at a time. Tea bags are convenient but comparatively expensive—48 bags equal about ¼ pound. Store tea in a tightly covered tin away from spices or other aromatic foods.

HOT TEA

Warm a china or earthenware pot (metal changes the flavor of the tea) by rinsing it with boiling water.

Measure the tea into the pot—½ to 1 teaspoon per cup according to the quality of the tea and the strength you like. Pour in just enough boiling water so that the tea leaves float freely. Cover and let stand 3 minutes. Longer steeping develops a bitter taste in tea. Strain, and dilute with boiling water.

To make tea with tea bags. Pour fresh boiling water into a cup or pot and add the tea bags immediately. Cover, let steep 3 minutes, and remove the tea bags.

To serve with tea. Serve cube sugar or rock candy, cream or milk (English tea lovers insist on milk), and thin slices of lemon, studded with two or three cloves for a spicy flavor.

Serve delicate China tea or smoky Souchong tea clear, with nothing to detract from the distinctive bouquet.

An Austrian fashion is to serve tea with sugar and rum.

TEA FOR FIFTY

Bring 1½ quarts water to the boiling point. Add ¼ pound tea, stir, cover, and let stand 4 minutes. Strain into a warmed pot. Dilute with fresh boiling water as you serve it.

ICED TEA

Use inexpensive tea for iced tea, since the flavor will be blended with mint and lemon.

Pour strong hot tea over cracked ice or ice cubes in glasses or a large pitcher. Add more ice, if needed. Garnish with sprigs of mint and slices of lemon or orange. Serve very fine sugar and lemon juice with iced tea. Do not use confectioners' sugar because it makes the tea cloudy.

Cold-water Iced Tea. *An easy way to make very clear sparkling tea.* Put 1 teaspoon tea for each cup of water in a large pitcher. Add cold water. Cover. Let stand in the refrigerator 12 hours. Strain.

Madeleine's Iced Tea. *Somewhat cloudy but delicious.* Allow 1 teaspoon sugar and 1 sprig mint for each glass to be made. Measure into a large pitcher and add strong hot tea. Stir to dissolve the sugar. Dilute with ice cubes to make the required amount. Add lemon juice to taste. Strain.

HOT COCOA

Dutch-type cocoa has the richest flavor.

Mix in a saucepan
1½ tablespoons cocoa
2 tablespoons sugar
Few grains salt

Add
½ cup boiling water
Boil 3 minutes. Add
4 cups milk
Heat slowly to just below the boiling point. Beat well with an egg beater or wire whisk. Flavor with
Few drops vanilla
Makes 6 cups.

Mexican Chocolate. Add 2 teaspoons instant coffee. Flavor with vanilla or cinnamon to taste.

HOT CHOCOLATE

Put in a saucepan
4 cups milk
2 ounces sweet chocolate *or* 1½ ounces unsweetened chocolate and ¼ cup sugar
Few grains salt
Heat until the chocolate melts. Beat until smooth and foamy. Add
1 teaspoon vanilla
Serve with
Whipped cream
Makes 6 cups.

Iced Chocolate. Chill. Pour over crushed ice, stir well, and sweeten to taste. Serve with whipped cream.

FRENCH CHOCOLATE

Put in a saucepan
2 ounces unsweetened chocolate
½ cup cold water
Stir over low heat until the chocolate melts. Add
¾ cup sugar
Few grains salt
Cook until thick (about 10 minutes). Cool. When cold, fold in
½ cup heavy cream, whipped
When ready to serve, heat
1 quart milk
Pour hot milk into each cup, and top with a spoonful of the chocolate cream. *Serves 6.*

CHOCOLATE SYRUP

For flavoring milk shakes.

Put in a saucepan

- **2 cups boiling water**
- **2 cups sugar**
- **⅛ teaspoon salt**
- **6 ounces unsweetened chocolate *or* 1 cup cocoa**

Cook and stir over moderate heat until smooth. Cool. Add

- **1 teaspoon vanilla**

Store in a covered jar. *Makes 3 cups.*

CHOCOLATE MILK SHAKE

If the ingredients have been thoroughly chilled in the refrigerator, you will not need ice.

For each milk shake, beat together with an egg beater, or put in a shaker and shake thoroughly

- **2 tablespoons finely crushed ice**
- **⅔ cup milk**
- **2½ tablespoons Chocolate Syrup (above)**

Strain into a glass. A few gratings of nutmeg or a few grains of cinnamon may be sprinkled on top.

REDUCER'S COFFEE MILK SHAKE

For each milk shake, beat in an electric blender until creamy

- **1 cup skim milk**
- **1 ice cube**
- **1 teaspoon instant coffee**
- **1 table saccharin, crushed, *or* Sucaryl to taste**

MOLASSES *or* MAPLE MILK SHAKE

For each milk shake, blend or shake together

- **1 glass milk**
- **2 tablespoons molasses *or* maple syrup**

CORNELL MILK SHAKE (HIGH PROTEIN)

Sometimes called "Tiger's Milk," this is a wonderful source of energy to serve at breakfast or luncheon or as a between-meal pick-me-up. With an electric blender, you may flavor the milk shake with fruits such as bananas, strawberries, apricots or pineapple.

For each milk shake, shake together thoroughly, or mix in an electric blender

- **1 cup milk**
- **1 teaspoon powdered brewer's yeast**
- **2 tablespoons (or more) powdered skim milk**
- **1 teaspoon molasses, maple syrup, frozen orange juice concentrate *or* apricot nectar**

CHOCOLATE ICE CREAM SODA

Cream makes a superlative soda.

For each soda, put in a tall glass

- **3 tablespoons Chocolate Syrup (above)**
- **1 tablespoon heavy cream**

Mix well. Add

- **Small scoop chocolate, mint or vanilla ice cream**
- **Soda water to fill the glass**

Stir thoroughly.

FRUIT JUICES

Fresh or canned fruit juices are refreshing additions to the menu. Serve them at breakfast, as a between-meal pick-me-up, as the first course at luncheon or dinner, as an after-school treat or as a party drink. Blend several juices for an interesting flavor. If the juice is not tart enough, add lemon juice. Sweeten drinks with Sugar Syrup. Dry sugar may settle in the bottom of the glass.

Sugar Syrup. Boil 2 cups sugar with 2 cups water 5 minutes. Chill and store in a covered jar.

FRUIT JUICE COCKTAIL

Garnish orange or pineapple juice with a sprig of mint. Or pour fruit juice over a spoonful of sherbet. Apricot nectar with orange sherbet and cranberry juice with lemon sherbet are two delicious combinations.

THREE-FRUIT COCKTAIL

For each glassful, mix
- **5 tablespoons grapefruit juice**
- **2 tablespoons orange juice**
- **1 tablespoon lemon juice**
- **3 tablespoons Sugar Syrup (above)**
- **Few grains salt**
- **½ cup soda water**
- **Crushed ice**

Pour into glasses and garnish each with
- **A sprig of mint**

SAUERKRAUT JUICE COCKTAIL

Season sauerkraut juice with lemon juice. Serve very cold.

TOMATO JUICE COCKTAIL

Season plain tomato juice, canned or homemade (p. 553), to taste with lemon juice, sugar and a few drops of onion juice. If it needs more flavor, add a stalk of celery, a bit of bay leaf or basil. Let stand an hour, chill, and strain.

Tomato and Clam Juice Cocktail. Combine tomato juice and clam juice, using two-thirds clam juice and one-third tomato or half of each.

CLAM JUICE COCKTAIL

Season canned clam juice with salt, celery salt, and a few drops of Tabasco sauce and lemon juice. Chill or pour over crushed ice.

LEMONADE

Frozen concentrated lemonade is easy but may be too sweet for your taste. Improve it by adding fresh lemon juice.

For each serving, mix
- **2 tablespoons lemon juice**
- **2 tablespoons sugar *or* ¼ cup Sugar Syrup (above)**

Stir thoroughly to dissolve the sugar. Add
- **1 cup ice water *or* water and crushed ice *or* ice cubes**

Stir well. Decorate with
- **Maraschino cherries *or* sprigs of fresh mint**

To frost glasses. Set the glasses on a tray and put them in the freezer compartment until they are covered with frost. Dip the rims in sugar. Return to the compartment to refrost, if necessary.

Pineapple Lemonade. Add ½ cup pineapple juice.

Limeade. Instead of lemon juice, use 4 tablespoons lime juice. Garnish with a thin slice of lime.

ORANGEADE

For each tall glass, prepare ¾ cup orange juice or dilute ¼ cup frozen concentrated juice with ½ cup water. Sweeten, if necessary, with Sugar Syrup (above) or add lemon juice to make more tart. Fill glasses half full of crushed ice. Pour in the orange juice and stir well.

APRICOT NECTAR

Add lemon juice to taste to canned apricot juice. Pour over crushed ice.

GRAPE JUICE FIZZ

Mix
- **1 quart ginger ale**
- **1 pint grape juice, frozen or bottled**

Pour into glasses half filled with finely crushed ice. *Serves 8.*

Grapefruit Fizz. Use grapefruit juice in place of grape juice.

COFFEE PUNCH

Put in a large bowl
- **1½ pints ice cream (vanilla *or* chocolate), frozen hard**

Pour over the ice cream
- **4 cups hot coffee**

Beat lightly with a wire whisk until the ice cream is partially melted. Pour into punch glasses and sprinkle with
- **Grated nutmeg**

Serves 8.

FRUIT PUNCH

Blend fresh, canned or frozen fruit juices. Sweeten to taste, if necessary, with Sugar Syrup (p. 37) and sharpen with lemon juice. Pineapple juice is particularly delicious combined with orange juice, grape juice or lime juice. Chill thoroughly. When ready to serve, dilute with water or ginger ale and pour over ice cubes or a block of ice in a punch bowl.

Garnish with lemon or orange slices, bits of pineapple, strawberries or raspberries or mint leaves.

Vodka Fruit Punch. Add 80-proof vodka to any fruit punch combination. Vodka has no flavor of its own. Use about 1 cup vodka for each 4 cups of fruit juice.

SHERBET PUNCH

Pour fruit juice over sherbet in a punch bowl or individual punch cups. Stir to blend and chill, but serve before the sherbet is entirely melted. Some good combinations are grape juice with lemon sherbet, orange juice, pineapple juice or ginger ale with lemon or lime sherbet. *One quart of juice with 1 pint of sherbet makes 8 to 10 servings.*

FRUIT PUNCH FOR FIFTY

Boil together 5 minutes
- **1 cup water**
- **2 cups sugar**

Add
- **1 cup strong hot tea**
- **2 cups fruit syrup (such as strawberry *or* loganberry)**
- **1 cup lemon juice**
- **2 cups orange juice**
- **2 cups pineapple juice**

Let stand 30 minutes. Add
- **4 quarts ice water**
- **1 cup maraschino cherries**
- **1 quart soda water**

Pour over ice in a punch bowl. *Serves 50.*

TEA PUNCH

Mix
- **1 cup sugar**
- **1 cup strong hot tea**

When the sugar is dissolved, add
- **⅓ cup lemon juice**
- **¾ cup orange juice**

Pour over ice in a punch bowl. Just before serving add
- **1 pint ginger ale**
- **1 pint soda water**

Garnish with
- **Few slices orange**

Serves 12.

HARVARD PUNCH

Mix
3 cups orange juice
1 cup lemon juice
1 cup pineapple juice
1 cup raspberry syrup
1½ cups strong hot tea
Boil 5 minutes
1 cup water
1¼ cups sugar
Add to the fruit juices and tea. Chill thoroughly. Just before serving add
1 quart soda water
Pour over ice in a punch bowl. *Serves 30.*

MINT TULIP

Discard the stems and injured leaves of
1 bunch fresh mint
Cover the perfect leaves with
1½ cups sugar
½ cup water
1 cup lemon juice
Let stand 30 minutes. Pour over ice in a large pitcher. Add
3 pints ginger ale
Serves 10.

MULLED CIDER

Serve in mugs with hot doughnuts for a winter party.

Mix in a saucepan
1 quart cider
2 whole allspice
2 whole cloves
1 stick cinnamon (3 inches long)
Boil 5 minutes. Add
⅜ cup brown sugar
Boil 5 minutes longer. *Serves 6.*

HOT SPICED CRANBERRY PUNCH

Serve in mugs or punch glasses.

Heat slowly until the sugar dissolves
1 quart cider *or* grape juice
1 quart cranberry juice
6 cloves
1 stick cinnamon (3-inch)
4 whole allspice
½ cup brown sugar
Taste and add more sugar if needed. *Serves 12.*

ICED CRANBERRY PUNCH

Mix
1 quart cranberry juice, canned *or* homemade
Sugar Syrup (p. 37) to taste
2 cups water
1 cup orange juice
Juice of ½ lemon
Chill. Just before serving, add
1 quart ginger ale *or* soda water
Serves 20.

CRANBERRY JUICE

Cook 1 pound cranberries in 4 cups water until soft. Crush. Drain through cheesecloth to make crystal-clear.

ORANGE SYRUP FOR PUNCH

Buy the citric acid crystals at a drugstore. Dilute the syrup with 3 or 4 gallons of plain or carbonated water to make punch for a big party—a school dance, for example. Store in four quart jars in the refrigerator and use as needed.

Cut into pieces without peeling or removing the seeds
6 oranges
2 lemons
Put through a food chopper or blender. Add
9 cups boiling water
Let stand until cool. Squeeze through cheesecloth. Add
6 cups sugar
Stir well. Stir together
2½ ounces citric acid crystals
1 cup boiling water
When dissolved, add to the

orange syrup. *Makes the base for 5 or 6 gallons of punch.*

RHUBARB JUICE

Make rhubarb juice in quantity and can it to have ready for refreshing summer drinks.

Cut in small pieces
1½ pounds rhubarb
Add
1 quart water
Cook until the fruit is soft. Squeeze through a double thickness of cheesecloth. Add
1 cup sugar
Stir and heat to the boiling point. *Makes about 3 pints.*

RHUBARB PUNCH

Stir and heat to the boiling point
1½ quarts Rhubarb Juice (above)
½ cup sugar
Cool. Add
⅓ cup orange juice
4 tablespoons lemon juice
Few grains salt
Chill. Just before serving add
1 quart soda water *or* ginger ale
Pour over ice in a large pitcher or punch bowl. *Serves 12.*

HOLIDAY EGGNOG

Make at least a week before serving so that it will mellow.

Beat until stiff
12 egg whites
Beat in
½ cup sugar
Beat until very light
12 egg yokes
1 cup sugar
¼ teaspoon salt
Combine the egg mixtures and stir until thoroughly blended. Add
1 quart heavy cream, beaten
1 quart milk
1 quart bourbon whiskey
Beat well. Add
1 cup rum
Pour into a gallon jug (put the extra in a quart jar). Store in a cool cellar. Shake or stir thoroughly before serving. Ladle from a big punch bowl into small cups and sprinkle with
Nutmeg
Serves 30.

MINT JULEP

Allow 1 jigger (2 ounces) bourbon or rye whiskey for each julep. Set tall thin glasses or silver julep cups on saucers or a tray so that you will not have to touch them and disturb the frost as it forms. Set in the refrigerator or freezer compartment. When ready to serve, put in each glass a sprig of mint, a lump of sugar and a teaspoon of whiskey. Crush with a spoon. Fill to the brim with finely shaved ice. Tamp down hard. Pour in part of the whiskey and stir gently with a long-handled spoon. Add more ice, tamp down, add whiskey, and continue until the glass is full of ice, packed hard. Garnish with a generous bouquet of mint.

RUM SWIZZLE

Almond-flavored falernum gives a swizzle its special character.

Mix in a big pitcher or a punch bowl
3 parts light rum
1 part falernum
1 part lime juice
Dash of bitters
Add
1 or 2 squeezed halves of lime
Add plenty of ice cubes. Mix hard with a swizzle stick, or stir with a spoon. A swizzle is still delicious as the ice melts and dilutes it.

RUM PUNCH

Mix
1½ cups lemon juice
1½ cups grapefruit juice
5 cups orange juice
6 cups unsweetened pineapple juice
8 cups water
1 cup Sugar Syrup (p. 37)
1 bottle Jamaica rum
2 bottles West Indies rum
Let stand at least 1 hour to blend. Pour over ice in a punch bowl. *Makes about 75 glasses.*

HOT JAMAICA PUNCH

Simmer ½ hour
1 gallon cider
Few sticks cinnamon
½ teaspoon whole mace
½ teaspoon whole allspice
Add
1 cup Jamaica rum
1 cup brandy
Serve hot. *Makes about 40 glasses.*

REGENT PUNCH

Mix
1 quart rye whiskey
1 quart rum
1 quart strong tea
Juice 6 lemons
Juice 6 oranges
1 pound sugar
When ready to serve, pour over ice in a punch bowl. Add
1 quart champagne
1 quart soda water
Makes about 40 glasses.

CLUB PUNCH

Mix
1 quart Burgundy
1 cup rum
⅓ cup brandy
⅓ cup Benedictine
1 quart soda water
3 sliced oranges
½ cup crushed pineapple
Juice 2 lemons
1 cup strong hot tea
Sweeten to taste with
Sugar Syrup (p. 37)
Pour over ice in a punch bowl. *Makes about 25 glasses.*

CHAMPAGNE PUNCH

Modify these combinations as you like. For a more economical punch, add soda water and more tea. Sweeten to taste with Sugar Syrup (p. 37).

Mix
1 cup brandy
½ cup rum
½ cup Cointreau
2 cups strong tea
When ready to serve, pour over ice in a punch bowl. Add
1 gallon champagne
Stir with a ladle. *Makes about 50 glasses.*

DOVER RUM PUNCH

Mix
1 quart dark rum
1 quart ginger ale
¼ cup Cointreau
1 cup lemon juice
2 ounces brandy
1 cup Sugar Syrup (p. 37)
Pour over ice in a punch bowl. *Makes about 25 glasses.*

CLARET CUP

As an attractive garnish, add ¼ cup diced pineapple and ¼ cup fresh strawberries, halved.

Mix and stir well
1 quart claret
⅓ cup sugar
½ orange, sliced
½ lemon, sliced
Cover. Chill 1 hour. Add
1 quart soda water
Pour over ice in a large pitcher or punch bowl. *Serves 12.*

Claret Punch. Add 1 cup orange juice, 1 cup lemon juice, 2 cups Sugar Syrup (p. 37) and 1 quart water. *Serves 25.*

SAUTERNE CUP

Ripe strawberries are a perfect garnish.

Mix

¼ cup brandy
¼ cup curaçao
Rind ½ orange
Rind ½ lemon
¼ cup sugar

Cover and let stand 2 hours. Add

1 quart sauterne

Strain and chill. Just before serving, add

1 quart soda water *or* champagne, chilled

Garnish with

Mint leaves
Few slices orange

Serves 12.

WHISKEY CUP

Mix

2 quarts whiskey
1½ cups sugar
Juice of 3 lemons
2 oranges, sliced thin

Stir until the sugar dissolves. Add

¼ bottle grenadine
2 quarts soda water

Pour over ice in a punch bowl. *Serves 25.*

Cocktail Tidbits, Snacks and Hors d'Oeuvres

Appetizing tidbits and snacks are very popular in these days of informal entertaining. In addition to the recipes in this section, browse through the book for other suggestions—such as cheese (p. 116), fruits (p. 363), small pastries (pp. 457–459) and sandwiches (p. 356).

COCKTAIL TIDBITS

Before a hearty dinner, cocktail accompaniments should be very simple. Serve at least one thing which is not a wafer or a canapé. Many recipes are in this section. Other suggestions are:

- Packaged wafers (crisp in the oven if necessary)
- Potato chips
- Cheese Wafers (p. 335)
- Corn Crisps (p. 334)

If the cocktail hour is to take the place of the first course at table, you may like to serve something heartier such as:

- Seafood canapés
- Shrimp with cocktail sauce
- Tiny hot Sausage Balls (p. 48)
- Oysters or Clams on the Half Shell (p. 55), arranged on crushed ice on a big platter
- Stuffed Eggs (p. 107)

COCKTAIL PARTY FARE

The food may be as hearty as for a buffet supper but it is usually "finger food." Pass everything on trays or arrange on a table. Have at least one hot dish such as Swedish Meat Balls (p. 177) and a "conversation piece" such as a Cocktail Checkerboard (p. 51), Cheese Ball (p. 51) or Quiche Lorraine (p. 121). A Cocktail Bowl (p. 51) is a pleasant contrast to heartier foods. Place bowls of salted nuts and simple wafers here and there to be nibbled.

SNACKS WITH BEER

Traditional are pretzels, pumpernickel and cheese. Pizzas (p. 349) are good too.

HORS D'OEUVRES AS A DINNER COURSE

See page 51.

NUTS WITH COCKTAILS

Unless the nuts are freshly toasted (p. 520), heat them in the oven at 350° long enough to make them crisp. Brazil Nut Chips (p. 520) are delicious.

CURRIED PEANUTS

Spread salted peanuts in a shallow pan. Sprinkle with curry powder and dot with butter. Heat in a 350° oven, stirring several times.

PECAN SURPRISES

Put perfect pecan halves together in pairs with a filling of anchovy paste, pâté de foie gras, Mock Pâté de Fois Gras (p. 54) or other canapé spread.

COCKTAIL GRAPES

Slit Malaga or Tokay grapes without cutting all the way through. Remove the seeds. Stuff with cream cheese blended with Roquefort and highly seasoned with onion juice, salt and Worcestershire. Smooth the filling along the cut. Chill.

COCKTAIL OLIVES

All sort of olives are good with drinks. As a special treat, stuff pitted olives with toasted almonds or filberts or with bits of anchovy.

GARLIC OLIVES

Pour out part of the juice from a pint jar of stuffed olives. Add to the jar the juice of 2 limes and a cut clove of garlic. Close the jar. Let stand 24 hours before using.

CREAM CHEESE BALLS

Mash cream cheese. Add any of the seasonings suggested below and shape in ¾-inch balls. Dust with paprika or roll in finely cut dried beef, chopped nuts or crushed potato chips. Serve on cocktail picks.

Walnuts, chopped fine, and brandy to taste
Onions or chives, chopped fine, and prepared mustard or horseradish to taste
Chopped ham or shrimp

CANAPÉS

A canapé is a tiny open sandwich spread with a savory mixture. The base may be a crisp cracker or a small piece of bread toasted on one side. The bread may be cut in squares, rounds, triangles or crescents.

Spread the base generously with Savory Butter (p. 45) or one of the spreads on pages 45 to 46. Spread toast canapés on the untoasted sides well to the edge.

Garnish, if at all, very simply with a shake of paprika, a leaf of parsley or watercress, a slice of stuffed olive or a bit of chopped egg white or crumbled egg yolk. Press the garnish into the spread so that it will not fall off.

SERVING COCKTAIL DIPS

Many savory mixtures are adaptable as dips. See the recipes which follow for dips and spreads and also cocktail sauces (p. 55) and sandwich fillings (p. 358). Thin, if necessary, with mayonnaise or sour cream. Prepared spreads are convenient, but liven them up with more seasoning.

Put the dip in a bowl. Have ready a plate of crisp packaged wafers or crackers, potato chips, Melba toast, pretzel sticks, small squares of hot toast or homemade Corn Crisps (p. 335). Each person dips his own.

SOUR CREAM DIP

Mix
½ pint sour cream
1 package dried onion soup mix *or* a small jar of red caviar *or* 1 cup drained canned minced clams
Stir well, cover, and chill at least 2 hours.

DEVILED HAM DIP

Mash together
1 small can deviled ham
2 hard-cooked eggs, chopped
Thin with
Mayonnaise, yogurt *or* sour cream
Season more highly, if you like, with
Curry *or* Worcestershire

MUSHROOM DIP

Chop fine
½ pound mushrooms
Melt
2 tablespoons butter
Add the mushrooms. Cook 5 minutes. Sprinkle with
1 teaspoon flour
Stir and add
½ cup heavy cream
Cook until thick. Season with
Salt, pepper and nutmeg
Serve hot with toast or crackers. Best of all, serve in a chafing dish or electric saucepan. Or use as the filling for Rolled Sandwiches (p. 361). Toast just before serving.

SAVORY BUTTER

Cream butter until it is soft and fluffy. Season with anchovy or sardine paste or other fish or meat pastes, minced shrimp or lobster, sieved pimiento, caviar, chutney, chopped pickle, grated horseradish, finely cut watercress or parsley. Season to taste with French dressing, prepared mustard, a few drops of onion juice or lemon juice or other seasoning.

ANCHOVY BUTTER

Mash
1 small package of cream cheese
Add
2 teaspoons capers
½ teaspoon grated onion
1 teaspoon anchovy paste
Few drops Worcestershire
Mix well. Stir in
Heavy cream *or* mayonnaise
until thin enough to spread. Thin more to use as a dip.

ROQUEFORT BUTTER

Cream butter. Add crumbs of Roquefort and a few drops of onion juice.

BLEU CHEESE BUTTER

Put in a small heavy bowl
½ pound Bleu cheese
¼ pound soft butter
Blend with a fork. Add
¼ cup port wine
Set in a pan of hot water and beat until smooth and creamy. Add
2 tablespoons chopped parsley
Few drops onion juice
Cover the bowl and chill several hours to blend the flavors. Take from the refrigerator long enough ahead of time to serve at room temperature, not icy cold.

CREAM CHEESE BUTTER

Mash cream cheese. Add cream or melted butter until soft enough to spread. Season highly to taste with grated onion, chopped chives, chopped stuffed or ripe olives or chopped parsley.

EDAM AND ROQUEFORT SPREAD

Scoop out the center of an Edam cheese. Measure and add an equal amount of Roquefort. Grind together in the food chopper. Add about half as much butter as cheese. Blend well and season with Worcestershire or brandy. Pile on a plate or spoon into the cheese shell.

SHERRIED CHEESE SPREAD

Serve with cocktails, with salad, or, in the English fashion, as the savory last course at dinner.

Put through the food chopper

½ pound Cheddar cheese

Add

3 tablespoons sherry
2 tablespoons butter, creamed
1 teaspoon prepared mustard
½ teaspoon salt
Few grains cayenne

AVOCADO AND BACON SPREAD

Mash avocado with a silver fork (to prevent discoloring). Mix with crumbled crisply cooked bacon. Season with lemon juice, salt and pepper to taste.

GUACAMOLE

Mash avocado with a silver fork. Season highly with onion juice or onion salt, lemon juice, salt and pepper. Beat in mayonnaise, tomato pulp or tomato catsup until the consistency of whipped cream. If you like it very highly seasoned, add chili powder. Pile in a bowl and serve with corn wafers or homemade Corn Crisps (p. 334).

RIPE OLIVE SPREAD

Moisten chopped ripe olives with mayonnaise or mix with cream cheese and mayonnaise. Season highly with Worcestershire, chopped parsley and paprika.

RIPE OLIVE CANAPÉS

Put in a jar

1 small tin chopped ripe olives
2 drops olive oil
1 clove garlic

Close the jar. Refrigerate at least 1 day. Spread

Toast rounds or wafers

with

Cream cheese

Top each with a dab of the olive mixture.

LIVER SAUSAGE SPREAD

Mash liver sausage. Moisten with melted butter and season with port or brandy.

CHICKEN LIVER SPREAD

Sauté livers in butter 5 minutes. Mash with a fork and add crumbled cooked bacon, chopped hard-cooked egg or chopped cooked or canned mushrooms. Season highly with minced onion, salt and pepper. Add mayonnaise until thin enough to spread.

Chicken Liver Balls. Keep the mixture firm enough to shape in small balls. Roll in chopped pickled beets and serve on cocktail picks.

LOBSTER, SHRIMP *or* TUNA SPREAD

Chop the fish fine. For 1 cupful, hard-cook 4 eggs. Mash the yolks and add to the fish. Moisten with melted butter and a little cream, sweet or sour. Season with salt, cayenne, mustard and a few drops of beef extract.

LIPTAUER CHEESE

Serve with beer, cocktails or salad.

Cream together
- **2 small packages cream cheese**
- **¼ cup butter**

Add
- **1 teaspoon capers**
- **1 teaspoon paprika**
- **2 anchovies, chopped fine**
- **1 shallot *or* 1 slice onion, minced**
- **½ teaspoon caraway seed**
- **½ teaspoon salt**

Mix thoroughly and press into a small mold or form in a roll and wrap in wax paper. Let stand several hours in the refrigerator to blend the flavors.

HOT CANAPÉS

Prepare toasted canapé bases (p. 44). Spread the untoasted side with any of the mixtures suggested below or invent your own savory spread. Put on a cooky sheet. Just before serving, broil or bake at 400° until thoroughly heated or until the bacon crisps or the cheese melts. Serve immediately on a warm plate.

Uncooked bacon, minced and mixed with chopped ripe olives or with grated cheese seasoned with mustard and paprika.

Cheese, sliced and cut slightly smaller than the canapés. Sprinkle with paprika.

Parmesan cheese, grated and moistened with heavy cream and seasoned to taste.

Mayonnaise mixed with chopped onion. Top or not with grated cheese before baking.

Mushroom Dip (p. 45) with a square of bacon on top.

Peanut butter, with bits of bacon on top.

FINNAN HADDIE CANAPÉS

Piping hot, these are excellent with drinks.

Melt
- **3 tablespoons butter**

Add and cook 5 minutes
- **2 teaspoons finely chopped onion**
- **2 mushroom caps, chopped fine**

Sprinkle with
- **2 tablespoons flour**

Stir in
- **⅔ cup thin cream**

Bring to a boil. Add
- **2 tablespoons grated cheese**
- **2 egg yolks, slightly beaten**
- **1 cup cooked shredded finnan haddie (p. 140)**

Season to taste with salt and cayenne. Pile on
- **Circular pieces of hot toast**

Sprinkle with
- **Grated cheese**
- **Buttered bread crumbs**

Just before serving, bake at 375° until brown. *Makes 24 or more.*

HOT SEAFOOD CANAPÉS

Spread canapé bases with any of the following and bake or broil (above).

Minced clams (fresh or canned), mixed with mayonnaise and seasoned with curry.

Chopped crabmeat, lobster, shrimp or tuna, creamed or mixed with mayonnaise. Season highly. Sprinkle with grated cheese before baking.

DEVILED HAM CANAPÉS

Prepare toasted canapé bases (p. 44). Spread with deviled ham. Add onion soup mix to mayonnaise (1 teaspoon or more for 1/4 cup mayonnaise). Spread over the ham. Just before serving, heat in a 450° oven or in the broiler until delicately brown.

BEEF TARTARE

This raw beef is also delicious made into larger sandwiches for lunch.

Remove all the fat from high-grade lean raw beef (top round or sirloin). Put twice through the grinder so that it will be very fine. Season to taste with onion juice, salt, pepper and A-1 sauce or Worcestershire. Serve with squares of toast or sliced and buttered party rye.

COCKTAIL SAUSAGES *or* MEAT BALLS

Pan-fry or broil small sausages or tiny balls of sausage meat or hamburger. Keep hot in a chafing dish or electric saucepan or put on picks and stick in a bright red apple. Swedish Meat Balls (p. 177) are popular, too, with drinks.

COCKTAIL CROQUETTES

Make tiny (1-inch) Chicken (p. 236) or Lobster (p. 152) Croquettes. Serve very hot on picks.

COCKTAIL FISH BALLS

Make 1-inch Codfish Balls (p. 139). Serve hot with a Cocktail Sauce (p. 55).

COCKTAIL PUFFS

Fill tiny Cream Puffs or Éclair Shells (p. 408) with shrimp mixed with mayonnaise, or with Chicken, Lobster, Shrimp or Crab Meat Salad (pp. 296–297), or with cream cheese blended with Roquefort and beaten with a little heavy cream. See also Cheese Puffs (p. 334).

RISSOLETTES

Roll Plain Pastry (p. 438) or Puff Paste (p. 453) 1/4 inch thick. Shape with a small round cutter dipped in flour. Wet the edges of half the pieces and place in the center of each 1 teaspoon highly seasoned filling made of chopped meat, sausage, fish or cheese. Cover with the remaining pieces and press together. Prick well. Bake at 450° until pale brown (about 6 minutes).

Caviar Rissolettes. Fill with caviar seasoned with lemon juice.

SMOKED SALMON

Smoked salmon is marketed in tins or by the pound. The best is pale pink, fine-grained and not too salty. Serve with lemon wedges, black pepper (freshly ground or in a pepper mill) and thin slices of pumpernickel or dark rye bread spread with unsalted butter.

HAM, DRIED BEEF *or* SALMON ROLLS

Cut thin slices of ham, dried beef or smoked salmon in neat pieces. Spread with cream cheese highly seasoned with prepared mustard or horseradish. Roll up tightly and fasten with a cocktail pick.

Horns of Plenty. Shape in cornucopias. Fill as above or with caviar seasoned with lemon juice or with finely chopped cucumber mixed with mayonnaise.

COCKTAIL BACON STRIPS

Cook strips of lean bacon, keeping them as flat as possible. Drain well. Just before serving, sprinkle with grated Parmesan cheese and set in the broiler long enough to melt the cheese slightly. The strips should be crisp enough to take in the fingers.

BACON-WRAPPED OLIVES *or* OYSTERS

Cooked chicken livers, cooked cocktail sausages and pickled onions are good this way too.

Wrap stuffed olives or oysters in half-slices of bacon. Fasten with toothpicks. Grill in the broiler or bake at 425° until the bacon is crisp. Replace the toothpicks with fresh ones or with croquette sticks.

COCKTAIL ARTICHOKE LEAVES

Cook an artichoke (p. 240). Cool. Pull off the leaves and spread them, hollow side up, on a large plate or platter. (Save the base to add to a salad.) On the fleshy end of each leaf, put a shrimp and a bit of avocado. Top with a dab of mayonnaise delicately seasoned with curry.

STUFFED BRUSSELS SPROUTS

Cut the centers out of uncooked Brussels sprouts. (Save the centers to cook as a vegetable.) Soak the sprouts in ice water ½ hour. Drain thoroughly. Fill with cottage or cream cheese seasoned with chopped chives and mixed with heavy cream, sweet or sour.

STUFFED CARROT SLICES

Scrape a large even carrot. Cut off the ends and make a hole through the center with an apple corer. Stuff tightly with highly seasoned cream cheese mixed with finely cut chives. Chill until the cheese is firm. Cut in ¼-inch slices. Use to garnish a tray of canapés.

Stuffed Dill Pickle. Use a large pickle instead of a carrot.

STUFFED CELERY

Wash and dry pieces of celery from the heart. Leave on a bit of the foliage as decoration. If

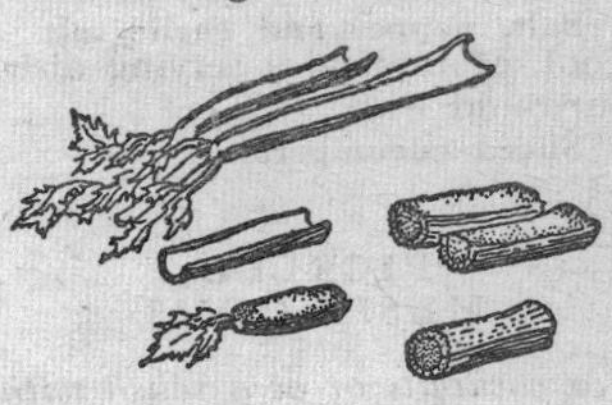

the pieces are large, cut in 1½-inch lengths after filling. Fill the grooves with:

Caviar sprinkled with a few drops of onion juice.
Cream cheese highly seasoned with French dressing, tomato catsup and Worcestershire sauce.
Cream cheese blended with Roquefort crumbs and softened with mayonnaise or sour cream.
Prepared cheese spread.

Chopped raw mushrooms seasoned with Worcestershire and garlic salt.

CELERY ROUNDS

Wash and dry two perfect stalks of celery. Fill with any cream cheese filling and press together. Wrap tightly in wax paper and chill. Cut in ½-inch slices and place on rounds of buttered brown bread.

EGGPLANT CAVIAR

Bake at 350° until soft
1 eggplant
Peel, chop fine, and set aside. Put in a pan
½ cup minced onion
¼ cup olive oil
Cook together slowly until the onion is soft. Add the eggplant. Add
4 tablespoons tomato paste
Cook and stir until thick (about 15 minutes). Add
1 tablespoon lemon juice
Season with
Salt, pepper and garlic salt
Cool. Mound on a serving dish. Surround with
Sliced cucumbers

PICKLED MUSHROOMS

For cocktails or as a relish with cold chicken or beef.

Wash
½ pound mushrooms
Cut the stems even with the caps. (Use the stems for soup or a sauce.) Peel if the skin is discolored. Slice very large mushrooms. Leave small ones whole. Cover with
2 cups boiling water
2 teaspoons salt
Simmer 5 minutes and drain. Mix and boil 10 minutes
⅔ cup mild cider vinegar *or* wine vinegar
6 peppercorns
1 slice onion
1 sprig parsley
1 bay leaf
3 celery leaves *or* 1 teaspoon celery salt
Pour over the mushrooms. Cool. Add
¼ cup olive oil
Put in a tightly covered jar. Shake well. Refrigerate at least 1 day before serving. Drain.

MUSHROOMS À LA GRECQUE

Peel perfect mushrooms. Leave small ones whole. Cut large ones in half. Cover with French dressing. Tuck in 2 bay leaves for each cup of mushrooms. Cover and chill 12 hours or more. Drain (saving the dressing to use on a salad). Serve the mushrooms on cocktail picks or add to a salad.

COCKTAIL MUSHROOMS

Fill perfect mushroom caps (raw or sautéed in butter) with highly seasoned cream cheese or chopped ham mixed with mayonnaise.

FRENCH-FRIED MUSHROOMS

See page 259.

CHEESE ROLL

Serve with cocktails, coffee or salad.

Put through the grinder
¼ pound American cheese
½ cup unblanched almonds
Sliver of garlic
Add and blend well
1 small package pimiento cream cheese
1 small package cream cheese

Pat into a roll. Sprinkle a thick layer of paprika on wax paper. Coat the cheese roll with paprika and roll tightly in the paper. Store in the refrigerator. Serve with crisp crackers.

PARTY CHEESE BALL

For a large cocktail party.

Prepare
1 cup chopped pecans *or* chopped parsley
Set aside half. Add the rest to
1 pound Roquefort
2 pounds cream cheese
1 small package processed sharp Cheddar
1 onion, minced fine
1 teaspoon Worcestershire
Salt to taste
Blend well and shape in a ball. Roll in the reserved parsley or pecans. Chill. Place on a large plate and surround with crisp crackers.

COCKTAIL BOWL

Season mayonnaise highly with curry or Worcestershire. Thin with a little cream, sweet or sour. Put in a small bowl on a large sandwich plate. Around the bowl put any of the following—on cocktail picks to make serving easier.

Artichoke hearts, cooked or canned
Asparagus tips, cooked or canned
Carrot sticks
Cauliflower flowerets, raw
Celery
Lobster meat, cut in neat pieces
Shrimp, cooked or canned

COCKTAIL CHECKERBOARD

The canapé tray never looks disorderly when arranged this way, even when it is nearly empty.

Make square canapés, measuring them with a ruler. Make two sorts in contrasting colors such as mushroom canapés and smoked salmon. Arrange like a checkerboard on a large tray. Along the edges place pastry sticks brushed with melted butter and sprinkled with chopped parsley.

HORS D'OEUVRES AS A DINNER COURSE

Served at the table, hors d'oeuvres may be more elaborate than those passed with cocktails in the living room. It is sometimes pleasant to serve the cocktails or sherry with them.

Make attractive arrangements on individual plates or pass a handsome tray of assorted tidbits. For special recipes, see pages 52–55.

Other delicious first courses are Fruit Cocktails (p. 364), tomato or fruit juices, and small servings in ramekins of highly seasoned shellfish such as Oysters Casino (p. 154), Oysters in Sherry Cream (p. 154), Deviled Crabs (p. 146) and Coquilles St. Jacques (p. 55).

HORS D'OEUVRES PLATTER

The first course for a dinner party or the main dish at lunch.

A special hors d'oeuvre dish is divided into sections, but any large platter or large round plate will do. Make an attractive arrangement with a variety of hors d'oeuvres and garnish it with sprigs of watercress or parsley. Include at least one hearty hors d'oeuvre, one salad, vegetable or fruit, and one highly seasoned relish. There are also special hors d'oeuvres recipes below.

Eggs. Eggs à la Mimosa (p. 106) or hard-cooked egg, sliced, marinated, and sprinkled with finely cut parsley, chives or watercress.

Fish. Anchovies, herring, smoked salmon, sardines (with wedges of lemon or thin slices of onion), flaked shrimp with mayonnaise, canned or cooked salmon with Tartare Sauce (p. 103) and cucumber dice, tiny cream puff or pastry shells filled with lobster or shrimp or crab salad.

Fruits. Avocado or melon in thin strips. Cantaloupe with thin slivers of prosciutto.

Relishes. Finely cut pickled beets, celery, green or ripe olives, pickled onions, radishes.

Salads and vegetables (marinated). Artichoke bottoms or hearts, fresh okra (boiled), cooked whole string beans or carrot slivers in French dressing, sprinkled with minced onion and parsley, asparagus tips, cauliflower flowerets, sliced cucumbers, canned or cooked mushrooms, sliced tomatoes (sprinkled with chopped parsley, chives or watercress), mixed vegetable salad.

PLATEAU PRUNIER

The pattern is from a famous restaurant; vary it as you like.

On each plate put 2 or 3 scallop shells or deep oyster shells. Fill each shell with a different hors d'oeuvre such as shrimp, crab or lobster in mayonnaise, Oyster Cocktail (p. 55, Seafood Cocktail) and Russian Salad (p. 284). On each plate put a tiny roll, split, buttered, and filled with smoked salmon.

ANTIPASTO

The Italian version of hors d'oeuvres. As a convenience, have on hand prepared antipasto, which is marketed in jars, ready to chill and serve.

Arrange on individual plates a small serving of each type of appetizer listed below. Garnish with Italian olives. Serve with crisp bread sticks.

A vegetable, such as Green Beans Fiesole (p. 53) Celery Remoulade (p. 53) or Artichokes Vinaigrette (p. 285).

Prosciutto, sliced cold chicken or veal, sardines, anchovies, chunks of lobster or tuna or Stuffed Egg Salad (p. 296). See also Prosciutto (with melon, p. 200).

Tomato chunks or sliced cucumber in French dressing or Russian Salad (p. 284).

JULIENNE OF ROAST BEEF

Cut lean roast beef in match-shaped pieces. Moisten with sour cream. Season highly with Worcestershire or A-1 sauce. Add bits of pimiento, chopped green pepper or chopped ripe olives, or a little of each. Serve with lemon wedges.

AVOCADO MOUSSE

An interesting first course, and hearty enough for the main dish at luncheon or a buffet supper, served with thin slivers of ham.

Sprinkle
  2 teaspoons gelatine
over
  ½ cup cold water
Let stand 5 minutes. Add
  ½ cup boiling water *or* stock
Stir until dissolved. Cool. Mix
  ½ cup cream, whipped
  ½ cup mayonnaise

Add the dissolved gelatine. Add

2 cups mashed avocado
1 teaspoon salt
1 teaspoon onion juice (or season with onion salt)

Pour into a lightly oiled ring mold (1 quart). Chill until firm. Turn out on a serving platter and garnish with

Sliced tomatoes sprinkled with French dressing

Serves 8 as a first course, 4 as the main dish.

To season more highly, add celery salt, a few drops of Worcestershire, a few grains cayenne and a tablespoon or more chopped pimiento.

GREEN BEANS FIESOLE

Tasty as an hors d'oeuvre, as an unusual relish, or in place of salad.

Wash and snip off the ends from

1 pound tender young green beans

Add

½ cup water

Cook until just tender (not more than 10 minutes). Drain, reserving the cooking water. To ⅓ cup of the water add

⅓ cup cider vinegar *or* wine vinegar
⅓ cup salad oil
1 teaspoon salt
1 onion, sliced thin
1 clove garlic, split
¼ teaspoon oregano

Pour over the beans. Cover and chill at least 6 hours.

CELERY ROOT REMOULADE

An hors d'oeuvre to serve as a first course or as one of the items for a buffet or smörgåsbord.

Cut celery root or celeriac in julienne strips. Cover with boiling water and cook 1 minute. Drain, cover with French dressing, and refrigerate at least 6 hours. Drain and moisten with mayonnaise highly seasoned with prepared mustard and chopped parsley. Add (for 2 cups) 1 sour pickle and 1 tablespoon capers, chopped fine.

TOMATO HORS D'OEUVRES

Peel small ripe tomatoes.

I. Scoop out the centers. Chill and stuff with caviar, any mixed vegetable salad or chicken, lobster, tuna or crab meat salad. Serve on lettuce.

II. Cut in half. Top with a spoonful of cottage cheese. Serve on lettuce with Russian dressing.

LIVER PÂTÉ

Serve with cocktails, as a first course, or as one item at a buffet supper.

Have ready

¼ pound bacon, sliced thin

Line a 1-pint mold with some of the bacon and set it in the refrigerator. Cut the rest in small pieces and cook 5 minutes with

1 tablespoon chopped shallots *or* 1 teaspoon grated onion
1 tablespoon chopped parsley

Add

½ pound sliced calves' liver cut in 2-inch pieces

Stir and cook until brown (5 minutes). Set aside until cool. Meantime let stand in a bowl

1 cup bread crumbs
1 cup milk *or* consommé

When the liver is cool, put through a very fine sieve, or if possible chop in an electric blender. Add

1 egg yolk

Drain the liquid from the crumbs and set aside. Add the

crumbs to the liver mixture. Season to taste with

Salt, pepper, allspice, marjoram and thyme

Add enough of the liquid to make a thick paste that will drop from a spoon. Pack into the mold. Cover. Set in a pan of hot water. Bake 2 hours at 300°. Cool. Turn out onto a serving dish. Garnish with

Watercress
Quartered tomatoes dipped in French dressing

MOCK FOIE GRAS

Remove the skin from

½ pound liver sausage

Mash the sausage with a fork. Add

1 small package cream cheese
1 tablespoon melted butter
1 tablespoon Worcestershire
Salt and paprika to taste

Blend well. Serve with crackers or thin dry toast, at the table or with cocktails.

As a variation, add ½ cup sliced mushrooms sautéed in butter or season with port or with curry powder.

CHICKEN LIVER PÂTÉ SUPRÊME

A delicacy to serve with drinks or with salad at a summer luncheon.

Put in a pan

2 tablespoons butter
2 onions, chopped fine

Cook slowly until the onion is soft. Add

½ pound chicken livers

Cook 10 minutes. Put in a bowl. Mash with a fork. Add to the pan juices

2 tablespoons dry sherry

Stir and scrape to get all the good brown bits and add to the liver. Cool. Cream

½ cup butter

Stir in the liver. Season with

Salt

and more sherry if needed. Pack into a small bowl or crock and serve with Melba toast or crackers.

PÂTÉ MAISON

An excellent and attractive way to use bits of leftover cooked meat.

Cut the meat in small pieces, add a few slices of raw carrot, and put through the meat grinder, using the finest knife. Season to taste with salt, pepper, melted butter and brandy or sherry. Pack in a small crock or bowl to serve with cocktails, or shape in a loaf to serve at luncheon or supper.

To vary, add a few finely chopped mushrooms or almonds.

Improve canned pâtés (liver, chicken or ham) by combining any two and seasoning as above.

BLACK CAVIAR

The best imported caviar is one of the great luxuries. Put it in a bowl set in a bed of crushed ice. The classic accompaniments are thin fingers of dry, unbuttered toast, lemon wedges, finely chopped hard-cooked egg white, crumbled hard-cooked egg yolk and finely minced onion.

RED CAVIAR

Red caviar is marketed in small jars. Spread on crackers or canapés on a layer of cream cheese or put it in a bowl, ready to dip out.

CAVIAR RING

Serve with wafers for a cocktail party or as a first course at dinner.

Rinse a ring mold with cold water. Sprinkle black or red caviar in it. Fill with highly seasoned Tomato Aspic (p. 290). Chill until firm. Turn out on a serving dish. Fill the center with mayonnaise or chopped hard-cooked egg mixed with mayonnaise.

OYSTERS *or* CLAMS ON THE HALF SHELL

Open the oysters (p. 153) or clams (p. 142), or have it done at the market if it can be done shortly before serving time. Leave the oyster or clam in the deep half of the shell. Put 4 or 6 on each plate. To keep them appetizingly cold, set them on a layer of finely crushed ice.

Serve with cocktail sauce, wedges of lemon, grated horseradish, Tabasco or Worcestershire. The cocktail sauce may be in tiny dishes in the middle of each plate.

For a cocktail party, put the oysters or clams on a large platter on a bed of crushed ice.

SEAFOOD COCKTAIL

Oysters, clams or cooked or canned crab meat, lobster, shrimp or scallops are good this way. Or combine two or more such as crab, lobster and shrimp.

Use about ⅓ cup of seafood for each serving. Mix with cocktail sauce or serve the sauce separately. Put on lettuce or watercress in chilled dessert glasses.

BASIC COCKTAIL SAUCE

Cocktail sauces, homemade or canned, may be used to add zest to various dishes. Stir a little into mayonnaise or cream cheese to use as a dip, or add a little to a casserole.

Mix and let stand at least 2 hours.

½ cup tomato catsup
3 tablespoons cider vinegar *or* lemon juice
10 drops Tabasco
Salt and pepper to taste

To vary, add 1 teaspoon each of chopped parsley, chopped chives and horseradish and season with prepared mustard and Worcestershire to taste. Or add finely chopped celery or parsley.

SAUCE REMOULADE

Perfect with shrimp or lobster. The mustard should be mild.

Mix

1 cup mayonnaise
1 teaspoon lemon juice
3 tablespoons chopped chives
3 tablespoons chopped parsley
Dijon or Louisiana mustard to taste

Let stand at least 2 hours to blend.

COQUILLES ST. JACQUES

Delicious, too, as the main course at luncheon.

Mix creamed diced lobster, shrimp, crab meat and sautéed sliced mushrooms. Season to taste with Worcestershire, sherry or brandy. Spoon into scallop shells or individual baking dishes. Sprinkle with a thick layer of grated Parmesan cheese. Put a square of butter (about 1 tablespoon) on each. Stick a toothpick through the butter to hold it in place until it melts. Brown in the broiler. Remove the toothpicks. Serve piping hot with small brown bread sandwiches.

SMÖRGÅSBORD

Actually a hearty buffet meal but much like a cocktail party. Many of the appetizers in this chapter may be included, but there should be a strong emphasis on fish, cheese and seasoned cold vegetables.

To be correct in the Swedish fashion, begin with hot boiled potatoes and herring, a surprisingly good combination. Serve with tiny glasses of aquavit or schnapps.

Provide at least two kinds of bread—crisp Swedish Knäckebrod (packaged) and dark sour rye; also pats of unsalted butter and a variety of cheese. Beer is the usual beverage.

Arrange on a table as many different items as convenient. Suggestions follow, but visit a delicatessen for other ideas.

Sardines in oil or tomato sauce
Herring, smoked or pickled
Lobster meat in chunks
Shrimp
Pickled eel
Finnan haddie
Smoked salmon
Tuna chunks
Sliced cold roast beef, veal, turkey or ham
Swedish Meat Balls (p. 177)
Stuffed Egg Salad (p. 296) on tomato slices
Mixed vegetable salads
Chopped pickled beets and chopped apple, covered with whipped cream seasoned with horseradish
Radishes
Cucumbers, sliced thin and covered with mild vinegar

Soups and Chowders

With simplified modern meals, soup is often omitted as an extra course, but it has come into its own as a main course and as a party beverage. It is often at its best the second day, so do not hesitate to make more than you need for one meal.

SOUP AS THE FIRST COURSE

As the first course at luncheon or dinner, soup is usually served at the table, but a pleasant way to simplify service is to pass cups of soup in the living room, either after cocktails or in place of them. Allow about ½ cup for each serving.

Chilled soup is delightfully refreshing in summer. Vichyssoise (p. 72), Madrilène (p. 69), Consommé (p. 61) and Gazpacho (p. 73) are the most popular, but there are many other possibilities. Experiment with chilling leftover soup as a way to serve it another day. A thickened soup becomes thicker as it cools; if it is too thick, add consommé or thin cream, season to taste, and chill.

SOUP AS THE MAIN COURSE

Hearty soups are successful main dishes at luncheon or supper. Thick steaming hot chowder is particularly attractive served in generous pottery bowls and accompanied by crisp and colorful salad on wooden plates and crusty French or Italian bread.

If the soup is light, add a hearty garnish (pp. 58–60) to provide a stouter meal, or supplement the menu with plain or toasted sandwiches or with crackers and cheese. Stir powdered skim milk into any cream soup to increase the protein.

Allow plenty of soup for second servings—at the least, a full cup per person.

Browsing in this chapter will give you other ideas, but all of these soups are appropriate for main courses.

- Chicken Gumbo (p. 74)
- Clam Chowders (pp. 78–79)
- Corn Chowder (p. 70)
- Fish Chowders (pp. 80–81)
- Lobster Stew (p. 79)
- Minestrone (p. 73)
- Mulligatawny Soup (p. 74)
- Oxtail Soup (p. 75)
- Oyster Stew (p. 79)
- Parsnip Stew (p. 71)
- Philadelphia Pepper Pot (p. 75)
- Queen Victoria Soup (p. 74)
- Scallop Stew (p. 80)
- Scotch Broth (p. 75)
- Split Pea (p. 71)

SOUP AS A BEVERAGE

A clear hot broth or bouillon is often a welcome substitute for coffee as a party beverage. Pour it from a handsome pot or coffee urn or serve it in cups. Good accompaniments are cheese wafers or individual pizzas or crackers with a variety of cheeses. Olives, celery and salted nuts too, if you like.

Soup is good too at a children's party served with plenty of tasty sandwiches or crackers and cheese. The best soups to serve this way are Chicken Broth (p. 62), Consommé (p. 61), Mushroom Bouillon (p. 67), Madrilène (p. 69) or Clam Broth (p. 76). If you use canned broth, improve the seasoning a bit by adding sherry or a trace of curry.

Soup on the Rocks. Put an ice cube or two in an old-fashioned glass. Pour over it any of the clear soups suggested above.

PREPARED SOUPS

Canned and frozen soups are not to be scorned by even the proudest cook. Many are delicious heated and served just as they come from the can. Others are improved by being diluted with top milk or consommé instead of water. Browse through this section for special recipes using canned soups, and see Canned Soups as Sauces (p. 92). Dehydrated soups are a convenience for the emergency shelf. Dehydrated onion soup is useful as added seasoning in a gravy, sauce or casserole.

Season canned soup critically to make it taste homemade. Add nutmeg to chicken or mushroom soup, curry to chicken soup with rice, oregano to tomato soup, chili powder to black bean soup and thyme to clam chowder. Heat tomato soup with a bay leaf.

Garnish as suggested on pages 58–60.

Combine two soups occasionally for an interesting effect. Some successful combinations are:

- Cream of pea and cream of tomato
- Cream of celery and cream of tomato
- Cream of pea and green turtle
- Cream of chicken and cream of mushroom or celery
- Chicken with rice and cream of tomato
- Scotch broth and consommé
- Tomato bouillon and clam broth
- Cream of celery and clam chowder

SOUP GARNISHES

Traditional garnishes are suggested with certain soups, but improve any soup by adding a colorful garnish such as:

- Paprika
- Parsley, chives or dill, cut fine
- Grated cheese
- Slivers of ham or chicken
- Avocado slices for consommé, green pea or tomato soup

CROUTONS

Packaged croutons, plain or seasoned, are available. Crisp them in the oven.

Cut the crusts from slices of day-old bread and cut the bread in even cubes. Sauté in a little butter, turning to brown on all sides. Drain on a paper towel. Another way is to spread sliced bread lightly with butter, cut it in cubes, spread on a cooky sheet, and bake at 350° until brown.

PARKER HOUSE CROUTONS

Toast on one side

4 slices stale bread, ¼ inch thick

Blend
1 egg yolk
2 tablespoons butter
4 tablespoons grated Parmesan cheese
Spread the mixture on the untoasted side of the bread. Cut in ¼-inch cubes. Arrange on a cooky sheet, toasted side down. Bake at 350° until golden-brown. Put a few on any cream soup.

SALTED WHIPPED CREAM

Beat heavy cream (sweet or sour) slightly or until stiff. Add a few grains of salt. Fold in grated cheese, if desired. Put a dab on each serving of soup, such as tomato, chicken or clam broth.

PIMIENTO CREAM

To add a bit of color to pallid soups like potato or cream of corn, top with a spoonful of this rosy cream.

Dry on a paper towel and force through a sieve
Canned pimientos (to make 2 tablespoons of purée)
Beat until stiff
½ cup heavy cream
Fold in the purée. Add
Few grains salt

ROYAL CUSTARD

Beat slightly
1 egg
3 egg yolks
Add
½ cup consommé or milk
⅛ teaspoon salt
Slight grating of nutmeg
Few grains cayenne
Pour the mixture into a small buttered cup. Put the cup in a pan of hot water and bake at 350° until the custard is firm. Cool. Remove the custard from the cup and slice it thin. Cut the slices in diamonds or fancy shapes and serve in consommé or chicken broth.

CHICKEN CUSTARD

Rub through a sieve
¼ cup chopped cooked chicken (white meat)
Add
¼ cup Chicken Stock (p. 62) *or* canned chicken broth
1 egg, slightly beaten
Season to taste with
Salt, pepper, celery salt
Nutmeg
Anchovy paste
Bake like Royal Custard (above). Cut in small cubes and serve in chicken, pea or tomato soup.

CRÊPES (FRITTATEN)

Mix
½ cup flour
1 egg, slightly beaten
½ cup milk *or* Chicken Stock (p. 62) *or* canned chicken broth
Pinch of salt
Make thin pancakes. Cut them into fine strips and put a spoonful in each soup cup.

To vary, add finely chopped chives or parsley to the batter.

BUTTER DUMPLINGS

Cream
2 tablespoons butter
Beat in
2 eggs
¼ teaspoon salt
6 tablespoons flour
Drop from a teaspoon into simmering clear soup and cook 5 minutes. Serve one or two in each bowlful of soup.

PÂTE À CHOUX PUFFS

This mixture is almost identical with Cream Puff batter. It is easy to save a little to use this way when you make cream puffs —¼ cupful will make about 20 tiny puffs.

Heat to the boiling point
2 tablespoons milk
1 teaspoon butter
Add
¼ cup flour
Few grains salt
Stir hard until the mixture forms a ball. Remove from the heat. Add
1 egg (medium size)
Beat until well mixed. Cool. Heat fat in a frying kettle to 370°. Drop bits of the pâte from the tip of a teaspoon into the fat. Fry until brown, turning once. Drain on a paper towel. Put 2 or 3 in each serving of soup. *Makes about 50.*

Parmesan Puffs. Add 2 tablespoons grated Parmesan cheese to the mixture.

EGG BALLS

To enrich any clear soup.

Rub through a sieve
1 hard-cooked egg yolk
Add
1 hard-cooked egg white, chopped fine
⅛ teaspoon salt
Few grains cayenne
½ teaspoon melted butter
Moisten with
Raw egg yolk
Use enough so that you can shape the mixture into marble-sized balls. Poach in boiling water or stock, or roll in flour and sauté in butter. Add 2 or 3 to each serving of soup.

BROWN STOCK
(Bouillon)

Stock is the basis for many good soups and sauces. Use it also as a clear broth for a first course or a beverage. Stock made with bouillon cubes (or canned consommé) is a convenience, but many good cooks take pride in having homemade stock on hand, and make it either from soup meat ordered for the purpose or from bones or bits of leftover cooked meat such as chops or roast beef, lamb, veal or fowl. Do not use bones from pork or mutton, and do not use burned pieces, smoked or corned meats or lamb surrounded by fat. When you order meat, ask the butcher to give you any bones and trimmings and use them for stock.

If it is not convenient to use marrow bones, brown the meat in 3 tablespoons of fat instead of the marrow.

Scrape the marrow from
1 to 2 pounds cracked marrow bones
Remove the lean meat from
6 pounds beef shin *or* other soup meat
Cut in 1-inch cubes. Melt the marrow (or fat if used) in a large kettle and brown half the meat cubes in it. Add the remaining meat and the bones and
3 quarts cold water
Cover and bring slowly to the boiling point. Skim off the scum. Add
8 peppercorns
6 cloves
½ bay leaf
3 sprigs thyme *or* pinch of dried thyme
1 sprig marjoram *or* pinch of dried marjoram
2 sprigs parsley
¼ cup diced carrot
¼ cup diced turnip
¼ cup diced onion
¼ cup diced celery
1 tablespoon salt
Simmer 3 hours or more or cook in a pressure saucepan about 1 hour. Skim occasionally. Strain. Cool quickly to prevent souring. *Makes about 2½ quarts.*

To store. Cover and refrigerate. Do not remove the cake of fat which forms on the stock when it is cold. This excludes air and aids in preserving the stock until it is to be used.

To clear. When the stock is cold, run a knife around the edge of the bowl and carefully lift off the fat. The small quantity of fat which remains may be removed by passing a cloth wrung out of hot water around the edge and over the top of the stock. To remove the fat before the stock has cooled, take off as much as possible with a spoon and remove the rest by passing crumpled paper towels over the surface, or drop a few ice cubes into the stock and take them out when the fat has collected on them. To clarify fat for other uses, see page 9 (To render fats).

If you are using only part of the stock, remove the fat and put the quantity to be cleared in a pan. Taste. If further seasoning is needed, add it at this point, not after clearing. For each quart add 1 egg white, beaten slightly with a fork and mixed with 2 teaspoons cold water. Add the eggshell broken in small pieces. Bring to the boiling point, stirring constantly, and boil 2 minutes. Let stand 20 minutes over very low heat. Strain through a fine strainer, lined with a double thickness of cheesecloth.

WHITE (VEAL) STOCK

A good basis for cream soups and many sauces. For white stock made of chicken, see page 62.

Cut in small pieces

4-pound knuckle of veal *or* 3-pound knuckle and 1 pound lean beef

Put in a kettle. Add

3 quarts cold water
1 tablespoon salt
10 peppercorns
1 onion
2 stalks celery
Blade of mace
1 carrot, sliced
½ bay leaf
2 sprigs thyme *or* pinch of dried thyme
2 cloves

Bring slowly to the boiling point, skimming frequently. Reduce the heat, cover, and simmer 4 or 5 hours. Pour through a strainer lined with a double thickness of cheesecloth. Further clearing should not be necessary. *Makes about 2 quarts.*

CONSOMMÉ

True consommé owes its distinctive flavor to the combination of beef, veal and chicken. It is seldom made at home these days because it is expensive and time-consuming to prepare. Canned consommé or consommé made from cubes or flakes is quite acceptable if you make it somewhat stronger than the directions on the can or package suggest. Also, combine consommé and chicken broth or stock to make a tastier soup.

Heat consommé and season to taste with lemon juice, sherry, celery salt or onion salt.

Garnish each serving with a leaf of parsley, a thin slice of lemon, cooked macaroni cut in ¼-inch rings, a few strands of cooked and drained fine noodles or a special garnish like Royal Custard (p. 59) or Parmesan Puffs (p. 60).

Consommé with Cream. Add a little top milk or cream. Season well with Maggi's seasoning or sherry or sprinkle with chopped chives.

Consommé with Avocado. Put 2 or 3 cubes of avocado in each bouillon cup. Pour hot consommé over them and serve immediately.

Consommé with Herbs. Simmer consommé ½ hour with a sprig or two of thyme, marjoram, bay leaf, parsley, chervil or chives. Strain and reheat.

Consommé Julienne. Add (for 1 quart) 2 tablespoons each of cooked peas and string beans and ¼ cup each of cooked carrots and turnips or leeks, cut in matchlike strips.

Consommé mit Ei (with Eggs). Have eggs at room temperature. Heat consommé to the boiling point and pour into heated bowls. Break an egg into each bowl. Cover immediately so that the eggs will be slightly poached. Each person stirs the egg into his bowl of soup.

Consommé Princess. Add cooked green peas and diced cooked chicken to the consommé.

Iced Consommé. Heat consommé. Season to taste with lemon juice or sherry. Chill. Pour into bouillon cups and garnish with a sprig of parsley or a thin slice of lemon.

Jellied Consommé. Chill consommé in a shallow dish until firm, or chill undiluted canned consommé in its can. Break up lightly with a fork and serve in chilled soup cups. Garnish.

Consommé à la Barigoule. Add to the consommé diced cooked chicken and thin slices of stuffed olives and raw mushrooms.

Consommé du Barry. For each cup, add a bit of cooked cauliflower, a teaspoon of hot cooked rice and a sprinkling of shredded toasted almonds.

CHICKEN STOCK, BROTH *or* BOUILLON

Homemade chicken stock is particularly delicious, but it will often be more convenient to use canned stock or bouillon or chicken bouillon cubes. Save the broth when you cook chicken in water, adding seasoning such as celery tops to improve the flavor. For superior flavor and darker color, brown the pieces of chicken first in fat.

Use the leftover cooked chicken meat in any way you like, such as creamed or in salad or sandwiches.

Clean and wipe

4-pound fowl (cut as for fricassee)

Put all except the breast in a deep kettle. Add

6 cups cold water
1 carrot, sliced
2 stalks celery (with leaves)
1 onion, sliced
½ bay leaf
6 peppercorns
1 teaspoon salt

Heat slowly to the boiling point and add the breast. Cover and cook slowly until the breast meat is tender. Cool. Remove the fat. Bring to the boiling point, strain and season. *Makes 1 quart.*

PRESSURE-COOKER CHICKEN STOCK

Use all the bones and bits of meat from broilers, roast chicken or fricassee, scraping the plates and the platter. Put into the pressure cooker. Add a slice each of onion and carrot and a few celery tops. You may like to add more onion and, for a spicier flavor, a bay leaf, 2 whole cloves, 6 peppercorns and ½ teaspoon whole allspice.

Add any leftover broth or gravy. If necessary, add enough water to make at least 2 cups of liquid. Adjust the cover, bring up to pressure, then cook 20 to 30 minutes. Let the pressure drop normally.

Strain the broth and add salt to taste. If there is enough fat to show on the surface, cool the broth until you can spoon off most of the fat.

BLENDER CHICKEN SOUP

Put chicken stock or broth in an electric blender, with a few bits of leftover cooked chicken and well-browned chicken skin. Blend until perfectly smooth. Add more broth or top milk until as thin as you like it. Season carefully. Serve hot or chilled.

Vary the flavor by blending with the chicken 1 tablespoon blanched almonds, 1/4 cup sautéed chopped mushrooms or 1/2 cup cooked peas.

CHICKEN SOUP

Season homemade or canned chicken stock to taste. If convenient, add 1 tablespoon chopped cooked chicken to each 2 cups of soup. For color and flavor, add finely diced pimiento or green pepper, or minced parsley.

Vary by adding cream or a little boiled rice. Or add 2 tablespoons uncooked rice or tapioca to the soup and cook about 15 minutes.

CREAM OF CHICKEN SOUP

Heat chicken stock (canned or homemade). For each pint of stock, heat 1/2 cup of cream or evaporated milk. Add it slowly to the soup. Season to taste with salt and a trace of nutmeg. Sprinkle each serving with chopped parsley or a shake of paprika.

Potage à la Reine. Add a few slivers of cooked white meat of chicken to each serving.

Cream of Chicken with Rice. Heat the stock to the boiling point. Before adding the cream, add 1/4 cup cooked rice for each pint of stock.

MOCK TURTLE SOUP

Mock turtle soup is impractical to make at home since it requires a calf's head and makes enough for twelve or more. Use canned soup, but improve the flavor with lemon juice, tomato juice and Madeira or sherry.

QUICK CURRY SOUP

An easy but unusual dinner party soup.

Chop
- **1 tart apple**
- **1 small onion**

Add to
- **4 cups canned consommé**

Simmer 20 minutes. Strain. Add
- **1 cup cream**
- **Salt, pepper and curry powder to taste**

Serve hot or chilled. *Serves 6.*

BORTSCH

Traditionally made with beets, but also very good made entirely of cabbage.

Put in a kettle
- **1 quart Brown Stock (p. 60) *or* canned consommé *or* beef broth**
- **2 cups raw beets, peeled and chopped or shredded**
- **1 onion, chopped fine**
- **1 to 2 cups cabbage, shredded**

Simmer, tightly covered, until the vegetables are very tender. Add
- **1 tablespoon lemon juice *or* vinegar**

Add enough water to make 1 1/2

quarts. Taste and season further, if necessary. Serve hot or chilled. Stir in

½ cup sour cream

or put a spoonful in each bowl. *Makes 4 to 6 big bowlfuls.*

QUICK BORTSCH

Season sieved canned beets (or prepared baby food) with onion juice, lemon juice, and a trace of sugar. Dilute as you like with canned consommé. Serve hot or chilled, with a spoonful of sour cream in each bowl.

CREOLE SOUP

As a garnish, cut strips of cooked macaroni to make tiny rings.

Melt in a saucepan

2 tablespoons bacon fat

Add

1 tablespoon chopped green pepper
1 tablespoon chopped onion

Cook 5 minutes. Stir in

2 tablespoons flour

Add

1 cup tomatoes
3 cups canned consommé *or* Brown Stock (p. 60)

Simmer 15 minutes. Strain. Season highly with

Salt, pepper, cayenne

Add enough water to make 4 cups. Just before serving, add

1 tablespoon grated horseradish
½ teaspoon vinegar

(If you use bottled horseradish, omit the vinegar.) *Serves 8.*

CREAM SOUPS

A cream soup may be thickened or not, as you like. If it is to be served as a first course, a more delicate soup is usually preferred, but if it is to be the main dish, a thicker soup is welcome. Do not make it too thick—it will be thicker as it begins to cool.

To bind (thicken) soups. *Potato flour is excellent for this as it cooks quickly and smoothly.* For each 2 cups of soup, melt 1 tablespoon butter and stir in 1 tablespoon flour or 1 teaspoon potato flour. Cook slowly until smooth, stirring constantly (about 5 minutes). Add a little of the hot soup, stir well and pour into the rest of the soup. Reheat, stirring constantly.

CREAM OF VEGETABLE SOUP

For any leftover vegetables or a combination of several. There are special recipes for many vegetable soups. Chopped parsley, chives or hard-cooked egg, or crisp croutons, add color and zest.

Put in a double boiler

½ cup cooked vegetable, mashed or chopped
1½ cups milk
1 slice onion

Heat 20 minutes. Rub through a sieve or food mill. Reheat. If desired, add

1 or 2 bouillon cubes

Bind (above) if you like a smoother, thicker soup. Season to taste with

Salt and pepper
Paprika *or* any herb seasoning

Serves 2 or 3.

Cream of Cauliflower Soup. Use cooked cauliflower. Keep out a few flowerets to add whole. Use part chicken stock and part milk.

Cream of Potato Soup. Scald 2 cups of milk with 1 slice onion. Add 1 cup mashed potato. Mix with a whisk or blending fork. Strain if you like, and pour into hot bowls. Put a dab of butter on each and sprinkle with chopped parsley, chives, or paprika.

Cream of Spinach Soup. Use cooked spinach. Use chicken stock in place of half the milk or add a chicken bouillon cube. Add a trace of nutmeg.

CREAM OF ALMOND SOUP

A delicate dinner party soup to serve either hot or chilled.

Chop very fine in a nut chopper or an electric blender

⅓ cup blanched almonds
3 bitter almonds (if available)

As you chop, add slowly

2 tablespoons cold water

Add to

2 cups Chicken Stock (p. 62) *or* canned chicken broth
1 slice onion
1 stalk celery, cut fine

Simmer 30 minutes. Rub through a sieve. Add more stock or water if it is needed to make 2 cups. When ready to serve, heat

2 cups top milk *or* milk and cream

Stir it into the hot soup. Do not boil. Season to taste with

Salt, pepper and mace

Serves 8.

CREAM OF ARTICHOKE SOUP

A party soup with an unusual flavor.

Bring to a boil

4 cups water

Add and cook until soft

6 Jerusalem artichokes

Rub through a sieve, without draining. Melt

2 tablespoons butter

Stir in

2 tablespoons flour
1 teaspoon salt
Few grains cayenne
Few gratings of nutmeg

Add the hot sieved artichoke and cooking water slowly, and cook 1 minute. Stir in

1 cup scalded cream
2 tablespoons sauterne
1 egg, slightly beaten

Pare and cut in cubes

2 cucumbers

Sauté in

Butter

Add to the soup. *Serves 8.*

CREAM OF ASPARAGUS SOUP

Cook

1 bunch asparagus (1 pound) *or* 1 package frozen asparagus

Drain, reserving the cooking water. Cut off the tips to add later. To the asparagus water, add the stalks and

1 thin slice onion
1½ cups chicken stock *or* water

Boil 5 minutes, and rub through a sieve or pureé in an electric blender. Melt

2 tablespoons butter

Blend in

2 tablespoons flour

Add the strained soup. Cook and stir 5 minutes. Measure and add

Scalded milk *or* cream (to make 3 cups in all)
Salt and pepper to taste

Put the asparagus tips in the soup plates and pour the soup over them. *Serves 6.*

CREAM OF CELERY SOUP

Cook together until the vegetables are soft

1 cup chopped celery, stalks and leaves
1 slice onion (or more)
2 cups chicken broth *or* water

Rub through a sieve, without draining, or whirl in an electric blender. Add

1½ cups top milk *or* cream
Salt and pepper to taste

Heat slowly. Bind (p. 64) if you

prefer a thicker, smoother soup. *Serves 4 to 6.*

CHEESE AND CELERY SOUP

Cook together 5 minutes

1 tablespoon butter
1 *or* 2 tablespoons chopped onion

Add

1 can celery soup
Milk (an equal amount)
1 small package pimiento cream cheese

Cook and stir until the cheese melts. *Serves 4 to 6.*

CHEESE SOUP

Melt in a large saucepan

1 tablespoon butter

Add

1 tablespoon chopped onion

Cook slowly until the onion is yellow. Stir in

1 tablespoon flour

Add slowly, stirring constantly

1 cup Brown Stock (p. 60) *or* canned consommé
2 cups milk

Bring to the boiling point. Strain. Add

¾ cup grated cheese

Stir until the cheese melts. Serve sprinkled with paprika, bits of canned pimiento or croutons. *Serves 4 to 6.*

To vary, add 2 tablespoons each of chopped cooked carrot and chopped cooked celery. Sprinkle with chopped parsley.

CREAM OF CHESTNUT SOUP

Bring to the boiling point

1 quart Chicken Stock (p. 62) *or* canned chicken broth

Add and simmer until soft

1 cup shelled chestnuts (p. 13)

Rub through a sieve or whirl in an electric blender. Add

1½ cups cream *or* top milk, heated
½ teaspoon salt
⅛ teaspoon paprika

Serves 8.

CREAM OF CORN SOUP

If you have an electric blender, use no flour. Put all the ingredients in the blender, whirl, heat, and season.

Combine and cook over very low heat or in a double boiler

1 cup cooked or canned corn (cream-style)
1 cup boiling water
1 cup milk
1 small slice onion

Bind (p. 64) with

1 tablespoon butter
1 tablespoon flour

Season to taste with

Salt and pepper

Serves 4 to 6.

Curried Corn Soup. Season delicately with curry powder.

CREAM OF CUCUMBER SOUP

An unusual dinner party soup.

Peel, slice and seed

3 large cucumbers

Cook 10 minutes in

2 tablespoons butter

Stir in

3 tablespoons flour

Add gradually

2 cups Chicken Stock (p. 62) *or* canned chicken broth

Scald together

1 cup milk
1 slice onion
Few grains mace *or* nutmeg

Combine the mixtures. Rub through a sieve or whirl in an electric blender. Reheat to the boiling point. Stir in

½ cup cream
2 egg yolks, slightly beaten

Season to taste with

Salt and pepper

Serves 8.

Chilled Cucumber Soup. Omit the egg yolks. Chill before adding the cream. Season with a few drops of Angostura bitters.

MUSHROOM BOUILLON

You may like to add ½ teaspoon caraway seeds and a tiny sprig of marjoram.

Simmer together 1 hour
- **½ pound mushrooms, chopped**
- **4 cups consommé *or* water**
- **½ teaspoon grated onion**
- **Salt to taste**

Let stand several hours or overnight. Strain. Serve hot or chilled. *Serves 6.*

To vary, put a spoonful of chopped or finely cut raw mushrooms in each cup, add a teaspoon of sherry, and fill with hot or cold soup.

CREAM OF MUSHROOM SOUP

Put ½ teaspoon sherry in each serving, if you like.

Melt in a deep pan
- **3 tablespoons butter**

Add
- **1 tablespoon chopped onion**
- **¼ pound mushrooms, chopped fine, *or* stems from ½ pound mushrooms, chopped fine**

Cook slowly 15 minutes. Stir in
- **1 tablespoon flour**

Add slowly
- **2 cups Chicken Stock (p. 62) *or* canned chicken broth *or* milk *or* water**

Bring to the boiling point. Cook slowly 2 minutes on an asbestos mat or in a double boiler. Strain the soup if you like, but it is delicious with bits of mushroom and onion in it. Season to taste with
- **Salt and pepper**
- **Lemon juice *or* grated nutmeg**

Just before serving add
- **½ cup cream *or* top milk**

Heat but do not boil. *Serves 4 to 6.*

For a richer soup, prepare the mushrooms with stock as above, then add ½ cup boiling water and 2 tablespoons quick-cooking tapioca. Cook until the tapioca is clear. Season. Just before serving, stir in 1 cup heavy cream and 2 egg yolks, slightly beaten. *Serves 8.*

For the easiest soup, blend chopped mushrooms and top milk in an electric blender, add more milk, heat and season. Put in a chicken bouillon cube, if you like.

CREAM OF ONION SOUP

Cook together for 10 minutes, stirring constantly
- **2 large mild onions, sliced thin**
- **4 tablespoons butter**

Add
- **4 cups Chicken Stock (p. 62) *or* canned chicken broth**

Cook slowly 30 minutes. Strain or not, as you prefer. Add
- **1 cup top milk *or* milk and cream**

Heat. Just before serving, add
- **1 tablespoon chopped green pepper *or* ¼ cup grated cheese**

Season to taste. *Serves 6 to 8.*

FRENCH ONION SOUP

Melt in a large pan
- **1 tablespoon butter**

Add and cook slowly until soft
- **¾ cup sliced onions (or more)**

Add
- **½ teaspoon sugar**
- **1 tablespoon flour**

Stir and cook 1 minute. Add
- **4 cups water *or* consommé**

Season to taste with
- **Salt and pepper**

Simmer at least 30 minutes. Add more water, if needed, to make 4 cups. (Let mellow a day to develop the finest flavor.) To serve, toast

4 thick slices French bread *or* rounds cut from sliced bread

Put a slice in each bowl. Pour the soup over the toast, and sprinkle with

Grated Italian cheese

Set the bowls in a 400° oven to melt and brown the cheese. Pass extra cheese to sprinkle over the soup. *Serves 4.*

Parker House Onion Soup. Use large mild onions and Chicken Stock (p. 62) or canned chicken broth. Just before serving, add a tablespoon of heavy cream for each bowlful.

CREAM OF PEA SOUP

If the peas are very young and tender, cook a few pods with them.

Cook together for 5 minutes

2 tablespoons butter
1 tablespoon chopped onion

Add

2 cups fresh or frozen peas
½ teaspoon salt
1 teaspoon sugar
2 cups water

Cook until the peas are soft (about 20 minutes). Put through a sieve or whirl in an electric blender. Add

1 cup top milk *or* milk and cream

Heat slowly. Season to taste with

Garlic salt *or* mace
Pepper

Sprinkle with

Chopped parsley

Serves 6.

Quick Pea Soup. Use cooked or canned peas the same way, but cooking will not be necessary after the onion is cooked.

Potage Longchamps. Reheat with a few sprigs of fresh mint. Remove the mint before serving.

Potage St. Germain. Add and cook with the peas 2 leaves of lettuce and 1 small carrot, sliced thin. Use chicken stock in place of water and use cream in place of top milk. Sprinkle with croutons.

PEA SOUP LOUISE

An elegant but easy-to-do dinner party soup.

Simmer together for ½ hour

1 can undiluted cream of pea soup
½ cup water
1 chicken bouillon cube
⅛ teaspoon mace
¼ teaspoon dried tarragon

When ready to serve, add

½ cup cream
½ cup dry white wine *or* champagne

Heat. Garnish with

Sprigs of fresh mint *or* tarragon

Serves 4.

BOULA

Combine, adding water according to the directions on the cans

1 can pea soup
1 can green turtle soup

Bring to the boiling point. Season to taste with

Salt and pepper
Sherry

Fill individual pottery bowls arranged on a cooky sheet. Whip

½ cup heavy cream
Few grains salt

Put a spoonful on each bowl. Set in the broiler a moment to brown the cream. Serve immediately. *Serves 4 to 6.*

Boula with Cheese. Sprinkle the whipped cream with grated Parmesan cheese before browning.

TOMATO SOUP

Use Garden Special (p. 554), Savory Tomato Juice (p. 553) or canned tomatoes as a basis for soup. Dilute with water or stock and add seasonings, such as a bit of bay leaf, a sprig of thyme and a few whole cloves. Simmer ½ hour. Strain or not, as you prefer.

Tomato Soup Portugaise. Put in each dish a tablespoon of cooked rice and a bit of tomato, peeled and sautéed in butter.

Thick Tomato Soup. For 1 pint of soup, cook 2 tablespoons butter until brown, add 2 tablespoons flour, and cook 5 minutes. Stir into the soup. Bring to the boiling point and strain.

TOMATO BOUILLON

Combine tomato juice with an equal amount of chicken stock or bouillon. Season with a little lemon juice, salt and a few grains of sugar. If you like a sharper flavor, heat with a bit of bay leaf or basil, chopped onion, one or two cloves, a few celery seeds, and peppercorns. Strain.

Heat. Float on each cup of bouillon a little chopped parsley or chives, a thin slice of lemon or orange or a spoonful of salted whipped cream.

TOMATO MADRILÈNE

Canned tomato madrilène is an excellent reserve item for summer. Keep a can or two in the refrigerator. If you make this soup with plain tomato juice, add extra seasoning.

Put in a saucepan
- **½ cup cold water**
- **1 tablespoon gelatine**

Let stand 5 minutes. Add
- **1 cup tomato bouillon *or* tomato juice cocktail**

Stir over moderate heat until the gelatine dissolves. Add
- **1 cup tomato bouillon *or* tomato juice cocktail**

Chill until slightly firm. Break up with a fork and pile in bouillon cups. Top with chopped chives or dill or a bit of caviar. *Serves 4.*

CREAM OF TOMATO SOUP

If you use canned tomato soup, follow the directions on the label but vary the soup by changing the seasoning. Add a bit of oregano or curry powder or a few gratings of nutmeg or a bouillon cube. To keep the soup smooth, add cold milk to the cold soup and heat slowly. Season to taste with salt, pepper and a trace of sugar. Crisp buttery croutons add the perfect touch.

Cream of Tomato and Corn. Add ¼ cup chopped canned corn for each cup of tomato soup.

TOMATO BISQUE

This old-fashioned cream of tomato soup was called a bisque because it resembled lobster or crab bisque in color.

Cut in pieces and put in a pan
- **2 cups tomatoes (drain canned tomatoes if used)**

Add
- **2 teaspoons sugar**

Cook 15 minutes. Rub through a sieve. Heat
- **4 cups top milk *or* milk and cream**
- **½ cup dry bread crumbs**
- **½ onion, stuck with 6 cloves**
- **Sprig of parsley**
- **Bit of bay leaf**

Remove the seasoning and rub the thickened milk through a

sieve. When ready to serve, combine the mixtures and heat to the boiling point. Season with

Salt and pepper

Stir in, bit by bit

⅓ cup butter

Serves 6 to 8.

CREAM OF WATERCRESS SOUP

Simmer together for 10 minutes

2 bunches watercress, cut fine
4 cups Chicken Stock (p. 62) *or* canned chicken broth

Strain to remove bits of stem and leaves. Melt

4 tablespoons butter

Stir in

2 tablespoons flour

Cook slowly 5 minutes. Add a little of the hot soup and stir until smooth. Add to the rest of the soup and bring to the boiling point, stirring constantly. Add

1 cup cream
Salt and pepper to taste

Color delicately with

Green vegetable coloring

Serves 6 to 8.

BAKED BEAN SOUP

The traditional garnishes for this soup are slices of hard-cooked egg and lemon.

Put in a deep pan

1 cup baked beans
1 slice onion
1 stalk celery
2 cups water

Simmer 30 minutes. Add

¾ cup stewed or canned tomatoes

Rub through a sieve or put through a food mill. Add

Water, consommé *or* Brown Stock (p. 60), to make 3 cups

Season to taste with

Chili sauce
Salt and pepper

Serves 4.

BLACK BEAN SOUP

To save time, use canned black bean soup, but season it critically and garnish as suggested below.

Put in a large kettle

2 cups dried black beans
2 quarts cold water

Bring to the boiling point, simmer 10 minutes, cover and set aside 1 hour. Add

1 small onion, sliced
2 stalks celery, chopped, *or* ¼ teaspoon celery salt
1 hambone (optional) *or* bits of leftover ham

Simmer until the beans are soft (3 to 4 hours). Add more water if needed, to make about 1½ quarts. Remove the bone. Rub the soup through a very fine sieve or blend in an electric blender. Add

2 teaspoons salt
½ teaspoon pepper
¼ teaspoon dry mustard
Few grains cayenne
Sherry, to taste, if liked

Garnish with

2 hard-cooked eggs, sliced thin
1 lemon, sliced thin

Serves 8 generously.

Black Bean Soup Guatemala Style. In place of egg and lemon, garnish with bits of alligator pear.

CORN CHOWDER

Use 3 tablespoons butter in place of salt pork, if it is more convenient.

Dice and put in a deep pan

1½-inch cube salt pork

Cook slowly until the fat is melted and the pork bits are crisp and brown. Add

1 small onion, sliced

Cook slowly 5 minutes, stirring often. Add

4 potatoes, cubed or sliced
2 cups water

Cook until the potatoes are tender. Add

2 cups cream-style corn
4 cups milk
Heat. Add
3 tablespoons butter
Salt and pepper to taste
Serves 6 to 8 generously.

VIENNA PEA SOUP

A satisfying lunch or supper dish.

Put in a pan
1 tablespoon butter
1 Vienna sausage *or* frankfurter, sliced
1 small onion, diced
Cook slowly 10 minutes. Add
1 can condensed split pea soup
1 can milk (using soup can as measure)
Heat thoroughly. *Serves 2 or 3.*

SPLIT PEA SOUP

Read the directions on the package of split peas to see if previous soaking is required.

Bring to the boil in a large kettle
1 quart water
Add
1 cup dried split peas (2 cups for a very thick soup)
Cover, remove from the heat and let stand 1 hour. Add
2-inch cube fat salt pork *or* a hambone
1 onion, sliced (or more)
For extra savor, add
½ cup chopped celery
¼ cup chopped parsley
Pinch of herbs such as thyme *or* rosemary
1 bay leaf
Simmer until the peas are soft (1 or 2 hours). Remove the pork or the bone. Rub the soup through a sieve or crush the peas with a blending fork. Dilute to the thickness you like with
Milk
Season to taste
Salt and pepper
As an attractive garnish, put on each cup
A few crisp croutons
A few cooked fresh green peas
As a thick soup, serves 4 or 5. Diluted further, it can serve 8 to 10 as a first course.

Jules' Split Pea Soup. Make the soup thick. After rubbing through sieve, add cooked carrot slivers and sliced frankfurters or Vienna sausage. Serve with rye bread as a hearty supper dish.

Lentil or Lima Bean Soup. Prepare like Split Pea Soup (above). Dried lentils will cook tender in a shorter time.

PARSNIP STEW

An old-fashioned lunch for a winter day.

Put in a kettle
1-inch cube salt pork, diced
Fry slowly until the fat melts and the scraps are crisp. Add
2 medium-sized parsnips, pared and diced
2 medium-sized potatoes, pared and diced
1 cup water
Cook until the vegetables are tender. Add
2 cups milk
Cook together
1 tablespoon butter
1 tablespoon flour
Thicken the soup with this mixture. Season to taste with
Salt and pepper
Serves 4 to 6.

PEANUT BUTTER SOUP

Sprinkle with chopped salted peanuts, if you like.

Put in a pan
1 tablespoon butter
3 tablespoons peanut butter
1 teaspoon minced onion
Cook 5 minutes. Add
2 tablespoons flour
Stir until smooth. Add slowly
3 cups milk, *or* milk and Chicken Stock (p. 62) *or* canned chicken broth

Cook 20 minutes in a double boiler. Season to taste with

Salt and pepper

Serves 6.

POTATO SOUP

For each bowl of soup, pare and dice 1 medium-sized potato. Add a slice of onion (or more) and cover with boiling water. Add salt, cover tightly, and cook slowly until the potatoes are very soft (about 15 minutes). Crush the potatoes with a fork without draining them. Add hot milk to make the soup as thin as you like it. Season to taste with salt, pepper, celery salt and cayenne.

LEEK AND POTATO SOUP

Put in a pan

1 bunch leeks, sliced very fine
3 stalks celery, sliced very fine
3 tablespoons butter

Cook 10 minutes, stirring constantly. Add

1 cup water

Cover. Cook 10 minutes. Add

2½ cups potatoes, diced
Water, to cover

Cover and cook 10 minutes longer. Add

3 cups milk

Simmer until the potatoes are tender. Season to taste with

Salt, pepper and cayenne

Strain, or serve for lunch as a chowder. *Serves 6.*

VICHYSSOISE

Purists demand unsalted butter for this soup. For perfectly blended flavor, prepare Vichyssoise the day before serving it. If you have some left over, eke it out with more top milk or chicken stock and season to taste.

Melt (preferably in an enamelware or glass saucepan)

4 tablespoons butter

Add, cut fine

4 leeks (white part only)
1 onion

Cook very slowly until the vegetables are tender but not brown. Add

4 cups Chicken Stock (p. 62) *or* canned chicken broth
2 sprigs parsley
2 small stalks celery
2 potatoes, sliced thin
Salt and pepper to taste
Few grains nutmeg *or* curry powder
Few drops Worcestershire

Cook until the potatoes are tender. Put through a very fine sieve or mix in an electric blender. Add more stock if necessary to make 2 cups. Just before serving, stir in

1 cup heavy cream

Serve hot, or chill in the refrigerator and serve icy cold. Sprinkle with

Finely chopped chives, dill *or* parsley

Serves 8.

Quick Vichyssoise. Use canned Vichyssoise, but season it critically as suggested above and add some heavy cream.

VEGETABLE SOUP

Add other vegetables as convenient—shredded cabbage, tomatoes, green beans or corn. For a heartier dish, serve grated cheese to sprinkle on the soup or add alphabet noodles.

Put in a deep pan

4 tablespoons butter
½ cup diced carrot
½ cup diced turnip
½ cup diced celery
½ onion, sliced thin

Cook 10 minutes, stirring constantly. Add

½ cup diced potatoes

Cover. Cook 2 minutes. Add

1 quart water, consommé *or* Brown Stock (p. 60)

Cook slowly 1 hour or until the vegetables are tender. Add more water, if needed, to make 1 quart. Season with

Salt and pepper

Add

1 tablespoon butter
1 tablespoon chopped parsley

Serves 6 to 8.

Pressure-cooked Vegetable Soup. Sauté the vegetables 5 minutes in the pressure saucepan. Add 2 cups water and cook at 15 pounds pressure for 3 minutes. Let the pressure drop normally. Add 1 cup stock or water and bouillon cubes or meat concentrate to taste. Add salt and pepper and parsley.

Petite Marmite. This hearty soup should be as thick as a chowder. Make Vegetable Soup (p. 72), using stock. Omit the potatoes. Add plenty of other vegetables, such as shredded cabbage and green beans. Serve in pottery bowls with a sprinkling of grated cheese on top.

GAZPACHO

An interesting Spanish soup. Refreshing for lunch with cottage cheese and whole-wheat wafers. Pleasant as the first course for a summer dinner.

Crush together

1 clove garlic, split
½ teaspoon salt

Add

2 tablespoons olive oil
5 ripe tomatoes, cut in pieces
1 chopped onion
¼ teaspoon pepper
¼ teaspoon paprika
1½ tablespoons vinegar
1½ cups cold water *or* bouillon

Let stand 1 hour. Put through a food mill or crush through a coarse strainer. Taste and add more salt if necessary. Stir in

¼ cup dry bread crumbs

Divide in 4 soup bowls or 6 bouillon cups. Put an ice cube in each. Pass (to sprinkle on the soup)

Croutons
Chopped cucumber
Chopped green pepper

Serves 4 to 6.

MINESTRONE

A treasure from the Italian cuisine. A satisfying main dish served with a green salad and crusty French or Italian bread.

Put in a large pan

1 cup dried white beans
1 quart water

Bring to the boiling point and boil 2 minutes. Cover, remove from the heat, and let stand 1 hour to soften the beans. Simmer until the beans are tender. Do not drain. Put in a soup kettle

2-inch cube salt pork, diced
1 onion, chopped fine
1 tablespoon minced parsley
½ clove garlic (or more)

Cook and stir 10 minutes. Stir in

1 can tomato paste
2 cups boiling water *or* consommé

Simmer 15 minutes. Add

1 cup coarsely chopped cabbage

Cook 10 minutes longer. Add the beans with their cooking water and stir gently to blend. Bring to the boiling point. Add

1 cup elbow macaroni

Cook until it is just tender (7 to 10 minutes). Season to taste with

Salt and pepper

Add more water or stock if needed to make about 1½ quarts. The soup should be very thick. Heat. Sprinkle each serving generously with

Grated Romano *or* Parmesan cheese

Serves 6 to 8 generously.

To vary, use almost any combination of vegetables, such as tomatoes, celery, carrots, onions, turnips, cabbage, peas, green peppers, potatoes, zucchini, summer squash and leeks. Add a little finely chopped ham to each serving, if convenient.

AMERICAN MINESTRONE

Use any of the vegetables suggested for Minestrone (p. 73).

Put in a large kettle

2 tablespoons olive oil *or* butter

Add

1½ cups thinly sliced vegetables

Sauté slowly 15 minutes. Add

1 quart boiling water *or* water and consommé
1 sprig parsley
½ bay leaf
Bit of thyme
Salt and pepper to taste
½ cup elbow macaroni *or* spaghetti

Boil 5 minutes, then reduce the heat and simmer 30 minutes. Sprinkle each serving generously with

Grated Parmesan *or* Romano cheese

Serves 3 or 4.

To make with frozen vegetables. Use 1 cup sliced celery, 1 chopped onion, and 1 package of frozen mixed vegetables. Increase the water to 6 cups and add 4 bouillon cubes.

CHICKEN GUMBO

For a heartier soup, add canned corn or cooked rice or both.

Put in a saucepan

4 tablespoons butter
1 onion, finely chopped

Cook and stir 5 minutes. Add

1 quart Chicken Stock (p. 62) *or* canned chicken broth
½ green pepper, chopped fine
1 cup cooked or canned okra
2 teaspoons salt
¼ teaspoon pepper
1 to 2 cups canned tomatoes

Bring to the boiling point and simmer 40 minutes. *Serves 6 to 8.*

MULLIGATAWNY SOUP

Serve fluffy boiled rice to spoon into the soup.

Put in a deep pan

4 tablespoons butter *or* other fat
¼ cup diced onion
¼ cup diced carrot
¼ cup diced celery
1 pepper, chopped fine
1 apple, sliced
1 cup diced raw chicken

Cook slowly until brown. Stir in

⅓ cup flour

Add

1 teaspoon curry powder
½ teaspoon nutmeg *or* mace
2 cloves
1 sprig parsley
Salt and pepper
1 cup tomatoes, canned or chopped
5 cups canned chicken broth *or* Chicken Stock (p. 62)

Simmer 1 hour. Strain, reserving the liquid. Pick out the bits of chicken and set aside. Rub the vegetables through a sieve. Add the puréed vegetables and the chicken to the soup, and season to taste. *Serves 6 to 8.*

QUEEN VICTORIA SOUP

A modern adaptation of a rich and famous English recipe. Hearty enough for the main dish at lunch or supper.

Put in a deep pan

1 tablespoon butter
1 teaspoon finely chopped onion

Cook slowly until the onion is yellow. Add

½ cup finely cut mushrooms
1 cup diced celery

Cook 10 minutes. Add

4 cups Chicken Stock (p. 62) *or* canned chicken broth
1 tablespoon quick tapioca

½ cup diced cooked chicken
½ cup diced cooked ham
Sage, nutmeg and onion salt to taste

Cook 20 minutes. Add

2 hard-cooked eggs, chopped fine
1 or 2 cups cream

Heat. Serve in large bowls. Garnish with

Chopped parsley

Serves 7 or 8.

To simplify. Use a can of mushroom soup in place of the fresh mushrooms and cream, and canned luncheon meat in place of ham. Not the same, but very good and a thought for the emergency shelf.

PHILADELPHIA PEPPER POT

Serve as the main dish for supper.

Put in a deep pan

3 tablespoons butter
¼ cup chopped onion
¼ cup chopped celery
½ cup chopped green pepper
1½ cups potato cubes

Cook slowly 15 minutes. Stir in

3 tablespoons flour

Stir and cook 5 minutes. Add

5 cups Chicken Stock (p. 62) *or* canned chicken broth
½ pound cooked honeycomb tripe, cut in ½-inch squares
½ teaspoon freshly ground pepper
2 teaspoons salt

Cover. Cook slowly 1 hour. Just before serving, add

½ cup heavy cream
1 tablespoon butter

Serves 6 to 8 as a main dish.

SCOTCH BROTH

Use rice in place of barley, if you prefer, adding it ½ hour before the soup is to be served.

Discard the fat and cut the lean meat in 1-inch cubes from

3 pounds lamb or mutton (bony cuts such as neck, flank or breast)

Put the meat and bones in a deep kettle. Cover with

Cold water

Bring quickly to the boiling point. Add

½ cup barley

(Soak old-fashioned barley 12 hours and drain.) Simmer 1½ hours or until the meat is tender. Remove the bones. Cool the soup and skim off the fat. Put in a pan

2 tablespoons butter
¼ cup each of finely cut carrot, celery, turnip and onion

Cook 5 minutes. Add to the soup. Season with

Salt and pepper to taste

Cook until the vegetables are soft. Just before serving, add

Chopped parsley

Add more water if the soup is too thick.
Serves 8 or more.

OXTAIL SOUP

A tablespoon of Madeira enhances the flavor of this good soup.

Have the butcher cut in 2-inch lengths

1½ pounds oxtail

Sprinkle with

Flour
Salt and pepper

Melt in a deep kettle

3 tablespoons fat

Add the oxtail. Cook 10 minutes, turning to brown on all sides. Add

2 quarts Brown Stock (p. 60), consommé *or* water

Simmer until the meat falls away from the bones (2 or 3 hours). Remove the bones. Add

½ cup each of diced carrots, turnip, onion and celery

Simmer until the vegetables are soft. Add

1 teaspoon lemon juice
1 teaspoon Worcestershire

Add enough water to make about 1½ quarts. *Serves 8.*

CLAM BROTH

Season homemade or canned clam broth to taste. Serve hot or chilled. Garnish each cup with chopped parsley or a spoonful of salted whipped cream or Pimiento Cream (p. 59).

To prepare broth. Wash clams in the shell, scrubbing them with a brush and changing the water several times. Put them in a kettle. Add ½ cup water for each quart of clams. Cover tightly and steam until the shells open wide (about 30 minutes). Let stand 15 minutes so that the sediment will settle. Strain carefully. Chop the cooked clams fine, season, and use as a canapé spread.

Clam and Tomato Broth. Combine clam broth and tomato bouillon or tomato juice. Season with celery salt. Serve hot or chilled.

Clam and Chicken Frappé. Mix 1⅔ cups clam broth and 2½ cups chicken stock or bouillon. Season highly. Freeze to a mush in an ice-cube tray. Stir with a fork. Serve in bouillon cups or small glass bowls as the first course at a summer luncheon or dinner. Garnish each serving with a dab of salted whipped cream.

CREAM OF CLAM SOUP

Heat
1 cup minced canned clams
Add to
2 cups scalded top milk
Season to taste. Top each serving with
Salted whipped cream
Paprika
Sprig of parsley
Serves 3 or 4.

MANHATTAN CLAM BISQUE

For each cup of clam broth, canned or homemade (above), brown 1 tablespoon butter, stir in 1 tablespoon flour, and brown well. Add the broth slowly and simmer 20 minutes. Add ¼ cup cream.

CLAM AND TOMATO BISQUE

Heat together
1 cup clam broth, canned or homemade (above)
1 cup canned tomato soup
1 cup top milk *or* cream
Do not boil. For added flavor, heat with the soup
Few grains mace *or* nutmeg
1 stalk celery
1 sprig parsley
Bit of bay leaf
Slice of onion
Strain, reheat and season to taste. *Serves 4 to 6.*

AMSTERDAM OYSTER SOUP

Put in a saucepan
1 pint oysters, cleaned (p. 153) and chopped
1 cup water
Simmer 20 minutes. Strain. Add enough water to make 1 pint. Melt
1 tablespoon butter
Cook until brown. Add
1 tablespoon flour
Stir until brown. Add the oyster liquor gradually, stirring constantly. Simmer ½ hour. Season with
Salt, paprika and celery salt
Just before serving, add
½ cup cream
Serves 4.

CHICKEN AND OYSTER CONSOMMÉ

Clean (p. 153)

1 pint oysters

Reserve the soft part of 12. Chop the rest and add to them

1 cup water

Simmer 25 minutes. Strain out the oysters and discard. Add to the liquid

3 cups Chicken Stock (p. 62) *or* canned chicken broth
Few grains cayenne
1 teaspoon salt

Remove from the heat. Just before serving, heat the reserved oysters in a shallow pan until plump. Heat the soup, add the oysters and

½ cup cream

Serves 6.

SHRIMP BISQUE

Put in a deep pan

3 tablespoons butter
2 tablespoons chopped celery
4 tablespoons chopped mushrooms
2 slices each of onion and carrot
Bit of bay leaf
Sprig of marjoram
Few grains mace *or* nutmeg
½ teaspoon peppercorns
½ teaspoon salt

Cook slowly 5 minutes. Add

1 tablespoon lemon juice
2 cups Chicken Stock (p. 62) *or* canned chicken broth

Simmer 15 minutes. Strain. Add

1 cup cooked or canned shrimp, cut small

Cook 5 minutes. Just before serving, add

1 cup heavy cream *or* top milk
Dry sherry *or* white wine to taste, if desired

Serves 6 to 8.

Nymph Aurore. Before adding the cream, strain the soup or put in an electric blender. Add half the cream. Color the soup pale green with food coloring. Whip the rest of the cream and put a spoonful on each serving.

QUICK CRAB *or* SHRIMP BISQUE

Mix

1 can pea soup
½ can tomato soup
2 cups milk *or* Chicken Stock (p. 62) *or* canned chicken broth
½ to 1 cup flaked crab meat *or* shrimp broken in pieces

Heat. Season to taste with

Rum, sherry *or* Worcestershire

Serves 4.

To vary, use a whole can of tomato soup and 1 cup cream in place of the milk or stock.

CHILLED MUSHROOM AND SHRIMP BISQUE

Mix

1 can cream of mushroom soup
2 cups milk
1 small can shrimp, cut small

Season to taste. Add (if you like)

Sherry

Chill. Top each serving with

Chopped chives

Serves 4 to 6.

LOBSTER BISQUE

Put in a pan

2 tablespoons butter
1 teaspoon chopped onion
1 sprig parsley

Cook slowly until the onion is yellow. Add

1½ cups finely chopped lobster meat (fresh-cooked, canned or frozen)

Cook and stir 5 minutes. Stir in

2 tablespoons flour
1 tablespoon tomato paste (for color, but omit it if you wish)

Add

2 cups Chicken Stock (p. 62) *or* canned chicken broth

Simmer 20 minutes. Remove the parsley. Add

2 cups thin cream *or* top milk

Heat but do not boil. Season with

Salt and cayenne to taste
Serves 6.

Crab Bisque. Substitute crab meat for lobster.

LOBSTER BISQUE DE LUXE

The classic version—more complicated than the preceding one and a superb creation. Order the lobster split at the market if you can cook it promptly.

Put in a deep kettle
2 cups Brown Stock (p. 60), canned consommé *or* water
¼ cup rice
Cook until the rice is very soft. Do not drain. In another pan, put
2 tablespoons butter *or* olive oil
1 carrot, sliced
1 onion, sliced
Cook slowly 5 minutes. Add
Bit of bay leaf
Sprig of thyme *or* ½ teaspoon dried thyme
1½-pound fresh lobster or 2 smaller ones, split (p. 150, Broiled Live Lobsters)
Cover and cook until the lobster shells are red. Add
1 teaspoon salt
¼ teaspoon pepper
1 cup dry white wine *or* ½ cup sherry
Cook slowly 15 minutes. Add
2 cups Chicken Stock (p. 62) *or* canned chicken broth
Remove the lobster. Strain the broth. Take the lobster meat out of the shells and set aside. Break up the shells and scrape out of them as much of the bits of meat as possible. Set aside. Put the shells and the strained hot broth in a pan, cover and simmer 1 hour (or cook 10 minutes in a pressure pan). Strain and add to the rice. Add the lobster meat, cut small, and
2 cups Chicken Stock (p. 62) *or* canned chicken broth
Put in a small pan
1 tablespoon butter *or* olive oil
1 tablespoon tomato paste
Lobster liver (and coral, if any)
Stir over low heat until smooth. Add slowly to the soup. Heat just before serving, and add
1 cup cream
Season. Sprinkle with
Croutons *or* chopped parsley
Serves 8 to 10.

MANHATTAN CLAM CHOWDER

The New York version always has tomatoes in it.

Put in a deep saucepan
1½-inch cube fat salt pork, diced
Cook slowly until the fat melts. Add
1 onion, sliced thin
Cook and stir 5 minutes. Add
1 cup cubed potatoes
1 teaspoon salt
2 cups boiling water
Boil 10 minutes. Add
2 cups stewed or canned tomatoes
Cook until the potatoes are soft (5 to 10 minutes). Add
1 pint fresh or canned clams, chopped fine
¼ teaspoon dried thyme
Salt and pepper to taste
Simmer 3 minutes. *Serves 4.*

To vary, cook with the onion ½ cup chopped celery, ½ teaspoon caraway seeds and a bit of bay leaf.

NEW ENGLAND CLAM CHOWDER

This is the traditional chowder. Old-fashioned cooks discarded the pork scraps, but they add a savory touch to the chowder.

Clean and pick over
1 quart clams
using
1 cup cold water
Drain, reserving the liquid. Strain it if it is sandy. Chop the

hard parts of the clams. Put in a deep pan

1½-inch cube fat salt pork, diced

Cook slowly until the fat melts and the scraps are crisp and brown. Remove the pork scraps and set them aside so they will be crisp when they are added. Add to the fat

1 onion, chopped fine

Cook slowly until the onion is golden. Prepare

3 cups cubed potatoes

Put the potatoes and the chopped clams into the pan in layers, dredging each layer with

Flour
Salt and pepper

Add

2½ cups boiling water

Simmer until the potatoes are tender (about 20 minutes). Add the soft part of the clams and cook 2 minutes. Add

4 cups hot milk
4 tablespoons butter
Salt and pepper to taste

Add at the last (to avoid curdling) the reserved clam water thickened with

1 tablespoon butter
1 tablespoon flour

Sprinkle some of the pork scraps on each serving. *Serves 8 generously.*

QUICK CLAM CHOWDER

Put in a deep pan

1-inch cube fat salt pork, cut small

Cook slowly until fat melts and the pork scraps are crisp and brown. Remove the bits of pork and set aside. Put into the pan

1 slice onion
1 cup cubed potatoes
2 cups boiling water

Simmer 20 minutes. When ready to serve, add

1 pint chopped clams, fresh or canned

Cook 2 minutes. Add

2 cups hot milk
3 tablespoons butter
Salt and pepper to taste

Sprinkle some of the pork scraps over each bowlful. *Serves 4.*

OYSTER STEW

For superior flavor, use top milk or part cream.

Put in a saucepan

2 tablespoons butter
¼ teaspoon Worcestershire
½ teaspoon celery salt

Cook slowly 5 minutes. Add

½ pint oysters (cleaned, p. 153)

Heat gently until the oyster edges start to curl. Add, if there is any, the

Oyster liquid

Add

2 cups hot milk
1 tablespoon butter

Season with

Salt and pepper

Pour into bowls and garnish with

Paprika, chopped parsley, chopped chives *or* chopped green onions

Serves 2.

Oyster Stew with Celery. Melt 1 tablespoon butter, add ½ cup celery, cut fine, and cook slowly until tender. Add to the stew and season delicately with sherry.

MILDRED'S OYSTER STEW

Heat in a double boiler

2 cups milk

Add

1 pint oysters (cleaned, p. 153)

Heat until the oysters curl. Add

Salt and pepper to taste
1 teaspoon butter (or more)

Serves 2.

LOBSTER STEW (CHOWDER)

The perfect lobster stew or chowder should "age" at least 5

hours, so prepare it well ahead of serving time.

Melt in a deep pan
3 tablespoons butter
Add
1 cup cooked or frozen lobster meat, cut in ¾-inch cubes
Cook and stir 5 minutes. Add very slowly, stirring constantly
1 quart milk (use part cream, if convenient)
Heat slowly but do not boil. Season to taste with
Salt and paprika *or* cayenne
Serves 4.

To simplify. Scald the milk. Add the lobster meat, cover and let stand 2 days in the refrigerator to develop flavor. Heat and season.

Marblehead Lobster Stew. Instead of using lobster meat, boil 2 small lobsters (p. 148) and remove the meat. Break up the shells and cook 10 minutes with 1 cup clam broth. Strain and add the broth to the stew.

SCALLOP STEW

Melt
1 tablespoon butter
Add
1 pint scallops, cleaned (p. 156), and cut in two if large
Cook 5 minutes. Add
2 cups milk or milk and cream
Salt and pepper to taste
Cook slowly 15 minutes. Add
1 tablespoon butter
Serves 3 or 4.

FISH CHOWDER

A simplified version of the classic recipe (see Old-fashioned Fish Chowder, below). Chowder is improved if you make it one day and serve it the next.

Put in a saucepan
1 pound fillet of haddock
1 cup water
Cook slowly until the fish flakes when tried with a fork. Remove the fish and separate it into flakes. Add to the cooking water
2 cups cubed potatoes
Cook until tender but still firm. Meanwhile, put in a pan
1-inch cube salt pork, diced, or 3 slices bacon, diced
Fry slowly until the fat melts. Add
1 small onion, diced
Cook slowly until the onion is golden-brown. Add to the potatoes. Add the fish. Put into the pan in which the onion was cooked
2 cups milk *or* milk and cream
Heat and stir to get all the flavor. Add to the chowder. Heat but do not boil. Add
Salt, pepper and butter to taste
If you made the chowder with top milk, you will not need butter. *Serves 4.*

To vary, cook the fish in clam juice instead of water, or add minced clams or oysters to the finished stew.

OLD-FASHIONED FISH CHOWDER

Fish stock made with bones improves the flavor of the chowder. There was a time when New Englanders always put into the chowder common or Boston crackers soaked in milk. Nowadays the crackers are usually omitted.

Order a
4-pound cod *or* haddock
Have the butcher skin it, remove the fish from the backbone and give you the head, tail and bone. Put the head, tail and bone (broken in pieces) in a deep kettle. Add
2 cups cold water
Simmer slowly 10 minutes. Drain and save the liquid. Put

in a small frying pan

1½-inch cube fat salt pork, diced

Cook slowly 5 minutes. Add

1 onion, sliced thin

Cook until the onion is soft (about 5 minutes). Strain the fat into a deep pan and set the crisp scraps aside. Add to the kettle

4 cups thinly sliced potatoes
2 cups boiling water

Cook 5 minutes. Add the fish, cut in 2-inch pieces, and the liquid drained from the bones. Cover and simmer 10 minutes. Add the scraps of onion and pork. Add

4 cups scalded milk *or* cream
1 tablespoon salt
⅛ teaspoon pepper
3 tablespoons butter

Heat but do not boil. *Serves 8 generously.*

CONNECTICUT FISH CHOWDER

Follow either recipe for Fish Chowder (p. 80), but instead of milk, add tomato juice. Season to taste. If you prefer a slightly thickened chowder, stir in ⅔ cup cracker crumbs just before serving.

BOUILLABAISSE

Serve this famous French dish in big bowls as the main course for Sunday night supper. Use at least three kinds of fish, such as flounder, whiting, sole, haddock, perch, whitefish or red mullet.

Put in a big kettle

½ cup olive oil
1 carrot, chopped
2 onions, chopped
2 leeks, cut small
1 clove garlic, crushed

Cook slowly until golden-brown. Add

3 pounds boned fish, cut in 3-inch squares
2 large tomatoes, cut in pieces, *or* 1 cup canned tomatoes
1 bay leaf
2 cups Fish Stock (p. 126), clam juice *or* water

Simmer 20 minutes. Add

½ cup shrimp, crab *or* lobster meat, cooked or canned
1 dozen oysters, clams *or* mussels (in the shell)
½ cup pimientos, cut small
Few grains saffron

Simmer until the shells open (about 5 minutes). Season to taste with

Salt and pepper

Add

Juice of 1 lemon
1 cup dry white wine

Put in a soup tureen or a large bowl

8 slices French bread, toasted

Pour the bouillabaisse over the bread. Sprinkle with

1 tablespoon chopped parsley

Serves 8.

Stuffings

Stuffing recipes serve as general guides, but you can vary them widely.

Crumbs for stuffing. Buy packaged crumbs, plain or seasoned, for dressing, or prepare crumbs as directed on page 6. For very dry stuffing, cut the bread in small cubes and toast in the oven until delicately brown.

How much stuffing to make. Birds vary, but as a general guide, allow 1 cup for each pound the bird weighs. Allow 2 to 4 tablespoons for a squab or Rock Cornish game hen and 1 or 2 cups for a 4-pound fish or for a roast prepared with a pocket for stuffing. The stuffing will expand as it cooks, so do not pack it in too firmly. If you have any left over, bake it separately in a greased pan.

Leftover dressing. Serve it cold with the leftover roast or spread it in a buttered pan, cover with sliced mushrooms, sprinkle with salt and pepper, dot with butter or cover with a thin layer of cream, and bake about 15 minutes at 400°.

BREAD STUFFING

This light and crumbly stuffing is delicate and buttery and so does not overwhelm the flavor of a young roast chicken. Your family may prefer a more savory dressing. If so, try any of the variations below. In a highly seasoned dressing, use bacon or sausage drippings or chicken fat in place of butter.

Mix lightly with a fork

4 cups dry bread crumbs
½ cup melted butter
½ teaspoon salt
⅛ teaspoon pepper
1 tablespoon minced onion

Makes 4 cups.

For a more savory dressing, season with sage, poultry seasoning or celery seed, or increase the onion to as much as ¾ cup.

STUFFING VARIATIONS

For a high-protein stuffing, mix toasted wheat germ, brewer's yeast and powdered milk with the crumbs.

Start with packaged crumbs or stuffing, or prepare Bread Stuffing (above). Add chopped chives, green pepper or pimiento, or leftovers such as chopped cooked meat or vegetables. Or make any of the variations given below or the special stuffings which follow.

Apricot Stuffing. Leave out the onion. Add 1 cup cooked apricots, cut in strips. Moisten with some of the water in which the apricots were cooked. Add ½ cup chopped celery.

Corn Bread Stuffing. Instead of using all white bread for crumbs, use dry corn bread for a third to a half of the crumbs. *Especially good for turkey.*

Corn Stuffing. Add to Corn Bread Stuffing 1 cup whole kernel corn, cooked or canned.

Cranberry Stuffing. Chop 1 cup raw cranberries. Cook 5 minutes in the fat, stir in 1/4 cup sugar, and add to the dressing.

Fruit Stuffing. Cut in small pieces drained fruit such as pineapple, mixed fruit cocktail, apricots, peaches, prunes or oranges. Add to plain stuffing and season to taste. For a richer stuffing, add chopped pecans, peanuts or other nuts.

Giblet Stuffing. Simmer the giblets in water until tender. Drain, reserving the broth, and chop. Add to the stuffing. Moisten with a little of the broth.

Herb Stuffing. Add thyme, sweet basil, summer savory or marjoram (1 tablespoon fresh or 1 teaspoon dried). Cut fresh herbs fine with scissors.

Mushroom Stuffing. For each cup of crumbs, add 1/2 cup chopped mushrooms, cooked 5 minutes in butter.

Savory Mushroom Stuffing. Add nutmeg, chopped parsley and chopped chives.

Onion Stuffing. Parboil 6 onions 10 minutes. Drain, chop fine. Add to dressing with 1 egg slightly beaten.

Oyster Stuffing. Wash 1 pint oysters and remove the tough muscles. Add whole if small, chopped if large. Moisten with 1/4 cup oyster liquid and lemon juice to taste. Season with salt, pepper and mace.

Parsley Stuffing. Add 1/4 to 1/2 cup finely cut parsley. Cooked parsley is more delicate in flavor than uncooked, so put in plenty and know that you are giving your family a food that is one of the richest in minerals and vitamins.

NEW ENGLAND STUFFING

Compact and lighter than Bread Stuffing.

Toast and crumble into coarse crumbs
- **12 slices bread**

Moisten with
- **Stock *or* water**

Add
- **2-inch cube fat salt pork, finely chopped, *or* 1/8 pound sausage meat**
- **1 egg, well beaten**
- **Salt and pepper**
- **Sage *or* poultry seasoning**

For chicken or turkey. Makes 3 cups.

To vary. Follow any of the suggestions above. Mashed potato or cooked rice may replace some of the bread.

APPLE STUFFING

Put in a saucepan
- **4 tablespoons bacon fat**
- **2 cups diced tart apples (unpeeled)**
- **2 teaspoons sugar**

Cook 5 minutes. Add
- **1/2 cup dry bread crumbs**
- **Salt, nutmeg and cinnamon to taste**

For duck or pork. Makes about 2 cups.

Savory Apple Stuffing. Cook 1/2 cup each of chopped celery, onion and parsley in the fat for 2 minutes before adding the apple. Omit the nutmeg and cinnamon and season with salt and pepper.

CELERY STUFFING

Put in a saucepan
- **2 tablespoons butter**
- **1/2 cup chopped celery**
- **2 tablespoons minced onion**
- **2 tablespoons parsley**

Cook 3 minutes. Add
- **2 cups fine dry bread crumbs**
- **1/4 teaspoon savory seasoning**

¼ teaspoon celery seed
½ teaspoon salt
Few grains pepper

For chicken, duck or fish. Makes 3 cups.

CHESTNUT STUFFING

Put through ricer or food mill
3 cups chestnuts, canned or cooked
Add
¼ cup cream
¼ cup butter
Salt and pepper
Mix
¼ cup melted butter
1 cup cracker crumbs
Combine mixtures. *For chicken or turkey. Makes 4 cups.*

MINT STUFFING

Put in a saucepan
3 tablespoons butter
1½ tablespoons chopped onion
3 tablespoons chopped celery
Cook 2 minutes. Add
¾ teaspoon salt
⅛ teaspoon pepper
½ cup fresh mint leaves, finely cut
Cook until the liquid evaporates. Mix
3 tablespoons melted butter
3 cups fine dry bread crumbs
Stir into the first mixture.
For chicken, lamb or fish. Makes 3 cups.

Watercress Stuffing. In place of mint use 1½ cups finely cut watercress.

ORANGE STUFFING

Toast lightly
3 cups bread cubes
Add
½ cup hot water *or* orange juice
Let stand 15 minutes. Add
2 teaspoons grated orange rind
⅔ cup orange sections, freed from membrane
2 cups finely cut celery
¼ cup butter, melted
1 egg, slightly beaten
½ teaspoon salt
⅛ teaspoon pepper

For duck. Makes 4 to 5 cups.

PRUNE AND APPLE STUFFING

Pour boiling water over
½ pound dried prunes
2 tablespoons seeded raisins
Let stand 5 minutes. Drain. Remove the pits; cut the prunes in pieces. Add
2 tablespoons cracker crumbs
⅛ teaspoon salt
¼ teaspoon sugar
1 egg yolk, beaten
1 large apple, peeled, cored, and sliced

For duck and pork. Makes 2 cups.

WILD RICE AND MUSHROOM STUFFING

Wild rice is such an expensive delicacy that you may prefer to stretch it by adding cooked brown rice, buckwheat, bread crumbs or more mushrooms. To save time, use canned cooked wild rice.

Steam
1 cup wild rice (or use 2 cups canned rice)
Cook together for 5 minutes
2 tablespoons butter *or* cooking oil
¼ pound chopped mushrooms
¼ cup chopped onion
Add to the rice. Season to taste with
Salt, pepper and nutmeg

Makes about 3 cups. Enough for 4- or 5-pound chicken or 4 squab or Rock Cornish game hens.

SAUSAGE STUFFING

Cook and stir until brown
1 pound pork sausage meat
Add
12 cups dry bread cubes
2 tablespoons minced onion
Salt to taste

1 teaspoon pepper
2 tablespoons minced parsley
Makes 12 cups. Enough for 12- to 14-pound turkey.

Sausage and Sweet Potato Dressing. Use 6 instead of 12 cups bread cubes and add 5 cups mashed sweet potatoes and 1 cup finely cut celery (with the tops).

SAUSAGE AND CHESTNUT STUFFING

Boil and shell (p. 13)
4 dozen Italian chestnuts
Mash half of them. Put in a pan
2 tablespoons butter
1 small onion, finely chopped
Cook 3 minutes. Add
½ pound sausage meat
Cook and stir 5 minutes. Add the mashed chestnuts and mix well. Season with
2 teaspoons salt
¼ teaspoon pepper
⅛ teaspoon powdered thyme
2 teaspoons finely chopped parsley
Add
1 cup fresh bread crumbs
Mix in the whole chestnuts. *For chicken or turkey. Makes 4 cups.*

Garnishes and Relishes

Elaborate decorations are out of style except for hotel or steamer meals. Often the prettiest of all is a sprig of parsley, mint or watercress or a sprinkling of paprika or chopped toasted nuts.

LEMON GARNISHES

Cut in thin slices, lengthwise sections, fan-shaped pieces, cups or baskets. Decorate with sprigs of parsley, finely chopped parsley, paprika, strips of canned pimiento, sliced radishes or the red part of radishes, chopped or cut in fancy shapes.

TRUFFLES

Add epicurean elegance to a molded salad or other cold entrée with these expensive imported delicacies, which are marketed in small tins or jars.

DEVILED ALMONDS

Blanch (p. 13) and shred

⅔ cup almond meats

Melt

1 tablespoon butter

Add the almonds. Sauté until well browned. Mix

1 tablespoon chutney
2 tablespoons chopped pickles
1 tablespoon Worcestershire
¼ teaspoon salt
Few grains cayenne

Pour over the nuts and heat. *For fish or chicken.*

DEVILED RAISINS

Stem large raisins and sauté in salad oil until plump. Drain on a paper towel. Sprinkle with salt and paprika or with a few drops of rum. *For chicken or veal.*

FRIED PARSLEY

Select perfect sprigs. Wash and pat dry on a paper towel. Fry 1 minute at 390° in fat deep enough to cover the parsley. Drain on a paper towel. *For fish or broiled chops or steak.*

FRESH VEGETABLE RELISHES

Crisp raw vegetables are welcome relishes with lunch or dinner, especially when no salad is served. They are popular, too, with pre-dinner drinks and as snacks for children. Prepare and put in ice water to crisp. Drain just before serving.

Carrots, cut in matchlike sticks or in curls (p. 280).

Cauliflower, separated into flowerets.

Celeriac (celery root), sliced and seasoned with salt and vinegar.

Celery, hearts or sticks (p. 280).

Cucumber, cut in sticks 4 inches long and as thick as a pencil.

Radishes, various ways (p. 281).

Relish Bowl. Fill a shallow bowl with crushed ice. Stick crisped celery stalks, carrot and cucumber sticks into the ice, upright.

FRUIT RELISHES

A fruit relish adds flavor and color to enhance what might otherwise be too bland a dish. Fruits go especially well with pork, veal and poultry, but try them with other foods as well. Many other recipes are in the fruit section (p. 363)—applesauce and cinnamon apples to serve with pork, sautéed bananas and hot fruit compotes, which are excellent with turkey and goose. Improvise a fruit relish, hot or cold, by using canned fruit, drained and seasoned with cinnamon, brandy or rum.

FRUIT KABOBS

String on skewers pineapple cubes, spiced apricot or peach halves and cooked and pitted prunes. Brush with butter and broil 5 minutes. *Serve hot with chicken or lamb chops. A good barbecue relish.*

FRIED APPLE RINGS

Core tart apples. Pare only if the skins are very tough. Cut in ½-inch slices. Sauté in butter or in bacon or sausage fat until just barely tender. Turn once with a broad spatula. When the apples are nearly tender, sprinkle lightly with brown sugar or grated cheese. Cover and cook until the sugar or cheese melts. *Serve with sausage, ham or pork.*

SPICED CRABAPPLES

Put in a saucepan

1 cup sugar
2 cups boiling water
24 whole cloves
6 allspice berries
2-inch stick of cinnamon
Few grains salt

Add

1 pound crabapples (washed)

Simmer gently until the apples are tender. Skim out the fruit and pour a little of the juice over it. If it is to be stored overnight, cover with the juice and drain off most of it when you serve the fruit. *For ham or pork.*

Spiced Cranberries or Carrots. Add raw cranberries or tiny new carrots to the syrup in place of crabapples and cook as above.

Spiced Apricots or Peaches. Pour the syrup over cooked or canned pitted apricots or peach halves. Do not cook but let stand until the syrup is cold.

CRANBERRY SAUCE

Put in a saucepan

1 pound cranberries (washed)
1½ cups sugar
2 cups boiling water

Cook 10 minutes. Watch to prevent boiling over. Skim off the white froth. Cool. *Serves 6.*

BAKED CRANBERRIES

Put in a baking dish

1 pound cranberries (washed)

Sprinkle with

1½ cups sugar

Cover. Bake 1 hour at 350°. *Serves 6.*

CRANBERRY JELLY

Put in a saucepan

1 pound cranberries (washed)
2 cups boiling water

Boil 20 minutes. Rub through a sieve and cook 3 minutes. Add

2 cups sugar
Few grains salt

Cook 2 minutes. Pour into a

mold or bowl or in Orange Baskets (p. 371). Chill. *Serves 8.*

Spiced Cranberry Jelly. Cook the cranberries with a 2-inch piece of stick cinnamon, 24 whole cloves and 6 allspice berries.

Cranberry Jelly with Celery. When the jelly begins to thicken, fold in 1½ cups celery, cut crosswise in ⅛-inch slices.

FRESH CRANBERRY MOLD

Wash and drain
3 cups perfect cranberries
Make a slit part way through each berry. Add
1 cup sugar
1 cup cold water
Bring very slowly to the boiling point, stirring gently. Boil 1 minute. Remove from the heat. Stir in
½ bottle liquid pectin
Skim off the foam. Pour into a mold. *For chicken, turkey or pork.*

CRANBERRY AND ORANGE RELISH

Wash
2 cups cranberries
Cut in pieces and remove the seeds from
1 small orange
Put the fruit through a food chopper. Add
¾ cup sugar
Mix thoroughly. Let stand 30 minutes or more. *Serves 6 to 8.*

CRANBERRY CATSUP

A quickly made relish to serve with pork, veal, chicken or turkey.

Put in a saucepan
1 pound cranberries
½ cup mild vinegar
⅔ cup water
Boil until the berries are soft (about 5 minutes). Put through a food mill. Add
1 cup brown sugar
½ teaspoon each of clove, ginger and paprika
1 teaspoon cinnamon
½ teaspoon salt
¼ teaspoon pepper
Simmer 3 minutes. Add
2 teaspoons butter
Pour into a jar. Store at room temperature. *Makes 1 pint.*

ORANGE SLICES

Slice a whole orange. Dot the slices with currant or mint jelly. Arrange on the platter around *roast lamb, roast duck or chicken.*

BROILED ORANGE SLICES

Slice a whole orange. Dot the slices with butter and sprinkle lightly with brown sugar and a trace of curry powder. Broil until the sugar melts. *Serve with lamb chops, roast lamb, veal or chicken.*

BAKED ORANGES

Cover small oranges with cold water. Bring to the boiling point, simmer ½ hour and drain. Cut a slice off the top of each orange, put in a teaspoon of sugar, and bake in the pan with *roast turkey or duck.*

BROILED PEACHES *or* APRICOTS

Also delicious as dessert.

Put fresh or canned peach or apricot halves in a shallow pan, cut side up. Dot with butter

Simple Garnishes
Carrot Sticks and Curls
Watercress
Radish Slices and Roses
Parsley
Lemon Shapes
Hard-Boiled Eggs
Cucumber
Pepper Rings
Tomatoes
Mushrooms and Truffles
Croutons, Nuts, and Cheese Balls
Pickles and Olives

and sprinkle with brown sugar. Broil until the sugar melts. *For turkey or duck.*

Broiled Peaches with Blueberries. Put a spoonful of blueberries in each half, dot with butter and sprinkle with sugar. Broil slowly.

Broiled Brandied Peaches. Put ½ teaspoon brandy in each peach.

GLAZED PINEAPPLE

Drain canned pineapple slices. Put in a single layer in a shallow baking pan. Place over very slow heat or in a 250° oven. Cook until the pineapple is almost transparent (2 or 3 hours). Garnish each slice with a candied cherry. *For ham.*

SAUTÉED PINEAPPLE

Drain canned sliced pineapple. Dry on a paper towel. Sauté in butter until delicately browned. *For lamb chops or ham.*

PRUNES IN BACON

Cook prunes until plump and tender but not soft. Drain and remove the pits. Wrap in half-slices of bacon. String on skewers, put in a shallow pan, and bake at 450° until the bacon is crisp. Remove from the skewers and serve on the platter around *turkey, ham or pork.*

Chutney Prunes. Stuff with chutney before wrapping in bacon.

PICKLES AND RELISHES

See page 541.

JELLIES

See page 532.

BEET RELISH

If you use bottled horseradish, drain it well.

Mix well
- **1 cup chopped cooked or canned beets**
- **3 tablespoons grated horseradish root**
- **2 tablespoons lemon juice**
- **2 teaspoons powdered sugar**
- **1 teaspoon salt**

See also Pickled Beets (pp. 246, 549). *Makes 1 cup.*

CELERY RELISH

Mix
- **1½ cups chopped celery, including small tender leaves**
- **4 teaspoons powdered sugar**
- **1 teaspoon salt**
- **½ teaspoon mustard**
- **¼ cup vinegar**

Cover and let stand in a cold place 1½ hours. Drain off the liquid before serving. *Serves 6.*

QUICK CHILI SAUCE

Combine
- **2 cups canned tomatoes**
- **1 onion, chopped**
- **½ teaspoon salt**
- **Few grains cayenne**
- **⅛ teaspoon each of ground cloves and ground cinnamon**
- **⅛ cup sugar (or more)**
- **½ cup mild vinegar**

Simmer 1 hour. Add
- **2 tablespoons chopped green pepper**

Simmer ½ hour longer. *Makes about 1½ cups.*

QUICK MUSTARD RELISH

Mix
- **2 cups shredded cabbage**
- **1 pimiento, chopped fine**

½ large green pepper, chopped fine
⅓ cup chopped onion
1 cup vinegar
1½ cups water
2 tablespoons salt

Let stand. Mix

¼ cup sugar
3 tablespoons flour
2 teaspoons mustard
¼ teaspoon turmeric
¼ teaspoon celery salt
½ teaspoon salt

Add slowly, stirring constantly

½ cup cold water
½ cup vinegar

Stir and cook over hot water or low heat until thick. Cover and cook 10 minutes. Bring the vegetables to the boiling point and drain off the liquid. Add them to the dressing and simmer 5 minutes. Serve cold. *Makes about 3 cups.*

PHILADELPHIA RELISH

Mix

2 cups finely shredded cabbage
2 green peppers, finely chopped
1 teaspoon celery seed
¼ teaspoon mustard seed
½ teaspoon salt
2 tablespoons brown sugar
¼ cup vinegar

Let stand at least an hour before serving. *Makes 2½ cups.*

FRESH SUMMER RELISH

Chop and mix

1 cored apple
1 onion
3 tomatoes
3 stalks celery

Add

1 tablespoon finely chopped mint leaves
1½ cup raisins
2 tablespoons vinegar
¼ teaspoon cardamon seeds
1 clove garlic, crushed
1 teaspoon salt
1 fresh chili, seeded and chopped, *or* ½ teaspoon cayenne

Heat to the boiling point. Serve either hot or cold. *Makes 2 cups.*

CRANBERRY FRAPPÉ

Cook together 8 minutes

1 quart cranberries
2 cups water

Put through a sieve. Add

2 cups sugar
Juice 2 lemons

Cool. Pour the mixture into a refrigerator tray and freeze without stirring until firm. When ready to use, stir or beat slightly and serve with the main course in individual chilled sherbet glasses. Frappés should be slightly icy. *For chicken or turkey.*

CURRANT ICE

Boil together 5 minutes

2 cups water
¾ cup sugar

Add

1 cup currant juice

Cool. Freeze like Cranberry Frappé (above). *For roast lamb, chicken or turkey.*

TOMATO FRAPPÉ

Combine

1¾ cups tomatoes, cut small
3 apples, cored, pared and chopped
2 cups water
1 cup sugar
3 tablespoons lemon juice
Piece ginger root *or* ¼ teaspoon ginger

Cook 35 minutes. Rub through a sieve and freeze to a mush. Makes 1 quart. *For roast lamb, ham or turkey.*

Sauces for Fish, Meat and Vegetables

A delicious sauce can make a simple dish a memorable one. Make it carefully so that it will be satin-smooth. Season a sauce subtly so that it will enhance the flavor of the dish it completes but will not overwhelm it.

THICKENING SAUCES

Flour is the most commonly used thickener. Blend it smoothly with the melted fat before adding the liquid. Frequent stirring keeps the sauce velvety as it cooks. The mixture of fat and flour is called a "roux." White roux is made without browning, brown roux by browning the fat and flour before adding the liquid, as in a brown gravy.

Potato flour and cornstarch cook quickly and smoothly and are particularly successful as the thickening for a clear sauce. To substitute for flour, use 1 teaspoon potato flour or cornstarch for each tablespoon of flour in any sauce recipe.

CANNED AND FROZEN SOUPS AS SAUCES

Condensed canned or frozen soups make tasty sauces to serve over fish, meat, vegetables, rice, toasted sandwiches, toast or crackers. They are also useful as the basis for casseroles. Heat the undiluted soup slowly and thin it with a little top milk or consommé if it is too thick. Season to taste. Here are a few suggestions, but experiment with others.

Celery Sauce. Add a bouillon cube to condensed cream of celery soup. Heat and season to taste.

Chicken Sauce. Heat condensed cream of chicken soup. Add extra bits of chicken, if at hand, or a few sliced sautéed mushrooms. Season to taste with thyme. Dilute with cream or top milk.

Mushroom Sauce. Heat condensed cream of mushroom soup. Add sliced sautéed mushrooms, if convenient. Add a trace of freshly ground nutmeg.

Onion Soup. Heat condensed onion soup. Taste. If too salty, add a trace of sugar and a little cream.

Shrimp *or* Lobster Sauce. Heat canned or frozen shrimp or lobster bisque. Thin slightly with cream and season with sherry.

Tomato Sauce. Heat condensed cream of tomato soup. Add 2 tablespoons butter. For a more savory sauce, add a pinch of oregano or a shake of garlic salt.

Tomato Cheese Sauce. Add 1 cup grated cheese to Tomato Sauce and stir until the cheese melts.

SPAGHETTI SAUCES

See pages 313–314.

MARINADES AND BARBECUE SAUCES

Meats, fish and vegetables are sometimes soaked in a savory sauce (marinade) before cooking or serving. A marinade is a blend of seasonings, oil, and an acid such as lemon juice, tomato juice or wine. The simplest is French dressing, seasoned more highly, if you like, with herbs, chopped onion, Worcestershire or soy sauce. The marinade is also used as a basting sauce while the meat is cooking. The recipes below suggest the basic combinations, which can easily be varied. In addition, special mixtures are given with the recipes for certain dishes.

FRENCH DRESSING MARINADE

Mix

1 cup French dressing, preferably made with wine
1 clove garlic, crushed
1 teaspoon chopped parsley
⅛ teaspoon each of dried tarragon and thyme

For chicken, lamb or veal.

WINE MARINADE

Mix

1 cup wine (white for poultry and veal, red for other meats)
1 cup olive oil
2 or 3 cloves garlic, split
2 teaspoons dried herbs, such as rosemary, thyme and marjoram
¼ cup chopped parsley
½ teaspoon freshly ground pepper

To vary. Add Worcestershire and chopped onion. Or, for chicken or duck, add ½ cup orange or pineapple juice.

BARBECUE SAUCE

Mix

1 teaspoon salt
1 teaspoon chili powder
1 teaspoon celery seed
¼ cup (or less) brown sugar
¼ cup vinegar
¼ cup Worcestershire
1 cup tomato catsup
2 cups water
Few drops Tabasco

Simmer half an hour.

To vary. Cook 1 grated onion and 1 minced clove of garlic 5 minutes in butter and add to the sauce.

SMOKY BARBECUE SAUCE

Mix in a small saucepan

3 tablespoons Worcestershire
1 tablespoon meat glaze such as B-V
½ cup catsup
2 tablespoons butter
3 tablespoons shortening
1 tablespoon sugar
1 tablespoon vinegar
2 teaspoons liquid smoke
1 medium onion, grated
1 teaspoon salt
Few drops Tabasco

Heat to the boiling point. *For beef or lamb.*

CHICKEN BARBECUE SAUCE

Mix

1 egg, well beaten
½ cup cooking oil
1 cup cider vinegar
2 tablespoons salt

1½ teaspoons poultry seasoning
¼ teaspoon pepper

If you like, use other seasonings in place of poultry seasoning, such as finely chopped onion and chopped parsley, with a shake of celery salt and a pinch of tarragon or thyme. Ginger is good, too. *Enough for 6 half broilers.*

HERBED BARBECUE SAUCE

Mix

1 cup dry white wine
¼ cup olive oil
2 tablespoons butter
1 medium onion, minced
1 crushed clove of garlic
1 teaspoon salt
¼ teaspoon paprika
2 teaspoons fresh rosemary, minced
1 teaspoon parsley, minced

Simmer half an hour. *For chicken, caponettes or turkey.*

CREAM SAUCE (BASIC WHITE SAUCE)

Keep a jar in the refrigerator ready for hurry-up dishes such as scalloped eggs, creamed tuna, crab meat or chicken. Canned cream sauce is on the market.

Melt in a double boiler top or a small heavy saucepan

2 tablespoons butter

Stir in

2 tablespoons flour

Blend well over low heat. Stir in

1 cup cold milk *or* milk and cream

A blending fork or a wire whisk helps keep a sauce smooth as it cooks. Bring slowly to the boiling point. Cook 2 minutes, stirring constantly. Season to taste with

Salt and pepper

Makes 1 cup.

Croquette Sauce (the basis for most croquette mixtures). Increase the butter and flour to 4 tablespoons each.

A blending fork

Thin Cream Sauce (to combine with puréed vegetables to make a soup). Reduce the flour to 1 tablespoon.

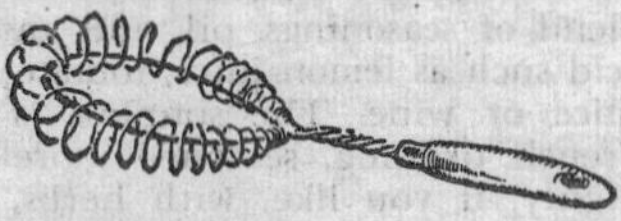

A wire whisk

CREAM SAUCE VARIATIONS

Season more highly with paprika, meat extract, onion juice, onion salt or herbs, or with ¼ teaspoon dry mustard mixed with the flour. For a richer sauce, stir in a slightly beaten egg yolk just before serving.

Brown Almond Sauce. Add to the melted butter ¼ cup (or more) chopped blanched almonds. Cook and stir until delicately brown.

Curry Cream Sauce. Add to the flour 1 teaspoon curry powder and ¼ teaspoon ground ginger. Season highly to taste with onion juice and paprika.

Lobster Sauce. Add 1 teaspoon meat extract and ½ cup diced cooked or canned lobster meat. Add the lobster coral if you are using fresh lobster. See also Lobster Velouté Sauce (p. 96).

Mock Hollandaise. Just before serving, stir in 2 egg yolks, 6 tablespoons butter (a tablespoon at a time) and 1 tablespoon lemon juice.

Onion Sauce. Add to the butter 3 tablespoons chopped onion and cook 3 minutes. For a richer sauce, stir in 1 egg yolk, slightly beaten, just before serving.

Parsley Cream Sauce. Add 1 to 4 tablespoons chopped parsley.

Truffle Sauce. Add 1 tablespoon chopped canned truffles and 1 tablespoon Madeira wine.

CHEESE SAUCE

Make Cream Sauce and add to it ¼ to ¾ cup mild or sharp cheese, grated or cut in small cubes. Heat in a double boiler or over very low heat until the cheese melts.

Sauce Mornay. This French sauce is usually made with a combination of two kinds of cheese such as Parmesan and Swiss. One-fourth cup will be enough for this delicate sauce. Just before serving, stir in an egg yolk, slightly beaten, and 2 tablespoons butter, bit by bit. Taste and add more salt, if necessary.

JIFFY CHEESE SAUCE

This sauce will keep well in the refrigerator. Make a larger amount and keep it on hand for hurry-up meals such as cheese toast or sliced cooked eggs in cheese sauce.

Heat in double boiler or in a saucepan over very low heat
1 small can evaporated milk (1 cup)
Add
½ cup mild or sharp cheese, cut small
Stir until the sauce is smooth. Season to taste with
Salt, paprika, dry mustard, curry powder *or* bits of pimiento
If the sauce is too thick, add
A little milk *or* cream
Makes about 1½ cups.

BÉCHAMEL SAUCE

A tasty cream sauce made with part stock and part milk. Use it with any of the variations suggested on pages 94–95.

Cook together 20 minutes
1½ cups chicken stock
1 slice onion
1 slice carrot
Bit of bay leaf
Sprig of parsley
6 peppercorns
Strain. There should be 1 cupful. Melt
¼ cup butter
Add and blend
¼ cup flour
Add gradually, stirring constantly, the strained chicken stock and
1 cup milk *or* milk and cream
Season with
Salt and pepper
Makes 2 cups.

Yellow Béchamel Sauce. Just before serving, add 1 egg yolk, slightly beaten and mixed with a small quantity of the hot sauce.

BERÇY SAUCE

Melt
1 tablespoon butter
Add
1 tablespoon finely chopped shallot *or* 1 teaspoon finely chopped onion
Cook 5 minutes. Add
2 tablespoons flour
Blend well. Add gradually, stirring constantly
1 cup Chicken Stock (p. 62) *or* canned chicken broth
Simmer 15 minutes and strain.

Add
2 tablespoons butter
Season to taste with
Salt and pepper
For chicken or fish. Makes 1 cup.

DRAWN BUTTER SAUCE

Melt
2 tablespoons butter
Add
2 tablespoons flour
½ teaspoon salt
⅛ teaspoon pepper
Stir until smooth. Add, stirring constantly
1 cup hot water *or* Fish Stock (p. 126)
Boil 5 minutes. Add
1 teaspoon lemon juice
2 tablespoons butter, bit by bit
For fish. Makes 1 cup.

For a richer sauce, stir in a slightly beaten egg yolk just before serving.

To vary, season to taste with anchovy paste or add a tablespoon of drained capers.

Egg Sauce. Add 2 hard-cooked eggs, sliced ¼ inch thick.

Shrimp Sauce. Add ½ cup cooked or canned shrimps, cut in pieces.

VELOUTÉ SAUCE

Many famous sauces are actually Velouté Sauce with special seasoning added. Strong chicken stock makes all the difference. All these sauces are delicious poured over steamed or panbroiled fish fillets.

Melt
2 tablespoons butter
Add
3 tablespoons flour
¼ teaspoon salt
Few grains pepper
Blend well. Add slowly, stirring constantly
1 cup Chicken Stock (p. 62) *or* canned chicken broth
Bring to the boiling point and boil 2 minutes. Add
⅓ cup cream
Makes about 1 cup.

For a simpler sauce, use 2 tablespoons flour and omit the cream.

As a variation, use only ½ cup chicken stock and add ½ cup white wine.

Suprême Sauce (Poulette Sauce). Just before serving, stir in 1 or 2 egg yolks, slightly beaten. Season to taste with a few grains of nutmeg and a dash of lemon juice.

Allemande Sauce. Add 3 tablespoons grated Parmesan to Suprême Sauce.

Lobster Velouté Sauce. Cover lobster shells with water. Cover and simmer 1 hour or cook 20 minutes in a pressure cooker. Strain off the liquid and boil until it is reduced to 1 cupful. Use this stock as the liquid for Velouté Sauce. Season with salt, paprika and lemon juice. Just before serving, add ½ cup diced cooked lobster. For a richer sauce, stir in 2 egg yolks, slightly beaten, and remove the sauce from the heat.

Olive and Almond Sauce. Just before serving, add ¼ cup shredded toasted almonds, 1 teaspoon beef extract, 8 olives, pitted and quartered, and ½ tablespoon lemon juice.

Russian Sauce. Before adding the cream, add ½ teaspoon finely chopped chives, ½ teaspoon prepared mustard, and 1 teaspoon grated horseradish. Cook 2 minutes. Strain, add the cream and 1 teaspoon lemon juice. Reheat.

Soubise Sauce. Cook 2 cups sliced onions 5 minutes in boiling water to cover. Drain. Cover with boiling water and cook until soft. Drain, rub through sieve, and add to the sauce. Season.

Mushroom Sauce. Add ¼ cup sliced mushroom caps to Velouté or Suprême Sauce. Cook 5 minutes. Season. Add chopped truffle, if desired.

NORMANDY SAUCE

Melt in a small saucepan
2 tablespoons butter
Blend in
2 tablespoons flour
Stir in slowly
1 cup Fish Stock (p. 126) *or* clam juice
Bring to the boiling point. Pour slowly over
2 egg yolks, well beaten
Beat thoroughly. Add
1 tablespoon lemon juice
Salt, cayenne and pepper to taste
For steamed or baked fish. Makes 1 cup.

To vary, season to taste with grated cheese and with Madeira instead of lemon juice.

ROBERTS SAUCE

Melt in a small saucepan
1 tablespoon butter
Add
3 shallots, finely chopped, *or* 2 tablespoons chopped mild onion
1 teaspoon flour
Cook 5 minutes. Add
1 tablespoon vinegar
½ cup Chicken Stock (p. 62) *or* canned chicken broth
2 chopped pickles
½ tablespoon chopped capers
1 teaspoon chopped olives
½ teaspoon prepared mustard
½ teaspoon salt
Few grains cayenne
Cook 10 minutes, stirring constantly. *For fish. Makes about 1 cup.*

SPANISH SAUCE
(Espagnole Sauce)

A well-seasoned brown sauce which is one of the basic French sauces.

Put in a saucepan
2 tablespoons finely chopped lean raw ham or bacon
2 tablespoons chopped celery
2 tablespoons chopped carrot
1 tablespoon chopped onion
4 tablespoons butter (or 2 tablespoons, if bacon is used)
Cook until the butter is well browned. Stir in
4 tablespoons flour
Add
1⅓ cups consommé *or* stock
⅓ to ⅔ cup stewed tomatoes
Cook 5 minutes. Strain or not, as you prefer. *For eggs, fish or sweetbreads. Makes about 1½ cups.*

CREOLE SAUCE

Put in a saucepan
2 tablespoons chopped onion
4 tablespoons finely chopped green pepper
2 tablespoons butter
Cook 5 minutes. Add
2 tomatoes or ½ cup canned tomatoes
¼ cup sliced mushrooms
6 pitted or stuffed olives, cut in pieces
Cook 2 minutes. Add
1⅓ cups Brown Sauce (below) *or* gravy *or* water and 2 bouillon cubes
Bring to the boiling point. Season to taste with salt, pepper and sherry. *For eggs or fish. Makes about 2 cups.*

BROWN SAUCE

See also Brown Gravy (p. 164).

Melt
2 tablespoons butter *or* bacon fat
Add
½ slice onion (if desired)

Cook slowly until the fat is well browned but not black. Add

- **2 tablespoons flour *or* 2 teaspoons potato flour**
- **½ teaspoon salt**
- **⅛ teaspoon pepper**
- **Few grains sugar**

Add gradually

- **1 cup Brown Stock (p. 60), consommé *or* water**

Bring to boiling point. Boil 2 minutes. Strain or remove the bit of onion. Cook 15 minutes in double boiler or over very low heat. *Makes about 1 cup.*

For a thinner sauce, add more boiling water or stock and stir thoroughly. Taste and correct the seasoning.

For a stronger onion flavor, mince the onion and leave it in the sauce, or add a few drops of onion juice.

Anchovy Sauce. Season with anchovy essence or paste. *For fish.*

Bordelaise Sauce. Cook with the onion 1 shallot, chopped fine, 2 slices of carrot, a sprig of parsley, a bit of bay leaf and a whole clove. Some French recipes also call for a tablespoon of chopped ham and for a split clove of garlic. Bordelaise Sauce is always highly seasoned, so add Worcestershire, catsup or sherry to taste.

Brown Curry Sauce. Season highly with curry powder and dry mustard.

Chestnut Sauce. Add ½ cup boiled French chestnuts, chopped or broken in pieces.

Currant Jelly Sauce. Omit the onion. Melt ¼ glass currant jelly in the sauce. Season with 2 tablespoons sherry or port.

Olive Sauce. Add 1 or 2 tablespoons chopped ripe or stuffed olives.

Sauce Piquante. Add 1 tablespoon vinegar, ½ small shallot, finely chopped, 1 tablespoon capers, 1 tablespoon chopped pickle and a few grains cayenne.

Brown Russian Sauce. Stir in ¼ cup tomato catsup and ½ cup sour cream.

HOT TARTARE SAUCE

Mix

- **½ cup Cream Sauce (p. 94)**
- **⅓ cup mayonnaise**
- **½ shallot, finely chopped *or* ¼ tablespoon finely chopped onion**
- **½ teaspoon vinegar *or* tarragon vinegar**
- **½ tablespoon each of finely chopped pickles, olives and parsley**
- **1 tablespoon capers**

Set over low heat. Stir constantly until thoroughly heated, but do not bring to the boiling point. *For fish. Makes about 1 cup.*

NEWBURG SAUCE

Many cooks use only sherry, but brandy and sherry together make an even better sauce.

Melt

- **1 tablespoon butter**

Add

- **1 teaspoon flour**
- **1 cup cream**

Cook and stir until thickened. If you are heating lobster, shrimp or other food in the sauce, add it at this point and keep warm in a double boiler or over very low heat. Just before serving, add

- **2 egg yolks, slightly beaten**
- **2 tablespoons sherry *or* 1 tablespoon sherry and 1 tablespoon brandy**

Season to taste. *Makes 1 cup, or enough for 2 cups shrimp, lobster or flaked fish.*

MUSHROOM SAUCE

Another good mushroom sauce is gravy thick with sliced sautéed mushrooms. See also Mushroom Sauce (p. 97) and Tomato and Mushroom Sauce (below).

Melt
3 tablespoons butter
Add
½ pound mushrooms, sliced
Cook 5 minutes. Stir in
3 tablespoons flour
Few drops onion juice
Cook 5 minutes over low heat. Add gradually, stirring constantly
1 cup cream
Season with
1 teaspoon beef extract
Salt and paprika
Makes 1½ to 2 cups.

OYSTER SAUCE

Put in a pan
1 pint shelled oysters
Cook slowly until the oysters are plump (about 5 minutes). Remove the oysters. Measure the liquid in the pan and add to it
Milk, water, Chicken Stock (p. 62) *or* canned chicken broth (enough to make 1¾ cups)
Melt
4 tablespoons butter
Blend in
4 tablespoons flour
Stir well and add the oyster liquid gradually, stirring constantly. Boil 2 minutes. Add the oysters. Season with
Salt and pepper
For fish. Makes about 2 cups.

RUSSIAN OYSTER SAUCE

Put in a pan
1 cup chopped shelled oysters
Cook 5 minutes. Strain and measure the liquid in the pan. Add
Chicken Stock (p. 62) *or* canned chicken broth (to make 1 cup)
Melt
3 tablespoons butter
Blend in
4 tablespoons flour
Stir in slowly
½ cup cream
Add the oyster liquid. Bring to the boiling point. Add the oysters. Stir in
2 egg yolks
½ tablespoon vinegar
1 tablespoon lemon juice
2 tablespoons capers
1 tablespoon grated horseradish
Salt and pepper to taste
For fish. Makes about 2 cups.

TOMATO SAUCE

Melt until brown
2 tablespoons butter
Stir in
2 tablespoons flour
Add slowly
1 cup tomato juice *or* tomato cocktail *or* strained cooked or canned tomatoes
Cook and stir over low heat until thick. Season to taste with
Salt and pepper
Onion salt
Oregano *or* nutmeg
Makes about 1 cup.

Tomato and Mushroom Sauce. Add 1 cup sliced mushrooms, canned or sautéed in butter.

TOMATO PASTE SAUCE

Mix in a saucepan
1 can tomato paste
3 cans water
Stir over moderate heat until smooth. Tomato paste has seasonings in it, but add more to taste for a more piquant sauce. *Makes about 2 cups.*

MEXICAN TOMATO SAUCE

Cook together 5 minutes
1 onion, chopped fine
2 tablespoons butter

Add
1 red pepper, chopped fine
1 green pepper, chopped fine
1 clove garlic, minced
2 tomatoes, peeled and cut in pieces
Cook 15 minutes. Season with
1 teaspoon Worcestershire
¼ teaspoon celery salt
Salt
Makes about 1 cup.

SAUCE FINISTE

Cook until well browned
3 tablespoons butter
Stir in
½ teaspoon mustard
Few grains cayenne
1 teaspoon lemon juice
1½ teaspoons Worcestershire sauce
¾ cup stewed and strained tomatoes
For steak, hamburg or fish. Makes about 1 cup.

BREAD SAUCE

The English custom is to serve both bread sauce and a thin dish gravy with fowl or game. This sauce should be almost as thick as mayonnaise.

Heat in a double boiler
2 cups milk
Add
⅓ cup fine stale bread crumbs
1 onion stuck with 6 cloves
Cook slowly 30 minutes. Remove the onion. Stir in
1 teaspoon salt
Few grains cayenne
2 tablespoons butter
Put in a frying pan
1 tablespoon butter
½ cup coarse dry bread crumbs
Stir over moderate heat until brown. Put the sauce in a serving bowl and sprinkle with the coarse crumbs. *Makes about 2 cups.*

HOLLANDAISE

This queen of sauces is superb with artichokes, asparagus, broccoli, green beans, fish, veal or broiled chicken, or in special dishes such as Eggs Benedict. Canned Hollandaise saves a little time and is a useful addition to the emergency shelf. See also Mock Hollandaise (p. 95).

Put in a small heavy saucepan or double boiler top
3 egg yolks
Beat with a wooden spoon or wire whisk until smooth but not fluffy. Add
2 tablespoons lemon juice *or* mild vinegar
½ cup butter *or* margarine, melted
2 tablespoons hot water
¼ teaspoon salt
Few grains cayenne
Set over very low heat or over hot water and beat until the sauce begins to thicken (about 5 minutes). The sauce will be thicker as it cools. *Makes about 1 cup.*

EDIE'S HOLLANDAISE

Less rich than classic Hollandaise, and easier to make.

Beat until thick and set aside
2 egg yolks
Heat in a double boiler top
¾ cup water
2 tablespoons lemon juice
¼ teaspoon salt
Stir together until smooth
2 tablespoons cornstarch
¼ cup water
Add to the first mixture and stir to mix well. Pour slowly over the egg yolks, stirring constantly. Pour back into the double boiler top and set over hot water. Add
2 tablespoons butter
Cook and stir until thick. *Serves 4.*

HOLLANDAISE VARIATIONS

Season homemade or canned Hollandaise with sherry (Sauce

Trianon), grated horseradish or anchovy paste, or add ¼ cup heavy cream, plain or whipped. Or make any of the following variations.

Béarnaise Sauce. Add 1 teaspoon finely chopped parsley and 1 teaspoon chopped fresh tarragon or ½ tablespoon tarragon vinegar. Or make Hollandaise with tarragon vinegar and add 1 teaspoon finely chopped parsley.

Cucumber Hollandaise Sauce. Pare cucumber. Chop and squeeze in a piece of cheesecloth to drain thoroughly. Add ¼ to ½ cup to the Hollandaise. Add a few grains of cayenne.

Sauce Henriette. Add 1 tablespoon each of tomato paste and finely chopped parsley. For **Sauce Figaro,** add Worcestershire to taste.

Victor Hugo Sauce. Stir 1 teaspoon meat extract into the melted butter. To the finished sauce add 1 tablespoon grated horseradish and a few drops of onion juice.

AIOLI

A famous French sauce of the mayonnaise type with a strong garlic flavor.

Have ready
1 cup olive oil
Peel and split
8 cloves garlic
Mash in a mortar or as described on page 17. Mix with
1 egg yolk
¼ teaspoon salt
Few grains pepper
Stir in, drop by drop, 3 tablespoons of the olive oil and
Juice of 1 lemon
Stir in the rest of the oil, a little at a time. *For bland-flavored fish such as sole, flounder or halibut. Makes about 1 cup.*

HOT MAYONNAISE

Put in a very heavy pan or double boiler top
2 egg yolks
Beat slightly. Stir in slowly
2 tablespoons olive oil
Stir in, a little at a time
1 tablespoon vinegar
¼ cup hot water
Stir and cook over very low heat or over hot water until thickened. Season with
Salt and a few grains cayenne
Add
1 teaspoon finely chopped parsley
For fish or vegetables. Makes about ½ cup.

GUAYMAS SAUCE

Mix just before serving
⅓ cup tomato juice, canned or homemade
1 cup mayonnaise
2 tablespoons olives, cut in slivers
For fish. Makes about 1½ cups.

LITTLETON SAUCE

Mix in a heavy pan or double boiler top
1 teaspoon flour
1 teaspoon mustard
Add
1 tablespoon butter
1 tablespoon vinegar
½ cup boiling water
3 egg yolks, well beaten
Cook over boiling water or very low heat until thickened, stirring constantly. Season with
¼ teaspoon salt
Few grains pepper
Few grains cayenne
Just before serving, stir in
1 tablespoon currant jelly
For fish. Makes about 1 cup.

CURRANT CHILI SAUCE

Mix 1 cup chili sauce with a 6-ounce glass of currant jelly.

Season with 4 tablespoons prepared horseradish. *For ham or tongue.*

ROCHESTER SAUCE

Mix 1 cup chili sauce, ½ cup sherry and ½ cup brown sugar. *For ham or tongue.*

HORSERADISH SAUCE

Mix

½ cup cracker *or* bread crumbs
½ cup grated horseradish
1½ cups milk *or* milk and cream

Let stand 2 hours. Cook 20 minutes over hot water or very low heat. Add

3 tablespoons butter
½ teaspoon salt
⅛ teaspoon pepper

For ham or boiled beef. Makes about 2 cups.

HORSERADISH CREAM

Beat until stiff

½ cup heavy cream

Stir in

½ teaspoon salt
Few grains cayenne
2 to 4 tablespoons grated horseradish
4 teaspoons vinegar

For roast beef or boiled beef. Makes about ¾ cup.

Epicurean Sauce. Omit the vinegar. Add ½ teaspoon prepared mustard and 3 tablespoons mayonnaise.

MUSTARD SAUCE

See also Prepared Mustard (p. 16).

Mix

2 tablespoons dry mustard
1 teaspoon flour
¼ teaspoon salt
¼ cup evaporated milk *or* cream

Put in a heavy pan or double boiler top

¾ cup evaporated milk *or* cream
¼ cup sugar

Heat. Stir in the mustard mixture. Add

1 egg yolk beaten until thick

Cook and stir until thick. Stir in

½ cup vinegar, heated

For fish, beef, ham or spinach. Makes 1½ to 2 cups.

COLONY MUSTARD SAUCE

Melt

2 tablespoons butter

Add

1 teaspoon mustard
1 teaspoon Worcestershire
2 tablespoons Escoffier sauce

Stir until smooth. Just before serving, add

2 tablespoons heavy cream

Thin with more cream, if you like. Serve hot with *broiled steak, hamburg or lamb chops. Makes about ½ cup.*

CUCUMBER SAUCE

Pare cucumbers. Grate or chop and drain thoroughly. Season to taste with salt, pepper and vinegar. *For fish.*

CUCUMBER CREAM

Pare and chop

1 cucumber

Drain thoroughly. Add

¼ teaspoon salt
Few grains pepper

Chill. Fold in

½ cup sour cream *or* sweet cream beaten stiff and seasoned with 2 tablespoons vinegar

Taste and add more seasoning if necessary. *For fish. Makes about ¾ cup.*

TARTARE SAUCE

Mix well

- **¾ cup mayonnaise**
- **½ shallot, chopped fine, *or* 1 teaspoon chopped onion**
- **1 teaspoon capers**
- **1 teaspoon finely chopped pickles**
- **1 teaspoon chopped olives**
- **1 teaspoon chopped parsley**
- **1 tablespoon tarragon vinegar**

For fish and shellfish, especially fried shrimps or scallops. Makes about 1 cup.

VINAIGRETTE SAUCE

Mix well

- **1 teaspoon salt**
- **¼ teaspoon paprika**
- **1 tablespoon tarragon vinegar**
- **2 tablespoons cider vinegar**
- **6 tablespoons olive oil**
- **1 tablespoon chopped green pepper**
- **1 tablespoon chopped cucumber pickle**
- **1 teaspoon finely chopped parsley**
- **1 teaspoon finely chopped chives**

Change the proportions or add other herbs, if you like. *For fish. Makes about 1½ cups.*

LEMON BUTTER

Cream butter until very light and fluffy. Season with a few drops of lemon juice. *For canapés and sandwiches as well as for fish.*

Savory Butter. See page 45.

LOBSTER CORAL BUTTER

Put lobster coral through a fine sieve. Work it into ½ cup creamed butter. Use to color and season lobster soups and sauces or as a canapé spread.

MAÎTRE D'HÔTEL BUTTER (PARSLEY BUTTER)

Cream

- **½ cup butter**

Beat in

- **½ teaspoon salt**
- **⅛ teaspoon pepper**
- **2 tablespoons finely chopped parsley**

Beat in, drop by drop

- **1 tablespoon lemon juice**

For steak, chops or broiled fish. Makes about ½ cup.

Herb Butter. Add 1 teaspoon dried thyme or marjoram and 1 teaspoon dried basil. Or add fresh herbs, chopped fine. Add ¼ teaspoon garlic salt. *Spread on broiled lamb chops.*

Parsley Butter Pats. Put Maître d'Hôtel Butter on a piece of wax paper. Shape into a cylinder about 1 inch thick. Wrap and chill. When ready to serve, slice and place a pat on each serving of *steak, lamb chops or broiled fish.*

BEURRE NOIR (BLACK BUTTER)

Instead of using all butter, you may use the fat remaining in the pan after frying fish or meat and add enough butter to make about ⅓ cup.

Put in a small pan

- **⅓ cup butter**

Stir over low heat until melted and dark brown. Add

- **1 teaspoon lemon juice *or* mild vinegar**
- **Salt and pepper**

For fish or meat.

Tart Black Butter. Add 1 tablespoon vinegar and 1 tablespoon Worcestershire.

Black Butter Almond Sauce. When the butter begins to brown, stir in ⅓ cup blanched almonds, cut in pieces.

MARCHAND DE VIN SAUCE

Melt
  4 tablespoons butter
Stir in
  6 scallions, minced, *or* ½ cup minced onion
Cook 5 minutes. Add
  ¾ cup red wine
Simmer 20 minutes. Add
  1¼ cups (or 1 can) brown gravy
  2 tablespoons lemon juice
Just before serving, heat and stir in bit by bit
  2 tablespoons butter
For steak or roast beef. Makes about 2½ cups.

SWEET AND SOUR SAUCE

Traditionally, sliced tongue is heated in this sauce, but it is delicious, too, with hot or cold ham. If used with tongue, use the water in which the tongue was cooked for added flavor.

Simmer together
  4 cups water
  ⅓ cup mild vinegar
  2 small onions, sliced thin
  ½ cup raisins
  1 lemon, sliced paper-thin
  ½ cup brown sugar
  1 teaspoon allspice
  Cayenne, salt, ginger
  2 bay leaves
Simmer until the lemon and onions are tender. Add
  1 cup fine ginger snap crumbs
Stir until smooth and slightly thickened. *Makes about 4 cups.*

RAISIN SAUCE

Mix
  ½ cup brown sugar
  ½ tablespoon mustard
  ½ tablespoon flour
Add
  ¼ cup seedless raisins
  ¼ cup vinegar
  1¾ cups water
Cook slowly to a syrup. *For ham or tongue. Makes about 1½ cups.*

SPICY RAISIN SAUCE

Cook together 5 minutes
  1 cup sugar
  ½ cup water
Add
  1 cup seedless raisins
  2 tablespoons butter
  3 tablespoons vinegar
  ½ tablespoon Worcestershire
  ½ teaspoon salt
  ¼ teaspoon cloves
  Few grains each of mace and pepper
  1 glass tart fruit jelly
Cook until the jelly melts. *For ham or tongue. Makes 1 to 1½ cups.*

SPICED FRUIT SAUCE

Simmer 15 minutes
  ¾ cup claret
Add
  1 cup grape jelly
  ⅛ teaspoon cinnamon
  ⅛ teaspoon nutmeg
  Salt and pepper
Slice in thin strips
  Peel of 1 orange (removing the white membrane)
Add to the sauce, with
  Slices of orange, seeded
For ham, tongue or duck. Makes about 1½ cups.

COLD ORANGE SAUCE

Mix
  6 tablespoons currant jelly
  3 tablespoons sugar
  Grated rind 2 oranges
Beat 5 minutes. Add
  2 tablespoons port wine
  2 tablespoons orange juice
  2 tablespoons lemon juice
  ¼ teaspoon salt
  Few grains cayenne
Stir until well blended. *For duck or lamb. Makes about 1½ cups.*

GREEN HERB SAUCE

Whatever herbs your garden offers will make a delicious

sauce. Select perfect leaves and discard the stems.

Chop lettuce, celery and plenty of fresh herbs until very fine. You should have about 1 cupful. Stir in olive oil (¼ cup or more according to the greens used) drop by drop until the sauce is as thick as mayonnaise. Season with salt and vinegar. *For broiled or steamed fish, cold salmon or cold sliced lamb.*

MINT SAUCE

Heat together

½ cup mild vinegar
¼ cup sugar

Pour over

½ cup chopped mint leaves (no stems)

Let stand 1 hour or more. If you like a sweeter sauce, add more sugar. *For lamb. Makes about ½ cup.*

CURRANT MINT SAUCE

Separate a glass of currant jelly into small pieces with a fork. Do not beat. Sprinkle with 1 tablespoon grated orange rind and stick in a few perfect sprigs of mint. *For lamb.*

Eggs

Among the most versatile of foods, eggs are an excellent and comparatively inexpensive way to step up the protein in family meals. Use eggs as freely as possible in desserts and sauces and serve them often in place of meat or fish. Vary the ways you serve them so that your family will continue to enjoy them. Note the suggestions following Scrambled Eggs (p. 110) and Omelets (pp. 111–114). Then invent others of your own.

Buying and storing eggs (pp. 6–7).
Separating and beating eggs (p. 7).
Using extra whites and yolks (pp. 7–8).

"BOILED" EGGS

Not actually "boiled," since the water should be kept below the boiling point.

Have ready a pan of boiling water deep enough to cover the eggs. Have the eggs at room temperature; eggs icy cold from the refrigerator may crack when they touch the water. Slip each one carefully from a tablespoon into the pan. Reduce the heat so that the water just simmers.

Cook 3 to 5 minutes for soft-cooked eggs, 5 to 10 for medium, and 15 to 20 for hard-cooked. If the eggs are very small or very large, modify the time slightly.

You can also start the eggs in cold water. Bring slowly to the boiling point. For very soft eggs, take from the water immediately. Cover and simmer 2 minutes for soft-cooked eggs, 3 to 5 for medium, and 12 to 15 for hard.

Eggs with Cheese Sauce. Cook 10 minutes so that the white is firm but the center still creamy. Shell carefully and cover with hot Cheese Sauce (p. 95).

CODDLED EGGS

Let eggs stand in warm room long enough to lose chill. Put into a heavy pan filled with boiling water. Cover very closely and turn off the heat. Let stand 4 to 8 minutes, according to individual preference.

EGGS À LA MIMOSA

An attractive cold dish for a summer luncheon.

Cut hard-cooked eggs in half lengthwise. Remove the yolks and fill the white with chopped lobster, crab, tuna or ham. Cover with mayonnaise and sprinkle with egg yolk, crumbled evenly with a fork.

CREAMED EGGS

A useful basic recipe which helps with the problem of left-overs. Add chopped cooked ham, veal, chicken, lobster or shrimp, boned and mashed sardines, finely cut pimientos, cooked peas or asparagus tips. Undiluted canned soups (such as tomato, chicken or pea) make excellent sauces.

Cut in slices, quarters or eighths or chop fine

4 hard-cooked eggs

Prepare

1½ cups Cream Sauce (p. 94)

Add the eggs. Season to taste. Serve over

Toast, waffles *or* pancakes

Dust with paprika or decorate with a sprig of parsley or a few buttered crumbs or toasted wheat germ. *Serves 4.*

Curried Eggs. Season highly with curry powder or use Curry Sauce (p. 94). Add ½ cup cooked rice to the sauce.

Goldenrod Eggs. Separate the whites of the cooked eggs and chop them fine. Add to the sauce and pour it over the toast. Crumble the yolks over the top.

Scotch Woodcock. Chop the eggs fine. Season the sauce with anchovy paste.

SCALLOPED EGGS

A tasty "second day" dish. Add more protein by mixing toasted wheat germ with the crumbs.

Prepare

¾ to 1 cup cooked ham, chicken, veal *or* fish
2 hard-cooked eggs, chopped
2 cups Cream Sauce (p. 94)
¾ cup buttered fine bread crumbs

Butter a casserole and sprinkle with crumbs. Cover with half the eggs, then half the sauce and half the meat or fish. Repeat and cover with the rest of the crumbs. Bake at 375° until the crumbs are brown. *Serves 6.*

For a complete casserole dish, add peas, sliced cooked potatoes and more sauce or milk.

STUFFED EGGS

Stuffed egg halves, put together in pairs, are good picnic or lunchbox fare. They are also excellent as a salad on any salad green.

Hard-cook eggs. Crack and drop immediately into cold water to reduce darkening of the yolks. Shell and cut in half. Mash the yolks, moisten with melted butter or mayonnaise. Season to taste with salt, pepper, vinegar, lemon juice, mustard and cayenne. Refill the whites with the mixture.

Anchovy Eggs. Add anchovy paste to taste. Omit the mustard.

Deviled Eggs. Season highly. If you like, add 1 teaspoon grated cheese or minced pickles or olives for each egg.

Chicken, Ham *or* Veal Stuffed Eggs. Add chopped cooked chicken, ham or veal to the mashed yolks. Season to taste.

Eggs en Casserole. Arrange in a baking dish. Cover with Cheese (p. 95), Tomato (p. 99) or Mushroom Sauce (p. 98), or undiluted canned tomato, mushroom, celery or cream of chicken soup. Sprinkle with grated cheese or buttered crumbs. Bake at 350° until brown.

FRIED EGGS

Heat a heavy frying pan. Put in 1 tablespoon butter or bacon fat. Heat until the fat sizzles but doesn't smoke. Break an egg into a saucer. Turn into the pan, reduce the heat and cook slowly until the white is firm. Cook one or more at a time. Add a little more fat as needed, using just enough to keep the egg from sticking. During cooking, spoon the fat over the egg. Serve without turning ("sunny side up"), or turn and cook the other side, or slide the pan under the broiler to cook the top a little. Another way is to turn the eggs into the pan, as above, add 1 teaspoon of hot water, then cover closely, turn off the heat and let stand until as firm as you like.

Buttered Eggs à la Roberts. Fry 6 eggs in butter on one side only. Arrange on a hot platter. Pour around Roberts Sauce (p. 97).

Buttered Eggs with Tomatoes. Serve eggs fried in butter on tomato slices seasoned and sautéed in butter.

Eggs au Beurre Noir. In the same pan, brown 2 tablespoons butter quickly, add 1 tablespoon vinegar, and pour over the eggs.

EGG WITH A HAT

Plenty of butter makes this dish perfect.

Cut a round out of a slice of bread with a 2½-inch cooky cutter. Melt 2 tablespoons butter in a heavy frying pan. Put in both pieces of bread and cook over moderate heat until they begin to brown.

Break an egg into the hole and sprinkle it with salt and pepper. Continue cooking until the bread is brown, turn and brown the other side. Add butter as needed to keep the bread from sticking to the pan. Serve with the cut-out piece on top.

SHIRRED EGGS (OEUFS SUR LE PLAT)

Traditionally cooked and served in shallow baking dishes ("shirrers") just large enough for one or two eggs.

Set the oven at 400°. Put ½ teaspoon butter in each dish and heat until the butter melts. Break one or two eggs into each dish. Sprinkle with salt and add a teaspoon of cream or melted butter. Bake until the white is firm (4 or 5 minutes).

For a heartier luncheon dish, put in each dish any of the following and heat 5 minutes before adding the eggs.

- **Mushrooms,** sliced or chopped and sautéed in butter.
- **Cooked vegetables,** such as asparagus tips, peas, spinach, sliced carrots or tiny whole ones.
- **Bits of cooked ham, fish or seafood.**

Shirred Eggs with Crumbs. Butter the shirrers. Cover the bottoms and sides with fine cracker crumbs. Slip in the eggs. Cover with buttered crumbs. Bake as above.

Eggs Shirred in Cream. For each egg, mix 1½ tablespoons heavy cream with 2 tablespoons fine bread crumbs and ¼ teaspoon salt. Put half in the shirrer, slip in the egg, cover with the rest of the mixture and bake.

Shirred Eggs with Sausages. Cut 6 small pork sausages in ½-inch pieces. Cook 10 minutes in 1 teaspoon butter. Add 1 cup Tomato Sauce (p. 99) or canned tomato soup and divide in 6 egg shirrers. Break 1 or 2 eggs into each and bake.

Eggs Mornay. For 6 eggs, make Mornay Sauce (p. 95). When the eggs are ready to bake, cover with the sauce and sprinkle with grated cheese. Bake as above.

EGGS FLORENTINE

Set the oven at 350°. Butter individual casseroles. Put in each a tablespoon of chopped cooked spinach, seasoned with salt and butter. Sprinkle with grated Parmesan cheese. Break an egg into each casserole and cover with 1 tablespoon cream. Sprinkle with more cheese. Bake until the eggs are set (about 8 minutes).

POACHED EGGS

Perfect poached eggs have firm whites and creamy soft yolks. To keep them in attractive rounds, use an egg poacher.

Fill a heavy frying pan two-thirds full of boiling salted water. Break each egg separately into a saucer and slip carefully into the water. Cover the pan and turn off the heat. Let stand 5 minutes. Test by pressing the yolk lightly with the back of the fork. If you like eggs firmer, turn on the heat again and cook slowly a minute or two more. Take out of the water very carefully with a skimmer. Serve on buttered toast or sautéed rounds of bread.

To vary, spoon over the eggs sautéed mushrooms or any mushroom or tomato sauce, or put on the toast a sautéed chicken liver or a thin slice of ham, or spread the toast with mashed liver sausage or foie gras.

Poached Eggs on Tomatoes. For each egg, sauté a thick slice of tomato in olive oil seasoned with salt and pepper and a pinch of basil or oregano. Cook a sliver of garlic with the tomato, if you like. Put a poached egg on each slice.

Poached Eggs au Gratin. Set the oven at 350°. Butter a shallow baking dish. Put poached eggs in it. Sprinkle with grated Parmesan cheese. Cover with Tomato (p. 99), Cream (p. 94) or Yellow Béchamel Sauce (p. 95). Sprinkle with more cheese. Bake until the top is brown.

EGGS BENEDICT

Split and toast English muffins. Put on each piece a thin round of ham, sautéed 5 minutes. Put a poached egg on each. Cover with Hollandaise Sauce (p. 100), thinned with cream.

FRENCH POACHED EGGS

Eggs poached this way are perfectly symmetrical and look very attractive.

Bring 3 pints of water to a full boil in a deep saucepan. Add 1 tablespoon vinegar and ½ tablespoon salt. Break an egg into a saucer. Stir the boiling water vigorously around and around the edge of the pan with a wooden spoon held almost upright. As soon as a well forms in the middle of the water, stop stirring and slip the egg into the center of the well. Lower the heat and cook until the white is set. Take out with a skimmer and trim evenly. Repeat until the desired number of eggs is prepared. Serve in any of the ways suggested under Poached Eggs.

EGGS MOLLET CHASSEUR

Poached eggs in a wonderful sauce.

Cook and stir 3 minutes

1 tablespoon butter
1 shallot, chopped fine, *or* 1 teaspoon chopped onion

Add

3 mushrooms, chopped

Cook 5 minutes. Add

¼ cup chicken stock *or* bouillon
1 tablespoon sherry
⅛ teaspoon salt
Pepper and cayenne to taste

Bring to the boiling point. Simmer 10 minutes. Pour into a shallow baking dish. Poach about 5 minutes

4 eggs

Put the eggs in the sauce in the baking dish. Sprinkle over them

2 tablespoons cream
1 tablespoon grated Parmesan cheese

Bake at 400° until the cheese melts. *Serves 4.*

EGGS À LA SUISSE

Melt in a small omelet pan

1 tablespoon butter

Add

½ cup cream

Slip in, one at a time

4 eggs

Sprinkle with

Salt, pepper and cayenne

Cook slowly until the whites are nearly firm. Sprinkle with

2 tablespoons grated cheese

Continue cooking until the whites are firm. Serve on

Buttered toast

Pour the cream from the pan over the eggs. For an extra touch, season the cream with

Sherry to taste

Serves 4.

Eggs in White Wine. Use dry white wine in place of cream.

Eggs in Tomato Sauce. Use Tomato Sauce (p. 99) in place of cream. Season it to taste with minced thyme, basil or parsley, or a combination of herbs. Heat a piece of garlic in the sauce, if desired.

SCRAMBLED EGGS

Soft, creamy scrambled eggs, served piping hot with a slice or two of boiled ham or crisp bacon, can be an epicurean dish. Cook slowly and be sure not to let the eggs brown at all. An easy but slow way is to scramble eggs in a double boiler, stirring them occasionally.

Mix

5 eggs, slightly beaten
½ teaspoon salt
⅛ teaspoon pepper
½ cup top milk *or* cream

Heat an omelet pan. Melt in it

2 tablespoons butter

Add the eggs. Cook over low heat until creamy, constantly stirring and scraping from the bottom and sides of the pan. Do not overcook. *Serves 4.*

To vary, use sour cream, or when nearly done, stir in 1 cup cottage cheese, or 1 small cream cheese, crumbled.

Scrambled Eggs with Mushrooms. Sauté 1 cup sliced mushrooms in butter, sprinkle lightly with flour, add a few drops onion juice, salt and cayenne, and cook 8 minutes. Add the eggs and milk and cook.

Scrambled Eggs New York Style. Cook 1 cup match-shaped pieces of ham (1 thin slice) with 2

tablespoons chopped onion and $1\frac{1}{2}$ tablespoons butter. After 5 minutes, add 5 mushroom caps, peeled and sliced, and cook 5 minutes longer. Serve as a border around the eggs.

SCRAMBLED EGGS CREOLE

Put in a skillet
2 tablespoons butter
1 slice onion, diced
Cook 5 minutes. Add
1 cup tomatoes
1 teaspoon sugar
Salt and pepper
Cook 5 minutes. Add
5 eggs, beaten slightly
¼ cup grated cheese (if desired)
Stir and cook until creamy. *Serves 4.*

SCRAMBLED EGGS COUNTRY STYLE

Melt in an omelet pan
2 tablespoons butter
Turn in
4 eggs, unbeaten
Add
½ cup top milk, *or* sweet *or* sour cream
Stir, using a fork, and cook over very slow heat until as firm as you like. Season with
Salt and pepper
Serves 2 or 3.

EGGS À LA CARACAS

Cut fine, with scissors
2 ounces dried beef
Add
1 cup tomatoes, canned or fresh, cut small
¼ cup grated cheese
Few drops onion juice
Few grains cinnamon and cayenne
Melt in an omelet pan
2 tablespoons butter
Add the mixture and heat 3 minutes. Add
3 eggs, well beaten
Stir and cook over direct heat until creamy. *Serves 4.*

FRENCH OMELET

Never make an omelet with more than 4 eggs. Make several small ones instead. Select an omelet pan carefully. Heavy cast aluminum is excellent because it heats evenly.

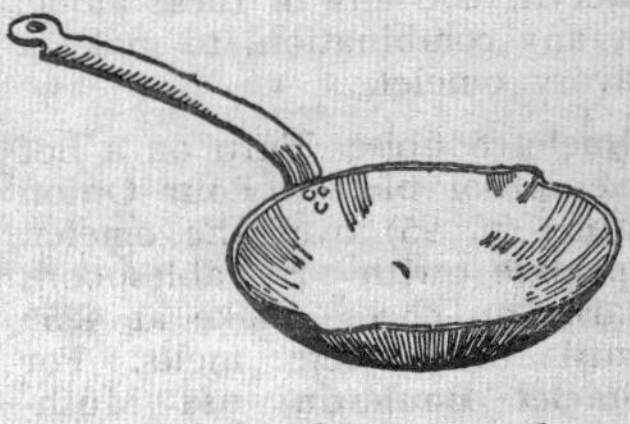

Beat slightly, just enough to blend the yolks and whites
4 eggs
Add
4 tablespoons water
½ teaspoon salt
⅛ teaspoon pepper
Melt in a hot omelet pan
2 tablespoons butter
When the butter begins to sizzle, add the eggs and reduce the heat slightly. As the omelet cooks, lift it with a spatula, letting the uncooked part run under, until the whole is creamy. Increase the heat to brown slightly underneath. A perfect omelet is creamy inside, or what the French call *baveuse.* Fold double and turn onto a hot platter. *Serves 2 or 3.*

To vary, add to the eggs ¼ cup croutons (p. 58), or sauté in the butter 1 teaspoon minced parsley or 2 tablespoons minced green or red peppers.

Cheese Omelet. Add to the eggs 4 tablespoons grated cheese and cook as above. Gruyère is especially good.

Sweet Omelet. Omit the pepper. Add 1½ tablespoons very fine sugar and ½ teaspoon vanilla. Cook as above. Spread with jam, tart jelly or marmalade before folding. Sprinkle with sugar. As a fancy touch, score with a hot skewer. Serve as dessert.

Omelet aux Fines Herbes. Add to the egg mixture ½ teaspoon each of finely cut parsley, watercress, chives, and tarragon or chervil. Use any of these alone, or any combination, to make a savory omelet.

Omelet Soubise. Turn on a hot oven-proof platter. Pour Onion Sauce (p. 95) over the omelet. Sprinkle with 2 tablespoons Parmesan cheese. Bake at 425° until the cheese melts. For **Omelet Boulestin,** use Mushroom Sauce (p. 98).

Omelet Paysanne. Cut thin strips of bacon in small squares to make ½ cup. Fry until crisp and brown. Drain off the fat and in it fry 1 cup ¼-inch potato cubes until delicately brown. Drain and mix with the bacon. Fold half into the omelet and put the rest around the edge.

FILLED OMELETS

An excellent way to present leftovers.

Make a French Omelet (p. 111), but before folding it, spread with 2 tablespoons heavy sweet or sour cream, grated cheese, crumbled cooked bacon or chopped cooked ham or sausage. Or fill with any of the following, heated so that the omelet will not be cooled.

Chicken, cooked, chopped and creamed or seasoned.
Fish, cooked and flaked or creamed.
Kidney, cooked and minced.
Lobster, shrimp, tuna or crab meat, cooked or canned, cut small and creamed or heated in butter.
Mushrooms, creamed or sautéed.
Tomato, fresh or canned, cut small and seasoned to taste.
Cooked vegetables, cut small and heated in butter. Asparagus tips, peas and chopped spinach are especially good.

CHICKEN NOODLE OMELET

Mix
- **5 eggs, beaten slightly**
- **1 can concentrated chicken noodle soup**

Cook like French Omelet (p. 111) for an emergency supper dish *for 4.*

SPINACH OMELET À LA MARTIN

Mix
- **3 eggs, slightly beaten**
- **3 tablespoons hot water**
- **½ teaspoon salt**
- **1 tablespoon red pepper, cut in strips**
- **1 tablespoon green pepper, cut in strips**
- **1 tablespoon cooked ham, cut in tiny pieces**

Put in a heated omelet pan
- **1½ tablespoons olive oil**

Pour in the egg mixture. Cook like French Omelet (p. 111). Serve on a layer of
- **Spinach, cooked and seasoned**

Garnish with
- **Parsley**

Serves 3.

LOBSTER OMELET

Cook together 5 minutes
- **1 teaspoon butter**
- **1 small onion, sliced thin**

Add

1 stalk celery, diced
⅛ teaspoon sugar
2 tablespoons Chicken Stock (p. 62) *or* canned chicken broth
1 teaspoon soy sauce
⅓ cup diced cooked lobster

Turn the mixture into a buttered omelet pan. Add

2 eggs, slightly beaten

Spread evenly and cook until the eggs are set. Turn and fold. *Serves 2.*

OMELET SAVOYARDE

A savory French peasant dish.

Wash and boil until soft

2 potatoes

Cool, pare, cut in ½-inch cubes, and set aside. Melt in a small frying pan

1 tablespoon butter

Add

1 cup potato cubes
¾ teaspoon onion juice
¼ teaspoon salt
Few grains pepper

Cook until the potatoes are slightly browned. Cut in thin slices crosswise

½ cup leeks (white part)

Cook in boiling water until soft. Drain and set aside. Melt in an omelet pan

2 tablespoons butter

Mix

5 eggs, slightly beaten
⅔ cup cream
½ teaspoon salt
⅛ teaspoon pepper

Pour into the pan. Cook 5 minutes, pricking and picking up with a fork. Add the potatoes, leeks and

1 tablespoon chopped parsley

Continue cooking until creamy. Add

3 tablespoons grated cheese

Increase the heat to brown the omelet quickly underneath. Fold and turn out on a hot serving dish. Garnish with

A sprig of parsley

Serves 6.

SPANISH OMELET

Sliced mushrooms and a few capers may be added to the sauce for extra zest.

Put in a saucepan

3 tablespoons butter *or* bacon fat
1 tablespoon finely chopped onion
1 tablespoon finely chopped red or green pepper

Cook until the onion is yellow. Add

1¼ cups tomatoes, cut in quarters

Cook until thick. Season to taste. Make a French Omelet (p. 111), using

4 eggs

Pour the sauce around it. *Serves 2 or 3.*

Piperade Basque. Prepare the sauce, using 3 onions and 2 peppers. Add it to the eggs and cook like Scrambled Eggs (p. 110).

PUFFY OMELET

Milk is sometimes used in place of hot water, but hot water makes a more tender omelet.

Put in a bowl

4 egg yolks

Beat until thick and lemon-colored. Add

4 tablespoons hot water
½ teaspoon salt
Few grains pepper

Beat until stiff

4 egg whites

Cut and fold the whites into the yolks, until the mixture is well blended. Heat an omelet pan with a metal or heatproof handle. Butter the sides and bottom. Spoon the omelet mixture into the pan and spread it evenly. Cook slowly, occasionally turning the pan to brown the omelet evenly. When well-puffed and delicately browned underneath, put the pan in a 375° oven to finish cooking the top. If you like, sprinkle with

Grated cheese

The omelet is cooked if it is firm to the touch when pressed with a finger. If it clings like beaten egg white, the omelet needs to be cooked longer. Fold and turn onto a hot platter. *Serves 4.*

Vary in any of the ways suggested for French Omelet (p. 111).

Almond Omelet with Caramel Sauce. Prepare 1 cup Caramel Sauce (p. 430) and add ¼ cup to the beaten yolks. Add ½ teaspoon vanilla and fold in the beaten whites. Sprinkle the buttered omelet pan with ½ cup shredded almonds before pouring in the omelet mixture. Cook as above. Pour the rest of the sauce around the omelet. Serve as dessert.

Bread Crumb Omelet. Soak ½ cup dry crumbs 15 minutes in ½ cup milk. Add to the beaten yolks.

FRITTATA

This Italian dish makes good use of bits of leftover cooked vegetables such as asparagus tips, peas, green beans, chopped spinach or bits of zucchini or artichoke bottoms.

Put in an 8- or 9-inch frying pan
1 tablespoon olive oil
½ clove garlic (on a toothpick)
1 tablespoon minced onion
Cook slowly until the onion is yellow. Remove the garlic. Mix
4 eggs, slightly beaten
1 cup cooked vegetable
⅓ cup grated crumbs, soaked in ¼ cup tomato juice, milk, consommé *or* water
Heat the frying pan containing the onion and add to it
1 tablespoon olive oil
Pour in the egg mixture. Cover and cook slowly until the frittata shrinks from the side of the pan. Prick the center if it puffs up. Set in the broiler to brown the top. Cut in wedges like a pie. *Serves 4.*

EGGS FOO YUNG

Beat together
5 eggs
½ cup water
Add
¼ cup slivered onions
½ cup bean sprouts *or* finely cut celery
½ cup chopped cooked lean meat, chicken, lobster *or* shrimp
½ cup sliced water chestnuts *or* mushrooms
Salt and pepper
Soy sauce to taste
Spread in a thin layer in a well-buttered, heated omelet pan. Brown on both sides. *Serves 4.*

· LUNCHEON CUSTARD

Mix
4 eggs, slightly beaten
1 cup milk
½ teaspoon salt
⅛ teaspoon pepper
Few grains cayenne
Few drops onion juice
Fill buttered timbale molds or small custard cups. Set in a pan of hot water. Bake at 350° until firm (about 25 minutes). Unmold and serve with
Tomato (p. 99) *or* Mushroom Sauce (p. 98)
Serves 4.

Custard Ring. Bake in a ring mold. Turn out onto a serving dish. Fill the center with buttered peas or creamed mushrooms.

Cheese Custard. Add ½ cup grated cheese and 2 tablespoons melted butter to the custard mixture.

Egg and Pimiento Timbales. Line the buttered custard cups or timbale molds with canned pimientos.

GARDEN CLUB SOUFFLÉ

Melt
2 tablespoons butter
Stir in
2 tablespoons flour
Add slowly
2 cups milk *or* milk and cream
Stir and cook 5 minutes. Beat
4 egg yolks
until thick and lemon-colored. Stir into the sauce. Remove from the heat. Add
1 teaspoon salt
Few grains cayenne
1 tablespoon grated onion
1 teaspoon each of chopped fresh herbs (basil, tarragon and parsley, for example)
Cool slightly. Beat
4 egg whites
until stiff. Stir 1 tablespoon beaten white thoroughly into the soufflé mixture. Fold in the rest. Turn into an unbuttered straight-sided dish and set in a pan of hot water. Bake at 350° until as firm as liked (45 to 60 minutes). Serve from the baking dish. *Serves 4 to 6.*

EGG TIMBALES

Melt
1 tablespoon butter
Blend in
1 tablespoon flour
Add slowly
⅔ cup milk
Stir until thick and smooth. Remove from the heat. Stir in
3 egg yolks, beaten until thick
1 tablespoon chopped parsley
½ teaspoon salt
⅛ teaspoon pepper
Few grains celery salt
Few grains cayenne
Cut and fold in
3 egg whites, beaten until stiff
Turn into buttered custard cups. Set in pan of hot water. Bake at 350° until firm (35 to 45 minutes). Unmold and serve with any tomato or mushroom sauce. *Serves 4.*

Cheese

Cheese is an appetizing source of protein, calcium and vitamins. Enrich the family diet by serving it often. Main dishes made with cheese are highly satisfying as a substitute for meat.

All cheeses are made of milk or cream, but vary widely in flavor due to various methods of aging. Many of the types once produced only in foreign countries are now made in the United States.

Process cheese is blended with milk and pressed into brick form. It is also sold with added seasonings.

The following list gives the principal types of cheese. There are many other delicious ones to be found in provision stores which cater to persons of cosmopolitan tastes.

American: semi-hard; mild to sharp
Bel Paese: semi-hard; mild
Blue (Bleu): marbled; strong, salty flavor
Brie: soft, almost liquid center; sharp
Camembert: soft, almost liquid center; sharp
Cheddar: semi-hard to hard; mild to sharp
Cheshire: hard Cheddar type; sharp
Cottage: soft; mild
Cream: soft; mild
Edam: hard, somewhat crumbly; mild
Gorgonzola: semi-soft, marbled; sharp
Gouda: semi-hard; mild
Gruyère: semi-hard; mild
Liederkranz: soft; sharp, pungent
Limburger: soft; sharp, pungent
Mozzarella: soft, semi-dry; mild
Munster: soft, semi-dry; mild
Neufchâtel: soft; like cream cheese but slightly less mild
Parmesan: hard; sharp
Pineapple: hard; moderately sharp
Pont l'Évêque: soft, almost liquid; similar to Brie
Poona: soft, almost liquid; similar to Brie but sharper
Port du Salut: semi-hard; moderately sharp
Provolone: semi-hard; mild, smoky
Ricotta: similar to cottage but drier; used in distinctive Italian dishes
Romano: hard; moderately sharp
Roquefort: semi-hard, marbled; strong, pungent
Scandinavian: hard or semi-hard; distinctive sandy texture—mild to pungent
Stilton: hard, marbled; pungent
Swiss: semi-hard; mild

COOKING CHEESE

Cook cheese at low temperature. Cooking too fast or too long makes cheese tough or stringy. Cheddar cheese, often called "American" or "store" cheese, is the standard cooking cheese. It may be mild or sharp in flavor. Process cheeses melt to creamy smoothness in sauces but are often somewhat bland in flavor. Other good cheeses for cooking are the Italian types such as Mozzarella and Provolone. Some recipes call for special cheeses—cottage, Ricotta, cream, Swiss or Roquefort.

GRATING CHEESE

Use dry hard cheese, such as Cheddar, Gruyère, pineapple, Parmesan or Romano. Grate it as needed on a grater, in a cheese grater or in an electric blender, or buy freshly grated cheese in small quantities. One pound of cheese yields 4 to 5 cups, grated.

STORING CHEESE

Put in a tightly covered container or wrap in aluminum foil. Store in a cool dry cupboard or in the refrigerator.

SERVING CHEESE

Cheese often adds the satisfying final touch or balances an otherwise light meal. Any cheese that is not too hard to cut is good for snacks or for dessert.

Some of the best are the soft uncooked cheeses such as cottage, cream and Neufchâtel. Vary cottage cheese by moistening with melted butter and sweet or sour cream, and season to taste with salt and, if you like, finely cut chives or herbs. Serve cream cheese with jam or Bar-le-Duc currants and toasted crackers for a simple but satisfying dessert. To dress it up a bit, mold in a cone, cover with whipped cream or sour cream, and pour the jam or Bar-le-Duc around it.

To serve cheese at its best, let it stand at room temperature several hours. Put Camembert, Pont l'Évêque and Brie in a slightly warm place (on a radiator or near the stove) so that the soft center will be almost liquid.

Serve a bright Edam or Gouda cheese whole. Cut a slice off the top and serve from the shell with a cheese scoop. Cut Swiss cheese in thin slices. Cut other cheeses in slices or neat cubes or leave in one large piece to be cut as needed.

Crackers and cheese is an obvious combination. Have the crackers very fresh and crisp, preferably unsalted—like hard pilot biscuit. Hot toasted ones are especially good. So is crusty French bread, toasted or not. Cheese, especially Provolone, and fine pears or apples go superbly together. Cheese and pie need no comment.

Cheese spreads are marketed ready to use. Or you can prepare your own (p. 45).

Recipes featuring cheese. Cheese appears in many recipes throughout the book. Here are some of the most popular; consult the index for others.

Macaroni and Cheese (p. 312)
Cheese Soufflé (p. 121)
Toasted Cheese Sandwiches (p. 362)
Cheese Soup (p. 66)
Pizza (p. 349)
Cheese Cake (p. 450)

COEUR À LA CRÈME

An easy but festive dessert. To present it in the classic French fashion, mold it in a special heart-shaped basket.

Put through a coarse sieve
¼ pound cottage cheese

Add and beat together until smooth

- **¼ pound cream cheese**
- **½ cup sweet *or* sour cream**
- **½ teaspoon confectioners' sugar**

Pack in a mold lined with damp cheesecloth. Chill 2 hours. Turn out onto a plate and serve with cream and sugar or with strawberry jam.

PETIT SUISSE

Imported petit suisse is very perishable and so is rarely available, but it is simple to prepare a delicious substitute.

Mash a package of cream cheese with a fork and add ½ teaspoon granulated sugar. Stir in heavy cream, a little at a time, until the cheese is softened but still firm enough to shape into a cylinder about 1½ inches across. Roll in wax paper. Chill, turn out onto a plate, and serve like Coeur à la Crème.

FROZEN CHEESE ALEXANDRA

A tasty last course at dinner or, with salad and hot biscuits, the main course for a party luncheon.

Cream

- **½ cup butter**

Add and work until well blended

- **¼ pound Roquefort, crumbled**

Mix in

- **1 teaspoon salt**
- **½ teaspoon paprika**
- **1 teaspoon minced chives**
- **2 tablespoons sherry**

Pack in a small mold and freeze.

HOT CHEESE SAVORY

Rich hot cheese to serve at lunch with a generous green salad, or in the English fashion as the savory last course at dinner.

Mix

- **2 eggs, slightly beaten**
- **⅔ cup heavy cream**
- **½ cup Swiss cheese, cut small**
- **½ cup grated Parmesan cheese**
- **Salt and pepper**
- **Cayenne**
- **Nutmeg**

Spoon into a small casserole or into 6 small ramekins. Bake 15 minutes at 450°.

SPRING SALAD

To carry on a picnic, pack in individual paper cartons. It need not be icy cold to be refreshing, nor does it need to be served on lettuce.

Add to cottage cheese finely cut olives, celery, radishes and raw carrot. Moisten with mayonnaise and season to taste.

CHEESE PIMIENTOS

A colorful and delicious luncheon dish. Quick, too!

Drain canned pimientos thoroughly. Cut mild cheese in slices ⅓ inch thick and sprinkle with salt and cayenne. Put a slice of cheese in each pimiento, sprinkle with flour, and sauté in butter until the cheese melts.

CHEESE TOAST

The cheese may be a tasty Cheddar or a combination of cheeses. Season more highly, if you like, with Worcestershire or curry.

Melt

- **2 tablespoons butter**

Stir in

- **1 tablespoon flour**
- **¼ teaspoon salt**
- **Few grains pepper**

Add

1 cup milk

Cook and stir until thick. Add

¾ cup grated cheese

Cook until the cheese melts. Add

2 egg yolks, slightly beaten

Cook and stir until thick. Fold in

2 egg whites, beaten stiff

Stir just enough to blend. Pour over

6 slices toast

Garnish as you like with

A shake of paprika, a bit of crisp bacon, a sprig of parsley or watercress, *or* a few slices of stuffed olive

Serves 3.

WELSH RABBIT (RAREBIT)

Which is correct? Nobody knows and it really doesn't matter. The secret of perfection is the quality of the cheese—an honest Cheddar or Cheshire type, either mild or sharp as you prefer.

Put in a double boiler or chafing dish or in a pan over low heat

½ pound cheese, cut small
1 tablespoon butter
¼ teaspoon salt
½ teaspoon dry mustard
Few grains cayenne *or* 1 teaspoon paprika

Cook slowly until the cheese melts, stirring occasionally. Add

½ cup ale *or* beer
1 egg, slightly beaten

Stir constantly until thick (a wooden spoon is best). Taste and add more seasoning if you like, such as a few drops of Worcestershire. Pour over toast, Saltines or broiled tomato slices. *Serves 4.*

Cream Rarebit. Omit the butter and the ale. Instead, melt the cheese with ¾ cup cream.

Ways to serve Welsh Rabbit. As a simple but satisfying luncheon or supper dish, spoon over any of these:

Slices of chicken or turkey breast on buttered toast. Top with a strip of bacon and set under the broiler until the bacon crisps.

Slices of tomato on toast.

Broccoli, cauliflower, or asparagus on toast or on sliced ham.

Sliced hard-cooked eggs or poached eggs on toast.

Toast spread with deviled ham.

Bits of cooked lobster, shrimp, crab meat or tuna on rice or toast.

ENGLISH MONKEY

A simple luncheon or supper dish. Also delicious as a hot cocktail dip.

Mix in a double boiler

1 cup crumbled bread (not too fresh)
1 cup milk
1 cup sharp or mild cheese, cut small

Cook until the cheese is melted, stirring occasionally. (It can be left several hours or ½ hour, whichever is convenient.) Season to taste with

Salt, pepper and prepared mustard

Pour over

Crackers, toasted and spread with butter

Serves 4.

RUM TUM TIDDY

A quickie for the teen-age crowd.

Mix

1 can condensed tomato soup
½ pound sharp cheese, cut in small pieces

Cook and stir over low heat or in a double boiler until the cheese melts. Season to taste with

Salt, pepper, mustard

Serve hot on crackers or toast. *Serves 4.*

For a heartier dish, add 1 cup cooked rice or 1 can drained whole kernel corn.

CHILALY

For luncheon or supper with a salad or a green vegetable.

Melt
1 tablespoon butter
Add
2 tablespoons chopped green pepper
1 tablespoon chopped onion
Cook slowly 3 minutes. Add
½ cup drained canned tomatoes
Cook 5 minutes. Add
¾ pound soft mild cheese, cut in small pieces
½ teaspoon salt
Few grains cayenne
Cook slowly or over hot water until the cheese melts. Stir in
2 tablespoons milk
1 egg, slightly beaten
Spoon over toast or crackers. *Serves 4 to 6.*

QUICK FONDUE

Mix
1 can evaporated milk
½ pound sharp cheese, cut in small pieces
Cook and stir over low heat or in a double boiler until the cheese melts. Remove from the heat. Stir in
¼ teaspoon dry mustard *or* prepared mustard to taste
1 egg, slightly beaten
Salt and pepper to taste
Mix thoroughly and serve hot on crackers or toast. *Serves 4.*

SWISS FONDUE

A conversation piece served in a chafing dish or a heavy casserole with thick cubes of crusty French bread to dip (on forks) directly into the fondue. If you prefer, ladle the fondue into well-heated individual pottery bowls. For the authentic Swiss touch, flavor with Kirsch just before serving.

Use either a chafing dish or a heavy casserole on an asbestos mat over very low heat. Rub the dish with
A clove of garlic, split
Pour in
¾ cup dry white wine *or* vermouth
Heat just until it bubbles. Add
1 pound well-aged Swiss cheese, diced
Cook and stir until melted and smooth. Season to taste with
Salt, nutmeg and pepper
Serves 4.

AMERICAN FONDUE

Firmer than a Swiss fondue and easier to make. It can wait, too.

Mix
1 cup scalded milk
¼ cup soft bread crumbs
¼ pound mild cheese, cut in small pieces (1 cup)
1 tablespoon butter
½ teaspoon salt
Cook over low heat until smooth, stirring with a fork. Remove from the heat. Stir in
2 or 3 egg yolks, beaten thick
Cut and fold in
2 or 3 egg whites, beaten stiff
Pour into a buttered 1-quart casserole. Bake 20 minutes at 350°. For a firmer fondue, bake 30 minutes. *Serves 4.*

FONDUE CELESTINE

An adaptable recipe. You will think of other fillings to use—chopped hard-cooked eggs, crab meat, tuna or ham.

Mix
1 pound cooked *or* canned lobster meat, chopped
1 cup finely cut celery
2 tablespoons chopped onion
½ cup mayonnaise

1 tablespoon mustard
½ teaspoon paprika
Remove the crusts from
16 thin slices of bread
Make into sandwiches using the prepared filling. Cut in quarters. Butter a baking dish and put in layers of the sandwiches, alternating with layers of
Sliced or grated cheese (about ¾ pound in all)
Mix
1 egg, slightly beaten
2 cups scalded milk
Salt and pepper
Pour over the sandwiches. Set in a pan of hot water. Bake at 325° until firm (about ½ hour). *Serves 8.*

CHEESE SOUFFLÉ

Rush a soufflé to the table the minute it is done, especially if it is baked the French way—crusty outside but soft and creamy within. Vary the cheese sometimes by using a combination of Camembert and grated Parmesan or Swiss and bleu cheeses.

Melt
4 tablespoons butter
Blend in
4 tablespoons flour
Add gradually
1 cup milk
Stir until thick and smooth. Add
½ teaspoon salt
Few grains cayenne
½ to 1 cup grated cheese
Stir until smooth and remove from the heat. Add
4 egg yolks, beaten until light
Cool. Just before baking beat until stiff
4 egg whites (5 for a very fluffy soufflé)
Stir a tablespoon of the white into the yolk mixture. Fold in the rest. Spoon into an unbuttered 1½-quart straight-sided baking dish. Set in a pan of hot water. **For a firm soufflé,** bake 30 to 45 minutes at 325°. **For a creamy soufflé** (French fashion), bake 25 minutes at 375°. *Serves 4.*

For a heartier soufflé, add diced ham and sautéed mushrooms, or diced turkey or chicken, or diced ham with whole kernel corn.

Tomato Soufflé. Use tomato juice instead of milk. Season with oregano if you like.

Seafood Soufflé. Mix cooked or canned lobster or shrimp with sautéed mushrooms and enough mayonnaise to moisten. Put a layer in the baking dish before spooning in the soufflé mixture.

TAPIOCA CHEESE SOUFFLÉ

Mix in a saucepan
3 tablespoons quick tapioca
1 teaspoon salt
1 cup milk
Cook and stir until the mixture boils. Add
1 cup grated cheese
Stir until the cheese melts. Beat until stiff and set aside
3 egg whites
Without washing the beater, beat
3 egg yolks
Stir into the tapioca mixture. Fold in the egg whites. Bake 20 to 25 minutes at 375°. *Serves 4.*

QUICHE LORRAINE

A luncheon or supper dish and also—in bite-sized pieces—a perfect tidbit with drinks. Serve it warm, but not piping hot.

Cook until crisp
½ pound bacon
Crumble it and put aside. Put in a pan
1 tablespoon butter
½ cup finely chopped onion
Cook 5 minutes. Mix

3 eggs, slightly beaten
2 cups cream *or* top milk
1 teaspoon salt
½ pound Swiss cheese, cut small

Add the bacon and the onion. Season with

Cayenne and nutmeg

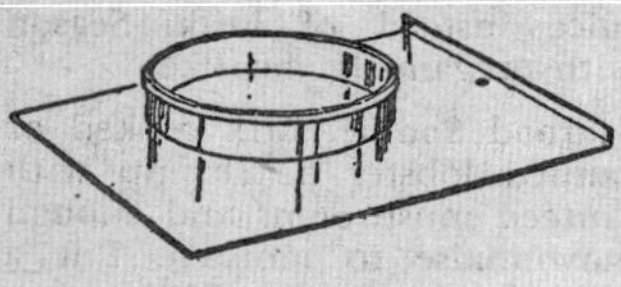

Line a 9-inch pie pan or flan ring with

Plain Pastry, homemade (p. 438) or from a mix

Pour in the mixture. Bake 10 minutes at 450°, then reduce the heat to 325° and cook until firm (about 20 minutes). Cut in wedges. *Serves 6.*

Quiche Lorraine with Ham. Substitute ¼ pound diced ham for the bacon.

SHAPLEIGH LUNCHEON CHEESE

Spread with butter

4 slices dry bread about ⅓ inch thick

Cut each slice in 8 strips. Put a layer in a buttered baking dish. Arrange the rest of the strips upright around the sides. Mix and pour into the dish

2 eggs, slightly beaten
1 cup thin cream
1 teaspoon salt
½ teaspoon mustard
¼ teaspoon paprika
Few grains cayenne
½ pound mild cheese, cut in small pieces

Bake 30 minutes at 350°. *Serves 4.*

CHEESE AND OLIVE CASSEROLE

An adaptable recipe. Use cooked chicken or tuna in place of the olives or with them.

Butter

5 slices bread

Cut off the crusts in thin strips. Cut the centers into 1-inch squares. Mix the squares with

1 cup grated cheese
3 eggs, slightly beaten
2 cups scalded milk
½ cup sliced stuffed olives

Season to taste and pour into a casserole. Sauté the bread strips in butter until golden-brown and put over the top. Bake at 300° until firm (40 to 60 minutes). *Serves 4 to 6.*

CHEESE CROQUETTES

Perfect with chicken or ham or with creamed mushrooms as the main dish for lunch or supper.

Melt

3 tablespoons butter

Add

¼ cup flour
⅔ cup milk

Stir until thick and smooth. Add

2 egg yolks, unbeaten

Mix well. Add

½ cup Swiss or Gruyère cheese, cut in small pieces

Stir over the heat until the cheese melts. Remove from the heat. Fold in

1 cup mild cheese, cut in small cubes

Season with

Salt, pepper and cayenne

Spread in a shallow pan, 8 by 8 inches, and cool. Turn out onto a board, cut in small squares or strips. Roll in

Crumbs

Fry (p. 4). *Serves 6.*

Fish

Fish cookery is an especially useful art to acquire because fish, although usually less expensive, has protein values at least equal to and in some cases greater than the best meats and it is also rich in iodine and in the B vitamins. Improved shipping and freezing are bringing more varieties to all parts of the country, even far from the sea.

SHOPPING FOR FISH

If you buy fish whole or with the bones, allow 3/4 pound for each generous serving. Steaks or fillets will provide two or three servings to the pound. Leftover cooked fish can be used in many tasty dishes (p. 136).

Fresh fish has firm elastic flesh, bright eyes and gills, and a characteristic odor which can only be described as "fresh" but which is easily learned. Wrap tightly in wax paper or foil and store in the coldest part of the refrigerator but not in the freezer.

Frozen fish should be hard-frozen when bought. Store in the freezer or the ice-cube compartment. Fillets may be cooked frozen or thawed, but a large piece of fish cooks more evenly if it is thawed just before cooking. Never refreeze frozen fish.

PREPARING FISH FOR COOKING

Fish bought in markets is usually ready to cook. Have the head and tail removed or not according to the way the fish is to be cooked. Keep the head and tail to make a savory Fish Stock (p. 126) as the basis for soup or a sauce.

To scale and clean fish. Place the fish on a piece of paper and hold it firmly with a clean cloth. Scrape off the scales with a fish scaler or a straight sharp knife. Work from the tail toward the head and slant the knife slightly toward you to keep the scales from flying. Make a gash on the under side of the fish with scissors or a sharp knife. Remove the entrails and any clotted blood which clings to the backbone. Wipe inside and out with a paper towel or a damp cloth.

To skin fish. Remove the fins along the back with a sharp knife. Cut off a narrow strip of skin the entire length of the back. Loosen the skin on one side from the bony part of the gills. If the flesh is very firm, the skin will peel off easily. If it is soft, work slowly and carefully, pushing the flesh away from the skin with the back of the knife to keep from tearing. Turn the fish and skin the other side.

To bone fish. Clean and skin. Beginning at the tail, run a long sharp knife under the flesh close to the backbone. Follow the bone (making as clean a cut as possible) its entire length to remove half the flesh. Turn and cut the flesh from the other side. Pick out any small bones that remain.

FISH COOKERY

Fish may be cooked successfully at either a very high temperature for a short period or at a low temperature for a longer period. By either method, cook until the fish flakes when tested with a fork but is still slightly moist. Do not overcook or the flesh will be dry and will lose its delicate flavor.

SAUCES FOR FISH

Lean fish is often served with a rich sauce, although the juice in the pan, plus chopped parsley and more butter, if needed, serves very well. Look through the chapter on Sauces (pp. 92–105) for ideas, such as the various cream sauces, Hot Tartare Sauce, Oyster Sauce, Shrimp Sauce, Tomato Sauce, the Hollandaise family and the strongly garlic-flavored Aioli.

The lean (dry-meated) fish are: Carp, cod, flounder (all varieties), haddock, hake, halibut (in steaks), pickerel, pike, red snapper, rockfish, salmon (in steaks), smelt, sturgeon, swordfish, weakfish and whiting.

Fat (oily-meated) fish requires only wedges of lemon or the simplest thin sharp sauce, such as Sauce Finiste, Cucumber Sauce, Vinaigrette, or the classic Beurre Noir (Black Butter) made of the juices in the pan.

The fat (oily-meated) fish are: Bass, bluefish, butterfish, eel, halibut (with fat), herring, mackerel, millet, pompano, rosefish, salmon, shad, tilefish, trout, tuna and whitefish.

GARNISHES FOR FISH

Sprigs of parsley or watercress are attractive with any fish. See pages 86 and 89 for the various ways to cut lemons prettily. Chopped toasted almonds add a pleasant crunchiness. For other garnishes, see pages 86 ff.

BAKED STUFFED FISH

Use whole bass, bluefish, cod, haddock or other fish weighing 3 to 5 pounds. Stuff cleaned fish not more than two-thirds full with Bread (p. 82), Mushroom (p. 83), Celery (p. 83) or Oyster Stuffing (p. 83). Oyster Stuffing is especially good with cod. Close the opening with skewers or toothpicks laced together with string.

Put on an oiled ovenproof platter or on buttered or oiled unglazed paper or cooking parchment in a shallow baking pan. Cut 3 or 4 gashes through the skin on each side to keep the fish in shape during baking. Sprinkle lean fish with cream, French dressing, or melted butter in an equal amount of hot water, and baste with the same mixture every 10 minutes during baking. Bake at 400° until the fish flakes when tried with a fork (30 to 45 minutes, according to thickness).

Place, whole, on a heated platter. To serve, make a deep cut along the backbone, then cut in pieces at right angles to the backbone. Serve with Cream Sauce (p. 94), Mock Hollandaise (p. 95) or Drawn Butter Sauce (p. 96).

Baked Stuffed Fish Fillets. Put fillets or slices of fish on oiled baking dish. Sprinkle with salt. Cover with stuffing and put another fillet or slice on top. Brush with oil or melted butter and bake.

QUICK-BAKED FISH

As good as broiled fish—and no broiler to wash!

Have ready
 1 pound fish fillets ¾ inch thick *or* small whole fish
Let stand at room temperature 15 minutes so that the fish will not be icy cold. Set the oven at 500°. Mix
 ½ cup milk
 2 teaspoons salt
Dip the fish in it, then in plenty of
 Dry bread crumbs
to make a thick coating. Put in an oiled baking pan or on an ovenproof platter. Sprinkle with
 1 tablespoon salad oil *or* melted butter
Bake, uncovered, until the fish flakes when tested with a fork (about 10 minutes). Serve with
 Cucumber Sauce (p. 103), Olive Sauce (p. 98) *or* Sauce Finiste (p. 100)

Baked Fish with Welsh Rabbit. Especially good for halibut fillets. Pour hot Welsh Rabbit (p. 119) over the baked fish. *Serves 3.*

BROILED FISH

Use small whole fish such as smelts or brook trout, or split and cleaned bluefish, mackerel, pompano or scrod, or fillets or steaks from larger fish.

Rinse the fish in cold water and pat dry on a paper towel. Dip small whole fish in olive oil. Preheat the broiler 10 minutes at 500°. Put the fish on the broiler rack (split fish with the skin side down). Sprinkle with salt and pepper. Brush dry-meated fish with oil or butter. Sprinkle lightly with flour or buttered crumbs. Set the rack 4 inches from the heat if the fish is about 2 inches thick, closer for thinner pieces. Cook until the fish flakes when tried with a fork (15 minutes or more). Unless the fish is very thick, it will not need to be turned to brown the skin. Move the fish carefully to a hot platter, using two pancake turners or broad spatulas so that it will not break apart.

PAN-FRIED FISH

Small whole fish, fillets or slices of larger fish—all may be pan-fried quickly and easily. Sliced haddock is particularly good done this way.

Wipe the fish dry with a paper towel. For 1 pound of fish, put ½ cup flour, fine cracker crumbs, cracker meal or corn meal on a piece of wax paper and mix with it 1 teaspoon salt (no salt if you use bacon fat or other salty fat for the frying). Roll each piece of fish in the flour.

In a shallow frying pan heat 4 tablespoons of fat, which may be any vegetable shortening, butter, half butter and half olive oil, bacon fat or fat salt pork (cut small and heated until enough melts to keep the fish from sticking).

Put the fish in the pan, one layer deep, and cook slowly until brown on one side. Turn carefully with a broad spatula or pancake turner and brown on the other side. Test with a fork. When the fish flakes, it is cooked enough—about 10 minutes for a piece ½ inch thick.

FRENCH-FRIED FISH

Pat dry with a paper towel small whole fish or fillets cut from larger fish. Sprinkle with salt, dip in flour, slightly beaten egg, then in fine cracker crumbs. Fry (p. 4) in fat heated to 370°.

POACHED FISH

Cooking fish in a shallow liquid kept below the boiling point preserves its fine flavor better than the old-fashioned method of boiling. Poach any fish except very oily ones like mackerel.

Poach a large piece of fish in salted water or Court Bouillon (below). Wrap the fish in cheesecloth so that you can lift it out after cooking without breaking it apart. Set on the rack in a large kettle, add water or Court Bouillon to a depth of 2 inches. Cover closely and simmer until the fish flakes when tried with a fork. Allow 8 to 12 minutes to the pound according to thickness of the fish.

Lift the fish out carefully. Strain the liquid and use in place of Fish Stock (below) in making sauce or as a base for soups. Put the fish on a heated platter. Garnish and serve with Cream Sauce (p. 94), Brown Almond Sauce (p. 94), Egg Sauce (p. 96) or Berçy Sauce (p. 95).

COURT BOUILLON

For poaching fish.

Melt

1 tablespoon butter

Add

1 sprig parsley
1 tablespoon each of finely cut carrot, onion and celery

Cook 3 minutes. Add

3 peppercorns
1 whole clove
Bit of bay leaf
1 teaspoon salt
1 tablespoon vinegar
1 quart water

Bring to the boiling point. Simmer 15 minutes.

Court Bouillon with Wine. Omit the vinegar and add 2 cups dry red or white wine.

FISH STOCK

Cover fish bones and scraps with Court Bouillon. Simmer 30 minutes and strain. Use as the liquid in making a sauce to serve with the fish or in fish or vegetable soup.

POACHED FISH FILLETS

Fill a frying pan 1 inch deep with milk or white wine and heat to just below the boiling point. Add 1 pound fish fillets, sprinkled with salt. Reduce the heat and cook gently until the fish flakes when tried with a fork. Lift out the fish and serve it with a sauce made of the juices in the pan. *Serves 3.*

Sauce for Poached Fish. Melt 2 tablespoons butter, add 2 tablespoons flour and stir until smooth. Add 1 cup juices from the pan, adding cold water if necessary. Cook and stir 5 minutes. Season to taste, adding salt, pepper and a teaspoon of lemon juice. Just before serving, add 2 tablespoons butter, bit by bit.

Fish Fillets Poached in Cream. Dip fillets in salted flour. Arrange in a shallow baking dish. Cover with cream. Bake 15 minutes at 400°. Put the fish on a hot platter. Season the cream delicately with beef extract or anchovy essence, a chicken bouillon cube or finely cut parsley. Or season with salt and pepper only, and after you have poured the sauce over the fish, sprinkle with finely cut salted almonds or halved seedless white grapes.

Fish Fillets Poached in Tomato Sauce. Cook fillets either way suggested above, using tomato sauce as the liquid. Sprinkle with parsley.

POACHED FISH FILLETS SUPRÊME

Heat 1 can frozen oyster stew or shrimp bisque. Add 1 cup sliced mushrooms (fresh or canned). Add 1 pound fish fillets and cook as above. Just before serving, add lemon juice to taste. Serve with fluffy steamed rice.

STEAMED FISH

Unless the fish is to be garnished whole, cut it in pieces so that it will be sure to cook evenly. Sprinkle it with salt and put it on the rack in a steamer. Put boiling water in the lower part. Cover closely and steam 10 or 15 minutes to the pound, or until the fish flakes when tested with a fork. If the fish is thick, turn once during steaming. To serve, see Poached Fish (p. 126). See also Molded Salmon (p. 295).

If you are steaming a whole fish or a large piece, wrap it in a piece of cheesecloth so that it will be less likely to break apart when you move it to a platter.

To steam fish in the oven. Set on the rack in a roasting pan. Pour in hot water 2 inches deep. Cover and steam in 350° oven.

BAKED BLUEFISH BRESLIN

Cook other fish this way, too.

Split and bone
Bluefish (about 4 pounds)
Place on a well-buttered baking pan or an ovenproof platter. Bake 20 minutes at 400°. Mix
¼ cup butter, creamed
2 egg yolks
2 tablespoons finely chopped onion
2 tablespoons chopped pickle
2 tablespoons chopped parsley
2 tablespoons capers
2 tablespoons lemon juice
1 tablespoon vinegar
½ teaspoon salt
¼ teaspoon paprika
Spread over the fish. Continue baking until the fish flakes when tried with a fork (about 30 minutes). *Serves 6 to 8.*

BLUEFISH À L'ITALIENNE

Split and bone
Bluefish (about 4 pounds)
Put on a buttered baking pan or ovenproof platter. Sprinkle with
Salt and pepper
3 tablespoons dry white wine
3 tablespoons mushroom liquid (below)
½ onion, chopped fine
8 mushroom caps, chopped
Add enough water for basting. Bake 45 minutes at 375°, basting every 10 minutes. Serve with
Brown Sauce (p. 97), made with stock *or* water.
Serves 6 to 8.

To prepare mushroom liquid. Chop the stems, barely cover them with water and simmer 20 minutes. Strain. If you are using canned mushrooms, use the liquid in the can.

FILLETS OF SOLE BAKED IN CREAM

"Sole" is usually flounder in the United States, but English sole

is sometimes available in metropolitan markets.

Dip the fillets in salted flour. Arrange them in a baking dish and cover with cream. Bakc 15 minutes at 450°. Remove the fish to a heated platter. Season the pan juices delicately with anchovy paste or beef extract and pour it over the fish. *One pound serves 3.*

Fillets of Sole Berçy. In place of cream sprinkle the fillets with dry white wine, dry vermouth or lemon juice mixed with an equal amount of water. Serve with Berçy Sauce (p. 95) made with the liquid in the baking pan.

Fillets of Sole Véronique. Sprinkle seeded or seedless white grapes over Fillets of Sole Berçy (above) and reheat before serving.

FILLETS OF SOLE À LA MEUNIÈRE

Dip the fillets lightly in salted flour. Melt butter in a heavy frying pan. Put in the fillets and cook until delicately brown. Squeeze a little lemon juice into the liquid in the pan and pour it over the fish. *One pound serves 3.*

For a very rich and delicate flavor, have the butter deep enough to cover the fish. Remove the cooked fish to a warm platter. For each ½ cup of juice in the pan, stir in 2 tablespoons flour, ½ cup chicken stock, a few drops of lemon juice and 1 tablespoon chopped parsley. Blend well and pour over the fish.

Fillets of Sole Amandine. Sprinkle with sliced almonds sautéed in butter.

FILLETS EN PAPILLOTE (IN PAPER CASES)

If parchment paper is not available, use aluminum foil. The effect will not be as festive as the prettily browned paper, but the fish will be just as tasty.

For each serving, put a neat piece of flounder fillet on a thin slice of cooked ham trimmed slightly larger than the fillet. Put on a piece of parchment paper. Dot with butter and sprinkle with salt, pepper, thyme and chopped parsley. Wrap like a package, folding the edges to keep in the juice. Put in a shallow pan. Brush the paper with melted butter. Bake 15 minutes at 400°. Serve without removing the paper so that each person opens his own. Serve with melted butter seasoned with lemon juice.

To vary, put in each package 2 or 3 cooked or canned mushroom caps or tiny onions.

FILLETS OF SOLE MARGUÉRY

A gourmet dish for lunch. Serve a simple salad and French bread with it.

Have ready

- **8 fillets of sole *or* flounder**
- **1 boiled lobster, with the meat removed and the shell cracked**
- **18 littleneck clams**

Put in a pan the bones and trimmings of the fish, if available, the lobster shell and 6 of the clams. Cover with cold water and simmer until the liquid is reduced to make about 1 cup fish stock. Put the fillets in a shallow baking dish. Sprinkle with

- **Salt and paprika**
- **½ cup dry white wine**

Cover the pan with foil. Bake

15 minutes at 350°. Meanwhile, melt

3 tablespoons butter

Stir in

3 tablespoons flour

Add the strained fish stock slowly. Bring to the boiling point and stir in 1/4 cup of the liquid from the baking pan. Season to taste with

Salt and pepper

Arrange the fillets on an ovenproof platter. Strain the sauce over them. Garnish with the rest of the clams and the lobster meat, cut in slices. Sprinkle with

4 tablespoons grated Parmesan cheese

Bake until thoroughly heated. *Serves 6 to 8.*

Fillets of Sole St. Mâlo. In place of lobsters and clams, garnish with 1/2 pint oysters. Parboil the oysters (p. 153), drain off the liquid, and add it to the stock made of the fish trimmings and bones. If you prefer, use water or chicken or clam broth in place of stock.

Sole Normande. In place of lobster and clams, garnish with 1/2 pound shrimp, cooked or canned. Add to the sauce 1/2 pound mushrooms, sliced and sautéed in butter.

STUFFED TURBANS OF FLOUNDER

Trim into neat pieces

8 fillets of flounder

Coil inside 8 buttered muffin rings placed in a buttered pan. Put in a pan

3/4 cup chopped mushroom stems
Few drops onion juice
3 tablespoons butter

Cook 1 minute. Stir in

4 tablespoons flour

Add gradually, stirring constantly

1/2 cup cream

Stir until the mixture boils. Add

Chopped soft part of 12 oysters *or* 1/2 cup crab meat

Season to taste with

Salt, pepper, cayenne and mace

Fill the muffin rings with the mixture. Cover with foil. Bake 20 minutes at 375°. Remove the foil. Sprinkle with

Buttered bread crumbs

Bake until the crumbs are brown. Slip from the rings onto a hot platter. *Serves 8.*

BAKED FISH FILLETS

Put fillets of cod, flounder, haddock, halibut or scrod on an ovenproof platter. Sprinkle with salt, pepper and lemon juice. Dot with butter or cover with buttered crumbs. Bake at 400° until the fish flakes when tried with a fork (12 to 30 minutes, according to the thickness of the fish).

Fish Fillets Vermouth. Instead of lemon juice, sprinkle generously with dry vermouth. Especially delicious for fillets of flounder or halibut.

FISH FILLETS À LA PRESTON

Put 2 fillets together with Mushroom Stuffing (p. 83). Put on an ovenproof platter. Pour 2/3 cup cream or top milk over the fish. Bake 25 minutes at 375°. Sprinkle with buttered crumbs. Bake until brown.

OYSTER-STUFFED FISH FILLETS

Put fillets together with a layer of oysters. Brush the top with a slightly beaten egg, then cover with buttered cracker crumbs. Bake 50 minutes at 350°. Serve with Hollandaise (p. 100).

FISH FILLETS MÉTROPOLE

Put in a baking dish in a single layer

2 pounds fish fillets

Cover with

Normandy Sauce (p. 97)

Bake at 400° until the fish flakes when tried with a fork (about 15 minutes). Beat until stiff

½ cup heavy cream

Add to the cream

1½ tablespoons pimiento, rubbed through a sieve
½ tablespoon chopped chives
¼ teaspoon salt

Spread over the fish. Sprinkle with

½ cup buttered coarse bread crumbs

Bake until delicately brown. Serve with

Hollandaise (p. 100)

Serves 6.

HOLLENDEN HALIBUT

Cut in very thin slices

⅛ pound fat salt pork

Put 6 slices on an ovenproof platter or a shallow baking dish. Over the pork put

1 small onion, sliced thin
Bit of bay leaf
2 pounds halibut in one piece

Cream together

3 tablespoons butter
3 tablespoons flour

Spread on the fish. Cover with the rest of the pork, cut in narrow strips, and

½ cup buttered crumbs

Cover with foil and bake 55 minutes at 350°. Remove the foil and bake 15 minutes longer to brown the crumbs. Garnish with

Sliced lemon

Sprinkle with

Chopped parsley
Paprika

Serve with

Cream Sauce (p. 94)

made with the fat in the pan instead of butter. *Serves 6.*

HALIBUT À LA SUISSE

Set the oven at 375°. Put in a buttered baking pan

2 pounds halibut, in one piece or cut in slices

Sprinkle with

Salt and pepper

Dot with

½ cup butter

Bake whole piece 15 minutes, slices 10 minutes, basting twice with the juices in the pan. Cover with

¼ pound mushrooms, cut in pieces
1 cup cream

Bake another 15 minutes for whole piece, 10 minutes for slices. Stir into the pan juices

1 teaspoon beef extract

Bake 10 minutes longer, basting twice. *Serves 6.*

BAKED HALIBUT SWEDISH STYLE

Remove the skin from

1½-pound slice halibut

Put in a shallow casserole. Sprinkle with

Salt and pepper

Brush over with

Melted butter

Mix and spread over the fish

1 cup drained canned tomatoes
½ teaspoon powdered sugar

Cover with

1 onion, sliced thin

Bake 20 minutes at 375°. Pour over the top

½ cup heavy cream

Bake 10 minutes longer. *Serves 4.*

HALIBUT CREOLE

Wipe and put on a buttered ovenproof platter or baking pan

1½ pounds halibut in one slice

Sprinkle with

Salt and pepper

Put over the fish

5 thick slices peeled tomato

½ green pepper, chopped
2 teaspoons chopped onion
Bake 25 minutes at 400°. Baste 3 times during the baking with the juices in the pan and with
⅓ cup melted butter
Serves 4.

HALIBUT À LA POULETTE

Prepare
1½ cups Béchamel Sauce (p. 95)
2 hard-cooked eggs
Clean and cut in 8 fillets
1½ pounds halibut
Melt
¼ cup butter
Add
¼ teaspoon salt
⅛ teaspoon pepper
2 teaspoons lemon juice
Few drops onion juice
Set over low heat or over hot water to keep the butter melted. Take up each fillet on a fork, dip in the butter, roll and fasten with a toothpick. Put in a shallow pan. Sprinkle with
Flour
Bake 12 minutes at 400°. Take out the toothpicks. Put the fish on a platter and pour the sauce around it. Garnish with the egg yolks rubbed through a sieve, the whites cut in strips, and
1 lemon, cut in fan-shaped pieces
Parsley
Serves 4.

FISH MOUSSE (NORWEGIAN FISH PUDDING)

Halibut or flounder makes a very delicate mousse. Salmon Mousse is excellent, too, served with Normandy Sauce (p. 97) or Cucumber Hollandaise (p. 101).

Put through a food chopper, using a fine knife
1 pound halibut *or* other delicate fish
(*To make even smoother, pound in a mortar or in a double boiler top with a wooden potato masher or prepare in an electric blender, starting with one-third of the cream and one-third of the fish, cut in small pieces.*)
Put in a bowl set in a pan of ice water. Stir in very slowly
3 egg whites
beating with a wire whisk to keep the mixture very smooth. Stir in very slowly
1 cup heavy cream *or* evaporated milk
1 teaspoon salt
½ teaspoon pepper
Season to taste with
Cayenne, nutmeg *or* celery salt
Few drops of onion juice
Let stand 1 hour. Stir well. Butter or oil a 1½-quart mold or a set of small timbale molds. Pour in the mixture. Set in a pan of hot water 1 inch deep. Cover with foil. Bake at 350° until firm or cook on top of the stove over low heat so that the water barely simmers. Do not overcook. Turn out onto a serving dish. Pour over the mousse
Lobster (p. 94), Shrimp (p. 96) *or* Mushroom Sauce (p. 98)
If you like, season the sauce with
Sherry
Serves 4 to 6.

Jean's Fish Mousse. Not quite so delicate but simpler. Heat the cream and add 1 cup dry bread crumbs and the chopped fish. Season. Beat the egg whites stiff and fold into the fish mixture. Bake and serve as above. *Serves 8.*

Swedish Fish Balls. Shape the mixture in ovals in a buttered tablespoon. Slip from the spoon into boiling water. Cook 8 minutes. Cover with Normandy Sauce (p. 97) and sprinkle with chopped parsley.

HALIBUT TIMBALES

Grind very fine

1 pound halibut

Rub through a sieve. Add

1 egg yolk
1 teaspoon salt
¼ teaspoon pepper
Few grains cayenne
¾ teaspoon cornstarch

Add, gradually

⅔ cup milk
⅓ cup heavy cream, beaten stiff

Fill buttered timbale molds or a ring mold. Set in pan of hot water. Bake and serve like Fish Mousse (p. 131). *Serves 4.*

Halibut Timbales Farci. Line small molds with Fish Mousse (p. 131). Fill with Creamed Lobster (p. 151), Shrimp (p. 159) or Crab Meat (p. 146), and cover with mousse. Set in a pan of hot water and bake as above. Serve with Lobster Sauce (p. 94) or Béchamel Sauce (p. 95). Before filling the molds, sprinkle, if desired, with lobster coral rubbed through a sieve.

MACKEREL BAKED IN MILK

Split the fish, clean, and remove the head and tail. Put in a buttered baking pan. Sprinkle with salt and pepper, dot with butter (1 tablespoon to a medium-sized fish), and pour ⅔ cup milk over the fish. Bake 25 minutes at 400°.

POMPANO

A delicious fish native to South Atlantic and Gulf waters.

Split and broil or bake whole, or remove the bones and broil, sauté or poach the fillets. Cucumber Hollandaise (p. 101) and Brown Almond Sauce (p. 94) are excellent with pompano.

ROYAL POINCIANA POMPANO

Split and clean

1 pompano (about 2 pounds)

Put in a buttered baking dish. Beat together

2 eggs
½ cup heavy cream

Add

2 cups shrimp, chopped fine
½ teaspoon salt
½ cup chopped mushrooms
¼ cup sherry

Spread over the fish. Pour around the fish

½ cup heavy cream

Bake 45 minutes at 350°. Garnish with

Sliced cucumber
Sliced lemon

Serves 4 or 5.

STEAMED SALMON

Steam the salmon (p. 127). Serve hot with Egg Sauce (p. 96) or Hollandaise (p. 100). Serve cold with Mayonnaise (p. 302), Cucumber Hollandaise (p. 101), Ravigote Mayonnaise (p. 303), or Cucumber Sauce (p. 102). See also Molded Salmon (p. 295). A salad of cooked peas, lima beans, and carrots (cut small), mixed with mayonnaise, is a good accompaniment for cold salmon.

BROILED SCROD

Scrod is young cod or haddock split down the back and with most of the backbone removed. Creamed or hashed brown potatoes are traditional with it.

Sprinkle with melted butter, fine crumbs, and salt and pepper. Broil (p. 125) skin side down until it flakes (about 10 minutes). *A small scrod (½ to ¾ pound) serves 1 or 2.*

BAKED or PLANKED SHAD

Shad is at its best in the spring. Buy it with the roe if you can.

Put the fish in a shallow baking dish or on a buttered plank, skin side down. Sprinkle with salt and pepper. Brush with melted butter. Bake 25 minutes at 400° or broil about 15. Spread with butter, garnish with parsley and lemon, and serve on the plank. *A 3-pound shad serves 6.*

Baked Shad with Creamed Roe. Spread Creamed Roe (below) over the thin part of baked shad. Cover with ½ cup buttered crumbs and return to the oven to brown the crumbs.

SHAD ROE

Fresh roe is usually served with the shad, either baked with it or Creamed (below) or made into Roe Sauce. However, it is delicious served as a separate dish. Canned roe is very satisfactory and may be used in place of parboiled fresh roe. Roe from 1 shad gives 2 servings.

To parboil roe, cover the roe with boiling water, add 1 tablespoon salt and 1 tablespoon vinegar or lemon juice, and simmer 15 minutes (2 minutes for small, young roe). Drain, cover with cold water, and let stand 5 minutes. Drain.

Broiled Shad Roe. Arrange the parboiled roe in a lightly buttered shallow pan. Broil quickly until golden-brown, turning once and sprinkling several times with melted butter. Properly cooked roe is firm but not dry or hard.

Fried Shad Roe. Cut parboiled roe in pieces. Sprinkle with salt and pepper. Brush with lemon juice. Dip in crumbs, egg, and crumbs. Fry in deep fat heated to 390°. Serve with Tartare Sauce (p. 103).

Sautéed Shad Roe. Cut parboiled roe in pieces. Melt 3 tablespoons butter, add the roe, and cook 10 minutes. Serve plain or with broiled bacon. Or make a sauce by adding to the fat in the pan 1 tablespoon butter, ½ cup chopped celery, a few drops onion juice, a few drops lemon juice, salt and pepper. Serve with the roe.

CREAMED SHAD ROE

Parboil and mash with a fork
1 shad roe (above)
Melt
3 tablespoons butter
Add
1 teaspoon chopped shallot *or* mild onion
Cook 5 minutes. Add the roe. Sprinkle with
1½ tablespoons flour
Stir in
⅓ cup cream
Cook slowly 5 minutes. Season highly with
Salt, pepper and lemon juice
Serves 2.

ROE SAUCE

Put in a small shallow baking dish
½ shad roe
Sprinkle with
Salt, pepper, cayenne and nutmeg
Dot with
2 tablespoons butter
Add
2 tablespoons sherry
2 tablespoons white wine
Cover with foil. Bake 30 minutes at 350°. Pick out the membranes. Melt until brown
3 tablespoons butter
Stir in
4 tablespoons flour
Cook until brown. Pour on gradually

1 cup Chicken Stock (p. 62)
***or* canned chicken broth**

Bring to the boiling point, stirring constantly. Add

¼ teaspoon beef extract
Salt to taste

Stir in the roe. Serve with Planked or Baked Shad (p. 133).

SAUTÉED SMELTS

Split and clean smelts, allowing 1 or 2 per person. Cut 5 diagonal gashes on each side. Sprinkle with salt, pepper and lemon juice. Cover and let stand 10 minutes. Roll in flour. Sauté in butter or olive oil.

Smelts à la Meunière. Pour the juices from the pan over the cooked smelts. If you like a bit more sauce, add a little butter to the pan juices and stir in a teaspoon of anchovy paste and a few drops of lemon juice. Sprinkle with chopped parsley. Serve with lemon.

Smelts Amandine. Sprinkle with sliced almonds sautéed in olive oil.

Smelts au Beurre Noir. Put the cooked fish on a hot platter. Add enough butter to the pan juices to make about ⅓ cup. Stir until dark brown. Add 1 teaspoon lemon juice, salt and pepper. Pour over the fish. Sprinkle with chopped parsley.

FRIED SMELTS

Split and clean the smelts. Sprinkle with salt and pepper. Dip in crumbs, then in slightly beaten egg, and then in crumbs again. Fry 3 to 5 minutes in deep fat heated to 370°. As soon as the smelts are put into the fat, reduce the heat so that they will not become too brown before being cooked through. Serve with Tartare Sauce (p. 103).

RED SNAPPER FLORIDA

Put in a buttered baking dish

1½ pounds red snapper fillets

Sprinkle over them

1 teaspoon salt
⅛ teaspoon pepper
1½ teaspoons grated orange rind
1 teaspoon grated grapefruit rind
Few grains nutmeg

Cover with foil. Bake 15 minutes at 400°. *Serves 4 to 6.*

BROILED SWORDFISH

Swordfish is especially dry-meated, so do not broil a thin slice. Order slices cut 2 inches thick, preferably from the center of the fish.

Place the fish on a buttered shallow pan. Sprinkle with salt and pepper. Dot generously with butter. Cook 15 minutes in a broiler 3 inches from the heat. Turn, season, dot with butter, and cook 10 minutes longer or until the fish flakes. *Two pounds serves 6.*

BROOK TROUT MEUNIÈRE

Clean and wipe the fish. Sprinkle with salt and pepper. Dip in flour. Sauté in butter until delicately brown. Squeeze a little lemon juice into the pan juices and pour over the fish. Sprinkle with chopped parsley. *One pound serves 3.*

FRIED WHITEBAIT

The perfect fish course for a formal dinner. Serve with wedges of lemon or lime, sliced cucumbers or tomatoes and thin sandwiches of brown bread and sweet butter. As a luncheon dish, combine with shrimp.

Wash the whitebait thoroughly. Dry carefully in a clean cloth. Shake it to remove moisture. Sprinkle with salt and pepper, roll in flour, and shake lightly in a sieve to remove extra flour. Sauté in butter or fry in deep fat heated to 370°, using a frying basket with very fine mesh. Whitebait are so tiny that they cook in 1 to 3 minutes. *One pound serves 6 to 8.*

BAKED *or* PLANKED WHITEFISH

Split and bone the fish. Put skin side down on a buttered plank or baking dish. Sprinkle with salt and pepper. Dot with butter. Bake 25 minutes at 400° without turning. Broil, if you prefer, about 15 minutes.

FRIED FROGS' LEGS

As sweet and tender as young chicken. Allow ½ pound per person.

Sprinkle frogs' legs with salt, pepper and lemon juice. Dip in crumbs, egg, and again in crumbs. Chill 1 hour. Sauté in butter until brown, or fry 3 minutes in deep fat heated to 375°.

FROGS' LEGS NEWBURG

Serve on thin toast or in patty shells.

Cut in ¼-inch strips

½ pound mushroom caps

Sauté 3 minutes in

1 tablespoon butter

Steam until tender

2 pounds frogs' legs

Add

½ pound crab meat
2 tablespoons melted butter
½ cup sherry

Cover and let stand 30 minutes. Cook 5 minutes. Pour off about half the liquid in the pan. Add the mushrooms. Scald in a double boiler

1⅓ cups cream

Mix and stir into the cream

1 tablespoon cornstarch
1 tablespoon cold water

Cook 20 minutes, stirring constantly until thick. Stir in

1 egg yolk, slightly beaten

Add to the first mixture, reheat, and season to taste. *Serves 6.*

TERRAPIN

Terrapin is always a luxury. The diamond-back terrapin of Chesapeake Bay is considered the choicest. Terrapin should be alive when bought. Allow one 6- or 7-inch terrapin for 2 persons. Canned terrapin is also available.

Plunge the terrapin, alive, into boiling water and boil 5 minutes. Lift out of the water with a skimmer and remove the skin from the feet and tail by rubbing with a towel. Draw out the head with a skewer so that you can rub off the skin.

Cover with boiling salted water and cook slowly until the feet fall off and the shell cracks (1 to 1½ hours). Add to the cooking water 2 slices each of carrot and onion and 1 stalk of celery. Remove from the water, lay on its back, and cool only enough to handle. Draw out the nails from the feet, cut under the shell close to upper shell, and remove. Empty the upper shell and carefully remove and discard the gall bladder, sandbags, and thick, heavy part of intestines. Any of the gall bladder would give a bitter flavor to the dish. Serve the liver, small intestines, cut small, and eggs with the meat. Cut the meat into pieces about 1½ inches long.

Most terrapin gourmets make no attempt to remove the bones.

Terrapin Baltimore Style. Add cooked terrapin meat and intestines to ¾ cup chicken stock. Simmer until liquid is reduced one half. Add liver separated in pieces, 2 egg yolks, 3 tablespoons butter, salt, pepper, and cayenne. Egg yolks may be omitted and ½ cup butter added bit by bit. If liked, season with sherry just before serving, but many Baltimoreans prefer to serve sherry with this dish, not in it.

Terrapin Washington Style. Make a sauce of 1½ tablespoons butter, 1½ tablespoons flour, and 1 cup cream. Add cooked terrapin and ½ cup sautéed chopped mushrooms. Season to taste. Just before serving, stir in 2 eggs, slightly beaten.

RECIPES USING COOKED FISH

Many of the following recipes may be used for either cooked or canned fish, such as tuna or salmon. Serve any of the creamed dishes over toast or with rice or noodles. Or fill a casserole, individual baking dishes or scallop shells, cover with buttered crumbs, and heat in a 350° oven until the crumbs are brown.

KEDGEREE

A famous English breakfast dish which is also delicious hot or cold for luncheon or supper.

Mix in a double boiler

2 cups cooked rice
4 hard-cooked eggs, chopped
3 tablespoons chopped parsley
2 cups flaked cooked fish
½ cup cream
Salt, pepper and curry, if liked

Heat thoroughly. *Serves 6.*

FISH HASH

Mix equal parts of cold flaked fish (especially halibut) and cold boiled potatoes chopped fine. Season with salt and pepper. Try out fat salt pork and remove the scraps, leaving enough fat in the pan to moisten the fish and potatoes. Put in the fish and potatoes and stir until heated. Cook until well browned underneath, fold, and turn like an omelet.

CREAMED FISH

Flake cooked fish, removing the bones and bits of skin, or use canned tuna or salmon. Add to Cream Sauce (p. 94), using 1 cup of sauce for each ½ to 1 cup of fish. Heat in a double boiler. Season highly to taste. Serve on toast or in a border of cooked rice or mashed potato. Sprinkle with paprika and/or chopped parsley.

Variations. (1) Make a richer sauce by stirring in an egg yolk just before serving.
(2) Add a few sautéed mushrooms.
(3) Use part fish stock or chicken stock in making the sauce.
(4) Add crumbled hard-cooked egg yolks and season with anchovy essence.
(5) Use concentrated mushroom soup as a sauce, diluting it to the right consistency with cream or water.

SCALLOPED FISH (FISH AU GRATIN)

Use the recipe for Scalloped Eggs (p. 107) and vary it as you like. Or put creamed fish in a buttered casserole, ramekins or scallop shells. Cover with buttered cracker crumbs (½ cup to

2 cups of the scallop). Bake at 450° until the crumbs are brown.

Other toppings to use are crushed potato chips, corn flakes, grated cheese mixed with crumbs, or toasted wheat germ.

Scalloped Fish with Cheese Meringue. Beat 2 egg whites until stiff and fold in 1/4 cup grated cheese. Spread over the filled casserole or ramekins. Sprinkle with grated cheese. Bake at 450° until browned.

HUNTINGTON SCALLOPED FISH

A leftover dish with a flair—so good that you will often cook a fillet of fish especially for it.

Melt
3 tablespoons butter
Add
1 green pepper, cut fine
Cook until the pepper is soft. Stir in
2 tablespoons flour
Blend until smooth. Add
1 1/2 cups cream *or* top milk
Cook and stir until thick and smooth. Add
1 cup flaked cooked haddock *or* halibut
1/2 cup soft bread crumbs
Salt, pepper and sherry to taste
Put in a baking dish. Cover with
1/2 cup buttered crumbs
Bake at 375° until brown (about 30 minutes). *Serves 4.*

To vary. Add 1/2 to 1 cup sautéed sliced mushrooms.

FISH SOUFFLÉ

Prepare by removing bits of bone and skin and separating into flakes
2 cups cooked *or* canned salmon, tuna *or* other fish
Add
1/4 teaspoon salt
1/8 teaspoon paprika
2 teaspoons lemon juice
Cook together 5 minutes
1/2 cup dry bread crumbs
1/2 cup milk
Add the fish and
3 egg yolks, beaten thick
Fold in
3 egg whites, beaten stiff
Spoon into a buttered baking dish. Set in a pan of hot water and bake at 350° until firm (about 30 minutes). Serve with
Hollandaise (p. 100) *or* Spanish Sauce (p. 97)
Serves 6.

FISH MOUSSE

Made with cooked fish. See also page 131.

Prepare
2 cups finely chopped cooked fish
Season with
Salt to taste
Few grains cayenne
1 1/2 teaspoons lemon juice
Fold in gently
1/3 cup cream, whipped
3 egg whites, beaten stiff
Spoon into a buttered 1-quart mold or into individual molds. Set in a pan of hot water 1 inch deep. Cover with foil. Bake at 350° until firm (about 20 minutes) or cook slowly over moderate heat. Take out of the molds. Cover with
Béchamel (p. 95) *or* Lobster Sauce (p. 94)
Garnish with
Parsley
Serves 6.

SALMON LOAF

Vary this recipe according to the amount of salmon on hand. One cup of salmon may be combined with a cup of crumbs and a cup of hot milk.

Mix
2 cups flaked cooked or canned salmon
1/2 cup fine bread crumbs

4 tablespoons butter
2 eggs, slightly beaten
1 tablespoon chopped parsley
Salt, pepper and Worcestershire to taste
Chopped onion, green pepper *or* celery, if convenient

Put in a buttered baking dish. Set in a pan of hot water 1 inch deep. Bake at 350° until firm (about 30 minutes). Serve hot with

Mustard Sauce (p. 102)

or cold with

Cucumber Sauce (p. 102)

Serves 6.

Tuna Loaf. Use tuna in place of salmon. Add 1 tablespoon pimiento cut in tiny pieces.

SALMON CHEESE LOAF

Mix

2 cups flaked cooked or canned salmon
1½ cups grated cheese
1 egg, well beaten
3 tablespoons milk
1 tablespoon melted butter
½ teaspoon salt
Few grains pepper
Cracker *or* bread crumbs to make a stiff mixture

Pack into a loaf pan. Cover the top with

Buttered crumbs

Bake at 375° until golden-brown. *Serves 6.*

Tuna Cheese Loaf. Use tuna in place of salmon.

SPICED SALMON

For a summer supper with a mixed vegetable salad and pumpernickel.

Prepare (rinsing canned salmon with hot water to remove the oil and freeing fresh salmon of bones and skin)

2 cups canned or cooked salmon

Mix in a small pan

1 cup mild vinegar
1 teaspoon whole cloves
½ teaspoon allspice berries
8 peppercorns
¼ teaspoon salt

Bring to the boiling point. Pour over the fish. Cover and let stand 2 hours. Drain and separate into flakes. *Serves 4.*

TUNA

There are various grades of canned tuna. The most expensive is light-colored and in large chunks. Use it in salads or in scalloped dishes in which appearance is of importance. Sliced or grated tuna, light or dark, is less expensive but has equal food value. Use it in any recipe in which the tuna is to be cut in small pieces or mixed with other ingredients, as in sandwich fillings.

Consult the index for tuna recipes in other sections of the book. Use tuna in any of the following recipes, or substitute tuna for cooked chicken in any of the recipes listed under Recipes Using Cooked Chicken (p. 232).

Kedgeree (p. 136)
Creamed Fish (p. 136)
Scalloped Fish (p. 136)
Fish Soufflé (p. 137)
Fish Sandwich Fillings (p. 359)
Savory Meat *or* Chicken Roll (p. 213)

TUNA NOODLE CASSEROLE

Use condensed cream of mushroom soup, if you like, instead of cheese sauce and mushrooms.

Butter a 1-quart casserole. Put in it

1 7-ounce can tuna fish, drained
2 cups cooked noodles
3 hard-cooked eggs, sliced
2 cups Cheese Sauce (p. 95)
½ cup sliced mushrooms

Salt, pepper and celery salt
Few drops onion juice
Mix gently. Cover with
Buttered crumbs
Bake at 375° until the sauce bubbles and the crumbs are brown (about 20 minutes). *Serves 4.*

TUNA FISH RICE

A simple dish but very popular.

Melt in a large saucepan
3 tablespoons butter
Add
¼ cup chopped onion
¼ cup chopped celery
Cook slowly until tender. Stir in gently
1 7-ounce can tuna fish, drained and flaked
2 cups cooked rice
¼ cup chopped parsley
Salt and paprika to taste
Heat thoroughly, stirring lightly to keep from sticking. *Serves 4.*

TUNA FISH PIE

Also attractive baked in individual pottery bowls. Bake plenty of extra pastry rounds or squares to serve with second helpings.

Combine
2 7-ounce cans tuna fish, drained and flaked
2 cups Cream Sauce (p. 94)
1 teaspoon Worcestershire
1 tablespoon sherry, if liked
1 tablespoon chopped parsley
Salt, pepper and celery salt to taste
Pour into a buttered 2-quart casserole. Roll out
Plain Pastry (p. 438)
Shape it to fit the top of the casserole. Put on the crust and slit or prick it. Bake at 425° until brown (about 25 minutes). *Serves 6.*

CODFISH BALLS

Canned fish ball mix and frozen fish balls are convenient.

Freshen, following directions on the package
½ pound salt codfish
Wash, pare and cube potatoes to make
2½ cups potato cubes
Put the fish and potatoes in a pan. Add boiling water to cover and cook until the potatoes are nearly soft. Drain thoroughly and shake over the heat until completely dry. Mash well. Add
½ tablespoon butter
1 egg, well beaten
⅛ teaspoon pepper
Taste and add salt, if necessary. Beat with a fork until smooth and light (about 2 minutes). Fry or sauté. *Serves 6.*

To fry. Heat fat to 375°. Take up the fish ball mixture by spoonfuls and fry 1 minute. Fry six at a time. Drain on paper towels.

To sauté. Shape in flat patties and brown in butter.

Codfish Hash. Dice a 2-inch cube of fat salt pork. Heat it in a frying pan until the fat melts. Remove the crisp bits of pork to use as a garnish on the hash. Pour off some of the fat, leaving enough to grease the pan well. Spread the codfish mixture in the pan and cook slowly until well browned underneath. Fold like an omelet. *Serves 6.*

CREAMED SALT CODFISH

Following directions on the package, freshen
½ pound salt codfish
Add to
1½ cups Cream Sauce (p. 94) *or* cream
Heat. Just before serving, stir in
1 egg, well beaten
Garnish with
Sliced hard-cooked egg
Serve with baked potatoes. *Serves 4.*

SPANISH CODFISH

Following directions on the package, freshen

½ pound salt codfish

Separate into small pieces. Slice

4 cold boiled potatoes

Put alternate layers of fish and potatoes in a buttered casserole. Sprinkle with

3 canned pimientos, cut in strips
Salt and pepper

Pour over the top

1 cup Tomato Sauce, homemade (p. 99) or canned

Cover with

½ cup buttered crumbs

Bake at 350° until the crumbs are brown. *Serves 6.*

COD CHEEKS AND TONGUES

If salted, soak overnight in water to cover. Drain, cover with fresh water, simmer 5 minutes and drain. Sauté in butter until delicately brown (about 10 minutes). Pour over browned butter, seasoned with lemon juice. Sprinkle with chopped parsley. *One pound serves 4.*

Scalloped Cod Cheeks *or* Tongues. Place in a baking dish. Pour over 1 cup Cream Sauce (p. 94) seasoned with lemon juice. Spread with buttered crumbs. Bake at 350° until the crumbs are brown.

KIPPERED HERRING

A typical English breakfast dish —good for brunch, too.

Arrange herring on an ovenproof platter. Sprinkle with pepper, brush over with lemon juice and melted butter, and cover with the liquid from the can. Heat and garnish with parsley and slices of lemon.

FINNAN HADDIE

Finnan haddie is haddock, dried, smoked and salted.

Finnan Haddie in Milk. Cover with milk and cook (covered) over moderate heat 25 minutes. Drain, dot with butter and sprinkle with pepper.

Broiled Finnan Haddie. Broil until brown on both sides. Put in a pan, cover with hot water and let stand 10 minutes. Drain, spread with butter and sprinkle with pepper.

FINNAN HADDIE RABBIT

Put in a double boiler top

½ pound Cheddar cheese, cut small
1 cup heavy cream *or* evaporated milk
½ pound finnan haddie, flaked

Cook over hot water until well blended. Stir in

1 egg, slightly beaten

Serve on

Toast

Serves 6.

FINNAN HADDIE DELMONICO

Put in a skillet

1 pound finnan haddie, in strips

Cover with cold water, place over low heat and bring to the boiling point. Reduce the heat and simmer 25 minutes. Drain and rinse thoroughly. Separate into flakes. Add

½ cup heavy cream
4 hard-cooked eggs, sliced thin
1 tablespoon butter
Cayenne to taste

Sprinkle with

Finely chopped parsley

Serves 4.

SAVORY FINNAN HADDIE

Put in a shallow pan
½ pound finnan haddie
Cover with
Milk
Let stand 1 hour. Cook until tender, drain and separate into flakes. Cook until tender and drain
1½ cups small potato balls or cubes
Cut in tiny cubes
⅛ pound fat salt pork
Cook slowly until brown and crisp. Set the scraps aside. Put 2 tablespoons of the fat in a pan. Add
2 tablespoons flour
Stir until well blended. Add slowly
1 cup milk
Bring to the boiling point, stirring constantly. Add the finnan haddie, pork scraps and potatoes. Stir in
2 eggs, slightly beaten
Serves 4.

EPICUREAN FINNAN HADDIE

Prepared in advance, this is an ideal supper party dish. Have it ready for the final heating and browning.

Put in a shallow baking dish
1 pound finnan haddie
Cover with
Milk
Let stand 1 hour. Bake 30 minutes at 350°. Separate into flakes. There should be about 2 cups. Put in a pan
¼ cup butter
1 tablespoon finely chopped green pepper
½ tablespoon finely chopped shallot *or* mild onion
½ tablespoon finely chopped red pepper
Cook 5 minutes. Add
4 tablespoons flour
1 teaspoon salt
½ teaspoon paprika
Few grains cayenne
Stir until well blended. Add gradually, stirring constantly
1 cup milk
1 cup cream
Bring to the boiling point. Add the finnan haddie and spoon into a buttered baking dish. Cover with
Buttered crumbs
Bake at 350° until the crumbs are brown. *Serves 6.*

To vary. Add ¼ pound mushrooms, sliced and sautéed in butter. Instead of the peppers, add 1 pimiento, cut in small pieces.

CREAMED SARDINES

For lunch or as an evening snack.

Drain
1 small tin sardines
Remove the backbones and mash the fish. Melt
4 tablespoons butter
Add
4 tablespoons bread crumbs
1 cup cream
Heat thoroughly. Stir in the sardines and
2 hard-cooked eggs, chopped fine
Season to taste with
Salt and paprika
Serve on
Toast
Serves 2 or 3.

GRILLED SARDINES

Drain canned sardines and cook in an omelet pan until heated, turning frequently. Place on small oblong pieces of dry toast and serve with Maître d'Hôtel (p. 103) or Lemon Butter (p. 103).

Grilled Sardines with Anchovy Sauce. Serve with sauce made of 1½ tablespoons sardine oil (from the can), 2 tablespoons flour, and 1 cup Brown Stock (p. 60) or canned consommé. Season to taste with anchovy sauce or paste.

Shellfish

Shellfish—quick-frozen, canned or refrigerated—are high in minerals and vitamins and low in calories compared with other protein foods. There are many epicurean ways to serve them.

ABALONE

Abalone is a large mollusk, native to California waters and not available elsewhere. Buy it sliced, by the pound. *One pound serves 2 or 3.*

PAN-FRIED ABALONE

Pound slices thoroughly with a wooden mallet. Pat dry with a paper towel. Sprinkle with salt and pepper. Egg and crumb (p. 4), using cracker crumbs. Brown quickly in olive oil or butter, allowing about 1 minute on each side. Do not cook longer, as overcooking toughens abalone.

ABALONE CHOWDER

Vary the vegetables by adding parsley or carrots and omitting green pepper or leek. Vary the seasoning, too.

Put through the food chopper

1 pound sliced abalone

Put in a deep kettle

2 tablespoons butter
2 tablespoons chopped onion
1 tablespoon chopped leek
1 tablespoon chopped celery
1 tablespoon chopped green pepper

Cook slowly until the vegetables are soft. Stir in

1 tablespoon flour

Add the chopped abalone and

½ cup fresh or canned tomatoes
4 cups water
Salt, pepper, and Worcestershire and Tabasco to taste

Cover and cook slowly 1 hour. Add enough more water or tomato juice to make 4 cups of chowder. Add

1 or 2 potatoes, diced

Cook until the potatoes are just barely soft (about 10 minutes). Season to taste. *Serves 4.*

Abalone Chowder with Cream. Omit the tomatoes. Just before serving, add ½ cup cream.

CLAMS

Buy clams in the shell by the dozen or by the quart or peck. See that the shells are tightly closed. This shows that the clams are alive and therefore fresh. If they are to be served raw, order them opened at the market, or open them with a special heavy knife. For Clam Chowder (p. 78), buy shelled clams by the pint or in cans.

There are three principal varieties in American markets: soft-shelled, hard-shelled and the delicious razor clams which come from the Pacific. Soft-shelled New England clams are oval-shaped. Hard-shelled are round and come in three types: littlenecks (small), cherrystones (medium), and quahogs or chowder clams (large).

Clam Chowder is on page 78, Clams on the Half Shell on page 55.

SEASHORE CLAMBAKE

Have at least 1 quart of clams for each person, preferably soft or long-necked variety. Live lobsters, too, and corn on the cob in its husks, if you are planning a hearty bake.

Dig a pit in the sand about 1 foot deep. Put a layer of stones in it. Build a wood fire on the stones and burn until it dies down and the stones are white-hot (about 1 hour). Meanwhile, wash the clams well in sea water, kill the lobsters (p. 150, Broiled Live Lobster) and dip the corn in sea water. Rake off the ashes and spread a thin layer of rockweed on the stones. Put a piece of chicken wire over the rockweed and pile the clams, lobsters and corn on it. Cover with more rockweed and a piece of canvas to keep in the steam. Work quickly so that the rocks will not cool. Steam about 1 hour.

STEAMED CLAMS

Soft-shelled clams are best for steaming. Allow 1 quart of clams per serving.

Scrub the shells thoroughly with a brush, changing the water until there is no trace of sand. Put in a deep kettle. Add 2 tablespoons water for each quart of clams. Cover closely and cook over low heat until the shells open a little (about 15 minutes). Do not overcook.

Remove with a perforated spoon to large soup plates. Serve with individual dishes of melted butter. If liked, add a few drops of lemon juice or vinegar to the butter. If a small quantity of boiling water is put into the dishes, the melted butter will float on top and remain hot much longer.

Strain the broth left in the kettle into small glasses and serve with the clams. Lift each clam from the shell by the black neck. Dip in the clam broth, then into the butter, and eat all but the neck.

BROILED CLAMS

Remove top shell from hard-shelled clams (medium size). Sprinkle with fine bread crumbs and a bit of butter. Broil 5 to 8 minutes. Serve very hot.

FRIED CLAMS

Allow about 6 soft-shelled clams per serving.

If the clams are in the shell, remove them. Clean and drain dry on paper towels. Dip in seasoned flour or in Fritter Batter (p. 409), using no sugar. Fry in deep fat heated to 375°. Drain on paper towels. Serve with Tartare Sauce (p. 103).

STUFFED CLAMS UNION LEAGUE

Put in a kettle

4 tablespoons butter
½ teaspoon finely chopped shallot *or* onion

Cook 5 minutes. Add

18 small clams (in the shell)
½ cup dry white wine *or* water

Cover and cook until the shells open. Remove the clams from the shells and chop. Cook the liquid in the kettle down to ⅓ cup. In a saucepan, melt

2 tablespoons butter

Blend in

2 tablespoons flour

Stir in the clam liquid, little by little. Add the clams and

¼ cup cream

Season with salt and pepper. Spoon into the shells. Sprinkle with

Chopped parsley

Put on each

Bacon, diced, *or* buttered crumbs mixed with grated cheese

Bake at 400° until the bacon is crisp or the crumbs are brown. *Serves 3, or 6 as a first course.*

FRICASSEE OF CLAMS

Delicious as a first course for a party dinner or as an evening snack after bridge or the theater.

Put in a saucepan

2 tablespoons butter
1 pint chopped clams, fresh or canned
2 tablespoons flour

Stir in gradually

½ cup cream

Stir and cook 1 minute. Add

Salt and cayenne to taste

Stir in

1 egg yolk, slightly beaten

Season with

Sherry *or* Madeira

Serve on

Toast *or* in pastry cases

Serves 4.

CLAM FRITTERS

To serve as hors d'oeuvres with cocktails, measure with an after-dinner coffee spoon.

Drain

1 cup chopped clams, fresh or canned

Measure the juice and to it add

Milk (to make ⅓ cup liquid)

In a mixing bowl, beat

1 egg

Add the clam juice and milk. Sift together

⅔ cup flour
1 teaspoon baking powder
½ teaspoon salt
Pepper

Add to the liquids and blend well. Add the clams. Sauté by spoonfuls in bacon fat, or fry 3 to 5 minutes in deep fat heated to 375°. *Makes 12 large fritters or 30 cocktail size.*

CRABS AND CRAB MEAT

Allow 1 or 2 crabs per serving, according to size. Buy them alive and active to be sure they are fresh. Or buy frozen crabs, ready to cook.

Soft-shelled crabs may be ordered cleaned at market. Otherwise, kill by sticking a small sharp knife into the body between the eyes, then lift and fold back the tapering points on each side of the back shell and remove the spongy substance under them. Turn the crab on its back, and with a pointed knife remove the small piece at the back of shell which ends in a point; this is called the apron. Soft-shelled crabs are eaten shell and all.

Hard-shelled crabs are cooked like boiled lobsters (p. 149) for 25 minutes. The edible crab meat is in the top of the back and in the claws. Discard the spongy fiber. Crack the claws with a nutcracker.

Crab meat may be bought fresh, by the pound, or in cans. Use fresh crab meat as soon after purchasing as possible. Remove the stiff tendons from canned crab meat.

SAUTÉED CRABS À LA MEUNIÈRE

Sprinkle soft-shelled crabs with salt, pepper and lemon juice.

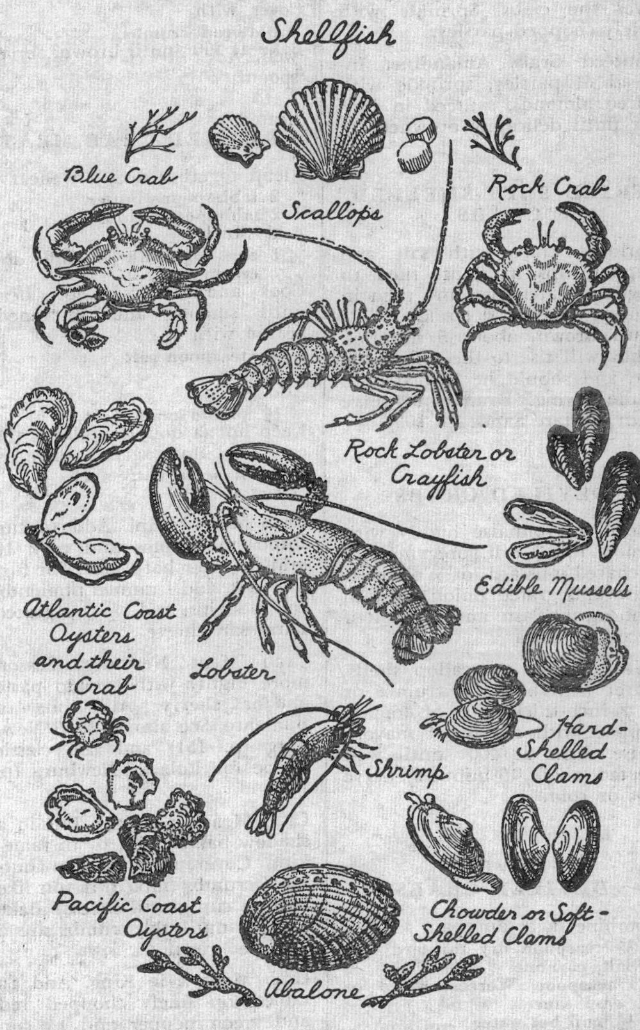
Shellfish
Blue Crab
Scallops
Rock Crab
Rock Lobster or Crayfish
Edible Mussels
Atlantic Coast Oysters and their Crab
Lobster
Hard-Shelled Clams
Shrimp
Pacific Coast Oysters
Chowder or Soft-Shelled Clams
Abalone

Sauté in butter 5 minutes on each side. Pour the pan juices over the crabs. Sprinkle with finely chopped parsley.

Sautéed Crabs Amandine. Instead of parsley, sprinkle with sliced almonds, sautéed in butter until delicately browned.

FRIED SOFT-SHELLED CRABS

Sprinkle crabs with salt and pepper, dip in flour, then in slightly beaten egg, and then in crumbs. Fry in deep fat (375°) until brown, about 5 minutes. They will rise to the top of the fat, and should be turned once while frying. Drain and serve with Tartare Sauce (p. 103).

DEVILED CRABS

Season mayonnaise highly with lemon juice, dill, oregano and prepared mustard (or Worcestershire and grated onion). Stir in crab meat. Taste and add salt if necessary.

Fill ramekins or scallop shells. Cover with buttered crumbs or a ½-inch-thick slice of tomato topped with a dab of mayonnaise. Bake at 400° until well heated (about 15 minutes). Serve hot or cold.

IPSWICH DEVILED CRABS

Combine in a saucepan
- **¼ teaspoon dry mustard**
- **Salt, cayenne**
- **1 teaspoon Worcestershire *or* A-1 sauce**
- **½ cup hot water**
- **½ cup soft bread crumbs**
- **1 tablespoon cream**
- **1 tablespoon butter**

Simmer 5 minutes. Stir in
- **1 cup crab meat**
- **¼ cup chopped stuffed olives**

Fill ramekins or scallop shells. Cover with
- **Buttered crumbs**

Bake at 350° until brown. *Serves 6.*

CREAMED CRAB MEAT

Blend together over low heat
- **2 tablespoons butter**
- **2 tablespoons flour**

Add slowly
- **1 cup top milk *or* milk and cream**

Cook and stir over low heat until smooth and thickened. Season with
- **¼ teaspoon salt**
- **Pepper**

Add
- **½ pound crab meat**

Keep hot (a double boiler is the easy way) until served. Serve on
- **Toast *or* in patty shells**

Serves 4.

Crab Meat Urzini. Add ½ cup sliced mushrooms and cook 10 minutes over hot water. For further zest, add 1 canned pimiento, cut in strips, and ½ cup grated Parmesan cheese.

Crab Meat Newburg. Season more highly with tomato paste and/or sherry. Add bits of pimiento. See also Seafood Newburg (p. 151) and the classic recipe for Lobster Newburg (p. 151).

Crab Meat au Gratin. Put in a shallow baking dish or in ramekins. Cover with ⅓ cup buttered crumbs (mixed, if you like with ¼ cup grated cheese). Bake at 350° until the crumbs are a delicate brown.

Crab Meat à la King. Add ½ tablespoon finely chopped red and green pepper and ½ cup sliced mushrooms. Season to taste with sherry.

Crab Meat de Luxe. Season with a dash of Worcestershire. Use only ½ cup crab meat, and add ½ cup each of sliced mushrooms and blanched, shredded or whole almonds, and 1 hard-cooked egg, chopped.

CRAB MEAT DIVAN

Put a layer of well-seasoned, chopped cooked spinach in a shallow baking dish. Spread over it 1 cup of cooked or canned crab meat. Over the top pour 1 cup hot Cheese Sauce (p. 95). Bake at 350° until well heated and lightly browned. *Serves 4.*

CRAB MEAT TERRAPIN STYLE

Put in a pan

2 tablespoons butter
½ small onion, sliced thin

Cook until the onion is yellow, remove it and stir into the butter

1 cup crab meat
2 tablespoons sherry

Cook 3 minutes. Stir in

⅓ cup heavy cream
2 egg yolks

Season with

Salt and cayenne

Serves 2 to 4.

CRAB MEAT INDIENNE

Put in a pan

2 tablespoons butter
1 teaspoon onion, chopped fine

Cook 3 minutes. Mix

3 tablespoons flour
2 teaspoons curry powder

Stir into the onion mixture. Add

1 cup chicken broth *or* Chicken Stock (p. 62)

Bring to the boiling point. Add

1 cup crab meat

Season to taste. *Serves 4.*

CRAB MEAT MORNAY

As a first course, bake in eight or more small ramekin dishes.

Blend in a saucepan over low heat

4 tablespoons butter
3 tablespoons flour
2½ tablespoons cornstarch

Add gradually

1 cup chicken broth *or* Chicken Stock (p. 62)

Boil 3 minutes, stirring constantly. Add

1 cup milk

Blend and bring to a boil. Stir in

2 egg yolks, slightly beaten
¾ teaspoon salt
1 pound crab meat, cooked or canned

Spoon into a buttered 1½-quart casserole. Sprinkle with

½ cup grated cheese

Cook under the broiler until the cheese melts and browns. *Serves 6.*

CRAB CAKES

Put in a saucepan

2 tablespoons butter
2 tablespoons minced onion

Cook until the onion is yellow. Remove from the heat. Add

1 cup soft bread crumbs
1 pound crab meat, cooked or canned
1 egg, well beaten
1 teaspoon dry mustard
Salt and paprika to taste

If the mixture seems dry, moisten with

Milk

Shape in flat cakes. Sprinkle with

Flour

Brown quickly in

Butter

Reduce the heat and cook slowly 5 minutes. *Serves 4.*

CRAB MEAT TEMPURA

A Japanese specialty. The sauce should be served in tiny individual bowls into which the pieces of crab are dipped.

Prepare

1 pound cooked or canned crab meat

Keep the large chunks whole and reserve to use later. Flake the small pieces of crab meat and mix with

1 egg, well beaten
4 tablespoons cracker crumbs

Shape into 1-inch balls. Chill. Make a batter by mixing

1 egg, slightly beaten
½ cup water
½ cup flour

Heat to 370°

2 cups peanut oil

Dip the crab meat chunks and the balls into the batter and cook them in the hot oil until brown. Drain on a paper towel and serve with sauce (below). *Serves 4.*

PIQUANT SAUCE FOR TEMPURA

Mix

½ cup hot bouillon
2 tablespoons soy sauce
1 teaspoon sugar
1 teaspoon prepared horse-radish
½ teaspoon monosodium glutamate

Serves 4.

OYSTER CRABS

Oyster crabs are sold by the pound at specialty shops in a few large cities. They live in the oyster shell and are very small. They are eaten whole, shells and all. One pound serves 8 as the fish course in a formal dinner.

FRIED OYSTER CRABS

Wash and drain. Roll in flour and shake in a sieve to remove excess flour. Sauté 5 minutes in unsalted butter or fry in a basket in deep fat heated to 390°. Garnish with parsley and slices of lemon. Serve with tiny boiled potato balls and sliced tomatoes with French dressing and chopped parsley. Or serve with cucumber sandwiches made with brown bread.

Fried Oyster Crabs and White-bait. Mix fried oyster crabs and whitebait (p. 134) as a de luxe luncheon dish. *One half pound of each will serve 4.*

OYSTER CRABS NEWBURG

Mix

1 cup mushroom caps, broken in pieces
1 cup oyster crabs
⅓ cup sherry

Cover and let stand 1 hour. Melt in a saucepan

¼ cup butter

Add the first mixture and cook 8 minutes. Stir in

1 tablespoon flour

Cook 2 minutes. Season with

Salt, cayenne and nutmeg to taste

Add

¾ cup heavy cream

Just before serving, heat and stir in

2 egg yolks, slightly beaten
1 tablespoon brandy

Serves 4.

LOBSTERS

Allow 1 small lobster per person or, if the lobsters are larger, about 1 pound in the shell per person. Buy lobsters alive or already boiled at the market. Buy cooked lobster meat fresh, canned or frozen.

Lobster tails or rock lobster are increasingly popular as a substitute for lobster. To kill live lobster (p. 150, Broiled Live Lobster). Cook immediately after killing.

BOILED LOBSTERS

Fill a large kettle three-quarters full of water. Bring it to a rapid boil. Add 2 tablespoons salt for each quart of water or use sea water.

Put in the live lobsters, one at a time, grasping just behind the claws. Let the water boil again after putting in each lobster. Lower the heat, cover the kettle and simmer 15 minutes for small lobsters (3/4 to 1 pound), 20 minutes for medium-sized (1 1/2 to 2 pounds), and 40 for very large ones.

Cool in the broth, or, if the lobster is to be served hot, lift from the broth and drain.

To shell a cooked lobster and remove the meat. Place the lobster on its back. Twist off the claws. Separate the tail from the body. Break off the flippers. Stick a fork into the base of the tail meat and push the meat out in one piece. Remove and discard the black line which runs its entire length. Crack the body shell. Lobster meat lies in the four pockets where the small claws are attached.

Pushing out the meat from a lobster tail and removing the black central fibre

The green part is tomally or liver, the coral is roe, and both are edible. Discard other portions.

Break open the large claws with a hammer or nutcracker, and remove the meat. Use the small claws for garnishing.

To serve boiled lobster. Split the lobster and serve hot with melted butter or cold with mayonnaise. If desired, remove the meat from the shell, arrange attractively on a platter and garnish with small claws.

BOILED LOBSTER TAILS

Allow 1 or 2 per person.

Cover with boiling salted water. Bring to the boiling point and simmer 5 minutes. Serve with melted butter and lemon wedges or use the meat in any of the recipes calling for cooked lobster meat.

BUTTERED LOBSTER

This simple dish is also delicious heated with grated Cheddar cheese and a sprinkling of rum.

Cut cooked, canned or frozen lobster meat in pieces. Sauté slowly in melted butter until well heated. Sprinkle with salt, pepper, and lemon juice.

FRIED LOBSTER

Sprinkle large chunks of cooked, canned or frozen lobster meat with salt, pepper and lemon juice. Dip in crumbs, egg, and again in crumbs. Fry in deep fat, heated to 385°. Drain. Serve with Tartare Sauce (p. 103).

BROILED LOBSTER TAILS

Allow 1 or 2 per person.

Thaw, if frozen. Cut lengthwise along each side of the membrane and remove it. Bend the tail backward to crack the shell. Broil 15 minutes on the shell side, turn, spread with butter and broil 10 minutes. Serve with melted butter and lemon wedges.

BROILED LIVE LOBSTER

Allow 1 small or ½ large lobster per person.

Kill by inserting a sharp knife between the body and shell at the tail to sever the spinal cord. Put the lobster on its back and make a deep, sharp cut through the entire length of the body and tail with a heavy sharp-pointed knife or lobster shears. Spread open and remove the black line and the stomach. Crack the claw shells with a mallet.

Place in the broiler, shell side down. Sprinkle with olive oil or melted butter. Broil slowly about 20 minutes or until the flesh is brown. Serve with melted butter.

LIVE LOBSTER EN BROCHETTE

Allow 1 small or ½ large lobster per person.

Split the lobster (see Broiled Live Lobster). Remove the meat from the tail and large claws, cut it in pieces, and arrange on skewers, alternating the pieces with small slices of bacon. Fry in deep fat heated to 375°. Drain.

Cook the green lobster liver with 1 tablespoon butter 3 minutes, season highly with mustard and cayenne, and serve with the lobster.

LOBSTER À L'AMÉRICAINE

Sometimes called Armoricaine. A de luxe dish for a special occasion.

Kill and split (see Broiled Live Lobster, above)

1½-pound live lobster

Cut in pieces. Remove the liver and coral and set aside. In a large frying pan heat

1 tablespoon salad oil
1 tablespoon butter
½ bay leaf
Pinch of thyme

Put the pieces of lobster into the pan. Sprinkle with

1 tablespoon chopped onion *or* shallot
Few grains cayenne

Cover and cook 5 minutes. Mix

2 tablespoons tomato paste
2 tablespoons sherry *or* ¼ cup dry white wine

Add to the lobster. Cover and cook over low heat until the lobster is tender and the shells are red (10 to 15 minutes). Take out the pieces of lobster and remove the meat. Strain the liquid. Put back in the pan. Add the liver and the coral. Cook and stir until thick. Add

Sherry to taste

Add the lobster. *Serves 2.*

Lobster Flambé. Just before serving, pour ¼ cup warmed brandy or Pernod over the lobster. Light with a match and stir until the flame dies down.

LOBSTER THERMIDOR

Boil and split

4 small or 2 large lobsters

Remove the meat and cut it in neat pieces. Cook together 5 minutes

2 tablespoons butter
½ pound mushrooms, sliced

Melt

4 tablespoons butter

Add the lobster and cook 5 minutes. Sprinkle over the lobster

2 tablespoons flour

Stir until smooth. Add gradually

1 pint heavy cream *or* milk and cream *or* evaporated milk

Stir well. Heat slowly until smooth. Add the mushrooms. Season to taste with

Salt and paprika *or* cayenne
Sherry

Spoon into the lobster shells. Set in a baking pan. Sprinkle with

¼ cup grated Parmesan cheese

Bake at 450° until browned or brown in the broiler. *Serves 4.*

CREAMED LOBSTER

Most people call this Lobster Newburg but see the classic recipe, below. Add, if you like, chopped parsley, strips of canned pimiento or sliced sautéed mushrooms.

Cook 3 minutes over moderate heat

1 cup cooked lobster, cut small
3 tablespoons butter

Sprinkle with

2 tablespoons flour

Stir well. Add

1 cup top milk *or* milk and cream

Cook slowly and stir until well heated and thickened. Season to taste with

Salt, nutmeg and cayenne
Lemon juice
Tomato catsup *or* tomato paste (if you like)

Serve on toast, in patty shells or with fluffy boiled rice. *Serves 3 or 4.*

Deviled Lobster. Add mustard to taste. Season highly.

Curried Lobster. Season with curry instead of catsup or tomato paste.

Scalloped Lobster. Put in buttered scallop shells or a baking dish. Cover with buttered crumbs. Bake at 350° until the crumbs are brown.

Baked Stuffed Lobster. Put in the lobster shell which has been brushed with olive oil to help keep its bright color. Sprinkle with fresh bread crumbs mixed with grated cheese. Bake at 350° until the crumbs are brown.

LOBSTER NEWBURG

This is the classic version, very rich and delicious. For a modified version, make Creamed Lobster (above) and season it with sherry and brandy.

Cook together 3 minutes

2 cups cooked lobster meat, sliced
¼ cup melted butter

Add

1 tablespoon sherry
1 tablespoon brandy

Cook 1 minute and add

1 cup cream
Salt, cayenne, nutmeg
3 egg yolks, slightly beaten

Stir over low heat until slightly thickened. Serve on toast or with triangles of Puff Paste (p. 453). *Serves 4 or 5.*

SEAFOOD NEWBURG

Follow the recipe for Lobster Newburg or Creamed Lobster using other shellfish, separately or in combinations such as scallops (cut in half unless they are tiny) and shrimp, lobster and scallops or crab meat, lobster and scallops.

LOBSTER PIE

Prepare Creamed Lobster (above) or Lobster Newburg (above). Put in a baking dish or in individual dishes. Cover with a generous layer of buttered crumbs mixed with grated cheese. Bake at 375° until the crumbs are brown.

LOBSTER MOUSSE

Follow the recipe for Fish Mousse (p. 131), using 1½ cups

lobster meat and ¼ pound flounder fillet, both ground fine in the food chopper or blender. Season with sherry. Serve with Normandy Sauce (p. 97) or Hollandaise (p. 100).

LOBSTER TIMBALES

Luncheon party fare.

Cook together 5 minutes
1 cup chopped cooked lobster meat
1 tablespoon butter
Stir in
1 tablespoon flour
1 teaspoon salt
⅛ teaspoon paprika
Few drops onion juice
2 egg yolks
⅓ cup milk
Fold in
⅓ cup cream, beaten stiff
1 egg white, beaten stiff
Bake like Egg Timbales (p. 115). Serve with Lobster Sauce (p. 94). *Fills 6 or more molds.*

LOBSTER CROQUETTES

To vary seasonings, omit the mustard and add a few gratings of nutmeg and 1 teaspoon parsley, chopped fine.

Mix
2 cups chopped lobster meat
½ teaspoon salt
¼ teaspoon mustard
Few grains cayenne
1 teaspoon lemon juice
1 cup Croquette Sauce (p. 94)
Chill. Shape, crumb, and fry in deep fat heated to 375° (p. 4). *Makes 12 or more.*

Lobster Cutlets. Add 1 egg yolk to the mixture. Shape in flat ovals and fry or sauté in butter.

MUSSELS

To prepare mussels. The shells should be tightly closed. Let stand 20 minutes in cold water with 1 tablespoon dry mustard. Scrub thoroughly under running water until all bits of sand are removed. Some specialty shops sell imported canned mussels.

STEAMED MUSSELS

Allow 6 to 12 mussels per person.

Prepare (above). Put in a deep kettle. Add 2 tablespoons water for each dozen mussels. Cover and steam until the shells open (5 to 10 minutes).

Serve with melted butter seasoned with garlic and chopped parsley or with Poulette Sauce (p. 96) made with the broth from the kettle.

MOULES MARINIÈRE

Simmer together
1 cup dry white wine
6 shallots, finely chopped, *or* 3 tablespoons finely chopped onion
1 tablespoon chopped parsley
½ bay leaf
Few grains cayenne
When reduced to about ½ cup, strain into a large kettle. Add
4 dozen mussels, prepared (above)
Cover tightly. Heat 5 to 10 minutes, or until the shells open, shaking the pan from time to time. Remove the mussels carefully to deep soup plates and keep hot. To the sauce in the kettle, add
2 tablespoons butter
Salt, if needed
Pour carefully over the mussels, leaving any sediment in the bottom of the pan. Sprinkle with
Chopped parsley
Serves 6.

To vary, add fresh herbs, garlic, celery, or 1 or 2 slices of carrot.

OYSTERS

Fresh oysters in the shell are marketed by the dozen, or, if shelled, by the pint, quart or gallon. Be sure the shells are tightly closed, and that shelled oysters are plump and shiny and fresh-smelling. Oysters are in season all year on the Pacific Coast and from September through April on the Atlantic and Gulf coasts. Quick-frozen shelled oysters are available all year.

Long cooking toughens oysters. Prepare them just before serving to develop the best flavor.

To open oysters. Insert the tip of a thin sharp knife between the halves of the shell, just back of the muscle. Cut through the muscle. Lift off the shallow shell. Loosen the oyster from the shell with the point of the knife. Save the oyster liquid.

To clean oysters. Put the shelled oysters in a sieve placed over a bowl to catch the liquid. Pour cold water over oysters, allowing ½ cup water to each quart of oysters. This is to loosen the bits of shell. Lift the oysters one by one and remove any bits of shell. Strain the water in the bowl to use in cooking the oysters.

To parboil oysters. Put the cleaned oysters in a saucepan with the water and liquid drained from them. Heat and cook only until the oysters are plump and the edges begin to curl. Drain and add water, if necessary, to make up the amount of oyster liquid called for in the recipe. Strain the liquid through cheesecloth or a very fine sieve.

OYSTER COCKTAIL

See page 55, Seafood Cocktail.

OYSTER STEW

See page 79.

PIGS IN BLANKETS

Serve for lunch or supper or with drinks.

Wrap cleaned and dried oysters in thin strips of bacon. Fasten with toothpicks. Arrange on a rack in a shallow pan. Bake at 425° until the bacon is crisp and brown. Turn once to cook evenly. Drain on a paper towel.

BROILED *or* SAUTÉED OYSTERS

Clean (above)

1 pint large oysters (about 30)

Pat dry on a paper towel. Mix

⅔ cup cracker crumbs
½ teaspoon salt
⅛ teaspoon pepper

Dip oysters in

¼ cup melted butter

then in crumb mixture. Broil on a greased broiling rack, 2 inches from the heat, or sauté in

2 tablespoons butter

Turn once while cooking. Serve on toast with Maître d'Hôtel Butter (p. 103) or sprinkle with sherry. *Serves 4.*

FRIED OYSTERS

Allow 6 to 8 oysters per serving.

Clean (above) and dry. For about 2 dozen oysters, make a

batter by beating 2 eggs slightly and stirring in 2 tablespoons milk, 1 teaspoon salt and 1/8 teaspoon pepper. Dip oysters in the batter, then in fine dry bread crumbs or cornmeal.

Sauté in butter in a single layer or fry in deep fat heated to 375°. Drain on a paper towel. Serve with Tartare Sauce (p. 103) or Philadelphia Relish (p. 91).

Oven-fried oysters. Arrange in a shallow baking pan in a single layer. Sprinkle with olive oil. Bake at 400° until nicely browned (about 15 minutes).

FANCY ROAST

The traditional New England name for a very simple dish.

Clean 1 pint oysters (p. 153). Cook with their liquid in a chafing dish or omelet pan until the oysters are plump and the edges begin to curl. Shake the pan to keep the oysters from sticking. Season with salt, pepper and 2 tablespoons butter. Serve on small pieces of toast. Garnish with parsley. *Serves 2 or 3.*

Oysters à la Thorndike. Add a slight grating of nutmeg and 1/4 cup thin cream. Add 2 egg yolks, slightly beaten, and cook and stir until slightly thickened.

OYSTERS IN SHERRY CREAM

Put in a shallow baking dish
- **1 dozen oysters, shelled and cleaned (p. 153)**

Sprinkle with
- **Salt and pepper**

Cover with
- **1/2 cup coarse bread crumbs**
- **1 tablespoon sherry**
- **1/2 cup cream**

Cook 2 minutes under the broiler, or just long enough to heat the cream and curl the edges of the oysters. *Serves 3 or 4 as a first course or 2 as a luncheon dish.*

OYSTERS CASINO

Allow 6 to 8 oysters per serving.

Open carefully to keep the juice. Remove the flat shell, leaving the oysters in the deeper half. Sprinkle each with a few drops of lemon juice and a bit of finely minced green pepper. Season with salt and pepper and put a 1/2-inch square of bacon on each.

Arrange in a shallow pan on a bed of rock salt (salt holds the heat well). Bake at 450°, or under the broiler until the bacon is crisp.

PANNED OYSTERS

Clean (p. 153) 1 pint large oysters. Arrange small oblong pieces of toast in a shallow baking pan. Put an oyster on each piece. Sprinkle with salt and pepper.

Bake at 400° until the oysters are plump. Serve with Lemon Butter (1/4 cup creamed butter with 1 tablespoon lemon juice beaten in drop by drop). *Serves 4.*

Oysters Algonquin. Instead of toast, put the oysters on sautéed mushroom caps, smooth side down. For a richer dish, serve with Béchamel Sauce (p. 95).

ROASTED OYSTERS

Scrub oysters in the shell thoroughly with a brush. Put in a shallow baking pan, with the deep side of the shells down.

Bake at 450° until the shells part. Open, sprinkle with salt and pepper, and serve in the deep halves of the shells.

OYSTERS ROCKEFELLER

If you have an electric blender, use it to blend the butter and the greens. There are many versions of this dish, so vary it to suit yourself, such as by adding a few drops of Pernod, which has the flavor of licorice.

Chop fine

3 green onions, stalks and tips
¼ cup chopped celery
1 teaspoon minced chervil
1 teaspoon minced tarragon leaves
3 sprigs parsley
½ cup young spinach leaves

Add

⅛ cup soft bread crumbs

Season to taste with

Salt and pepper
Few drops Tabasco, Worcestershire and anchovy sauce

Pound in a mortar until smooth. Blend well with

1 cup butter, creamed

Force through a sieve. Put a bed of damp rock salt (which holds the heat well) in a large pan. Arrange on the salt

2 dozen large oysters, on the half shell

Put a tablespoon of the butter mixture on each. Bake at 450° until thoroughly heated (about 10 minutes). *Serves 6.*

OYSTERS FRICASSEE (CREAMED OYSTERS)

Parboil (p. 153)

1 pint oysters

To the liquid, add

Milk *or* cream (enough to make 1 cup)

Melt over low heat

2 tablespoons butter

Add

2 tablespoons flour

Stir until smooth. Add the liquid gradually and stir until thickened. Season with

¼ teaspoon salt
Few grains cayenne
1 teaspoon chopped parsley

Add the oysters and

1 egg, slightly beaten

Cook 1 minute. Serve on

Toast, in timbale cases *or* patty shells

Serves 4.

Savory Oysters. Brown the butter in making the sauce. Season with 1½ teaspoons lemon juice, 1½ teaspoons vinegar, ½ teaspoon beef extract, and 1 teaspoon Worcestershire, or with anchovy paste to taste.

Oysters à la d'Uxelles. Cook 2 tablespoons chopped mushrooms (or more) 5 minutes in the butter before stirring in the flour.

SCALLOPED OYSTERS

For a pleasantly subtle flavor, sprinkle each layer with a few gratings of nutmeg.

Clean, reserving the liquid

1 pint oysters

Mix

½ cup bread crumbs
1 cup cracker crumbs
½ cup melted butter

Put a thin layer in a shallow buttered baking dish. Cover with half the oysters. Sprinkle with

Salt and pepper

Add

2 tablespoons oyster liquid *or* clam juice
1 tablespoon milk *or* cream

Repeat. Cover the top with the rest of the crumbs. Bake 20 minutes at 450°. *Serves 4.*

DEVILED OYSTERS

Clean (p. 153) and chop

1 pint oysters

Cook together 3 minutes

3 shallots, chopped fine
1 tablespoon butter

Add

2 tablespoons flour

Stir until well blended. Add

½ cup milk
¼ cup cream

Bring to the boiling point, stirring to keep smooth. Add the chopped oysters. Season with

½ teaspoon salt
⅛ teaspoon nutmeg
Few grains cayenne
½ teaspoon prepared mustard
½ tablespoon Worcestershire sauce
3 chopped mushroom caps
½ teaspoon chopped parsley

Simmer 12 minutes. Stir in

1 egg yolk

Put the mixture in the deep halves of the oyster shells or in scallop shells. Cover with

Buttered crumbs

Bake 15 minutes at 400°. *Serves 6 as a first course, 3 or 4 as a luncheon or supper dish.*

OYSTERS LOUISIANE

Parboil (p. 153)

1 quart oysters

Reserve the liquid and add enough

Water to make 1½ cups

Cook together 5 minutes

3 tablespoons butter
2 tablespoons chopped red pepper
½ tablespoon chopped shallot

Stir in

4 tablespoons flour

Add the oyster liquid gradually, stirring constantly. Bring to the boiling point and season with

½ teaspoon salt
⅛ teaspoon paprika
Few grains cayenne

Put the oysters in large buttered scallop shells or in individual baking dishes. Cover with the sauce and sprinkle with

½ cup grated Parmesan cheese

Bake at 400° until thoroughly heated. *Serves 6 to 8.*

OYSTERS CAPE COD

Sift together

1½ cups flour
3 teaspoons baking powder
½ teaspoon salt

Cut in

1 tablespoon butter

Add

1 cup drained chopped oysters
6 tablespoons oyster liquid

Spread in a buttered shallow pan. Over the top, arrange

8 pork sausages

Bake 30 minutes at 450°, turning the sausages once to brown. *Serves 4.*

OYSTER PIE

Line a shallow pie plate with pastry. Put in two layers of oysters. If you have more than two layers, the middle ones will be underdone. Sprinkle with salt and pepper. Dot with butter, cover with pastry, and prick well.

Bake at 400° until brown (about 20 minutes). Serve with ham, hot or cold.

SCALLOPS

Small bay or cape scallops are more delicate than large deep-sea scallops. One pint or 1 pound sautéed or fried serves 3, scalloped or in a sauce serves 6.

To clean scallops. Dip quickly in cold water. Remove any bits of shell or sand.

To parboil scallops. Barely cover with boiling water. Cook 5 minutes and drain.

SCALLOP STEW

See page 80.

SAUTÉED SCALLOPS

Clean. Brush with melted butter and roll in salted flour. Sauté in butter about 5 minutes.

Arrange on a serving dish. Pour the butter from the pan over them. Sprinkle with lemon juice and finely chopped parsley. *One pound serves 3.*

FRIED SCALLOPS

Clean the scallops, drain, and pat dry on paper towels. Season with salt and pepper. Dip in slightly beaten egg, then in crumbs. Let stand 20 minutes to dry the coating. Fry 2 minutes in deep fat heated to 375°, or pan-fry not more than 5 minutes in melted butter or other cooking fat.

FRIED SCALLOPS HUNTINGTON

Clean
  1 quart scallops
Add
  Juice 1 lemon
  1 tablespoon olive oil
  1 teaspoon finely chopped parsley
  1 teaspoon salt
  ½ teaspoon pepper
Cover and let stand 30 minutes. Drain. Mix
  3 tablespoons chopped cooked ham
  4 tablespoons soft bread crumbs
  2 tablespoons grated Parmesan cheese
  1 teaspoon finely cut chives
Egg and crumb the scallops (p. 4), using the prepared crumb mixture. Fry at 385°. Serve with
  Tartare Sauce (p. 103)
Serves 6.

DEVILED SCALLOPS

Barely cover with boiling water
  1 pint scallops
Simmer 5 minutes. Drain (reserving the liquid). Chop the scallops. Cream together
  3 tablespoons butter
  ¼ teaspoon prepared mustard
  ½ teaspoon salt
  Few grains cayenne
Add ⅓ cup of the reserved liquid and the scallops. Let stand ½ hour. Put in a baking dish or in scallop shells. Cover with
  ⅓ cup buttered cracker crumbs
Bake 20 minutes at 375°. *Serves 3.*

SCALLOPS À LA NEWBURG

If desired, add ½ cup shrimps or ½ pound sliced sautéed mushrooms—or both. For a simple version, follow the recipe for Creamed Lobster (p. 151), using scallops instead of lobster.

Cut in half
  1 pint scallops
Cook 3 minutes with
  2 tablespoons butter
Add
  1 teaspoon lemon juice
Cook 1 minute and set aside. Blend in a saucepan, over low heat
  1 tablespoon butter
  1 teaspoon flour
  ½ cup cream
Stir constantly and bring to the boiling point. Add
  2 egg yolks, slightly beaten
  2 tablespoons sherry
Add the scallops. Reduce the heat and stir well. If the mixture curdles from overcooking, add a little milk and stir until smooth again. Season to taste with
  Salt and cayenne
Serves 6.

SAVOY SCALLOPS

Cut into quarters
  1 quart scallops, parboiled (p. 156)

Reserve the scallop liquid and add enough

Water to make 1⅓ cups

Melt over low heat

3 tablespoons butter

Stir in

3 tablespoons flour

Blend well. Add the liquid slowly, stirring constantly. Bring to the boiling point and lower the heat. Stir in, a little at a time

½ cup mayonnaise

Add the scallops and

½ teaspoon dried thyme

Keep hot in a double boiler, or over very low heat so that the mixture does not boil. *Serves 6.*

SCALLOPED SCALLOPS

Clean

1 pint scallops

Melt in a saucepan

3 tablespoons butter

Add the scallops. Cook and stir 5 minutes. Stir in

3 tablespoons flour

Blend well. Add, a little at a time

1 cup cream
¾ cup milk

Cook and stir until slightly thick. Season to taste with

Salt and pepper

Put in a buttered casserole. Cover with

½ cup buttered crumbs

Bake at 400° until the crumbs are brown (about 10 minutes). *Serves 4 to 6.*

Savory Scalloped Scallops. Cut fine 1 small onion and 1 green pepper. Cook in the butter until the onion is yellow. Add 1 cup sliced mushrooms. Cook 5 minutes. Add the scallops and continue as above.

SHRIMP

Buy fresh shrimp in the shell, raw, cooked or frozen, or buy peeled shrimp cooked, canned or frozen. To serve 4, buy 1 pound in the shell or ½ pound cooked and peeled.

To prepare shrimp for cooking. Wash shrimp (cover frozen shrimp with cold water and let stand 15 minutes). Peel off the shells with your fingers. Take out the black line. The most convenient tool is a beer can opener because it has a firm but somewhat dull point. Or use the point of a knife or a toothpick or a special shrimp cleaner.

To cook shrimp. Put 1 cup boiling water in a pan. Add ½ teaspoon salt. To season more highly, add a sprig of parsley, a slice of onion, a tiny piece of bay leaf, a clove and 1 teaspoon vinegar. Add the shrimp, cover closely, and simmer until tender (5 to 12 minutes). Cool the shrimp in the water in which they were cooked. Drain and save the liquid to use in a soup or sauce.

FRIED SHRIMP

Shell and clean raw shrimp (above). Sprinkle with lemon juice, rum or brandy. Let stand 15 minutes. Dip in Fritter Batter (p. 409), made without sugar, or egg and crumb (p. 4). Fry 1 minute in deep fat heated to 370°. Drain on a paper towel. Serve with mayonnaise seasoned with horseradish, capers or catsup with grated onion and lemon juice.

SAUTÉED SHRIMP

Sauté canned or cooked shrimp lightly in melted butter. Pour the butter over the shrimp. Sprinkle with finely chopped parsley.

To serve Sautéed Shrimp with drinks. Serve on toothpicks. Dip in Mustard Sauce (p. 102) or melted butter, highly seasoned with lemon or lime juice and pepper. Or serve with any of the dips suggested for Fried Shrimp (p. 158).

SHRIMP NEWBURG

For a simpler version, prepare Creamed Shrimp (below) and season with sherry and brandy.

Cook together 3 minutes
2 cups cooked or canned shrimp
2 tablespoons butter
Add
1 teaspoon lemon juice
Cook 1 minute and set aside. Melt in a saucepan over low heat
1 tablespoon butter
Add
1 teaspoon flour
Mix well. Add gradually, stirring constantly
½ cup cream
Cook until thickened. Remove from the heat. Add
2 egg yolks, slightly beaten
1 tablespoon sherry
1 tablespoon brandy
Add the shrimp. Season with
Salt and pepper to taste
Reheat but do not boil. *Serves 4.*

CREAMED SHRIMP

Heat 1 pint canned or cooked shrimp in Cream Sauce (p. 94) or in heavy cream lightly salted. Serve with boiled rice. *Serves 4.*

Creamed Shrimp with Curaçao. Add ¼ teaspoon celery salt, few gratings nutmeg and ½ teaspoon curaçao.

Creamed Shrimp with Dill. Add 1 teaspoon finely cut dill to the cream or sauce.

Curried Shrimp. Heat in Curry Cream Sauce (p. 94) or Brown Curry Sauce (p. 98) seasoned with 3 tablespoons tomato catsup.

SHRIMP WIGGLE

Vary the seasoning by adding lemon juice to taste, a tablespoon or two of chopped ripe olives or toasted chopped almonds.

Melt over low heat
2 tablespoons butter
Stir in
2 tablespoons flour
Blend well. Add gradually
1 cup milk *or* milk and cream
Cook until smooth. Add
Salt and pepper to taste
½ to 1 cup cooked or canned shrimp
½ cup cooked peas
Keep hot over boiling water or over very low heat. Pour over toast or crackers. *Serves 4.*

For a richer sauce, stir in an egg yolk before serving.

SHRIMP JAMBALAYA

For variety, add 12 parboiled oysters (p. 153). Use this recipe also with cooked ham, chicken, sausage or tongue in place of shrimp. For a less highly seasoned dish, omit the chili powder.

Cook until the fat melts
3 slices bacon, diced
Add
3 tablespoons chopped onion
2 tablespoons chopped celery
2 tablespoons chopped parsley
3 tablespoons chopped green pepper
Cook and stir until the onion is yellow. Add
1 tablespoon flour
Stir until the flour is slightly brown. Add
4 cups tomatoes, cooked or canned
1 teaspoon salt
Few grains cayenne
1 teaspoon chili powder

Cook until thick. Add

3 cups cooked rice
2 cups cooked shrimp, broken in pieces

Stir well. Heat. Taste and add more seasonings, if needed. *Serves 8.*

SHRIMP LOUISIANA STYLE

Cook together 5 minutes

2 tablespoons butter
1 teaspoon chopped onion

Add

⅔ cup cooked or canned shrimp (1 small can), broken in pieces
⅔ cup hot boiled rice
⅔ cup heavy cream

Heat well. Add

½ teaspoon salt
¼ teaspoon celery salt
Few grains cayenne
3 tablespoons tomato catsup, if desired

Serves 4.

GEORGIA SHRIMP MULL

Use canned shrimp if more convenient.

Clean, cook, and peel

2 pounds raw shrimp

Cook slowly

1 can tomatoes (about 2½ cups)

until the liquid is almost evaporated. Put in a saucepan

4 tablespoons bacon fat
1 large onion, chopped

Cook until the onion is soft. Stir in

4 tablespoons flour

Add the tomatoes. Add

1½ cups finely cut celery
1 large or 2 small green peppers, cut fine

Cook until the vegetables are tender. Add

Salt to taste
1 tablespoon Worcestershire

Add the shrimp. Cook slowly 20 minutes. Put in a baking dish. Prepare

Baking Powder Biscuit dough (p. 326)

Cut out small biscuits and put over the shrimp, close together. Put the rest of the biscuits on a cooky sheet. Bake at 450° about 15 minutes. Use the extra biscuits for the second serving. *Serves 6.*

SHRIMP POLONAISE

Sometimes called Shrimp de Jonghe, this is a superb dish to serve at lunch or supper or in smaller portions as a first course at dinner. It can be prepared in advance—even the day before.

Use canned shrimp or clean, cook, and peel

1½ pounds shrimp

Cream together

½ cup butter
1 clove garlic, crushed

Stir in

½ cup bread crumbs
¼ cup finely cut parsley
¼ cup dry sherry

Taste and add more seasoning if you like—salt, a drop or two of Worcestershire, a shake of mace or nutmeg. Spread the shrimp in a shallow baking dish. Dot with the butter mixture. Bake 25 minutes at 400°. *Serves 4 or 5.*

Meats

In most families, meat is the favorite main dish for the principal meal of the day. It is more expensive than other protein foods, so it is especially important to select it wisely and cook it to perfection.

SHOPPING FOR MEAT

Deal regularly with a reliable butcher and depend upon his advice as to the best cuts available. If you have a freezer or a freezer compartment, you can often take advantage of a special value even though you may not use it immediately. As a general rule, 1 pound of meat free of bones gives 3 or 4 servings. With the bone left in, count on 2 servings to the pound. But appetites vary with the individual, the type of meal and even with the season. Also, it is possible to increase the number of servings if the meat is prepared with a sauce or combined with vegetables or other foods in a casserole or stew.

Boned meat is easier to carve than meat with the bone in. The flavor is just as fine, contrary to the old belief, but of course an unboned roast looks handsome on the platter. If you order a roast boned, ask the butcher to give you the bones and the scraps to use for stock or soup.

Tender and less tender cuts have the same food value. Use the tender, expensive cuts for roasting and broiling and the less tender ones for stews and for dishes using chopped meat.

STORING MEAT BEFORE COOKING

Remove the wrapping paper. Put the meat on a plate and cover loosely with wax paper. Store in the refrigerator. Use chopped meat within a day or two. A roast keeps fresh longer —four or five days. If you plan to keep meat longer than this before cooking, wrap it in freezer paper or self-sealing wax paper and set it in the freezing compartment or in the ice tray section.

MEAT COOKERY

Meat cooks more evenly if it is at room temperature when you start, so take it out of the refrigerator long enough before cooking to remove the chill—at least 1 hour. **Frozen roasts** should be thawed completely before cooking begins — otherwise they will cook unevenly, with the center scarcely warmed through when the outside is thoroughly done. **Frozen steaks and chops** may be thawed or not, as convenient. If you start cooking while the meat is still solidly frozen, allow at least 10 minutes longer and test by making a cut into the meat to be sure it is done to your taste before you serve it.

ROASTING

Roasting is the easiest method of cooking meat. With the low-temperature method, a roast requires little or no attention. Times given for roasting are only approximate because roasts of the same weight differ in shape and in the amount of fat. A chunky roast takes longer than a thin one. A lean roast takes longer than a fat one. However, it is simple, as serving time approaches, to adjust the oven temperature up or down to speed or slow the roasting. A roast will continue to cook somewhat after it is out of the oven.

Preheat the oven at the temperature suggested in the recipe—325° for most meats, 350° for pork.

Use a shallow roasting pan without a cover. Set a rack in the pan so that the roast will not stick. Put the roast on the rack, fat side up. If the meat is very lean, put a piece of suet, bacon or salt pork on top and hold it in place with a toothpick.

A roast thermometer makes for carefree roasting. Make an incision with a skewer into the center of the roast, push in the thermometer, and make sure it does not rest against a bone. When the meat is done the dial will show the proper temperature.

Do not sprinkle with flour or salt. Do not baste, unless the recipe requires it. Add no water at any time. As the fat melts, it will moisten the meat.

Roast the required time. For a crisp brown surface, increase the heat to 400° for the last 15 minutes. Plan to have the roast ready at least 20 minutes before time to start carving. The meat will slice much more easily. Place it on a carving board or heated platter and cover it with aluminum foil to keep warm while you make the gravy.

BARBECUING

Meat cooked out of doors over a charcoal or wood fire has a wonderful flavor. A simple portable grill is a practical piece of equipment for the backyard or patio. A more elaborate one with an electrically operated rotating spit will make it possible to cook such tasty fare as Barbecued Leg of Lamb (p. 182). Any meat that can be broiled or pan-fried may be cooked on the grill. For delicious flavor, baste with a Barbecue Sauce (p. 93) during the cooking. Skewer cooking is successful for beef or lamb (see Shaslik, p. 186) but not for veal or pork, which need slow cooking.

BROILING

Take the broiler pan and rack out of the oven. Preheat the oven 10 minutes. To save washing the pan, line it with aluminum foil. Grease the broiling rack lightly by rubbing it with a piece of the fat from the meat or with other fat. Arrange the meat on the rack and set it in place about two inches from the heat. Cook half the required time on one side, then turn and complete cooking on the other side. Season with salt and pepper. Dot with bits of butter or spoon over the meat a small amount of the juices from the pan.

PAN-BROILING

A heavy frying pan cooks meat more evenly and with less danger of burning than a thin one. If you must use a thin one, set it on an asbestos mat.

If the meat is very lean, such as calves' liver or veal cutlets, grease the pan very lightly, just enough to keep the meat from sticking. When you pan-broil lamb or pork chops or ham, rub the pan with the fat around the edge of the meat. For other meats, merely sprinkle the pan generously with salt. Put in the meat and cook on one side until brown. Turn and brown on the other side. Reduce the heat and cook the required time. If any fat accumulates in the pan, pour it off so that the meat will cook by dry heat.

Serve the meat on a heated platter or plates. Season with salt and pepper. If you like, add just enough water or red wine to the pan juices to loosen the tasty brown glaze, stir well and pour over the meat. Vary by seasoning the pan juices with vinegar, lemon juice, mustard, Worcestershire or other table sauce. Sour cream or yogurt stirred into the pan juices makes a delicious sauce which can be varied by adding finely cut parsley.

STEWING AND POT-ROASTING

Cooking by moist heat softens the fibers of the less tender cuts of meat. There are special recipes including all the delicious variations of ragouts and fricassees, made with wine or tomato juice as the liquid, and with a whole range of interesting additions such as mushrooms, herbs, curry or saffron.

BEEF

The favorite American meat is undoubtedly beef, whether the traditional Sunday roast, a savory stew or one of the innumerable hamburger variations.

Shopping for beef. Top-grade beef is dull red, firm and fine-grained. It should have a good coating of fat and should be well marbled—that is, showing threadlike lines of fat throughout the lean. The fat should be white or creamy. Yellow fat means that the animal was range-fed and therefore the flesh will be less tender. Suet (the fat around the loin) should be dry and crumbly.

ROAST BEEF
(Rib, Sirloin, Rump, Eye of the Round)

Allow ½ to 1 pound per person if the bone is left in. A boned roast yields 3 or 4 servings to the pound. But appetites vary! Select a compact, chunky piece which will roast evenly. To cook well, a boned roast should weigh at least 3 pounds, an unboned one 4. A smaller roast is likely to be too dry to be appetizing. If a roast is very lean (such as the eye of the round) put a piece of suet on it so that it will melt and baste the meat while it is roasting.

See Roasting (p. 162). Set the oven at 325°. Put the meat on a rack in a shallow roasting pan without a cover. No rack is needed for an unboned rib roast —the bones will keep the meat out of the pan juices. Roast without basting to the desired stage (p. 164). Times given are approximate. Chunky roasts take longer than flat ones. Even a very large roast takes no more than 3 hours.

Rib Roast (with bone)

	STAGE	HOURS
4 to 6 pounds	Rare (140°)	1¾
	Medium (160°)	2
	Well done (180°)	2½
8 pounds or more	Rare (140°)	2¼
	Medium (160°)	2½
	Well done (180°)	3

Boned Rib Roast, Sirloin, Rump *or* Eye of the Round. Add 10 minutes per pound to the times given above.

Roast Beef Gravy. See Brown Gravy (p. 164).

CARVING ROAST BEEF

Place the roast on a heated platter, fat side up. If a rib roast does not stand firmly, place it on its side and cut slices off the top. With a pointed, thin-bladed, sharp knife, cut a sir-

loin or rib roast in thin slices, then cut the slices from the ribs. If there is a section of tenderloin, remove it from under the bone and cut it in thin slices across the grain.

Carve a rump roast in thin slices with the grain of meat; by so doing, some of the less tender muscle will be served with that which is more tender. If you cut across the grain of the meat, the more tender portion is sliced by itself, as is the less tender portion.

BROWN GRAVY

Perfect gravy is rare, which is sad because it is not difficult to make. Avoid using too much fat, or the gravy will be greasy. Before adding any liquid, cook the flour thoroughly with the fat so that the gravy will be a rich brown. A blending fork will keep the gravy smooth and scrape all the savory glaze from the pan.

After taking out the roast, pour all the juices from the pan into a cup or a narrow jar so that the fat will rise quickly. Spoon

off the fat. Set the roasting pan on the stove over low heat. Put in it 4 tablespoons of the fat. Cook and stir to loosen the brown bits in the pan. Add (to help browning)

¼ teaspoon sugar

Cook and stir until brown. Add

4 tablespoons flour

Stir until rich, dark brown. Add slowly, stirring constantly

1½ cups cool liquid (pan juices plus water or consommé)

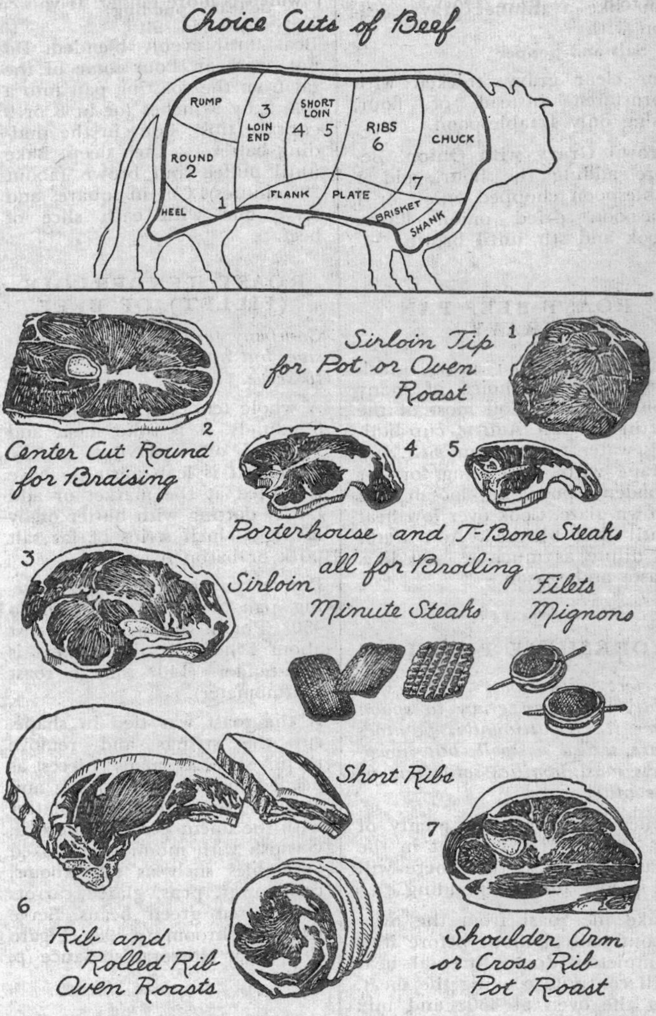
Choice Cuts of Beef
RUMP
3 LOIN END
SHORT LOIN 4 5
RIBS 6
CHUCK
ROUND 2
7
FLANK
PLATE
1
HEEL
BRISKET
SHANK
Sirloin Tip for Pot or Oven Roast 1
2 Center Cut Round for Braising
4 5
Porterhouse and T-Bone Steaks all for Broiling
3 Sirloin
Minute Steaks
Filets Mignons
Short Ribs
7
6 Rib and Rolled Rib Oven Roasts
Shoulder Arm or Cross Rib Pot Roast

Bring to the boiling point. Lower the heat and simmer 5 minutes. Add more liquid if you like a thinner gravy. Season with

Salt and pepper

For clear gravy, thicken with cornstarch instead of flour, using only 1 tablespoon.

Brown Gravy with Onion. Before adding the flour, add 1 tablespoon chopped onion or 1 teaspoon dried onion flakes. Cook and stir until brown.

ROAST BEEF PAN GRAVY

Unthickened pan gravy (dish gravy) is the choice of many epicures. Spoon off most of the fat in the pan. Add 1/4 cup boiling water to the pan. Stir and scrape with a blending fork or wooden spoon to loosen the brown glaze. Cook over low heat until well blended. Add water to dilute as much as you like. Taste and season.

YORKSHIRE PUDDING

Perfect with roast beef, especially with pan gravy to spoon over it. Traditionally, potatoes were served as well, but nowadays most families serve one or the other.

Unless the roast has plenty of fat on it, put extra suet in the roasting pan so that there will be plenty for the pudding.

Take the roast from the oven about half an hour before it is completely done. Internal heat will continue cooking the meat. Set the oven at 450° and mix the pudding batter.

Beat together until well blended

2 eggs
1 cup milk

Stir in

1 cup all-purpose or bread flour (or 1/2 cup for a very delicate pudding)
1/4 teaspoon salt

Beat until evenly blended. Do not overbeat. Pour some of the fat from the roasting pan into a pan 9 by 9 inches (or in 8 or 9 cupcake tins). Pour in the pudding batter, 1/2 inch deep. Bake until puffed and brown (about 30 minutes). Cut in squares and serve one with each slice of beef.

ROAST TENDERLOIN (FILLET) OF BEEF

Company fare, delicious, expensive, but quick to cook and easy to serve.

A whole tenderloin weighs 4 to 6 pounds. It is solid meat and yields 3 or 4 servings to the pound. It is lean meat, so have it larded at the market or add fat by dotting with butter or by laying 1/4-inch strips of fat salt pork or bacon over it.

Put on a rack in an open roasting pan. Preheat the oven to 450°. Put in the meat and roast about 1 hour until the meat is fork-tender (140° on a roast thermometer).

If the roast was tied in shape, cut the strings and remove them. Slice as many pieces as needed for the first serving and arrange them on the platter with the uncut piece at the end. Garnish with mounds of cooked vegetables such as mushrooms, cauliflower, peas, glazed carrots or slivered green beans. Serve with Mushroom (p. 98), Figaro (p. 101) or Horseradish Sauce (p. 102).

CHATEAUBRIAND OF BEEF

Another way to prepare this dinner-party cut of beef.

Order a whole tenderloin of beef and have it tied firmly. Sauté 10 minutes in olive oil or butter, turning it to brown well on all sides. Cover closely, reduce the heat and cook 15 minutes longer. If you prefer the meat less rare, cook it another 15 minutes.

Cut in thin slices and arrange overlapping on a hot platter. Pour Espagnole (p. 97) or Mushroom Sauce (p. 98) over the meat. *Serves 8 to 12.*

BARBECUED EYE OF ROUND

Select a roast weighing about 3½ pounds. Cut shallow gashes in the meat and tuck in slivers of onion. Sprinkle with thyme. Place on a spit and roast 1½ hours, basting frequently with Barbecue Sauce (p. 93). (Or roast in a 350° oven, basting frequently and turning the meat over so that it will be thoroughly seasoned.) Slice very thin. *Makes about 10 servings.*

POT ROAST OF BEEF

The usual cuts for a pot roast are chuck, shoulder, rump or round. The piece should weigh 4 or 5 pounds (a smaller piece is apt to dry out too much). Have it trimmed, rolled and tied firmly to make a compact piece that will cook evenly. The pan for pot-roasting should be a deep, heavy one with a tight cover.

Mix

2 tablespoons flour
2 teaspoons salt
¼ teaspoon pepper
½ teaspoon sugar (to help browning)

Pat into the surface of

4- or 5-pound piece of beef (see above)

Heat a deep, heavy pan over high heat, greasing it lightly if the beef is very lean. Put in the meat and brown it thoroughly on all sides. Cook with the meat

1 or 2 slices of onion (or add a package of onion soup mix with the liquid)

When the meat is a dark, rich brown (this may take 30 minutes or longer), put a low rack under it so that it will not stick. Add

½ cup water *or* tomato juice

Put on the cover, lower the heat and cook very slowly until the meat is fork-tender (3 to 4 hours). Add a little liquid from time to time as it cooks away, but never have the liquid more than 1 inch deep.

Put the meat on a heated platter to keep warm while you make the gravy (p. 164). There will be much more liquid than for oven-roasted beef, so pour it into a jar and cool it 10 minutes. You can then take off the fat easily, leaving plenty of clear juice. Add consommé or water to make plenty of gravy for second servings or for the next day. *Serves 10 to 12.*

To carve and serve. Cut pot roast in thin slices with a very sharp knife. Serve it with mashed or boiled potatoes and plenty of gravy. Horseradish Sauce (p. 102) is excellent with it.

For another meal, reheat the gravy, add thin slices of the meat, and serve on a platter edged with sautéed mushrooms or other vegetables; or heat the vegetables in the gravy with the meat.

Pressure-cooked Pot Roast. After browning, put the meat on a rack in a pressure pan. Add only enough water or tomato juice to cover the rack. Cover and bring the pressure to 15 pounds. Cook 45 minutes. Let the pressure drop, remove the meat and make the gravy.

Herbed Pot Roast. Add with the liquid ½ cup chopped celery, a few sprigs parsley and thyme or ½ teaspoon dried thyme. Experiment with other herbs, too (pp. 18–21).

Pot Roast with Vegetables. After cooking the pot roast 2 hours, add small whole peeled potatoes, tiny onions and small carrots. Or add canned potatoes and onions when the pot roast is almost done.

BEEF À LA MODE

This famous dish is a glorified pot roast.

Put in a deep glass or pottery bowl
- **4-pound piece of rump *or* round (larded at market)**

Add
- **1 tablespoon salt**
- **½ teaspoon pepper**
- **1 tablespoon mixed pickling spices**
- **3 onions, sliced**
- **3 carrots, sliced**
- **3 sprigs parsley**
- **2 bay leaves**
- **1½ cups red wine**

Cover and let stand 12 to 24 hours. Remove the meat and pat dry with a paper towel. Strain the liquid. Proceed as for Pot Roast (p. 167), using the liquid. When the meat is tender, remove it from the pan. Pour the liquid into a bowl and skim off as much of the fat as possible. Put the meat and the liquid back into the pan and cook very slowly 20 minutes longer, spooning the gravy over the meat. Taste and add
- **Salt (if necessary)**

Do not thicken the gravy—it should be thin and dark. Serve with
- **Tiny whole carrots and onions**

cooked separately but added to the dish long enough to heat thoroughly. *Serves 10 to 12.*

SAUERBRATEN

A glorified pot roast, European style. Tender and tasty, it may be company fare. Even better reheated.

Put in a deep glass or pottery bowl
- **4- to 6-pound piece of stewing beef (eye of the round is the best cut)**

Sprinkle with
- **1½ tablespoons salt**
- **10 peppercorns**

Pour over the meat
- **1 cup mild vinegar *or* red wine**
- **Boiling water (to cover)**

Add
- **1 sliced onion**
- **2 bay leaves**
- **2 tablespoons mixed spices**
- **2 tablespoons sugar**

Cover. Let stand at least 2 days, turning twice a day with 2 wooden spoons. Take the meat out of the liquid. Brown and cook like Pot Roast (p. 167), using 2 cups of the strained liquid. Add more liquid as the meat cooks. Mix
- **1 tablespoon flour *or* 5 ginger snaps, rolled fine**
- **½ cup sour cream**

Stir into the liquid to thicken. Serve with Potato Dumplings (below). *Serves 10 to 12.*

To season more highly, put a cheesecloth bag of mixed spices in the kettle while the meat is cooking.

POTATO DUMPLINGS

Especially to serve with Sauerbraten but good with other stews as well.

Boil, peel and mash
- **2 pounds potatoes**

Add
- **½ cup flour**

1 egg
Salt, pepper and nutmeg to taste

Have ready a deep pan of boiling salted water. Drop a tablespoon of the batter into the water. If it breaks apart as it cooks, add a little more flour and test again. Flatten a tablespoon of the mixture on your hand. Put 4 or 5 croutons, homemade (p. 58) or packaged, on the dumpling. Roll into a ball. Repeat until the mixture is used. Drop into the boiling water, lower the heat and cook, uncovered, about 6 minutes. Remove with a slotted spoon. Serve plain or roll in buttered crumbs.

SWISS STEAK

Rump, round or chuck. Have it cut about 1½ inches thick. A pound provides 3 servings, but prepare more at a time if you like—this dish reheats successfully.

Leave the meat in one piece or cut it in pieces for serving. Season with salt and pepper and sprinkle with flour, using about 3 tablespoons for each pound of meat. To make the meat very tender, pound the flour into it with a meat tenderizer or the edge of a heavy plate. Heat a heavy frying pan. Grease it thoroughly with suet or other fat. Put in the meat and brown it well on both sides. Add stewed tomatoes to cover (about 1 cup for each pound of meat). Cover and cook very slowly until the meat is fork-tender (2 hours or more). Add a little water from time to time if necessary to keep the meat from sticking. Cook either on top of the stove or in the oven.

Vary by adding minced green peppers, sliced onions or mushrooms, or herbs.

To cook in a pressure saucepan. Have the meat cut about 1 inch thick. Brown in the pressure pan, add tomatoes, bring the pressure to 15 pounds and process 15 minutes. Let the pressure drop. If the gravy is too thin, thicken it with flour or cornstarch (p. 164).

BROILED STEAK

Use sirloin, porterhouse, T-bone, club, tenderloin or rib. Allow ⅓ to ¾ pound per person. Have steaks cut 1 to 2 inches thick.

For details about broiling and pan-broiling, see page 162.

Take the steaks out of the refrigerator at least ½ hour before broiling them. Cook half the time on each side. A steak 1½ inches thick cooks rare in 25 minutes, medium in 30 to 35 minutes and well-done in 40. If the meat browns very rapidly, move the rack farther from the heat. When the steak is done, put it on a heated platter and sprinkle with salt and pepper. Serve immediately.

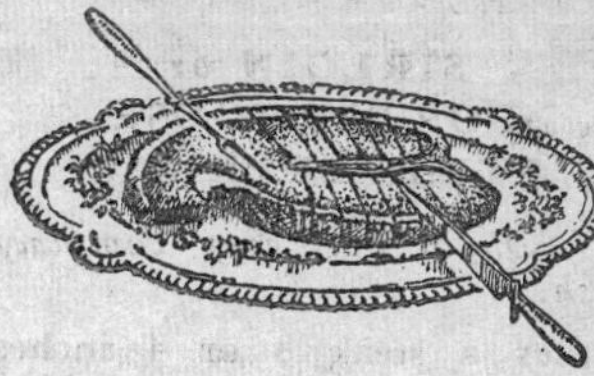

To carve steak. Make cuts close to the bone to free all the meat. Cut a thick steak in narrow strips, slanting from top to bottom. Serve two or three strips at a time.

SAUCES TO SERVE WITH STEAK

A perfect steak needs no sauce, but you may like to dot it with butter for extra goodness or add one of these sauces.

Platter Sauce. Put 2 tablespoons butter on a hot platter and add 1 teaspoon dry mustard, a few drops Worcestershire or A–1 sauce, salt and paprika. Put the broiled steak on the platter and slice it. Stir the beef juices with the seasonings and pour a spoonful over the steak as you serve it.

Other steak sauces

- Black Butter (p. 103).
- Mushroom Sauce (p. 98).
- Mustard Sauce (p. 102).
- Tomato and Mushroom Sauce (p. 99).
- Bordelaise (p. 98).
- Victor Hugo Sauce (p. 101).
- Hollandaise (p. 100) to which add a few drops of onion juice and ½ tablespoon chopped parsley.
- Henriette Sauce (p. 101), half spread under the steak and half on top.
- Marchand de Vin Sauce (p. 104).
- Velouté (p. 96), flavored with catsup.
- Sauce Trianon (p. 100).

SIRLOIN *or* PORTERHOUSE STEAK SUPRÊME

A superb but easy company dish.

Order a steak 3 or 4 inches thick. One hour before cooking sprinkle it with bourbon or crushed garlic. Broil until brown (about 10 minutes on each side). Put in a shallow roasting pan and roast at 300° about 1 hour.

PLANKED STEAK

An impressive company dish which combines the meat and vegetables in a handsome picture.

Broil or pan-broil a tender steak 1¾ inches thick for 5 minutes on each side or until nicely browned. Butter or oil a plank. Arrange, close to the edge, a border of Duchess Potatoes (p. 267), preparing three times the recipe. If any of the wood is not covered, oil it well so that it will not burn. Put the steak on the platter. Bake at 375° until the steak is cooked and the potatoes are brown (about 15 minutes). Sprinkle the steak with salt and pepper. Garnish the platter as suggested below.

To season a new plank. Planks for oven use are 1 inch thick, of oak, hickory or pine. Soak overnight in cold water. Brush thoroughly with oil. Warm 1 hour in a 250° oven.

To clean a plank after use, scrape it thoroughly but do not wash it. Wipe with a paper towel. Wrap in wax paper and store in a cool, dry spot.

Garnishes for Planked Steak

- Cauliflower, peas and stuffed mushrooms.
- Sautéed mushroom caps, broiled tomatoes topped with cucumber slices.
- Glazed onions, buttered carrots in thin strips, sautéed mushroom caps.
- Glazed onions, sautéed strips of green pepper.
- Slices of cucumber and sections of tomato in French dressing.
- Anchovies, stuffed tomatoes, asparagus tips.

BROILED TENDERLOIN

Also called Filet Mignon or Tournedos. Expensive, delicious, easy—especially succulent served with Béarnaise Sauce (p. 101) in the classic French style.

Order slices cut ¾ to 1½ inches thick. Allow 1 slice per serving. To serve plain or with a simple sauce, wrap each slice into a neat round, wrap a slice of bacon around the edge and fasten firmly with a toothpick. Sauté in butter 10 to 15 minutes or until cooked to your taste. The meat is so tender that it does not need long cooking. Serve with any of the sauces suggested for Broiled Steak (pp. 169–170).

Broiled Tenderloin with Stuffed Mushroom Caps. Make Espagnole Sauce (p. 97), using stock or consommé. Prepare a large Stuffed Mushroom (p. 259) for each serving, using some of the sauce to moisten the stuffing mixture. Broil the meat 10 minutes and put in a baking dish. Put a mushroom on each piece and bake at 425° until the crumbs are brown. Put on a serving dish, surround with sauce and garnish with strips of red and green pepper.

LONDON BROIL (FLANK STEAK)

Flank steak must be top quality to cook tender by this method. Unless you are sure, braise it (p. 3) or treat it with meat tenderizer.

Peel and split

1 clove garlic

Rub it over both sides of

1 pound flank steak

Sprinkle the steak with salad oil. Place in a preheated broiler, 1½ inches from the heat. Broil 5 minutes, turn and broil 5 minutes on the other side. Spread with butter and sprinkle with salt and pepper. Cut in thin slanting slices against the grain. *Serves 3 or 4.*

DELMONICO (CLUB) STEAKS

These are cut from the rib about ½ inch thick. They weigh 7 to 10 ounces and are usually boned. Sauté in butter about 3 minutes on each side.

SKEWER-COOKED BEEF

Follow the recipe for Shaslik (p. 186), substituting cubes of lean tender beef for lamb.

MINUTE (CUBE) STEAKS

Melt just enough fat in a skillet to keep the meat from sticking. Add the steaks and cook 2 or 3 minutes on each side, or slightly longer if you prefer meat well done. Add a bit more fat if necessary to keep the meat from sticking. Spread with butter and sprinkle with salt and pepper and chopped parsley.

BRAISED MINUTE *or* FLANK STEAKS

Sprinkle lightly with flour, brown well in a greased frying pan and add enough boiling water to just cover the meat. Cook very slowly, covered, until fork-tender. Season with salt and pepper and sprinkle with chopped parsley.

BEEF STROGANOFF

For a less expensive version, use round steak and cook it slowly about 20 minutes so that it will be tender before adding the mushrooms and cream. But made with tenderloin, the meat is tender after only brief cook-

ing and is still pink and rare when served.

Cut in strips about 2½ by 1 inch

2 pounds beef tenderloin

Melt in a heavy frying pan

2 tablespoons butter

Add

1 tablespoon minced onion

Cook and stir until the onion is yellow. Add the beef. Cook quickly about 5 minutes, turning the meat to brown on all sides. Set aside. Melt

2 tablespoons butter

Slice into it the caps from

½ pound mushrooms (keep the stems for soup)

Cook and stir 5 minutes. Season with

Salt and a trace of nutmeg

Add to the beef. Add

½ pint sour cream

Season delicately to taste. Serve with a border of

Brown *or* wild rice

Serves 6.

Roast Beef Stroganoff. Cut rare roast beef in neat strips, removing all the fat. Add to the cooked onion, as above, but set aside without further cooking. Add the cooked mushrooms and sour cream and heat.

OLD-FASHIONED BEEF STEW

Long slow cooking develops the fine flavor of a perfect beef stew. That makes it a practical dish to prepare well in advance —even the day before serving— since reheating improves it. Allow ¼ to ½ pound lean meat per person.

Use chuck, round, rump or shin. Have all the gristle and most of the fat cut off. Keep the fat and use some of it to brown the meat. Cook a piece of the cracked bone with the meat for good flavor, removing it before serving the stew.

Cut the meat in 1½-inch cubes. Sprinkle with salt and pepper and roll in flour. Melt some of the fat from the meat in a deep heavy pan. Brown the meat cubes thoroughly in the fat to a rich dark color. For added flavor, cook a slice or two of onion with the meat.

Cover with boiling water, stock or part tomato juice or red wine. The amount to use depends on the amount of gravy you want. For 2 pounds of meat, the usual amount is 1 quart. Bring to the boiling point. Cover, reduce the heat, and cook very slowly until the meat is fork-tender. This will take 2 to 3 hours.

Skim, if fat collects on the surface of the stew. Remove any pieces of fat. If the gravy is not as thick as you like it, mix 2 tablespoons flour (for about 2 cups of gravy) with ¼ cup water until it is smooth (or shake it in a swirl mixer), stir it into the stew, bring to a boil, and cook 3 minutes.

Season to taste with salt and pepper and any added seasonings you like such as thyme, Worcestershire or chopped parsley. Serve with rice, noodles or dumplings.

Beef and Vegetable Stew. After cooking the stew 1½ hours add, for each serving, 2 small whole carrots or 1 large carrot, sliced or cubed, and 3 tiny onions. One half hour later add 2 small whole potatoes or ½ cup sliced potatoes. Add, if you like, peas, whole green beans, cauliflowerets, or mushrooms.

Pressure-cooked Beef Stew. Brown the meat in a pressure saucepan. For 2 pounds of meat, add 2 cups of liquid. Adjust the cover. Bring to 15 pounds pressure. Cook 15 minutes and reduce the pressure immediately. Finish the stew as on page 172. If you are cooking vegetables in the stew, reduce the pressure after 11 minutes, add the vegetables, raise again to 15 pounds and cook 4 minutes.

Oven-cooked Beef Stew. After browning the meat, put it in a casserole or bean pot. For 2 pounds meat, add only 2 cups liquid, which may be all water, or half red wine or tomatoes. Cover and bake 3½ hours at 250°. Add more liquid from time to time, if necessary. Finish the stew as on page 172.

DUMPLINGS

For beef stew and other dishes.

Sift together
1 cup flour
2 teaspoons baking powder
½ teaspoon sugar
½ teaspoon salt
Stir in slowly
Milk (about ½ cup)
until the batter is thin enough to take up by rounded spoonfuls with a wet tablespoon.

Bring the finished stew to the boiling point. The gravy should be shallow enough so that the dumplings rest on meat or vegetables as they cook. Put spoonfuls of batter on the stew. Cook, uncovered, 10 minutes. Cover and cook 10 minutes longer. A glass cover will let you watch the cooking without uncovering the stew. *Makes 6 to 8.*

Steamed Dumplings. These cook more evenly than dumplings cooked in the stew. Mix the batter, using only enough milk to make the dough as stiff as for baking powder biscuits. Pat, roll out ½ inch thick and cut with a biscuit cutter. Arrange, close together, in the buttered top part of a small steamer. Cover and cook 12 minutes. Place on the finished stew.

Rich Dumplings. Before adding the milk, cut in 2 tablespoons butter or other shortening as in making baking powder biscuits. Add a well-beaten egg and 1 tablespoon finely chopped parsley, if you like.

Savory Dumplings. Add to the batter ½ teaspoon poultry seasoning, ½ teaspoon celery seed, 1 teaspoon dried onion flakes and 2 tablespoons salad oil.

Crunchy Dumplings. Mix ½ cup bread crumbs with 2 tablespoons melted butter. Roll tablespoons of the dough in this mixture and cook as directed above.

BRAISED BEEF

Richer than beef stew because the gravy cooks down more in a shallow pan than in a deep one.

Remove the fat from
2 pounds bottom round steak *or* chuck
Cut the meat in 2-inch cubes. Dip in
Flour
Brown on all sides in a heavy frying pan greased with the fat just enough to keep the meat from sticking. Add
2 cups boiling water
Cover tightly. Simmer over very low heat until the meat is fork-tender and the gravy very thick and dark (about 3 hours). Add more water from time to time as needed. Season with
Salt and pepper to taste
Put in a frying pan
1 tablespoon butter
½ pound mushrooms, sliced
Cook and stir 5 minutes. Add to the beef. *Serves 4.*

To vary. Omit the sliced mushrooms and garnish the platter with a row of broiled mushroom caps.

BEEF BOURGUIGNONNE

Put in a deep heavy pan
⅛ pound salt pork *or* suet, diced
12 small white onions
Cook and stir until the onions are brown. Remove the onions and set them aside. Add
2 pounds round steak, in 2-inch cubes
Brown well. Sprinkle with
2 tablespoons flour
Salt, pepper, marjoram and thyme
Stir and add
1 cup red wine
1 cup bouillon *or* water
Cover and cook over lowest possible heat 4 or 5 hours or in a casserole or bean pot in a 250° oven. Add the onions and
12 small potatoes
½ pound sliced mushrooms
Cook until the vegetables are tender (about 45 minutes). Season to taste. *Serves 6.*

HUNGARIAN GOULASH

Use the best paprika for this famous dish. Never use pepper because it would change the flavor of the paprika. Meat for goulash may be all beef (shin has an excellent flavor) or half beef, one-quarter veal and one-quarter pork.

Remove any fat from
2 pounds lean meat
Cut the meat in 1½-inch cubes. Melt in a heavy skillet
3 tablespoons bacon fat *or* beef suet
Add and cook until slightly browned
2 large onions, chopped fine
Add the meat and brown thoroughly on all sides. Add
3 tablespoons flour
2 teaspoons paprika
2 cloves garlic (on toothpicks)
Stir thoroughly. Add
1 quart boiling water, stock *or* stock and Burgundy *or* tomato juice
Cover and cook slowly until fork-tender (about 2 hours). Remove the garlic. Add enough more liquid to make about 2 cups, stir and heat. The sauce should be dark and thick. *Serves 4 to 6.*

Pressure-cooked Goulash. Brown the meat in a pressure cooker. Add only 1 cup of liquid. Bring to 15 pounds pressure and cook 15 minutes.

Goulash with Sour Cream. Add ½ cup sour cream and reheat.

Goulash with Vegetables. Twenty minutes before serving, add potato balls, tiny whole carrots, whole green beans, small cooked beans, small cooked onions or cooked lima beans. Season with marjoram. Five minutes before serving, add tomato wedges or 1 cup stewed tomatoes. If desired, cook 1 tablespoon chopped green pepper and 1 tablespoon chopped parsley with the onion.

GOULASH SOUP

More like a thin stew than a soup. But serve it in the traditional way in deep bowls as a savory supper dish. Add marjoram and caraway seeds for further flavoring.

For each 2 cups of Goulash (above), fresh-made or leftover, add 3 cups boiling water and 1 cup diced peeled potatoes. Cover and cook until the potatoes are soft (about 10 minutes).

To add more color, melt a tablespoon of fat, add ½ teaspoon paprika, 2 tablespoons water and 1 tablespoon tomato paste, bring to a boil, and stir into the soup.

STEAK AND KIDNEY PIE

Remove the fat from

2 pounds round steak

Cut the lean meat in ¾-inch cubes. Skin and split

4 lamb kidneys *or* piece of beef kidney

Cut out and discard the fat and hard parts. Cut in ¼-inch cubes. Put the fat from the steak in a frying pan. Heat until the fat melts. Add

2 onions, sliced

Cook and stir until the onions are brown. Add the cubed meat and

1 tablespoon butter

Brown well on all sides. Pick out and discard any bits of hard fat. Add

2 cups boiling water
1½ tablespoons Worcestershire
2 tablespoons chopped parsley
Salt and pepper to taste

Cover and cook very slowly until the meat is very tender (about 1½ hours). Add a little water from time to time as the juices cook away. Mix together and stir in

2 tablespoons butter
2 tablespoons flour

Cook and stir until thick. Put in a casserole and cover with

Pastry, baking powder biscuits *or* mashed potatoes

Bake at 400° until brown. *Serves 8.*

BRAISED SHORT RIBS

Allow at least 1 pound per person and select as meaty pieces as possible.

Brown thoroughly in a heavy skillet, pouring off the fat as it melts. Cover and cook slowly until fork-tender. Add vegetables, if you like, such as chopped or sliced onion and cook until tender. Season to taste.

BRAISED OXTAIL

Add ½ pound sliced mushrooms with the vegetables, if you like. This dish is even better when reheated, so do not hesitate to make more than you need for one meal.

Wash and drain

2 pounds oxtail, in 2-inch pieces

Roll in

Flour

Melt in a heavy skillet

2 tablespoons butter *or* other fat

Add the oxtail and

2 onions, sliced

Cook until well browned. Add

2 cups stock *or* consommé
2 cups water
2 cups canned tomatoes
1 teaspoon salt
½ teaspoon pepper
1 bay leaf
1 clove garlic (on a toothpick)

Cover and cook over very low heat (or in a casserole in a 300° oven) until the meat is fork-tender (about 3 hours). Remove the bay leaf and garlic. Add

4 carrots, cubed
1 small turnip, cubed

Cook until the vegetables are tender. Season to taste. *Serves 6.*

CORNED BEEF

Choose cuts that are not too fat. The best cuts are from the ribs and brisket.

Wash under running cold water to remove the brine on the surface. Cover with cold water and bring slowly to the boiling point. Boil 5 minutes, remove the scum, reduce the heat, cover and simmer until tender (3 or 4 hours). Cool slightly in the water in which it was cooked. Drain. Serve hot or cold with Horseradish Sauce (p. 102) or Mustard Sauce (p. 102). *A 4-pound piece serves 8.*

Pressed Corned Beef. Cool completely in the broth. Drain.

Cover with wax paper and put a weight on top to press the meat firmly. Chill and slice.

Corned Beef and Cabbage. When meat is nearly tender, remove 2 cups of the cooking water to another pan. In it cook a small cabbage, quartered and cored. Drain and serve on the platter with the beef.

NEW ENGLAND BOILED DINNER

Cook Corned Beef (p. 175). Remove the meat from the kettle. To the cooking broth add pared potatoes, carrots and turnips. If they are small, leave them whole. Otherwise, cut them in slices. Cook 15 minutes. Add cabbage, quartered and cored. (Some prefer to cook the cabbage separately instead of in the kettle with the other vegetables.) Cook until all the vegetables are tender (10 to 20 minutes longer). Put the meat back in the kettle long enough to reheat it.

Put the meat on a platter. Arrange the vegetables neatly around it. For added color and flavor, serve hot buttered beets or pickled beets. Serve with Horseradish Sauce (p. 102) and Mustard Pickle (p. 547).

CORNED BEEF HASH

Vary homemade or canned hash by adding chopped parsley, green or red pepper or pimientos.

Mix

1½ cups chopped cooked or canned corn beef
2 cups chopped boiled potatoes
1 tablespoon chopped onion
⅓ cup cream, milk *or* stock
Salt and pepper to taste

Melt in a heavy skillet

2 tablespoons butter

Put in the hash and spread evenly. Cook very slowly until browned on the bottom (about 40 minutes). If you like crisp brown bits throughout the hash, stir and scrape along the bottom from time to time. Fold like an omelet and turn out onto a hot platter. *Serves 4.*

Red Flannel Hash. Add 1 cup finely chopped cooked or canned beets.

Baked Corned Beef Hash. Spread hash in buttered casserole. Bake 20 minutes at 325°. Serve from the casserole.

Eggs on Corned Beef Hash. Shape the hash in 3-inch patties, 1 inch thick. Arrange in a buttered baking pan, or put in individual casseroles. Press a hollow in each and break an egg into it. Sprinkle with salt and pepper. Cover. Bake at 325° until the egg white is set—about 25 minutes.

GROUND BEEF

A whole cookbook could well be devoted to the multitude of good recipes using ground beef. Since there is no waste, it is comparatively economical, even when you buy the better grade, such as shoulder, bottom round or chuck ground to your order so that it will not be dried out. For the best flavor, see that some fat is ground with the meat, but not so much that the meat looks heavily flecked with white. Salt pork (⅛ pound to 1 pound beef) adds flavor and juiciness. Have the meat ground medium fine, not too fine, unless you are making a special dish such as Spaghetti with Meat Balls (p. 178) or Swedish Meat Balls (p. 177).

HAMBURGERS

Shape ground beef into round patties about ½ inch thick.

Handle lightly so that the meat will not be pressed solidly together. Sprinkle a cold frying pan with salt. Put in the patties and cook over moderate heat until done to your taste (about 5 minutes on each side unless the meat is icy cold).

To the tasty juices remaining in the pan, add ¼ cup hot water or sour cream, stir, bring to the boiling point and pour over the meat. As a variation, rinse out the pan with a tablespoon or two of sherry or bourbon and pour it over the patties.

Broiled Hamburgers. Broil 2 inches from the heat, 5 minutes on each side. Sprinkle with salt and pepper.

Cheeseburgers. Cook patties on one side. Put on toasted split buns, cooked side down. Sprinkle with salt and pepper. Put thin slice of cheese on each. Put under the broiler and cook until the cheese melts. For more piquant flavor, dot hamburgs with prepared mustard, chili sauce or both.

Cincinnati Hamburgers. For 1 pound of ground beef, add 1 egg, slightly beaten, ¼ cup milk or tomato juice, 1 teaspoon prepared mustard, 1 teaspoon salt, ¼ teaspoon pepper and a few grains of nutmeg. Mix well and shape in 8 patties.

Hamburgers with Corn Flakes. To 1 pound of ground beef add 1 cup corn flakes (crushed fine), 1 teaspoon salt, ½ teaspoon pepper, ¼ teaspoon poultry seasoning and ½ cup milk. Shape in 10 patties and cook as above. To vary, use ⅔ cup oatmeal in place of the corn flakes. This is also an excellent recipe to enrich with toasted wheat germ—use it in place of half the crumbs.

SALISBURY STEAK

Pat ground beef gently into one oval cake about 1 inch thick. Pan-broil or broil, turning carefully with two spatulas when half done. Sprinkle with salt and pepper. Garnish with parsley or watercress. Serve with Mushroom Sauce (p. 98) or Brown Gravy (p. 164) made with consommé.

HAMBURGER TOAST

Toast slices of bread on one side. Spread untoasted side well to the edges with a layer of ground beef about ¼ inch thick. Sprinkle with salt and pepper. Put under the broiler about 2 inches from the heat. Broil about 5 minutes (or to your taste), dot with butter and serve immediately.

BEEF À LA LINDSTROM

A popular luncheon or supper dish from Sweden.

Boil and mash
- **2 potatoes**

Add
- **1¼ pounds ground beef**
- **2 egg yolks, slightly beaten**
- **½ cup cream**
- **2 pickled beets, diced**
- **1 tablespoon minced onion**
- **2 tablespoons capers**
- **Salt, pepper and paprika**

Mix well. Shape in 8 or more patties. Melt in a large frying pan
- **2 tablespoons butter**

Add the patties and cook about 15 minutes, turning once. *Serves 4 or 5.*

SWEDISH MEAT BALLS

A combination of tomato and consommé is excellent, too. Use

1 can of consommé and ½ can concentrated tomato soup or 1 can tomatoes. You may like to make a larger quantity, since it reheats well. Broad noodles are good with meat balls.

Put through the meat grinder twice

1 pound lean beef, preferably shoulder
¼ pound salt pork
6 slices whole wheat bread

Add

1 egg, slightly beaten
½ teaspoon sugar
½ teaspoon allspice
½ teaspoon nutmeg
1 teaspoon salt

Mix well. Shape lightly with your fingers into 1-inch balls. Brown on all sides in a lightly greased skillet. Put in a deep pan.

2 cups consommé or stock

Heat and add the meat balls. Cover and cook over very low heat 1½ hours. Add extra consommé or water from time to time if necessary to keep the meat balls from sticking. *Serves 4 to 6.*

If you like more gravy with this dish, add extra consommé and thicken the gravy with flour stirred with a little water until smooth. Or add a can of beef gravy.

SPAGHETTI AND MEAT BALLS

Mix

1 pound finely chopped beef
1 cup buttered bread crumbs
2 tablespoons finely cut parsley
1 tablespoon scraped onion *or* 1 teaspoon dried onion flakes

Season to taste with

Salt and pepper

Shape in 1-inch balls and brown well in

Butter

Prepare, omitting the meat

2 cups Italian Tomato Sauce (p. 313) (or use canned sauce)

Add the meat balls. Heat. Serve with

Spaghetti (p. 313)

using an 8-ounce package *to serve 4 to 6.*

HAMBURG STROGANOFF

Not the classic recipe but excellent. You can "stretch" it by serving it in a rice ring.

Melt in a heavy skillet

¼ cup butter

Add and cook slowly until soft

½ cup minced onion

Add

1 pound ground beef
1 clove garlic, peeled

Stir until slightly browned. Stir in

2 tablespoons flour
2 teaspoons salt
¼ teaspoon pepper
½ pound mushrooms, sliced

Cook 5 minutes. Add

1 can condensed cream of chicken *or* mushroom soup

Simmer 10 minutes. Stir in

1 cup sour cream

Heat and sprinkle with minced parsley, chives or dill. *Serves 4.*

TEXAS HASH

Do this in an electric skillet at the table or prepare it ahead of time and serve it in a casserole.

Chop

1 onion
3 stalks celery

Melt in a skillet

1 tablespoon butter

Add the onion and celery and cook until soft. Add

1½ pounds chopped beef

Cook and stir until brown. Add

1 cup cooked rice
1 cup canned tomatoes

Cook and stir over low heat 15 minutes. Season to taste with

Worcestershire, Tabasco *or* chili sauce

Serves 4.

BEEF AND CORN CASSEROLE

Melt in a frying pan
2 tablespoons butter *or* bacon fat
Add
1 green pepper, chopped
2 onions, chopped
Cook until the onions are brown. Add
1 pound ground beef
Cook and stir until brown. Place in a buttered baking dish in alternate layers with
Cream-style canned corn (1 large can)
Sprinkle the layers with
Salt and pepper
Put over the top a layer of
Sliced tomatoes
Sprinkle with
Buttered crumbs *or* toasted wheat germ
Bake at 350° until the crumbs are brown. *Serves 6.*

BEEF DOVES

This useful recipe is an excellent way to use up leftovers. Any cooked meat may provide the filling. Or use corned beef hash or sausage meat. Vary the seasoning by adding minced onion, chopped celery or pickle, or poultry seasoning.

Mix
½ pound ground beef
⅓ cup quick-cooking rice *or* ½ cup cooked rice
½ teaspoon salt
¼ teaspoon pepper
Few grains cayenne
Moisten with
1 tablespoon condensed tomato soup
Cook 2 minutes in boiling water
8 cabbage leaves
Drain and put 2 tablespoons of the meat mixture on each leaf. Fold to enclose the meat, fasten with toothpicks or tie with thread to make a tight bundle. Put in a deep pan, add the rest of the can of soup and a canful of water. Cover and simmer 1½ hours, or 20 minutes if you are using cooked meat and cooked rice. *Serves 4.*

CHILI CON CARNE

Heat in a skillet
3 tablespoons bacon fat *or* salad oil
Add
1 onion, sliced
Cook 2 minutes. Add
1 pound ground beef
1 clove garlic on a toothpick
Cook and stir 5 minutes. Add
1 can red kidney *or* chili beans
2 cups (or more) stewed or canned tomatoes *or* tomato juice
1 tablespoon chili powder
Simmer until thick (about 1 hour). Season to taste with
Salt and paprika
Remove the garlic. *Serves 6.*

Chili con Carne with Dried Beans. Cook ½ pound dried beans (p. 244) and use in place of canned beans.

Corn Pone Pie. Put in a 1½-quart casserole. Over the top spoon Corn Bread batter (p. 329) or batter from ½ package corn bread mix. Bake 20 minutes at 400°.

CHOP SUEY

Melt
2 tablespoons butter
Add
1 cup finely cut celery
½ cup minced onion
Cook slowly until tender. Add
1 pound ground beef
Cook and stir 5 minutes. Add
1 teaspoon thick soy sauce
1 can bean sprouts
Mix well and heat. Serve with thin soy sauce as a condiment. *Serves 4.*

AMERICAN CHOP SUEY

Cook and drain
½ package egg noodles

Add

2 cups canned tomatoes
¼ pound grated cheese

Cook and stir until the cheese melts. Heat

4 tablespoons salad oil

Add

1 large onion, sliced

Cook until soft. Add

1 pound ground beef

Cook and stir until browned. Add

1 stalk celery, cut in fine strips 2 inches long

Add to the noodles, heat, and season to taste with

Soy sauce, salt and pepper

Serves 6.

REVOLTILLOS

A highly seasoned Mexican dish to serve immediately or to make ahead of time and reheat.

Steam (p. 309)

1 cup rice

in

2 cups bouillon

Heat in a heavy frying pan

¼ cup salad oil

Add

3 green peppers, chopped
3 onions, chopped
2 cloves garlic, mashed

Cook until tender. Add

2 pounds chopped beef

Cook and stir until brown. Add

¾ cup raisins
¾ cup ripe olives, pitted or not
½ box bay leaves

Cover and cook slowly ½ hour. Pick out most of the bay leaves. Stir in the rice. Season to taste. *Serves 6.*

MEAT LOAF

This basic recipe is a fixture in most families. The variations are many and it can be served hot or cold. It is an appetizing way to use leftovers. See also other recipes for meat loaf on pages 194, 202–203, 209–210.

Mix

1 egg, slightly beaten
2 teaspoons salt
¾ cup water *or* milk
1 cup soft bread crumbs
2 tablespoons minced onion *or* dried onion soup mix *or* flakes
2 pounds ground beef

Taste and season more highly if you like. Pat into a greased loaf pan. Over the top lay

4 strips bacon

Bake 1 hour at 350°. Serve hot with Tomato Sauce (p. 99) or Mushroom Sauce (p. 98). Or serve cold with pepper relish or chili sauce. *Serves 8.*

WAYS TO VARY MEAT LOAF

In place of milk or water, use canned tomatoes, gravy, undiluted mushroom, celery, tomato or vegetable soup, or ½ cup catsup and ½ cup water.

For added flavor, add up to ½ cup grated cheese, chopped ripe or green olives, chopped pimientos, or chopped celery, both stalk and leaves.

Season to taste with Worcestershire or Tabasco or a pinch of thyme and/or basil or other herbs.

In place of bread crumbs, use 2 cups rice flakes.

To step up the protein, use toasted wheat germ in place of crumbs. Add ½ cup powdered milk and increase the liquid to 1 cup. Add 1 tablespoon brewer's yeast and 2 tablespoons catsup or chili sauce to disguise the pronounced yeast flavor.

To use leftovers, add as part of the meat chopped cooked ham, beef, lamb, chicken or turkey. Add up to 1 cup cooked peas, diced carrots or other cooked vegetables.

MISS DANIELL'S MEAT LOAF

Follow the recipe for Meat Loaf (p. 180), but in place of 2 pounds ground beef use 1 pound of beef mixed with ½ pound each of chopped fresh pork and veal.

CANNELON OF BEEF

Use high-grade beef such as top round.

Mix

2 pounds ground beef
Grated rind ½ lemon
1 tablespoon finely cut parsley
1 egg, slightly beaten
½ teaspoon lemon juice
2 tablespoons melted butter
Few gratings nutmeg
1 teaspoon salt
¼ teaspoon pepper

Shape in a roll 6 inches long. Put on a rack in a baking pan. Lay over the top

5 slices salt pork *or* bacon

Bake 1 hour at 350° and serve with

Mushroom Sauce (p. 98)

Serves 6.

CHIPPED BEEF

If the beef is very salty, cover with warm water and drain immediately. Separate the slices and remove any stringy bits. For ¼ pound, melt 4 tablespoons butter in a frying pan. Add the beef and cook until the edges curl (2 or 3 minutes). Serve like bacon.

Creamed Chipped Beef. Tear ¼ pound dried beef in pieces and cook as above. Sprinkle with 3 tablespoons of flour. Stir and add 2 cups top milk or milk and cream. Cook and stir over low heat until thickened. Season and pour over toast or serve with baked potatoes or rice.

Nancy's Creamed Chipped Beef. Cook in the butter 1 tablespoon chopped onion and ¼ cup chopped celery until the onion is yellow. Continue as directed above, season with thyme and sprinkle with chopped parsley.

FRANKFURTERS

See page 205.

LAMB AND MUTTON

Lamb is from young animals. The flesh should be pinkish, firm and fine-grained, the fat white, solid and flaky.

Mutton comes from mature animals. Young mutton has a mild, delicious flavor and may be as tender as lamb. Older mutton is darker red and has a stronger, distinctive flavor.

ROAST LAMB

Cuts for roasting are the leg, the loin, the saddle or whole loin, crown roast (p. 184) and shoulder or cushion. Except the crown roast, all these cuts may be boned at the market for easier carving. For stuffed roasts, see page 182.

Do not try to roast a piece weighing less than 3 pounds. It will be too dry. A whole leg provides 10 to 16 servings. For a smaller roast, order a half leg, a strip of the loin or a piece of the shoulder. A heavy roast is a wise buy, since there is more meat in proportion to bone. There are many delicious recipes using leftover lamb (pp. 188–189, 213–215).

Do not sprinkle with salt, pepper or flour, but if you like garlic as a seasoning, make about 10 shallow slits in the roast with a sharp knife and tuck in each a thin sliver of garlic. There are many other ways to season lamb —sprinkle with caraway seed, ginger, thyme or marjoram, or top with a few lemon slices. Experiment to find what you like best.

Put the roast on a rack in a shallow roasting pan without a cover. If the fat covering is very thin, lay several strips of bacon on top. Turn loin and saddle cuts over during the last half-hour of roasting so that they will brown.

Roast at 325° 25 to 35 minutes per pound according to whether you like lamb pinkish or well done. If the roast is boned, allow 5 minutes more per pound. A meat thermometer registers 170° for pinkish lamb, 175° for medium, and 180° for well done. A 6-pound leg of lamb takes about 3 hours. A saddle or loin of lamb should always be pinkish—roast it about 2 hours.

Lamb Gravy. Follow directions for making Brown Gravy (p. 164). Season with thyme, marjoram, lemon juice, red wine or a trace of instant coffee.

CARVING LAMB

Leg. Cut a slice from the flatter side so that the roast will rest firmly on the platter. Slice thin at right angles to the bone.

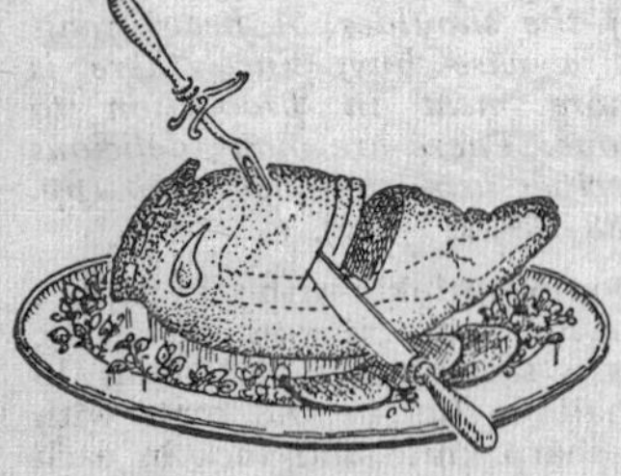

Loin and crown. Cut between the chops or, if boned, cut in slices ½ inch thick.

Saddle. Make a cut along the backbone on each side to loosen the meat and slice at right angles to the bone, slipping the knife underneath to free the meat from the rib bones.

To serve with roast lamb
- Littleton Sauce (p. 101)
- Mint Sauce (p. 105)
- Currant Mint Sauce (p. 105)
- Cold Orange Sauce (p. 104)
- Currant Jelly Sauce (p. 98)
- Brown Sauce (p. 97) flavored with tarragon
- Mint Jelly
- Currant Jelly

GLAZED ROAST LAMB

Baste roast lamb (p. 5) during the last hour of roasting with ½ cup currant or grape jelly in ½ cup boiling water, or with mint-apricot glaze. **To prepare the glaze,** cook 1 cup sugar with 2 cups water and ½ bunch mint 5 minutes, strain, add ⅔ cup cooked sieved apricots, continue cooking until well blended, and add 2 tablespoons butter.

STUFFED ROAST LAMB

Have a leg or shoulder of lamb prepared at the market for stuffing.

Sprinkle inside with salt and pepper. Stuff lightly with Bread (p. 82), Onion (p. 83) or Celery Stuffing (p. 83). Sew edges together or fasten with skewers. Roast (p. 181) at 325° about 35 minutes per pound for well-done lamb (180° on a meat thermometer). Place on a very hot platter. Slice and serve with any of the accompaniments suggested for Roast Lamb (p. 181).

BARBECUED LEG OF LAMB

Have the butcher bone a leg of lamb and tie it firmly in shape.

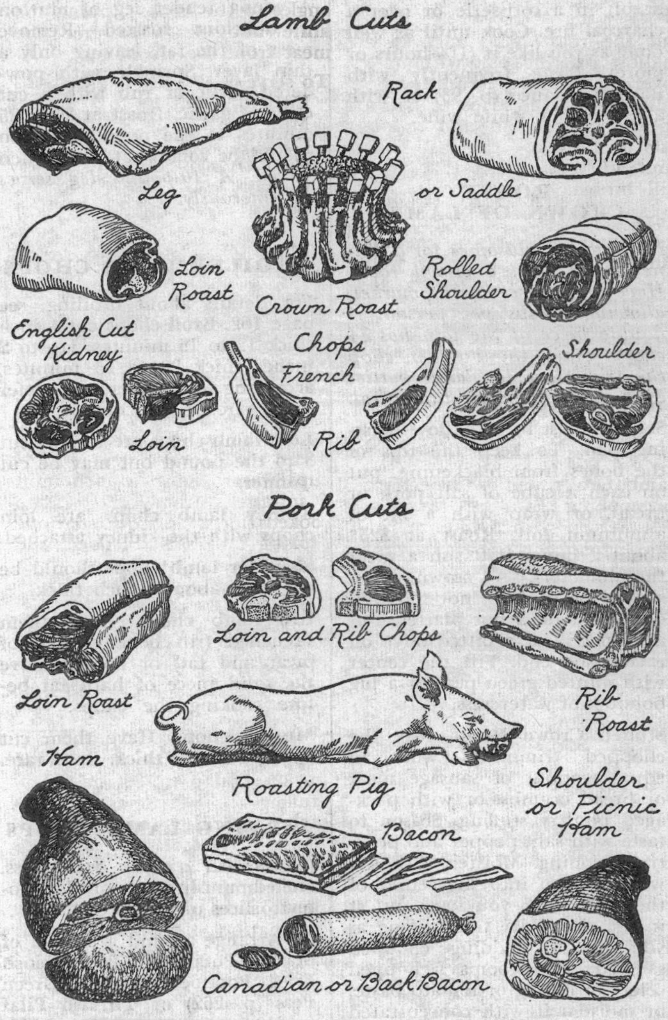
Lamb Cuts
Leg
Rack
or Saddle
Loin Roast
Crown Roast
Rolled Shoulder
English Cut Kidney
Chops
French
Shoulder
Loin
Rib
Pork Cuts
Loin and Rib Chops
Loin Roast
Rib Roast
Ham
Roasting Pig
Shoulder or Picnic Ham
Bacon
Canadian or Back Bacon

Make several shallow cuts in it and tuck into them bits of peeled garlic. Put the lamb on a spit in a rotisserie or over a charcoal fire. Cook until as well done as you like it (1½ hours or more). Baste frequently with Barbecue Sauce (p. 93) or with a dry red or white wine.

ROAST CROWN OF LAMB

Nothing is handsomer for a dinner party than a crown roast. Have it prepared at the market, allowing 2 ribs per person. A double piece of the loin has 14 chops. Have the butcher chop the trimmings for lamb patties or meat loaf for another meal.

Set the roast in a shallow roasting pan. To keep the tips of the bones from blackening, put on each a cube of salt pork or bread, or wrap with a bit of aluminum foil. Roast at 325° about 2 hours (170° on a meat thermometer). A crown roast should be pinkish, not too well done. Put on a hot platter. Put a chop frill or a pitted olive on each bone end. Fill the center with minted green peas or a big bouquet of watercress.

Stuffed Crown Roast. Mix the chopped trimmings with an equal amount of sausage meat or bread crumbs, or with packaged poultry stuffing. Season to taste with salt, pepper and poultry seasoning. Moisten with hot water. Spoon into the center of the roast after you have put it in the pan. Vary this stuffing as you like by adding chopped sautéed mushrooms, chopped celery or onion, or tomato paste, or moisten it with concentrated mushroom, celery or tomato soup in place of water. Roast ½ hour longer than the unstuffed roast.

ROAST LEG OF MUTTON

A young tender leg of mutton is delicious roasted. Remove most of the fat, leaving only a thin layer. Sprinkle with powdered garlic or rub with a cut clove of garlic. Roast at 350°, 25 minutes to the pound. Mutton should be somewhat pink when served. *A 10-pound leg serves 12 generously.*

BROILED LAMB CHOPS

For details about broiling, see page 162. Broil chops cut 1 inch thick 12 to 15 minutes, 1½ to 2 inches thick 20 to 35 minutes, according to whether you prefer them rare or well done.

Loin lamb chops are usually cut 3 to the pound but may be cut thinner.

Kidney lamb chops are loin chops with the kidney attached.

Shoulder lamb chops should be cut thin, about 1 inch thick.

Rib lamb chops. Have them Frenched (rib bone cleared of meat and fat) or not. Remove the solid piece of hard fat before cooking the chops.

Mutton chops. Have them cut 1½ to 2 inches thick. Broil rare.

SERVING LAMB CHOPS

(1) Garnish with watercress, stuffed mushroom, broiled tomato slices or slivers of ham.

(2) Arrange around a mound of Mashed Potatoes (p. 266), French Fried Potatoes (p. 269), Green Peas (p. 262) or Turkish Pilaf (p. 310).

(3) Serve on thin slices of Broiled Ham (p. 201), Fried Eggplant (p. 255) or toast.

(4) Serve with any of the following:
- Tomato Sauce (p. 99)
- Mushroom Sauce (p. 98)
- Soubise Sauce (p. 96)
- Currant Mint Sauce (p. 105)
- Spanish Sauce (p. 97)
- Mint Jelly
- Currant Jelly

TOURNEDOS OF LAMB

Have loin chops boned and wrapped in strips of bacon. Broil or pan-broil. Sprinkle with salt and pepper. Top each with a sautéed mushroom cap or a slice of tomato sprinkled with chopped parsley.

STUFFED LAMB CHOPS

Split thick (2 inch) lamb chops to the bone. Stuff with sausage meat or any stuffing (p. 82). Press together lightly. Dip in crumbs, eggs and crumbs (p. 4). Arrange in a shallow pan and bake 30 to 40 minutes at 450°. Turn after baking 15 minutes.

ROASTED LAMB CHOPS

No last-minute attention for these chops. They are actually individual roasts of lamb.

Order loin lamb chops cut 2½ inches thick, boned and wrapped in bacon. Sprinkle with salt, pepper and flour. Brown well in a heavy frying pan. Transfer to a rack on a baking pan and bake at 350° until tender (about 40 minutes).

BRAISED LAMB CHOPS WITH VEGETABLES

Brown boned chops in a heavy frying pan. Put in a casserole and sprinkle with salt and pepper. Over the chops arrange small potato balls, tiny new carrots and tiny onions or other vegetables such as mushrooms and quartered tomatoes. Sprinkle with salt and pepper. Add canned tomatoes, stock or consommé (1 cup for 6 chops). Cover and bake at 350° until the chops are tender (about 40 minutes). If you use canned potatoes and onions, add them after the chops have cooked 20 minutes so that they will not be too soft.

Pressure-cooked Braised Lamb Chops. Brown the chops in a pressure cooker (uncovered). Slip the rack under them, add the vegetables and enough liquid to cover the rack. Adjust the cover, bring the pressure to 15 pounds and cook 10 minutes. Reduce the pressure immediately.

MIXED GRILL

Heat the broiler. Rub the rack with fat. For each person, put on the rack a lamb chop, cut 1 inch thick, and a split lamb kidney or 2 small pork sausages which have been parboiled 5 minutes and drained. Broil 7 minutes.

Turn the chops over and put on the broiler with them strips of bacon and vegetables such as tomato halves, mushroom caps, cooked or canned artichoke bottoms and slices of cooked potatoes or frozen potato puffs. Brush the vegetables with butter or salad oil and sprinkle with salt and pepper. Broil until the bacon is crisp, turning it to cook both sides (about 7 minutes).

LAMB STEAKS

Order 1-inch slices of lamb cut from the leg. Cut in serving-size pieces or in strips. Pan-broil like chops (p. 184). *One pound serves 3.*

PAN-BROILED FILLETS OF LAMB

Order

2 pounds lamb steaks (p. 185)

Have the butcher pound them so that they will be ¾ inch thick. Mix and pour over the lamb

3 tablespoons olive oil
3 tablespoons vinegar
½ teaspoon salt
½ onion, sliced
1 tablespoon chopped parsley

Let stand several hours, turning the meat so that it will be well seasoned. Heat a heavy frying pan. Put in it

2 tablespoons butter *or* salad oil

Put in the meat and cook about 3 minutes on each side. *Serves 4 or 5.*

SHASLIK (SHISH KEBAB)

Best of all cooked over a charcoal fire. Lean tender beef may be cooked this way, too.

Thread 1-inch cubes of lean lamb (shoulder, breast or leg) on long skewers or smooth green sticks (not dry ones, which might burn). Brush with olive oil. Broil until fork-tender, turning to brown evenly. Sprinkle with salt and pepper.

To marinate before broiling. Put the cubed lamb in a bowl and cover with French dressing, Burgundy or a Marinade (p. 93). Let stand several hours and drain. Baste with the marinade during the cooking.

Shaslik with Vegetables. Prepare pieces of vegetable about the same size as the lamb cubes. Alternate on the skewers. Some good combinations are:

(1) Halved or quartered tomatoes, small cooked onions and squares of green pepper.
(2) Mushroom caps, sliced potatoes and carrots.
(3) Sweet potato chunks and pineapple cubes or wedges.
(4) Bacon squares, mushroom caps and eggplant.

IRISH STEW

Authentic Irish Stew needs no thickening except the potato cooked in it, but if you prefer a thicker gravy, mix ¼ cup flour with ¼ cup cold water, pour into the finished stew and cook and stir until the gravy is smooth and thick.

Cube or cut into serving-size pieces

2 pounds stewing lamb

Cover with boiling water, cover, and simmer 1 hour. Add

½ cup cubed carrot
½ cup cubed turnip
1 onion, sliced
1 potato, cubed

Cover and simmer ½ hour. Add

2 cups sliced potato

Cover, simmer ½ hour and season to taste with

Salt and pepper

Serves 6.

Irish Stew with Dumplings. See Dumplings, page 173.

FRICASSEE OF LAMB

Cut in 1½-inch cubes

2 pounds stewing lamb

Dip in

Flour

Heat a deep pan and grease it lightly with

Salad oil *or* butter

Put in the meat and brown well on all sides. Add

2 cups boiling water, tomato juice *or* tomato juice cocktail

¼ cup chopped onion *or* 1 package onion soup mix
2 small carrots, chopped
4 sprigs parsley
Bit of bay leaf
8 peppercorns
4 whole cloves
2 teaspoons salt (less if you use soup mix instead of onion)

Cover. Reduce the heat and simmer until the meat is fork-tender (about 2 hours). Add a little more liquid if needed to keep the meat from sticking. *Serves 6.*

To thin the gravy. Add water or Burgundy and reheat.

To thicken the gravy. Mix 1 tablespoon flour with ¼ cup water, add slowly to the fricassee, and cook and stir 5 minutes.

To season more highly. Add Worcestershire or garlic salt or cook a split clove of garlic in the fricassee.

Fricassee of Lamb with Vegetables. After the meat has been cooking for 1½ hours, add 2 cups diced potatoes (sweet potatoes are surprisingly good with lamb) and 2 cups of other vegetables such as small whole green beans, peas, cubed turnips, tiny onions and diced celery. Add more water, if necessary, and continue cooking until the meat and vegetables are tender. If you prefer, cook the vegetables separately and arrange them around the fricassee on the platter. As a time-saver, add canned new potatoes and canned onions to the finished stew, and simmer about 5 minutes to heat thoroughly.

Lamb Printanière. Make the fricassee with spring lamb. Add perfect young vegetables, such as tiny new potatoes, green beans, fresh peas, baby carrots and small onions. Season delicately.

BRAISED LAMB SHANKS

Lamb shanks weigh about ½ pound each. Allow 1 or 2 per person.

Roll in flour. Brown well in fat or oil in a heavy pan. Add a bit of bay leaf, sliced onion, salt and pepper. Add just enough boiling water to cover the meat. Reduce the heat, cover and simmer until tender (1½ to 2 hours). If more convenient, cook in the oven at 300°.

Lamb Shanks Savory Style. Brown shanks as above. For 4 shanks, mix 1 tablespoon cornstarch, 2 teaspoons salt, ½ teaspoon dry mustard and ¼ teaspoon each of pepper, ginger, cloves and onion salt. Add 3 cups hot water and pour over the meat. Simmer or bake. Season to taste. Sprinkle with chopped parsley.

GROUND LAMB

Ground lamb may be used in many ways as well as in the recipes which follow. See, for example, Meat Loaf (p. 180).

LAMB PATTIES

Buy prepared lamb patties or season ground lamb with salt and pepper and shape like hamburgers. Wrap each patty in a strip of bacon and fasten with a toothpick. Broil or pan-broil about 12 minutes, turning often.

SAVORY LAMB PATTIES

Mix well
1 pound ground lean lamb
1 teaspoon salt
¼ teaspoon pepper
1 egg

¼ cup chopped celery
½ cup chili sauce
¾ cup dry bread crumbs

Shape in flat patties or roll in croquette shape. Brown well on all sides in

Shortening, any kind

Put on a rack in a shallow pan. Bake 40 minutes at 300°. Serve with

Tomato sauce *or* relishes

Serves 4 or 5.

MOUSSAKA

A Greek dish, with many possible variations.

Put in a deep pan

3 tablespoons salad oil

Add and cook until brown

3 tablespoons chopped onion

Add

1 pound chopped lamb, veal or beef

Cook until the meat is brown and crumbly. Add

1 cup tomato sauce *or* 1 can tomato paste and water to make 1 cup
2 tablespoons chopped parsley
1 cup dry white wine
1 cup water

Season to taste with

Salt, pepper and plenty of nutmeg

Cover and cook slowly 1 hour. While the meat is cooking, cut in ¼-inch slices

3 *or* 4 small egg plants

Brown on both sides in

2 tablespoons salad oil

Place in a large baking dish and set aside. Melt

¼ cup butter

Stir in

1 cup flour

Add slowly, stirring constantly

4 cups scalded milk

Stir until smooth. Cook over hot water 15 minutes. Add

2 eggs, slightly beaten

Prepare

1 cup grated cheese
½ cup dry bread crumbs (and a few more for the top)
¼ cup melted butter

Stir half the cheese and half the bread crumbs into the cooked meat mixture. Divide the rest of the crumbs into two parts, and sprinkle one part over the egg plant. Spread the meat mixture over the egg plant, sprinkle with the rest of the cheese and another layer of crumbs. Spoon in the thick sauce, top with a few crumbs and sprinkle with the melted butter. Bake at 350° about ½ hour. *Serves 6.*

LAMB BURGUNDY

A tasty way to present leftover roast lamb.

Cook 5 minutes

2 tablespoons butter
¼ cup chopped onion

Add

1 tomato, cut small, *or* 1 tablespoon tomato paste
2 or 3 cups diced cooked lamb
1 cup lamb gravy
½ cup Burgundy *or* claret

Season to taste with

Salt, garlic salt, Worcestershire *or* rosemary

Simmer ½ hour, stirring occasionally. *Serves 3 or 4.*

To vary. Omit the tomato and season with prepared mustard and cayenne.

Parmesan Lamb. Make a border of mashed or Duchess Potatoes (p. 267) on a baking platter or in a shallow casserole. Sprinkle with melted butter. Pour the meat and gravy in the center. Sprinkle generously with grated Parmesan cheese. Bake at 400° until the potatoes are browned.

CURRY OF LAMB

If the dish is made the day before or must stand several hours before serving, it may need more curry. Taste and see. Lamb is traditional, but other meats can be prepared the same way—beef, pork, veal or mutton.

Melt in a deep pan

2 tablespoons bacon fat *or* salad oil

Add and cook slowly until golden

2 large onions, chopped

Stir in

2 tablespoons flour
½ teaspoon sugar
½ teaspoon salt
1 tablespoon curry powder (or more)

Add

Gravy *or* consommé, to make 2 cups

Cook and stir until thick. Taste and, if needed, add

Salt and pepper

Add

3 to 4 cups cubed cooked meat

Heat, but do not let the gravy boil. Serve with

Fluffy rice
Small bowls of at least 4 of the condiments listed below

Each person spoons the curry over the rice and sprinkles some of the condiments over the top. *Serves 6.*

To vary. Add ½ cup diced celery or 1 tablespoon chopped parsley. Or tuck in a bay leaf.

To serve with curry

Crisp bacon
French-fried onions
Toasted coconut flakes
Sliced bananas, sautéed in butter
Mango chutney
Chopped salted peanuts or almonds
Chopped cooked egg whites
Crumbled cooked egg yolks
Sliced pineapple
Green pepper, chopped fine
Chopped ham

LAMB HASH

Remove the fat from cooked lamb. Cut the meat in small even pieces. Mix with an equal amount of cooked potatoes, cut small. Moisten with gravy and season to taste. Put in a shallow baking dish and bake at 350° until thoroughly heated (about ½ hour). Sprinkle the top with cream, then with grated Parmesan cheese, and set under the broiler until the cheese melts.

ZUCCHINI STUFFED WITH LAMB

Make lengthwise holes in small zucchini with an apple corer. Stuff with well-seasoned chopped cooked lamb mixed with cooked rice and moistened with gravy. Put in a casserole. Cover with any tomato sauce. Bake at 350° until tender (about 30 minutes).

LAMB À LA BRECK

Butter a casserole. In it put

1 cup cooked and drained macaroni

Mix and spread over the macaroni

1 cup cooked lamb, chopped fine
½ teaspoon salt
⅛ teaspoon celery salt
⅛ teaspoon pepper
Few drops onion juice

Mix and pour over the meat

2 eggs, slightly beaten
1½ cups milk

Bake at 350° until firm (to test custard, p. 385, Baked Custard). *Serves 4 to 6.*

VEAL

Veal is young beef. It is almost as delicately flavored as chicken and so combines well with other foods. It is usually very lean and needs to be cooked by moist heat or with some added fat.

ROAST VEAL

The cuts used for roasting are the leg, cushion (upper part of the leg), loin, rump, shoulder and breast. Veal is usually boned at the market and cut in a piece of the desired size, 4 to 6 pounds or more.

If you wish to stuff the roast, use Onion (p. 83), Mushroom (p. 83) or other savory stuffing. For added flavor, rub lightly with a cut clove of garlic or make shallow gashes in the meat and squeeze into them small amounts of anchovy paste.

Place on a rack in a shallow roasting pan. Place strips of fat salt pork on the meat. Roast 40 minutes to the pound at 325°. A roast thermometer will read 180° when the veal is done. Veal should always be well done.

Serve with Brown Gravy (p. 164) made with the fat in the pan and either milk or water as the liquid. Add chopped parsley to the gravy.

BRAISED LEG OF VEAL

Veal done this way is tender and moist.

Cream together
- **2 tablespoons shortening**
- **1 clove garlic, crushed**
- **1 teaspoon salt**
- **¼ teaspoon sage**
- **¼ teaspoon pepper**

Spread over
- **Leg of veal (boned and tied)**

Put in a heavy Dutch oven or casserole
- **½ cup butter**
- **2 onions, sliced**
- **2 stalks celery**

Put in the meat, cover, and bake at 375° until the meat is fork-tender (about 2 hours). Turn the meat several times. Add a little water as needed to keep the meat from sticking. Remove the meat. Strain the broth, measure it, and add enough
- **Water to make 2 cups**

Mix
- **1 tablespoon cornstarch**
- **¼ cup sherry or Marsala**

Add to the broth and cook and stir until smooth. Put the meat back in the pan. Add the gravy and heat, turning the meat to glaze the surface. *Serves 8 to 10.*

BROILED VEAL CHOPS

Veal chops are usually cooked like cutlets (below) since they are apt to be lean and need fat to keep them from drying out as they cook.

Broil only young tender chops which will not take too long to cook. Have them cut 1 to 1½ inches thick. Sprinkle with salad oil and broil 10 minutes on one side, turn and sprinkle with more oil or top with a strip of bacon, and cook until thoroughly done (test by making a tiny slit in the meat).

Cheese-topped Veal Chops. After turning, sprinkle with salt, pepper and oregano and top with a slice of cheese. Broil until the cheese melts.

SAUTÉED VEAL CUTLETS

In Europe, veal is much more generally available than beef, and the many delicious ways of preparing it are among the famous dishes of the finest restaurants. Veal cutlets are usually slices from the leg cut ½ inch thick. One pound serves 3.

Remove any bits of the bone and skin. Cut in pieces for serving. Pound with a meat tenderizer or the edge of a heavy saucer until ¼ inch thick. Roll up irregular pieces and fasten with toothpicks. Sprinkle with salt, pepper and flour.

Sauté slowly until evenly browned and tender, in butter, olive oil, or in mixture of one-third butter and two-thirds bacon fat. Cook 2 split garlic cloves and/or ¼ cup chopped onion with the cutlets if you like.

Veal Cutlets with Mushrooms. Cut the meat in 3-inch pieces. Sauté a few at a time with sliced mushrooms. When all are cooked, put back into the pan and add ½ cup cream for 1 pound meat. Heat and season.

Veal Cutlets aux Fines Herbes. Sprinkle with chopped parsley and chives (3 tablespoons parsley to 1 teaspoon chives). Sprinkle with lemon juice.

Veal Cutlets Flambé. Sauté wafer-thin pieces, sprinkle with warm brandy, light with a match, and ladle the juice over the meat. Serve with Béarnaise Sauce (p. 101).

Veal Cutlets with Cheese Soufflé. Arrange cooked cutlets in a casserole. Pour Cheese Soufflé mixture (p. 121) over the meat and bake.

Veal Cutlets Hollandaise. Sauté. When almost tender, sprinkle with dry vermouth, cover and simmer 10 minutes longer. Serve with Hollandaise (p. 100).

Veal Cazapra. Sauté. When almost tender, sprinkle with dry vermouth (¼ cup for each pound). Cover and simmer 10 minutes. Sprinkle with pine nuts (pignolia), cover and cook 5 minutes longer.

Veal Cutlets Paradiso. Spread tomato paste in a baking dish. Put in the sautéed cutlets. Put a slice of cheese on each. Set under the broiler until the cheese melts.

VEAL CUTLETS AU VIN

Prepare for sautéing (p. 190)
1 pound veal cutlets
Melt in a heavy skillet
1 tablespoon butter
Add the cutlets and cook 5 minutes on each side. Add
1 tablespoon chopped onion
1 teaspoon chopped parsley
1 tablespoon chopped ham
1 clove garlic, split
Cover and cook slowly 20 minutes. Remove the garlic. Add
¼ cup dry wine, white or red
Cover and cook slowly 10 minutes. Put the meat on a hot platter. Add to the pan
¼ cup water
Boil, season with
Salt and pepper
Pour over the meat. *Serves 3.*

BRAISED VEAL CUTLETS

Follow the recipe for Sautéed Veal Cutlets (p. 190), but after browning, surround with stock, gravy, sour cream, tomato sauce or canned tomato soup. Cover and cook slowly on top of the stove or bake in a casserole at 300° until tender—35 to 60 minutes. Add more liquid from time to time as it cooks away. Season the sauce to taste, adding salt, pepper, onion juice, and sherry or Marsala.

Veal Cutlets with Claret Sauce. Without browning, put the cutlets in a baking dish, cover with claret, and let stand 30 minutes. Take out, dip in flour, and put in a buttered pan. Add the claret, an equal amount of stock or consommé, and (for 1 pound meat) the juice of ½ lemon.

Scallopini alla Marsala. Before browning, sprinkle with grated Parmesan cheese. Brown in olive oil. Braise in a mixture of one-third Marsala wine and two-thirds stock or consommé. Add a pinch of marjoram or oregano. As a variation, add sautéed mushrooms and tiny cubes of ham.

Veal Paprika. Never use pepper in a paprika-flavored dish. Sauté a cut clove of garlic with the meat. Simmer in water or stock. Remove the garlic. Put the meat on a hot platter. Add sour cream (½ cup for 1 pound meat) to the pan and enough paprika to make the sauce very pink. Cook and stir until well heated and pour over the meat.

BREADED VEAL CUTLETS

Cover cutlets with boiling water. Cover and simmer until tender (about 35 minutes). Add various seasonings to the cooking water if you like—a slice or two of onion and carrot, a stalk of celery, a few peppercorns and whole cloves. Drain. Save the broth to use in a soup or a sauce. Dip the cutlets in flour, egg and crumbs (p. 4). Chill 20 minutes or longer to make the coating firmer. This helps keep the coating from slipping off as the cutlets cook. Sauté or fry in deep fat heated to 385°.

VEAL HOLSTEIN

Dip cutlets in flour, egg, and crumbs (p. 4). Sauté slowly until brown in mixture of two-thirds bacon fat and one-third butter. Cover with Brown Sauce (p. 97). Cover and simmer until tender. For traditional German service, top each piece with poached egg. Garnish with cucumber pickles, pickled beets, sliced lemon and olives stuffed with capers and anchovies.

VEAL CORDON BLEU

Pound veal cutlets until very thin. Cut in even pieces and put together like a sandwich with a thin slice of ham and a slice of cheese as the filling. Dip in egg, beaten slightly with a tablespoon of water, then in grated cheese. Let stand 20 minutes. Sauté slowly in a mixture of half olive oil and half butter until brown (about 20 minutes).

VEAL BIRDS

Cut well-pounded veal cutlets in pieces about 2 by 4 inches. Spread with packaged stuffing, Bread Stuffing (p. 82) or a variation. Roll up and fasten with toothpicks or skewers. Sprinkle with salt, pepper and flour. Sauté in butter or bacon fat until brown. Add enough cream or gravy to half cover the meat. Cover and cook slowly until tender. Cook on top of the stove or bake in a casserole at 350°.

Veal Birds with Meat Stuffing. Grind the trimmings with a small piece of salt pork or bacon. Measure. Add half the quantity of crumbs. Season to taste. Moisten with beaten egg and hot water. Spread on the meat.

Veal Olives. Do not stuff the cutlets. Wrap the pieces of meat in strips of bacon or prosciutto ham. Brown. Cook in water or stock. Make a Brown Sauce (p. 97), using the stock in the pan.

CITY CHICKENS

Allow 1 pound lean veal and 1 pound lean pork for 6.

Have the meat cut in 1½-inch cubes. Alternate cubes of veal and pork on skewers, 4 or 5 cubes to each. Sprinkle with salt and pepper, dip in flour, then in slightly beaten egg, and then in crumbs. Sauté in butter, bacon fat or other shortening until well browned. Add ½ cup water to the pan, cover closely and cook until tender (about 30 minutes).

BLANQUETTE OF VEAL

On the platter with the veal, arrange sliced sautéed mushrooms, tiny potato balls and well-seasoned whole green beans or young carrots. Use any leftovers to make a veal and vegetable stew for another meal.

Put in a deep pan
3 pounds stewing veal, cut in 2-inch squares
Cover with
Cold water *or* cold water and white wine
Add
6 small white onions
4 sprigs parsley
1 stalk celery with tops
½ bay leaf
1 spring thyme
2 cloves
1 teaspoon salt
¼ teaspoon pepper
Cover and cook slowly until the meat is fork-tender (about 40 minutes). Remove the meat and strain the broth. Melt
3 tablespoons butter
Add
3 tablespoons flour
Stir well and add 3 cups of the strained broth. Cook 5 minutes. Just before serving, heat the sauce to the boiling point and pour slowly over
3 egg yolks, beaten with the juice of 1 lemon
Season with
A few grains nutmeg
Put the meat in a heated serving dish and pour the sauce over it. *Serves 6.*

VEAL AND ONION CASSEROLE

Mix
2 tablespoons flour
2 teaspoons salt
⅛ teaspoon pepper
Roll in it
1½ pounds veal cutlets, cut in cubes
Heat 5 minutes
2 tablespoons fat *or* salad oil
1 clove garlic, split
Remove the garlic. Add the meat and
1½ cups chopped onions
Cook and stir over low heat until the onions are golden. Put in a casserole. Add
1 cup sour cream
Cover and bake at 350° until the veal is fork-tender (1½ to 2 hours). *Serves 4 or 5.*

ENGLISH VEAL PIE

Remove the meat from
A knuckle of veal (about 5 pounds) *or* other piece for stewing
Cover the bones with
Cold water
Add
1 slice onion
1 slice carrot
Bit of bay leaf
Sprig of parsley
12 peppercorns
Blade of mace *or* ½ teaspoon ground mace
2 teaspoons salt
Heat slowly to the boiling point. Add the veal and
½-pound piece lean ham
Cover and simmer until the meat is fork-tender (about 1½ hours). Take out the veal and ham and cook the broth until it is reduced to 2 cups. Melt
4 tablespoons butter
Cook until brown. Add
4 tablespoons flour
Cook and stir until again well browned. Add the broth. Cut the veal and ham in neat cubes and add to the sauce. Simmer 20 minutes. Taste and add more seasonings if needed. Put in a casserole. Put on
Pastry top (Plain or Puff, pp. 438, 453), baked separately
Serves 8 or more.

CHOPPED VEAL

Chopped veal is usually combined with other more highly flavored foods in such recipes as Miss Daniell's Meat Loaf (p. 181) and Ham and Veal Loaf (p. 202). Use it also in Moussaka (p. 188) or in place of beef in Beef Doves (p. 179). Herbs add zest to this bland meat. Try adding a trace of chervil, marjoram, rosemary, tarragon or thyme.

VEAL AND ALMOND PATTIES

Cover with water
1½ pounds lean veal
Add
1 teaspoon salt
Cook slowly 30 minutes. Drain, reserving the liquid. Chop the meat fine. Add to 1 cup of the liquid
4 slices bread, broken in pieces
2 tablespoons butter
Cool and add the meat and
¼ cup sliced almonds
Season to taste. Shape in flat oval patties about 2½ inches long. Dip in
Egg and cracker crumbs (p. 4)
Sauté in
Butter
over low heat until well browned, turning once. Serve with
Mushroom Sauce (p. 98)
Serves 6.

VIENNA STEAKS

Stuffed or broiled mushrooms add the right touch.

Mix
½ pound ground veal
½ pound ground beef
1½ teaspoons salt
¼ teaspoon paprika
½ teaspoon celery salt
Few gratings nutmeg
1 teaspoon lemon juice
Few drops onion juice
1 egg, well beaten
Shape in 12 oval cakes, ½ inch thick. Cook like hamburgers. Remove the meat to a heated serving dish. Heat in the pan and pour over the meat
½ cup sour cream
Serves 3 or 4.

ZUCCHINI STUFFED WITH VEAL

Cover with boiling salted water
2 or 3 zucchini
Cook 10 minutes, drain, cool and cut in half lengthwise. Scoop out the pulp and chop it. Heat in a skillet
2 tablespoons olive oil
Add
½ pound lean veal
Cook until well browned. Take out the veal and chop it. Put in the skillet
2 tablespoons chopped onion
1 clove garlic, crushed
Cook until the onion is yellow. Add the zucchini pulp and cook 5 minutes. Cool slightly and add the chopped veal and
2 eggs, well beaten
⅓ cup grated Italian cheese
Season to taste with
Salt and pepper
Marjoram *or* thyme
Minced parsley
Fill the zucchini shells. Sprinkle with
Buttered crumbs
Bake at 350° until the zucchini is tender (about 30 minutes).
Serves 4 to 6.

VEAL LOAF

See also Miss Daniell's Meat Loaf (p. 181) and Ham and Veal Loaf (p. 202).

Mix
2 pounds veal, ground
½ pound fresh pork, ground
½ green pepper, cut fine
1 onion, chopped
1 tablespoon lemon juice
1 teaspoon salt

½ cup cracker meal *or* wheat germ
1 egg
½ cup milk
1 teaspoon Worcestershire

Press firmly into a loaf pan. Lay over the top

6 strips bacon

Cover with a piece of foil and bake 40 minutes at 300°. Uncover and bake 30 minutes longer. Serve with

Mushroom Sauce (p. 98)

Serves 8.

PRESSED VEAL

A handsome dish for a summer buffet.

Cover with boiling water

Knuckle *or* shin of veal (about 4 pounds)
1 pound lean veal
1 onion

Cover and cook slowly until the meat is tender (about 1½ hours). Drain, reserving the broth. Grind the meat and season it with

Salt, pepper and marjoram

Hard-cook, cool, and slice

3 eggs

Garnish the bottom of a mold or loaf pan with slices of egg and

Chopped parsley

Put in a layer of the meat and a layer of sliced egg, sprinkle with parsley and cover with the rest of the meat. Cook the broth until it is reduced to 1 cup and pour it over the meat. Press down firmly and chill. Turn out onto a serving dish and garnish with

Sprigs of parsley
Quartered tomatoes

Serves 6.

VEAL TETRAZZINI

Follow the recipe for Chicken Tetrazzini (p. 234), using veal in place of chicken and seasoning with thyme, tarragon or grated lemon rind instead of nutmeg.

VENISON

The meat from fresh-killed venison is apt to be tough. It will be tenderer and of better flavor if you have your butcher hang it at least 2 weeks in his refrigerator before you cook it. He will cut it in pieces for you. They may be used immediately or wrapped, frozen and stored for later use.

BROILED VENISON

Cut ½-inch slices from the loin. Sprinkle with salt and pepper. Brush with melted butter or olive oil. Broil or sauté 5 minutes on each side. Serve with Maître d'Hôtel Butter (p. 103), Chestnut (p. 98) or Currant Jelly Sauce (p. 98), seasoned to taste with port or Madeira.

ROAST VENISON
(Leg, Loin, Saddle)

Put the meat in a pottery bowl or an enameled dish. Cover with French dressing made with lemon juice or with a special marinade (below). Cover and refrigerate 12 to 24 hours to tenderize the meat and improve the flavor. Turn occasionally so that the marinade reaches all parts of the meat. Drain and put in a shallow baking pan. Put slices of bacon over the meat. Roast like lamb (p. 181). Allow 20 minutes per pound for rare venison, 22 minutes for medium rare. Increase the heat to 450° for the last 15 minutes to brown the surface.

Marinade for venison. Heat 1 cup red wine or cider with 2 tablespoons oil, a slice of onion,

2 bay leaves and ½ teaspoon salt. For a more savory marinade, add sliced celery, onions or carrot and a sprig of thyme or rosemary. Cool.

PORK

High-grade pork is fine-grained and firm. Lean pork from a young animal is nearly white, from an older animal, pinkish. The fat is white and softer than beef fat.

ROAST PORK

The cuts for roasting are the loin, shoulder and fresh ham or pork leg. Allow ½ to 1 pound per person. Do not roast a piece weighing less than 3 pounds.

Put the roast, fat side up, in a shallow roasting pan. Roast at 350° until the meat is fork-tender (35 minutes per pound for large roasts, 45 for small ones). Pork is always cooked to the well-done stage (185° on a roast thermometer).

Make gravy (p. 164), using the fat in the pan.

Roast Shoulder of Pork. A whole shoulder weighs 8 to 12 pounds but is usually cut into smaller pieces called the butt and picnic shoulder or shoulder cushion. It may be boned to make carving easier or to be stuffed.

Roast Fresh Ham or Pork Leg. This large roast weighs 8 to 12 pounds. It may be boned or not.

Roast Loin of Pork. A whole loin weighs 10 to 14 pounds, but a smaller roast can be cut off. The center cut is the most expensive per pound, but there is less waste. To make carving easier, have the butcher separate the backbone from the ribs and saw through the bones.

Roast Crown of Pork. See Crown of Lamb (p. 184), but roast to the well-done stage. Allow 2 chops per person.

Stuffed Roast Pork. Have fresh ham, butt or shoulder boned at the market. Stuff with Bread (p. 82), Apple (p. 83) or Celery Stuffing (p. 83). Skewer or sew together.

TO SERVE WITH PORK

Sweet potatoes, onions and tomatoes are particularly good with pork. Serve them in any of the ways suggested in the vegetable chapter (p. 238).

Serve a tart fruit relish to heighten the bland flavor of fine pork:

Applesauce (p. 366)
Fried Apple Rings (p. 87)
Cinnamon Apples (p. 366)
Glazed Pineapple (p. 90)
Sautéed Pineapple (p. 90)

LITTLE ROAST PIG

This unusual roast is handsome holiday fare. A 10 to 12 pound pig serves 12 or more.

Prepare 8 cups Onion Stuffing (p. 83). Stuff the cleaned pig and sew or skewer together. Skewer the legs in position, stretching the hind legs backward, the forelegs forward. Make 4 parallel gashes, 3 inches long, through the skin on each side of the backbone. Put on a rack in a shallow pan. Brush all over with melted butter and sprinkle with flour.

Roast at 350° until tender (4 hours or longer). For a crusty skin, baste every 15 minutes with melted butter or salad oil and sprinkle with flour. Put a small red apple in the mouth, raisins or cranberries in the eyes, and a wreath of laurel or holly around the neck.

PORK CHOPS

One pound serves 3.

Have rib, loin or shoulder chops cut about 1 inch thick. Sprinkle with salt and pepper. Dust lightly with flour.

Pan-broiled. Brown on both sides in a well-heated, heavy frying pan (greased lightly, if the chops are lean). Pour off the fat. Reduce the heat, cover, and cook slowly 40 to 60 minutes or until tender, turning occasionally to cook evenly.

Baked. Arrange the chops on an oven-proof platter. Put 1 tablespoon moist stuffing on each. Onion (p. 83), Apple (p. 83), Celery (p. 83) or Corn Stuffing (p. 83) are all delicious with pork. Bake at 350° about 2 hours or until very tender. Baste with water from time to time if the chops seem dry.

Stuffed. Stuff thick chops (see Stuffed Lamb Chops, p. 185) with Celery (p. 83), Apple (p. 83) or Apple and Prune Stuffing (p. 84). Bake as above.

Pressure - cooked (stuffed or plain). Brown on both sides in hot fat in a pressure cooker. Put a rack under the chops. Add 1/4 cup water. Put on the cover. Bring to 15 pounds pressure. Cook 15 minutes and reduce the pressure.

BROILED PORK TENDERLOIN

One pound serves 3.

Cut tenderloin in slices 1/2 inch thick. Pound with a potato masher to flatten to about 1/4 inch thick. Brush with melted butter. Pan-broil slowly until very tender (about 30 minutes).

BRAISED PORK CHOPS, STEAK *or* CUTLET

Allow 1 or 2 chops for each serving. One pound of pork from the leg, sliced 1 1/2 inches thick, serves 3.

Brown meat on both sides in a heavy skillet. Pour off the fat. Sprinkle with salt and pepper. Cover with a liquid—water, Barbecue Sauce (p. 93), consommé or Sweet and Sour Sauce (p. 104). For heightened flavor, add chopped onion or a pinch of marjoram, sage, savory or thyme. Cover and cook slowly until very tender (1 to 1 1/2 hours). Or cook in a casserole at 350°.

PORK GOULASH

Follow the recipe for Goulash (p. 174), using pork.

CITY CHICKENS

See page 192.

SPARERIBS

Spareribs are bony, so allow 1 pound per person. Loin ribs are meatier than regular ribs and so are more expensive. Spareribs are usually fresh pork, but in some parts of the country cured ribs are also marketed. Cured ribs must be cooked in water and drained to remove some of the salt before cooking in other ways.

Baked Spareribs. Cut into 2-rib pieces. Arrange in a shallow baking pan. Sprinkle with salt and pepper. On each piece put a slice of lemon and a teaspoon of chopped onion. Bake 1½ hours at 350°, basting several times with Barbecue Sauce (p. 93). Turn meat occasionally so that it will cook evenly.

Spareribs Chinese Style. Cut in single-rib pieces. For 2 strips of spareribs, prepare a sauce by mixing 1 teaspoon cornstarch, 1 cup vinegar, 1 teaspoon sugar, 1 cup sherry, 1 teaspoon thin soy sauce and 2 teaspoons salt. Beat 1 egg, add half the sauce, and dip each rib into the mixture. Sauté slowly until brown and tender in hot peanut oil, ½ inch deep. Put the meat on a hot platter. Add the remaining sauce and 1 cup water to the pan. Cook and stir until thick. Serve with the meat.

STUFFED SPARERIBS

Order a pair of spareribs and have them cracked to make carving easier. Put one section on a rack in a baking pan. Cover with sauerkraut or Apple (p. 83), Onion (p. 83) or Bread Stuffing (p. 82). Put the other section on top. Bake at 350° until tender (about 1¼ hours). Baste several times during the baking, using the fat in the pan.

PIGS' FEET (HOCKS)

Often available already boiled or pickled. Allow 1 or 2 per person.

Clean thoroughly. Leave whole or split in half. To keep in shape, wrap tightly in cheesecloth. Put in a pan and cover with cold water. Add (for 8 pigs' feet) ½ onion, sliced, ½ carrot, sliced, ⅛ teaspoon whole peppercorns, a sprig of parsley, a bit of bay leaf and ½ teaspoon salt. Bring to the boiling point and simmer until tender. Do not cook so long that the meat falls apart.

Broiled Pigs' Feet. Wipe boiled pigs' feet. Sprinkle with salt and pepper. Broil 6 to 8 minutes. Serve with prepared mustard, Maître d'Hôtel Butter (p. 103) or Sauce Piquante (p. 98).

Pickled Pigs' Feet. Cook the pigs' feet in vinegar and water, allowing 1 cup vinegar to each 3 cups water and adding the seasonings suggested above.

Jellied Pigs' Feet. Prepare pickled pigs' feet. Strain the broth and remove the meat, discarding the skin and bones. Taste the broth and add more salt if needed. Add the meat, pour into a mold and chill until firm.

GROUND PORK

Ground pork is used in many tasty recipes such as the various meat loaf recipes (p. 180). It may replace the beef in Beef Doves (p. 181).

JO MAZZOTTI

Excellent for a buffet supper. Even better if you make the sauce the day before and let it season. Use other meats in place of pork if more convenient—ground beef or pork sausage. If you use sausage you will not need extra fat.

Cook together until well browned

¼ cup butter *or* other cooking fat
1½ pounds lean pork, ground
8 large onions, sliced

Add

3 cans concentrated tomato soup *or* 1 can tomato paste and 2 cups water
1 pound mushrooms, sliced
1 bunch celery, diced
2 green peppers, cut fine
Juice of ½ lemon
Salt and pepper
1 pound sharp cheese, cut small

Simmer 15 minutes to make a rich sauce. Meanwhile, in a deep kettle of boiling salted water (1 teaspoon to each quart of water), cook until just tender

1 large package broad noodles

Drain and mix with the sauce. Cover closely and cook slowly 1 hour on top of the stove or in a 350° oven. *Serves 12 to 16.*

SMOKED HAMS

A whole ham weighs from 8 to 24 pounds. For a small family, buy a half ham (the butt end is meatier), a 5- or 6-pound "picnic" or "cottage" ham, or a piece of Canadian-style bacon (boned and smoked loin). One pound with the bone serves 2, boneless it serves 3 or 4.

Tenderized or precooked hams need no soaking or boiling. The flavor is improved by baking (below).

Home-cured, Smithfield and Virginia hams are especially salty. Scrub well with a brush under running water. Cover with cold water and soak overnight before cooking.

Polish or Polish-style hams have a distinctive flavor due to special feeding and aging. Follow the directions on the wrapping or tin.

Canned hams are excellent reserve items. Store in the refrigerator. Serve hot or cold with any of the sauces suggested for Baked Ham (below).

BOILED HAM
(Home-cured, Virginia *or* Smithfield)

Most hams are ready to bake without boiling first. Read the label.

Soak (above). Put in a large kettle. Cover completely with boiling water. Reduce the heat so that the water barely simmers. Cover. Cook until the small bone is loose enough to pull out easily (20 to 30 minutes to the pound). Cool the ham in the water in which it was cooked. Remove from the water and peel off the outer skin. Cut off most of the fat, leaving a ¼-inch layer. Bake (below).

For added flavor, replace part of the water with cider, wine or pineapple juice. Or add to the water ½ cup vinegar or 1 onion, 2 stalks celery, 4 cloves, a bit of bay leaf, 2 carrots and a few sprigs of parsley.

BAKED HAM

Precooked hams are baked or glazed without boiling beforehand. Follow the directions on the wrapper.

Place the ham on a rack in a shallow roasting pan, fat side up, and bake at 325°. A meat thermometer will register 150° when the ham is done.

Precooked hams take about 10 minutes per pound to heat thoroughly.

Mild-cured hams (bone in) take about 2½ hours for a 5-pound half ham or shank or butt, 3½ hours for a 9- to 12-pound ham, and 4 hours for a 15- to 20-

pound ham. A 5-pound boned piece takes 2½ hours, an 8-pound piece 3 hours.

Baked Daisy ham, canned ham, Canadian-type bacon. Since these hams are already cooked, they need only an hour in a 350° oven to heat thoroughly. Follow any of the suggestions given for basting, glazing and serving Baked Ham (below). **For easy serving,** have your butcher cut a canned ham or a piece of Canadian bacon in thin slices and tie it firmly in shape. After baking, put on a hot platter, snip the string and remove it carefully.

TO GLAZE BAKED HAM

Cut off all the skin from a precooked boiled or baked ham. Place the ham on a rack in a shallow roasting pan. With a long sharp knife, score the fat (make cuts about ¼ inch deep) in a diamond pattern. Spread with a glaze (below). Stick a whole clove in each square. Bake at 400° about 30 minutes. Baste several times during the glazing with cider, cider mixed with brandy, or a special basting sauce (below). To make slicing easier, remove from oven about 15 minutes before serving.

To make the glaze, mix 1 cup brown sugar with ¼ cup strained honey, maple syrup, cider or fruit juice. Mix a little mustard with the sugar, if you like, or spread the ham with prepared mustard and pat on brown sugar mixed with fine cracker crumbs.

For basting sauce, mix 1 cup brown sugar with 1 teaspoon dry mustard and ½ cup mild vinegar or with 1 teaspoon ginger and ½ cup ginger ale or with 1 cup honey and 1 cup orange juice.

TO SERVE WITH HAM

If you have basted the ham with a savory sauce, you may need no other accompaniment than prepared mustard. Otherwise, serve any of these.

Raisin Sauce (p. 104)
Spiced Fruit Sauce (p. 104)
Rochester Sauce (p. 102)
Crushed pineapple
Mustard Sauce (p. 102)
Mustard Pickle (p. 547)
Piccalilli (p. 545)
Cole Slaw (p. 285)
Fruit Relishes (p. 87)

CARVING A HAM

Make a cut at right angles to the bone with a long straight knife. Cut several parallel slices. Slip the knife beneath to free the slices from the bone.

DAISY HAM ON A SPIT

For out-of-door cooking.

Select a long, narrow daisy ham. Put it on a spit and wrap foil around it, folding the ends to keep in the juices. Cook over hot coals at least 1 hour or until tender. Serve with a tasty sauce (above).

PROSCIUTTO (PRAGUE-STYLE HAM)

Slice paper-thin. Serve as cocktail tidbits or as a first course with sliced cantaloupe or honeydew melon.

BROILED HAM

One pound serves 3.

Cut gashes in the fat so that it will not curl during the cooking. Broil ½-inch slices 3 minutes on each side.

Broiled Ham Epicurean Style. Have the ham cut in 1-inch slices. Broil on one side, turn and spread with a thick layer of brown sugar. Broil until the sugar melts, reducing the heat so that the sugar will not scorch. Serve with sautéed pineapple slices.

PAN-BROILED HAM

Grease a frying pan with a little of the ham fat. Put in the ham and cook 3 minutes on each side. Thin slices of Canadian bacon take only 1 or 2 minutes on each side.

Ham with Mushrooms. Pile sliced sautéed mushrooms on the ham.

Barbecued Ham. When the ham is cooked, add to the fat in the pan 3 tablespoons vinegar, 1½ teaspoons mustard, ½ teaspoon sugar, ⅛ teaspoon paprika and 1 tablespoon currant jelly. Heat and pour over the ham.

Ham and Eggs. When the ham is cooked, fry eggs in the ham fat and serve on or with the ham.

HAM ROLL

Spread a 1-inch-thick slice of ham (1½ to 2 pounds) with Celery Stuffing (p. 83) or Bread Stuffing (p. 82). Roll up and skewer or tie in shape. Put in a baking dish. Cover with stock, consommé or canned tomatoes. Cover. Bake 1½ to 2 hours at 350°. *Serves 6.*

HAM STEAK WITH GLACÉED PINEAPPLE

Put in a baking dish
1 slice ham, 1 inch thick (about 1½ pounds)
Spread with
Prepared mustard
Pour over it
1 cup syrup from canned pineapple
Sprinkle with
½ cup brown sugar
Stick with
Whole cloves
Bake at 350° until tender (about 1 hour). Over the ham lay
6 slices canned pineapple
Bake until the pineapple is delicately brown, basting frequently with the juices in the pan. *Serves 4 or 5.*

HAM CASSEROLE COUNTRY STYLE

Equally good made with bits of leftover ham. Put the ham and potatoes in layers.

Cut off the outside edge of fat from
1 slice ham, 2 inches thick (about 2 pounds)
Put in a casserole and cover with
1½ cups thinly sliced potatoes
1 onion, sliced
Sprinkle with
Thyme
Add
2 cups milk
Cover and bake 1½ hours at 350°. *Serves 6.*

HAM AND ONION CASSEROLE

Good variations are many—add herbs, chopped parsley or mush-

rooms to this basic dish. Or make it with bits of leftover ham.

Put in a casserole
3 large onions, sliced thin
Lay over the onions
1 slice ham, 1 inch thick (about 1½ pounds)
Pour over the ham
1 can undiluted cream of celery soup *or* 1½ cups canned tomatoes
Bake 1 hour at 350°. *Serves 4.*

GROUND HAM

Ground ham is a major ingredient in tasty meat loaf recipes (below), but it is also a savory addition to many others. Add it to sauces and salads for extra flavor.

HAM PATTIES

Mix
1 cup ground ham (about ½ pound)
1 egg
¼ cup dry bread crumbs
Season to taste with
Prepared mustard *or* Worcestershire
Chopped parsley, stuffed olives *or* onion
Add
Milk or water (enough so that you can shape the mixture)
Shape into patties. Brown on both sides in
Bacon fat
Serve with
Mustard Sauce (p. 102)
Serves 2 or 3.

HAM AND VEAL LOAF

Order chopped together
2 pounds ham
1 pound veal
Add
1 cup bread crumbs
2 eggs, slightly beaten
2 cups milk
Salt and pepper to taste
Mix well. Shape in a roll. Put on a flat baking dish. Bake 2 hours at 350°. Serve with
Tomato (p. 99) *or* Horseradish Sauce (p. 102)
Serves 8.

HAM LOAF

Grind together (or have it done at the market)
1½ pounds ham
1 pound fresh pork
Add
¼ teaspoon pepper
¼ teaspoon salt
2 eggs, well beaten
1 cup milk
1 cup cracker crumbs
Mix well and shape into a loaf. Put in a shallow baking pan. Bake 2 hours at 350°. During the baking, baste frequently with the following basting sauce.

BASTING SAUCE FOR HAM LOAF

Cook and stir together for 5 minutes
½ cup brown sugar
1 tablespoon prepared mustard
½ cup boiling water
½ cup mild vinegar

NANCY'S HAM LOAF

Delicious hot or cold.

Order ground together
1 pound ham
½ pound beef
½ pound pork
Add
1 cup bread, cut in ¼-inch cubes
¾ cup powdered milk
⅛ teaspoon pepper
2 tablespoons minced onion
1 egg, beaten
1 cup tomato juice
Mix well. Pack into a loaf pan. Bake 1½ hours at 350°. *Serves 8.*

GERMAN LOAF

Fussier than some recipes but delicious. Cuts in handsome thin slices.

Cut off the fat from
1 pound ham
Set the fat aside. Grind the ham with
1 pound fresh pork
1 clove garlic
1 small onion
Add
1 tablespoon salt
1 teaspoon pepper
2 teaspoons curry powder
1½ tablespoons sage
Grind again. Add
1 egg white
½ cup cream
Mix thoroughly. Put 4 strips of the ham fat on a square of cheesecloth. Press the meat mixture into a loaf shape and place on the fat. Fold the cheesecloth tightly around the meat and tie firmly. Put on a trivet in a deep kettle. Add
3 quarts boiling water
¼ cup vinegar
1 teaspoon salt
Cover and simmer 2½ hours. Drain, cool and press under a weight.

HAM MOUSSE ALEXANDRIA

Party fare for lunch or supper.

Butter lightly 6 to 8 small molds. Set the oven at 350°.
Mix to a smooth paste
½ pound ham, ground fine
4 egg whites
Rub through a sieve or whirl in an electric blender. Add
⅛ teaspoon pepper
Few gratings nutmeg
Stir in, a little at a time
½ cup heavy cream
Fill the molds. Set in a pan of hot water. Bake until firm (30 to 45 minutes). Turn out onto a platter or plates. Coat with
Allemande Sauce (p. 96)
Garnish with
Parsley

HAM AND SPINACH SOUFFLÉ

Put in a bowl
½ cup dry bread crumbs
Milk (enough to cover the crumbs)
Let stand until the crumbs are soft. Drain off the milk. Add to the crumbs
3 tablespoons butter
Cook and stir until smooth. Add
1 cup chopped cooked spinach
2 tablespoons finely chopped onion
¾ cup diced cooked ham
⅛ teaspoon pepper
3 egg yolks, beaten until thick
Salt to taste
Fold in
3 egg whites, beaten stiff
Spoon into a straight-sided unbuttered baking dish. Set in a pan. Put hot water in the pan so that it is 1 inch deep. Bake at 350° until firm (about 40 minutes). Serve with
Hollandaise (p. 100)
Serves 4 as a luncheon dish or 6 as a vegetable.

Vary by adding more ham or chopped mushrooms or herbs.

USING LEFTOVER HAM

Ham is one of the most versatile of leftovers. Chop and add to vegetable soups, sauces, mashed potato, potato salad, Welsh rabbit, scrambled eggs, omelets, soufflés or macaroni and cheese, or mix it with cottage or cream cheese, pickle relish or peanut butter for sandwiches or cocktail canapés. Consult the index for further suggestions.

A few special recipes using ham:

Ham Casserole Country Style (p. 201)
Ham and Onion Casserole (p. 201)
Ham and Spinach Soufflé (p. 203)
Scalloped Eggs (p. 107)

SCRAPPLE

It is seldom worth while to make scrapple for a small family. It is marketed by the pound or in cans.

Put in a deep pan

1 pound pork (inexpensive bony cut)
2 fresh pigs' feet
1 quart boiling water
2 teaspoons salt

Cover the pan, reduce the heat and cook until the meat drops from the bones. Strain the broth into a large double boiler top. Grind the meat. Stir into the broth

⅔ cup corn meal *or* buckwheat flour

Cook and stir over direct heat 5 minutes. Add the meat and

2 tablespoons chopped onion

Season to taste with

Salt and pepper

Cook over boiling water 1 hour. Pack into a small loaf pan rinsed with cold water. Chill.

FRIED SCRAPPLE

Cut scrapple in slices ½ inch thick. Pan-fry until crisp and brown. Unless the pork is very lean you will need no added fat in the pan. Serve hot with syrup for a satisfying winter breakfast or lunch.

BACON

Bacon varies in flavor and in leanness. It is marketed in one piece (slab bacon) or in thick or thin slices. Buy only enough for a week at a time because bacon is at its savory best when it is fresh. It does not freeze well.

Bacon drippings. Store in a can or covered jar in the refrigerator. Use (within two weeks) for frying eggs or potatoes or for seasoning vegetables.

PAN-BROILED BACON

Arrange strips of bacon in a single layer in a cold frying pan. If the strips are too cold to separate easily, put the bacon in the pan and separate the slices as it warms. Occasionally pour off the fat as it accumulates. Drain the bacon on a paper towel.

OVEN-BROILED (BAKED) BACON

Place thin slices of bacon close together on a rack in a shallow pan or on a special bacon cooker. Bake at 425° until crisp and brown, turning once.

CANADIAN BACON

See Broiled Canadian Bacon (p. 201, Pan-broiled Ham) and Baked Canadian Bacon (p. 200).

FRIED SALT PORK COUNTRY STYLE

Dip in flour to coat well

¼ pound lean salt pork (about 9 thin slices)

Heat a heavy frying pan. Put in the pork, lower the heat and cook until crisp and brown, turning frequently. Remove the pork from the pan and put in a warm serving dish. If there is more than about 2 tablespoons of fat in the pan, pour off the extra. Stir in and blend well

2 tablespoons flour

Add

1 cup milk

Cook and stir until thickened. Add

Worcestershire, Tabasco *or* a few grains of pepper

Pour into a bowl. Serve with

Hot boiled potatoes

Serves 3.

For a richer gravy, add a little cream or butter just before serving.

SAUSAGES AND SAUSAGE MEAT

The delicatessen counter offers a wide range of sausages, varying in shape and in ingredients.

Bologna, salami (smoked and cooked), Cervelat and other distinctively seasoned sausages are sold by the piece or in thin slices ready for sandwiches, a platter of mixed cold meats or a salad.

Liver sausage (liverwurst) discolors when sliced. Buy it in a piece and slice it as you serve it. See also Mock Foie Gras (p. 54).

Link sausages (frankfurters or pork) are sold by the pound or in packages.

Sausage meat is sold by the pound.

Store sausage in the refrigerator. For the finest flavor, use within a few days of purchasing.

FRANKFURTERS (WIENERS)

Frankfurters may be all beef or a mixture of beef, pork and veal. There is no cereal in the best ones. They are already cooked but need brief heating to be appetizing.

Pan-broiled Frankfurters. Heat slowly in just enough butter to keep them from sticking. Turn with tongs to keep from pricking the skin.

"Boiled" Frankfurters. Cover with boiling water. Cover the pan and lower the heat or turn it off so that the water no longer boils. Let stand 5 minutes and drain.

Frankfurters Grilled with Cheese. Cut a long slit in each frankfurter. Tuck in a piece of cheese. Broil, cheese side up, until the cheese melts.

FRANKFURTERS IN BUNS

Standard fare for picnics and cookouts but good any time.

Split buns without cutting all the way through. Toast on the cut side and tuck in a heated frankfurter. Serve with prepared mustard or piccalilli or both.

FRANKFURTERS AND SAUERKRAUT

Simmer sauerkraut until thoroughly heated. Lay frankfurters over it and serve as soon as they are hot.

Frankfurters with Caraway Seeds. For each pound of sauerkraut, add 1 teaspoon caraway seeds and 1 tablespoon water.

FRANKFURTERS SOUTHERN STYLE

Melt

1 tablespoon butter *or* bacon fat

Add

1 medium onion, diced
½ cup diced celery
½ green pepper, diced

Cook slowly until the vegetables are tender. Add

1 pound frankfurters, cut in pieces
1 large can tomatoes (2½ cups)

Season to taste with

Thyme and oregano

Simmer 10 minutes. Pour into a large casserole. Set the oven at 425°. Mix and spread over the top of the casserole

Corn bread batter (p. 329) *or* batter made with 1 package corn bread mix

Bake until the corn bread is brown and crusty (about 25 minutes). *Serves 6.*

PAN-BROILED SAUSAGES

Some sausages need only browning. Follow directions on the package.

Cut sausages apart but do not prick. Put in a cold frying pan. Cook about 10 minutes over moderate heat, turning with tongs to brown evenly. Pour off the fat as it accumulates. Serve with eggs, pancakes or waffles or on squares of corn bread or a bed of mashed potatoes. Any of the accompaniments suggested for pork (p. 196) are good with sausage.

To reduce the fat, cover the sausages with boiling water, simmer 5 minutes and drain before browning.

CORNELL SAUSAGE MEAT

Meat for sausage should not be too lean. One-third fat is about right. If you make more than enough for one meal, store it in the freezer and use it within two or three weeks.

Mix thoroughly
- **1 pound pork chopped for sausage**
- **1 teaspoon salt**
- **½ teaspoon freshly ground pepper**
- **½ teaspoon sage**

SAUSAGE CAKES

Shape sausage meat in flat round cakes like small hamburgers. Put in a cold frying pan. Set over moderate heat. Cook about 10 minutes on one side, turn and cook 10 minutes on the other side. Pour off the fat as it accumulates. Sausage cakes should be well browned and thoroughly cooked but not dry.

To remove some of the fat before browning, cover the patties with boiling water, cover and simmer 5 minutes. Drain and cook as above.

SAUSAGE-STUFFED APPLES

Cook together 15 minutes
- **1 pound sausage meat**
- **1 clove garlic, crushed**
- **1 tablespoon chopped onion**

Stir with a fork. Core and stuff with the sausage
- **8 apples**

Put in a baking dish. Sprinkle with
- **Brown sugar**

On each apple put a strip of
- **Bacon**

Bake at 350° until the apples are soft (about 40 minutes).

SAUSAGE AND APPLE CASSEROLE

Shape into 8 balls
- **1 pound sausage meat**

Cook in a skillet until brown. Core and peel halfway down
- **8 small tart apples**

Fill with
- **Cinnamon sugar**

Pare and cut in quarters
- **2 large sweet potatoes**

Put in the center of a casserole
- **Bread Stuffing (p. 82)**

Arrange around it the sausage, apples and sweet potatoes. Bake at 350° about 1 hour. *Serves 4.*

SAUSAGE-STUFFED PRUNES

A good luncheon dish or an attractive garnish on the turkey platter.

Put in a saucepan
- **½ pound large prunes**

Cover with water. Cook until just tender. Drain and pit. Mix
- **½ pound sausage meat**

½ cup soft bread crumbs
Salt and pepper to taste

Stuff the prunes generously. Put in a lightly greased pan. Bake at 400° until the sausage is well browned (about 25 minutes). As a luncheon dish, serve with the prunes the sauce below. *Serves 3 or 4.*

To make the sauce. Mix 1 tablespoon fat with 1 tablespoon flour. Add 1 cup prune juice, 1 tablespoon lemon juice, 1 teaspoon grated lemon rind and salt to taste. Cook and stir until the sauce boils.

PINEAPPLE RABBIT WITH SAUSAGE CAKES

Spread
6 slices canned pineapple
with
Horseradish
Shape in 6 flat patties
1 pound sausage meat
Put a patty on each slice of pineapple. Put in a baking dish. Add
1 cup sherry
Bake 30 minutes at 350°, basting 4 times. Put on each patty a slice of
Cheese
Bake until the cheese begins to melt. Dust with
Paprika
Serves 6.

BUBBLE-AND-SQUEAK

An old-fashioned English supper dish.

Put in layers in a casserole
1 pound cooked sausage meat
2 cups cooked chopped cabbage
Pour over the top
2 cups Cream Sauce (p. 94)
Sprinkle with
Bread crumbs
Bake at 350° for 30 minutes. *Serves 4 to 6.*

VARIETY MEATS

Brains, hearts, kidneys, liver and sweetbreads are far higher than other meats in the best protein, minerals and vitamins and therefore should be served frequently. It is important that these meats be absolutely fresh, so cook them promptly.

BRAINS

Calves' brains are considered the choicest, but there is very little difference in the flavor of calves', beef, lamb or pork brains. Allow about ¼ pound for each serving.

Precook before using in the following recipes. Hold under running water and remove the membranes. Cover brains with boiling water. Add 1 teaspoon salt and 1 tablespoon vinegar. Cover and simmer 20 minutes. Drain, cover with cold water, let stand 10 minutes, and drain again. Use at once or store in the refrigerator, well wrapped.

Brains with Black Butter. Slice cooked brains. Sauté in butter until delicately brown. Put on a hot platter. Add a little more butter to the pan and heat until it is dark brown. Add a little lemon juice and pour over the brains.

Brains Sautéed with Bacon. Slice cooked brains and sauté in bacon fat until delicately brown. Serve with crisp bacon. Watercress is an attractive garnish.

Scrambled Brains. Beat 4 eggs slightly. Add ½ pound cooked brains, broken in ½-inch pieces. Add 1 teaspoon salt, ¼ teaspoon pepper, 1 tablespoon Worcestershire and 2 tablespoons tomato catsup. Melt 2 tablespoons butter, add the mixture, and cook and stir over low heat until just firm.

Brains à la York. Break cooked brains in ½-inch pieces. Sprinkle with sherry (½ cup for 1 pound), cover and let stand 1 hour. Add to 1½ cups Mushroom Sauce (p. 98). Serve on toast.

HEARTS

Veal hearts weigh about ¾ pound, beef hearts 3 to 3½, lamb hearts ¼ pound and pork hearts ½ pound. Allow about ⅓ pound per serving.

To prepare for cooking, cut out the coarse fibers at the top and inside the heart. Wash in cold water. A large beef heart may be tough—soak it overnight in 1 quart water and 2 tablespoons vinegar.

Hearts on Toast. Cover with boiling salted water. Simmer until tender. Drain, chop, season to taste and serve on toast.

Pan-broiled Hearts. Slice ½ inch thick. Sprinkle with flour or crumbs and cook slowly in butter (about 15 minutes).

STUFFED HEART

Prepare
2 veal hearts *or* 1 beef heart (above)
Stuff with
Bread Stuffing (p. 82)
Sprinkle with
Salt and pepper
Roll in
Flour
Brown evenly in
Bacon fat
Put in a casserole. Add
½ cup boiling water
Cover. Bake 2 hours at 350°, adding more water from time to time if the liquid cooks away. Put the heart on a serving dish and keep warm. Pour the broth into a saucepan. Stir in
1 tablespoon flour, mixed with ¼ cup cold water

Bring to the boiling point. Season to taste and pour around the heart. *Serves 4 or 5.*

Fruit Stuffed Heart. Instead of Bread Stuffing, fill with a mixture of pitted prunes and diced apricots.

KIDNEYS

For each serving, allow 1 veal kidney or 1½ lamb kidneys.

To prepare for cooking, split and remove the white tubes and the fat. Cover with cold water and let stand 30 minutes. Drain and pat dry with paper towel. Cook kidneys briefly—overcooking toughens them.

Broiled Kidneys. Dip in French dressing. Broil 10 minutes, turning frequently. Serve on toast. Season melted butter with salt, cayenne and lemon juice and pour over the kidneys.

Pan-broiled Kidneys. Cut in ¼-inch slices. Sprinkle with salt and pepper. Cook in butter until tender (about 5 minutes). Add a little lemon juice or wine to the butter in the pan and pour it over the kidneys.

Kidneys en Brochette. Cover with stock or consommé and cook 10 minutes. Drain, reserving the stock. Slice and arrange on skewers with squares of bacon, mushroom caps and quartered small tomatoes. Broil until the bacon is crisp, turning to cook evenly. Baste with French dressing several times. Serve with slices of lemon or with Brown Sauce (p. 97) made with the stock.

KIDNEY STEW

See also Steak and Kidney Pie (p. 175).

Prepare

1½ pounds veal *or* lamb kidneys

Cut veal kidneys in ½-inch slices. Split lamb kidneys. Roll in flour. Heat in a skillet

2 tablespoons bacon fat

Add and cook until onion is yellow

¼ cup chopped onion
1 clove garlic, split

Add the kidneys and cook and stir until lightly browned. Add

4 peppercorns *or* ¼ teaspoon pepper
½ teaspoon salt
1 can consommé
½ cup red wine *or* Madeira

Cover and simmer until the kidneys are tender (about 30 minutes). *Serves 4.*

To cook in a pressure saucepan. Brown the kidneys in the pressure pan and add the other ingredients as above. Put on the cover and cook 12 minutes at 15 pounds pressure. Turn off the heat and let the pressure drop to normal.

LIVER

Liver is an excellent source of Vitamin A, iron, copper, riboflavin, niacin and thiamine. It is marketed both fresh and frozen. Store fresh liver in the refrigerator, loosely wrapped, and use within 24 hours. Store frozen liver in the freezer and thaw in the refrigerator before cooking. Calves' liver is the most expensive, but young beef, pork and lamb liver are excellent and equally nutritious. One pound serves 4.

To prepare for cooking, wipe with a damp cloth and remove the thin outside skin and veins. If beef liver is tough, cover with boiling water, simmer 5 minutes, and drain.

Broiled Liver. Cut in slices ¼ to ½ inch thick. Broil 5 minutes. Spread with butter and sprinkle with salt and pepper.

Liver Sautéed in Butter. Sprinkle with salt and pepper. Dip in flour. Sauté in butter, allowing 2 tablespoons for 1 pound liver. Turn frequently. Cook ½-inch slices about 5 minutes (overcooking toughens liver) or until red color is gone. Serve with crisp bacon or add a little sour cream to juices in the pan, heat and pour over liver.

Liver and Bacon. Pan-fry bacon and drain on paper towel. Cook sliced liver (seasoned and dipped in flour) in bacon fat and serve with a piece of bacon on each slice.

LIVER VENETIAN STYLE

Popular even with those who think they don't like liver.

Heat in a skillet

2 tablespoons salad oil

Add

4 onions, sliced thin

Cook slowly until the onions are soft and golden. Add

1 pound liver, cut with scissors in matchlike pieces

Cook and stir until the liver is just browned (about 3 minutes). Season to taste with

Salt and pepper

Serves 4.

LIVER LOAF

Cover with hot water

1 pound beef liver

Simmer 5 minutes, drain, and reserve the stock. Chop the liver with

½ pound fresh pork
1 onion

Add

1 cup bread crumbs
1 egg, well beaten
1 teaspoon salt
¼ teaspoon pepper

2 tablespoons tomato catsup
Juice ½ lemon
Tomato juice *or* stock (p. 209) to moisten

Mix thoroughly. Line a loaf pan with

Bacon

Pack in the mixture. Lay bacon over the top. Bake 1 hour at 350°. Serve hot or cold. *Serves 6.*

LIVER PÂTÉ

Serve cold on a platter garnished with watercress and quartered tomatoes. Good, too, as an hors d'oeuvre with cocktails.

Cover

1 cup bread crumbs

with

Milk *or* consommé

Grind together, using fine knife

1 pound beef *or* calves' liver
3 slices bacon

Drain the crumbs, reserving the liquid, and add to the liver. Season to taste with

Salt, pepper, allspice and mixed spices

Stir in

1 egg

Mix thoroughly and add enough of the reserved liquid to make a smooth paste. Line a pan with

Bacon slices

Fill with the liver mixture. Bake 1 hour at 350°. Chill and turn out onto a serving dish. *Serves 6.*

SWEETBREADS

Sweetbreads are as tender and delicate as chicken and combine pleasantly with other ingredients. Veal sweetbreads are the most expensive, but lamb and beef sweetbreads are also good. They are marketed fresh or frozen. Use fresh sweetbreads promptly. Store frozen sweetbreads in the freezer. It is not necessary to thaw before cooking. One pound serves 4.

To prepare for cooking. Cover with boiling water. For each quart of water, add 1 teaspoon salt and 2 tablespoons vinegar or lemon juice. Cover and simmer 20 minutes. Drain. Cover with cold water and let stand until chilled. Drain. Slip off the thin membrane with the fingers and cut out the dark tubes and the thick membrane.

Sautéed Sweetbreads. Prepare (above). Pan-fry in melted butter until brown on all sides (about 5 minutes).

Braised Sweetbreads. Prepare (above). Cut in slices. Sauté. Cover with Brown Gravy (p. 164), canned or made with consommé (1 cup for each pound). Heat. Season with sherry. Add, if you like, sautéed mushrooms, cooked vegetables or sliced olives.

Broiled Sweetbreads. Prepare (above) and split. Brush with melted butter. Broil 5 minutes, turning once.

Sweetbreads en Brochette. Prepare (above). Cut in cubes and put on skewers, alternating with squares of bacon. Brush with melted butter or olive oil. Sprinkle with crumbs. Set the skewers on a cake tin so that the ends rest on the rim of the tin. Broil slowly 10 minutes or until the bacon is crisp, turning to brown evenly. Serve on the skewers or push off onto plates.

SWEETBREADS COUNTRY STYLE

Prepare sweetbreads (above). Split or slice. Sprinkle with salt, pepper and flour. Put in a casserole. Brush with melted butter, allowing 2 tablespoons to a pound of sweetbreads. Cover with thin slices of salt pork or bacon. Bake 25 minutes at 450°, basting twice during the cooking with the juices in the pan.

CREAMED SWEETBREADS

Sweetbreads are delicious in place of chicken in any of the variations of Creamed Chicken (p. 232).

Prepare sweetbreads (p. 210). Cut in small pieces. For 1 pound of sweetbreads, prepare 1 cup of Cream Sauce (p. 94) or Velouté Sauce (p. 96) and season it highly with meat extract such as B–V. Heat the sweetbreads in the sauce. Serve on toast, in patty shells or on thin slices of broiled or baked ham, or fill individual baking dishes, sprinkle with buttered crumbs and bake at 375° until the crumbs are brown.

Vary by doubling the amount of sauce and adding 1 cup cooked peas, sautéed mushrooms, asparagus tips, chopped ham or chicken. Sprinkle over the top toasted slivered almonds or buttered crumbs or toasted wheat germ. The sauce may be concentrated cream of mushroom or chicken soup, diluted with milk or cream.

SWEETBREAD AND SPINACH SOUFFLÉ

Substitute cooked sweetbreads for ham in Ham and Spinach Soufflé (p. 203).

TONGUE

Tongue is marketed in many ways—fresh, smoked, corned or pickled—to serve hot or cold. In cans or jars, it is a very convenient emergency shelf item. It is solid meat and yields 4 to 6 servings to the pound.

Follow directions on the wrapper in preparing smoked or pickled tongue.

To cook fresh tongue. Scrub with warm water. Cover with boiling water. Add 1 sliced onion, 2 bay leaves, 1 teaspoon salt, 6 peppercorns and 6 cloves. Cover and simmer until tender (2 to 4 hours, according to size). Drain, dip in cold water, slit the skin and peel it off. Cut off the bones and gristle at the thick end.

SLICED COLD TONGUE

Arrange thin slices of cooked or canned tongue on a platter. Garnish with watercress, cole slaw in lettuce cups, sliced tomatoes or stuffed olives. Other meats may be served with the tongue, such as sliced ham, chicken or cold roast meats. Serve with any of the sauces suggested for ham (p. 200) or with mustard, horseradish, currant jelly or sliced fruit.

SWEET AND SOUR TONGUE

An excellent dish for a buffet supper.

Put in a shallow pan

- **1 lemon, sliced paper-thin**
- **1 cup mild cider vinegar**
- **1 cup dark brown sugar**
- **12 ginger snaps, rolled**
- **1 bay leaf**
- **½ cup raisins**
- **1 cinnamon stick**
- **8 whole cloves**
- **⅓ cup blanched almonds, halved**
- **1 small onion, sliced thin**

Cook slowly 10 minutes. Add

- **1 cooked or canned beef tongue, cut in thin slices**

Heat thoroughly. *Serves 8 to 10.*

BRAISED TONGUE

Cook (above)

- **1 fresh tongue**

Reserve the liquid for the sauce.

Put the tongue in a deep pan. Add

1/3 cup diced carrot
1/3 cup diced celery
1/3 cup chopped onion
1 sprig parsley

Melt

4 tablespoons butter

Cook until brown. Add

4 tablespoons flour

Brown well. Add 4 cups of the reserved liquid (or part tomato juice). Stir well. Season with

Salt, pepper and Worcestershire

Pour over the tongue. Cover and bake 2 hours at 300°, turning after the first hour. Remove the tongue and put it on a hot platter. Strain the sauce (or not), and serve it with the tongue. *Serves 8 to 10.*

TONGUE-MUSHROOM CASSEROLE

Melt

2 tablespoons butter

Add

1 pound mushrooms, sliced

Cook 5 minutes. Add

2 cans undiluted mushroom soup

Heat. If you like a thinner sauce, add

A little water

Season to taste with

Nutmeg and sherry *or* brandy

Slice and put in a shallow baking dish

1 pound cooked *or* canned tongue

Cover with the sauce and keep warm in a 300° oven. *Serves 6.*

To vary the seasoning, add herbs instead of nutmeg.

TRIPE

There are three kinds of tripe—honeycomb (the choicest), pocket and smooth. It is marketed fresh, pickled or canned. Fresh and pickled tripe need further cooking. Use fresh tripe within 24 hours. Store it, covered, in the refrigerator. Canned tripe is ready to heat and serve. One pound serves 4 or 5.

Cover with cold water, bring to the boiling point and drain. Cover with boiling salted water. Simmer until tender (1 hour or more). For additional flavor, add, after the first half-hour, 1 clove garlic (split) or 1/4 cup chopped onion, a few sprigs parsley and 1/2 cup chopped celery. Drain, reserving the liquid. Serve with Tomato Sauce (p. 99) or Espagnole Sauce (p. 97) made with the reserved liquid.

Broiled Tripe. Cut cooked tripe in pieces for serving. Dip in fine cracker dust, then in olive oil or melted butter. Place, smooth side up, on the broiler rack 3 inches from the heat. Broil 5 minutes. Turn and broil until lightly browned (about 5 minutes). Serve, honeycomb side up, spread with butter and seasoned with salt and pepper. Good with broiled tomato slices and bacon as a mixed grill.

TRIPE LYONNAISE

Cook 5 minutes over moderate heat

2 tablespoons butter
1 tablespoon chopped onion

Add

1 pound cooked tripe, cut in pieces about 1/2 by 2 inches

Cook 5 minutes. Sprinkle with

Salt, pepper, lemon juice and chopped parsley

Serves 4.

TRIPE IN BATTER

Cut cooked fresh or pickled tripe (above) in 1 1/2-inch squares. Dip in batter (p. 213). Sauté in bacon fat or fry in deep fat at 370°. Serve with sliced lemon and chili sauce.

Batter for tripe. Sift 1 cup flour with 1/4 teaspoon salt and 1 teaspoon baking powder. Beat 1 egg, add 1/3 cup milk or water and 1 teaspoon salad oil or melted butter. Stir into the flour and beat until smooth.

WAYS TO USE COOKED OR CANNED MEATS

Cooked or canned meats can be presented in many appetizing ways. They are especially convenient for meals which must be made ready ahead of time with no last-minute tasks for the hostess. Cut the meat in neat, attractive pieces, free of bits of skin, fat, gristle and bone.

There are special recipes in the following section, but consider also suggestions such as Veal Tetrazzini (p. 195), which can be adapted to other meats, and general recipes such as:

- Rissoles (p. 458)
- Omelets (p. 111)
- Sandwiches (p. 358)
- Fashion Park Salad (p. 282)
- Filled Biscuits (p. 327)
- Stuffed Peppers (p. 264)
- Stuffed Tomatoes (p. 277)
- Stuffed Zucchini (p. 279)
- Scalloped Eggs (p. 107)
- Pilaf (p. 310)

ROAST BEEF HASH

Follow the recipe for Corned Beef Hash (p. 176), using chopped roast beef.

SLICED ROAST MEAT

Cut roast or canned meat in neat slices and serve cold, attractively garnished with watercress, sliced tomatoes or pickled fruits. Or heat gravy or tomato sauce piping hot and pour it over the meat. Do not warm meat in the gravy over high heat as that toughens it.

LAMB CARDINAL

Mix in a saucepan
- **1/4 cup tarragon vinegar**
- **1/4 cup currant jelly**
- **1/2 cup tomato catsup**

Add
- **1 cup cubed cooked or canned meat**

Simmer about 20 minutes and season to taste with
- **Salt and paprika *or* cayenne**

Serves 2 or 3.

Veal or Ham Cardinal. Substitute veal or ham for lamb.

LAMB MILANESE

Put a layer of well-seasoned chopped cooked spinach in a shallow baking dish. Put sliced cooked meat on the spinach. Pour Cheese Sauce (p. 95) over the meat. Bake at 350° until well heated and lightly browned (20 to 30 minutes).

Veal or Ham Milanese. Substitute veal or ham for lamb.

SAVORY MEAT *or* CHICKEN ROLL

Prepare
- **Baking Powder Biscuit dough, homemade (p. 326) or a mix**

Roll it into an oblong 1/4 inch thick. Mix
- **Chopped cooked chicken or meat (1 cup or more)**
- **Gravy *or* cream, to moisten**
- **Chopped onion, green pepper *or* olives**
- **Salt and pepper to taste**

Spread over the dough. Roll up and put in a buttered baking pan with the fold underneath. Bake at 425° until well browned (20 to 30 minutes). Cut in slices and serve with
- **Gravy *or* Mushroom Sauce (p. 98) *or* Tomato Sauce (p. 99)**

Serves 4 to 6.

RAGOUT OF BEEF, LAMB, PORK *or* VEAL

Vary by seasoning with claret or Marsala or by adding sliced sautéed mushrooms, tiny whole onions or sliced olives.

Heat
1½ cups Brown Sauce (p. 97) *or* gravy *or* 1 can undiluted mushroom *or* celery soup
Add
2 cups cubed cooked meat
Season to taste with
Worcestershire, onion juice and cayenne
Heat but do not let the sauce boil. *Serves 4.*

CASSEROLE OF MEAT PROVENÇALE

Cook and drain
2 to 4 ounces noodles
Melt
2 tablespoons fat
Add
½ cup sliced onion
½ cup diced green pepper
1 cup sliced mushrooms
Cook until tender. Add
1 to 2 cups cubed cooked meat
Cook slowly 10 minutes. Add
2 small tomatoes cut in pieces
1½ cups gravy
Heat. Season to taste with
Salt and pepper
Add the noodles. Put in a casserole. Sprinkle with
Grated cheese
Bake 30 minutes at 325° or 20 minutes at 375°. *Serves 3 to 6, according to the amount of meat and noodles used.*

BASIC CASSEROLE RECIPE

With this good basic recipe, you can create a tasty dish no matter what you have on hand in the way of cooked or canned meat, fish, chicken or turkey.

Cut in small, neat pieces
Cooked or canned meat, fish, chicken *or* turkey
Add to it an equal amount of
Cooked vegetable
Add also, if you like,
Cooked rice *or* diced boiled potato
Mix well and moisten with
Gravy, Cream Sauce (p. 94) *or* undiluted canned cream soup
If the mixture seems too thin, stir in
Bread crumbs *or* cracker crumbs
If it is too thick, add
Gravy, milk *or* tomato juice
Season to taste with
Salt and pepper
Or season more highly with
Onion juice *or* herbs
Spoon into a casserole. Put on the cover or sprinkle over the top
Buttered crumbs, crushed corn flakes *or* potato chips
Bake at 375° about 30 minutes.

COTTAGE PIE

Also called Shepherd's Pie.

Chop or cube cooked beef or lamb. Season with salt, pepper and onion juice or onion salt. Moisten with gravy. Put in a baking dish. Cover with a thin layer of mashed potato. Bake at 425° until thoroughly heated.

Beef, Lamb *or* Veal Creole. Add chopped green pepper and tomatoes, quartered. Arrange the mashed potato in a border in the baking dish.

MEAT PIE

Vary the amount of meat according to what you have on hand. Cooked vegetables are a tasty addition—mushrooms, peas, carrots, okra or green beans, for example.

Remove the fat from cooked meat. Cut the meat in neat

cubes. Cover with gravy, adding water or consommé if needed. Add, if you like, chopped onion, celery or parsley. Cook slowly until the meat is very tender. If the gravy is too thin, blend 2 tablespoons flour and ¼ cup water, stir it in, and cook and stir until smooth. Cover with a topping (below). Bake at 450° until brown (about 15 minutes).

Biscuit Topping. Cover with 2-inch rounds made from Baking Powder Biscuit dough (p. 326) or a mix. Or cover with packaged biscuits.

Pastry Topping. Roll out Plain Pastry (p. 438) or pastry mix. Cut to fit the top of the pie. Place on the pie and make slits to let out the steam. Or cut the pastry in strips and lay them over the pie. Or bake the top separately and put it on the heated pie when you serve it.

RICE AND MEAT LOAF

Melt
2 tablespoons butter
Stir in
2 tablespoons flour
Add
¾ cup gravy *or* consommé
Cook and stir until thick. Add
2 cups chopped cooked meat
3 tablespoons chili sauce
1 tablespoon chopped onion
Season more highly, if you like, with
Worcestershire *or* Tabasco
Cook and drain
¾ cup rice (1½ cups, cooked)
Spread half the rice in a well-greased loaf pan. Spread the meat over the rice. Cover with the rest of the rice. Press down firmly. Set in a pan of hot water ½ inch deep. Bake 40 minutes at 350°. Turn out on a platter and serve with
Tomato Sauce, homemade (p. 99) or canned
Serves 6.

MEAT CROQUETTES AND TIMBALES

Follow the recipe for Chicken Croquettes (p. 236) and Chicken Timbales (p. 235), using chopped cooked or canned meat. Season the mixture to taste, adding more parsley and onion or herbs, if you like.

Poultry and Game

Poultry can be prepared in so many ways that it is one of our most valuable foods. Eat it often because it is so delicious and also because it is a rich source of protein, iron, thiamine and riboflavin. It is available at popular prices throughout the year—fresh or frozen, whole or in parts.

Top-quality birds are plump, with broad meaty breasts. Young poultry has soft thin skin, older birds have coarse thick skin. Capons and caponettes are especially tender and meaty. Fowl is a good buy for salads and creamed dishes, but must be cooked by moist heat to become tender.

For each person to be served, buy 3/4 to 1 pound of chicken, guinea chicken or turkey, 1 to 1½ pounds of duck or goose, and 1 pigeon, squab or small Cornish game hen. Larger birds have more meat in proportion to bone and so are often a more economical buy.

Leftovers are no problem. There are many easy and delectable recipes using cooked chicken or turkey (pp. 232–237).

Modern markets sell poultry ready to cook, so that the old and tedious task of plucking and cleaning a bird is over for most of us. However, the United States Department of Agriculture and State Extension Services have bulletins describing the process and also telling how to cut up a bird for fricasseeing or broiling. Poultry shears are a convenience for cutting poultry in pieces.

Game birds include grouse, partridge, pheasant, wild duck, wild goose, quail, snipe and plover. The flesh of game birds, except partridge and quail, is dark in color, and all, except some wild ducks and geese, contain less fat than domestic poultry.

Rabbit is included here because it is cooked like chicken. Young and tender rabbits, domesticated or wild, have soft ears and paws, short necks and smooth sharp claws.

TO PREPARE POULTRY FOR COOKING

If all the feathers have not been removed, pull them out with tweezers or a small sharp knife and burn off the fine hairs over the gas flame or with burning paper. Remove every particle of the lungs (red, spongy bits along the backbone). Cut out the small oil bag at the base of the tail.

Let cold water run through the bird, but do not soak it in water. Wipe inside and outside, looking carefully to see that everything has been withdrawn. If there is a slightly stale odor, freshen the bird by washing inside and out with soda water (1 teaspoon baking soda to 1 cup water).

If the giblets have not been cleaned at the market, remove the thin membrane, the arteries, veins and clotted blood around the heart. Separate the gall bladder from the liver, cutting off and discarding any of the liver which has a greenish tinge. Cut the fat and membranes from the gizzard. Make a gash through the thickest part of the gizzard, and cut as far as the inner lining, being careful not to pierce it. Remove the inner sack and discard it. Wash the giblets.

TO STUFF POULTRY

Stuffing recipes are on pages 82–85. Packaged stuffings are convenient and good. Prepare the stuffing the day before, if you like, but do not stuff the bird until just before you roast it.

Put the stuffing into the neck opening by spoonfuls, using enough to fill the skin so that the bird will look plump when served. Cracker stuffing expands during cooking, so fill more loosely. Put the rest of the stuffing in the body. Sew the opening together or fasten with skewers and lace with string.

TO TRUSS POULTRY

Draw the thighs close to the body. Tie firmly to the tail with string. Lace the string along the skewers and tie. Place the wings close to the body and hold them in place with a long skewer. Draw the neck skin under the back and fasten it with a toothpick. To keep a large capon or turkey firm during roasting, insert a long skewer under the middle joint, run it through the body and under the middle joint on the other side.

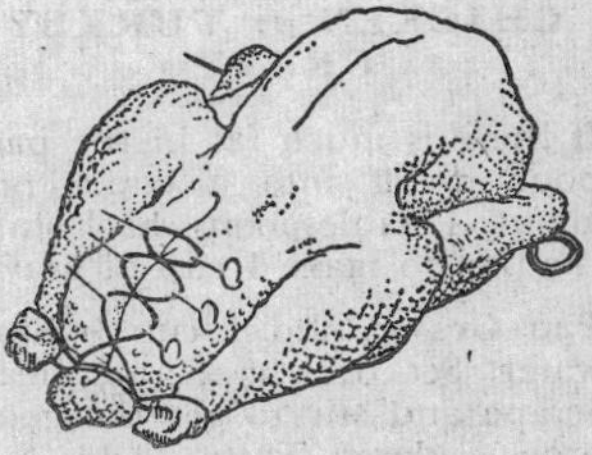

ROAST CHICKEN *or* CAPON

Allow ¾ to 1 pound as purchased per person.

Select a plump, meaty bird for roasting, either a young roasting chicken or a capon. Clean (details p. 216), stuff and truss (above). Allow about 4 cups of stuffing for a 4-pound chicken. Celery (p. 83), Corn Bread (p. 82) and Savory Mushroom Stuffing (p. 83) are particularly delicious for chicken.

Place, breast side up, on a rack in an open roasting pan. Rub the skin with soft butter or salad oil. Put over the bird a piece of aluminum foil large enough to cover it loosely. Do not let the foil touch the heating unit in an electric oven.

Roast at 325° until tender. Test by moving the drumstick gently. When the bird is done, the joint will move easily. A 3-pound chicken will take about 2½ hours, a 4-pound chicken about 3 hours, and a 6-pound chicken about 4. Half an hour before the roasting time is up, turn back the foil so that the skin will brown prettily.

Keep the bird warm while you make the gravy. It will be easier to carve if it stands 20 minutes or so after roasting.

CHICKEN *or* TURKEY GRAVY

If there is much fat in the pan, pour it off into a cup. Pour about 4 tablespoons back into the pan to make 1 cup of gravy.

Pan Gravy. Add 1 cup boiling water. Set over moderate heat. Scrape and stir to get the good brown glaze. Taste. Add salt and pepper, if needed. Strain.

Thickened Gravy. Stir in 2 tablespoons flour. Set the pan over moderate heat and stir and scrape until the flour and fat are smoothly blended and nicely browned. Add 1 cup cold water, milk or cream. Cook and stir until smooth. Season to taste. Strain or not, as you prefer.

Giblet Gravy. Cover the giblets, neck and wing tips with cold water. Add ½ teaspoon salt. Bring quickly to the boiling point. Cook until the giblets are tender. Discard the neck and wings. Cut the giblets small. Drain off the stock to use in making thickened gravy (above). Add the giblets to the finished gravy.

TO CARVE CHICKEN *or* TURKEY

Place the bird on the platter, breast up. Set before the carver with the bird's legs to his right. Insert the carving fork across the breastbone, hold it firmly in the left hand, and with the carving knife in the right hand cut through the skin between the leg and body, close to the body. Hold the leg by the bone and pull it away from the body. Find the joint with the tip of the knife and cut through it. Cut through the joint which separates the drumstick from the second joint. Cut off the wing.

Carve the breast meat in thin slices. Just above the tail, on

each side of the backbone, are two small, oyster-shaped pieces of dark meat, which are delicious tidbits. For a small family, carve one side completely, leaving the other side untouched so that it will look just as attractive for serving the second day.

HERBED ROAST CHICKEN

This French method of roasting is delicious. Vary it by using dill in place of thyme.

Prepare for roasting
- **2½- to 3-pound chicken**

Put in the chicken
- **1 carrot, sliced**
- **1 teaspoon thyme**
- **⅓ teaspoon salt**
- **1 tablespoon butter**

Tie or skewer the legs and wings to the body. Put the chicken in a shallow roasting pan. Lay over the breast
- **3 slices bacon**

Dot the chicken with
- **2 tablespoons butter**

Dust with
- **Salt, paprika and thyme**

Roast at 450° until lightly browned (about 15 minutes). Reduce the heat to 350° and roast until tender (about 1¾ hours). Mix

½ cup beef bouillon
¼ cup water

Spoon some over the chicken every 15 minutes during the cooking. Put the roasted chicken on a hot platter and remove the skewers or string. To the drippings in the pan add

Juice of 1 lemon

Scrape and stir, heat, season to taste, and serve as a sauce with the chicken. *Serves 4.*

ROAST TURKEY

Allow 1 pound per person. This is a generous amount which will usually provide leftovers for another meal.

New breeds have been developed so that you can buy a meaty turkey even if you buy a small one. A hen turkey has more breast meat than a tom. A half turkey is often an economy buy. Roast it cut side down. Thaw frozen turkeys to room temperature overnight before stuffing.

Stuff and truss (p. 217). Allow 8 cups of stuffing for a 10-pound turkey. Use any of the following:

- Bread Stuffing (p. 82)
- New England Stuffing (p. 83)
- Giblet Stuffing (p. 83)
- Celery Stuffing (p. 83)
- Oyster Stuffing (p. 83)
- Sausage and Chestnut Stuffing (p. 85)
- Apple and Prune Stuffing (p. 84)
- Chestnut Stuffing (p. 84)

Follow directions for roasting chicken (p. 217). Carving will be easier if the roasting is finished a half-hour before serving time. Set the roasted turkey in a warm place while you make the gravy (p. 218).

TIMETABLE FOR ROASTING TURKEYS AT 325°

Weight in pounds	*Hours*
4 to 6	3 to 4
8 to 12	4 to 4½
12 to 16	4½ to 5
16 to 20	6 to 8
20 to 24	8 to 9

ROAST DUCK

Allow at least 1 pound per person.

Roast with a stuffing or not; either way is good. Apple (p. 83) and Onion Stuffing (p. 83) are excellent with duck. Instead of stuffing, put inside 2 cored and quartered apples or a handful of celery leaves. It is not necessary to truss ducks as they have short legs and wings.

Place on a rack in an open roasting pan. Roast at 325° until tender (about 30 minutes per pound). Do not baste, since ducks are fat. Prick in several places so that some of the fat will drain off. Turn often to brown evenly. Pour off the fat as it accumulates. Serve with Gravy (p. 218) or with Olive Sauce (p. 98). Traditional with duck are Applesauce, Stewed or Brandied Apples (pp. 366–367). Also a tart jelly such as currant or cranberry.

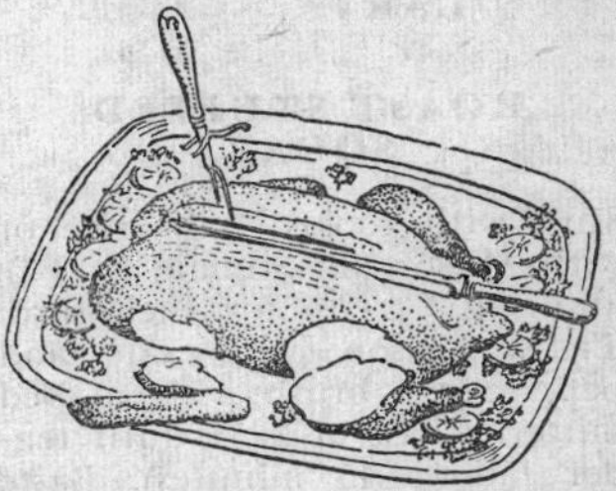

To carve roast duck. Cut off the legs and wings. Slice the breast meat at right angles to the surface.

Roast Duck Bigarade. Put a sliced orange in the duck. Make the gravy with one-third orange juice and two-thirds water. Cook the peel of 1 orange in boiling water 3 minutes, drain, scrape out the white pulp, cut the peel in thin strips and add to the gravy. Season to taste. Garnish the platter with thin slices of orange.

Salmi of Duck. Cut roast duck in pieces for serving. Reheat in Spanish Sauce (p. 97).

ROAST GOOSE

Allow 1 pound or more per person as there is much bone and fat in proportion to the meat.

Stuff (preparing 8 cups stuffing for 10-pound goose). Use Bread (p. 82), Apple (p. 83) or Apple and Prune Stuffing (p. 84). Roast like Roast Duck (p. 219).

Wild Goose. Do not stuff. Put celery leaves inside. Allow 3 hours or more, as wild geese are often old and very tough.

ROAST GUINEA HEN

Roast like Roast Chicken (p. 217).

ROAST STUFFED SQUAB

Stuff with cooked wild rice or with Mushroom Stuffing (p. 83), allowing ⅓ cup for each bird. Truss. Season with salt and pepper and brush with melted butter. Roast at 325° until tender (about 45 minutes). Baste frequently with ⅓ cup butter melted in ⅔ cup boiling water or with melted currant jelly.

ROAST GAME BIRDS

Prepare for roasting. Tie the legs together and fasten close to the body with skewers. Do not stuff, but sprinkle inside with salt. Serve on toast. Garnish with watercress.

Duck. Stuff with sliced apple, onion or celery tops. Put slices of bacon or fat salt pork over the breast. Roast at 450° for 12 minutes for very rare duck with the juice still red. For well-done duck, roast at 350° for 15 minutes to the pound. Baste frequently during the roasting with melted butter, red wine or a mixture of the two.

Grouse, Quail *or* Partridge. Brush with butter. Roast at 350° until tender (12 to 20 minutes). Baste 3 times with melted butter during roasting.

Pheasant. Put strips of bacon over the breast. Roast 30 to 40 minutes at 350° (or longer if you like pheasant well done). Remove the bacon.

BROILED CHICKEN

Allow ½ or ¼ chicken per person, depending on the size of the bird.

Order young chicken split or quartered for broiling. Preheat the broiler oven to 550°. Place the broiler rack so that the top of the chicken will be 4 inches from the heat. Place the chicken on the rack, skin side down. Sprinkle with salt and pepper. Brush with salad oil or melted butter or other fat. Broil 10 minutes. Turn over, brush with fat, and broil 10 minutes. Turn again and continue cooking until the chicken is very tender (35 to 60 minutes in all, depending on size of chicken). Dot with butter 3 times during broiling.

Put on a hot platter. Pour the drippings from the pan over the chickens.

To vary flavor. Sprinkle each broiler with a few drops of onion juice and a few grains of ginger before broiling, or spread sparingly with anchovy paste mixed with a little prepared mustard, or slice ripe olives over chickens.

Sally's Broiled Chicken. Broil on each side only long enough to brown, then transfer to a baking pan. Add enough water or chicken stock to the pan to keep the chicken from burning. Dot with butter or put strips of bacon on each piece of chicken. Cover. Bake at 300° until tender (30 minutes or longer). Baste several times with the liquid in the pan. The chicken will be very tender.

Orange Broiled Chicken. Make a basting sauce of ½ cup orange juice, ½ cup salad oil, 3 tablespoons grated orange rind, and salt, mustard, paprika and Tabasco to taste. Brush the chickens with it before broiling and when you turn them. Baste with the sauce several times during broiling.

DELMONICO'S DEVILED CHICKEN

Broil the chicken 8 minutes (p. 220). For each broiler, cream 4 tablespoons butter with 1 teaspoon prepared mustard, ½ teaspoon salt, 1 teaspoon vinegar and ½ teaspoon paprika. Spread over the bird. Put in a baking pan. Sprinkle with ¾ cup soft buttered crumbs. Bake at 350° until the chicken is tender and the crumbs are brown (about 30 minutes).

BARBECUED BROILERS

Allow ½ broiler or ¼ (or more) frying chicken per person.

Broiler halves or quartered frying chickens are tasty and tender cooked this way. Dip each piece in Chicken Barbecue Sauce (p. 93) and put them on the grill, skin side up. Turn about every 8 minutes. Each time you turn them, brush a little of the sauce over them. They will be done in about 45 minutes. To test, take hold of the leg bone and twist slightly. If the joint moves easily, the chicken is done.

OVEN-BROILED CHICKEN (Fat-free)

Put pieces of chicken in a shallow baking dish in a single layer, skin side up. Cover tightly with a piece of heavy aluminum foil. Bake 30 minutes at 325°. Remove the foil and broil the chicken two inches from the heat until it is browned (about 15 minutes). Sprinkle with salt, pepper and, if you like, a little ginger.

For a crisp topping, sprinkle the chicken before broiling with toasted wheat germ.

BROILED DUCKLINGS

Use the same directions for guinea hens, squabs and turkey broilers.

Follow directions for Broiled Chicken (p. 220). Turkey broilers are cut in quarters for broiling.

BROILED GAME BIRDS

Game birds (quail, plover, young pheasant, partridge, grouse, young duck) tend to be dry, so rub well with butter or oil and baste often during broiling. Split and broil like chicken (p. 201), allowing 8 to 20 minutes according to size.

BARBECUED CHICKEN

For outdoor cooking.

Take the bird out of the refrigerator 2 or 3 hours before cooking. Truss securely. Rub all over with fat or oil. Put on a revolving spit or turn often during cooking. Roast over hot coals about 30 minutes to the pound, basting often with Herbed Barbecue Sauce (p. 94).

Barbecued Caponette *or* **Turkey** may be cooked the same way.

FRIED CHICKEN

Order young broilers cut in halves, fryers or small young roasting chicken cut in serving-size pieces. Dip in cold water or milk. Drain but do not wipe dry. Sprinkle with salt and pepper. Coat with flour by shaking in a paper bag with about ½ cup flour.

Melt fat in a heavy frying pan to a depth of ½ to 1 inch. For delicious flavor use ⅓ butter and ⅔ olive oil, lard or vegetable fat, but any cooking fat or salad oil is satisfactory. Heat fat well but not so hot that it smokes.

Put in the chicken. Brown quickly on all sides. Cook until tender (30 minutes to 1 hour, depending on the size of the bird). **For a crisp crust,** cover, cook half the required time, and remove the cover for the last half of cooking. **For a tender crust,** cook uncovered half the time, then cover to finish cooking.

Southern Fried Chicken. Dip pieces of chicken in batter (p. 409). Or, for a very crisp crust, dip in water or milk, then coat as thickly as possible with flour to which has been added baking powder (½ teaspoon to each cup of flour). Have the fat 1½ to 2 inches deep.

Maryland Fried Chicken. Dip floured chicken in slightly beaten egg mixed with 2 tablespoons cold water, then in soft bread crumbs. Have the fat 1½ to 2 inches deep.

Baked Crisp Chicken. Brown the chicken quickly on both sides. Place in a single layer in a baking dish. Brush generously with melted butter or salad oil. Bake at 350° until tender (about 40 minutes). After the first 15 minutes, brush with butter or oil and again when the chicken is ready to serve.

FRIED CHICKEN (In Deep Fat)

Sprinkle chicken halves (if very small) or quarters with salt and pepper. Dip in Fritter Batter (p. 409). Fry until golden-brown in deep fat heated to 350° (about 15 minutes). Drain on a paper towel.

For very tender chicken, but not as crisp, fry only 10 minutes, drain, put on a rack in a baking pan, cover, and bake 1 hour at 325°.

SAUCES FOR FRIED CHICKEN

Chicken Gravy (p. 218), made with chicken stock and cream or tomato juice.

Cream Gravy (*traditional with Southern Fried Chicken*). Use half milk and half cream as the liquid.

Hungarian Sauce. Cook 2 sliced onions in 4 tablespoons butter until yellow, stir in 1 tablespoon flour, ½ teaspoon salt and 1 tablespoon paprika. Stir in 1 cup sour cream and cook until smooth.

SAVORY FRIED CHICKEN

Dip in flour
  2 young chickens, cut in pieces
Fry in oil (p. 222). Put the pieces in a casserole and cover with
  ¼ cup chopped onion
  ¼ cup chopped celery
  1 tablespoon chopped green pepper
  1½ cups milk, tomatoes *or* tomato juice
Sprinkle with
  Salt and pepper
  Oregano *or* thyme, if liked
Cover and bake 1 hour at 325°. Uncover and bake 10 minutes longer. *Serves 4 or 5.*

Fried Chicken with Mushrooms. Slice and sauté ½ pound mushrooms and add to the casserole 20 minutes before the chicken is done.

SAUTÉED CHICKEN *or* TURKEY BREASTS

One pound serves 2 or 3.

Cut chicken breasts in half, turkey breasts in serving-size pieces. Pound to flatten slightly. Sprinkle with salt and pepper. Roll in flour and sauté in butter or salad oil until delicately browned. Cover and cook slowly until tender. Or put in a baking pan and dot with 2 tablespoons butter. Cover with foil and bake at 375° until tender (about 20 minutes).

Pressure-cooked. Brown in butter or bacon fat in a pressure saucepan. Season with salt and pepper. Add ¼ cup boiling water. Bring to 15 pounds pressure and cook 5 minutes. Let the pressure drop normally. Add ½ cup cream to the juices and pour over the fillets.

Suprême of Chicken. Serve on cutlet-shaped pieces of hot broiled ham. Garnish the top of each with 3 asparagus tips or a large broiled mushroom cap. Surround with Suprême Sauce (p. 96).

Chicken Lake Como. After dipping in flour, dip in slightly beaten egg mixed with 1 tablespoon water, then in ¼ cup grated Parmesan cheese mixed with ½ cup dry bread crumbs. Sauté the chicken and serve on a layer of chopped spinach seasoned with lemon juice and nutmeg. Add a little cream or wine to the juices in the pan, heat and pour over the chicken.

SMOTHERED CHICKEN

Most of the interesting foreign ways of cooking chicken are based on browning fryers or young roasting chickens in oil or fat, then adding a liquid and cooking slowly until tender. The liquid may be water, sour cream, stock, wine, tomato juice, or a mixture of several. Seasonings vary as well. Mexican chicken emphasizes pimientos. Italian recipes use herbs, tomatoes and garlic. Thoughtful seasoning of the sauce makes each dish distinctive.

Any one of these is excellent party fare, since you can prepare the chicken in advance and keep it warm in a casserole. Serving is simple too, and you need only to add a tossed salad and crusty rolls or French bread for an interesting and savory meal.

If you have a freezer, you may like to brown several chickens at a time, using more than one pan. It is almost as simple to watch four pans at a time as one! Browned chickens will be ready to finish in any of the ways suggested.

Select split broilers or fryers or young roasting chickens cut in pieces. Sprinkle with salt, pepper and flour. Melt butter or salad oil in a heavy pan, using about ½ cup for 2 broilers. Put in the pieces of chicken and brown well on all sides. Cover and cook slowly until tender (30 to 60 minutes).

Smothered Chicken with Sour Cream. Take the cooked chicken out of the pan. To the juices in the pan add sour cream (1 cup for 2 broilers). Stir well. Heat quickly, season to taste, and pour over the chicken.

Smothered Chicken Swedish Style. Omit the butter. Sprinkle the chicken sparingly with flour and cook in 1 cup heavy cream (adding more cream if needed, while browning). Serve with gravy made with 3 tablespoons of the fat remaining in the pan, 3 tablespoons flour, 1½ cups chicken stock and ½ cup heavy cream.

CHICKEN À LA CONTADINE

Put in a large pan

2 onions, chopped fine
½ cup butter *or* salad oil

Cook slowly until the onions are soft. Add

2 young chickens, quartered

Cook slowly until the chickens are browned. Remove the pieces of chicken and add

½ cup Italian vermouth

Light with a match, and when the flame dies down, add

1 teaspoon tomato paste
⅛ teaspoon cinnamon
1 teaspoon salt

Stir well, add the chicken, cover, and cook slowly until tender (30 to 60 minutes). *Serves 6.*

CHICKEN ALLA CACCIATORA

A famous Italian dish with many possible variations. Add chopped green peppers, mushrooms or pimientos, if you like. Add rosemary, thyme, a bit of bay leaf or chopped parsley to vary the seasoning.

Have ready

2 young chickens, quartered, *or* 4-pound chicken, cut in pieces

Sprinkle with

Salt, pepper and flour

Brown lightly in

4 tablespoons olive *or* salad oil, butter *or* chicken fat

Take the chicken out of the pan. To the juices in the pan add

1 large onion, chopped fine
1 stalk celery, chopped fine
1 clove garlic

Stir and cook until the onion is yellow. Add the chicken and

¼ teaspoon sugar
Pinch of allspice *or* cinnamon
¼ cup sherry *or* ½ cup red wine

Cook and stir 5 minutes. Remove the garlic. Add

1 cup tomato juice *or* 3 tomatoes, cut in pieces

Cover and cook slowly until the chicken is tender (40 to 60 minutes). If necessary, add more liquid from time to time, using

Chicken broth, tomato juice *or* water

Season to taste. *Serves 6.*

CHICKEN MARENGO

Have ready

4-pound chicken, cut in pieces

Sprinkle with

Salt, pepper and flour

Brown in

4 tablespoons olive *or* salad oil

Take the chicken out of the pan and set aside. Cook in the pan juices

1 chopped onion
½ clove garlic

Add the pieces of chicken and

¼ cup dry white wine
½ cup stewed *or* chopped fresh tomatoes
8 mushrooms

Cover closely and cook slowly until tender (40 to 60 minutes). *Serves 6.*

COQ AU VIN

Melt in a large pan

¼ pound butter

Dredge with flour

5-pound roasting chicken, cut in serving pieces

Add to the butter and brown thoroughly. Put the chicken and juices in a large casserole. Add

½ cup chopped ham
10 small white onions
1 crushed clove garlic
¼ teaspoon thyme
1 sprig parsley
1 bay leaf
8 whole mushrooms
Salt and pepper to taste

Pour over the chicken

2 ounces warm cognac

Light the cognac with a match. When the flame dies down add

1 cup red wine

Cover. Bake at 275° until the chicken is tender (about 2½ hours). *Serves 6.*

MEXICAN CHICKEN

Have ready

2 young chickens, cut in pieces

Sprinkle with

Salt and pepper

Brown in

3 tablespoons oil *or* chicken fat

Add

1 teaspoon salt
8 canned pimientos, puréed
1 chopped onion
2 crushed cloves garlic
Boiling water to cover

Cover and cook until the chicken is tender (about 1 hour). Put the chicken on a serving dish. Cook together until smooth

3 tablespoons butter
3 tablespoons flour

Thicken the juices in the pan with this mixture and pour over the chicken. *Serves 6.*

CHOP SUEY

Specialty shops and Chinese groceries sell water chestnuts, bamboo shoots, soy sauce and Chinese almonds.

Cube the lean meat from

2 pork chops

Prepare

2 cups cubed cooked *or* raw chicken

Heat in a heavy frying pan

¼ cup peanut oil

Add the meat and stir over low heat until the meat is white (about 10 minutes). Add

½ cup chicken stock *or* water
1 cup celery, in julienne strips
½ teaspoon thin soy sauce
½ teaspoon sugar
Salt to taste

Cover and cook slowly until the celery is tender but still crisp. Mix

1 teaspoon cornstarch
½ cup chicken stock *or* water

Stir into the pan. Bring to the boiling point and add

1½ cups water chestnuts, sliced paper-thin
1½ cups bamboo shoots, in julienne strips

Cover and heat well. Season to taste. Serve with

Chinese almonds
Chinese fried noodles (canned)

Serves 6.

CHINESE CHICKEN

One secret of fine Chinese cooking is to cut everything small, so that it cooks rapidly and is still crisp and fresh when served.

Cut in matchlike pieces the meat from

6 raw chicken breasts

Cook slowly until the meat is white in

¼ cup butter *or* salad oil

Add

1 cup sliced water chestnuts
1 cup bamboo shoots
2 cups sliced celery
½ pound green beans, slivered
3 cups boiling chicken broth *or* stock
¼ cup soy sauce
2 teaspoons salt
2 teaspoons monosodium glutamate
1 teaspoon sugar
1 teaspoon pepper

Cover and cook 5 minutes. Taste and add more salt, if necessary. Mix with a little of the broth

2 tablespoons cornstarch

Pour it into the pan and stir until the sauce thickens. *Serves 6 to 8.*

Chinese Chicken with Nuts. Sauté 1 cup Chinese almonds or walnut meats quickly in butter and scatter over the finished dish.

HAWAIIAN CHICKEN

Canned or cooked chicken may be prepared this way, too.

Heat in a frying pan

1 tablespoon salad oil

Add

1 cup uncooked rice

Stir until the rice is brown. Put into a 2-quart casserole. Stir in

1¼ cups chicken broth *or* stock

Cover and bake 1 hour at 350° (adding a little broth if the rice dries). Put in the frying pan

2 tablespoons salad oil

Add

1½ cups uncooked chicken, cut in small strips

Cook and stir until the chicken is white. Add

2 cups sliced celery
1 cup coarsely chopped onion
½ cup coarsely chopped green pepper
1 tablespoon soy sauce

Heat

1 cup syrup from a can of pineapple

Dissolve in this

1 chicken bouillon cube

Add to the chicken, cover and simmer 5 minutes. Mix this into the rice. Put over the top

Pineapple slices

Heat thoroughly in the oven. *Serves 6.*

BOILED CHICKEN *or* CAPON

In a salad, boiled chicken is less dry than roast chicken. It is also delicious served hot with a sauce.

Truss but do not stuff. Put in a deep kettle. Add boiling water to half cover the bird. Cover and simmer until tender (2 to 3 hours). Turn occasionally. Add salt the last hour of cooking. Drain, reserving the liquid to use in the sauce or in soup.

Chicken à la Providence. Remove the cooked chicken and boil the liquid until it is reduced to 2 cups. Thicken with 2 tablespoons each of butter and flour cooked together. Just before serving, stir in 2 egg yolks, slightly beaten, and 1 teaspoon lemon juice. Season with salt, pepper and nutmeg.

Place the chicken on a hot platter, pour the sauce around it, and sprinkle with chopped parsley. Carve like roast chicken. If you like, add to the sauce sliced sautéed mushrooms or ½ cup cubed cooked carrots and ½ cup cooked peas.

Herbed Chicken. Add to the cooking water ½ onion, sliced, 1 small carrot, cubed, 2 sprigs thyme, 1 sprig parsley and 1 bay leaf.

CHICKEN FRICASSEE

Browning the chicken first improves both flavor and appearance, but many cooks omit this step. For the most appetizing flavor, make the fricassee the day before you serve it.

Melt in a deep pan
4 tablespoons fat
Add
5-pound stewing chicken, cut for fricassee
Brown the pieces evenly on all sides, adding more fat if necessary. Add
Boiling water to cover
½ small onion, sliced
Few stalks *or* tops celery
1 small carrot, sliced
Bay leaf
3 peppercorns *or* ⅛ teaspoon pepper
Cover and simmer over low heat until the chicken is tender when tried with a fork (1½ hours or more). Add, after the chicken has cooked 45 minutes
2 teaspoons salt
Remove from the heat and let stand until the fat collects on the surface. Spoon off the fat and set it aside. Remove the chicken and keep it warm. Melt
4 tablespoons chicken fat
Blend in
4 tablespoons flour
Add slowly, stirring constantly
2 cups chicken broth *or* broth and milk *or* cream
Heat to the boiling point, stirring so that it will thicken evenly. Season to taste with
Salt and pepper
Few drops Worcestershire *or* lemon juice, if liked
Pour some of the sauce over the chicken and pass the rest in a bowl. Serve with hot Baking Powder Biscuits (p. 326), Dumplings (p. 173), toast, fluffy rice or mashed potatoes. *Serves 6.*

For a richer sauce, beat 1 or 2 egg yolks slightly, add ½ cup cream, and stir in just before serving.

Chicken Fricassee with Mushrooms. Add 1 cup sliced sautéed mushrooms or put a row of sautéed mushroom caps around the platter.

Chicken Fricassee with Meat Balls. Mix ½ pound chopped beef with 1 slice bread (½ inch thick) soaked in water, ½ teaspoon salt, few drops onion juice and a few grains of ginger. Form into small balls. Bring the sauce to the boiling point, add the meat balls, cover closely, turn off the heat, and let stand 15 minutes. Reheat, if necessary.

CHICKEN PIE

Follow the recipe for Chicken Fricassee (above) without browning the chicken. Before making the sauce, remove the skin and bones from the pieces of chicken. Put the chicken in a baking dish not more than 3 inches deep. Add cooked vegetables, if you like, such as potato balls, peas or carrots, and pour the sauce over the chicken. Cool to room temperature but do not chill.

Roll out Plain Pastry (p. 438). Cut a piece to fit the top of the casserole and make cuts in it to let out the steam as the pie bakes. Lay it over the pie or cover the pie with crisscross strips of pastry. Bake extra pastry in rounds or diamonds to serve with second helpings.

Bake 10 minutes at 450°. Reduce the heat to 350° and bake 15 minutes longer or until the pastry is a delicate brown. *Serves 6.*

Louisburg Chicken Pie. Add 12 mushroom caps, sliced and sautéed in butter, ½ pound sausage meat, made into tiny balls and sautéed, and 1 cup tiny potato balls, cooked. *Serves 8.*

Chicken Pie Country Style. Instead of a pastry top, cover with Baking Powder Biscuit mixture (p. 326) rolled ½ inch thick. Cut a 2-inch round from the center to allow the steam to escape during the baking. Biscuit mixture may be cut in small rounds and placed close together over the top of the pie. Bake extra biscuits for second servings. Bake at 450° until brown (15 to 20 minutes).

CHICKEN CASSEROLE

Cut in pieces for serving
2 small chickens
Put in a casserole. Sprinkle with
Salt and pepper
Melted butter
Add boiling water until 1 inch deep. Cover. Bake at 375° until tender (1 hour or more). Pour over the chicken
1 cup chicken gravy, cream *or* undiluted canned mushroom *or* chicken soup
Cook 10 minutes. Season to taste. *Serves 4 or 5.*

To vary, add sliced sautéed mushrooms or strips of pimiento.

Chicken and Vegetable Casserole. After baking ½ hour, add young whole carrots, peas, potato balls or whole green beans, or a combination of several vegetables. Parboil carrots, potatoes and beans 10 minutes before adding to the casserole.

SQUABS EN CASSEROLE

Truss squabs. Put in a casserole. Brush with melted butter. Cover. Bake 10 minutes at 375°. Add chicken stock (½ cup for 2 or 3 squabs). Cover, reduce heat to 325° and cook until the squabs are tender (about 45 minutes). When they are almost tender, add any cooked vegetables you like—potato balls, whole green beans, tiny carrots, onions or asparagus tips. Malaga grapes are delicious with squab. Split, seed and add 5 minutes before squabs are done.

CHICKEN AND ONION STEW

Put in a large pan
1 chicken, cut for fricassee
12 tiny onions
Barely cover with water. Cover and cook slowly until tender (1 to 1½ hours). Take the chicken and onions out of the stock and keep them warm. Boil the stock until it is reduced to one cup. Melt
1 tablespoon butter *or* chicken fat
Add
2 tablespoons flour
Stir in slowly the stock and
½ cup heavy cream
Just before serving, add
1 egg yolk, slightly beaten
Salt and pepper to taste
Lemon juice to taste
Heat thoroughly and pour the sauce over the chicken and onions. *Serves 4 or 5.*

For a more savory stew, add chopped parsley, chopped celery and a pinch of thyme or marjoram.

BRUNSWICK STEW

This famous Southern dish can be varied many ways. It is often made in huge quantities for an out-of-doors get-together and can be made of squirrel and rabbit as well as stewing chicken. Sometimes pork spareribs and pieces of stewing beef are cooked with the chicken, and other vegetables are added, such as green beans, okra, diced potatoes and peas.

Cover with boiling water
1 stewing chicken, cut in pieces

Cover and simmer until tender (about $1\frac{1}{2}$ hours). After cooking 45 minutes, add

2 teaspoons salt

Take out the pieces of chicken. Remove the bones and cut the meat in 1-inch pieces. Put back in the kettle. Add

1 can condensed tomato soup,
3 tomatoes *or* 1 cup canned tomatoes
1 onion, sliced thin
1 cup green lima beans
3 potatoes, sliced thin
1 tablespoon sugar
Salt and pepper

Cook until the beans and potatoes are tender. Add

1 cup corn, cut from the cob *or* canned whole-kernel corn
¼ pound butter

Cook 5 minutes. *Serves 6 to 8.*

HUNGARIAN CHICKEN PAPRIKA

Cook together 10 minutes

1 tablespoon chicken fat *or* butter
3 red onions, cut fine

Stir in

1 tablespoon paprika

Cook until red. Add

1 young roasting chicken, cut in pieces *or* 2 broilers, quartered
1 teaspoon vinegar
¼ teaspoon sugar
Salt to taste

Cover and cook slowly 20 minutes. Sprinkle with

2 teaspoons flour

Add

½ cup chicken stock *or* tomato juice

Cover and cook slowly until the chicken is tender (20 to 30 minutes), adding more stock or water if necessary to keep the chicken from sticking. Remove the chicken and take off the skin. Strain the sauce. Add the pieces of chicken. Stir in

½ cup sour cream

Reheat. Season to taste. *Serves 4 to 6.*

VIENNESE CHICKEN

Cook together in a large pan

2 tablespoons butter
1 minced onion

When the onion is yellow, add

1 roasting chicken, cut in serving pieces

Cook until the chicken is brown, turning to brown evenly. Add

1 green pepper, chopped
2 carrots, chopped
6 mushrooms, chopped
1 fresh tomato *or* ¼ cup canned tomatoes
1 cup water
Salt

Cover and simmer until tender (about 1 hour). Mix together

1 tablespoon flour
½ cup sour cream

Stir it into the chicken and sauce. Cook and stir 3 minutes. *Serves 6.*

CHICKEN CALIFORNIAN

For added zest, add ⅓ cup capers.

Put in a deep pan

½ cup salad oil

Heat until it sizzles. Add

4 to 5 pounds chicken, cut in pieces
1 tablespoon chopped parsley

Cook until the chicken is nicely browned on all sides. Remove the chicken and set it aside. Add to the pan

2 cups uncooked rice

Cook and stir until the rice is brown. Add

2 cups water
1 can consommé
2 teaspoons salt
2 bay leaves

Put in the chicken, cover and simmer until the rice and chicken are tender (about 1 hour). Add

½ cup green olives
½ cup black olives
2 cups cooked peas

Serves 6.

PAELLA

This tasty Spanish dish is an ideal casserole supper for company. Vary it by adding canned chick peas and cooked green peas. Add other meats and shellfish as convenient.

Heat in a large pan

¼ cup olive oil

Add

3 to 5 pounds chicken, cut in serving pieces

Brown well on all sides. Add

¼ cup water

Cover and cook until the chicken is tender (30 minutes or more). Remove the pieces of chicken and set them aside. To the juices in the pan, add

½ cup chopped onion
1 split clove garlic

Cook slowly 5 minutes. Melt in a saucepan

3 tablespoons butter

Add

2 cups uncooked rice
Few bits of saffron (not more than ¼ teaspoon)

Stir over low heat 5 minutes. Add

4 cups chicken broth *or* water

Bring to the boiling point, cover, and cook slowly 17 minutes. Stir into the pan with the onion. Arrange in layers in a 4-quart casserole the rice, the chicken and

1 pound shrimp, cooked and shelled
12 thin slices Italian or Spanish sausage *or* 1 cup chopped ham
2 dozen cherrystone clams (in the shell)

Have a few of the clams on top. Bake at 350° until thoroughly heated and the clams are open. *Serves 8 generously.*

BRAISED DUCK A L'ORANGE

Prepare for cooking

1 duck (about 6 pounds)

Rub with

Salt and pepper

Brown in a heavy pan in

4 tablespoons butter

Peel and cut in quarters

2 oranges

Scrape the white inner pulp from the peel and cut enough peel in thin strips to make 1 tablespoonful. Add to the duck with the orange quarters and

½ cup stock *or* strong consommé

Cover closely and simmer until tender (about 1½ hours). Remove the duck and keep it warm while you make the sauce. Pour off all but ½ cup of the juice in the pan. Add

½ cup white wine, Italian vermouth *or* orange juice

Heat to the boiling point. Mix

1 teaspoon cornstarch
Water (enough to pour)

Add to the sauce and stir until slightly thickened. Pour it over the duck. Garnish with

Thin slices of unpeeled orange

Serves 6.

BRAISED GAME BIRDS

Split small birds. Cut larger ones in serving-size pieces. Sprinkle with salt, pepper and flour. Brown well in butter or bacon fat. Cover with cream to a depth of 1 inch. Cover closely and cook over low heat or in a 325° oven until tender.

Thicken the juices in the pan with potato flour or cornstarch. Season to taste with salt, pepper and sherry.

Game Birds Chasseur or Hunter's Style. Add to each cup of sauce ⅓ cup tomato juice, lemon juice to taste, 1 teaspoon chopped parsley and ⅓ cup sliced sautéed mushrooms.

RABBIT AND HARE

Allow 1 pound per person.

A rabbit weighs 1½ to 4 pounds, a hare 4 to 10. The meat is like chicken or veal. Soak wild rabbit 1 hour in salted water to which has been added 2 tablespoons vinegar. Cut in pieces. Fricassee (p. 227) or fry (p. 222) like chicken, using bacon fat.

BRAISED HARE WITH SOUR CREAM SAUCE

Ask the butcher to lard the hind legs and back of the hare, or lay strips of salt pork over it as it cooks.

Prepare for cooking
1 hare (5 to 6 pounds), split
Sprinkle it with
Salt and pepper
Melt in a saucepan
2 tablespoons bacon fat
Add
1 carrot, cut in small pieces
½ small onion
Cook 5 minutes. Add
1 cup Brown Stock (p. 60) *or* consommé
Pour around the hare in a baking pan. Bake at 400° until tender (45 minutes or more), basting 4 times with the pan juice. Add
1 cup heavy cream
Juice 1 lemon
Cook 15 minutes longer, basting every 5 minutes. Take the hare out of the pan and keep it warm. Strain the sauce. Cook together
2 tablespoons butter
2 tablespoons flour
Thicken the sauce with this mixture and season to taste with
Salt and pepper
Pour around the hare. *Serves 6.*

CHICKEN GUMBO

Prepare for cooking
3-pound chicken, cut in pieces
Sprinkle with
Salt and pepper
Melt in a large pan
3 tablespoons bacon fat
Brown the chicken thoroughly and set it aside. Add to the pan
½ onion, chopped
Cook until yellow. Add
Sprig parsley
4 cups sliced okra, cooked or canned
¼ sweet red pepper, chopped, *or* 1 pimiento, chopped
Cover and cook slowly 15 minutes. Add the chicken pieces and
1½ cups chopped tomatoes, fresh or canned
3 cups boiling water
1½ teaspoons salt
Cover and cook slowly until the chicken is tender (40 minutes or more). Stir in
1 cup boiled rice
Serves 4.

CHICKEN MOUSSE

Follow the recipe for Fish Mousse (p. 131), using chicken breasts in place of fish. You will need two or three whole breasts, according to their size. There should be 2 cups of chicken after it has been ground.

For mousse made with cooked chicken, see Chicken Loaf (p. 235) and Macédoine Loaf (p. 236).

CHICKEN LIVERS

One pound serves 4.

Cut in half. Sprinkle with salt and pepper.

Sautéed Chicken Livers. Dip in flour or in fine crumbs, or egg and crumbs (p. 4). Sauté in butter or bacon fat until tender (about 10 minutes). Do not overcook. Serve on toast with strips of crisp bacon or on broiled tomato halves. Or reheat in Brown Sauce (p. 97), seasoned to taste with Madeira or sherry and sliced olives.

Curried Chicken Livers. Reheat sautéed livers in Curry Sauce

(p. 98) made with chicken stock. Serve with steamed rice.

Chicken Livers en Brochette. Cut the livers in quarters. Alternate on skewers with squares of sliced bacon. Arrangc on a rack in a baking pan. Bake at 425° until the bacon is crisp. Serve on skewers.

CHICKEN LIVERS WITH MUSHROOMS

Cook together for 5 minutes
1 slice bacon, cut in pieces
2 tablespoons butter
Remove the bacon bits. Add
1 shallot, chopped, *or* ½ tablespoon chopped onion
Cook 2 minutes. Add
1 pound chicken livers
Cook 2 minutes. Add
2 tablespoons flour
1 cup Brown Stock (p. 60) *or* bouillon
1 teaspoon lemon juice
¼ cup sliced mushrooms
Cook 2 minutes more. Sprinkle with
Chopped parsley
Serves 4.

USING COOKED CHICKEN *or* TURKEY

Cooked chicken is one of the most useful of leftovers. If there is only a small amount to use, combine it with chopped ham or hard-cooked eggs in a casserole dish such as Scalloped Eggs (p. 107) or add it to a salad or sandwich filling. If there is enough chicken to slice into neat pieces, you may prefer to arrange a cold platter with an attractive garnish of small whole tomatoes or asparagus tips topped with mayonnaise. If the cooked chicken is to be cut in pieces, remove all the skin and bits of gristle or fat.

White meat is more attractive in any creamed dish in fairly large pieces or in neat, even cubes. Chop dark meat unless the directions with the recipe suggest another method. In an electric blender, you can grind the skin very fine and add it to the sauce or gravy to deepen the flavor. In addition to the recipes which follow, use cooked chicken in any of the following ways.

Filled Biscuits (p. 327)
Chicken Roll (p. 213)
Crêpes Nicholas (p. 320)
Turnovers (p. 458)
Stuffed Peppers (p. 264)
Stuffed Tomatoes (p. 277)
Scalloped Eggs (p. 107)
Filled Omelet (p. 112)
Chicken Salads (p. 296)
Fashion Park Salad (p. 282)
Pilaf (p. 310)
Rissoles (p. 458)

CREAMED CHICKEN

The sauce must be perfect—satin-smooth, thoughtfully seasoned and not too thick. Stir frequently as you make it and add more liquid if necessary.

In a large saucepan or double boiler top, melt
2 tablespoons butter *or* chicken fat
Add
3 tablespoons flour
Stir until evenly blended. Add gradually, stirring constantly
1 cup milk *or* chicken broth, *or* half each
Cook and stir over low heat until the sauce thickens. Bring to the boiling point and cook 2 minutes. Add
⅓ cup cream
1½ cups cubed cooked chicken
Salt and pepper to taste
Heat at least ½ hour over low heat on an asbestos mat or in the double boiler, so that the chicken will absorb some of the sauce and be moist. Serve on toast, waffles or hot biscuits or

with rice. Add a curl of crisp bacon or a sprig of parsley or watercress. Or decorate with paprika or a strip of pimiento. *Serves 4.*

To vary. Add diced cooked ham, chopped hard-cooked eggs, sliced cooked celery, cooked peas or sautéed mushrooms.

Blanquette of Chicken. Just before serving, stir in 1 egg yolk slightly beaten with 1 tablespoon milk or cream. Sprinkle with minced parsley.

Scalloped Chicken. Spoon into a buttered baking dish. Sprinkle with buttered crumbs. Bake at 375° until the crumbs are brown.

CREAMED CHICKEN AND MUSHROOMS

Cook and stir together for 5 minutes

2 tablespoons butter
6 mushrooms, cut in pieces
1 cup cubed cooked chicken

Blend in

2 tablespoons flour

Add

1 cup chicken stock *or* broth

Simmer 10 minutes. Season with

Salt, cayenne and nutmeg

Mix

1 slightly beaten egg
1 tablespoon cream
1 tablespoon sherry

Stir in and heat 1 minute. *Serves 4.*

CHICKEN CURRY

Follow recipe for Curry of Lamb (p. 188), using chicken in place of lamb and chicken stock as the liquid. Or season Creamed Chicken with curry powder and onion salt.

CHICKEN SCALLOP

Fill a buttered baking dish with alternate layers of sliced cooked chicken and cooked macaroni or rice. Over the top, pour hot Cream (p. 94), Brown (p. 97) or Tomato Sauce (p. 99), or undiluted cream of chicken, mushroom or celery soup. Sprinkle with buttered crumbs. Bake at 375° until the crumbs are brown.

CHICKEN À LA KING

Heat in a double boiler

1½ cups Velouté Sauce (p. 96)
1 cup cubed cooked chicken
½ cup sliced sautéed mushrooms
¼ cup canned pimientos, cut in strips

Just before serving, beat together and stir in

1 egg yolk
2 tablespoons sherry

Serve in Patty Shells (p. 454) or on toast. *Serves 2 or 3.*

CHICKEN POULETTE

Put slices of cooked chicken in a shallow baking dish. Add sliced sautéed mushroom caps. Make Velouté Sauce (p. 96), omitting the cream. Pour it over the chicken.

Bake 15 minutes at 375°. Mix 1 egg yolk with ⅓ cup cream and stir into the mixture. Bake 10 minutes longer. Just before serving, stir in ½ teaspoon lemon juice.

CHICKEN ALMOND SUPRÊME

If Chinese almonds are available, sprinkle them over the top without slivering them.

Put in a shallow baking dish

2 cups cooked chicken, cut in fairly large pieces

Spread over the chicken

1 cup sliced *or* whole sautéed mushrooms
Make another layer of
1 cup water chestnuts, sliced paper-thin
Pour over the top
2 cups Suprême Sauce (p. 96)
Cover the top with
Slivered almonds
Bake at 375° until thoroughly heated and the almonds are browned. *Serves 4 or 5.*

DEVILED CHICKEN BONES

For extra zest add 1 tablespoon walnut catsup to the sauce.

Mix in a large saucepan
2 tablespoons butter, melted
1 tablespoon chili sauce
1 tablespoon Worcestershire
1 teaspoon prepared mustard
Few grains cayenne
Cut 4 small gashes in
Drumsticks, second joints and wings of a cooked chicken
Sprinkle them with
Salt, pepper and flour
Brown thoroughly in the prepared mixture. Add
1 cup chicken stock
Simmer 5 minutes. Sprinkle with
Chopped parsley
Serves 4.

CHICKEN HOLLANDAISE

Cook together for 5 minutes
1½ tablespoons butter
1 teaspoon onion, chopped fine
Stir in
2 tablespoons cornstarch
Add gradually
1 cup chicken broth *or* stock
Add
1 teaspoon lemon juice
⅓ cup chopped celery
¼ teaspoon salt
Few grains paprika
1 cup cubed cooked chicken
Heat thoroughly. Add
1 egg yolk, slightly beaten
Cook 1 minute. *Serves 4.*

CHICKEN TETRAZZINI

Equally good with turkey, veal or lobster.

Have ready
4 or more slices cooked chicken breast
2 cups Velouté Sauce (p. 96)
Cook and drain
¼ pound spaghetti, in ¼-inch pieces
Melt
2 tablespoons butter
Add
½ cup sliced mushrooms
Cook 5 minutes. Season with
Few grains nutmeg
1 tablespoon sherry
Salt to taste
Put the spaghetti in a shallow baking dish. Pour half the sauce over it. Arrange the mushrooms and chicken on top of this and cover with the rest of the sauce. Sprinkle with
⅓ cup grated Italian cheese
Bake at 400° until well heated and browned. *Serves 4.*

CHICKEN AND NOODLES

Cook according to directions on the package
½ pound broad egg noodles
Drain. Stir in (reserving 2 tablespoons for the top)
¼ pound grated Parmesan cheese
Add
Salt and pepper to taste
Put in a buttered baking dish. Place on the noodles
2 cups cubed cooked chicken
Blend together in a saucepan over low heat
2 tablespoons butter
2 tablespoons flour
Add gradually
1 cup cream
1 cup chicken stock *or* broth
Bring to the boiling point, stirring constantly. Add
2 egg yolks, slightly beaten
Pour the sauce over the chicken. Sprinkle with the reserved

cheese. Bake at 375° until thoroughly heated and well browned. *Serves 6.*

CHICKEN CHARTREUSE

Follow the recipe for Rice and Meat Loaf (p. 215), using chicken in place of meat. Season the chicken with salt, pepper, celery salt, onion juice and ½ teaspoon finely chopped parsley.

CHICKEN *or* TURKEY HASH

Chop cooked chicken or turkey. Moisten with gravy. Season to taste. Add finely chopped parsley or pimiento, if you like. Cook in a hot buttered omelet pan or a shallow baking dish until thoroughly heated but not dry. Serve from the baking dish or turn out onto a serving dish and surround with peas, asparagus tips or broiled pork sausages.

Charleston Chicken Hash. Cube white meat of cooked chicken and put in a shallow baking dish. Sprinkle with salt, pepper and nutmeg. Pour enough heavy cream over the chicken to just barely cover it. Sprinkle with grated Parmesan. Bake at 350° until the cheese melts (about 15 minutes).

MINCED TURKEY

Put in a saucepan
1 cup turkey gravy
Add
1 cup minced cooked turkey
⅓ cup soft stale bread crumbs
Few drops onion juice
Salt and pepper to taste
Heat thoroughly. Serve on
Toast or cooked rice
Serves 2 or 3.

CHICKEN *or* TURKEY CAKES

Chop cooked chicken or turkey. To each cup add 1 tablespoon cream and 1 egg, slightly beaten. Season to taste. Shape in 2-inch flat cakes. Dip in flour or egg and crumbs (p. 4). Sauté in butter until well browned. Serve with Mushroom Sauce (p. 98).

CHICKEN SOUFFLÉ

Add diced pimientos or sliced sautéed mushrooms to the mixture, if you like. To make a particularly fluffy soufflé, use an extra egg white and stir a spoonful of the beaten white in thoroughly before folding in the rest.

Cook together until the onion is yellow
1 tablespoon chopped onion
2 tablespoons butter *or* chicken fat
Stir in
2 tablespoons flour
Add
2 cups chicken stock *or* stock and milk *or* cream
Cook and stir until smooth. Add
½ cup soft bread crumbs
Cook 2 minutes. Season to taste with
Salt and pepper
Worcestershire
Add
2 cups chopped cooked chicken
3 egg yolks, well beaten
1 tablespoon chopped parsley
Fold in
3 egg whites, beaten stiff
Pour into an unbuttered straight-sided baking dish. Bake 35 minutes at 325°. Serve with
Mushroom Sauce (p. 98)
Serves 6.

CHICKEN LOAF, RING *or* TIMBALES

Season with ¼ teaspoon marjoram or thyme if you like a delicate herb flavor.

Mix thoroughly

1 cup soft stale bread crumbs
2 cups milk
2 eggs, slightly beaten *or* 3 egg yolks
½ teaspoon salt
¼ teaspoon paprika
1 teaspoon Worcestershire
3 cups diced cooked chicken
½ cup chopped celery
1 green pepper, chopped
Juice of ½ lemon

Pack into a buttered 1½-quart mold or 6 or 8 timbale molds. Set in a pan of hot water. Bake at 325° until firm (about 40 minutes). Let stand 10 minutes before unmolding. *Serves 6 or more.*

MACÉDOINE LOAF

Mix thoroughly

1 cup undiluted cream of mushroom soup
½ cup soft bread crumbs
2 egg yolks
1 cup cooked macaroni, in ½-inch pieces
½ cup cubed cooked chicken
1 tablespoon canned pimiento, cut small
½ cup heavy cream, beaten stiff
1½ teaspoons salt
1 teaspoon chopped parsley

Fold in

2 egg whites, beaten stiff

Bake like Chicken Loaf (p. 000). Serve with

Tomato (p. 00) *or* Mushroom Sauce (p. 00)

Serves 6.

CHICKEN CROQUETTES

For delicious flavor, make the sauce of ¾ cup chicken stock and ¼ cup heavy cream and season with curry to taste.

Mix thoroughly

2 cups chopped cooked chicken
½ teaspoon salt
¼ teaspoon celery salt
Few grains cayenne
1 teaspoon lemon juice
Few drops onion juice
1 teaspoon finely chopped parsley
About 1 cup Croquette Sauce (p. 94)

Use enough sauce to keep the mixture soft but stiff enough to hold its shape. White meat will absorb more sauce than dark. Chill. Shape, egg and crumb, and fry (p. 4). Serve with

Cream Sauce (p. 94) *or* Sauterne Jelly (p. 397)

Serves 6.

Chicken and Almond Croquettes. Add ½ cup chopped nut meats to the mixture. Serve with Brown Almond Sauce (p. 94).

Chcken and Mushroom Croquettes. Use 1⅓ cups chicken and ⅔ cup chopped mushrooms.

CHICKEN CROQUETTES MACÉDOINE

Cook together 3 minutes, stirring constantly

3 tablespoons butter
1 shallot, chopped fine, *or* 1 tablespoon chopped onion

Blend in

¼ cup flour
1 teaspoon salt
¼ teaspoon paprika
Few gratings nutmeg

Add gradually, stirring constantly

1 cup chicken stock *or* broth

Bring to the boiling point and add

3 egg yolks
1 cup diced cooked chicken
½ cup diced cooked ham
¼ cup chopped mushrooms

Cook 5 minutes. Chill. Shape, egg and crumb, and fry (p. 4). Serve with

Cream Sauce (p. 94) *or* Velouté Sauce (p. 96)

Serves 6.

CHICKEN *or* TURKEY DIVAN

Put in a shallow oblong baking dish

4 stalks cooked broccoli *or* 8 stalks cooked asparagus

Sprinkle with

1 tablespoon melted butter
1 tablespoon grated Parmesan *or* Romano cheese
2tablespoons sherry

Lay over the vegetable

4 thick slices cooked turkey *or* chicken breast

Sprinkle with

1 tablespoon grated Parmesan *or* Romano cheese
2 tablespoons sherry

Beat together

1 cup Cream Sauce (p. 94)
2 egg yolks

Season to taste with

Salt and pepper

Fold in

1 tablespoon whipped cream

Pour over the chicken or turkey.
Sprinkle with

1 tablespoon grated Romano *or* Parmesan cheese
2 tablespoons sherry

Bake at 350° until delicately brown (about 12 minutes). *Serves 3 or 4.*

Vegetables

Vegetables deserve the best efforts of every cook because of their fresh flavor and superior food values. Give your family three servings a day. Potatoes are a valuable source of protein and minerals, so serve them often. Leafy green vegetables are low in calories but rich in minerals and vitamins, so include one a day, cooked or as a relish or salad. Choose the third vegetable according to the season and your family's preferences.

MARKETING FOR VEGETABLES

If possible, deal with a vegetable man who does his own marketing. He will take pride in selling you vegetables at their freshest and best. If he is foreign-born, he may tell you an exotic way to cook some familiar vegetable. For the small family, quantity buying is not an economy. Buy small amounts at a time, store them in a cool place and use them promptly.

Frozen vegetables vary in quality. Insist upon the brand you find most consistently high-grade.

Canned vegetables are graded as to quality, so read the labels carefully. Save all the liquid, which contains valuable minerals and vitamins. Drain it off, cook it down, add the vegetable and heat. If you prefer, drain it off and store it in a covered jar to use as part of the liquid in making soup or gravy. Commercially canned vegetables are richer in food values than home-canned ones, since oxygen reduces or destroys some food values and home canning is usually done in an open kettle.

PREPARING FRESH VEGETABLES

Wash thoroughly. Prepare just before cooking whenever possible, since air on the cut surfaces destroys some of the food values. If you must prepare them ahead of time, cover them tightly and store in the refrigerator until time to cook them. To retain the highest food values, pare vegetables after cooking, or eat the vegetable, skin and all, unless the skin is very tough.

VEGETABLE COOKING

In boiling water. Have the water boiling hard and use as little as possible. Do not discard the cooking water or you will be throwing away valuable vitamins and minerals. Cook it down, if necessary, and serve it on the vegetables or save it to use in soups, sauces, gravies, gelatine salads, vegetable juice cocktails, or as the liquid in cooked salad dressings. Cook the vegetables briefly, until just tender. Overcooking destroys some vitamins and much flavor.

In a pressure saucepan. Read the directions with your saucepan, and then use your judgment. It is all too easy to overcook a young tender vegetable. If the vegetable is very fresh and juicy, you may be able to use even less water than the directions say. In any case, keep every drop of the liquid, either to serve on the vegetable or in a soup or sauce.

In a casserole. Frozen vegetables and many fresh ones are excellent cooked in the oven, and it is often convenient to bake them while you are doing other baking. Pare vegetables and cut small. Put in a casserole. Sprinkle with salt and pepper and dot with butter. If you need liquid, use no more than 1 tablespoon water or consommé. Cover tightly. Bake until tender (30 to 40 minutes at 350°; 50 to 60 minutes at 325°). If vegetables are cooked sufficiently before you are ready to serve them, take the casserole out of the oven and let it stand, covered, until 10 minutes before serving; then reheat in the oven.

Foil cooking is often a convenience, especially for outdoor cooking. Prepare frozen or fresh vegetables as for cooking in a casserole and wrap in foil. Cook in the oven or on a grill.

Frozen vegetables need less time to cook because they have been precooked slightly in blanching. Follow directions on the package.

Use a double boiler for squash, mashed potatoes or other vegetables cooked before freezing. Cook corn in a double boiler with a tablespoon or two of top milk or cream. Cook asparagus in butter in a tightly covered frying pan until just tender—5 to 8 minutes. Defrost corn on the cob before cooking. Cook any vegetable in a casserole (above), allowing slightly less time than for fresh vegetables.

SEASONING VEGETABLES

Taste vegetables before you serve them. They vary in flavor, so that a recipe can only suggest the average amount of salt or other seasoning to use. Let your imagination suggest an occasional change in seasoning—add curry or nutmeg, sherry or brandy, or a suggestion of herbs. But remember that seasoning should enhance, not overwhelm!

SERVING VEGETABLES

Make vegetables more attractive by serving them in various ways. Provide a contrast in color or texture by sprinkling with croutons or toasted wheat germ, or by garnishing with sprigs of watercress or parsley or bits of pimiento, chopped toasted almonds or fried onion rings (canned ones are delicious). Eat the garnish—watercress and parsley are especially high in vitamins and minerals.

USING LEFTOVER VEGETABLES

See the general recipes for Cream of Vegetable Soup (p. 64) and for Vegetable Salads (p. 284). Serve vegetables in a sauce within a ring made of another vegetable—such as Spinach (p. 274) or Carrot Ring (p. 250). Or use them in one of the recipes which follow.

VEGETABLE CASSEROLE

Make a casserole dish with a mixture of vegetables and serve it as a main dish. Scraped onion or onion juice is almost a "must" as a seasoning. Alternate layers of well-seasoned cooked rice and cooked vegetables. Pour consommé over the vegetables, dot with butter, and bake until thoroughly heated at any convenient temperature. Sprinkle with crumbled cooked bacon, cheese or paprika.

VEGETABLE FRITTERS

Dip neat pieces of cooked vegetables in Fritter Batter (p. 409) and fry in deep fat at 390°. See special recipe for Corn Fritters (p. 253).

VEGETABLES À LA POULETTE

Heat a combination of cooked vegetables in Suprême Sauce (p. 96). Peas with cubed carrots and turnips is a good combination.

VEGETABLE SOUFFLÉ

In place of milk or cream, use part stock or the water in which the vegetable was cooked. Mix leftover vegetables if you like, such as peas and carrots, celery and carrots, or mushrooms and cauliflower.

Put in a saucepan

3 tablespoons butter
1 teaspoon chopped onion

Cook slowly until yellow. Add

3 tablespoons flour

Blend well. Add

1 cup top milk *or* cream

Cook and stir until thick. Add

1 cup cooked vegetable, mashed or chopped fine

Stir in

3 egg yolks, well beaten

Cook slowly 1 minute. Season to taste, adding more onion if needed. Cool at least 10 minutes. Beat until stiff

3 egg whites

Fold gently into the vegetable mixture. Spoon into a baking dish. Do not butter the dish unless the soufflé is to be turned out on a serving dish (as in a ring mold). Bake at 350° until firm (about 30 minutes). *Serves 6.*

GLOBE ARTICHOKES

Also called French or Italian artichokes. Allow 1 to a person (or half, if they are very large). Choose smooth, dark green, tightly closed heads.

Wash thoroughly. Cut off the stem close to the leaves. Pull off the tough outer leaves. Cut off the prickly tops with scissors. Put in a deep saucepan with 1½ inches of boiling water. Add 2 tablespoons lemon juice or vinegar. Cover the pan. Cook until you can easily pull off an outer leaf (25 to 45 minutes). Drain upside down. Set upright on a serving dish. Serve hot with individual dishes of melted butter or Hollandaise (p. 100) in which to dip each leaf as it is eaten. Or serve cold with Vinaigrette Sauce (p. 103) or mayonnaise seasoned highly with lemon juice and prepared mustard.

Stuffed Artichokes. *A good luncheon dish.* Cook until just barely tender. Cut out the prickly center (choke) with a teaspoon. Spread the leaves apart to make a cup. Fill with creamed chicken, crab meat or lobster. Sprinkle with buttered crumbs or grated cheese. Bake in a covered dish 30 minutes at 350°. Uncover to brown the tops.

USING CANNED ARTICHOKE HEARTS

Sautéed Artichoke Hearts. Drain. Sauté in butter until deli-

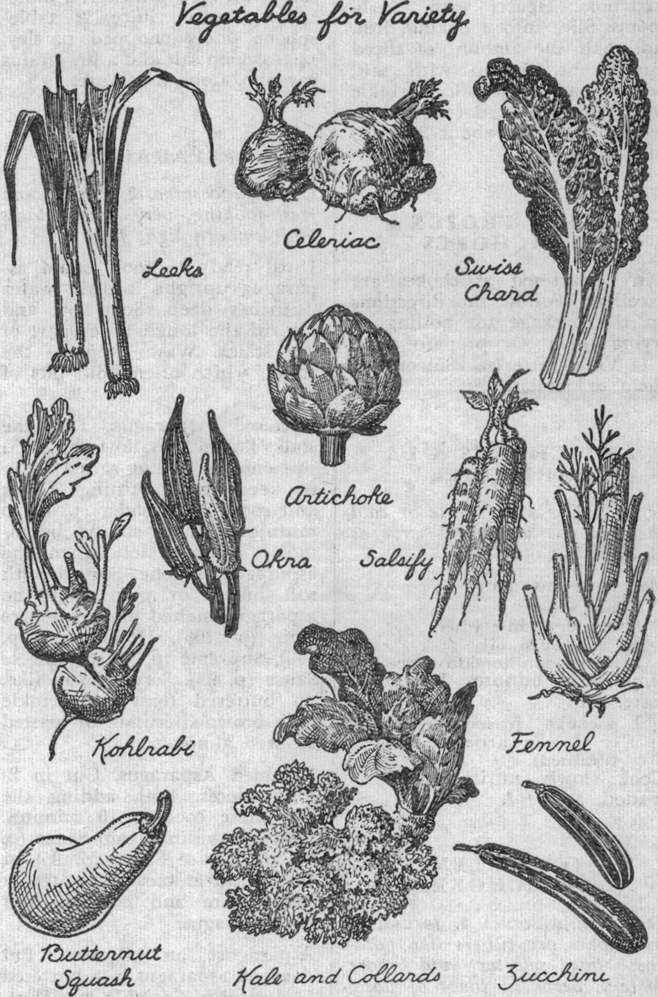
Vegetables for Variety
Celeriac
Leeks
Swiss Chard
Artichoke
Okra
Salsify
Kohlrabi
Fennel
Butternut Squash
Kale and Collards
Zucchini

cately brown. Sprinkle with salt, pepper, lemon juice and chopped parsley.

Artichoke Hearts with Mushrooms. Slice into a baking dish. Add half the amount of sliced mushrooms. Season with salt, pepper and garlic salt. Sprinkle with salad oil or dot with butter. Cover. Bake about 20 minutes at 350°.

USING FROZEN ARTICHOKES

Tiny quartered artichokes are excellent. Follow the directions on the package for boiling or frying them. Or prepare them à la Vinaigrette (p. 285) or add them to a salad.

ARTICHOKES À LA BARIGOULE

Serve hot as a vegetable or cool them in the sauce and serve as an appetizer or salad.

Mix in a saucepan

- **1 cup water**
- **1 cup dry white wine**
- **⅓ cup olive oil**
- **1 tablespoon tomato sauce**

Simmer 10 minutes. Season to taste. Add

- **1 package frozen artichokes *or* 1 can artichoke hearts (drained)**

Cook slowly until thoroughly heated. *Serves 4.*

JERUSALEM ARTICHOKES

One pound serves 6. Jerusalem artichokes are tubers like potatoes but sweeter and more watery. Serve in place of potatoes.

Scrub. Leave whole or pare and slice. Cook, covered, 15 to 35 minutes in boiling salted water or 2 minutes in a pressure saucepan. Overcooking toughens this vegetable. Drain. Pare if necessary. Add ½ cup butter, 2 tablespoons lemon juice, 2 tablespoons finely chopped parsley, ¼ teaspoon salt and a few grains cayenne. Cook 3 minutes.

ASPARAGUS

One pound serves 2 or 3. Choose fresh-looking, very green stalks with smooth tight tips.

Until ready to cook, stand asparagus upright in cold water 2 inches deep. Snap off and discard the tough lower part of the stalks. Wash. Remove the scales, which often hold bits of sand.

Buttered Asparagus. Lay the stalks flat in a shallow pan. Add just enough boiling salted water to keep from burning. Cover and cook until tender (15 to 20 minutes). There should be almost no water left when the asparagus is done. Spread with soft butter or pour over the asparagus melted butter, Beurre Noir (p. 103), Hollandaise (p. 100), Suprême (p. 96) or Cheese Sauce (p. 95). Serve if you like, on buttered toast or sprinkle with browned crumbs or toasted slivered almonds.

Creamed Asparagus. Cut in 2-inch pieces. Boil, adding the tips after cooking 10 minutes. Drain. Serve in Cream Sauce (p. 94) or Cheese Sauce (p. 95) or heat a little cream, yogurt or sour cream and pour it over the asparagus.

Asparagus au Gratin. Put creamed asparagus in a buttered baking dish. Sprinkle with buttered crumbs or with crumbs mixed with grated cheese. Bake at 350° until the crumbs are brown.

Asparagus Vinaigrette. Serve hot or cold with Vinaigrette Sauce (p. 103).

ASPARAGUS CANTON STYLE

Crisp and flavorful. Do not overcook.

Cut in thin slanted slices

1 pound asparagus

Melt in a frying pan over low heat or in an electric skillet at the table

1 tablespoon butter

Add the asparagus. Put on the cover. Cook gently until the asparagus is just barely tender (about 5 minutes). Season and add more butter if you like. *Serves 3 or 4.*

FRENCH-FRIED ASPARAGUS

Drain fresh-cooked or canned asparagus tips. Dip in egg and fine crumbs or flour (p. 4). Chill. Fry, a few at a time, for about 3 minutes in deep fat heated to 380°. Drain on a paper towel.

French-fried Asparagus with Cheese. Mix grated Parmesan with the crumbs for dipping, using half cheese and half crumbs.

GREEN *or* WAX BEANS

One pound serves 4. Select beans that are crisp enough to snap when broken and are fresh-looking, with a bright, clear color. Pods should look young and smooth, not too thick or well filled.

Wash thoroughly. Cut off the ends. Cut with a sharp knife or scissors in 1-inch pieces. You can work very fast if you cut off all the ends first, then put the beans on a cutting board in neat bunches and cut through with a long sharp knife. Or cut in very thin diagonal strips with a bean cutter, or cut lengthwise and then crosswise in thin pieces about 1½ inches long. Cook about 2 minutes in a pressure saucepan, or 15 to 20 minutes in a covered pan in boiling salted water ½ inch deep. Drain, if necessary. Add salt and butter to taste.

Green Beans Amandine. Sprinkle slivered toasted almonds over the buttered cooked beans. For a delicious flavor, cook the slivered almonds in butter until the butter is brown, and pour over the beans.

Green Beans au Gratin. Put 2 cups cooked green beans in a buttered baking dish. Season with salt and cayenne. Add ½ cup grated cheese, 1 tablespoon butter and ¼ cup heavy cream. Stir until well mixed. Sprinkle with grated cheese. Dot with 1 tablespoon butter. Bake at 400° until the cheese melts.

Green Beans with Mushrooms. Add sliced sautéed mushrooms.

Green Beans Polonaise. Reheat beans with ¼ cup cream and sprinkle with croutons or toasted wheat germ, or corn flakes, crushed fine.

Green Beans Texas Style. Season cooked beans with chili sauce to taste. Reheat and sprinkle crumbled crisp bacon over the top.

Uruguayan Green Beans. Sprinkle with chopped parsley and lemon juice.

PANNED GREEN BEANS

Cut in lengthwise strips

1 pound green beans (ends snipped off)

Melt in a heavy frying pan or electric skillet

1½ tablespoons butter

Add the beans. Cover and cook over low heat until just tender. Season to taste with

Salt and pepper

Serves 4.

BEANS PANACHÉ

A different way with frozen vegetables.

Melt in a frying pan or electric skillet

1 tablespoon butter

Add

½ cup water
1 package frozen baby limas
¼ teaspoon salt

Cover. Cook 5 minutes. Add

1 package frozen French-style green beans
1 package frozen green peas

Cover and cook until all the vegetables are tender (about 15 minutes). Stir in

1 tablespoon butter

Season to taste. *Serves 6 to 8.*

FRESH SHELL BEANS
(Lima, Green Soy, Fava, etc.)

One and a half pounds in the shell (a half-pound, shelled) serves 2.

Cut off the thin outer edge of the pods with a sharp knife. Squeeze out the beans. Wash. Cook 1 minute in a pressure saucepan or 15 to 25 minutes, tightly covered, in boiling salted water, 1 inch deep. Season with butter, salt and pepper. Add a little cream or top milk or sprinkle with chopped parsley or chives.

To shell soy beans. Drop into boiling water, cover, and let stand 5 minutes. Drain. Press the beans out of the pods with thumb and finger. Old soy beans (brownish pods) take longer to cook than other beans.

DRIED BEANS
(Lima, Kidney, Navy, Soy, Pinto and Black-eyed Peas)

Dried beans swell to double or more in bulk when cooked. One cup serves 4. After the beans or peas are tender, they may be seasoned and served in a great variety of ways so you may wish to cook more than enough for one meal.

Wash. Pick over and discard discolored beans. Cover with boiling water, cook 2 minutes, and remove from the heat. Let soak 1 hour or more. Bring to the boiling point and simmer until tender but not mushy (about 45 minutes for limas, 2 to 3 hours for soy beans and the others). Add more water from time to time as it boils away. Add salt when the beans are about half done. Drain. Season with salt, pepper and butter. Save some for Bean Soup (p. 70), Beans Bretonne (below) or Boston Baked Beans (p. 245).

BEANS BRETONNE

Put in a baking dish

1½ cups cooked pea beans

Add

1 cup stewed and strained tomatoes
1 cup Chicken Stock (p. 62) or canned chicken broth
6 pimientos, puréed
1 onion, chopped fine
¼ cup butter
2 teaspoons salt

Cover. Bake at 300° until the beans have nearly absorbed the sauce. *Serves 6.*

LIMA BEANS FERMIÈRE

Put in a casserole

2 cups cooked dried lima beans

Season to taste. Put in a small frying pan

2-inch cube fat salt pork, diced

Cook slowly until the fat melts and the lean bits are crisp and brown. Add

1 small onion, sliced thin
½ carrot, cubed

Cook and stir until the onion is brown. Add to the beans. Cover. Bake at 300° until the beans are soft. *Serves 4.*

BOSTON BAKED BEANS

Boston baked beans are always flavored with molasses and baked to a rich dark brown. The preferred beans to use are small California or New York pea beans, but kidney beans are delicious, too, baked in the same fashion.

Wash, discarding imperfect ones

2 pounds California *or* New York pea beans

Cover with

2 quarts water

Bring to the boiling point, boil 2 minutes, and soak 1 hour or more. Without draining, cook slowly until the skins burst when you take a few on the tip of a spoon and blow on them. Drain, reserving the cooking water. Cover with boiling water

½ pound fat salt pork

Let stand 2 minutes, drain, and cut 1-inch gashes every ½ inch without cutting through the rind. Put the beans in the bean pot. Push the pork down into the beans until all but the rind is covered. Mix

2 teaspoons salt
1 cup molasses
1 teaspoon dry mustard
2 tablespoons sugar, brown *or* white

Add 1 cup of the reserved water and bring to boiling point. Pour over the beans and add enough more water to cover the beans. Cover the bean pot. Bake 6 to 8 hours at 250°. Add water as needed to keep the beans moist. Uncover the last hour of baking so that the rind will be brown and crisp. *10 or more servings.*

To flavor the beans with onion, rub the inside of the pot with onion and add a few slivers of onion. If you like a pronounced onion flavor, put a peeled onion in the pot with the beans and remove it when you serve the beans.

Baked Beans New York Style. Omit the molasses and sugar. Bake uncovered in a shallow pan. Arrange the slices of salt pork over the top. Do not add water during the last hour of baking.

USING CANNED *or* FROZEN BAKED BEANS

The beans may suit you just as they are. Otherwise, season to taste with salt, mustard and molasses. Heat in a bean pot for a homemade look.

BEETS

One pound serves 3 or 4. Select beets with fresh-looking leaves.

Wash and cut off all but 1 inch of the tops. Do not cut off the root. Cook beets whole, without salt, until tender (5 to 10 minutes in pressure saucepan, 30 to 60 minutes in boiling water to cover). Very old, woody beets will never cook tender.

Drain, drop in cold water for a moment, and slip off the skins with your fingers. Leave whole, cut in quarters, or slice. Dot with butter, and season, or serve in one of the following ways.

Sugared Beets. Cut 4 hot boiled beets in thin slices. Add 3 tablespoons butter, 1½ tablespoons sugar and ½ teaspoon salt. Reheat.

Pickled Beets. Slice cooked beets and cover with mild cider vinegar or 1 cup vinegar boiled 5 minutes with ½ cup sugar. Add a few caraway seeds for extra zest. Serve lukewarm or cold in small individual sauce dishes.

SHREDDED BEETS

Wash but do not pare. Shred into a frying pan. For 1 pound of beets add 3 tablespoons butter, bacon fat or oil, and 1 tablespoon boiling water, lemon juice or vinegar. Cover. Cook over moderate heat until tender (5 to 10 minutes). Season.

BAKED BEETS

Wash. Cut off the tops. Brush with oil. Bake at 350° until tender (1 hour or more). Peel or not. Slice or chop. Season with butter, salt and pepper.

BEETS IN SOUR SAUCE

Melt in a saucepan

2 tablespoons butter

Blend in

2 tablespoons flour

Stir in

½ cup water in which the beets were cooked *or* liquid from the can
¼ cup vinegar
¼ cup cream
1 teaspoon sugar
½ teaspoon salt
Few grains pepper

Cook until smooth, stirring constantly. Add

2 cups cooked or canned beets, drained and cubed

Heat thoroughly. *Servcs 4.*

HARVARD BEETS

Mix in a saucepan

½ cup sugar
1½ teaspoons cornstarch

Add

¼ cup mild vinegar
¼ cup water

Boil 5 minutes. Add

12 small beets, cooked and sliced or cubed

Let stand 30 minutes or more. Just before serving, bring to the boiling point. Add

2 tablespoons butter

Serves 6.

BEETS AND GREENS

When beets are very young—no larger than marbles—they are delicious cooked with their tender leaves.

Wash thoroughly to remove every trace of sand. Cut off the tips of the roots. Cook, covered, with just enough water added to the pan to keep them from burning. Sprinkle with salt and cook until the beets are tender. Drain, if necessary. Cut the greens coarsely with the kitchen scissors. Add salt and butter to taste.

BROCCOLI

One pound serves 2 to 4. Select stalks with dark green, tightly closed buds and short crisp stems.

Cover with cold salted water. Soak 30 minutes. Drain. Cut off the tough part of the stalk and the coarse outer leaves. Peel the stalks and slit large ones lengthwise for an inch or two so they will cook evenly. If the stalks are too large for individual portions, split into pieces of attractive size and shape. Cook about 1½ minutes in a pressure saucepan or about 15 minutes in 1 inch of boiling water in a tightly covered pan. Do not ovrecook.

Serve with melted butter, Hollandaise (p. 100) or Cheese Sauce

p. 95). Sprinkle with buttered bread crumbs, if desired.

Puréed Broccoli. Chop fine or put through a purée strainer. Cover with Hollandaise (p. 100).

Broccoli au Gratin. Mix puréed broccoli with Cream Sauce (1 cup to 1 pound of broccoli). Season highly. Place in a baking dish. Sprinkle with buttered crumbs or crushed corn flakes and grated cheese. Bake 15 minutes at 350°.

BROCCOLI IN CHEESE CUSTARD

Cook, drain and chop

1 package frozen broccoli or 1 pound fresh broccoli

Put in a buttered casserole. Mix

2 eggs, slightly beaten
1½ cups milk *or* ¾ cup dried milk in 1¼ cups water
½ cup grated Cheddar cheese
2 tablespoons lemon juice
1 teaspoon salt
⅛ teaspoon pepper

If you used dried milk, add

3 tablespoons melted butter

Pour over the broccoli. Set the casserole in a pan of hot water and bake at 325° until the custard is firm (about 35 minutes). *Serves 6.*

BRUSSELS SPROUTS

One pound serves 3 or 4. Select light green, compact heads with no yellow spots.

Remove wilted leaves, cut off stems, and soak 15 minutes in cold salted water. Drain. Cook, covered, in boiling salted water 10 to 20 minutes or until just tender. Drain. Serve with melted butter or Hollandaise (p. 100).

Brussels Sprouts with Grapes. Add ½ cup peeled and seeded Malaga grapes to 1 pound cooked sprouts.

Brussels Sprouts with Mushrooms. Add 1 cup sliced sautéed mushrooms.

Brussels Sprouts with Celery. Cook 1 cup diced celery 2 minutes in 2 tablespoons butter. Stir in 2 tablespoons flour. Add 1 cup milk slowly. Bring to the boiling point, add the cooked sprouts and season to taste.

Brussels Sprouts with Chestnuts. Cook 2 tablespoons butter with 1 teaspoon sugar until golden brown. Add ½ cup cooked or canned chestnuts (p. 252) and brown well. Add 1 pound cooked sprouts which have been sautéed in butter. Moisten with stock or the water in which the sprouts were cooked. Season to taste.

Brussels Sprouts en Casserole. Season cooked sprouts with melted butter. Put in a casserole. Sprinkle with buttered crumbs. Bake at 350° until the crumbs are brown. Or follow the recipe for Madeleine's Scalloped Cabbage (p. 248), using cooked sprouts in place of cabbage.

CABBAGE

Young green cabbage, solid white cabbage, loose crinkly Savoy, deep red cabbage, pale mild Chinese—each has its special characteristics. Use them as table decorations, too. Nutritionists say the greener the cabbage, the richer in vitamins. Select a firm head, heavy for its size. One small head serves 4 to 6, or 1 pound serves 3.

BUTTERED CABBAGE

Take off the outside leaves, cut in quarters and remove the tough center. Hold firmly, cut side down, on a board and slice into shreds with a long sharp knife. Cook quickly in a covered pan with just enough water to keep from burning. Cook until just tender but still crisp—5 to 15 minutes for green or white cabbage, 20 to 25 minutes for red. Drain. Season with butter, salt and pepper.

Creamed Cabbage. Heat in cream or Cream Sauce (p. 94). Curry powder or grated cheese are tasty additions.

Scalloped Cabbage. Put Creamed Cabbage in a buttered baking dish. Cover with buttered crumbs. Bake at 350° until brown. If desired, add grated cheese to crumbs.

MADELEINE'S SCALLOPED CABBAGE

Cook as for Buttered Cabbage (p. 247)

1 small cabbage

Drain thoroughly. Season with

Salt and pepper

Put in a saucepan

2 tablespoons butter
¼ cup finely cut celery (or more)

Cook slowly 5 minutes. Stir in

2 tablespoons flour

Stir in gradually

1 cup top milk *or* milk and cream

Cook until thick, stirring constantly (about 5 minutes). Season to taste. Add the cabbage. Spoon into a baking dish. Cover with

Buttered crumbs

Bake at any convenient temperature (325° to 400°) until well heated and browned on top. *Serves 4 or 5.*

BRAISED RED CABBAGE AND APPLES

Caramelized chopped onion gives this dish its special flavor. To season more highly, add nutmeg and cayenne or allspice and clove.

Melt in a frying pan

4 tablespoons bacon fat *or* fat salt pork

Add

2 tablespoons sugar

Stir until brown. Add

1 small onion, chopped

Cook slowly until golden. Add

4 cups shredded red cabbage
2 tart apples, sliced
2 tablespoons mild vinegar
½ teaspoon caraway seeds
Salt and pepper

Cook slowly until very tender, adding

A little water, stock *or* red wine

as necessary to keep from sticking. *Serves 4 to 6.*

Braised White Cabbage. Use ¼ cup sugar and only 1 tablespoon vinegar.

CHINESE CABBAGE

Shred and set aside

1 head Chinese cabbage

Cook in a large frying pan until crisp

8 strips bacon

Remove the bacon and drain on a paper towel. Add the cabbage to the fat in the pan, cover and cook until just tender (5 to 10 minutes). Crumble the bacon and stir it into the cabbage. Season to taste. Serve with soy sauce. *Serves 4 to 6.*

CHINESE CABBAGE AND TOMATOES

To 4 cups shredded Chinese cabbage add ½ cup cooked or canned tomatoes and 1 small onion, chopped fine. Cook until tender, adding a little water if necessary to keep the cabbage from sticking. Season to taste. *Serves 4.*

HOT SLAW

Shred

½ cabbage

Mix in a double boiler top

2 egg yolks

¼ cup cold water
1 tablespoon butter
¼ cup hot vinegar
½ teaspoon salt

Cook over hot water, stirring constantly, until thick. Add the cabbage and reheat. *Serves 4.*

COLE SLAW

See page 285.

SAUERKRAUT

For an old-fashioned meal, serve sauerkraut with spareribs, ham or wieners.

Sauerkraut is marketed uncooked or cooked, ready to heat, season and serve. *One pound serves 4.*

To cook, cover with boiling water, stock or consommé. Cook slowly at least 35 minutes. Drain. Season to taste with salt, if needed, and pepper.

Many old German recipes suggest cooking with the sauerkraut a raw potato, grated, or a tart apple, cut fine. For an interesting flavor, add ¼ to 1 teaspoon caraway seeds, or season to taste with vinegar or brown sugar, or both.

Sauerkraut with Onions. Dice 1 onion and sauté in 2 tablespoons fat until soft. Add drained sauerkraut, stir well, cover, and cook slowly at least 30 minutes over moderate heat or in a 300° oven. Season to taste.

Sauerkraut with Wine. Cook sauerkraut with white or red wine, using 1½ cups to a pound. Use onion or not, as preferred.

CARDOON

Like coarse, prickly celery.

Wash and scrape. Cut in 2 or 3 inch lengths. Cook until tender in a pressure saucepan (2 minutes) or in boiling salted water in a covered pan (20 minutes). Drain. Serve with melted butter.

CARROTS

One pound serves 3 or 4. Carrots are one of the best sources of vitamin C, especially when cooked. Young carrots have fresh green tops. Winter carrots should be firm and unblemished.

Wash. Scrub young carrots with a stiff brush. Scrape old carrots with a wire brush, metal sponge, or with a vegetable parer. Slice, cube, cut in slivers, or leave whole, if they are small. Cook until tender (2 to 4 minutes in pressure saucepan or 10 to 25 minutes in boiling salted water). Season with butter, salt, pepper, a trace of sugar and a shake of nutmeg. Chopped mint or parsley is delicious with carrots, stirred in or sprinkled on top.

Carrots with Onion Butter. Cook 2 tablespoons butter with 2 tablespoons finely cut onion until the onion is yellow. Add to cooked chopped or sliced carrots.

Carrots and Peas. Combine finely cut cooked carrots with an equal quantity of cooked green peas, and season with butter, salt and pepper. Heat thoroughly.

Creamed Carrots and Celery. Cube cooked carrots, add finely cut cooked celery, and heat in Cream Sauce (p. 94) or a little heavy cream.

Riced Carrots. Put cooked carrots through a potato ricer. Season with butter, salt and pepper. Sprinkle with chopped parsley.

Candied Carrots. Cut in halves or quarters, if large. Melt ½ cup butter in a heavy pan and add ½ cup brown sugar. Stir until melted, add the cooked carrots, and cook slowly until the carrots are well glazed.

Carrots Poulette. Reheat in Suprême Sauce (p. 96) made with carrot water instead of stock.

Sweet and Sour Carrots. Make a sauce of the water in which the carrots were cooked, using 1 tablespoon fat and 1 tablespoon flour to each cup. Season the sauce to taste with brown sugar and vinegar or lemon juice. Add the sliced or cubed carrots and reheat.

MINT-GLAZED CARROTS WITH PEAS

Slice lengthwise, ¼ inch thick
3 medium-sized carrots
Cut in strips. Cook (p. 249) and drain. Add
½ cup butter
½ cup sugar
1 tablespoon chopped fresh mint leaves
Cook slowly until well glazed. Add
2 cups peas, cooked or canned
Heat and season to taste. *Serves 4.*

SLIVERED CARROTS

Easy to prepare at the table in an electric skillet.

Cut carrots in thin shavings with a "knee-action" peeler. Sprinkle with salt. Cook 5 minutes in a covered pan with just enough water to keep from burning. Add melted butter and plenty of chopped parsley.

BAKED CARROTS

Prepare
2 cups shredded scraped carrots
Melt
3 tablespoons butter
Add
¼ cup chopped onion
Cook slowly until soft. Add the carrots. Add
1 teaspoon sugar
Salt to taste
Put in a casserole. Add
½ cup water
Cover and bake at 350° until tender (about 30 minutes). *Serves 4.*

HUNTINGTON CARROTS

Melt in a heavy pan
½ cup butter
Add
4 cups carrots, cut in 1½-inch strips
Turn over and over in the butter until well coated. Sprinkle with
Salt
½ teaspoon sugar
Cover and cook slowly until tender (about 35 minutes). Turn occasionally. Season to taste. Just before serving, add
½ cup cream
Reheat. *Serves 4.*

Carrots Vichy. Use tiny young carrots and leave them whole. Instead of adding cream, sprinkle with lemon juice and chopped parsley.

CARROT RING *or* MOLD

Fill the ring with peas, Brussels sprouts or green beans, or with creamed chicken, ham or tuna as a main dish.

Mix
2½ cups mashed cooked carrots
2 tablespoons onion juice *or* minced onion
2 tablespoons melted butter
2 eggs, well beaten
1 tablespoon flour
1 cup top milk *or* cream

Season to taste with

Salt, pepper and paprika

Pack into a butter 1-quart ring mold. Set in a shallow pan of hot water. Bake at 350° until firm (40 to 50 minutes). *Serves 6.*

Carrot Ring with Cheese. Use 2 cups carrots and 1½ cups grated Parmesan cheese. Add 1 cup bread crumbs.

CAULIFLOWER

Choose a white head with fresh green leaves and no spots or bruises. Save out a few uncooked flowerets to use in a salad (p. 285) or on a relish tray. A medium-sized head serves 4 to 6.

BUTTERED CAULIFLOWER

Remove the leaves and cut off the stalk. Wash well. Leave whole or separate into flowerets. Cook in boiling salted water, not more than 12 to 15 minutes for flowerets, 20 to 25 for a whole head. Drain. Pour over the cauliflower melted butter, seasoned with lemon juice and finely chopped parsley, or Hollandaise (p. 100), thin Cream Sauce (p. 94) or Cheese Sauce (p. 95).

Cauliflower au Gratin. Place a whole cooked cauliflower on an ovenproof dish. Cover with buttered crumbs and place in 350° oven to brown the crumbs. Remove and pour over it 1 cup Cream Sauce (p. 94). If desired, sprinkle with grated cheese before covering with crumbs.

Cauliflower Allemande. Place cooked cauliflower in a baking dish. Cover with Allemande Sauce (p. 96), sprinkle with ¼ cup grated Parmesan cheese, and bake at 350° until the cheese is melted.

French-fried Cauliflower. Separate the cooked cauliflower into flowerets, dip in egg and crumbs (p. 4), and fry in deep fat heated to 370° until brown (about 5 minutes).

Cauliflower with Mushrooms. Separate cooked cauliflower into flowerets. Cover with Mushroom Sauce (p. 98). If desired, omit the onion and beef extract and season with ¼ teaspoon nutmeg.

CELERIAC (CELERY ROOT)

A variety of celery with a large turnip-like root. One pound serves 4.

Scrub thoroughly. Scrape or pare. Slice lengthwise or dice. Cook 2 minutes in a pressure saucepan or 20 minutes in a covered pan in boiling salted water. Drain. Mash or not, and serve with melted butter or Hollandaise (p. 100).

CELERY

Green pascal celery has a more pungent flavor than white celery. A pound serves 2 or 3. If you like, save some of the small tender hearts to use as a relish or in salad.

BUTTERED CELERY

Wash thoroughly. Cut off any discolored parts. Cut in 1-inch to 3-inch pieces. Cook 2 minutes in a pressure saucepan or 15 to 20 minutes, covered, in just enough boiling salted water to keep the celery from burning. Drain, if necessary. Add butter to taste.

Creamed Celery. Heat 2 cups cooked celery in 1 cup Cream Sauce (p. 94).

To vary, add 1 or 2 green peppers, seeded, parboiled and cut in small pieces. *Serves 4 to 6.*

BRAISED CELERY

Wash. Cut off the leaves. If the bunches are small, split the stalks in half or cut in even lengths. Put in a frying pan. Add just enough boiling salted water, consommé or stock to keep the celery from burning. Cover and cook until tender (15 to 20 minutes). Take out the celery. Add a little water, consommé or cream to the juices in the pan. Pour over the celery.

Braised Celery au Gratin. Arrange the cooked celery in a shallow baking dish. Sprinkle with melted butter, salt, pepper and plenty of grated Italian cheese. Broil or bake until the cheese melts.

CHAYOTE

This pale green member of the cucumber family is similar to summer squash. One pound serves 4.

Cut in half or in quarters or slice without removing the edible seed. Peel after cooking. Cover with boiling salted water. Cover the pan and cook until tender (15 to 20 minutes). Drain. Serve with melted butter or Tomato Sauce (p. 99).

FRENCH *or* ITALIAN CHESTNUTS

Canned cooked chestnuts are a convenience. One pound serves 3, but often there are imperfect nuts, so allow a little more to be sure.

Shell chestnuts (p. 13). Cover with boiling salted water. Cover the pan and cook gently until tender when tested with a toothpick (15 to 20 minutes). Drain.

Creamed Chestnuts. Heat in a small amount of heavy cream. Season to taste.

Riced Chestnuts. Put through a ricer or strainer. Pile lightly on a serving dish or beat until light with hot milk or cream. Season to taste.

Sautéed Chestnuts. Cook 5 minutes in butter. Serve as a garnish with ham or roast turkey.

CORN

Corn is at its best fresh-picked just before cooking. Fresh corn looks moist and juicy. The kernels are well filled but still soft and milky. Old corn looks hard and dull. Keep ears of corn in the refrigerator until cooking time. Husk just before cooking time.

CORN ON THE COB

Husk, pull off the silky threads and cut out any blemishes with a pointed knife. Defrost frozen corn on the cob. Have ready a deep kettle of unsalted water or half milk and half water. Bring to the boiling point and put in enough ears of corn for the first serving. Let the water come to the boiling point again and boil 5 minutes. (If you are boiling a large quantity of corn, it will be cooked enough as soon as the boiling point is reached.) Lift out with tongs, place on a platter covered with a napkin, and pull the corners over the corn. Serve with plenty of butter.

Buttered Corn. Cut freshly cooked corn from the cob with a long sharp knife and season with butter and salt.

Steamed Corn. Put the ears in the upper section of a steamer, not more than two layers deep. Steam 5 minutes.

Foil-roasted Corn. Wrap husked ears of corn individually in foil. Bake at 400° about 15 minutes. **At a picnic or barbecue,** roast over hot coals, turning once after 10 minutes.

Broiled Corn. Turn the husks back without removing them. Pull off the silky threads. Dip the corn in cold water and replace the husks. Broil on the grill over a picnic fire, turning often, until thoroughly heated (about 15 minutes).

SUCCOTASH

Heat together equal quantities of cooked corn and lima or shell beans. Season with salt and butter. Fresh corn cut from the cob or frozen corn is better for succotash than canned corn.

SCRAPED CORN

Cut uncooked corn from the cob with a long sharp knife. Scrape the cob with the dull edge of the knife to get all the sweet "milk." Add a small amount of cream or top milk, cover and simmer until just tender (about 5 minutes). Watch carefully so that the corn will not scorch. Season with salt, pepper and butter.

MILDRED'S CORN PUDDING

Rich and irresistible with ham or chicken.

Beat for 3 minutes
- **2 cups raw scraped corn**
- **1 cup heavy cream**
- **½ teaspoon salt**

Pour into a baking dish and bake at 325° until firm (about 45 minutes). *Serves 4.*

CORN SOUFFLÉ

Melt
- **1 tablespoon butter**

Stir in
- **2 tablespoons flour**

Add gradually
- **1 cup milk**

Stir and bring to the boiling point. Add
- **2 cups corn, fresh grated, canned, frozen or cooked**
- **2 egg yolks, beaten thick**

Season with
- **1¼ teaspoon salt**
- **Few grains pepper**

Cook 10 minutes or longer. Fold in
- **2 egg whites, beaten stiff**

Spoon into an unbuttered baking dish. Bake 30 minutes at 350°. *Serves 6.*

SOUTHERN CORN PUDDING

Mix
- **2 cups fresh grated corn or chopped canned, frozen or cooked corn**
- **2 eggs, slightly beaten**
- **1 teaspoon sugar**
- **1½ tablespoons melted butter**
- **2 cups scalded milk**
- **1 teaspoon salt**
- **⅛ teaspoon pepper**

Put in a buttered baking dish. Set in a pan of hot water. Bake at 325° until firm (about 45 minutes). *Serves 4 to 6.*

CORN FRITTERS

Chop and drain
- **1 cup fresh or whole-kernel canned corn**

Add
- **1 egg yolk, beaten thick**

Sift together
- **½ cup plus 2 tablespoons flour**

½ teaspoon baking powder
½ teaspoon salt
Few grains paprika

Stir into the corn. Fold in

1 egg white, beaten stiff

Drop from a tablespoon into fat heated to 370°. Cook until delicately brown. Drain on a paper towel. *Serves 4 to 6.*

Corn Oysters. Make the batter with only ¼ cup flour or ½ cup soft bread crumbs. Cook by spoonfuls on a hot griddle in bacon fat or drippings.

SCALLOPED CORN

Put in a saucepan

2 tablespoons butter
½ onion, chopped fine

Cook 5 minutes. Mix

2 tablespoons flour
1 teaspoon salt
¼ teaspoon paprika
¼ teaspoon mustard
Few grains cayenne

Stir into the butter and onion. Add, stirring constantly

½ cup milk

Bring to the boiling point. Stir in

1 cup fresh or drained canned whole-kernel corn
1 egg yolk, slightly beaten

Melt

1 tablespoon butter

Add

½ cup dried bread, broken in small pieces

Stir until brown. Add to the corn mixture. Put in a buttered baking dish. Cover with

⅔ cup buttered cracker crumbs

Bake at 400° until the crumbs are brown. *Serves 4 to 6.*

To season more highly, add a few drops of Worcestershire or Tabasco, or chop a small green pepper and cook it with the onion.

CUCUMBERS

Select firm slender cucumbers, dark green and glossy. Yellow spots show they are too mature and will be seedy and spongy.

Cucumbers in salads (p. 286). On the relish tray (p. 86). Wilted Cucumbers (p. 286).

STEWED CUCUMBERS

Pare the cucumbers unless they are very young and tender. Cut in pieces. Add just enough water, chicken stock or bouillon to keep from burning. Cover closely and stew gently until tender (5 to 15 minutes). Season with butter, salt and pepper.

FRIED CUCUMBERS

One large cucumber serves 3.

Wipe, pare, and cut in slices at least ¼ inch thick. Dry on a paper towel. Sprinkle with salt, pepper and flour. Sauté in butter or dip in crumbs, egg and crumbs (p. 4), and fry in deep fat heated to 390°. Drain on paper towels.

STUFFED CUCUMBERS

Wipe the cucumbers. Pare if the skin is tough. Cut in 2-inch pieces, crosswise. Remove the seeds. Stuff with bread crumbs mixed with finely chopped ham and cheese and moistened with tomato sauce or canned tomato soup. Or stuff with any well-seasoned mixture of bread crumbs or cooked rice combined with bits of cooked meat, chicken, lobster, crab meat or cheese. Put in a baking dish. Surround with stock or consommé. Bake about 30 minutes at 350°. Cover with buttered crumbs and bake until brown.

DANDELION GREENS

See Greens (p. 257).

DASHEENS

This rather uncommon vegetable is violet-colored when cooked. One pound serves 4.

Scrub thoroughly with a brush. Do not pare before cooking, as the raw juice is irritating to the skin. Cover dasheens with boiling salted water. Cook until tender (15 to 30 minutes). Peel. Put through a ricer or vegetable mill. Season with salt and pepper and plenty of butter.

EGGPLANT

Choose one that is satin-smooth and firm. A medium-sized eggplant (1½ pounds) serves 4.

Peel only if skin is very tough. Cut in slices ¼ to ½ inch thick. Dry on paper towel.

Pan-fried or Sautéed Eggplant. Dip in seasoned flour or fine bread crumbs. Brown slowly in butter or bacon fat, turning to cook evenly. Or dip in flour, egg and fine crumbs and fry in fat about ½ inch deep, using bacon fat or oil.

Oven-fried Eggplant. Prepare as for pan-frying but bake at 450° until tender (about 20 minutes). During the baking, sprinkle three times with melted butter or salad oil.

Baked Eggplant. Marinate 15 minutes in French dressing and drain. Or spread with softened butter. Bake until tender at 400° (about 15 minutes), turning once. Sprinkle with lemon juice.

French-fried Eggplant. Dip in Fritter Batter (p. 409), or flour, egg and crumbs (p. 4). Fry at 370°. Delicious cut in julienne strips instead of slices.

SCALLOPED EGGPLANT

Pare and cut in ½-inch cubes

1 eggplant

Cover with boiling water, cook until soft and drain. Melt

2 tablespoons butter

Add

½ onion, chopped fine

Cook until yellow. Add the eggplant and

1 tablespoon finely chopped parsley

Put in a buttered baking dish. Cover with

Buttered crumbs

Bake at 375° until the crumbs are brown. *Serves 4 to 6, according to the size of the eggplant.*

EGGPLANT AND MUSHROOMS

Put in a saucepan

1 tablespoon butter
1 large onion, minced

Cook until yellow. Add

½ pound mushrooms, cut small

Cover and cook 5 minutes. Add

1 eggplant, peeled and cubed
½ cup bouillon
½ clove garlic
Salt to taste

Cover and cook slowly 1 hour. Remove the garlic. *Serves 4.*

EGGPLANT ISTANBUL

Serve with lemon wedges or spoon over fluffy steamed rice and add an extra squeeze of lemon juice. Perfect with roast lamb.

Put in a saucepan

½ cup salad oil
1 eggplant, peeled and cubed
1 onion, chopped fine

Cook 10 minutes. Add

2 cloves garlic, crushed
2 tomatoes, peeled and cut in eighths
1 can tomato paste
Juice of 1 lemon

Simmer 15 minutes. Add

Salt to taste

Serves 6.

EGGPLANT AND OKRA

Put in a saucepan

1 eggplant, peeled and cubed
1 onion, sliced
3 tomatoes, quartered
12 okra pods, sliced
Salt and pepper

Cover. Cook slowly 30 minutes. Sprinkle with

1 tablespoon finely chopped parsley

Serves 4 to 6.

EGGPLANT SOUFFLÉ

Peel and cube

2 eggplants (about 3 pounds)

Cover with boiling salted water. Add

1 slice onion

Cover and cook until soft. Remove the onion. Drain and mash the eggplant. Add

2 tablespoons butter
½ cup bread crumbs
½ cup milk

Season to taste with

Salt, pepper and nutmeg

Stir in

3 egg yolks, slightly beaten

Cool. When ready to bake, fold in

3 egg whites, beaten stiff

Put in an unbuttered baking dish and sprinkle with

2 tablespoons buttered crumbs
2 tablespoons shredded toasted almonds

Bake 30 minutes at 400°. *Serves 6 to 8.*

Eggplant and Mushroom Soufflé. Add ½ cup chopped sautéed mushrooms.

BAKED STUFFED EGGPLANT

Cover with boiling salted water

1 eggplant

Cook 15 minutes. Drain. Cut in half lengthwise. Carefully remove the pulp with a spoon so that you will not break the skin. Chop the pulp and add

1 cup soft bread crumbs

Melt

2 tablespoons butter *or* bacon fat

Add

½ tablespoon finely chopped onion (or more)

Cook 5 minutes. Add to the pulp, season to taste and, if necessary, moisten with

A little stock *or* water

Cook 5 minutes. Cool. Add

1 egg, well beaten

Refill the eggplant. Cover with

Buttered crumbs

Bake at 375° for 25 minutes. *Serves 4 (or 6, if the eggplant is large).*

To vary. Add finely chopped ham, mushrooms or toasted almonds.

RATATOUILLE NIÇOISE

Vary this French luncheon or supper dish to suit your taste or your garden. There should always be tomatoes and cheese with eggplant or zucchini or both.

Peel and cube

1 eggplant

Peel (if skin is tough) and cube

1 zucchini *or* summer squash

Cook 10 minutes in boiling water and drain. Peel and cut in pieces

6 tomatoes

Put in a saucepan

4 tablespoons oil

Add

1 onion, chopped fine

Cook until brown. Add the vegetables and

1 clove garlic, crushed
1 tablespoon chopped parsley
1 bay leaf
Salt and pepper

Cook until the vegetables are tender (about 20 minutes). Season to taste. Place in a shallow baking dish, and sprinkle with

½ cup grated Italian cheese

Brown under the broiler. *Serves 6.*

BRAISED FRENCH ENDIVE

Allow 1 or 2 stalks per person.

Wash under running water and cut off any discolored parts. Leave stalks whole unless they are very large, in which case split them in two pieces. Place in a skillet, add bouillon or chicken broth until ½ inch deep. Sprinkle with salt, cover and cook slowly until tender (about 20 minutes). Drain, if necessary. Add butter, cover, and cook 10 minutes longer.

FENNEL (ANISE)

Fennel is like celery with a licorice flavor. Serve it raw as a relish or cooked. One pound serves 3.

Peel and slice the bulb and as much of the stalk as is tender. Wash and drain. Cook in a covered pan in salted boiling water until tender (15 to 25 minutes). Drain. Sprinkle with salt and pepper and melted butter or olive oil and lemon juice.

FERN FRONDS (FIDDLEHEADS)

Cut young fern shoots at the "fiddlehead" stage. Wash. Peel off the woolly skin. Cook as you would asparagus (about 5 minutes) and season with salt and melted butter.

GREENS

Young tender beet tops, Swiss chard, dandelion greens, collards, kale, chicory, escarole, lettuce, spinach, turnip tops, mustard greens. One pound serves 3, though some greens cook down more than others.

Remove any discolored leaves. Wash greens thoroughly, using slightly warm water at first. Cut off the roots and tough stems and wash again, lifting the greens out of the water to let the sand settle in the pan. Sprinkle with salt. Cook, covered tightly, until just barely tender, in a steamer or in the smallest amount of boiling water possible. The water that clings to the leaves from washing is usually enough. Drain if necessary. Chop fine or cut through a few times. Season with butter, pepper and salt.

KOHLRABI

Allow 1 or 2 to a person. Select small, pale green bulbs.

Cut off the tops, peel and slice. Cook uncovered, in boiling salted water until tender (25 to 35 minutes). Drain thoroughly. Season with melted butter, salt and pepper. If the tops are young and tender, cook in boiling salted water, drain, chop, and add to the sliced bulbs.

LEEKS

One large bunch serves 4.

Wash and trim, leaving about 1½ inches of the green top. Cook until tender 2 or 3 minutes in pressure saucepan or 15 to 20 minutes in boiling salted water. Drain. Serve with melted butter.

Leeks au Gratin. Arrange 8 cooked stalks in a baking dish, sprinkle with salt, pepper and 6 tablespoons grated cheese. Set under the broiler to melt the cheese.

DRIED LENTILS

Follow directions for cooking Dried Beans (p. 244). See also Lentil Soup (p. 71).

BRAISED LETTUCE

Soak in cold water 1 hour

3 small lettuce hearts *or* 1 large heart, quartered

Drain. Tie firmly with string. Cook 10 minutes in boiling salted water. Drain and cut off the string. Melt in a heavy frying pan

2 tablespoons butter

Add the lettuce. Season with

Salt, pepper and nutmeg

Cook slowly 35 minutes. Pour over the lettuce

1 tablespoon lemon juice

Serves 2 or 3.

WILTED LETTUCE

Add onion juice, if you like, or sprinkle the lettuce with 1 teaspoon finely cut onion. Use the same dressing for endive or dandelion greens or for young cabbage, shredded and cooked 5 minutes in boiling water and drained.

Wash and dry thoroughly

2 small heads tender lettuce (not iceberg)

Tear into pieces and put in a large salad bowl. Fry until crisp

4 strips bacon

Drain on a paper towel and crumble into bits. Add to the fat in the pan

2 tablespoons vinegar
2 tablespoons water
Salt and pepper
1 tablespoon brown sugar

Heat to the boiling point. Add the bacon and pour the hot dressing over the lettuce. Toss to wilt the lettuce. Slice hot hard-cooked eggs over the top if you like. *Serves 4.*

VEGETABLE MARROW

See summer squash recipes, page 274.

MUSHROOMS

One pound serves 4 (or 2, if served as main dish). Select firm, unspotted mushrooms. Most city markets have only one variety to offer. Try to find some of the others or learn which ones you can pick, wild, in your part of the country.

Wash. Do not peel unless the skin is tough and brown. If you do have to peel, save the skin to make mushroom soup. Cut off discolored parts and the tough ends of the stems.

SAUTÉED MUSHROOMS

Put in a heavy frying pan

¼ cup butter
1 pound mushrooms, washed and sliced

Season with

Salt, pepper and nutmeg

Cover and cook 10 minutes, stirring occasionally.

Creamed Mushrooms. Sprinkle with 1 tablespoon flour, stir, and add 1 cup of cream or top milk. Cook until slightly thickened. Season to taste with more nutmeg or sherry.

Mushrooms Flambé. Just before serving, add ⅓ cup warmed brandy and light with a match. Serve with steak or chicken. Add ½ cup heavy cream to make a rich sauce.

BROILED MUSHROOMS

Reserve the stems for soup. Dip the caps in milk, oil or melted butter and let stand ½ hour. Arrange in a shallow pan, smooth side up. Broil 3 minutes on each side. Put a small piece of butter in each cap. Sprinkle with salt and pepper. Serve on buttered toast or as a border on the meat platter. Pour juices from the pan over the mushrooms.

Sausage-stuffed Mushrooms. After turning the mushrooms, fill with sausage meat, and broil or bake at 375° until the sausage is cooked (about 20 minutes). Serve as a luncheon or supper dish or with roast turkey.

MUSHROOMS BAKED IN CREAM

Brush or wash and dry large mushrooms. Remove the stems (keep them for soup). Put the caps in a shallow buttered pan, smooth side down. Sprinkle with salt and pepper. Dot with butter and pour a little cream or top milk around them. Bake 10 minutes at 450°. Place on dry toast. Pour the juices over the mushrooms.

FRENCH-FRIED MUSHROOMS

Wash and dry perfect mushrooms. Cut off the stems and keep them for soup. Beat an egg with 1 tablespoon water. Dip each cap in the beaten egg, then in salted bread crumbs. Let stand 1 hour. Fry until brown in deep fat heated to 375°. Serve as a vegetable, as a garnish or appetizer, or for lunch with strips of crisp bacon.

For a thicker coating, dip the mushrooms in Fritter Batter (p. 409).

STUFFED MUSHROOMS

Brush or wash and dry on a paper towel

12 large mushrooms

Cut off the stems and chop them fine. Melt

3 tablespoons butter

Add the mushroom stems and

½ tablespoon finely chopped shallot *or* onion

Cook 10 minutes. Add

1½ tablespoons flour
Chicken stock, tomato juice *or* cream to moisten
Few gratings nutmeg
½ teaspoon finely chopped parsley
Salt and pepper

Cool. Fill the caps, rounding well over the top. Cover with

Buttered cracker crumbs

Bake 15 minutes at 425°.

To vary. Add finely chopped cooked chicken or turkey liver, ham, celery or cheese.

MUSHROOM RING

Melt in a frying pan

2 tablespoons butter

Add

1 tablespoon chopped onion

Cook slowly until golden. Add

½ pound mushrooms, chopped

Cook and stir 5 minutes. Add

½ teaspoon salt
⅛ teaspoon nutmeg
Few grains pepper
2 tablespoons flour

Add slowly, stirring constantly

½ cup milk

Cook and stir until thickened. Add

2 beaten eggs

Pour into a buttered ring mold. Bake at 350° until firm (about 30 minutes). Serve with buttered green peas or beans in the center of the ring. *Serves 6.*

Mushroom Flan. Most attractive done in a flan ring, but a pie plate will do. Flan rings are available in shops selling French cooking equipment. Increase the onion to one whole chopped onion. Pour the filling into an 8-inch pie plate or flan ring lined with Plain Pastry (p. 438). Bake at 400° until delicately browned (about 30 minutes). *Serves 6.*

OKRA (GUMBO)

One pound serves 6. Select small, crisp green pods.

Wash well and cut off the stems. If very young and small, leave whole. Otherwise, cut in ½-inch slices.

Stewed Okra. Cook 3 minutes in a pressure saucepan or until tender in salted boiling water to cover (10 to 20 minutes). Drain. Season with salt, pepper, butter and vinegar.

Okra with Tomatoes. Stew ½ pound okra (or 1 can) with 2 cups stewed or canned tomatoes. Season to taste.

Okra Baked in Tomato Sauce. Brown 1 sliced onion in 2 tablespoons butter. Add 1 pound sliced okra. Cook 3 minutes. Season. Put in a casserole, pour over the okra 1 cup tomato sauce or concentrated tomato soup. Bake 30 minutes at 350°.

ONIONS

Scallions, young green onions, tiny button onions, white, yellow and red cooking onions, mild Italian, Spanish and Bermuda onions—all are good. Select firm onions with dry crackly skins and no green sprouts. Buy a few at a time unless you have a cool dry place to store them.

BOILED ONIONS

One pound serves 4.

Peel, holding the onion under running water to keep the eyes from watering, or cover with boiling water, drain, dip in cold water, and slip off the skins. Make two crossed gashes on the root end. Cook until tender (10 minutes in a pressure saucepan or 20 to 40 in boiling salted water in a deep, uncovered pan). Drain. Add a little top milk or cream, cook 5 minutes and season with butter, salt and pepper.

Creamed Silverskins. Cook small onions 15 minutes. Drain. Add thin cream (1 cup for 3 cups onions) and cook in a double boiler until soft. Add salt to taste when the onions are nearly done.

Scalloped Onions. Put in a buttered baking dish 2 cups cooked onions (quartered). Cover with 1 cup Cream Sauce (p. 94) or canned cream of celery or mushroom soup. Sprinkle with buttered crumbs. Bake at 400° until brown. Mix grated cheese with the sauce if you like.

GREEN ONIONS *or* SCALLIONS ON TOAST

Trim off any wilted parts. Cook in boiling salted water until just tender (about 10 minutes). Drain. Serve on buttered toast. Season melted butter with salt and pepper and pour it over the onions.

BROILED ONIONS

Cut large mild onions in ½-inch slices. Put in a shallow pan. Season with salt and pepper. Dot with butter. Broil until tender (about 15 minutes), turning once.

ONIONS AND GREEN PEPPERS

Remove the seeds and the white membrane from

1 or 2 green peppers

Cut in very thin slivers. Sauté slowly until tender in

2 tablespoons butter

Stir in

2 tablespoons flour

Blend well. Add

1 cup rich milk *or* thin cream

Cook and stir until thickened. Add

1 pound small onions, cooked or canned

Heat slowly. Season to taste with

Salt and pepper

Serves 6.

FRENCH-FRIED ONIONS

Canned and frozen fried onion rings are very good—heat them in the oven before serving.

Peel 4 large mild sweet onions. Cut in ¼-inch slices and separate into rings. Dip in milk, drain, and dip in ½ cup flour mixed with ½ teaspoon salt. Fry 4 to 6 minutes in deep fat heated to 370° (p. 4). Drain on a paper towel and sprinkle with salt. Serve with cocktails or on steak.

SMOTHERED ONIONS

Peel 4 medium-sized onions and cut in thin slices. Sauté very slowly in butter until delicately brown. Turn occasionally with a fork so that the onions will not burn. Sprinkle with salt. *Serves 4.*

ONIONS BAKED IN CREAM

Two large onions serve 4 to 6.

Cut large sweet onions in thin slices. Arrange in a baking dish. Sprinkle with salt and pepper. Add enough cream to cover. Bake at 325° until tender.

GLAZED ONIONS

Drain cooked or canned tiny onions. For each cupful, melt 1 tablespoon butter with 2 teaspoons sugar or 1 tablespoon honey. Add the onions. Cook slowly until brown (about 20 minutes), turning occasionally. Cook on an asbestos mat over low heat or in a 350° oven. *1 cup serves 2.*

ONION SOUFFLÉ

See page 240, Vegetable Soufflé.

GREEN ONION PIE

Wonderful with sliced ham or tongue. If you prefer, bake as you would custard, without bothering with the pastry shell, and spoon it from the baking dish.

Put in a saucepan

3 tablespoons butter
3 cups sliced green onions *or* scallions

Cook slowly until tender. Put in an

Unbaked pie shell 8 or 9 inches

Mix

2 eggs, slightly beaten
½ cup cream
1 teaspoon salt
Pepper *or* nutmeg to taste

Pour over the onions. Bake at 425° until firm (about 20 minutes). *Serves 6.*

CHEESE AND ONION CASSEROLE

Cut in quarters

6 slices bread

Have ready

2 cups drained small white onions, cooked or canned
1 cup grated Cheddar cheese

Put the bread, onions and cheese in a buttered casserole in layers. Mix

4 eggs, beaten slightly
2 cups milk
½ teaspoon salt
Few grains pepper

Pour over the mixture in the

casserole. Set in a pan of hot water and bake at 350° until firm (about 45 minutes). *Serves 6.*

STUFFED ONIONS

An excellent way to use left-overs or to prepare a casserole dish well in advance. Do only the final browning at the last.

Cook large flat onions until tender in deep boiling salted water (about 30 minutes). Drain and cool. Take out part of the centers to make cups. Fill with sausage meat or with any well-seasoned mixture of cooked meat or chicken, chopped mushrooms and soft bread crumbs, moistened with cream or melted butter. Place in a baking dish with a small amount of water or stock. Sprinkle with buttered crumbs. Cover. Bake at 350° until soft, removing the cover the last 10 minutes. *Serves 6.*

OYSTER PLANT (SALSIFY)

Similar to parsnips but darker, with a flavor somewhat like oysters. One bunch (about 6 roots) serves 6.

Wash, scrape and put in cold water with a little vinegar or lemon juice to prevent discoloration. Cut in inch slices or strips. Do not salt before cooking. Cook until tender (10 minutes in pressure saucepan or 20 to 45 minutes in boiling water in a covered pan). Drain. Season with butter, salt and pepper.

Oyster Plant aux Fines Herbes. Add 1 teaspoon finely chopped parsley and 1/4 teaspoon finely chopped chives. Sprinkle with salt and pepper.

Oyster Plant Fritters. Mash. Season with butter, salt and pepper. Shape in small flat cakes, roll in flour, and brown in butter.

PARSNIPS

One pound serves 3 or 4. Parsnips are at their best in the spring. Large ones may have woody cores.

Wash, scrape and slice or cut in strips. Remove the cores, if woody. Cook until tender (30 to 40 minutes in boiling salted water, 4 to 10 minutes in a pressure saucepan). Drain and season with salt, nutmeg and butter.

Sautéed Parsnips. Boil small whole parsnips. Drain and cut in eighths lengthwise. Brown delicately in butter. Sprinkle with salt and pepper. **To candy,** sprinkle with brown sugar before sautéeing.

Parsnip Fritters. Mash. Season with butter, salt and pepper. Shape in 3-inch patties. Dip in flour and sauté on both sides in butter.

Caramel Parsnips. Scrape small whole parsnips. Cook 20 minutes and drain. Put in a shallow baking dish. Dot with butter. Sprinkle with brown sugar. Bake at 400° about 20 minutes.

Parsnip Soufflé. Follow recipe for Vegetable Soufflé (p. 240).

GREEN PEAS

Fresh peas have shiny green pods. Open a pod and taste to see if the peas are young and sweet. Do not shell until time to cook them. Store in the refrigerator. Young peas from a nearby farm—or your own garden—are best of all. Frozen peas are good, too, and so are canned tiny French peas which are very tender and delicious. One pound serves 2.

BUTTERED PEAS

Shell the peas. Put in a saucepan. Add just enough water to keep the peas from burning. Cover and cook until tender but not mushy. A pressure cooker is too fast for young peas. Season with salt, pepper and butter. Add a trace of sugar if the peas are not young and sweet.

Peas on Artichoke Bottoms. Serve on canned artichoke bottoms, sprinkled with lemon juice. Pour a little heated cream over them.

PETITS POIS À LA FRANÇAISE

Very young and tender peas are perfect cooked this way.

Put in a deep pan
- **1 tablespoon butter**
- **2 pound peas, shelled**

Lay over the peas
- **2 or 3 leaves of lettuce, rinsed in cold water**

Cover. Cook over low heat until the peas are just tender (10 minutes or more). Season with
- **Salt and pepper**
- **Butter**

Serves 4 or 5.

Petits Pois with Onions. Brown 12 tiny cooked or canned onions lightly in butter. Over them lay ½ head of lettuce, shredded, and the shelled peas. Vary by adding a few sliced sautéed mushrooms. Moisten, when cooked, with a little heavy cream. *Serves 6.*

PURÉE OF GREEN PEAS

Put cooked or canned peas through a vegetable mill or strainer or whirl in a blender. Beat until light and smooth with hot milk or cream. Season to taste. Keep hot in a double boiler. Dust with paprika. This is an excellent way to use old or tough peas. Vary the seasoning by cooking a slice of onion and a sprig or two of parsley with the peas.

Ring Mold of Green Peas. To 2 cups of puréed peas, add 2 well-beaten eggs and 2 tablespoons of melted butter. For a fluffier mixture, add the beaten whites last. Fill a buttered ring mold. Set in a shallow pan of hot water and cover with buttered paper. Bake at 350° until firm (about 25 minutes). Fill the center with creamed shrimp, chicken or mushrooms or Carrots Vichy (p. 250).

SNOW PEAS

Snow peas have tender edible pods. The tiny ones are delicious cooked, covered with French dressing, chilled and served as a salad.

Wash but do not shell. Cook them, shells and all, until tender (15 minutes or longer) in a covered pan in just enough salted water to keep them from burning. Drain, if necessary, and serve with Hollandaise (p. 100) or melted butter.

PURÉE OF SPLIT PEAS

Cover 1 pound of split peas with boiling water and cook 2 minutes. Remove from the heat and let stand 1 hour or more. Add a hambone or a piece of salt pork and cook slowly, covered, until the peas are soft. Drain and remove the bone or pork. Put the peas through a purée strainer. Season to taste. Add butter or heavy cream. *Serves 6.*

PEPPERS

Sweet (bell) peppers, green or red, are the ones usually cooked as a vegetable. The sharp green or red or chili peppers are used chiefly for seasoning. Pimientos are sweet red peppers preserved in oil. Peppers (especially the red ones) are one of the richest sources of vitamins A and C.

SAUTÉED BELL (SWEET) PEPPERS

Cut in half. Remove the seeds and the tough white membrane. Cut in small pieces. Put in a frying pan with butter, salad oil or bacon fat (2 tablespoons for 4 to 6 persons), cover, and cook over moderate heat 5 to 10 minutes. Sprinkle with salt and pepper. Serve as a vegetable or as a garnish.

FRENCH-FRIED PEPPER RINGS

Slice green sweet peppers in thin rings. Cover with boiling water, cook 5 minutes, and drain on a paper towel. Dip in egg slightly beaten with 1 tablespoon water, then in fine crumbs. Fry, a few at a time, in deep fat, heated to 370° (p. 4). Drain on a paper towel.

STUFFED GREEN PEPPERS

If the peppers are small, leave them whole and cut off a slice from the stem end. Cut large peppers in half. Remove the seeds and tough white membrane. Cook in boiling water 5 minutes and drain. Sprinkle with salt. Cool. Fill generously, as suggested below. Cover with grated cheese or buttered bread crumbs. Bake 15 minutes at 350°. Raise the temperature to 400° and bake until the tops are brown.

FILLINGS FOR PEPPERS

Scraped Corn (p. 253) or canned corn, sprinkled with salt and pepper.

Cheese. Mix grated cheese with an equal quantity of bread crumbs. Season to taste with salt, pepper, paprika and chopped onion or onion salt.

Chicken, Ham or Veal. Chop cooked meat. Mix with an equal quantity of bread crumbs. Season to taste. Add chopped sautéed mushrooms, if you like.

Hamburg and Rice (*to fill 4 peppers*). Sauté in 2 tablespoons butter 1 small onion, chopped, ½ pound ground beef, and 2 peeled and diced tomatoes (or ½ cup canned tomatoes). Add 1 cup cooked rice and season with salt and pepper.

Sweetbreads. Parboil (p. 210). Chop and mix with hot cooked rice. Moisten with concentrated tomato soup, and season to taste.

POTATOES

Potatoes rank with wheat in their combination of high food value and low cost. They are rich in minerals and vitamins and are a valuable daily item on the family menu.

Choose firm large potatoes for baking, French-frying and mashing. Small new potatoes are at their best boiled or steamed.

For a small family buy only enough potatoes for one or two weeks at a time. To store in quantity, keep in a dry cellar, cool but not freezing. Look over frequently and remove sprouts as they appear. Or dust with a commercial powder which prevents sprouting.

BAKED POTATOES

Use firm smooth potatoes with no blemishes. New potatoes will not bake well. Bake potatoes of uniform size, or start the larger ones earlier. Scrub with a vegetable brush. Place in a shallow pan, on a potato baker or directly on an oven rack. (It is easier to take them out if they are in a pan or on a baker.)

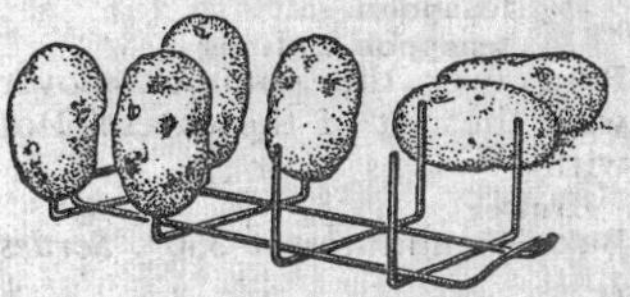

Baking potatoes on spikes

Bake until soft at any convenient temperature from 350° to 450°. At 350° medium-sized potatoes take about 1 hour and 10 minutes, at 450° about 40 minutes. To test, pick up one potato in a folded towel and squeeze gently. If it feels soft, the potatoes are done.

Cut a cross in the top of each and press the sides of the potato so that steam will escape. Put a bit of butter in each or serve plain. Potatoes will remain dry and fluffy if the serving dish is left uncovered.

West Coast Baked Potatoes. Serve with the potatoes a bowl of sour cream, a dish of chopped chives, salt and pepper.

STUFFED BAKED POTATOES

Bake potatoes (above). Cut in half lengthwise. Scoop out and mash thoroughly. Beat well, adding hot milk until the mixture is soft and fluffy (1 teaspoon or more for each potato). Season to taste with butter, salt and pepper. Add, if you like, grated cheese, minced green pepper sautéed in butter, minced pimiento or ham. Refill the shells. Brush with butter or sprinkle with grated cheese. Set on a baking sheet. Shortly before serving time, put in a 450° oven to reheat and brown (8 to 10 minutes unless the potatoes are very cold).

BOILED POTATOES

Allow 1 medium-sized potato per serving or 1 pound new potatoes for 5.

Scrub well. Do not peel. Leave small potatoes whole. Cut large ones in half. Put in a pan with about 1 inch of boiling water. Sprinkle with salt, cover and cook quickly until just tender (12 minutes for tiny new potatoes, 20 minutes or more for old ones). Add more water from time to time to keep the potatoes from burning.

Drain, if necessary, and shake over the heat a moment to dry. Peel old potatoes. Serve young potatoes unpeeled, peeled or with a band of peel.

Tuck a dish towel over the potatoes to keep them warm and to absorb steam so they will not be soggy. When ready to serve, put the potatoes in a heated serving dish. Pour melted butter over them and dust with paprika or chopped parsley, unless you are serving a sauce or gravy.

Parsley, Dill or Minted Potatoes. For 1 pound of potatoes, add 1 tablespoon lemon juice to ½ cup melted butter. Sprinkle the cooked potatoes with chopped parsley, fresh dill or mint, or roll small potatoes in parsley, dill or mint, and pour the melted butter around them.

STEAMED POTATOES

Prepare as for boiled potatoes (p. 265). Place in the perforated upper part of a steamer over boiling water. Cover tightly and steam until done. Or steam in a pressure cooker.

SPRING POTATOES WITH PEAS

Wash tiny new potatoes but do not pare. Steam for 10 minutes. Drain and add cream to half cover them. Cover and cook slowly until tender. Add an equal quantity of cooked peas. Season with salt, pepper and butter.

HOLLANDAISE POTATOES

Save the drained chicken broth to use in soup.

Slice or cube
 2 cups potatoes, pared or not
Cover with
 Chicken Stock (p. 62) *or* **canned chicken broth**
Cook until tender. Drain. Cream
 ½ cup butter
Beat in
 2 teaspoons lemon juice
Season with
 Salt and cayenne
Add to the potatoes. Stir and cook 5 minutes. Sprinkle with
 1 teaspoon chopped parsley
Serves 4.

POTATOES AU GRATIN

Rub a baking dish with
 1 clove garlic, split
 Butter
Grate
 ¼ pound Cheddar cheese
Sprinkle half of it in the baking dish. Cover evenly with
 2 cups sliced cooked peeled potatoes
Sprinkle with
 Salt and pepper
Mix
 2 eggs, beaten slightly
 1 cup milk
 ½ teaspoon salt
 ¼ teaspoon nutmeg
Pour over the potatoes. Cover with the rest of the cheese. Dot with
 Butter
Bake 45 minutes at 350°. *Serves 4.*

MASHED POTATOES

Peel the potatoes. Cut in pieces and cook, covered, in just enough boiling water to keep the potatoes from burning. Drain, reserving the water (there should be very little). Put the potatoes back in the pan and set over very low heat. Have ready about ½ cup hot milk or cream (for 6 potatoes). Crush the potatoes with a blending fork or a potato masher or put through a ricer. Beat until snowy white and as fluffy as whipped cream, adding the reserved cooking water and the hot milk, little by little, as you beat. Use enough milk so that the potatoes will not be dry, but be careful not to use so much that they are too soft to stand up in peaks.

For very fluffy potatoes, use a portable electric beater. Do not transfer potatoes to a bowl—beat them right in the pan over low heat.

Season to taste with salt and pepper. Spoon lightly into a heated dish and put a dab of butter on top. Serve immediately, if possible. If necessary, keep hot in a double boiler, uncovered.

To add extra protein. When the potatoes are fluffy, sprinkle powdered milk (1 or 2 tablespoons for each 1/4 cup of liquid used) over them and beat again. Season.

Riced Potatoes. Put the cooked potatoes through a ricer directly into a heated serving dish. Dot with butter and sprinkle with paprika.

Mashed Potato Border. Using a large tablespoon, put spoonfuls of potato around the platter to make a scalloped edge. Dust with paprika or sprinkle with chopped parsley or chives. Or, if you are using a heatproof platter, brush potato with egg yolk (slightly beaten with 1 tablespoon water) and brown 5 minutes at 400°.

Potatoes Fondante. Pile in a baking dish. For 5 potatoes, pour over 1/2 cup heavy cream. Sprinkle with 3/4 cup coarse dry bread crumbs. Bake at 425° until crumbs are brown. *Serves 6.*

Savory Potatoes. For each 2 potatoes, beat in 1 teaspoon chopped watercress and 1/8 teaspoon finely cut mint.

Spanish Potatoes. For each 2 potatoes, beat in 1 teaspoon canned pimiento, puréed or cut in small pieces.

POTATO CAKES

Shape cold mashed potato in small flat cakes. If the potatoes are too dry to make firm cakes, stir in an egg, slightly beaten. Roll lightly in flour. Brown on both sides in bacon fat or butter.

DUCHESS POTATOES

For planked steak or fish. See also Mashed Potato Border (above).

Mix
- **2 cups Riced Potatoes (above)**
- **2 tablespoons butter**
- **3 egg yolks, slightly beaten**

Beat well. Make a border on the plank or platter, using a pastry bag or a tablespoon.

CHANTILLY POTATOES

Spoon lightly into a baking dish
- **3 cups Mashed Potatoes (p. 266)**

Beat until stiff
- **1/2 cup heavy cream**

Fold in
- **1/2 cup grated cheese**

Season with
- **Salt and pepper**

Spread over the potatoes. Bake at 350° until delicately brown. *Serves 6.*

PITTSBURGH POTATOES

Cook in boiling salted water to cover
- **2 cups potato cubes**
- **1 teaspoon chopped onion (or more)**

Drain. Put in a buttered baking dish. Mix
- **1 or 2 canned pimientos, cut in small pieces**
- **1 cup Cheese Sauce (p. 95)**

Pour over the potatoes. Bake at 350° until the potatoes are soft. *Serves 6.*

FRANCONIA POTATOES
(Pan-roasted)

Pare medium potatoes. Cook 10 minutes in boiling salted water. Drain and place in the pan in which meat is roasting. Bake until soft (about 1 hour), basting several times with the fat in the pan.

BROILED NEW POTATOES

Pare small potatoes. Boil 10 minutes in salted water. Drain. Brush with melted butter. Broil until tender (10 to 15 minutes), turning to brown evenly.

SCALLOPED POTATOES

Melt
  2 tablespoons butter
Stir in
  1 tablespoon flour
Add slowly, stirring constantly
  1½ cups milk
Cook and stir over low heat until thickened. Season to taste with
  Salt and pepper
Put in a buttered baking dish
  4 potatoes, peeled and sliced
  1 onion, chopped fine
Pour the sauce over the top. Bake at 350° until tender (about 1¼ hours). *Serves 4 to 6.*

To vary, sprinkle grated cheese, buttered crumbs or toasted wheat germ over the top before baking.

SCALLOPED POTATOES COUNTRY STYLE

The easiest method, but the milk may curdle if you are making a large amount.

Pare the potatoes and cut in thin slices. Put a layer in a buttered baking dish. Sprinkle with salt, pepper and flour. Dot with butter. Repeat, having no more than 3 layers. Add milk until it can be seen through the top layer. Bake 1¼ hours at 350° or until the potatoes are tender.

Scalloped Potatoes with Onion. Sprinkle each layer with 1 teaspoon minced onion.

GERMAN-FRIED POTATOES

Allow 1 medium-sized potato per person.

Wash, pare, and slice thin, using a vegetable slicer. Let stand ½ hour in cold water. Drain and dry between towels. Heat fat ½ inch deep in a heavy frying pan. Put in the potatoes. Sprinkle with salt. Sauté slowly until evenly browned (about 15 minutes), turning occasionally. Cover and cook slowly 15 minutes longer or until tender.

To vary, cook minced onion in the fat before adding the potatoes.

Chambéry Potatoes. Instead of frying the sliced potatoes, arrange them in layers in a well-buttered shallow baking dish. Season each layer with salt and pepper and brush over with melted butter. Bake at 350° until tender and well browned (about 45 minutes).

HASHED BROWN POTATOES

Chop or dice raw or cooked potatoes. Season with salt and a few grains of pepper. For 2 cups potatoes, melt 3 tablespoons bacon fat or butter in a heavy pan. Put in the potatoes, stir and lift until the potatoes are well coated with fat. Reduce the heat and cook until the potatoes are tender and there is a crisp brown crust on the bottom (20 minutes for cooked potatoes, 30 or more for raw potatoes). Add more fat from time to time if necessary to keep the potatoes from sticking. Fold like an omelet and transfer to a hot platter.

POTATO PANCAKES

Grate and drain
3 medium-sized raw potatoes
Add
1 tablespoon flour *or* 2 tablespoons dry bread crumbs
1 tablespoon cream, sweet *or* sour
1 egg, beaten light
1 teaspoon salt
Grated onion *or* onion salt to taste
Stir well. Cook by spoonfuls in
Hot bacon or other fat
turning once. Or cook in one big pancake. Serve with meats, with
Applesauce, cranberry sauce *or* sour cream
to spoon over the pancakes. *Serves 4 or 5.*

FRENCH-FRIED POTATOES

To save time use packaged potatoes prepared for frying or frozen fried potatoes, which need only to be heated.

Wash and pare firm potatoes. Cut in eighths lengthwise, or with a special cutter or in balls or 1-inch cubes. Cover with cold water. Let stand at least 30 minutes. Drain. Dry thoroughly on a paper towel so that water will not make the fat sputter. Heat fat to 370° (p. 4). Put a single layer of potatoes in the frying basket. Fry 5 minutes. Keep the basket in motion so that the potatoes will fry evenly. Drain on a paper towel. Repeat until all are done. Just before time to serve, heat the fat to 390°. Put the potatoes in the

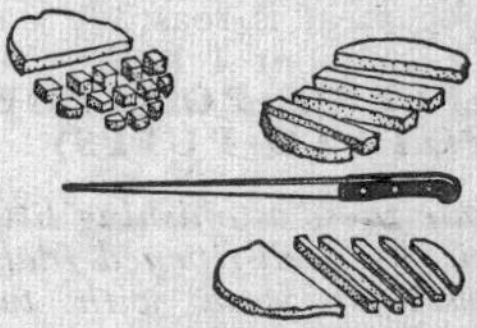

frying basket. Fry until crisp and brown. Keep the basket in motion. Drain; sprinkle with salt.

Oven-fried Potatoes. Dip the prepared potatoes in melted butter, bacon fat or suet. Put in a shallow pan. Bake at 400° for 40 minutes or till delicately brown, turning occasionally. Sprinkle with salt.

Potato Chips. Slice as thin as possible, using a vegetable cutter. Soak 2 hours in cold water, changing the water twice. Fry at 390°. Keep the chips warm but omit the second frying. Unpeeled sweet potatoes are delicious this way as a vegetable or as a cocktail tidbit.

Fried Potatoes Burgoyne. Melt 1 tablespoon butter in a heavy frying pan. Add 1 teaspoon finely cut chives and 2 cups French-fried potatoes. Stir gently until the butter is absorbed. *Serves 4.*

O'Brion Potatoes. Cook a slice of onion in 1 tablespoon butter

3 minutes. Remove the onion. Add 2 canned pimientos, cut small. Add 2 cups fried potato cubes. Stir gently to blend. Sprinkle with chopped parsley. *Serves 4.*

SOUFFLÉED POTATOES (POTATO PUFFS)

To create these astonishing little balloons, use well-ripened Idaho potatoes and work with two kettles of fat. Frozen potato puffs are ready for the second frying.

Pare potatoes. Cut in even slices, ⅛ inch thick, using a vegetable slicer. Do not use the ends of the potatoes, since it is necessary to have even pieces to make perfect puffs. If the slices seem large, cut out rounds with a small biscuit cutter. Soak in ice water 5 minutes, drain and dry thoroughly on paper towels.

Prepare two kettles of fat, one heated to 250°, the other to 425°. Fry the potato slices, a few at a time, at the lower temperature for 3 minutes. Keep well submerged during frying and turn at least once. At the end of 3 minutes, lift in a wire basket and put immediately into the 425° kettle. (The potatoes will puff instantly if they are the right type. If not, it is hopeless to try to prepare them this way. Cut the rest in strips and fry according to directions on page 4.) Continue to fry until delicately brown.

Remove and drain on paper toweling in a 350° oven until all are ready for serving. Salt and serve immediately.

POTATO CROQUETTES

Boil the potatoes. Drain, mash well or put through a ricer or food mill. For each cup (*1 cup serves 3*) add 1 tablespoon butter. Beat well and season to taste with salt, pepper and a few grains of cayenne. Season more highly, if you desire, by adding celery salt, onion salt or chopped parsley. For a richer mixture, stir in 1 egg yolk for each cup of potatoes.

Chill. Shape by tablespoonfuls into balls. Roll quickly into cylinders or cones. Egg and crumb. Fry in deep fat at 390° and drain (p. 4). Keep warm in 350° oven until ready to serve.

CREAMED POTATOES

Boil or bake potatoes. For additional seasoning put a stalk of celery in the water in which you boil the potatoes. If you bake them (for exceptionally delicious flavor) take the potatoes from the oven while they are still firm. Peel and cube. *One cup serves 2 or 3.*

For each cup of potatoes, heat ½ cup cream in a double boiler. (Or make Cream Sauce, p. 94, but cream is far more delicious.) Add the potatoes. Season to taste. Add, if you like, chopped pimiento, parsley or grated cheese. Cook at least 30 minutes to develop the best flavor.

To have ready ahead of time, put in a baking dish, sprinkle with buttered crumbs and/or grated cheese and bake at 350° until nicely browned.

QUICK CREAMED POTATOES

Peel and dice into a saucepan
4 or 5 potatoes
Add
½ cup boiling water
½ teaspoon salt
Cover and cook 10 minutes.

Uncover and simmer until the water has almost evaporated. Add

½ cup milk *or* cream

Season to taste. Cook until slightly thickened, stirring gently with a fork. Sprinkle with

2 tablespoons chopped parsley

Serves 4 or 5.

POTATOES HASHED IN CREAM

Bake at 350° until barely tender but still firm

4 medium-sized potatoes

Cool, peel and chop in a chopping bowl. Melt

2 tablespoons butter

Stir in

1 tablespoon flour

Add slowly

1 cup heavy cream

Cook and stir until the cream bubbles. Season with

Salt and freshly ground pepper

Add the potatoes, mix well, and spoon into a baking dish. Dot with

2 tablespoons butter

Bake at 350° until brown (about 30 minutes). *Serves 4.*

CURRIED POTATOES

Melt in a large saucepan

¼ cup butter

Add

1 small onion, chopped fine

Cook until yellow. Add

3 cups cold boiled potato cubes

Cook until the butter is absorbed. Add

½ cup Chicken Stock (p. 62) *or* canned chicken broth
½ tablespoon curry powder
½ tablespoon lemon juice
Salt and pepper

Cook until the potatoes have absorbed the stock. *Serves 6.*

LYONNAISE POTATOES

Put in a large frying pan

3 tablespoons butter
1 small onion, chopped fine

Cook until yellow. Add

2 cups cold boiled potato cubes
Salt and pepper

Stir until well mixed. Add

2 tablespoons consommé *or* stock

Cover and cook slowly until the potato is brown underneath. Fold like an omelet. Sprinkle with

Finely chopped parsley

Serves 6.

ALPHONSO POTATOES

Cook 6 minutes in boiling water

1 green pepper, seeded

Drain and mince. Add to

2 cups cold cooked potato cubes

Add

¾ cup milk
½ teaspoon salt

Simmer 15 minutes. Put in a buttered baking dish. Sprinkle with

1½ tablespoons grated Parmesan cheese

Bake 10 minutes at 400°. *Serves 6.*

COTTAGE-FRIED POTATOES

Dice or slice cold boiled potatoes. Season with salt and pepper. Brown on both sides in well-greased heavy frying pan. See also Hashed Brown Potatoes (p. 268).

BROILED POTATOES WITH CHEESE

Cut cooked peeled or unpeeled potatoes in thick slices. Brush with butter and broil on the buttered side until brown. Turn, brush with butter and put a thin wedge of Mozzarella cheese on each slice. Broil until the cheese melts and bubbles.

SWEET POTATOES AND YAMS

Sweet potatoes belong to a different species than white potatoes. They contain more sugar and fat and are a good source of vitamin A. They are particularly delicious with ham, roast pork and roast goose. Yams are sweeter and juicier than sweet potatoes. Canned sweet potatoes are satisfactory especially when fresh sweet potatoes are out of season.

Baked Sweet Potatoes. Scrub. Bake at 375° until soft (about 50 minutes).

Boiled Sweet Potatoes. Scrub. Cover with boiling salted water. Cover. Cook until soft (about 20 minutes). Drain. Peel.

Fried Sweet Potatoes. Boil 10 minutes. Drain, peel, and cut in strips. Fry in deep fat at 375° (p. 4). Drain on a paper towel. Sprinkle with salt. Yams are too soft to fry successfully.

Sautéed Sweet Potatoes. Boil, drain, and dice or slice. Sauté in butter until lightly browned. Sprinkle with orange juice and grated orange rind.

Franconia Sweet Potatoes. Pare. Cover with boiling salted water. Cook 10 minutes. Drain and put in the pan with roasting meat about 1 hour before it is done. Baste every 10 minutes with the fat in the pan.

SHERRIED SWEET POTATOES

Bake potatoes. Scoop out and mash. Moisten with cream. Season with salt, butter and sherry to taste. Refill the skins. Bake 5 minutes at 425°.

MASHED SWEET POTATOES

Allow 1 potato per serving.

Boil, drain and mash sweet potatoes. Moisten with hot milk or orange juice and beat until light. Add salt and butter to taste. If desired, add a few grains of nutmeg, allspice and cinnamon, or a few grains of ginger. Chopped candied ginger is delicious in any sweet potato dish.

Sweet Potatoes Calypso. Moisten with rum and add ½ teaspoon vanilla (for 6 potatoes).

Sweet Potatoes de Luxe. To 6 potatoes add ½ cup drained crushed pineapple or ½ cup chopped pecan nut meats. Put in a buttered baking dish. Dot with marshmallows. Bake at 375° until the marshmallows melt and brown.

Sweet Potatoes Georgian Style. Put in a buttered baking dish, leaving a rough surface. Boil 2 tablespoons molasses and 1 teaspoon butter 5 minutes. Pour over the potatoes. Bake at 400° until delicately brown.

Sweet Potatoes in Orange Cups. Cut oranges in half. Remove the pulp and white membrane. Use orange juice to moisten the potatoes. Add some orange pulp, cut small, if liked. Flavor with sherry or rum. Fill the orange shells and sprinkle with brown sugar. Bake at 350° until slightly glazed.

Sweet Potato Puffs. Shape in 2-inch balls. Brush with melted butter. Roll in corn flakes, chopped crisp bacon, or chopped almonds. Arrange on a baking sheet. Bake at 350° until brown. **To vary,** mold the balls around marshmallow halves. When baked, the marshmallow melts and blends with the potato to make a soft creamy center.

SWEET POTATO AND APPLE SCALLOP

Have ready

2 cups boiled sweet potatoes, sliced thin
1½ cups tart apples, sliced thin
½ cup brown sugar
4 tablespoons butter
1 teaspoon salt

Put half the potatoes in a buttered baking dish. Cover with half the apples, sprinkle with half the sugar, dot with half the butter, and sprinkle with half the salt. Repeat. Cover and bake ½ hour at 350°. Uncover and bake until the apples are soft and the top is brown. *Serves 6.*

To vary. In place of apple use 1 cup pineapple, chunk-style or crushed. Add ¾ cup pineapple juice before baking.

CANDIED SWEET POTATOES

Canned sweet potatoes are usually too soft to prepare this way. Instead, make a syrup of the butter, sugar and water, add the sliced potatoes and heat.

Boil until tender but still firm

4 medium-sized sweet potatoes

Pare and cut in half lengthwise. Heat in a heavy frying pan

¼ cup butter
⅓ cup brown sugar

Add the potatoes and turn until brown on both sides. Add

¼ cup water

Cover closely, reduce the heat, and cook until tender and delicately brown. If you prefer, bake at 300°. *Serves 4.*

Sweet Potatoes Flambé. Pour ½ cup brandy over the potatoes, light with a match and serve flaming.

Vermont Candied Sweet Potatoes. Heat ½ cup maple syrup with ¼ cup butter and 1 teaspoon Angostura bitters. Add the potatoes and simmer until tender.

SWEET POTATO CROQUETTES

Mix

2 cups hot riced sweet potatoes
2 tablespoons butter
½ teaspoon salt
Few grains pepper
1 egg, slightly beaten

If very dry, moisten with

Hot milk *or* cream

Shape in croquettes. Roll in flour or dip in crumbs, egg and crumbs. Fry in deep fat at 375° (p. 4) or sauté in butter. *Serves 6.*

Sweet Potato Balls. Shape in small balls instead of croquettes.

Sweet Potatoes Amandine. Add to the mixture ¼ cup chopped almonds, ⅛ teaspoon nutmeg and 1 teaspoon sugar. Croquettes may be rolled in chopped almonds instead of crumbs.

RADISHES

Piquant and unusual as a cooked vegetable. Allow about ⅓ cup per person. As a relish (pp. 86, 281).

Creamed Radishes. Slice. Add to Cream Sauce (p. 94), using 1 cup sauce for 1 to 1½ cups radishes. Cook over hot water until the radishes are tender (about 25 minutes).

Radishes Hollandaise. Cover sliced radishes with boiling salted water. Cover and cook until tender but still crisp (about 25 minutes). Drain. Serve with Hollandaise (p. 100).

SALSIFY

Another name for Oyster Plant (p. 262).

SPINACH

Select spinach with small, dark green, fresh-looking leaves. Frozen or canned spinach is less crisp than fresh spinach. One pound serves 2 or 3.

BUTTERED SPINACH

Prepare and cook like other greens (p. 257). Chop or leave in sprays or cut through several times. Season to taste with butter, salt and pepper or with French dressing. Add, if you like, a trace of sugar, a sprinkling of nutmeg or grated lemon peel. Serve with Hollandaise (p. 100) or garnish with toast points or sliced, hard-cooked eggs, cut in eighths or chopped fine.

CREAMED SPINACH FRENCH STYLE

Melt
3 tablespoons butter
Add
2 cups finely chopped cooked spinach
Cook 3 minutes. Sprinkle with
1 tablespoon flour
Stir well. Add
½ cup cream
Cook 5 minutes. Season to taste with
Salt, pepper, nutmeg and a trace of sugar
Garnish with
Pastry crescents *or* chopped sautéed almonds
Serves 4 or 5.

To prepare in a blender. Drain cooked spinach thoroughly. Whirl in an electric blender until smooth. Add powdered cream and seasonings to taste.

Spinach à la Béchamel. Instead of cream, use canned chicken broth or Chicken Stock (p. 62).

SPINACH RING

Spoon hot chopped cooked spinach or creamed spinach into a serving dish. Push to the edge to make a ring. Fill with tiny buttered beets or creamed mushrooms, chicken, fish or eggs. Or bake Spinach Custard (below) in a 1-quart ring mold, turn out onto a serving dish, and fill as suggested.

SPINACH CUSTARD

Mix
2 cups cooked spinach, chopped fine
2 tablespoons butter, melted
2 eggs, slightly beaten
1 cup milk
⅛ teaspoon sugar
Few drops onion juice
Few grains nutmeg
Salt and pepper
Vinegar *or* lemon juice to taste
Put in a buttered casserole. Bake at 300° until firm (about 25 minutes). *Serves 4.*

Spinach Soufflé. Beat the egg whites until stiff and fold them in last.

SUMMER SQUASH

Select small young squash of any of the many types available—smooth yellow crooknecks, dark green zucchini, striped vegetable marrow, or scalloped, pale green pattypan squash. One pound serves 3.

Wash, quarter or cut squash in thick slices. Do not peel unless rough and old. Cook until tender (2 minutes in pressure saucepan) 10 to 20 minutes in a covered pan with just enough water to keep from burning. Drain thoroughly. Mash. Season with butter, salt and pepper.

Creamed Summer Squash. Cut in cubes, cook until nearly done but still firm drain, and reheat in cream. Season.

BAKED SUMMER SQUASH AND ONIONS

Slice squash into a baking dish (removing the seeds if they are large). Add sliced onion, separated into rings. Dot with butter, salt and pepper. Repeat. Cover and bake 30 minutes at 400°. Uncover and add cream (½ cup for about 2 pounds of squash). Bake until delicately brown (about 10 minutes).

FRIED SUMMER SQUASH

One pound serves 3.

Cut in ½-inch pieces. Sprinkle with salt and pepper. Dip in crumbs, eggs and crumbs (p. 4), fry in hot fat (375°), and drain.

SAUTÉED SUMMER SQUASH

One pound serves 3.

Slice. Sprinkle with salt, pepper and flour. Sauté slowly in salad oil or butter until crisp and brown. Especially with zucchini, you will like the flavor if you put a clove of garlic in the pan. If you like tomato with squash or zucchini, add a spoonful or two of catsup, cover and heat 5 minutes, then serve.

SQUASH RING

Mix

- **3 cups cooked summer squash (drained and put through a coarse sieve before measuring)**
- **¼ cup melted butter**
- **¼ cup milk**
- **3 eggs, well beaten**
- **Salt, pepper, cayenne**
- **1 tablespoon grated onion**
- **¼ cup buttered crumbs**

Spoon into a buttered 1-quart ring mold. Set in a pan of hot water. Bake at 350° until firm (about 25 minutes). Turn onto a serving dish. Fill with buttered peas, tiny white onions or creamed mushrooms. *Serves 6.*

WINTER SQUASH

Hubbard squash weigh 5 pounds or more. Buy a whole squash or part of one. Butternut squash weigh 2 or 3 pounds and are very dry and mealy. Acorn squash weigh 1 pound or less and are perfect for the small family or for individual service. Allow ½ pound per person. If you cook more than you need for one meal, you will have some for a spicy Squash Pie (p. 451).

Mashed Winter Squash. Cut in pieces. Remove the seeds and fibers. Pare. Cook until tender (6 to 10 minutes in a pressure saucepan, 20 to 30 minutes in boiling salted water in a covered pan). Drain and mash. Season with butter, salt and pepper and a trace of sugar. If you like, put in a baking dish, cover with marshmallows or strips of bacon and bake at 400° until the marshmallows melt or the bacon crisps.

Baked Hubbard Squash. Put a whole squash in a large pan, a half squash cut side down. Bake at 350° until soft (2 hours or more). Cut in half. Remove the seeds. Scoop the squash out of the shell. Mash and season with butter, salt and pepper.

Baked Squash in Squares. Cut in 2-inch squares. Remove the seeds and fibers. Put in a baking pan, skin side down. Brush with butter or bacon fat. Sprinkle with salt and pepper. Put ½ teaspoon molasses on each piece or sprinkle with brown sugar. Bake at 350° until soft (about 50 minutes). Cover for the first half hour of the baking. Serve in the shell.

BAKED ACORN SQUASH

Cut in half but do not remove the seeds. Put on a cooky sheet, cut side up. Bake at 400° until soft (30 to 45 minutes). Scrape out the seeds and fibers and discard. Sprinkle with salt and pepper. Put a bit of butter in each. *Allow 1 or 2 halves per person.*

Glazed Acorn Squash. Just before serving, sprinkle with brown or maple sugar. Bake until the sugar melts.

Stuffed Acorn Squash. Fill the baked squash with Tomatoes Creole (p. 272) or, as a lunch or supper dish, with creamed chicken or ham. Sprinkle with buttered crumbs. Bake until brown.

TOMATOES

Tomatoes are at their succulent best when they are vine-ripened to a brilliant red or yellow but are still firm. Tiny round or pear-shaped ones are attractive additions to a salad or a relish tray. Broiled or curried green tomatoes are delicious. Hothouse tomatoes add color to a salad but are often disappointing in flavor. If the skins are tender, you do not need to peel them.

To peel. Wash. Dip in boiling water for 1 minute, then into cold water, and slip off the skin.

SAUTÉED TOMATOES

Cut ripe or green tomatoes in thick slices. Dip in flour seasoned with salt, pepper and a trace of sugar. Pan-fry in salad oil, bacon fat or butter. Turn once with a wide spatula. Add a little sour cream or evaporated milk to the pan juices, heat, season and pour over the tomatoes.

BAKED *or* BROILED TOMATOES

Serve as a relish on the meat platter, as an important part of a vegetable plate, or as the main dish at luncheon or supper with a curlicue of bacon on top.

Cut unpeeled tomatoes in half. Put in a buttered shallow pan. Season with salt, pepper, a trace of sugar and chopped onion or onion salt, or a few grains of curry powder or oregano. Dot with a bit of butter or cheese, or sprinkle buttered crumbs on top. Bake (at whatever temperature you are using for other baking) until thoroughly heated and brown. Or broil 6 to 8 minutes (cut side toward the heat) with whatever meat or fish you are broiling.

Tomatoes à la Crème. Heat sweet or sour cream, season highly to taste, and pour it over broiled tomatoes.

Deviled Tomatoes. Mix 2 teaspoons confectioners' sugar, 1 teaspoon mustard, ¼ teaspoon salt, few grains cayenne and 1 hard-cooked egg yolk. Add to 4 tablespoons creamed butter. Add 1 egg, slightly beaten, and 2 tablespoons vinegar. Cook and stir over hot water until thick. Pour over baked or broiled tomatoes.

BAKED STUFFED TOMATOES

Cut a thin slice from the stem end of smooth medium-size tomatoes. Take out the seeds and pulp and discard the seeds. Drain off most of the juice. Sprinkle with salt, invert and let stand 30 minutes or longer.

Add an equal quantity of bread crumbs to the pulp. Season with salt, pepper and a few drops onion juice. Add chopped green pepper and onion, if you like. Stuff tomatoes with the mixture. Place in a buttered pan. Sprinkle with buttered crumbs. Bake 20 minutes at 400°.

This is an excellent way to use a bit of leftover chicken or meat. Cook a little chopped onion in butter, add the meat, some of the tomato pulp and crumbs. Season well. For a firmer stuffing, stir in 1 egg, slightly beaten. For other suggestions, see Stuffed Peppers (p. 264).

Tomatoes Stuffed with Mushrooms. Stuff with finely chopped mushrooms, mixed with thick Cream Sauce (p. 94) or tomato pulp, season to taste.

Tomatoes Stuffed with Crab Meat. Stuff with Crab Meat à la King (p. 146) and sprinkle with buttered coarse bread crumbs.

WHOLE TOMATOES AUX FINES HERBES

Simmer chopped green onion in butter with an assortment of finely chopped herbs—parsley and basil, thyme or marjoram—chosen with discretion. Add small peeled tomatoes, sprinkle with salt and pepper, cover, and cook very slowly 15 or 20 minutes. Lift out carefully to keep the tomatoes whole. Pour the pan juice over the tomatoes.

STEWED TOMATOES

Allow 1 to 2 tomatoes per person.

Wipe the tomatoes, peel, cut in pieces, and cook slowly 20 minutes, stirring occasionally. Season with butter, salt, pepper and a few grains of sugar. Sprinkle with croutons.

TOMATOES CREOLE

Melt in a large pan
2 tablespoons butter
Add
1 green pepper, seeded and cut in tiny shreds
1 large onion, chopped fine
Cook slowly until the onion is yellow. Add
6 to 8 tomatoes
Cook slowly 20 minutes. Season to taste with
Salt and pepper
Serves 4 or 5.

SCALLOPED TOMATOES

Season stewed or canned tomatoes to taste with salt, pepper and onion juice. Oregano adds a pleasant flavor. Many like to add a little white or brown sugar. For 4 cups of tomatoes, prepare 1 cup of buttered bread crumbs or croutons. Put a layer of crumbs in a buttered casserole and cover with tomatoes. Repeat. Sprinkle the top with a thick layer of crumbs. Bake at 400° until the crumbs are brown. *Serves 6.*

TOMATO CURRY

Put in a large frying pan
2 tablespoons butter
½ tablespoon chopped onion
Cook until the onion is yellow. Add
1 tart apple, pared, cored, and

cut in small pieces
Cook 8 minutes. Add
½ cup stock *or* consommé
2 cups tomatoes, cut in pieces, *or* canned tomatoes
½ tablespoon curry powder
1 teaspoon vinegar
Salt and pepper
Bring to the boiling point. Add
1 cup boiled rice
Cook 5 minutes. *Serves 4.*

CURRIED GREEN TOMATOES

Melt in a saucepan
2 tablespoons butter
Add
2 tablespoons minced onion
Cook slowly until yellow. Add
1 teaspoon curry powder
2 cups green tomatoes, sliced or cut in pieces
Cook slowly until well heated. Season with
Salt and pepper
Serves 4.

TOMATO FRITTERS

Put in a saucepan
1 can tomatoes (about 3½ cups)
6 cloves
½ cup sugar
3 slices onion
Cook 20 minutes. Rub through a sieve to strain out the seeds. Add
1 teaspoon salt
Few grains pepper
Melt
½ cup butter
Stir in
½ cup cornstarch
Add the tomato slowly, stirring constantly. Cook 2 minutes. Stir in
1 egg, slightly beaten
Pour into a buttered pan about 7 by 7 inches. Cool. Turn out onto a board. Cut in squares, diamonds or strips. Roll in crumbs, egg and crumbs (p. 4), and fry in deep fat at 385°. Drain. *Serves 6 to 8.*

TOMATO SOUFFLÉ À LA NAPOLI

Melt in a saucepan
2 tablespoons butter
Stir in
2 tablespoons flour
Add slowly, stirring constantly
½ cup top milk
1 can tomato paste
Bring to the boiling point and simmer 2 minutes. Add
⅔ cup grated cheese
½ teaspoon salt
Few grains pepper
Cook in boiling salted water until soft
½ cup macaroni, in 1-inch pieces
Drain. Add
1 tablespoon butter
Add to the tomato mixture. Beat until stiff and set aside
3 egg whites
Without washing the beater, beat until thick
3 egg yolks
Stir into the tomato mixture and fold in the beaten whites. Turn into an unbuttered casserole. Bake at 300° until firm (about 45 to 60 minutes). Serve immediately. *Serves 6.*

MASHED TURNIPS

White turnips are milder than yellow rutabagas and cook in a shorter time. Select clean firm roots. One pound serves 3.

Wash and pare. Slice, dice or quarter. Cook until tender (5 minutes in pressure saucepan, 10 to 30 minutes in boiling water in covered pan). Drain off the liquid. Mash and cook a minute or two to dry thoroughly. Season with butter, salt and pepper. For variety, fold in ¼ cup heavy cream, whipped, and season delicately with rum or sherry.

Creamed Turnip. Reheat diced cooked turnip in a little heavy cream.

Turnip Soufflé. Follow recipe for Vegetable Soufflé (p. 240).

ZUCCHINI ITALIAN STYLE

For other ways to cook zucchini, see Summer Squash (p. 274). See *also Ratatouille Niçoise (p. 256).*

Sauté 1 sliced onion in butter until yellow, add 1 pound zucchini, sliced, and cook and stir 5 minutes. Add 1 cup fresh or canned tomatoes, season with salt and pepper, cover and cook 5 minutes. Reduce the heat and cook until tender (25 minutes), or put in a casserole, sprinkle with grated cheese and bake at 375° until brown. *Serves 4.*

BAKED ZUCCHINI

Allow 1 small zucchini per person.

Cut in half lengthwise. Put in a buttered baking dish cut side up. Dot with butter or bits of bacon. Sprinkle with salt and pepper. Bake at 375° until tender. Serve with Tomato Sauce (p. 99) or Hollandaise (p. 100).

Zucchini with Tomato. Scoop out some of the center. Fill with tomato, cut in pieces. Season and bake as above.

STUFFED ZUCCHINI

Allow ½ small zucchini per person.

Cook 10 minutes in boiling salted water. Drain. Cool. Cut in two lengthwise. Scoop out the pulp and chop and add to it an equal quantity of bread crumbs or crumbs and chopped sautéed mushrooms. Moisten with stock, consommé or gravy, and season with salt and pepper. Add grated cheese, minced parsley, marjoram or thyme to taste.

Stuff the zucchini with the mixture. Sprinkle with buttered crumbs and grated cheese. Bake at 350° until the zucchini is tender (about 30 minutes).

See also Zucchini Stuffed with Veal (p. 194) and Zucchini Stuffed with Lamb (p. 189).

Salads

Salad may appear at almost any point in the menu for lunch or dinner. Serve it as the first course in the California fashion, with the main course or immediately following it. A colorful fruit salad, especially a frozen one, is often served as dessert. A hearty salad is perfect for a buffet meal, summer or winter. In any case, suit the salad to the situation—the rest of the menu, the weather and your guests. Serve from a generous bowl or on chilled plates.

SALAD GARNISHES

Garnish a salad casually, so that the effect is natural and not ornate.

For vegetable salads. Sprays of watercress, mint or parsley, thin strips of pimiento or green pepper, grated raw carrot, chopped olives, chopped truffles or capers.

For fruit salads. Tiny canned grapes, red or green cherries, chopped candied orange peel or candied fruits.

CARROT CURLS

Make thin shavings with a "knee action" knife. Drop into ice water to crisp. Drain. Good with cocktails or as a relish with fish or meat.

CELERY

Save the tough outer stalks for soup or to cook as a vegetable. Serve the hearts whole ("club style") or separate into individual stalks. Crisp in a covered container in the refrigerator or in ice water with a little lemon juice, a lemon rind or a dash of vinegar.

CELERY CURLS

Cut celery hearts in 3-inch pieces. Beginning at one end, make 5 parallel cuts, one-third the length of the piece. Make cuts at both ends if you like. Cover with ice water. Let stand overnight or several hours. Drain. The cut ends will curl back and the celery will be very crisp.

GREEN *or* RED PEPPERS

Cut out the stem and remove all the seeds. Cut in thin rings or strips. Wash your hands at once—pepper juice is irritating.

RADISHES

Wash. Cut off the tip. Leave a bit of the stem and a tiny leaf, if you like. Crisp in ice water until serving time. Radishes may be cut to represent tulips or roses or in other fancy ways.

CHEESE WITH SALADS

Cheese is a natural complement to many salads. It provides a pleasantly contrasting flavor, especially for crisp greens and fresh fruit, and adds protein to make a light salad appropriate as a main dish. Assorted cheeses and crackers, Cheese Straws (p. 334), or Cheese Soufflé (p. 121) are often passed with a salad which is served as a separate course.

CREAM CHEESE BALLS

Mash ¼ pound cream cheese (1 small package). Moisten with cream or salad dressing. Season to taste with salt and paprika. Shape into balls about 1 inch in diameter.

Cheese and Nut Balls. Roll in finely chopped nut meats.

Ginger Cheese Balls. Add 2 teaspoons finely chopped Canton ginger. Moisten with ginger syrup.

Roquefort Cheese Balls. Blend in crumbs of Roquefort cheese. Season with a few drops of onion juice.

Chive Cheese Balls. Roll in finely cut chives. Or use chive cream cheese.

STUFFED FIGS *or* PRUNES

Mash cream or cottage cheese, moisten with heavy cream, and season highly with salt and cayenne. If desired, add a few chopped seedless raisins or blanched almonds. Wash and dry figs or pit cooked prunes. Stuff with the cheese mixture. Put one or two on each plate.

FRIED CHEESE BALLS

Mix
1 cup grated mild cheese
2 teaspoons flour
¼ teaspoon salt
Few grains cayenne
Add
2 egg whites, beaten stiff
Shape in small balls and roll in
Fine cracker meal
Fry in deep fat heated to 375°. Drain on paper towels. *Makes 24.*

SALAD GREENS

One of the joys of a kitchen garden is to have a variety of salad greens, many of which are seldom seen in a market—for example, peppergrass, oak leaf letttuce and mignonette lettuce.

Cut away any discolored or wilted parts. Wash gently but thoroughly. Dry with a clean soft towel. Chill. If you are not using all the greens immediately, store, unwashed, in a tightly covered container in the refrigerator and wash them as you need them.

Boston (Head) Lettuce. Cut off the root end and hold, head downward, under running water so that leaves are separated by water. Or, after cutting off the root end, let the lettuce stand in cold water.

Iceberg Lettuce. Wash and cut in halves, quarters or slices. To separate leaf by leaf, follow instructions for Boston lettuce or allow warm water to run briefly through the head. The lettuce cups will separate perfectly at once.

Romaine, Escarole, Watercress, Parsley, Spinach (tender young leaves), **Chicory, Dandelion.** Separate leaf by leaf. Remove any hard or discolored part. Wash.

Endive, French or Belgian, and Fennel. Wash under running water but do not let stand in water. Cut off the root end. Separate the leaves or cut in half lengthwise.

TOSSED GREEN SALAD

The classic salad is the simplest —lettuce or a combination of salad greens tossed in a wooden or pottery bowl with a perfect French dressing. You may arrange the salad on individual plates and pass the dressing, but there is no better style to the service than when the salad is mixed in a big bowl so that each leaf is well coated with the dressing.

Rub the bowl with a clove of garlic or toss a chapon with the salad. A **chapon** is a small piece of bread (traditionally, the end of a crusty French loaf) rubbed with a cut clove of garlic.

Prepare a variety of salad greens (p. 281). Dry gently and thoroughly so that no drops of water cling to them. Tear in bite-size pieces with the fingers and heap in the salad bowl. Pour French dressing over the greens and toss lightly with a fork and spoon (or two large forks) until all parts are well coated with dressing. Or sprinkle the salad lightly with olive oil, turning the leaves over and over until each glistens. Then dissolve salt and freshly ground pepper in vinegar (about 1/4 as much as there is oil) and mix lightly with the greens.

Improvise in making a tossed salad. Add any of these to the greens:

- Canned or cooked artichokes or artichoke hearts, cut small
- Avocado, in thin slices
- Carrot, grated raw
- Cauliflowerets, raw
- Cheese, crumbled
- Cucumber slices or sticks
- Ham, in slivers
- Mushrooms (uncooked), in thin slices
- Radish slices
- Red onion rings
- Shrimp, whole or broken in pieces
- Tiny Cheese Balls (p. 281)
- Tomato, in wedges

Chef's Salad. Add julienne-shaped pieces of ham, chicken or turkey, tongue and cheese, separately or in combination. Or use anchovies or bits of sardine.

Herb Salad. Before adding the dressing to the salad, add 1 tablespoon finely cut fresh herbs. Use any of the following, alone or in combination: anise, basil, borage, burnet, chervil, chives, mint, rue, sorrel, tarragon. Be careful! You can overdo herbs.

FASHION PARK SALAD

Arrange a bed of shredded iceberg lettuce in a big salad bowl. On it arrange neat piles of match-shaped pieces of ham or tongue, chicken or turkey, and plain Cheddar or American cheese. Have ready a generous bowl of Russian dressing. When ready to serve, pour the dressing over the salad and blend well.

CAESAR SALAD

Sometimes called California Salad.

Some Common Salad Greens

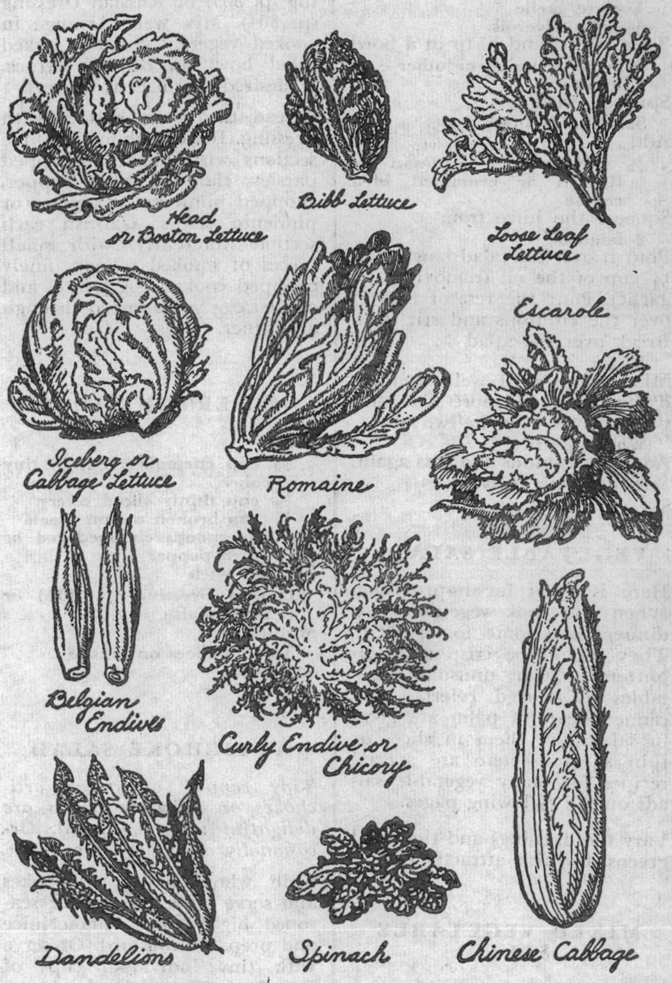

Have ready

1 cup croutons, packaged or homemade (p. 58)

Combine and let stand several hours

1 clove garlic
½ cup olive oil

Tear in bits and heap in a bowl

2 heads romaine or other lettuce

Sprinkle with

Salt and pepper

Add

½ cup grated Parmesan or Roman or crumbled bleu cheese

Squeeze the juice from

2 lemons

Pour it over the salad bowl. Add ¼ cup of the oil (removing the garlic). Pour the rest of the oil over the croutons and stir well. Break over the salad

1 egg

Mix gently until well blended. Taste and add more salt and pepper or a drop or two of

Worcestershire

Add the croutons and toss again. *Serves 6 generously.*

VEGETABLE SALADS

Here is room for improvising. When you cook vegetables for dinner, save some for a salad. They should be crisp and unbuttered. Such unusual vegetables as cooked celeriac and canned heart of palm are good in salad. Cut them in slices or thin slivers. There are special recipes for many vegetable salads on the following pages.

Vary the dressings and the salad greens. Garnish attractively.

MIXED VEGETABLE SALAD

Marinate cooked vegetables separately with French dressing. Chill and drain. Arrange attractively on a salad plate or in a salad bowl. Garnish. Serve with French dressing or mayonnaise.

Russian Salad. Combine any Dressing (p. 304), Cream Dressing (p. 305) or Russian Dressing (p. 304). Mix well. Arrange in cooked vegetables. Add Cooked salad bowl on bed of lettuce. If desired, garnish as follows.

Spread the entire surface with dressing. Divide the top in three sections with lines of chopped parsley, chopped green pepper, chopped pimiento or pepper or pimiento strips. Garnish each section differently, with small pieces of smoked salmon, finely chopped cooked egg white, and cooked egg yolks forced through a strainer.

ALLERTON SALAD

Mix

½ cup cucumber, cut in tiny cubes
½ cup thinly sliced celery
¼ cup broken walnut meats
3 tablespoons chopped red *or* green pepper

Moisten with

Cooked Dressing (p. 304) *or* mayonnaise

Mound on

Tomato slices on lettuce

Serves 6.

ARTICHOKE SALAD

Tiny canned or frozen artichokes or artichoke hearts are delightful in green salad. Occasionally available fresh.

Chill whole cooked artichokes and serve with mayonnaise seasoned highly with lemon juice and prepared mustard. Or serve with tiny individual cups of French dressing. Dip the leaves in the dressing as you eat them. Serve a whole artichoke to each person.

Artichokes Vinaigrette. Use Vinaigrette Sauce (p. 103) instead of dressing.

Stuffed Artichoke Salad. Fill the centers with a hearty salad—chicken, tuna or shrimp.

ASPARAGUS *or* BROCCOLI SALAD

Cover cooked asparagus tips or broccoli stalks with French dressing. Chill. Drain. Serve on any salad green, on a thick slice of tomato, if you wish. Pass French dressing or Vinaigrette Sauce (p. 103).

BEET SALAD

Cut cooked beets in thin slices. Put on lettuce and sprinkle with chopped mint. Serve with French dressing.

PICKLED BEET SALAD

Sprinkle Pickled Beets (p. 246) with caraway seed. Serve on lettuce.

GREEN BEAN *or* SNOW PEA SALAD

Marinate whole cooked green beans or snow peas in French dressing. Drain and arrange neatly on lettuce. Add a few rings of mild onion and/or crumbled crisp bacon. Serve with French dressing.

CABBAGE SALAD (COLE SLAW)

Shred cabbage or chop fine. Wrap or cover with a damp towel and chill in the refrigerator. Just before serving, mix with Cooked Dressing (p. 304) or Cream Dressing (p. 305), using ½ cup for 2 cups cabbage. If liked, add ½ teasoon caraway or celery seeds, or 1 tablespoon minced onion and ¼ cup finely cut green pepper. *Serves 4.*

For variety, add grated raw carrot or a few sliced stuffed olives. Finely cut celery, apple or drained crushed pineapple (a third to half the amount of cabbage) make tasty combinations.

CABBAGE SALAD BOWL

Remove the outside leaves from a small, solid white cabbage. Cut off the stalk close to the leaves. Cut out the center, leaving a shell three or four leaves thick. Cut the edge in points. Pin each point with a long clove. Fill with any cabbage or vegetable salad.

CARROT SALAD

Chop raw carrots. Add a few chopped toasted almonds or salted peanuts or raisins. Mix with mayonnaise. Serve on lettuce.

CAULIFLOWER SALAD

Slice raw cauliflower paper-thin or separate cooked cauliflower in flowerets. Serve on lettuce with French dressing or mayonnaise.

CELERY SALAD

Cut tender stalks lengthwise in narrow strips, then crosswise in fine pieces or short strips. Mix with mayonnaise or Cream Dressing (p. 305).

CUCUMBER SALAD

Pare if the skin is tough or discolored. Slice thin, dice or cut in julienne pieces.

To cut slices with a fancy edge, pare with a fluted knife or make parallel grooves lengthwise with a silver fork.

To crisp, soak ½ hour (no longer) in salted water and drain. Serve on lettuce with French dressing or a variation (p. 300).

WILTED CUCUMBERS

Pare and cut in paper-thin slices

1 cucumber

Mix and pour over the cucumber

1 cup cold water
1 tablespoon salt

Let stand 15 minutes. Drain and rinse with cold water. Pour over the cucumber

¼ cup French dressing

Sprinkle with

¼ teaspoon celery seed

Serves 3 or 4.

ONION SALAD

Cut in thin slices Bermuda, Italian or Spanish onions. Separate into rings, if you like. Serve on lettuce with French dressing.

Onion and Orange Salad. Alternate slices of onion with thin slices of unpeeled orange. Particularly good with duck.

POTATO SALAD

Vary the seasoning by adding chopped chives, parsley, olives or pickles. Use plenty of dressing so the salad will not be dry.

Mix and let stand several hours

2 cups cubed cooked potatoes
1 teaspoon grated onion
½ cup chopped celery
1 teaspoon salt
½ cup French dressing

Just before serving, add

1 hard-cooked egg, sliced
Mayonnaise *or* Cooked Dressing (p. 304)

Arrange in a large bowl on

Lettuce

Garnish with

Tomato sections, radishes *or* sliced hard-cooked egg

Serves 4.

Party Potato Salad. Put in a large bowl. Divide the top into quarters. Garnish one with finely chopped cooked egg white, the opposite one with crumbled egg yolk, and the others with chopped pickled beets. Mark the dividing lines with chopped parsley.

Bolivia Salad. Add 3 hard-cooked eggs, finely chopped, 1½ tablespoons minced pimientos and ½ tablespoon chopped olives. Mix with Cream Dressing (p. 305).

HOT POTATO SALAD

Cook, cool and slice into a baking dish

6 potatoes

Season with

Salt and pepper

Sprinkle with

¼ cup chopped celery
1 tablespoon chopped parsley

Mix

2 tablespoons tarragon vinegar
2 tablespoons cider vinegar
4 tablespoons olive oil *or* bacon fat
1 thick slice lemon

Heat to the boiling point. Remove the lemon and pour the dressing over the potatoes. Cover and let stand in a 350° oven until heated (about 10 minutes). *Serves 6.*

GERMAN POTATO SALAD

Cover with boiling water and cook until the potatoes are tender

2 cups diced potato
1 onion

Drain, remove the onion, and add

1 teaspoon grated onion
1 slice bacon, cooked and crumbled
2 tablespoons hot bacon fat

Let stand until cold. Mix with

French dressing

Season to taste and serve on

Lettuce

Serves 4.

TOMATO SALAD

If the skin is thin and tender, do not peel. Cut in slices, quarters or eighths. Leave tiny tomatoes whole or cut them in half. Serve on lettuce with French dressing, mayonnaise (add curry if you like) or Avocado Mayonnaise (p. 304). Garnish with watercress or parsley or sprinkle with chopped chives.

For a festive look, cut in eighths without cutting all the way through. Open like the petals of a flower. In the center put a spoonful of mayonnaise or any of the fillings suggested for Stuffed Tomato Salad (below).

STUFFED TOMATO SALAD

Peel tomatoes. Remove a thin slice from the top of each. Take out the seeds and some of the pulp. Sprinkle the inside with salt. Invert and let stand 30 minutes. Fill, garnish and serve on salad greens. Use any of these fillings:

Chicken (p. 296), Crab Meat (p. 297), Lobster (p. 297) or Shrimp Salad (p. 297).

Russian Salad (p. 284) or any mixed vegetable salad.

Shrimp, diced pineapple and cucumber with mayonnaise.

Diced cucumbers mixed with mayonnaise.

Shredded pineapple, fresh or canned, mixed with one-third the amount of nut meats and with mayonnaise.

Finely cut celery and apple mixed with mayonnaise.

Cottage cheese, well seasoned, mixed with chopped chives.

Roquefort and cream cheese worked together and moistened with French dressing.

Chopped broiled bacon, diced sardines and tomato.

Cream cheese, chopped stuffed olives and tomato pulp moistened with French dressing and seasoned with prepared mustard.

RUSSIAN TOMATO SALAD

A tasty way to use small amounts of cooked meats and vegetables.

Prepare as for Stuffed Tomato Salad (above), reserving the pulp

6 tomatoes

Drain ⅓ cup of the tomato pulp and mix with

⅓ cup diced cucumber
⅓ cup cooked peas *or* lima beans
¼ cup chopped pickles
2 tablespoons capers

Season with

Salt, pepper and vinegar

Add

½ cup diced cooked chicken, ham, pork or veal

Mix with

Mayonnaise *or* Russian Dressing

Stuff the tomatoes and serve on

Lettuce

Sprinkle with

Chopped parsley

Serves 6.

AVOCADO SALAD (ALLIGATOR PEAR)

To select, see page 367. Prepare just before using to avoid darkening.

Cut in half and peel. Slice or cut in wedges. Sprinkle with lemon juice. Serve on lettuce with French or Thousand Island Dressing (p. 301).

To vary, alternate slices of avocado with sliced cucumber or with orange or grapefruit sections.

STUFFED AVOCADO SALAD

Cut avocado in half and remove the seed. Serve a half to each person. Fill with a sharp French dressing or a simple fruit salad dressing (p. 302). Or stuff with diced orange and grapefruit sections mixed with French, Lime (p. 302) or Chutney Dressing (p. 301), or with Crab Meat, Chicken, Cooked Fish or Shrimp Salad (pp. 296 ff.), as a main luncheon dish.

BANANA SALAD

Cut bananas in 2-inch chunks. Roll in finely chopped salted peanuts. Put on lettuce and serve with French dressing or mayonnaise. Or slice on lettuce and serve with Peanut Butter Dressing (p. 305).

GRAPEFRUIT *or* ORANGE SALAD

Put sections on any salad green. Sprinkle with thin slices of sweet onion or with chopped ripe olives or chopped mint. Serve with French dressing. Or alternate sections of grapefruit and orange and serve with Lime Dressing (p. 302).

MELON SALAD

Cut cubes or balls of watermelon, cantaloupe or other melon. Sprinkle with salt and French dressing. Cover and chill at least 1 hour. A mixture of melons is excellent. Serve on lettuce with French dressing.

PEACH SALAD

Fill fresh or canned peach halves with chopped celery and nuts, well-seasoned cottage cheese or Cream Cheese Balls (p. 281). Place on lettuce and serve with French, Lime (p. 302) or Cream Dressing (p. 305).

PEAR SALAD

Peel and core ripe fresh pears or use canned pears. Slice or cut in halves. Serve on lettuce with French, Roquefort or Cream French Dressing (p. 301).

Stuffed Pear Salad. Fill halves with Waldorf Salad (p. 289) or chopped pecans, raisins and finely cut celery mixed with mayonnaise, or a cooked dressing.

TWO PEAR SALADS FOR CHILDREN

Bunny Salad. Put a pear half on a bed of shredded lettuce rounded side up. Insert blanched almonds for ears, cloves or pink candies for eyes and nose. Use a bit of marshmallow for the tail.

Sunbonnet Salad. Invert a pear half on a cup-shaped piece of lettuce with the small end of the pear on the stem end of the lettuce. Pin the lettuce to the pear with cloves on either side. Make a face on the pear with candies or cloves, or paint with vegetable color. Use strips of pimiento for bonnet strings.

PINEAPPLE SALAD

Put slices of fresh or canned pineapple on lettuce. Garnish with green pepper rings or Cream Cheese Balls (p. 281) or red or green cherries. Serve with French dressing.

PRUNE SALAD

Stuff cooked or canned pitted prunes with highly seasoned cream cheese or cottage cheese. Serve on any salad green with French dressing.

MIXED FRUIT SALAD

As the basis, prepare grapefruit or orange sections, or cut crisp tart (but not sour) apples in neat pieces. Small fruits add an attractive touch. Pit cherries. Leave strawberries and raspberries whole. Use seeded or seedless grapes, canned or fresh. Malaga, Tokay or Muscatel types are best. Slice kumquats very thin without peeling. Bits of dried fruits, raisins or candied orange peel are tasty additions. Add to the fresh fruit and let stand several hours to soften.

Chill the fruit. Mix or arrange in separate piles on a handsome glass or pottery serving plate. Add the dressing before serving or pass it in a bowl. French dressing is always good but sweet dressings are also popular, especially when the salad is to be served as a dessert. For suggestions, see page 302.

Some successful combinations are:

(1) Two oranges in sections, 3 bananas in thin slices, 1 cup seeded or seedless grapes and ¼ cup nut meats, broken in pieces. Cream Mayonnaise (p. 303).

(2) One grapefruit and 2 oranges in sections, ½ cup seeded or seedless grapes and ⅓ cup pecan meats, broken in pieces. Lakewood Dressing (p. 302).

(3) One cup each of orange and/or tangerine sections, banana slices and crushed or cubed pineapple. Nut Pascagoula Dressing (p. 302).

WALDORF SALAD

Cut well-flavored apple, peeled or not as you prefer, into small even cubes. To each cupful add ⅔ cup finely cut celery and 5 tablespoons mayonnaise or Cooked Dressing (p. 304). Mix well. Taste and season further, adding a shake of nutmeg or more salt or a little lemon juice. Add a few chopped walnut or pecan meats just before serving. Serve on lettuce.

Pineapple Waldorf Salad. Instead of celery, add cubed pineapple.

MOLDED SALADS

Molded salads are perfect for the buffet table. You can prepare them well in advance and serving them is very simple. There are special recipes for such dishes as Chicken and Almond Mousse (p. 295) and Molded Salmon (p. 295).

To mold. See page 12.

To garnish. Put a ½-inch layer of the jelly mixture in the mold and chill until the jelly begins to stiffen. Arrange on it any desired garnish, such as parsley sprigs, slices of stuffed olives, bits of pimiento or truffle or nut meats. Spoon the jelly carefully over the decorations and chill until firm before adding other ingredients. If the jelly has stiffened too much to pour, melt it in a double boiler.

To serve. Serve individual molds on any salad green. An attractive plate may be arranged with a small mold of a simple jelly (tomato or grapefruit), a few stalks of endive dressed with French dressing, and a spray of watercress.

Garnish a large mold with fruit or cooked vegetables, bits of pimiento or truffle or slices of stuffed olives. Fill the center of a ring mold with salad dressing or with another salad; for example, Tomato Aspic (below) with Chicken Salad (p. 296); Grapefruit Jelly (p. 291) with Mixed Fruit Salad (p. 289).

QUICK JELLIED SALADS

Dissolve 1 package flavored gelatine in 1 cup boiling water. Add 1 cup cold liquid (water, fruit juice, tomato juice, consommé or wine). Season to taste. Chill. When the jelly begins to thicken, fold in 1½ cups prepared fruit, vegetable (p. 290) or cooked meat or fish. Season to taste and mold.

Some suggested combinations are:

Lemon or lime gelatine with grated or diced cucumber and 1 teaspoon grated onion or 3 tablespoons chopped chives.

Apple gelatine with finely cut celery and ¼ cup chopped walnuts.

Lemon or apple gelatine with 1 cup uncooked cranberries chopped with 1 orange (seeded but not peeled). Add 2 tablespoons sugar.

Lemon gelatine with 1 cup diced or shredded cooked beets, 2 tablespoons minced onion, 1 tablespoon horseradish and ¾ cup diced celery. Use ¾ cup beet juice and 3 tablespoons vinegar as the required cup of cold liquid.

Lemon, lime or apple gelatine with 1 cup chopped nut meats and ½ cup sliced stuffed olives.

Lemon gelatine (made with tomato juice as the liquid) with shredded cabbage and celery, 1½ teaspoons chopped onion and 1½ tablespoons finely cut pimiento or green pepper (Quick Perfection Salad).

Aspic gelatine with chopped cooked ham, chicken, shrimp or lobster, and with or without vegetables such as finely cut celery or grated carrot.

TOMATO ASPIC (TOMATO JELLY)

A ring mold may be filled with lettuce, watercress, mayonnaise, diced celery mixed with mayon-

naise, or a mixture of chopped hard-cooked egg and sliced raw mushroom caps in mayonnaise.

Mix in a saucepan
  1 envelope gelatine (1 tablespoon)
  ½ teaspoon sugar
  ¾ cup tomato juice
Stir over moderate heat until the gelatine dissolves. Add
  1 cup tomato juice
Season to taste with
  Lemon juice, lime juice *or* vinegar
  Salt and pepper
  Few drops Worcestershire
Fill a 1-pint ring or other mold or a set of individual molds. Chill until firm. Turn out on a serving dish. *Serves 4.*

For a more highly seasoned jelly, use canned tomato juice cocktail or 1 cup canned tomato sauce diluted with ¾ cup water. Or heat the tomato juice first with oregano, a few sprigs of basil or thyme or a bay leaf, and strain it before mixing with the gelatine.

Anchovy Tomato Aspic. Fill the mold half full. Chill until firm. Spread with a thin layer of anchovy paste. Pour in the rest of the jelly and chill.

Caviar Tomato Aspic. Sprinkle caviar in the mold before pouring in the jelly.

Cottage Cheese Tomato Aspic. As the jelly begins to thicken, stir in ½ cup cottage cheese by the spoonful. Do not make the mixture too smooth.

Shrimp and Tomato Aspic. Put a layer of cooked or canned shrimp in the mold. Pour the aspic over them. Or break the shrimp in pieces and fold in as the aspic begins to thicken. Add cubed avocado, too, for color and flavor contrast. Make a lobster or crab meat aspic the same way.

PERFECTION SALAD

Chill Tomato Aspic (p. 290) in a bowl. As the jelly begins to thicken, fold in ½ cup each of shredded cabbage and celery, 1½ teaspoons chopped onion and 1½ tablespoons finely cut pimiento or green pepper. Mold.

For a heartier salad, add finely cut ham, chicken or cheese.

GRAPEFRUIT JELLY SALAD

Garnish with Cheese Balls (p. 281) or grapefruit sections and watercress.

Mix in a saucepan
  1 envelope gelatine (1 tablespoon)
  1 tablespoon sugar
Add
  ½ cup cold water
Cook and stir over low heat until the gelatine dissolves. Add
  1 cup grapefruit juice
  1 tablespoon lemon juice
  Sugar and salt to taste
Mold in a pint mold or 4 small molds. *Serves 4.*

Grapefruit and Cucumber Salad. Chill the jelly until it is as thick as unbeaten egg white. Stir in ½ cup each of grapefruit sections, cut small, and chopped drained cucumber.

Pineapple and Cucumber Salad. Use canned pineapple juice in place of grapefruit juice. As the jelly begins to stiffen, fold in ½ cup each of chopped drained cucumber and drained crushed pineapple.

Molded Fruit Salad. For each cup of jelly prepare 1 cup of fruit such as cubed apples, seeded or seedless grapes and pineapple cubes. Chopped celery is good, too. As the jelly begins to thicken, fold in the fruit. Serve with mayonnaise or any fruit salad dressing (pp. 302 ff).

Ginger Ale Fruit Salad. In place of grapefruit juice, use ⅔ cup ginger ale. Add an extra tablespoon of lemon juice. To heighten the ginger flavor, add 1 tablespoon chopped candied ginger.

AVOCADO MOUSSE

Put in a small saucepan
½ cup cold water
Sprinkle over it
1 teaspoon gelatine
Set over low heat and stir until the gelatine dissolves. Set aside. Peel
1 large avocado
Remove the pit and mash the pulp. Season with
½ teaspoon salt
Few drops onion juice
1 teaspoon Worcestershire
Mix gently together
¼ cup heavy cream, whipped
4 tablespoons mayonnaise
Add the dissolved gelatine and fold in the avocado pulp. Mold. Serve on
Lettuce
with
Mayonnaise
and a garnish of
Tomato wedges
Serves 4.

CHICKEN *or* TURKEY ASPIC

Eke out the chicken or turkey, if necessary, by adding chopped hard-cooked eggs or more celery.

Put in a small saucepan
¾ cup water
Sprinkle over it
1 envelope gelatine (1 tablespoon)
Stir over low heat until the gelatine melts. Cool. Stir into
¾ cup mayonnaise, Cooked *or* Cream Dressing (p. 305)
Blend well. Add
1 cup cooked chicken *or* turkey, cut in small pieces
½ cup chopped celery
¼ cup chopped green pepper, pimientos *or* stuffed olives
Mix well. Season to taste with
Salt and paprika
Mold and chill. *Serves 4 or 5.*

Molded Seafood Salad. In place of the chicken, use crab meat, lobster, shrimp, tuna, salmon or a combination of sea foods. Curry powder added to the mayonnaise is particularly good with it.

EPICUREAN HAM MOUSSE

Put in a small saucepan
¾ cup cold water
Sprinkle over it
1 envelope gelatine (1 tablespoon)
Stir over low heat until the gelatine dissolves. Mix
2 cups chopped cooked ham
1 teaspoon prepared mustard
Few grains cayenne
Stir in the gelatine. Fold in
½ cup heavy cream, beaten until stiff
Mold. Garnish with
Parsley
Serve with
Epicurean Sauce (p. 102)
Serves 4 to 6.

JELLIED VEGETABLE RING

Vary the vegetables according to what is on hand. For example, use 2 canned pimientos, cut small, in place of peas and beets.

Mix in a saucepan
1 envelope gelatine (1 tablespoon)
¼ cup sugar
Add
1 cup cold water
Stir over low heat until the gelatine dissolves. Add
¼ cup vinegar
3 tablespoons lemon juice
1 teaspoon salt
Chill until as thick as unbeaten egg white. Stir in

1 cup celery, cut in small strips
½ cup shredded cabbage
⅓ cup cucumber cubes
¼ cup cooked green peas
¼ cup cubed cooked beets
Mold. Serve on
Lettuce *or* watercress
with
Mayonnaise *or* Denver Cream Dressing (p. 305)
Serves 6.

JELLIED GARDEN SPECIAL

Pour off the liquid from
1 pint Garden Special (p. 554)
Measure the liquid and add enough water to make 1 cup. Put in a saucepan and sprinkle over it
1 envelope gelatine (1 tablespoon)
Stir over low heat until the gelatine dissolves. Chill until as thick as unbeaten egg white. Add the drained vegetables and mold. *Serves 4.*

CUCUMBER ASPIC

Put in a small saucepan
½ cup cold water
Sprinkle over it
1 envelope gelatine (1 tablespoon)
Stir over low heat until the gelatine dissolves. Put in an electric blender. Add
½ cup undiluted frozen orange juice
2 tablespoons lemon juice
2 cups sliced cucumber
½ small onion, sliced
4 sprigs parsley
1 teaspoon salt
Whirl until smooth. Chill until the mixture begins to set. Stir well and pour into an oiled mold. *Serves 4.*

CHEESE SALAD MOLD

Mash until smooth
½ pound cream cheese
Stir in
¼ cup milk *or* cream
½ cup grated Italian *or* Cheddar cheese
Whip and fold in
½ pint heavy cream
Put in a small saucepan
½ cup cold water
Sprinkle over it
1 envelope gelatine (1 tablespoon)
Stir over low heat until the gelatine dissolves. Stir into the cheese mixture. Season to taste with
Salt and paprika
Mold. Serve on
Lettuce
with
French dressing seasoned with curry
Serves 6.

BING CHERRY MOLD

Delicious with hot or cold chicken or turkey. Pretty, too.

Drain, reserving the juice
1 #2 can pitted Bing cherries
Put them in a ring mold. Add to the juice enough
Cold water to make 2 cups
Put ½ cup in a saucepan. Sprinkle over it
1 envelope gelatine (1 tablespoon)
Stir over low heat until the gelatine dissolves. Add the rest of the juice. Pour over the cherries. Chill until firm and unmold. Beat until as light as whipped cream
½ pound cream cheese
Pineapple juice (about ¼ cup)
Pile in the center of the ring. Garnish with
Watercress
Serves 6.

Walnut Cherry Mold. Stuff each cherry with a piece of walnut meat.

ASPIC

Classic aspic is made of homemade stock, but canned bouillon is what most of us use these days. Chicken broth is best if you are making a vegetable or chicken aspic.

Aspic-flavored gelatine is on the market. Before molding it, season it more highly by adding tomato paste, sherry, Burgundy or brandy.

Put in a saucepan
- **½ cup stock *or* bouillon**

Sprinkle over it
- **1 envelope gelatine (1 tablespoon)**

Stir over low heat until the gelatine dissolves. Add
- **1 cup stock *or* bouillon**
- **Lemon juice, sherry *or* brandy to taste**

Add enough more stock or water to make 2 cups in all. Mold. *Makes 1 pint.*

For a more savory aspic, add 1 teaspoon tomato paste or simmer the stock for 20 minutes with a sprig of parsley, a bit of thyme, a clove and a teaspoon each of diced carrot, onion and celery. Strain.

If the chilled stock is firm, you will need only 1 teaspoon gelatine. Soften the gelatine in cold water instead of stock.

EGGS IN ASPIC

The amount of aspic you need will depend on whether you arrange the eggs close together or not. It is simple to make more aspic and add it later to fill the mold.

Prepare highly seasoned Stuffed Eggs (p. 107), adding to the stuffing, if you like, chopped mushrooms, ham, crab meat or caviar.

Pour Aspic (p. 293) into a shallow serving dish or mold ½ inch deep. Chill until the jelly begins to stiffen. Arrange stuffed egg halves on it and add other garnishes, if you like, such as sprigs of parsley or watercress. Spoon in more aspic until the eggs are covered. Chill. Serve from the dish or unmold onto a serving dish.

COOKED MEAT IN ASPIC

Cooked meats in aspic are excellent as party fare or as a reserve for unexpected summer guests. The meat stays moist and appetizing even if you store it in the refrigerator for many days.

Prepare Aspic (p. 293). Pour it into a chilled mold until it is ½ inch deep. Chill until it begins to stiffen. Arrange the meat on it and fill the mold with another layer of aspic. If the aspic has become too stiff to pour, reheat it. Chill until firm.

Chicken *or* Turkey in Aspic. Arrange sliced breast meat in layers.

Ham in Aspic. Cut off the fat. Trim the slices in neat, even pieces.

Tongue in Aspic. Slice, or use a whole cooked tongue.

CHICKEN SALAD IN ASPIC

Cut cooked chicken in neat cubes. Prepare 1 cup Aspic (p. 293) for each cup of chicken and chill until it begins to stiffen. Fold in the chicken and season to taste. Mold in custard cups or individual molds. Serve on lettuce or other salad green with mayonnaise.

To vary. Use a combination of chicken and diced celery or chicken and chopped ham or hard-cooked egg. For added color and seasoning, add chopped green pepper, pimientos or a few capers.

CRANBERRY JELLY SALAD I

Mold Cranberry Jelly (p. 87) in cylindrical tin or use canned cranberry jelly. Slice 1 inch thick. Arrange on lettuce. Scoop out the centers to form rings. Fill with chopped apple and celery or other salad. Serve with Cream Dressing (p. 305) or mayonnaise.

CRANBERRY JELLY SALAD II

Prepare 2 cups Cranberry Jelly (p. 87) or melt canned cranberry jelly. Let stand to thicken slightly. Fold in ½ cup finely cut apple or celery and ¼ cup chopped nut meats. Mold. Chill. Serve on lettuce with Cream Dressing (p. 305) or mayonnaise. *Serves 4 to 6.*

CHICKEN AND ALMOND MOUSSE

Vary this party dish by adding chopped pimientos or sautéed mushrooms or by seasoning more highly.

Put in a saucepan
  1 cup cold chicken broth
Sprinkle over it
  1 envelope gelatine (1 tablespoon)
Stir over low heat until the gelatine dissolves. Pour it slowly over
  3 egg yolks, slightly beaten
Pour back into the saucepan and cook and stir until slightly thickened (about 5 minutes). Grind fine and add to the gelatine
  1 cup cooked chicken (white meat)
  ½ cup blanched almonds
Season highly to taste with
  Salt and cayenne
Chill until as thick as unbeaten egg white. Fold in
  ½ pint heavy cream, beaten stiff
Mold and chill. *Serves 6.*

JELLIED CRAB MEAT AND CELERY

Dissolve
  1 package lemon gelatine
in
  1 cup boiling water
Add
  1 can tomato sauce (8 ounces)
  1 teaspoon grated onion
  1½ tablespoons vinegar
  ½ teaspoon salt
  ⅛ teaspoon pepper
  1 can crab meat (8 ounces) *or* ½-pound fresh crab meat (flaked)
  1 cup diced celery
Stir well and mold. *Serves 4.*

JELLIED CUCUMBER AND SWEETBREADS

Parboil (p. 210)
  1 pair sweetbreads
  Bit of bay loaf
  1 slice onion
  1 blade mace
Drain and dice. Put in a small saucepan
  1 cup cold water
Sprinkle over it
  1 envelope gelatine (1 tablespoon)
Stir over low heat until the gelatine dissolves. Add
  3 tablespoons vinegar
Cool 10 minutes. Add to
  ½ pint heavy cream, whipped stiff
Add the sweetbreads and
  1½ cups cucumber cubes
Season to taste with
  Salt and paprika
Mold. Serve on
  Lettuce
with
  French dressing
Serves 6 to 8.

MOLDED SALMON, CUCUMBER SAUCE

Mix
  2 teaspoons salt
  2 tablespoons sugar

2 teaspoons flour
1 teaspoon mustard
Few grains cayenne
2 egg yolks
2 tablespoons melted butter
1 cup milk
¼ cup mild vinegar

Cook until thick over hot water (or in a heavy pan over low heat), stirring constantly. Put in a small saucepan

½ cup water

Sprinkle over it

1 envelope gelatine (1 tablespoon)

Stir over low heat until the gelatine dissolves. Stir into the sauce. Add

2 cups cooked or canned salmon, separated into flakes

Mold. Serve with

Cucumber Sauce (p. 102)

Serves 6.

CHICKEN SALAD

The meat of a plump boiled fowl (p. 226) is the tastiest for salad, but leftover roast chicken may be used, though it is less moist. For a small amount, steam a chicken breast or use canned chicken.

Prepare

2 cups cooked chicken, cut in neat cubes

Sprinkle over it

¼ cup French dressing *or* the juice of ½ lemon

Cover and let stand at least 1 hour. Add

¾ cup mayonnaise (mixed with chutney if desired) *or* Cream Dressing (p. 305)

Mix thoroughly. Serve on

Lettuce

and garnish with

Watercress *or* a dusting of paprika

Serves 2 or 3.

To vary, add diced celery or canned artichokes, cut small. A delicious combination is chicken, cubed cucumber, chopped nut meats and tiny canned peas.

Other garnishes are crumbled crisp bacon, sliced stuffed olives or toasted slivered almonds.

Sweetbread Salad. In place of chicken, use cooked sweetbreads with an equal amount of diced cucumber or celery.

CURRIED CHICKEN SALAD

Whip until stiff

¾ cup heavy cream

Blend into the cream

¾ cup mayonnaise
1 teaspoon curry powder
Salt and pepper to taste

Mix

2 cups diced cooked chicken
1 cup diced celery
1 cup diced peeled apple
2 tablespoons minced onion
½ cup diced drained cucumber

Add the dressing and mix well. Serve on

Lettuce

Serves 8.

STUFFED EGG SALAD

Cut hard-cooked eggs in half lengthwise. Remove the yolks, mash, and season with French dressing, mayonnaise or Cooked Dressing (p. 304). Refill the whites. Serve on lettuce with extra dressing.

Vary this basic pattern many ways. For example, add to the yolk mixture bits of crumbled crisp bacon, finely chopped chicken, chopped sweet pickles or Roquefort crumbs. Serve on slices of tomato or thin rounds of cooked ham.

CRAB *or* TUNA SALAD

Remove the hard tendons from crab meat. Measure and add about two-thirds as much finely cut celery. Mix with mayonnaise, season to taste and serve on lettuce or in avocado halves. Garnish with tomato wedges and watercress or sliced stuffed olives or pickles.

CRAB LOUIS

Remove the hard tendons from

2 cups crab meat

Heap on a bed of

Shredded lettuce

Mix

⅓ cup chili sauce
½ cup French dressing
2 tablespoons mayonnaise

Season to taste with

Salt, pepper and Worcestershire

Pour over the crab meat. *Serves 4.*

CRABS RAVIGOTE

Mix

2 cups crab meat (tendons removed)
1 teaspoon salt
⅛ teaspoon cayenne
1 teaspoon prepared mustard
½ teaspoon minced parsley
1 hard-cooked egg, chopped fine
3 tablespoons vinegar
1 tablespoon olive oil

Spoon into scallop shells, ramekins or other small dishes. Spread evenly with

Ravigote Mayonnaise (p. 303)

Serves 4.

HERRING SALAD

Mix

1 cup flaked cooked salt herring
1 cup cooked potato cubes
¼ cup chopped cooked egg white
¼ cup French dressing

Chill 1 hour. Beat until stiff

¼ cup heavy cream

Add

2 tablespoons pimiento purée (sieved canned pimiento)
¼ cup mayonnaise

Add the herring mixture. Serve on

Lettuce

Serves 4.

LOBSTER SALAD

At its luscious best made with lobster meat alone, but added celery makes a good salad, too. Allow ½ cup lobster meat for each serving or a little less if you are adding celery. Two pounds of lobster in the shell yields 1 cup.

Cut lobster meat, cooked or canned, in neat pieces. Sprinkle with lemon juice or French dressing, cover and let stand at least 1 hour. Add celery, cut fine, and mix with mayonnaise. Serve on lettuce.

LOBSTER SALAD (in the Shell)

Cook lobsters (p. 149). Remove the meat carefully, leaving the body and tail in one piece (p. 149). Make the salad (above) and pile it in the shells. Spread with mayonnaise and sprinkle with paprika.

To vary, mix the lobster liver and coral, rub it through a sieve, add a few drops of anchovy essence and enough mayonnaise to cover the top of the salad.

SHRIMP SALAD

Clean cooked or canned shrimp. Break in pieces and moisten with mayonnaise or Cream Dressing (p. 305). Arrange on lettuce or in avocado halves on lettuce. Garnish with whole shrimp, capers or sliced stuffed olives.

FROZEN SALADS

Prepared in advance, frozen salads can simplify summer entertaining.

To freeze. Fill oiled molds and seal tightly. Put in the freezer or in equal parts of crushed ice and salt. Let stand until firm (about 4 hours). Serve before the fruit is icy hard. Another way is to pack the salad in a refrigerator tray to freeze.

FROZEN FRUIT SALAD

Drain, reserving the juice

2 cups fruit, fresh or canned

Cut the fruit in small pieces. Put ½ cup of the fruit juice in a small saucepan. Sprinkle over it

1 envelope gelatine (1 tablespoon)

Stir over low heat until the gelatine dissolves. Add slowly to

⅓ cup mayonnaise

Stir in

⅔ cup heavy cream, beaten until stiff

Fold in the fruit. Season to taste with

Salt and paprika

Freeze (above). Serve on

Lettuce

with

French dressing

Serves 6.

FROZEN TROPICAL SALAD

Mix gently

1 cup mayonnaise *or* Cooked Dressing (p. 304)
1 cup heavy cream, whipped

Stir in

5 oranges, peeled and cut in small pieces
5 bananas, peeled and sliced
1 cup diced pineapple
½ cup Maraschino cherries, cut in pieces

Freeze (above). *Serves 6.*

FROZEN PEAR SALAD

Pack a large can of Bartlett pears in ice and salt or put in the freezer. Let stand 4 hours. Just before serving, open the can, slice the fruit or cut it in squares, and arrange on lettuce. Sprinkle with paprika. Garnish with cherries and cream cheese rosettes. Serve with French dressing or Cream Mayonnaise (p. 305). *Serves 6.*

FROZEN TOMATO CREAM

Season to taste

2 cups tomato sauce

Pour into a freezing tray. Freeze until icy. Fold in

½ cup heavy cream, beaten stiff

Freeze until firm. Serve on

Lettuce

Serves 6.

SALAD SANDWICH LOAF

A festive creation to prepare ahead of time for a company lunch or supper. The same salad may be used for all three layers or each layer may be different. Chop the ingredients fine, so that the layers will be firm enough to cut easily.

Prepare

3 cups salad, such as chicken, tuna, salmon *or* mixed vegetable

Remove the crusts from

1 small loaf firm bread, unsliced

Cut in 4 slices lengthwise. Spread 2 slices on one side (for the top and bottom) and 2 on both sides with

Creamed butter *or* mayonnaise

On 3 slices put a layer of

Lettuce, cut small

Spread prepared salad on the

lettuce. Put the layers together. Top with the fourth slice, buttered side down. Set a weight (a pan or platter) on top to press the loaf firmly. Mash

½ pound cream cheese

with enough

Mayonnaise *or* cream

to spread easily. Spread the top and sides of the loaf evenly. Garnish and chill. Cut in 1-inch slices. *Serves 6.*

Salad Dressings

Affinity between a salad and its dressing makes for perfection. A light French dressing (oil, vinegar or lemon juice, and seasonings) is right with almost any salad. Use mayonnaise, a cooked dressing or a whipped cream dressing with discretion. Vary the seasoning to suit the ingredients and your individual taste. Adventure a bit with your salad dressings—you may produce a masterpiece!

INGREDIENTS

Oils. To the epicure, high-grade olive oil is essential. Some prefer a fruity Italian oil, others the more delicate French type. Vegetable oils—made from corn, cotton seed, peanuts and soy beans—are excellent too, and are richer in food values than olive oil.

Vinegars vary in strength, so add gradually until the dressing is as sharp as you like. Old-fashioned cider vinegar has a mild, delicious flavor. Other vinegars add a distinctive taste to dressings — tarragon, wine, pear, garlic or other specially seasoned ones.

Seasonings. Use pure salt, since table salt has starch mixed with it so that it will not cake. Pepper is at its pungent best if you grind the whole peppercorns fresh in a pepper mill. To add garlic flavor, use cloves of garlic (to crush, see p. 16), garlic salt or powdered dry garlic. Fresh or dried herbs in discreet amounts are delicious with some salads. Special suggestions are given with the recipes.

FRENCH DRESSING

This is the classic formula, but modifications are many. With wine vinegar, garlic- or herb-flavored vinegar, you may need nothing more. If the vinegar is very sharp, add a trace of sugar. It is convenient to have French dressing on hand; make it in quantity but do not leave garlic in the dressing longer than a day.

Mix in a bottle or a jar with a cover

½ cup olive *or* salad oil
2 tablespoons mild vinegar
1 teaspoon salt
½ teaspoon freshly ground pepper
½ clove garlic

Cover. When ready to serve, remove the garlic and shake hard to blend. *Makes ½ cup.*

To vary. Add a few drops of onion juice, Tabasco or Worcestershire, or a teaspoon of strained tomato juice, or season delicately with mustard or curry powder or add Dijon mustard to taste. For a slightly thicker dressing add 1 tablespoon mayonnaise just before serving and shake well.

Chutney French Dressing. Add ¼ to 1 cup finely chopped chutney.

Cream French Dressing. Just before serving, add 1 tablespoon heavy cream or sour cream and shake well.

Martinique Dressing. Add 1 teaspoon finely chopped parsley and 1 tablespoon finely chopped green pepper.

Puerto Rico Dressing. Use half lemon juice and half vinegar. Add 2 tablespoons chopped olives and 1 tablespoon tomato catsup.

Roquefort *or* Bleu Cheese French Dressing. Add 1 to 4 tablespoons dry cheese crumbs and a few drops onion juice.

Russian French Dressing. Add 2 tablespoons chili sauce, 1 tablespoon finely chopped red or green pepper and a few drops onion juice.

Vermouth French Dressing. Use dry vermouth in place of vinegar.

Fruit Salad French Dressing. Use lemon juice or grapefruit juice in place of vinegar. Add finely chopped pistachio or other nuts, chopped candied fruit or fresh mint leaves. For a thicker dressing, add ½ cup strained honey or ⅓ cup sour cream, yogurt or heavy cream, whipped or not. See also the special dressings on page 302.

Cumberland French Dressing. Use lemon juice in place of vinegar. Add 1 tablespoon currant jelly and ¼ teaspoon grated lemon rind. *For fruit salads.*

HERB DRESSING

Add 1 teaspoon finely crushed dried marjoram and 1 tablespoon chopped parsley to French dressing made with lemon juice. Season more highly, if desired, with a few drops Angostura bitters, Worcestershire or A-1 sauce. Or omit marjoram and add 1 tablespoon finely chopped fresh herbs, using one of the following or a combination: anise leaves, basil, borage, burnet, chervil, chives, mint, rue, sorrel, tarragon.

CHIFFONADE DRESSING

Mix and chill

1 cup French dressing (double the recipe on page 300)
2 tablespoons chopped parsley
2 tablespoons chopped red pepper
1 teaspoon chopped onion *or* shallot
2 hard-cooked eggs, chopped fine

Shake well. *For green salads.*

INDIAN SALAD DRESSING

Mix and chill

1 cup French dressing
Yolks of 2 hard-cooked eggs, mashed
1 tablespoon each of finely chopped green pepper, red pepper, pickled beets and parsley

Shake well. *For green salads.*

THOUSAND ISLAND DRESSING

Mix and chill

⅓ cup olive *or* salad oil
Juice ½ orange
Juice ½ lemon
1 teaspoon salt
¼ teaspoon paprika
1 teaspoon onion juice
1 tablespoon chopped parsley
8 stuffed olives, sliced
1 teaspoon Worcestershire
¼ teaspoon mustard

Shake well. *For green salads.*

ASTORIA DRESSING

Mix
- ¼ **cup French dressing**
- ¼ **cup mayonnaise**
- 1 **tablespoon tomato catsup**
- **Tabasco to taste**

For green salads or as a cold sauce with fish and shellfish.

OHIO SALAD DRESSING

Mix and chill
- 1 **tablespoon sugar**
- 2 **teaspoons Worcestershire**
- 2 **teaspoons tomato catsup**
- 1 **tablespoon olive oil**
- ½ **teaspoon salt**
- ¼ **teaspoon mustard**
- **Few grains cayenne**
- 3 **drops Tabasco**
- 2 **tablespoons lemon juice**
- 1 **tablespoon vinegar**

Shake well. *For green salads.*

LIME DRESSING

Zestful on a fruit salad.

Mix and chill
- ¼ **cup olive *or* salad oil**
- 2 **tablespoons lime juice**
- 5 **drops Tabasco**
- **Few grains cayenne**
- ⅛ **teaspoon pepper**
- ¼ **teaspoon salt**
- 1 **teaspoon celery salt**
- 2 **teaspoons sugar**

Lakewood Dressing. Instead of lime juice, use 1 tablespoon grapefruit juice and 1 teaspoon vinegar. Add 1 tablespoon crumbled Roquefort cheese. *For fruit salads.*

NUT PASCAGOULA DRESSING

Pound into a paste (or whirl in a blender)
- 10 **pecan halves**
- 10 **blanched almonds**

Mix
- ¼ **teaspoon mustard**
- ¼ **teaspoon paprika**
- ¼ **teaspoon salt**
- ¼ **teaspoon sugar**

Add
- 1 **tablespoon vinegar**

Stir in slowly
- 5 **tablespoons olive *or* salad oil**

Add gradually to the nut mixture. *For fruit salads.*

PINEAPPLE HONEY DRESSING

Mix, chill and shake well
- ½ **cup honey**
- ¼ **cup lemon juice**
- ¼ **teaspoon salt**
- 3 **tablespoons crushed pineapple**

For fruit salads.

SOUR CREAM *or* YOGURT DRESSING

Season sour cream or yogurt with lemon juice, salt and pepper to taste. *For vegetable or fruit salads.*

Roquefort Cream Dressing. Add at least ¼ cup crumbled Roquefort to each cup of sour cream or yogurt. *Especially good stirred into iceberg lettuce, cut in small cubes.*

MAYONNAISE

Homemade mayonnaise is delicious, but commercial mayonnaise is good too, especially if you add a bit of seasoning to give it more zest (see Ways to Vary Mayonnaise, page 303).

Olive oil has a delicious flavor, but the mayonnaise is more likely to separate than if made with other oils. If you do not plan to use mayonnaise the day it is made, add 1 teaspoon of hot water. If mayonnaise separates (usually because the oil was added too rapidly) put an egg yolk in a bowl and add the mayonnaise to it, beating it in gradually. Add mayonnaise to a salad just before serving.

Have all the ingredients at room temperature, not icy cold. Have ready

¾ cup olive *or* salad oil

Sift into a small deep bowl

½ teaspoon mustard
½ teaspoon sugar
½ teaspoon salt
Few grains cayenne

Add

1 egg yolk

Mix thoroughly. Add, stirring constantly

1 tablespoon vinegar

Beat in 1 tablespoon oil, a drop or two at a time (using a small wooden spoon or an electric or hand beater). Beat in the rest of the oil, a teaspoonful at a time, until the dressing is as thick as whipped cream. Have the mixture perfectly smooth each time before you add more oil. Stir in

1 tablespoon lemon juice

Add more lemon juice if the mayonnaise is too thick.

WHOLE-EGG MAYONNAISE

The easiest method, especially with an electric mixer or blender.

Beat until thick

1 egg

Beat in

½ teaspoon mustard
½ teaspoon salt
2 tablespoons lemon juice *or* vinegar

Add, ¼ cup at a time

1½ cups olive *or* other oil

Beat until thick and smooth before adding each ¼ cup of oil.

To thin, stir in more lemon juice.

WAYS TO VARY MAYONNAISE

Season commercial or homemade mayonnaise by adding chutney or curry powder (especially for chicken salad) or by coloring it with tomato paste or tomato catsup. Or make one of the variations below.

To add more zest to "store" mayonnaise, add more seasonings or stir in a little lemon juice or heavy sweet or sour cream.

For a special variation, put in a jar ½ cup mayonnaise, ½ cup lemon juice and ¼ cup sugar (more seasonings if you like) and shake well.

CARLTON MAYONNAISE

Mix

1 cup mayonnaise
2 tablespoons tomato paste
½ tablespoon lemon juice
1½ teaspoons sugar
½ teaspoon Worcestershire
½ teaspoon A-1 sauce

For any meat or vegetable salad.

CREAM MAYONNAISE

Beat until stiff

⅓ cup cream

Stir gently into

1 cup mayonnaise

For fruit salads.

Chinese Mayonnaise. Before adding the cream, stir into the mayonnaise ¼ cup chopped almonds and ¼ cup currant jelly.

RAVIGOTE (GREEN MAYONNAISE)

Cover with boiling water

10 sprigs watercress
10 leaves spinach
4 sprigs parsley

Let stand 5 minutes. Drain, put

in cold water and drain again. Rub through a fine sieve and add to

1 cup mayonnaise

Season to taste with

Salt and nutmeg

For seafood salads.

RUSSIAN DRESSING

Mix

½ cup mayonnaise
½ cup chili sauce (drained)
¼ cup India relish *or* 1 tablespoon each of minced celery, pimiento and green pepper

Taste and add

Salt, if needed

For green salads or seafood salads.

Cream Russian Dressing. Just before serving, fold in ¼ cup cream, beaten stiff.

AVOCADO MAYONNAISE

Delicious on small whole tomatoes or shrimp or as a dip with cocktail wafers.

Mix

2 tablespoons evaporated milk
1 tablespoon lemon juice
1 teaspoon prepared mustard
¾ cup mashed avocado

Beat well. Season to taste with

Paprika, salt and Tabasco

CLEVELAND DRESSING

Mix

1 teaspoon salt
½ cup sugar
1 teaspoon dry mustard
1 teaspoon paprika
¼ cup vinegar

Chill overnight in the refrigerator. With an electric or rotary hand beater, beat in slowly

1 cup salad oil

Beat until as thick as honey. *For fruit salad.*

Poppyseed Dressing. Use lemon juice in place of vinegar and add 1 tablespoon poppyseed.

ROQUEFORT DRESSING

Mix

2 tablespoons mayonnaise
2 tablespoons crumbled Roquefort

Stir in slowly

¾ cup French dressing
½ teaspoon Worcestershire

For green salads.

GREEN GODDESS DRESSING

Mix in a bowl

1 egg yolk
½ teaspoon salt
2 tablespoons tarragon vinegar
1 tablespoon anchovy paste (or less)

Beat in, 2 tablespoons at a time

1 cup salad oil

Stir in

¼ cup cream
1 tablespoon lemon juice
1 teaspoon onion salt
Dash of garlic salt
2 tablespoons chopped chives
2 tablespoons chopped parsley

For green salads.

OLD-FASHIONED COOKED DRESSING

Sift into a double boiler top or a small heavy saucepan

½ teaspoon salt
1 teaspoon mustard
2 teaspoons sugar
Few grains cayenne
2 tablespoons flour

Stir in slowly

1 egg *or* 2 egg yolks
2 tablespoons butter
¾ cup milk
¼ cup vinegar

Stir and cook over boiling water or over low heat until slightly thick. Cool. *For vegetable and fruit salads.*

Cream Dressing. Use cream or evaporated milk in place of milk and butter.

Tango Dressing. Add ¼ teaspoon celery seed. Thin with orange juice.

SOUR CREAM COOKED DRESSING

Mix thoroughly
- **1 egg, slightly beaten**
- **¼ cup vinegar**
- **2 teaspoons salt**
- **2 teaspoons sugar**
- **1 teaspoon mustard**
- **⅛ teaspoon pepper**

Add to
- **1 cup sour cream**

Cook and stir until thick in a double boiler or in a small heavy pan over low heat. *For fruit salads.*

BACON DRESSING

Melt in a small heavy saucepan
- **3 tablespoons bacon fat**

Stir in
- **2 tablespoons flour**
- **1 teaspoon grated onion**

Cook and stir 1 minute. Add
- **½ teaspoon salt**
- **¼ teaspoon pepper**
- **¼ teaspoon sugar**
- **2 teaspoons prepared mustard**
- **2 teaspoons vinegar**

Cook until well blended. Add slowly
- **1 cup water**

Cook and stir until thick. Cool. *For vegetable salads.*

WHIPPED CREAM DRESSING

Beat until stiff
- **½ cup heavy cream, sweet *or* sour**

Beat in slowly
- **¼ teaspoon salt**
- **3 tablespoons vinegar *or* 2 tablespoons lemon juice**
- **Few grains pepper**
- **½ teaspoon sugar (if sour cream was used)**

For fruit salads.

Denver Cream Dressing. Add prepared mustard or grated horseradish to taste.

PEANUT BUTTEF DRESSING

Blend well
- **4 tablespoons evaporated milk**
- **4 tablespoons lemon juice**
- **4 tablespoons peanut butter**
- **Salt to taste**

For fruit salads, especially banana.

Cereals, Rice, Macaroni and Other Pastas

Cereals and grains are plant seeds, rich in protein, the B vitamins, iron and other minerals as well as starch. Wheat, cracked wheat (bulgur), oats, buckwheat, barley, rye, corn, rice, sago, soy and tapioca are all in this group of foods. They are especially valuable in their natural or whole-grain state, not stripped of the germ and the outer coat or husk. For most people whole grains are not indigestible, but if they are too rough, it is easy to compensate for the lost food values by adding wheat germ, which contains minerals and B vitamins but very little rough fiber. Nutritionists advise three servings daily from this group of foods, not only as breakfast foods but in puddings, breadstuffs of all sorts, cookies and cakes. Rice, corn meal, macaroni, spaghetti and noodles are popular to take the place of potatoes as accompaniments for meat, fish and poultry.

BREAKFAST CEREALS

It makes no difference nutritionally whether cereals are hot or cold. Some ready-to-eat cereals are made of whole grains. Some are enriched with added wheat germ, soy or other ingredients. Read the labels. Most people put plenty of milk on breakfast cereal, which adds protein and calcium to the meal.

Cook cereals according to directions on the package. Cook as briefly as possible and cook just enough for a meal. Long cooking and reheating destroy some of the vitamins. Cooking cereal in milk adds protein and calcium.

To enrich cooked cereal, sweeten it with unsulphured molasses and stir powdered skim milk into it. Brewer's yeast may be added too, but begin by adding only a teaspoon to 2 cups of cereal. Increase the amount as your family becomes accustomed to the unfamiliar taste.

Serving breakfast cereals. Brown sugar and shaved maple sugar are delicious on breakfast cereal. Sprinkle with toasted wheat germ for a tasty, crunchy topping full of protein and vitamins. Stir sliced dates, figs, prunes, apricots or raisins into cooked cereals. Slice bananas or peaches over cooked or ready-to-eat cereals.

CORN MEAL MUSH

Stir together until smooth

1 cup corn meal
1 cup cold water

1 teaspoon salt
In a heavy saucepan or double boiler top, bring to a boil
4 cups water
Add the soaked corn meal, stirring constantly. Cook and stir 2 minutes. Cover and reduce the heat, using an asbestos mat or cooking over hot water. Continue cooking until the mush tastes thoroughly cooked (30 to 45 minutes).

Hominy Grits. Substitute for corn meal.

FRIED MUSH

Cook corn meal, hominy grits or other cereal (pp. 306–307), using only 3 cups of water in all, so that the mush will be firm when it is cold.

Rinse a small loaf pan or a refrigerator storage dish with cold water. Fill with the cooked mush and cover to prevent a crust from forming. Chill. Cut in ½-inch slices. Dip in flour. Sauté slowly in butter or bacon fat.

Serve hot with maple syrup or Mock Maple Syrup (p. 431) as a breakfast dish, a dessert, or an accompaniment to ham or chicken.

Corn Meal *or* Hominy Cakes. Shape cooked corn meal or hominy grits in 3-inch patties. Dip in flour and cook as above. Serve in place of potato or other starchy vegetable.

HOMINY

Canned whole hominy is a convenience. Drain, season to taste with butter, salt and pepper, and heat over low heat or in a double boiler. Serve instead of potato. As a variation, serve hominy with tomato sauce.

For uncooked hominy and hominy grits, allow plenty of time for long slow cooking, as in Baked Hominy Southern Style.

BAKED HOMINY SOUTHERN STYLE

Put in a double boiler top
1 cup water
1 teaspoon salt
Set over direct heat and bring to a boil. Add, stirring constantly
¾ cup fine hominy grits
Boil 2 minutes, then set over hot water and continue cooking until thick. Add
1 cup milk
Stir thoroughly and cook 1 hour. Add
¼ cup butter
1 tablespoon sugar
1 egg, slightly beaten
1 cup milk
Turn into a buttered casserole. Bake 1 hour at 325°. *Serves 4 to 6.*

Buckwheat groats may be cooked in this same way.

HOMINY CROQUETTES

Put in a double boiler top
½ cup boiling water
Set over direct heat. Add slowly, stirring constantly
¼ cup fine hominy grits
Set over boiling water and cook until the hominy absorbs the water. Add
¾ cup milk
Cook until the hominy is tender. Add
2 tablespoons butter
½ teaspoon salt
Cool. Shape into croquettes. Roll in flour, dip in beaten egg, then in crumbs, and fry as for other croquettes (p. 4). *Serves 6.*

SPOON BREAD

White corn meal makes a crusty top and a soft center. Yellow corn meal gives an even texture throughout.

Butter a casserole and keep it warm. Put in a saucepan

2 cups boiling water

Add slowly

1 cup white or yellow corn meal
½ teaspoon salt

Cook and stir 1 minute. Remove from the heat. Add

2 tablespoons butter

Beat well. Beat in

4 eggs, well-beaten
1 cup milk

Pour into the casserole. Bake 25 minutes at 400°. *Serves 6.*

ALACE'S SPOON BREAD

Mix

2 eggs, well beaten
1 cup milk
1 cup water

Stir in

½ cup white *or* yellow corn meal
½ cup cooked hominy *or* rice
1 teaspoon baking powder
2 tablespoons butter
½ teaspoon salt

Put in a buttered casserole. Bake at 400° until the top is brown (30 to 40 minutes). *Serves 4.*

Buttermilk Spoon Bread. Use buttermilk in place of sweet milk and baking soda in place of baking powder.

BATTER BREAD

Beat until light

1 egg

Add

1 teaspoon salt
½ cup cold cooked hominy *or* rice
1 cup white corn meal

Stir in

Boiling water

to make the batter as thick as heavy cream. Put in a deep baking dish

1 tablespoon lard *or* bacon fat

Heat the dish until the fat smokes. Pour in the batter. Bake 40 minutes at 350°. *Serves 4.*

BULGUR

A special cracked wheat, which is widely used in Middle Eastern cooking. Good with chicken or lamb.

Follow the directions on the package. To make bulgur especially tasty, cook it in chicken broth.

Fried Bulgur. Put in a pan 2 tablespoons butter, 1 tablespoon chopped onion and 1 cup uncooked bulgur. Set over low heat and cook and stir until the onion is yellow. Add the required liquid and cook.

RICE

To preserve food values, do not wash packaged rice. Rice bought in bulk should be looked over and then washed quickly in a strainer without letting it soak in water.

Long-grain rice cooks into separate fluffy grains, and is excellent as an accompaniment to meat.

Short-grain rice is tender and moist when cooked. It is delicious in puddings.

Converted rice retains many of the food values lost in polished white rice.

Precooked rice is partially cooked before packaging and is handy for quick meals; read the directions on the package.

Brown or natural rice retains some of the outer coating. It is rich in food value and has a pleasant nutty flavor.

Wild rice is actually the seed of a marsh grass. It is a luxury item, but especially good with game and poultry.

STEAMED RICE

Put in a special rice cooker or a heavy saucepan with a tight-fitting cover

2 cups cold water
1 cup rice
1 teaspoon salt
1 teaspoon butter

Bring quickly to the boiling point. Reduce the heat so that the water just simmers, cover closely and cook 14 minutes. Uncover and let stand until the rice is dry and fluffy (about 5 minutes). Toss with a fork. *Makes 3 cups (5 or 6 servings).*

For more tender rice, use 2⅓ cups of water and cook 20 minutes.

Steamed brown rice takes 40 minutes or more after the water boils. To be sure it does not burn before it is tender, cook in a double boiler.

Rice Ring. Season Steamed Rice with butter and pack in a ring mold. Set in a pan of hot water to heat. Turn out onto serving dish.

GULLAH GOOBER RICE

Delicious with chicken or ham.

Mix

2 cups cooked rice
1 cup finely chopped celery
½ cup finely chopped salted peanuts

Cover. Set over low heat 10 minutes. *Serves 4.*

MUSHROOM RICE

Mix

2 cups steamed rice
½ cup sautéed chopped mushrooms
Few grains nutmeg

Serves 4.

SAUTERNE RICE

Put in a small pan

½ cup currants
Water to cover

Bring to a boil. Remove from the heat, let stand 5 minutes, and drain. Put in a large saucepan

⅓ cup butter
2 cloves garlic, split

Cook 5 minutes. Remove the garlic. Add

1½ cups dry white wine
3 cups water

Bring to a boil. Add slowly

2 cups rice
2½ teaspoons salt
¼ teaspoon pepper
¼ teaspoon nutmeg
¼ teaspoon allspice
2 teaspoons sugar

Bring to a boil again. Cover tightly. Reduce the heat. Simmer 25 minutes. Stir in the currants and

⅔ cup chopped or slivered Brazil nuts

Serves 8 generously.

FRIED RICE

Melt in a saucepan

4 tablespoons salad oil *or* butter

Add

1 cup rice

Cook and stir over low heat until the rice browns delicately (about 20 minutes). Add

2½ cups boiling water, stock *or* consommé
1½ teaspoons salt

Bring to the boiling point. Cover. Cook over low heat 20 minutes. Season to taste with

Salt and pepper

Serves 4.

SPANISH RICE

There is no "classic" recipe for Spanish rice. Start with cooked rice and add tomatoes, cheese, sautéed celery, onion, peppers and seasonings until the rice is as savory as you like. Or follow this recipe.

Put in a large frying pan
- **2 tablespoons bacon fat *or* butter**
- **2 onions, sliced thin**

Cook until the onion is soft. Add
- **1 cup uncooked rice *or* 1⅓ cups precooked rice**

Stir until the rice is lightly browned. Add
- **3 cups boiling water *or* stock (1⅓ cups for precooked rice)**
- **2 8-ounce cans tomato sauce *or* 2 chopped green peppers and 1 cup canned or fresh tomatoes**
- **Salt and pepper to taste**
- **Chili powder *or* prepared mustard to taste**

Stir well with a fork, cover and cook slowly until the rice is tender (10 minutes for precooked rice, 30 to 40 for uncooked rice). Season to taste. Spoon into a serving dish. Sprinkle with
- **Grated cheese**

Serves 4 to 6.

TURKISH PILAF

Put in a frying pan
- **2 tablespoons butter, bacon fat *or* chicken fat**
- **½ cup uncooked rice**

Cook and stir over moderate heat until the rice is brown (the rice will pop as it browns). Add
- **1 cup boiling water, tomato juice *or* canned bouillon**

Cook slowly until the liquid is absorbed. Add
- **1¾ cups drained canned tomatoes**

Cook until the rice is soft. Add
- **Salt and pepper to taste**

Serves 4 to 6.

Chicken *or* Lamb Pilaf. Add ½ cup (or more) diced cooked meat. Lamb and chicken are the traditional choice, but other meats are good, too. If you make the pilaf with chicken, cook the rice in chicken stock.

CURRIED RICE

Delicious with lamb or chicken.

Mix lightly with a fork
- **2 cups hot cooked rice**
- **1 egg yolk, slightly beaten**
- **1 teaspoon anchovy paste**
- **½ teaspoon curry powder**
- **Cayenne and salt to taste**

If convenient, add
- **1 chopped green chili**

Serves 4 or 5.

PARSLEY (GREEN) RICE

For a pretty luncheon dish, bake in a ring mold, turn onto a serving dish, and fill with creamed chicken or fish.

Mix and put in a buttered casserole
- **1 cup steamed rice**
- **1 cup milk**
- **4 tablespoons melted butter *or* olive oil**
- **½ cup grated cheese**
- **½ medium onion, chopped fine**
- **¼ to 1 cup chopped parsley**
- **1 egg, well beaten**
- **½ teaspoon salt**
- **¼ teaspoon paprika**
- **2 tablespoons chopped pimiento, if desired**

Bake at 350° until firm (about 45 minutes). *Serves 6.*

RICE WITH TOMATO SAUCE AND CHEESE

Melt in a heavy frying pan
- **2 tablespoons butter**

Add
- **3 cups steamed rice (p. 309)**

Cook until delicately browned,

stirring lightly with a fork. Spoon into a hot serving dish. Pour over the rice

1 cup hot tomato sauce

Sprinkle with

½ cup grated cheese

Lift the rice with a fork to coat each kernel with sauce and cheese. *Serves 6.*

BAKED RICE

Put in a buttered baking dish

2 cups cooked rice

Beat together and pour over the rice

1 egg
1 cup milk

Dot with

Butter

Sprinkle with

Salt, pepper and paprika

Bake until brown at 350° (about 20 minutes). *Serves 3 or 4.*

To season more highly, add chopped parsley, crumbled crisp bacon, bits of pimiento or sautéed mushrooms, or top with grated or sliced cheese.

BAKED RICE WITH CHEESE

A basic recipe which can be used as a main dish or to accompany meat or chicken.

Allow about ½ cup cooked rice per serving. Butter a baking dish. Put in it layers of the rice, dotting each layer with butter and thinly sliced mild cheese (about ⅛ pound for each 2 cups of rice). Add milk to about half the depth of the rice. Cover with crumbs and bake at 350° until the cheese melts and the crumbs are brown.

To vary, add chopped parsley, chopped pimiento or grated onion. For a heartier dish, add chopped ham, cooked chicken or hard-cooked eggs.

RICE CROQUETTES

As a luncheon or supper dish, serve with a tangy cheese sauce. Cook the rice in consommé if you prefer, but use less salt.

In a saucepan, put

½ cup boiling water
½ cup rice
1 teaspoon salt

Cover and cook slowly until the water is absorbed (about 10 minutes). Add

1 cup milk

Stir slightly with a fork, cover, and cook until the rice is tender. Stir in

2 egg yolks *or* 1 egg
1 tablespoon butter

Spread on a shallow plate to cool. Shape, egg and crumb and fry (p. 4). *Makes 6 or more.*

To season more highly, add tomato catsup and paprika to taste or use highly seasoned tomato juice in place of milk. Add ¼ cup grated cheese.

WILD RICE

Canned cooked wild rice saves the long cooking time.

Put in a double boiler top

1 cup wild rice, thoroughly washed
2 cups cold water
1 teaspoon salt

Set over direct heat and bring quickly to the boiling point. Cover and cook over hot water until tender but still firm (1 to 1½ hours). Serve plain or add butter or chopped sautéed mushrooms.

MACARONI, NOODLES AND SPAGHETTI

The best Italian pastes are creamy rather than white and break with a clean sharp edge. There are many attractive forms —elbows, shells, twists and letters as well as macaroni, spaghetti and vermicelli. Some types are available canned and ready to heat and season.

Noodles are usually enriched with eggs or egg yolks. Soy-enriched noodles are more like meat in food value because of the improved protein quality provided by the soy. Green noodles have spinach added to the dough to give them a fine color.

MACARONI

Allow 1 to 3 ounces per person, according to whether the macaroni is to be served as an accompaniment or as the main dish.

Break into 1 or 2 inch pieces. Have ready a deep kettle of rapidly boiling salted water (1 teaspoon salt to each quart). Add the macaroni slowly so that the boiling will not stop. Boil until just tender but still firm—*al dente,* as the Italians describe it. Be careful not to overcook, especially if there is to be further cooking in a sauce.

Drain in a strainer and rinse with cold water to remove excess starch which would make the paste sticky.

Reheat in cream, Cream Sauce (p. 94), Tomato Sauce (p. 99) or Cheese Sauce (p. 95), allowing ½ cup to each cup of macaroni.

Macaroni alla Milanese. Heat 2 cups cooked macaroni in 1 cup Italian Tomato Sauce (p. 313) with 6 sautéed sliced mushrooms and 2 slices cooked smoked tongue cut in strips. Serve with grated Parmesan cheese.

BAKED NOODLES

Cook like spaghetti (p. 313)

¼ pound noodles

Drain. Add

1 tablespoon butter
½ teaspoon salt
⅛ teaspoon pepper
Few grains nutmeg
¼ cup hot milk
2 egg yolks, well beaten

Mix lightly with a fork and spoon. Fold in

2 egg whites, beaten stiff

Pour into a buttered baking dish. Set in a pan of hot water. Bake 30 minutes at 325°. *Serves 4 to 6.*

Baked Noodles with Cheese. Increase the milk to ½ cup. Add ½ cup grated cheese (or ¼ cup grated cheese and ½ cup chopped cooked ham). Add 2 tablespoons each of shredded green pepper and finely cut celery.

BAKED MACARONI AND CHEESE

Cook and drain

1 9-ounce package macaroni

Put half of it in a buttered baking dish. Sprinkle with

½ cup grated cheese (or more)

Cover with the rest of the macaroni. Sprinkle with

½ cup grated cheese (or more)

Cover with

2 cups Cream Sauce (p. 94)

Sprinkle with

½ cup buttered bread crumbs

Bake at 400° until brown. *Serves 6.*

For a very creamy dish, make 2 cups Cheese Sauce (p. 95) and spread it on the layers of macaroni instead of cheese and cream sauce.

Macaroni and Cheese with Chipped Beef. Cover ¼ pound dried beef (separated in pieces) with boiling water. Drain. If the beef is very salty, let it stand a few minutes before draining. Put half the beef on each layer of macaroni.

Macaroni and Cheese with Spiced Ham. Cut canned spiced

ham in strips. Put half on each layer of macaroni. Other meats are good this way, too–sliced cooked frankfurters or bits of cooked ham or chicken.

MACARONI MOUSSE

Cook and drain

1 cup elbow macaroni

Add

1½ cups milk
¼ cup melted butter
2 eggs, well beaten
1 pimiento, chopped fine
1 sweet green pepper, chopped fine
1 tablespoon chopped onion
½ tablespoon salt
½ cup mild or sharp cheese, cut small
½ cup soft bread crumbs

Mix well. Put in a buttered loaf pan, 9 by 5 inches. Bake at 350° until firm (about 40 minutes). Turn out onto a serving plate. Serve with

Creamed Mushrooms (p. 258)

Serves 6.

Macaroni Ring. Bake in a 10-inch ring mold. Turn out onto a round serving dish. Fill with creamed mushrooms, chicken or seafood.

SPAGHETTI

1 package (8 or 9 ounces) serves 4 or 5 as the main dish.

Have ready a deep kettle of rapidly boiling salted water (1 teaspoon salt to each quart). Do not break spaghetti in pieces. Take a handful of it, dip the ends in the water, and as the ends soften, coil the spaghetti under the water. Cook until just tender (about 7 minutes). Drain in a colander. Arrange in layers in a heated serving dish, spreading each layer generously with sauce (below). Serve with extra sauce and plenty of freshly grated Parmesan or Romano

cheese. Spaghetti and Meat Balls (p. 178).

GARLIC SAUCE

Heat ¼ cup olive oil with 2 or 3 split cloves of garlic. Remove the garlic. Pour the oil over cooked spaghetti. Toss until well blended.

Garlic Sauce with Anchovies. Just before pouring the oil over the spaghetti, add 6 anchovies, cut in pieces.

Garlic Sauce with Mushrooms. Add ½ to 1 cup sliced sautéed mushrooms.

Garlic Sauce with Clams. Add ½ cup fresh or canned minced clams.

ITALIAN TOMATO SAUCE

Canned tomato sauce is a convenience. Add extra meat for a richer sauce. Leftover sauce is good over poached eggs or added to a soup or gravy.

Put in a large skillet or a saucepan

3 tablespoons olive oil *or* **2 tablespoons oil and 1 tablespoon butter**
1 or 2 onions, sliced thin
1 clove garlic, split

Cook until the onion is golden. Add

½ to 1 pound ground beef

Cook and stir 5 minutes. Add

1 can tomato paste
1 large can tomatoes (about 2½ cups)
1 tablespoon sugar
Salt, pepper, cayenne, oregano and basil to taste

Simmer at least 1 hour. Add water as needed, but the sauce should be thick and smooth. For the finest flavor, let the sauce mellow for a day before using it. *For ½ pound spaghetti.*

Variations. Add other seasonings such as thyme, chopped parsley, a few grains of mace or allspice or a few drops of Worcestershire or Tabasco.

Omit the meat for a simpler sauce.

Substitute for the tomatoes 2½ cups tomato juice, water or consommé.

In place of olive oil, use other salad oil, bacon fat or 2 slices bacon, diced.

Omit the onion, garlic and sugar.

TRUMAN'S SPAGHETTI SAUCE

Good also made with leftover chopped cooked lamb, pork, veal or beef.

Put in a large skillet or a heavy saucepan

2 slices bacon, diced
½ green pepper, chopped
1 or 2 onions, chopped
1 clove garlic, split

Cook until the onion is golden. Add

½ to 1 pound ground beef

Cook and stir until the meat is browned. Add

2 cans tomato paste
1 can consommé
1 tablespoon Worcestershire
2 tablespoons grated Parmesan *or* Romano cheese
Salt, pepper and oregano to taste

Simmer 2 or 3 hours, adding water if the sauce gets too thick. For finest flavor, let the sauce mellow a day. *For ½ pound spaghetti.*

QUICK TOMATO SAUCE

Empty a can or two of tomato paste into a pan. Stir in hot water until the sauce is as thin as you like it. Season to taste, adding a trace of sugar and a shake of powdered garlic.

MEAT BALLS FOR SPAGHETTI

See page 178.

HOMEMADE NOODLES

Beat slightly

1 egg
½ teaspoon salt

Mix in

Flour (about 2 cups)

to make a very stiff dough. Knead 5 minutes on a slightly floured board. Roll paper-thin. Cover with a towel and set aside 20 minutes.

For soup, cut in 3-inch strips. Pile the strips on each other and cut in fine shreds. **For broad noodles,** cut in strips of any desired width. Spread out on a table to dry.

Store in a tightly covered jar.

Cook like spaghetti (p. 313).

BUTTERED NOODLES

Cook noodles (p. 312). Stir in butter to taste and season with salt and pepper.

Noodles with Poppyseed. For ½ pound of noodles, melt 2 tablespoons butter, add 3 tablespoons poppyseed and ¼ cup chopped almonds. Cook and stir 5 minutes and stir into the cooked noodles.

SAUTÉED NOODLES

Cook ½ pound noodles according to the instructions on the package. Dry thoroughly on a towel. Melt 4 tablespoons butter, add the noodles and toss over moderate heat until the noodles are delicately brown. Serve sprinkled with croutons or arrange in a ring on a platter and fill with creamed chicken or other creamed dish. *Serves 6.*

ALFREDO'S NOODLES

Plenty of butter and plenty of cheese make this dish memorable.

Have ready a deep kettle of boiling salted water (1 teaspoon to each quart). Add slowly

½ pound broad noodles

Cook until the noodles are just barely tender. Drain. Add.

¼ pound unsalted butter, soft but not melted

Turn over and over with a large fork and spoon until the butter is melted and the noodles are well coated. Heap on a large heated platter. Sprinkle with

¼ pound grated Parmesan cheese

Toss with a fork and spoon until the cheese melts. *Serves 4 to 6.*

SOUR CREAM NOODLES

Cook like spaghetti (p. 313)

¼ pound broad noodles

Drain. Add

1 cup cottage cheese
1 cup sour cream
1 egg, slightly beaten
½ teaspoon salt
⅛ teaspoon pepper
¼ cup butter, melted

Mix. Put in a well-buttered baking dish. Bake 1½ hours at 300°. *Serves 4 to 6.*

Noodle Pudding. Add ½ cup raisins. Excellent with ham or chicken.

NOODLE RING

For a simple version, butter cooked noodles, pack into a ring mold and set in a pan of hot water in the oven until serving time.

Bake Sour Cream Noodles (above) or Baked Noodles (p. 312) in a well-buttered 1-quart ring mold. Turn out onto a serving dish. Fill with creamed chicken or seafood or with sautéed mushrooms or buttered green beans. *Serves 4 or 5.*

MARGERY'S NOODLES

For a more pungent flavor, add a clove of garlic, cut fine.

Cook like spaghetti (p. 313)

½ pound fine noodles

Mix

1 cup cottage cheese
1 cup sour cream
¾ cup finely chopped onion
1 teaspoon Worcestershire
Few drops Tabasco
Salt and pepper to taste

Add the noodles and mix well. Put in a buttered casserole. Bake 20 minutes at 350°. Spread over the top

½ cup grated Parmesan cheese
½ cup sour cream

Bake 10 minutes longer. *Serves 6.*

LASAGNE

Mix in a large kettle

1 large can tomato purée
2 cans tomato paste
2 cups water

1 teaspoon oregano
1 teaspoon sugar
1 teaspoon salt
¼ teaspoon fresh ground pepper

Simmer the mixture while you sauté in a skillet

2 tablespoons olive oil
1 cup minced onion
1 clove garlic, crushed

When the onion is golden, add

1½ pounds ground beef, preferably chuck
1 teaspoon salt

Cook until the meat has lost its red color and add to the kettle mixture. Simmer for about 2 hours or until the sauce is thick. Cook as directed on the package

1 pound lasagne noodles

Drain thoroughly, rinse and separate the noodles, spreading them on a towel to dry. Cut into thin slices

1 pound Mozzarella

Have ready

1 pound ricotta cheese
4 ounces fresh grated Romano cheese

Spoon some of the sauce into two 8-inch square pans or one large casserole. Put in a layer of noodles, then a layer of Mozzarella and a layer of ricotta. Put in another layer of noodles, crosswise, then more sauce, and layers of noodles, Mozzarella and ricotta. Top with a last layer of noodles and the rest of the sauce. Sprinkle generously with Romano cheese. Bake at 375° for 30 minutes. Let stand in a warm place for 15 minutes before serving. *Serves 8 to 10.*

CANELLONI

Cook like spaghetti

1 8-ounce package lasagne noodles

Drain. Spread on a cloth to dry. Mix

1 pound ricotta cheese
½ pound cream cheese
1 egg, slightly beaten
¼ cup chopped chives *or* parsley
¼ cup butter, creamed
Salt and pepper to taste

Spread a tablespoonful on each cooked noodle. Roll tight. Place the rolls, close together, on shallow baking dishes. Pour over the rolls

Italian Tomato Sauce (p. 313) *or* 2 cans tomato paste mixed with 3 cups water

Cut in thin slices

1 pound Mozzarella cheese

Put a slice of cheese on each roll. Sprinkle with

Grated Parmesan cheese

Bake 30 minutes at 375°. *Serves 4 to 6.*

For a heartier dish, add any chopped cooked meat to the filling.

RAVIOLI

Sift onto a bread board

1½ cups flour
½ teaspoon salt

Make a depression in the center. Drop in

1 egg yolk

Mix with a knife. Moisten with

Warm water

to make a stiff dough. Knead until smooth. Cover with a warm bowl. Let stand 30 minutes. Roll paper-thin. Cut in strips 3 inches wide. Put teaspoonfuls of

Filling (p. 317)

on half the strips, 2 inches apart. Cover with the other strips. Seal by pressing along the edges and

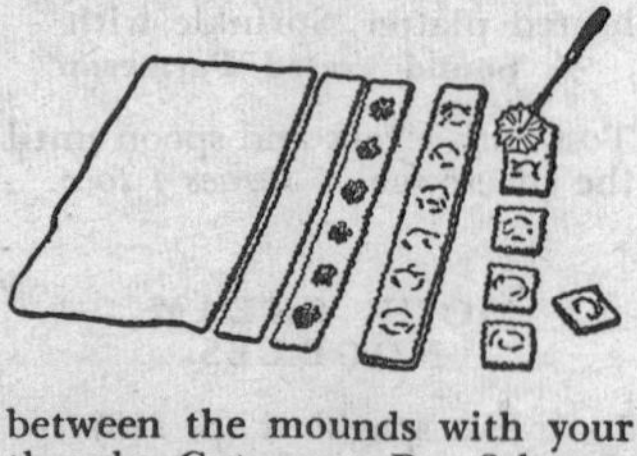

between the mounds with your thumbs. Cut apart. Dry 2 hours. Cook 20 minutes in

Rapidly boiling water, stock *or* bouillon

Take up with a skimmer. Arrange in layers in a heated serving dish. Sprinkle each layer generously with

Grated Parmesan cheese

Cover with

Italian Tomato Sauce (p. 313)

Serves 6.

Spinach and Cheese Filling. Mix ¼ cup cracker crumbs, ½ cup grated Parmesan or Romano cheese, ¼ cup chopped cooked spinch and 1 egg, slightly beaten. Moisten with chicken stock or broth. Season with salt and pepper.

Meat Filling. Mix ½ cup chopped meat or chicken, ½ cup chopped cooked spinach, 1 egg and 2 tablespoons grated Romano or Parmesan cheese. Season to taste with salt, pepper and oregano or nutmeg.

GNOCCHI ALLA ROMANA

Put in a saucepan

¼ cup butter

Melt until bubbling. Take from the heat. Add

¼ cup flour
¼ cup cornstarch
½ teaspoon salt

Stir well. Add slowly

2 cups milk

Cook 3 minutes over low heat, stirring constantly. Add

2 egg yolks, slightly beaten
½ cup grated Parmesan cheese

Pour into a buttered shallow pan, about 10 by 14 inches. Chill. Turn out on a board. Cut in squares, strips or diamonds. Place on a buttered ovenproof platter. Sprinkle with

¼ cup melted butter
¼ cup grated Parmesan cheese

Bake at 400° until brown (about 15 minutes). *Serves 6.*

Pancakes, Waffles and Doughnuts

Although traditionally served only at breakfast, pancakes, waffles and doughnuts now appear at other times as well. With crisp bacon or tasty country sausage, pancakes and waffles are hearty enough for lunch. Waffles are a welcome dessert after a simple main course. Pancake mixes and biscuit mixes are convenient.

TO COOK GRIDDLECAKES

To test the griddle for correct heat, pour a few drops of water on it. When the griddle is hot enough, the water will boil up immediately and form rapidly moving globules.

Heat the griddle or frying pan over moderate heat. Most modern griddles need no greasing, but if necessary, grease lightly with butter. To make pancakes all the same size, use a ¼-cup measure to dip the batter onto the griddle.

Cook until the cakes are full of bubbles and the undersurface is nicely browned. Lift with a pancake turner or spatula and brown the other side. Serve immediately.

TO SERVE WITH GRIDDLECAKES

Plenty of melted butter and warmed maple syrup are perfect, but other good accompaniments are Honey Sauce (p. 431) and Mock Maple Syrup (p. 431); and many like honey, molasses, sour cream, applesauce or other accompaniments. See also bacon (p. 204) and sausages and sausage cakes (pp. 205, 206).

GRIDDLECAKES

Put in a mixing bowl

- **½ cup milk**
- **2 tablespoons melted butter**
- **1 egg**

Beat lightly. Sift

- **1 cup all-purpose *or* pastry flour**
- **2 teaspoons baking powder**
- **2 tablespoons sugar**
- **½ teaspoon salt**

Add to the milk mixture all at once. Stir just enough to dampen the flour. Add more milk, if necessary, to make the batter about as thick as heavy cream. Cook (above). *Makes 6 or 8.*

To vary, use buttermilk, sour milk or yogurt in place of milk. Use ½ teaspoon baking soda instead of baking powder. Or sift a tablespoon of corn meal with the flour.

Whole-wheat Pancakes. Use ⅓ cup whole-wheat flour and ⅔

cup white flour. Sweeten with molasses instead of sugar.

Oatmeal Pancakes. Heat ½ cup milk, add ½ cup quick oatmeal and let stand 10 minutes. Add the rest of the ingredients but reduce the flour to 2 tablespoons.

Buckwheat Cakes. Use half buckwheat flour and half white flour.

Apple Pancakes. Peel 1 tart juicy apple. Quarter, cut in thin slices and stir into the batter.

Blueberry Pancakes. Add ½ cup blueberries to the batter. If you use canned blueberries, strain off the juice.

PANCAKE SANDWICHES

Put pancakes together sandwich fashion with any of the fillings suggested below. Serve immediately or keep warm in the oven. This is a tasty way to make leftovers into a hearty luncheon dish.

Creamed chicken or tuna.
Creamed mushrooms.
One can concentrated cream of chicken soup, diluted with about ¼ cup cream or top milk. Add extra chicken and mushrooms, if you like. Season to taste with nutmeg or sherry.
One can concentrated cream of celery soup, diluted with about ¼ cup cream or top milk. Add ½ cup chopped ham.

CORN MEAL GRIDDLECAKES

Put in a saucepan
¾ cup water
Bring to a boil. Stir in
4 tablespoons corn meal
Cook 5 minutes. Remove from heat. Stir in
¾ cup sour milk
Sift together
1 cup all-purpose flour
2 tablespoons sugar
½ teaspoon salt
½ teaspoon baking powder
¼ teaspoon baking soda
Add to the corn meal mixture. Stir in
1 egg, well beaten
1 tablespoon melted butter
Cook (p. 318). *Makes 12.*

To make with sweet milk. Omit the soda and use 1 teaspoon baking powder.

RICE GRIDDLECAKES

Mix
1 cup milk
1 cup warm cooked rice
½ teaspoon salt
Stir in
2 egg yolks, beaten until thick
1 tablespoon melted butter
⅞ cup all-purpose flour
Fold in
2 egg whites, beaten stiff
Cook (p. 318). *Makes 15 to 18.*

FRENCH PANCAKES

French pancakes are internationally famous for dessert. They are also the basis for some exceptional luncheon dishes and provide an epicurean way to use leftovers.

Put in a bowl
2 eggs, beaten
1 cup milk
½ teaspoon salt
1 cup all-purpose or pastry flour
Stir until smooth. Cover and let stand at least ½ hour. The batter should be thin—just thick enough to coat a spoon dipped in it. If the batter is too thick, stir in a little more milk. Heat a 5- or 6-inch frying pan. Grease lightly with salad oil. Pour in just enough batter to cover the pan with a very thin layer.

Tilt the pan so that the batter spreads evenly. Cook on one side, toss or turn with a spatula and brown the other side. Cook the pancakes one by one. Roll up or fold in quarters. Keep warm if you are serving them immediately, or set aside and reheat in the oven. *Makes 18 to 24.*

Normandy Pancakes. Cook small pork sausage links. Wrap one in each pancake. Heat in the oven. Serve with maple syrup and Fried Apple Rings (p. 87).

Crêpes Nicholas. Put a tablespoon of chopped cooked chicken on each pancake. Roll up and put close together in a shallow baking dish. When ready to serve, pour piping hot Cheese Sauce (p. 95) over the pancakes and brown slightly in the broiler.

Mushroom Crêpes. Slice 3/4 pound mushrooms thin. Cook 5 minutes in 3 tablespoons butter. Add 2 egg yolks beaten with 3/4 cup sour cream. Cook 2 minutes. Put a spoonful on each pancake and roll up. Put in a baking dish and reheat in a 350° oven.

Seafood Crêpes. Flake crab meat or tuna, or cut shrimp or lobster in small pieces. Mix with undiluted cream of celery soup. Season to taste with oregano, curry powder or paprika. Sherry, too, if you like. Put a spoonful on each pancake. Roll up and put in a buttered baking dish. Sprinkle with melted butter or salad oil. Bake at 350° until well heated (about 20 minutes). Serve with tomato sauce and grated Parmesan cheese.

Cocktail Crêpes. Cook the batter by teaspoonfuls on a large griddle. Put on each pancake a dab of any savory filling such as cheese, curried chicken, ham or lobster. Roll up, keep hot, and serve on toothpicks.

Crêpes Gruyère. Put a small piece of Gruyère cheese on each pancake. Fold to cover the cheese completely. Egg and crumb (p. 4) and fry in deep fat heated to 370° until lightly browned (about 1 minute). Serve with drinks or with tomato sauce for lunch.

BLINI

Make thin pancakes from a pancake mix (buckwheat mix is especially good), or follow the recipe for French Pancakes (p. 319). Serve with melted butter, sour cream and smoked salmon, smoked whitefish, caviar or salt herring.

Each person spreads his pancake with butter, then puts on a piece of fish, and tops the fish with a spoonful of sour cream.

Serve blini as a first course or as a supper or luncheon dish.

MANICOTTI

Make 8 French Pancakes (p. 319). Mix

- **1 pound ricotta *or* dry cottage cheese**
- **1 cup chopped cooked ham**
- **2 eggs, well beaten**
- **3 tablespoons chopped parsley**
- **1/4 cup grated Romano cheese**

Put one-eighth of this mixture on each pancake. Roll up and put close together in a baking dish. Mix

- **2 cans tomato paste**
- **2 cups water**

Pour over the pancakes. Sprinkle with

- **1/4 cup grated Romano cheese**

Bake about 30 minutes at 350°. *Serves 4.*

CRÊPES SUZETTE

For a gala effect, makes Crêpes Suzette at the table in a chafing dish or electric skillet. Other-

wise, put them on a warmed serving dish and pour the rest of the sauce over them. At serving time sprinkle with sugar and warmed brandy and light with a match.

Sift together
- **1 cup flour**
- **¼ cup powdered sugar**
- **½ teaspoon salt**

Put in a mixing bowl
- **2 eggs**
- **1 cup milk**
- **1 tablespoon brandy *or* 1 teaspoon vanilla**

Beat well. Stir in the flour mixture. Cover and let stand at least ½ hour. Follow the directions for cooking French Pancakes (p. 319). Heat
- **3 tablespoons Suzette Sauce I or II (below)**

in a chafing dish. Add 6 of the pancakes and heat slowly, spooning the sauce over the pancakes several times. Add more sauce as needed. When the sauce is syrupy and the pancakes are very hot, sprinkle with
- **Sugar and warmed brandy *or* curaçao**

Light with a match. Cook the rest of the crêpes the same way. *Makes 18 or more to serve 6.*

SUZETTE SAUCE I

Make the sauce ahead of time. It does not ned to be perfectly smooth.

Cream
- **½ cup sweet butter**

Beat in
- **½ cup powdered sugar**

Add
- **Grated rind and juice of 2 tangerines *or* 1 orange**
- **¼ cup cognac *or* curaçao *or* a mixture of maraschino, kirsch and curaçao**

SUZETTE SAUCE II

Mix
- **Grated peel and juice of 1 lemon**
- **Grated peel and juice of 1 orange**
- **1 cup sugar**
- **½ cup water**
- **¼ cup brandy**

JELLY PANCAKES

Make pancakes as for Crêpes Suzette (p. 320). Spread with jelly and roll up. Sprinkle with powdered sugar.

CRÊPES VERT GALANT

Make pancakes as for Crêpes Suzette (p. 320). Keep warm until all are made. Whip
- **½ cup heavy cream**

Fold in
- **½ cup chopped toasted almonds, hazelnuts *or* walnuts**

Sweeten to taste. Put a spoonful on each pancake, roll up, sprinkle with
- **Sugar**
- **Cointreau**

Serve immediately. *Serves 4 or 5.*

COTTAGE CHEESE PANCAKES

Best of all made on a table grill, so that you can serve them hot.

Put in a bowl
- **1 cup cottage cheese**
- **3 eggs, well beaten**
- **2 tablespoons butter**
- **¼ cup flour, sifted**
- **¼ teaspoon salt**

Beat only until well blended. Cook by tablespoons on a heated griddle. Spread with any tart jelly, roll up, and sprinkle with confectioners' sugar. Serve as dessert. *Makes 12.*

WAFFLES

Waffle mix and frozen waffles save a little time but the batter is easy to prepare.

Sift

1½ cups flour
3 teaspoons baking powder
2 teaspoons sugar
½ teaspoon salt

Put in a large shaker or a glass jar with a tight cover

1 cup milk *or* part cream
2 eggs, beaten
3 tablespoons melted butter *or* salad oil

Add the flour mixture and shake hard until well blended (10 or 15 times). Or put in a big pitcher and beat with a rotary or electric beater. The batter doesn't need to be perfectly smooth. If the batter is thicker than heavy cream, add a little more milk. A thin batter makes tender waffles.

Heat the waffle iron but do not grease it. Pour about 1 tablespoon of the batter into each compartment near the center (the batter will spread to fill the iron), cover and leave closed until steaming stops. Waffles should be well puffed and delicately brown. Lift from the iron with a fork. The first waffle is sometimes inclined to stick. Bake it a little longer to be sure you can lift it out easily. The others will be no problem.

Serve with melted butter and warmed maple syrup. For a heartier dish, serve with small broiled sausages, creamed chicken, mushrooms, bacon or fried chicken. *Makes 6 to 8.*

Sour Milk Waffles. Use 1¼ cups sour milk or cream, buttermilk or yogurt, and add ¼ teaspoon soda. Use only 2 tablespoons butter if you use sour cream.

Coconut Waffles. After pouring the batter onto the iron, sprinkle with a tablespoon or more of shredded coconut.

Ham Waffles. Add to the batter ½ to 1 cup chopped cooked ham.

Corn Waffles. Add to the batter 1 cup cooked corn or drained whole-kernel canned corn.

CIDER SYRUP FOR WAFFLES

Simmer 5 minutes

½ cup sugar
1 cup cider

RAISED WAFFLES

The best ever—crisp but tender. To serve at breakfast, start them the night before.

Put in a large mixing bowl

½ cup lukewarm water
1 package yeast

Let stand 5 minutes. Add

2 cups lukewarm milk
½ cup melted butter *or* salad oil
1 teaspoon salt
1 teaspoon sugar

Beat in

2 cups flour

Cover the bowl. Let stand overnight or at least 8 hours (not in the refrigerator). When time to cook the waffles, add

2 eggs
Pinch of baking soda

Beat well. The batter will be very thin. Cook on a waffle iron. *Makes 6 or more large waffles.*

Cornell Waffles. For high-protein and high-vitamin waffles, replace 1 cup of the flour with ½ cup whole-wheat flour or part soy flour, ½ cup powdered milk and ¼ cup toasted wheat germ. Add more milk, if necessary, to make the batter thin enough to pour.

CORN MEAL WAFFLES

Follow the recipe for Corn Meal Griddlecakes (p. 319), but fold in the egg white, beaten stiff, at the last. Cook on a waffle iron (p. 322). Good with sausage, bacon or ham.

RICE WAFFLES

Sift together into a mixing bowl

1¾ cups flour
4 teaspoons baking powder
¼ teaspoons salt
2 tablespoons sugar

Add

⅔ cup cold cooked rice

Mix evenly with a fork. Add

1½ cups milk
1 egg yolk, well beaten
1 tablespoon melted butter *or* salad oil

Stir thoroughly. Fold in

1 egg white, beaten stiff

Cook on a waffle iron (p. 322). *Makes 6 to 8.*

DOUGHNUTS

Sift

1¾ cups flour
2 tablespoons baking powder
¼ teaspoon nutmeg
½ teaspoon salt

Put in a mixing bowl

1 egg
½ cup milk
½ cup sugar
1 tablespoon melted butter *or* salad oil

Add the dry ingredients. Add enough more flour to make the dough just firm enough to handle, but keep the dough as soft as possible. Chill.

Put a third of the mixture on a floured board, knead slightly, pat, and roll out ⅓ inch thick. Shape with a floured doughnut cutter. Add the trimmings to half the remaining mixture. Roll and shape as before; repeat until all the dough is cut out. Put the doughnuts on a floured piece of wax paper. Let stand 5 or 10 minutes before frying.

Heat the fat to 360° (p. 4). Doughnuts will absorb fat if the fat is too cool, and will brown before they are done in the center if it is too hot. Lower the doughnuts gently into the fat and fry three or four at a time. When brown on one side, turn and brown on the other side. Lift from the fat with a fork or tongs (without piercing). Drain on paper towels. *Makes 18.*

To sugar. Roll in powdered sugar. Or put the sugar in a paper bag, add the doughnuts, two or three at a time, and shake gently until well coated.

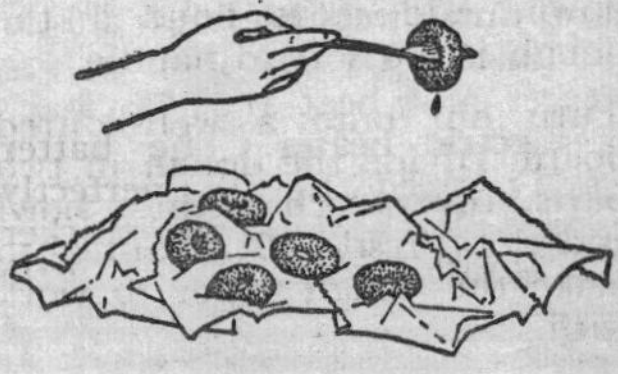

To frost. Spread one side with Portsmouth Frosting (p. 512), Sprinkle with chopped nut meats, if desired.

Sour Milk Doughnuts. *These doughnuts are especially tender.* Use half pastry flour and half all-purpose flour, and use sour milk or buttermilk in place of sweet milk. Add ½ teaspoon baking soda and use only ½ teaspoon baking powder.

Cream Doughnuts. Use cream in place of milk and butter. With sour cream (best of all) add ½ teaspoon baking soda and use only ½ teaspoon baking powder.

Lemon Doughnuts. In place of 1 whole egg, use 2 egg yolks. Add 1 tablespoon lemon juice and ½ teaspoon grated lemon rind. Season with nutmeg.

Chocolate Doughnuts. Sift ½ cup cocoa with the flour. Sugar the doughnuts or spread with Chocolate or Orange Portsmouth Frosting (p. 512).

RAISED DOUGHNUTS

Put in a mixing bowl

1 cup lukewarm milk
1 package yeast

1 teaspoon salt
2 cups all-purpose flour

Beat thoroughly. Cover and let rise ½ hour. Add

¼ cup melted butter *or* salad oil
1 cup light brown sugar
2 eggs, well beaten
½ teaspoon nutmeg
1½ cups flour

Beat well. Cover and let rise again until dough is light. Punch down. Add more flour if the dough is too soft to handle.

Turn out onto a well-floured board. Divide the dough in two parts, cover each with a bowl and let "rest" 10 minutes to make the dough easier to work with.

Roll about ½ inch thick. Cut with a floured biscuit cutter and shape into a ball, or cut with a 3-inch doughnut cutter. Set on the board, uncovered, and let rise about 1 hour. Fry (p. 323). Dip in granulated sugar. *Makes 24.*

Jelly Doughnuts. Cut out dough in 2½-inch rounds. On half of them place heaping teaspoons of jam or jelly. Brush the edges with slightly beaten egg white and cover with the other rounds. Press the edges together. Let rise, fry and dip in sugar.

CORNELL DOUGHNUTS

These delicious doughnuts are much richer nutritionally than standard doughnuts and provide a substantial amount of protein, calcium, phosphorus, iron, thiamine, riboflavin and niacin.

Follow the recipe for Raised Doughnuts (p. 323), but instead of using all white flour, use only 2½ cups flour with ½ cup soy flour, ½ cup powdered milk, 1 tablespoon brewer's yeast and 2 tablespoons wheat germ. Add ½ teaspoon cinnamon and 1 teaspoon vanilla.

AFTERNOON TEA DOUGHNUTS

Also delicious with coffee.

Beat until light

1 egg

Add

2 tablespoons sugar
½ teaspoon salt
3 tablespoons milk
1 tablespoon melted shortening *or* oil

Sift together

1 cup flour
2 teaspoons baking powder

Stir into the first mixture. Shape dough by teaspoonfuls, or force through a pastry bag with the small ladyfinger tube directly into deep fat, heated to 370°. Fry and drain. Serve with

Julienne strips of cheese

Makes 24 or more.

CRULLERS

Mix batter for Doughnuts (p. 323) or Raised Doughnuts. Roll it out ⅓ inch thick. Cut in strips 8 inches long and ¾ inch wide. Let rise (10 minutes for doughnut batter, 1 hour for raised doughnut batter). Twist several times and pinch the ends. Fry (p. 323) and roll in sugar. *Makes 3 dozen.*

JIFFY CRULLERS

Cut ready-to-bake packaged biscuits in half. Twist each piece to make a tiny cruller. Fry at 370°. Roll in sugar or sugar and cinnamon. These midget-sized crullers are perfect for a mid-morning coffee party.

FRENCH CRULLERS

See page 409.

DOUGHBOYS

Roll bread dough (p. 350) 1/8 inch thick. Cut in strips 2½ inches wide and cut the strips in squares or in diamond-shaped pieces. Cover and let stand 10 to 15 minutes. Fry like doughnuts (p. 323). Serve in place of hot rolls or with maple syrup or Mock Maple Syrup (p. 431) as a breakfast dish or a dessert.

Baking Powder Biscuits and Other Hot Breads

Hot breads give the menu a lift and you can make them in no time. If you use a packaged mix, give it a touch of your own—by adding a change of seasoning or a little more shortening. See the suggestions below (pp. 326–327).

Using baking powder and baking soda. See Leavening Agents (p. 10).

BAKING POWDER BISCUITS

The shortening may be all butter or margarine, all lard or other cooking fat or oil or half of each. Lard makes very flaky biscuits. For richer biscuits, double the amount of shortening or use cream or top milk. To add more protein, sift 1/4 cup dry milk or soy flour with the flour.

To serve piping hot, bake and serve in an oven-glass pie plate.

Split leftover biscuits, toast lightly, butter and serve for breakfast or tea.

Sift into a mixing bowl

2 cups all-purpose flour
4 teaspoons tartrate-type baking powder *or* 2 teaspoons "double-action" type
1 teaspoon salt

With finger tips or a pastry blender or fork, work in

2 tablespoons shortening

With a fork, quickly stir in

2/3 cup milk

Add more milk, little by little, until the dough is soft and light but not sticky. (Flours differ so much that it is impossible to tell exactly how much milk you will need.) Turn out onto a floured board. With floured hands, pat down or knead about 20 strokes until smooth. Roll lightly 3/4 inch thick. Shape with a biscuit cutter or roll out into an oblong and cut in diamonds with a knife.

Place on an ungreased cooky sheet (close together for soft biscuits, 1 inch apart for crusty ones). Prick with a fork. Bake 12 to 15 minutes at 450°. *Makes 12 to 15.*

Cheese Biscuits. Add 1/2 cup grated cheese to the dry ingredients.

Orange Biscuits. Before baking, put 1/2 teaspoon orange marmalade on each.

Peanut Butter Biscuits. Work in 2 tablespoons peanut butter, leaving it in large enough bits so that it will show when baked.

Butter Sticks. Melt 1/4 cup butter in an oblong pan about 12 by 10 inches. Roll the dough into an oblong about 1/2 inch thick. Cut in 16 finger-shaped pieces. Put in the pan and turn so that all sides are buttered.

Bacon Biscuits. Cook bacon until crisp. Crumble to make about ⅓ cupful. Add to the batter.

Buttermilk Biscuits. Use buttermilk in place of sweet milk and only 2 teaspoons baking powder. Add ¼ teaspoon baking soda.

Drop Biscuits. Increase the milk to 1¼ cups. Drop by spoonfuls in buttered muffin tins or on a buttered cooky sheet.

Filled Biscuits. Roll the dough ½ inch thick. Cut out rounds. Spread half of them with melted butter, then with chopped cooked ham, sausage meat, orange marmalade, shaved maple sugar or grated cheese. Press other rounds lightly on top. Brush with milk.

Cream Biscuits. Use 1 cup heavy cream in place of shortening and milk. Whip the cream stiff before adding.

Maple Tea Biscuits. Sprinkle Cream Biscuits with shaved maple sugar before baking.

PINWHEEL BISCUITS

Roll Baking Powder Biscuit (p. 326) dough into an oblong ¼ inch thick. Brush with melted butter. Roll up like a jelly roll. Cut off pieces ¾ inch thick. Set on a baking sheet, cut side down. Bake 15 minutes at 450°. *Makes 12 to 15.*

Orange Pinwheels. Cream ¼ cup butter with ½ cup sugar. Add ½ cup orange juice and 2 tablespoons grated orange rind. Distribute in 12 buttered muffin tins. Sprinkle the dough with ¼ cup sugar mixed with ½ teaspoon cinnamon before rolling it up. Arrange the pieces in the muffin tins.

Orange Marmalade Pinwheels. Roll out the dough. Spread with orange marmalade and roll up.

Cheese Pinwheels. Sprinkle with ½ cup grated cheese and roll.

Butterscotch Biscuits. Cream ½ cup butter with ¾ cup brown sugar. Spread part on the dough before rolling up. Spread remainder on bottom of 9-inch pan. Brush sides of biscuits with melted butter. Place close together in pan, flat side down. Sprinkle pecan nut meats on dough and in pan, if desired.

Onion Pinwheels. Spread with 1 cup finely chopped onion. Scatter sesame seed over the onion. Roll, cut and brush with slightly beaten egg white. Sprinkle a few more seeds on each. Bake. Serve hot, as an accompaniment for cocktails.

CREAM SCONES

Traditional English tea party fare.

Sift into a mixing bowl

- **2 cups flour**
- **4 teaspoons tartrate-type baking powder *or* 2 teaspoons "double-action" type**
- **2 teaspoons sugar**
- **½ teaspoon salt**

Using finger tips, a pastry mixer or fork, work in

- **4 tablespoons butter**

Into another bowl, break

- **2 eggs**

Reserve a small amount of the

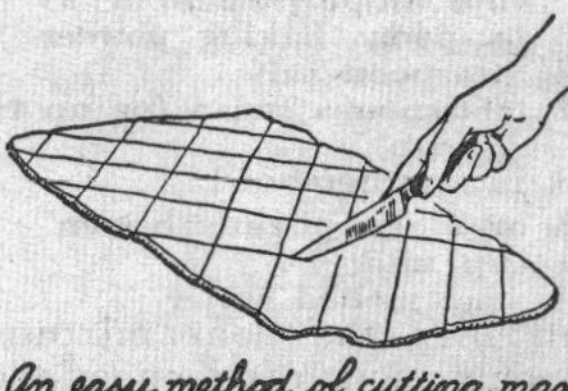

An easy method of cutting many biscuits and cookies.

egg white for the topping. Beat the rest and add to the flour mixture with

½ cup cream *or* milk

Add a little more cream or milk if needed to make the dough just firm enough to handle but still soft. Turn out onto a floured board. Knead ½ minute. Pat and roll into an oblong ¾ inch thick. Cut in diamonds by making diagonal cuts with a long sharp knife. Brush with the reserved egg white diluted with

1 teaspoon water

Sprinkle with

Sugar

Bake 15 minutes at 450°. *Makes 12 or more.*

IRISH BREAD

Follow the recipe for Baking Powder Biscuits (p. 326), adding 1 tablespoon shortening, 1 tablespoon sugar, ½ cup raisins, ½ cup currants and 1 tablespoon caraway seed. Spread in buttered heavy frying pan or 9-inch round tin. Bake about 30 minutes at 350°. Increase heat to 400° the last 5 minutes of baking. Serve in wedges.

MUFFINS

For the tenderest muffins, use pastry flour and avoid overbeating.

Sift into a mixing bowl

2 cups pastry flour *or* 1⅞ cups all-purpose flour
3 teaspoons baking powder
½ teaspoon salt
2 tablespoons sugar (or up to ½ cup)

Mix in another bowl

1 or 2 egg, slightly beaten
1 cup milk
¼ cup melted butter

Pour over the flour mixture. Stir only enough to dampen the flour. Spoon into buttered muffin tins, having the tins about two-

thirds full. Bake at 400° about 15 minutes. *Makes 12.*

Bacon Muffins. Use bacon fat as the shortening. Add 3 tablespoons cooked crumbled bacon.

Berry Muffins. Reserve ¼ cup of the flour. Sprinkle it over 1 cup blueberries or huckleberries. Stir into the batter last. Use ½ cup sugar.

Date *or* Raisin Muffins. Add ½ cup sliced pitted dates or ¼ cup raisins.

Orange Muffins. Add ¾ cup candied orange peel, cut in small pieces.

Peach Muffins. Add to the milk ¾ cup peaches, peeled and cut small.

Pecan Muffins. Use ¼ cup sugar. Add ½ cup chopped pecans. After filling the pans, sprinkle with sugar, cinnamon and more nuts.

Whole-wheat Muffins. Substitute ¾ cup coarse whole-wheat flour for 1 cup of the flour. Do not sift it. Add it after sifting the other dry ingredients.

Quick Sally Lunn. Spread in a buttered 8 or 9 inch square tin. Sprinkle with cinnamon sugar. Bake at 375° about 25 minutes. Cut in squares.

BRAN MUFFINS

Sift into a mixing bowl

1 cup all-purpose flour
3 teaspoons baking powder

¼ cup sugar
½ teaspoon salt
Mix in another bowl
1 egg, slightly beaten
1 cup milk
2 tablespoons melted butter
1 cup bran
Let stand 10 minutes. Add the flour mixture. Stir just long enough to dampen the flour. Spoon into buttered muffin tins. Bake at 400° about 25 minutes. *Makes 12.*

BERKSHIRE MUFFINS

Scald
⅔ cup milk
Pour slowly on
½ cup corn meal
Let stand 5 minutes. Add
½ cup cooked rice
Stir. Sift together
½ cup all-purpose flour
2 tablespoons sugar
3 teaspoons baking powder
½ teaspoon salt
Add to the first mixture with
1 egg yolk, well beaten
1 tablespoon melted butter
Stir and fold in
1 egg white, beaten stiff
Spoon into buttered muffin pans. Bake at 400° about 25 minutes. *Makes 12.*

POPOVERS

A perfect popover is crisp on the outside, tender and moist inside. The secret of success is simple—do not overbeat the batter, and be sure the popovers are thoroughly baked when you take them from the oven. Test one to be sure.

Set the oven at 450°. Butter muffin pans or glass or pottery custard cups. Beat until light
2 eggs
Add
1 cup milk
1 tablespoon melted butter
1 cup all-purpose flour
¼ teaspoon salt
Beat until evenly blended (30 seconds in an electric beater). The batter should be like heavy cream. Add more milk if necessary. Pour into the pans, having them ⅓ full. Bake 20 minutes. Reduce the heat to 350° and bake about 20 minutes longer. *Makes 8 to 12.*

Bacon Popovers. Add to the batter ¼ cup crumbled cooked, crisp bacon.

CORN BREAD

The shortening may be butter, bacon fat, chicken fat or beef drippings.

Mix and sift together
¾ cup corn meal
1 cup flour
⅓ cup sugar
3 teaspoons baking powder
¾ teaspoon salt
Add
1 cup milk
1 egg, well beaten
2 tablespoons shortening, melted
Bake in shallow buttered pan, 8 by 8 inches, at 425° for 20 minutes.

Rich Corncake. In place of baking powder, use 1 teaspoon soda and 2 teaspoons cream of tartar. In place of milk, use 1 cup heavy sour cream or yogurt and ¼ cup milk.

Molasses Corncake. Omit sugar. Use ¾ cup milk and ¼ cup molasses. If desired, add ½ to 1 cup ripe peaches, cut small.

Forest Hall Corn Sticks. Omit sugar. Add ½ cup hot boiled hominy to the mixture. Increase shortening to ¼ cup. Turn into buttered special bread stick pans. Bake 20 minutes at 350°.

JOHNNYCAKE

Mix
1 teaspoon salt
½ cup white corn meal

Gradually stir in

1 cup scalded milk *or* boiling water

Spread ¼ inch deep in buttered shallow pan or by spoonfuls in small buttered muffin pans. If desired, dot with bits of

Butter

Bake at 350° until crisp. Split and spread with butter.

WHITE CORNCAKE

Cream together

¼ cup butter
½ cup sugar

Add

½ cup milk

Mix and sift together

1¼ cups white corn meal
1¼ cups flour
4 teaspoons baking powder
1 teaspoon salt

Add one-fourth of the dry ingredients to the first mixture. Add the rest alternately with

1 cup milk

When all is added, beat thoroughly. Fold in

3 egg whites, beaten stiff

Spoon into a buttered pan 9 by 9 inches. Bake 30 minutes at 425°.

LITTLETON SPIDER CORNCAKE

Mix and sift together

1⅓ cups corn meal
⅓ cup flour
1 teaspoon baking soda

Add

1 cup sour milk
2 eggs, well beaten
1 cup sweet milk
¼ cup sugar
½ teaspoon salt

Stir in. In a heavy shallow baking dish, melt

1½ tablespoons butter

Pour in the mixture. Over the top, pour

1 cup sweet milk

Bake 50 minutes at 350°. Cut in wedges. *Serves 6.*

QUICK BREAD IN LOAVES

A recipe using about 2 cups of flour will fill a loaf pan 5 by 9 inches or, for party sandwich bread, two small pans. Butter the pans lightly, dust with flour, and fill. Let stand 20 minutes before baking to start the action of the baking powder or soda.

To cut in neat slices, make the bread the day before it is to be used. Very fresh bread crumbles easily.

QUICK GRAHAM BREAD

Sift into a bowl

½ cup all-purpose flour
1 teaspoon baking powder
1 teaspoon baking soda
1 teaspoon salt

Add

2 cups whole-wheat flour
4 tablespoons melted shortening
1½ cups sour milk
½ cup molasses

Stir well. Spoon into a buttered loaf pan, 9 by 5 inches. Let stand 20 minutes. Bake about 50 minutes at 375°.

Graham Nut Bread. Add ½ cup nut meats, broken in pieces.

NUT BREAD

Vary this good bread by substituting chopped dates or candied orange peel for the nuts. Bake in two small tins if you prefer.

Sift into a bowl

2 cups all-purpose flour
½ cup brown *or* white sugar
2 teaspoons baking powder
1 teaspoon salt

Add

1 egg
1 cup milk
2 tablespoons melted butter
½ cup walnut *or* pecan meats, broken in pieces

Beat thoroughly. Spoon into a buttered loaf pan 9 by 5 inches. Bake at 350° about 45 minutes.

Whole-wheat Nut Bread. Instead of all-purpose flour, use 1 cup whole-wheat flour and 1 cup pastry flour.

Orange Nut Bread. In place of sugar use ½ cup orange marmalade. Reduce the milk to ½ cup.

WINCHESTER NUT BREAD

Put in a bowl
- **½ cup brown sugar**
- **¾ cup cold water**

Stir until the sugar dissolves. Add
- **½ cup molasses**
- **¾ cup milk**

Sift together
- **1 cup all-purpose flour**
- **1 teaspoon salt**
- **2½ teaspoons baking powder**
- **¾ teaspoon baking soda**

Add to the dry ingredients
- **2 cups whole-wheat flour**

Combine the mixtures. Stir in
- **¾ cup walnut meats, in large pieces**

Spoon into two buttered pans 9 by 5 inches. Bake 2 hours at 275°.

APRICOT ALMOND BREAD

For tea sandwiches, bake in two small pans. If you make half the recipe, use 1 egg yolk in place of a whole egg.

Chop fine or put through food chopper
- **1½ cups dried apricots**

Add
- **1½ cups boiling water**
- **2 tablespoons butter**
- **1 cup sugar**
- **1 teaspoon salt**

Sift together
- **1½ cups pastry flour**
- **1 teaspoon baking soda**

Add to the apricot mixture. Add
- **1 cup whole-wheat flour**
- **1 cup almonds, chopped**
- **1 egg, well beaten**
- **1 teaspoon orange extract**

Stir well and put in a buttered loaf tin 9 by 5 inches. Bake 1¼ hours at 350°.

BANANA NUT BREAD

Some like to add 2 tablespoons melted butter to the batter.

Mix in a bowl
- **3 ripe bananas, well-mashed**
- **2 eggs, beaten until light**

Sift together
- **2 cups flour**
- **¾ cup sugar**
- **1 teaspoon salt**
- **1 teaspoon baking soda**

Add to the first mixture. Add
- **½ cup nut meats, chopped**

Stir well. Put in a buttered loaf pan 9 by 5 inches. Bake 1 hour at 350°.

ORANGE PEEL BREAD

When you double the recipe, use a whole egg.

Put in a small saucepan
- **½ cup prepared orange peel (below)**
- **Water to cover**

Cook until the peel is tender. Add
- **½ cup sugar**

Boil until the syrup is as thick as honey and the peel glossy and transparent. Put in a mixing bowl
- **1 tablespoon soft butter**
- **¼ cup sugar**
- **1 egg yolk**
- **1 cup milk**

Sift together and add
- **2 cups all-purpose flour**
- **2 teaspoons baking powder**
- **Few grains salt**

Beat well and add the orange peel and syrup. Spoon into a buttered loaf pan 9 by 5 inches. Bake about 45 minutes at 325°.

To prepare orange peel. Discard all the white part and cut the yellow part in small bits.

DATE AND NUT BREAD

For a sweeter, richer bread, double the amount of sugar and nuts. For an interesting flavor, add 1 tablespoon rum. Black walnuts are especially delicious in this bread.

Mix in a bowl
- **1 cup dates, cut fine**
- **½ cup sugar**
- **¼ cup butter**
- **¾ cup boiling water**

Stir until the butter melts. Cool. Stir in
- **1 egg, well beaten**
- **1 teaspoon baking soda**
- **1¾ cups flour**
- **½ teaspoon salt**
- **½ cup chopped nuts**

Put in a buttered loaf pan 9 by 5 inches. Bake about 50 minutes at 350°.

PECAN BREAD

Mix in a bowl
- **2 cups unsifted coarse whole-wheat flour**
- **1 cup pastry or cake flour**
- **¾ cup brown sugar**
- **1 teaspoon salt**
- **3 teaspoons baking powder**
- **1 teaspoon baking soda**

Add
- **2 cups buttermilk**
- **1 cup pecan meats, cut fine**

Stir well. Spoon into a buttered loaf pan 9 by 5 inches. Bake about 1 hour at 325°.

CRANBERRY BREAD

Grate the rind of
- **1 orange**

Squeeze the juice and add enough boiling water to make
- **¾ cup liquid**

Add the grated rind. Add
- **2 tablespoons butter**

Stir to melt the butter. Put in another bowl
- **1 egg**
- **1 cup sugar**

Beat well and stir into the orange mixture. Add
- **1 cup cranberries, chopped**
- **½ cup walnuts, chopped**

Sift together
- **2 cups flour**
- **½ teaspoon salt**
- **½ teaspoon baking soda**

Stir into the first mixture. Spoon into a buttered loaf pan 9 by 5 inches. Bake 1 hour at 325°.

HONEY BREAD

Long beating makes the fine texture which distinguishes this bread, the famous French pain d'épice. Add 1 tablespoon rum to the mixture, if you like.

Sift into a mixing bowl
- **2 cups all-purpose flour *or* half rye flour**
- **1 teaspoon baking powder**
- **1 teaspoon baking soda**
- **1 teaspoon salt**
- **½ teaspoon cinnamon**
- **1 teaspoon ginger**

Add
- **½ cup strained honey**
- **1 egg, slightly beaten**
- **1 cup milk**

Beat thoroughly, 15 minutes at the very least. If you have an electric beater, beat ½ hour. Spoon into a buttered loaf pan 9 by 5 inches, or into bread stick pans. Bake at 350°, about 50 minutes for the loaf pan, 25 for bread stick pans. Serve in thin slices with unsalted butter.

PEANUT BUTTER BREAD

Sift into a mixing bowl
- **2 cups all-purpose flour**
- **⅓ cup sugar**
- **2 teaspoons baking powder**
- **1 teaspoon salt**

Add
- **¾ cup peanut butter**

Blend with a fork. Stir in
- **1 cup milk**

Spoon into a buttered loaf pan 5 by 9 inches. Bake at 350° about 50 minutes.

PRUNE BREAD

Mix

1 cup sugar
2 tablespoons melted butter
1 egg, well beaten
1 cup cooked prunes, cut up
½ cup prune juice
1 cup sour milk *or* buttermilk

Sift together

1 cup fine whole-wheat flour *or* rye flour
2 cups all-purpose flour
1 teaspoon baking soda
¼ teaspoon baking powder
½ teaspoon salt

Add to the first mixture and mix thoroughly. Put in two buttered loaf pans 9 by 5 inches. Bake about 1 hour at 350°.

BOSTON BROWN BREAD

The classic New England recipe. Canned brown bread is good; heat it in a double boiler to serve it with baked beans.

Mix

½ cup rye meal *or* all-purpose flour
½ cup corn meal
½ cup coarse whole-wheat flour
1 teaspoon baking soda
½ teaspoon salt

Stir in

⅜ cup molasses
1 cup sour milk *or* ⅞ cup sweet milk *or* water

Mix well. Grease a mold (1 or 1½ quarts) or two smaller ones. Fill not more than two-thirds full. Put on the cover. Place on a rack in a deep kettle. Cover. Add boiling water to come halfway up around the mold. Set over the heat and steam 3½ hours in a large mold, 1½ to 2 in smaller ones. Keep the water boiling. Add more as needed to keep the water at the proper level. Take from the water, remove the cover, and set the mold in a 300° oven for 15 minutes to dry out somewhat. Remove from the mold.

To cut with string. Old-fashioned cooks make neat slices by drawing a string around the hot loaf, crossing the ends, and pulling them to cut off slices.

To cook in a pressure cooker. Set the mold on the rack in the cooker. Have the water 2 inches deep. Steam 15 minutes with the petcock open. Close and steam 1 hour longer for a large mold, 40 minutes for small ones.

Raisin Brown Bread. Add to the batter ½ cup seedless raisins.

PACKAGED CRACKERS AND WAFERS

Shape, size and seasoning vary endlessly. Some are tasty enough to serve as interesting accompaniments to beverages or salads. Others are simple and so are good with dips and spreads (pp. 44 ff.) or with cheese as a satisfying epilogue to a meal.

Store crackers in tightly closed packages or tins. If they lose their crispness, heat them in a moderate oven for a few minutes before you serve them.

Packaged crumbs are marketed, ready to use as a topping for casseroles or to make a crumb crust for pies (p. 441).

TOASTED CRACKERS

Spread simple crackers with butter. Sprinkle with grated cheese or not, as you like. Place on a cooky sheet. Brown delicately in the broiler or in a 350° oven.

SOUFFLÉED CRACKERS

Only old-fashioned unsalted crackers (usually called "common crackers") will puff up successfully. Cover them with ice water, soak 8 minutes and drain. Place on a cooky sheet and dot with butter. Bake at 500° until puffed (10 minutes). Reduce the heat to 375° and bake until the crackers are browned (about 45 minutes).

CORNELL WAFERS

High in protein and tasty, too.

Mix in a bowl
- **½ cup toasted wheat germ**
- **½ cup flour**
- **2 teaspoons baking powder**
- **1 teaspoon salt**

Cut in as for pastry
- **2 tablespoons butter**

Add
- **¼ cup ice water**

Stir until blended. Roll out ½ inch thick. Cut in rounds. Sprinkle half of them with
- **¼ cup toasted wheat germ**

and top with the other rounds. Press firmly together. Bake at 350° until brown (about 15 minutes).

CORN CRISPS

Wonderful with drinks, with soup or salads.

Set the oven at 425°. Butter 2 cooky sheets or use heavy unbuttered pans or lay pieces of foil on pans. Mix
- **½ cup corn meal (white or yellow)**
- **1 teaspoon salt**

Stir in
- **¾ cup boiling water**
- **2 tablespoons butter**

Arrange by teaspoonfuls on the cooky sheets, 10 to each, to leave plenty of room for spreading. Sprinkle with
- **Celery seed or poppy seed**

Bake until delicately brown (about 8 minutes). Let stand a moment to stiffen slightly, then remove carefully with a wide spatula. Repeat until all the batter is baked. *Makes 48 2-inch wafers.*

CHEESE STRAWS

Prepare pastry (homemade or from a mix) and roll into an oblong ¼ inch thick. Sprinkle lightly with grated Parmesan cheese or mixed Parmesan and Edam. Sprinkle with salt and a few grains of cayenne.

Fold double, press the edges firmly together, fold again and roll out as before. Again sprinkle with cheese, fold and roll. Repeat twice more so that you will have four layers of cheese and pastry. Cut in strips ¼ inch by 5 inches. Bake 8 minutes at 450°.

CHEESE PASTRIES

Prepare pastry (homemade or from a mix). Roll ¼ inch thick. Cut with a small cooky cutter or in oblongs or diamonds. Sprinkle with grated cheese and pat the cheese in lightly. Bake at 400° until the cheese melts and browns (about 10 minutes).

CHEESE PUFFS

Put in a small saucepan
- **½ cup boiling water**
- **2 tablespoons butter**

When the butter melts, add
- **¼ cup flour**
- **¼ cup grated cheese**
- **⅛ teaspoon salt**
- **Few grains paprika**

Stir and cook 3 minutes. Add
- **1 egg**

Beat with a wooden spoon until stiff. Arrange by half-teaspoonfuls on a buttered cooky sheet. Bake 15 minutes at 375°. Reduce the heat to 350° and bake until the puffs are dry (10 to 15 minutes). *Makes 30 1-inch puffs.*

CHEESE WAFERS

Blended nippy cheese in a roll is best for these rich and flaky wafers because it mixes easily with the butter. To substitute regular sharp cheese, put it through a chopper three times or whirl it in an electric blender to make it very smooth. Freshen leftover wafers by heating a few minutes in a 350° oven.

Put in a bowl and let stand to soften

1 roll blended sharp cheese (6 ounces)
½ cup butter

Cream together. Blend in

1 cup pastry flour
¼ teaspoon salt

Pat into a firm ball, cover and chill at least 1 hour. Roll, half at a time, about ⅛ inch thick. Cut out with a small cooky cutter and place on an unbuttered sheet or on sheets of aluminum foil on a cooky sheet. In warm weather, chill ½ hour or longer before baking.

Bake at 400° until delicately brown (about 5 minutes). Serve warm or not with drinks or salad. *Makes 60 or more wafers.*

Cheese Shortbreads. Roll ½ inch thick. Cut with a 1-inch biscuit cutter. Bake at 400°. These are surprisingly good sprinkled very delicately with powdered sugar while they are hot.

Savory Cheese Squares. Season more highly with cayenne, Worcestershire and garlic salt. Pat into an oblong ½ inch thick. Cut in 1-inch squares with a knife or pastry wheel and bake.

Rolls and Bread

Old-fashioned bread was truly the staff of life. It was made of unbleached flour, rich in vitamins, minerals and even some protein. Then came the era when many valuable nutrients were lost in the almost universal process of bleaching flour. Due to pressure by nutritionists and the informed public, bleached flour is now enriched by the restoration of at least some of the lost food values.

MIXES FOR MAKING BREAD AND ROLLS

Mixes are a tempting introduction to the art of bread-making. The saving in time is not great, but it is convenient to have all the ingredients in one small package. Follow the directions on the package. A plain mix may be made up in any of the ways suggested on page 341.

There are mixes for special breads such as corn bread. New mixes are constantly appearing —watch for them.

READY-TO-MAKE ROLLS

Among the most popular of the new "convenience foods," these rolls are marketed in many types. They need only brief baking to be ready to serve. Follow the package directions. Suggestions on page 342 may be used with plain rolls as well as Pinwheel Biscuits.

BAKER'S BREAD AND ROLLS

Buy unsliced bread if you do not use a whole loaf in a day or two. Sliced bread dries out quickly. Also you can then cut the slices as thick or thin as you like—thin slices for crisp toast and for afternoon sandwiches.

Heat baker's rolls (p. 339) so that they will be like fragrant home-baked ones. For an appetizing way to present a loaf of crusty French or Italian bread, see page 353.

Store bread, tightly wrapped, in the refrigerator or freezer.

MAKING ROLLS AND BREAD

Fragrant, crusty homemade rolls and bread are easy to make with modern yeast. Actually, yeast rolls, especially the type that is made without kneading or shaping, are simpler to make perfectly than baking powder biscuits. If you are a beginner, start with Feather Rolls, Raised Whole-Wheat Muffins and Brioche. As your courage and experience increase, make Dinner Rolls, Potato Biscuits, Sweet Rolls and Coffee Cakes, for these delicious breads rise quickly and so are easy to watch. When you feel confident in judging the amount of flour to use and the time dough needs to rise, you will be ready to venture to make that triumph of all baking —a handsome loaf of bread.

Since bread-making is a somewhat lengthy process, it pays to make the full amount in the recipes, even if your family is small. You can divide the dough and make it up in several different ways—part for a loaf of bread, part for tiny rolls or sweet buns, and part for a coffee cake. Bake them all at once and store them in the freezer. Reheat the stored breads before you serve them so that they will taste fresh-baked. Frost sweet buns and coffee cakes after they have been reheated.

INGREDIENTS FOR HOMEMADE BREAD

Yeast is a living plant which needs warmth and moisture to grow. Granular yeast and yeast cakes are equally satisfactory. Granular yeast may be kept on the pantry shelf, but yeast cakes must be stored in the refrigerator. Note the date on the package so that you will use the yeast while it is still at its best.

To soften yeast so that it will blend evenly with the dough, sprinkle or crumble it over lukewarm (110°) water or milk and allow to stand a few minutes while the other ingredients are measured. If the liquid is too cold, the yeast will not grow. If it is too hot, the yeast will be killed.

The standard amount is 1 package of yeast to each 2 cups of liquid in the recipe. This makes bread which is finished in 5 hours with two risings, or about 3½ hours with one rising. **To complete bread in 3 hours** (or in 2½ hours with one rising), use 2 packages of yeast. **To raise bread overnight,** use only ¼ package of yeast. Using the larger amount of yeast does not give bread a "yeasty" taste—overrising does.

For perfect rolls and bread, the yeast must be allowed to grow just the right amount. See page 338 for the description of this process.

Flours rich in gluten make the best bread because gluten makes the dough strong and elastic and able to expand with the growth of the yeast and the bubbles it makes. Bread flour is richest in gluten, but all-purpose flour is widely used and is quite satisfactory. Other flours, such as rye or buckwheat, need to be combined with wheat flour to make good bread. One secret of making deliciously tender rolls and bread is to use as little flour as you can and still be able to handle the dough.

Milk or potato water makes bread of better flavor than plain water. The bread browns better, keeps fresh longer and is more nutritious. If you use raw milk, scald it to destroy the enzymes which may affect the action of the yeast.

Shortening makes bread more tender and adds to its flavor and keeping quality. Use butter, lard or any bland-flavored cooking oil or fat. If the mixture is especially rich, with eggs or more shortening, the action of the yeast is slower.

Sugar makes the dough rise more quickly and helps the crust to brown, but too much sugar slows the action of the yeast.

Salt is added for flavor. It slows the action of the yeast somewhat, so if you are making salt-free bread, remember that it will rise more rapidly.

IMPROVING THE FOOD VALUE

Use unbleached or enriched flour. Replace part of the flour with soy flour, peanut flour or cottonseed flour. Health food stores can supply these flours. Buy in small quantities and store in a cool place. Add more protein, minerals and vitamins to any recipe by using some brewers' yeast, toasted wheat germ and dry skim milk. See also the special recipe for Cornell Bread (p. 352).

MIXING DOUGH

Thorough mixing at the start is important so that the yeast will be evenly distributed and the strength of the gluten in the flour developed. Beating in the flour with an electric mixer or a strong rotary egg beater is very successful.

Add the flour a little at a time until the dough is too stiff to beat. Then remove the beater and scrape the dough from the blades. If you are making a soft dough, add the rest of the flour and beat with a wooden spoon until thoroughly blended. If you are making a firm bread dough, add the rest of the flour and turn the dough out onto a pastry cloth and knead it.

KNEADING DOUGH

Watching an experienced person is the quickest way to learn to knead. But you can teach yourself by following directions carefully.

Dust the board very lightly with flour. Turn the ball of dough out onto the board. Cover it with an inverted bowl. Let it "rest" 10 minutes to make the dough easier to work with.

Rub your hands lightly with melted shortening. Fold the ball of dough double, then push it lightly and quickly away from you, using the "heel" of your hands. Pull it toward you again with your finger tips. Repeat these two motions, turning the dough as you work, until the surface is smooth and elastic (5 to 8 minutes). When the dough is light enough, you can hold the palm of your hand on it for 30 seconds without having the dough stick to your hand.

RAISING DOUGH

The time is based on dough made with 1 package of yeast to 2 cups of liquid.

Use a mixing bowl which will hold three times the bulk of the dough. Grease the mixing bowl lightly, put in the ball of kneaded dough, and turn it so that the top is greased. Cover with a clean, slightly damp cloth. Set in a warm place (80°–85°), and let rise until doubled in bulk (about 1½ hours). If your oven has a pilot light, it will be warm enough. Otherwise, set the mixing bowl in a cold oven with a pan of warm water on the shelf beneath it. Add warm (not hot) water from time to time to keep the temperature up to 80°. If the room is about 80°, keep the water at about 75°. The purpose is to keep the dough itself at 75° to 85°, the temperature at which yeast grows best. A higher temperature kills the yeast and a low temperature retards growth. You may insert a dairy or bath thermometer into the dough in order to watch the temperature precisely.

For perfect bread it is important to let the dough rise exactly the right amount. If you let it rise too long, the bread will be full of large holes; if not long enough, the bread will be heavy and soggy. To test it, press your finger into the dough. If the dent remains, the dough is just right.

If the dough rises before it is convenient for you to shape it, punch it down and let it rise again or store it in the refrigerator. Chilling the dough does no harm.

To punch down. When the dough has risen long enough, punch it down with your fist to let some of the gas escape and let fresh oxygen reach the yeast. Fold the edges toward the center. Put the dough on a floured mixing board and slap it hard to force out all the gas.

To make bread of very fine grain, put the dough back into the greased bowl, turn it so that the top is greased, and let it rise again (about 1 hour with 1 package of yeast, 30 to 45 minutes with 2).

Shaping and baking rolls and bread. Directions vary according to the type. See the individual recipes for details.

REHEATING ROLLS

Heat in a bun warmer or in the top part of a double boiler over hot water. Or put in a paper bag, sprinkle very lightly with water, close the bag tightly and set in a 400° oven for 5 minutes.

FEATHER ROLLS

These light and delicate rolls are very easy and quick to make and require no kneading or shaping. Try them for a Sunday brunch or supper.

Put in a mixing bowl

1 cup warm milk (not hot)
1 package yeast

Let stand 5 minutes. Stir well. Add

4 tablespoons soft butter *or* oil
2 tablespoons sugar
½ teaspoon salt
1 egg

Beat with a rotary egg beater or electric beater until the ingredients are thoroughly blended. Add

2 cups all-purpose flour

Continue to beat as long as possible, then finish mixing with a spoon. Cover the bowl, set in a warm place and let rise for about 45 minutes.

Stir down the batter and fill buttered muffin pans a little more than half full. Let rise in a warm place until the pans are full (about 30 to 45 minutes). Bake 15 to 20 minutes at 400°. *Makes 8 to 12 rolls.*

Grilled Muffins. Put buttered muffin rings on a hot greased griddle. Fill half full with the mixture and cook slowly until well risen and browned underneath. Turn the muffins and rings over and brown the muffins on the other side. Watch carefully and adjust the heat so the muffins do not brown too quickly.

Crumpets. Omit the sugar and egg and increase the butter to ½ cup. Cook like Grilled Muffins (above).

SOUR CREAM ROLLS

Put in a mixing bowl

¼ cup warm (not hot) water
1 package yeast

Let stand 5 minutes and stir. Add

¼ cup melted butter *or* oil
2 tablespoons sugar
1 teaspoon salt
1 egg
1 cup sour cream

Beat thoroughly. Beat in

3 cups sifted flour (about)

Add a little more flour if needed to make the dough stiff enough to handle. Grease the top lightly with

Melted butter *or* oil

Cover the dough and let rise until light and nearly double in size (about 50 minutes).

Put on a floured board, pat to ½ inch thick. Cut and shape in any of the ways suggested on page 307. Let rise and bake at 375° about 20 minutes. *Makes about 36 small rolls.*

RAISED WHOLE-WHEAT MUFFINS

Enriched with added protein and so just right with fruit salad as a complete luncheon. As a variation, add ½ cup chopped apple or chopped nuts or both.

Put in a mixing bowl

½ cup warm water (not hot)
2 packages yeast

Let stand 5 minutes. Stir well. Add

1 cup warm milk (not hot)
3 tablespoons dark molasses
1 egg
3 tablespoons bacon fat, melted butter *or* salad oil

Beat well. Sift together

1 cup whole-wheat flour
⅓ cup powdered milk
1 teaspoon salt

Stir into the yeast mixture. Stir in

½ cup wheat germ

When ingredients are blended well, spoon into 12 large greased muffin tins, filling them half full. Let rise until doubled (about 40 minutes). Bake about 20 minutes at 350°. *Makes 12.*

BRIOCHE

A touch of Continental elegance for Sunday breakfast or a morning or afternoon coffee party. The distinctive texture of brioche is due to its rising twice, once in the refrigerator.

Put in a mixing bowl

½ cup lukewarm milk (not hot)
1 package yeast

Let stand 5 minutes. Stir well. Add

⅓ cup butter *or* salad oil
1 egg
2 egg yolks
¼ cup sugar
¼ teaspoon salt
¼ teaspoon lemon extract *or* cardamon seeds
1¼ cups all-purpose flour

Beat thoroughly 10 minutes or 3 minutes in an electric beater. Add

1 cup flour

Mix thoroughly. Let the dough rise in the bowl for 3 hours. Stir down, chill in the refrigerator overnight or at least 3 hours. Butter heavy muffin pans and fill one-third full. Let rise until double in bulk. Bake about 15 minutes at 375°. *Makes 20.*

Flûtes. Shape the dough like Bread Sticks (p. 342). Place on a buttered sheet, cover, and let rise until light. Brush over with an egg white, slightly beaten and diluted with 1½ teaspoons cold water. Sprinkle with powdered sugar. Bake 10 minutes at 350°.

Apricot *or* Strawberry Buns. Put half the chilled dough on a pastry cloth dusted with flour. Pat it into a narrow rectangle ¼ inch thick. Spread with ¼ cup soft butter. Using the pastry cloth to help, roll into a long cylinder like a jelly roll. Cut off pieces ¾ inch wide. Place on a buttered pan and bake at 375° about 15 minutes. Spread with Lemon Frosting (p. 512) and top with a dab of apricot or strawberry jam. *Half the recipe makes 12 buns or 24 tiny ones.*

Coffee Twists. Shape like Apricot or Strawberry Buns. Instead of baking immediately, cover with a towel and let rise (about 1 hour). Twist each piece several times and shape into a coil. Place in buttered pans, cover, let rise, and bake. Spread with Lemon Frosting (p. 512).

HOT ROLLS

The basic recipe from which you can make many different types of rolls and buns according to the way they are shaped and seasoned.

Put in a mixing bowl
- **1 cup lukewarm milk**
- **1 package yeast**

Let stand 5 minutes. Stir. Add
- **2 tablespoons soft butter**
- **1 tablespoon sugar**
- **1 teaspoon salt**

Mix in gradually
- **2½ cups all-purpose or bread flour**

Beat thoroughly 5 minutes, or 2 minutes with an electric beater on slow speed. Add enough more flour to make the dough just barely firm enough to handle.

Knead (p. 338). Shape immediately in any of the ways suggested below, or let rise about 1 hour before shaping. The second rising makes rolls of finer grain, especially if you are using bread flour. Arrange in buttered pans. Brush with
- **Melted butter**

Cover with a clean dish towel. Let rise until double in bulk (about 1 hour). Bake at 425° until well browned (12 to 20 minutes). *Makes about 18.*

SHAPING ROLLS AND BISCUITS

Roll out the dough evenly with a rolling pin. Instead of making all the dough into rolls, you may prefer to make part of it into a small loaf of bread. To make rolls with plenty of crust, place them on the baking sheet with space between.

Biscuits. Roll about ⅛ inch thick. Cut with a small round cutter. If you prefer, shape the dough into a long thin rope and cut off small pieces. Fold the ends under to make smooth balls.

Clover Leaf Rolls. Shape bits of dough into 1-inch balls. Put three in each muffin tin.

Finger Rolls. Shape balls of dough, then roll under one hand on an unfloured board to the desired length.

Parker House Rolls. Cut with a special oval or round cutter. Let cut-out rolls "relax" on the board for 10 minutes. Crease through the center with a floured knife handle. Brush with melted butter and fold double.

Bowknots. Shape like Bread Sticks (p. 342) and tie loosely in knots.

Almond Wreaths. Shape like Bread Sticks (p. 342) in 6-inch lengths. Curve into rings. Brush with melted butter, then dip the upper surface in almonds, blanched, chopped and seasoned with salt.

Butter Rolls *or* Fantans. Roll the dough into a rectangle about 12 by 16 inches. Spread with softened butter. Cut in strips 2 inches wide. Stack evenly in a pile. Cut in 1-inch pieces and fit into buttered muffin tins.

Wings. Divide the dough in four parts. Roll each into an oblong 6 inches wide. Spread with soft butter. Roll up tightly like a jelly roll. Cut each roll in three pieces. Make a deep crease in the center of each with a floured knife handle. Each roll looks like a butterfly.

PINWHEEL BISCUITS

Prepare Hot Roll dough (p. 341). Roll 1/4 inch thick. Spread with softened butter. Roll up like a jelly roll. Cut in 3/4-inch pieces. Place in a buttered pan, cut side down. Bake at 375° about 25 minutes.

Cinnamon Rolls. After spreading with butter, sprinkle with 1/4 cup sugar mixed with 1 teaspoon cinnamon. Sprinkle with seeded raisins, chopped citron or nuts, if you like.

Butterscotch Biscuits. Cream 1/2 cup butter with 3/4 cup brown sugar. Spread part on the dough before rolling it up. Spread the rest in a 9-inch round pan. Brush the sides of the rolls with melted butter. Place close together in the pan, cut side down. Let rise until double in bulk. Bake. Remove from the pan immediately after baking, before the syrup hardens. Serve butterscotch side up.

HARD ROLLS

Prepare Hot Roll dough (p. 341), adding 1 egg white with first 1 1/2 cups flour. Sprinkle a pan with corn meal and arrange the shaped rolls on it 2 inches apart. Let rise and bake at 400° with a pan of boiling water on the shelf beneath the rolls. The oven should be kept steamy throughout the baking time.

Sesame *or* Poppyseed Rolls. Brush unbaked rolls with egg white blended with 2 tablespoons water, and sprinkle with sesame or poppyseed.

BREAD STICKS

Make Hot Roll dough (p. 341), adding 2 tablespoons butter and 1 egg white. When ready to shape, roll the dough into a rectangle about 8 by 12 inches. Cut in half lengthwise, then into 16 strips. Roll under the palms of your hands on an unfloured board to make smooth even sticks 8 to 10 inches long. Arrange 1 inch apart on a cooky sheet. Let rise. Bake 5 minutes at 425°, then reduce the heat to 350° and bake 15 minutes. The slower baking makes the sticks crisp and dry.

Twists. Tie loosely in knots.

Sesame *or* Poppyseed Sticks. Before baking, sprinkle with sesame or poppyseed.

Salt Sticks. Add 1 tablespoon salt to Hot Roll dough (p. 341). Shape and bake like Bread Sticks, but before baking, brush with an egg yolk, slightly beaten and diluted with 1/2 tablespoon cold water. Sprinkle with coarse salt or salt crystals. Bake about 20 minutes at 300° until crisp and dry.

CHEESE STICKS

Roll Hot Roll dough (p. 341) into a rectangle 1/4 inch thick. Spread with butter, sprinkle with flour, and fold from the ends to make 3 layers. Repeat three times and cut in finger-shaped pieces. Arrange on a cooky sheet, cover, and let stand 15 minutes. Bake at 425° for 10 minutes. Remove from the oven, brush the tops with egg white and dip in grated Parmesan cheese seasoned with salt and cayenne. Return to the oven and bake 4 minutes.

Making Rolls and Biscuits

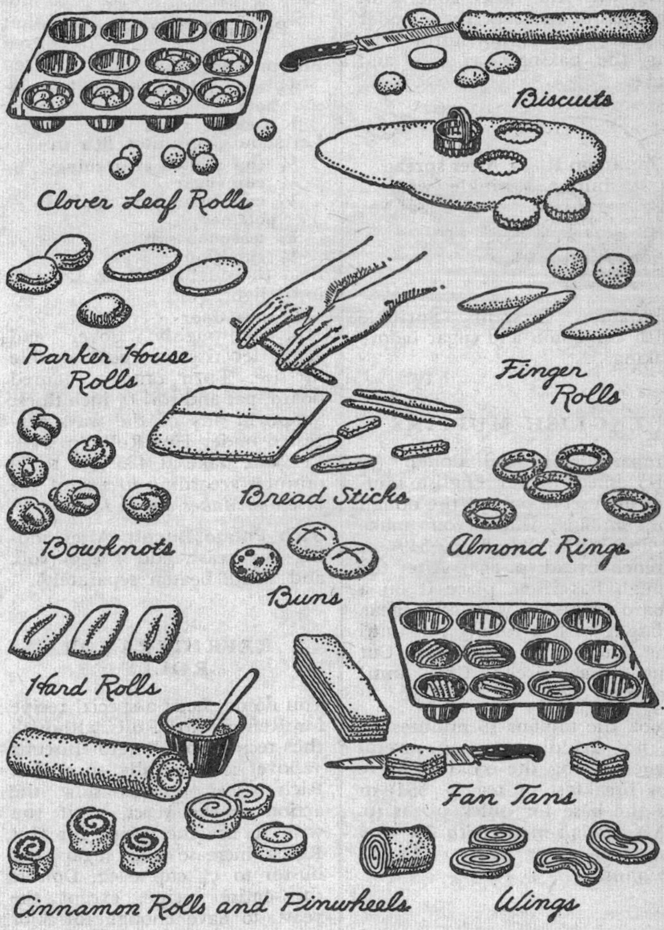

CRESCENT ROLLS

Divide Hot Roll dough (p. 341) in two parts. Roll each into a 12-inch circle. Spread lightly with soft butter. Cut like a pie into 12 parts. Roll each, beginning with the outer edge. Pull the points and tuck them under so that they will not unroll during the baking. Let rise and bake.

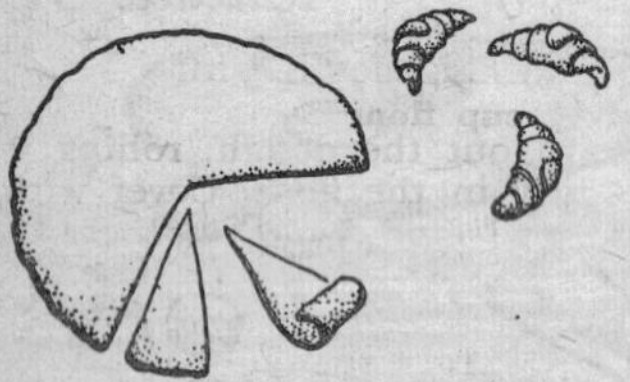

Cinnamon Crescents. Sprinkle with cinnamon and sugar before baking.

ENGLISH MUFFINS

Prepare Hot Roll dough (p. 341) especially for English muffins or reserve part of the dough for muffins when you make Rolls, White Bread (p. 349) or French Bread (p. 353). After the dough has risen, place it on a board sprinkled with corn meal. Flatten with a rolling pin until the dough is 1/2 inch thick. Cut out 3-inch circles. Chill until ready to cook.

Cook the muffins 15 minutes on a hot griddle, turning several times during the cooking. Serve for breakfast or tea (p. 354) or as the base for quick pizzas (p. 354). *Dough made with 2 1/2 to 3 cups of flour will make 12 muffins.*

BUTTERMILK ROLLS

Use buttermilk in place of milk in Hot Roll recipe (p. 341), sifting 1/2 teaspoon baking soda with the flour. These rolls have a delicious flavor and fine grain. **To make richer rolls,** use 1/4 cup sugar and 1/3 cup butter. Shape (p. 341).

POTATO BISCUITS

Put in a mixing bowl

- **1/2 cup lukewarm milk (not hot)**
- **1 package yeast**

Let stand 5 minutes. Stir in

- **1/4 cup melted shortening**
- **1/4 cup sugar**
- **1/2 cup lukewarm mashed potatoes**
- **3/4 teaspoon salt**
- **1/4 cup flour**

Beat thoroughly. Cover. Let rise until light. Add

- **2 cups flour**

Mix thoroughly. Cover and again let rise to about double in size. Turn onto a floured board, pat and roll 1/4 inch thick. Shape in any of the ways suggested under Hot Rolls (p. 341). Let rise. Bake at 425°, 12 to 20 minutes according to size of the biscuits. *Makes about 18.*

Rich Potato Biscuit. After adding the yeast, add 1 egg (yolk and white beaten separately).

REFRIGERATOR ROLLS

You do not need a special recipe for Refrigerator Rolls, although the recipe for Potato Biscuits (above) is especially successful. Rich sweet doughs slow the action of the yeast, so if you wish to use the recipe for Hot Rolls, increase the sugar and butter to 1/4 cup each. Double the entire recipe, except the yeast, to have enough for 3 or 4 dozen rolls. Put in a well-buttered bowl, turn the dough so that the top is greased, and cover tightly with wax paper or foil so that a crust will not form on top. Cover with a dampened towel. Store in the refrigerator. If the dough rises, cut through it with a knife, press it down, turn it over, and cover it again. Set a plate on top to help hold it down. A sweet dough will keep for 3 or 4 days.

When you wish to use some of the dough, cut off a piece, knead, shape, let rise and bake as usual. The dough may take longer to rise if it is very cold.

TWICE-BAKED ROLLS

These are the popular "brown and serve" rolls to finish baking at mealtime. Store on the pantry shelf for as long as 1 week, in the refrigerator 2 weeks, or in the freezer up to 3 months.

Put in a mixing bowl
3 cups lukewarm milk
2 packages yeast
Let stand 5 minutes. Stir well. Add
5 teaspoons salt
¼ cup sugar
6 cups flour
Beat as long as possible. Stir in
4 cups flour (about)
or enough to be able to knead the dough thoroughly. Let rise until about double in size. Shape like Hot Rolls (p. 341). Let rise until slightly less than doubled in bulk. Bake 40 minutes at 275°. Leave in the pans 20 minutes. Cool at room temperature and wrap in plastic freezer bags. *Makes 8 dozen rolls.*

When ready to serve, place on an unbuttered cooky sheet. Bake at 400° until brown (7 to 15 minutes according to the size you make).

FRENCH CROISSANTS

True croissants are almost as rich as pastry. Serve them for breakfast in Continental fashion or with coffee as an afternoon or evening treat.

Put in a mixing bowl
1 cup lukewarm milk
1 package yeast
Let stand 5 minutes. Stir. Add
1 tablespoon sugar
1 teaspoon salt
1 tablespoon soft lard *or* butter
1 cup all-purpose flour
Beat thoroughly. Mix in
1 cup flour
Pat the dough into a ball. Cover the mixing board with
½ cup flour
Turn out the dough, rolling it lightly in the flour. Cover with a bowl and let "rest" for 5 minutes. Knead the dough. Place in a greased bowl, cover, and let rise until doubled in bulk (about 1 hour). Punch down, cover and chill 1 hour or longer. Cream or wash (p. 8)
1 cup butter
Put the ball of dough on a slightly floured cloth or board and roll into a rectangle ¼ inch thick. Spread with 4 tablespoons of the butter and fold from the ends toward the center, making three layers. Turn a quarter way round, pat, roll out as before and again spread with 4 tablespoons butter. Repeat twice. Chill at least 2 hours.

Divide the dough in half. Shape like Crescent Rolls (p. 344), or shape half in crescents and chill the other half to make into a coffee cake or cheese squares for another meal.

Place on a cooky sheet. Chill 20 minutes. Bake 10 minutes at 400°, preheating the oven if necessary. Decrease the heat to 350° and bake 20 minutes longer. *Makes 24 crescents or 12 crescents and 1 coffee cake.*

Cheese Squares. Roll the dough as above, but use only half the amount of butter. Each time you spread the dough with butter, sprinkle it with any tasty cheese, grated or cut fine. Roll the finished dough into an oblong ½ inch thick. Cut in squares, tiny for cocktails, larger ones to serve as luncheon bread. Place on a cooky sheet and chill 20 minutes. Bake 10 minutes at 400°, then reduce the heat to 350° and bake 10 minutes longer.

SWEET ROLLS

The basic sweet dough to use for sweet buns and coffee cakes. It is a small recipe. You may like to double it and put some of the dough in the refrigerator to use another time or bake all of it and put some rolls in the freezer.

Put in a mixing bowl

1 cup lukewarm milk
1 package yeast

Let stand 5 minutes. Stir. Add

¼ cup sugar
1 teaspoon salt
¼ cup soft butter
2 eggs

Beat thoroughly with a heavy egg beater or electric mixer. Beat in

1½ cups all-purpose flour

Remove the beater. Let the dough rise about 40 minutes. Mix in about

1 cup flour

Use enough more flour to make the dough just barely firm enough to handle. Cover and chill ½ hour in the refrigerator. Knead and shape in any of the ways suggested below, or into tea rings, coffee cake, or rolls. See suggestions for using Hot Roll dough (p. 341). Arrange in buttered pans. Brush with

Melted butter

Cover with a clean dish towel. Let rise until double in bulk (about 1 hour). Bake at 400° until delicately brown (12 to 20 minutes, according to size). Frost with confectioners' sugar moistened with water and flavored with vanilla.

Sweet French Rolls. When the rolls are nearly done, brush with an egg white slightly beaten and mixed with 1 tablespoon water and ½ teaspoon vanilla. Sprinkle with sugar.

Cinnamon Buns. Flavor the dough with ½ teaspoon cinnamon. Cut out with a 3-inch cutter.

Raisin Buns. Add to Cinnamon Bun dough ¼ cup seeded raisins, cut small.

Hot Cross Buns. Mark hot Raisin Buns when they come from the oven with a cross of Portsmouth Frosting (p. 512).

Orange Rolls. Use orange juice in place of milk and add 1 tablespoon grated orange peel. Shape like Parker House Rolls. Put in each 1 navel orange section, drained and dipped in sugar. Fold and bake. Frost with Orange Confectioners' Frosting (p. 512).

For simpler orange rolls, roll out the dough and sprinkle with grated orange rind, roll lightly to press the rind into the dough, and cut out small rounds. Dip small sugar cubes in orange juice and press one into each roll. Let rise and bake.

COFFEE CAKES *or* KUCHEN

Prepare Sweet Roll dough. After kneading, divide it into two parts and spread in two buttered layer cake tins, or put the whole amount in a shallow pan about 9 by 15 inches, or make half into buns. Spread with desired topping. Let rise until double in bulk (about 1 hour). Bake at 375° (20 to 25 minutes).

Apple Kuchen. After spreading the dough in pans, brush with melted butter. Pare 5 tart apples and cut in eighths. Press close together into the dough, sharp edge down. Sprinkle with 1/4 cup sugar mixed with 1/2 teaspoon cinnamon and 2 tablespoons currants or seedless raisins. Cover and let rise. Bake 30 minutes at 350°.

Raisin Kuchen. Add to the dough 1/2 cup raisins, cut in pieces. Before baking, brush over with beaten egg and cover with following mixture: Melt 3 tablespoons butter, add 1/3 cup sugar and 1 teaspoon cinnamon. Stir and add 3 tablespoons flour.

Cincinnati Coffee Cake. Mix 4 tablespoons sugar, 1 1/2 teaspoons cinnamon, 1 cup soft stale bread crumbs, 4 tablespoons melted butter and 4 tablespoons chopped blanched almonds. Sprinkle over the dough after putting it in the pan.

Streusel Cake. Sift 1/3 cup sugar with 1/3 cup flour. Work in 1/3 cup butter and mix until all is crumbly. Spread over the coffee cake before the last rising, pressing in slightly with fingers.

Honey Twist. Add slightly more flour to make the dough firm enough to roll into a long cylinder about 1 inch in diameter. Coil in a buttered 9-inch layer cake tin, beginning at the outer

edge and covering the bottom. Cream 1/4 cup butter with 2 tablespoons honey and stir in 1 egg white and cup confectioners' sugar. Spread over the hot twist after it is baked.

Christmas Coffee Cake. Make a roll as for Honey Twist and shape on a cooky sheet like a Christmas tree. Bake. Frost and decorate with colored candies.

Ruth's Coffee Cake. Make a roll as for Honey Twist. Cut off 1-inch pieces, shape into balls, and dip in melted butter, then in sugar mixed with cinnamon (1/2 cup to 1 teaspoon). Arrange in 2 layers in a tube pan, sprinkling chopped nuts or raisins on each layer.

CHRISTMAS STOLLEN

Make Sweet Roll dough (p. 346). After mixing and raising, turn the dough onto a mixing board and pat or roll out flat. Cover with 1/2 cup slivered almonds, 1/2 cup candied fruit, 1 tablespoon grated lemon rind. Fold and knead the fruit into the dough. Flatten the dough into an oblong. Brush with melted butter and fold double lengthwise. Press the edges together. Place on a greased baking sheet. Let rise to double its size. Bake at 375° for 35 minutes. Frost with Confectioners' Frosting (p. 512) and decorate with almonds and candied fruit.

CINNAMON BREAD

Make Sweet Roll dough (p. 346), but increase the flour to about 3 cups. After the first rising, punch down and knead. Roll into a rectangle 1/2 inch thick. Spread with softened butter, sprinkle with 1/4 cup sugar mixed with 1 1/2 teaspoon cinnamon. Roll like a jelly roll. Place in a buttered loaf pan, brush with melted butter, cover with a clean cloth, and let rise. Bake 30 minutes at 400°.

DANISH PASTRY

Prepare Sweet Roll dough (p. 346), adding to it

- **¼ teaspoon vanilla**
- **¼ teaspoon mace**

After kneading the dough thoroughly, roll it into an oblong ¼ inch thick. Wash (p. 8)

- **⅞ cup butter**

Divide into small bits and place half in the center of the dough. Fold one end of the dough to cover the butter, place the remaining butter on top, and fold over the other end of the dough, pressing the edges firmly together. Turn a quarter way around, pat with a rolling pin, and roll as thin as possible, lifting it frequently to keep it from sticking. Fold each end to the center, pat, fold to make four layers, turn a quarter way around, pat, lift, roll and fold three times. Cover and let rise 20 minutes.

Roll ½ inch thick. Shape into pinwheels or horns (below). Arrange on a cooky sheet covered with brown paper. Brush with an egg, slightly beaten. Sprinkle with coarsely chopped nut meats, if desired. Let rise. Bake 25 minutes at 375°. Brush with Confestioners' Frosting (p. 512).

To shape pinwheels. Cut in 4-inch squares. Make a cut from each corner almost to the center. Fold each alternate point to the cente pressing them down firmly. Put a bit of jam in the center.

To shape horns. Cut in triangles 5 inches long and 3 inches wide at the base. Spread with a little jam or Cream Filling (p. 516). Press the long edges together and shape like horns.

SWEDISH BREAD

Put in a mixing bowl

- **1 cup lukewarm milk**
- **1 package yeast**

Let stand 5 minutes. Add

- **½ cup flour**

Beat well, cover and let rise. Add

- **2 cups flour**

Beat and let rise again. Add

- **¼ cup melted butter**
- **⅓ cup sugar**
- **1 egg, well beaten**
- **¼ teaspoon salt**
- **½ teaspoon almond extract**

Mix thoroughly. Add

- **Flour**

enough to knead the dough well. Let rise until about double in size. Shape in a braid or ring (below). Let rise. Bake about 20 minutes at 350°.

To shape braid. Divide the dough in thirds. Roll each part between the hands into long thin ropes of uniform size. Braid. Form in a ring, if desired. Put on a buttered cooky sheet, cover, and let rise. Beat an egg yolk with 1 teaspoon cold water. Brush it over the braid. Sprinkle with finely cut blanched almonds.

To shape ring. Shape with hands in a long roll. Roll as thin as possible on an unfloured board with a rolling pin. Lift with a knife to keep the dough from sticking to the board. Spread with melted butter. Sprinkle with sugar and chopped blanched almonds or cinnamon.

Roll like a jelly roll. Join the ends to form a ring. Place on a buttered cooky sheet. Snip with scissors, holding the scissors at right angles to the roll.

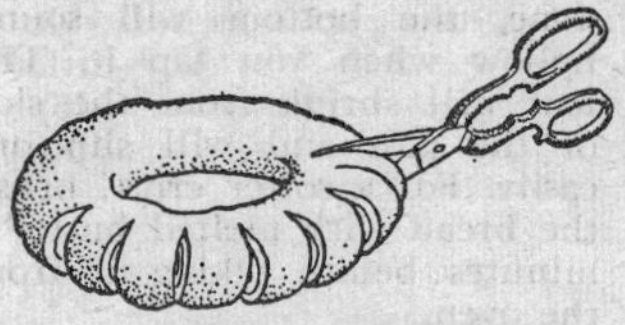

SALLY LUNN

Put in a mixing bowl
- **1 cup lukewarm milk**
- **1 package yeast**

Let stand five minutes. Stir. Add
- **½ cup softened butter *or* oil**
- **⅓ cup sugar**
- **½ teaspoon salt**
- **3 eggs**

Beat with a strong rotary beater or electric mixer, gradually adding
- **3½ cups flour**

Leave the mixture in the bowl and let rise until very light and about double in size. Spoon into a buttered 10-inch angel cake pan or Turk's head pan or 2 dozen 2-inch muffin pans. Let rise about 1 hour. Bake about 50 minutes at 350° in a large pan or 20 minutes at 425° in muffin pans.

To vary, add raisins and chopped citron or other fruits to the batter; or put a layer of brown sugar and pecans in the buttered pans; or sprinkle the top before baking with cinnamon sugar (½ cup sugar mixed with 2 teaspoons cinnamon) or with ½ cup sugar mixed with 1 teaspoon cinnamon and 1 teaspoon nutmeg.

PIZZA

Cut in wedges and serve hot as a luncheon dish or an evening snack with coffee, beer or red wine.

Put in a mixing bowl
- **1 cup lukewarm water**
- **1 package yeast**

Let stand 5 minutes. Stir. Add
- **1 teaspoon sugar**
- **1 teaspoon salt**
- **1 tablespoon shortening**

Beat well. Add
- **1½ cups all-purpose flour *or* bread flour**

Beat until smooth. Add another
- **1½ cups flour**

using enough to make a dough just barely firm enough to handle. Knead until smooth. Divide the dough in thirds. Knead each piece into a ball. Flatten, then pull and stretch gently to fit 9-inch layer cake tins, lightly greased. Press up around the edges to make a slight rim. Let rise 15 minutes. Brush lightly with
- **Olive oil**

Sprinkle with
- **Parmesan cheese, grated**

Cover with
- **Fresh tomatoes *or* drained canned tomatoes**
- **Slivers of Mozzarella *or* other Italian cheese**
- **Chopped anchovies *or* meat**
- **Sprinkling of oregano *or* basil**

Bake 25 minutes at 425°. *Makes three 9-inch pizzas.*

WHITE BREAD

Homemade bread is a joy and a satisfaction to the creative cook and to the conscientious home-maker who knows that it is far superior to most bakery products, not only in flavor but in food values.

As an introduction to bread-making, read pages 336 to 339, which describe the necessary ingredients and explain how to knead and raise the dough. It is essential to knead bread thoroughly and correctly, so that the yeast will be evenly distributed and the bread will have the perfect texture which marks the superior loaf.

Rinse a large mixing bowl with hot water (a cold bowl delays the action of the yeast). Put in it

- **½ cup lukewarm (110°) water**
- **1 package yeast**

Let stand 5 minutes, then stir to dissolve the yeast. Put in another bowl

- **1 cup milk**
- **1 cup boiling water**
- **2 tablespoons butter *or* other shortening**
- **2 tablespoons sugar**
- **1 tablespoon salt**

Stir until lukewarm. Add to the yeast mixture. Add

- **3 cups bread *or* all-purpose flour**

Mix thoroughly with a spoon or knife. Add another

- **3 cups flour**

Stir vigorously. Add a little more flour if needed to make the dough firm enough to keep it from sticking to the bowl.

Put ½ cup flour on the mixing board or cloth and use some of it to dust the board very lightly, pushing the rest aside to work into the dough if needed. Turn the ball of dough out onto the board, leaving a clean bowl. Cover with the inverted bowl and let "rest" 10 minutes, which makes the dough easier to work with. Knead and let rise as described on page 338.

To shape. Divide the dough into two equal parts. Knead each part to make a smooth ball. Cover with a cloth and let "rest" 10 or 15 minutes. Fold and pull to shape into loaves. Put into two greased bread pans with the "seam" underneath. Cover and let rise until doubled in bulk (about 1 hour). Do not have the pans in a place warmer than 80° or there will be a heavy streak near the bottom of the loaf.

To bake. Heat the oven to 400°. Bake the bread 40 to 60 minutes. Bake at 350° if you are using oven-glass bread pans, since oven-glass holds heat longer than metal. The loaf should begin to brown after the first 15 minutes. When the bread is done, the bottom will sound hollow when you tap it. The loaf will shrink from the side of the pan and will slip out easily. For a softer crust, brush the bread with melted butter 3 minutes before taking it from the oven.

To vary. Add fruit or nuts or shape part of the dough into rolls, braids or twists.

CARE OF BREAD AFTER BAKING

Remove the loaves at once from the pans and place, side down, on a wire cooling rack. Otherwise the crust will be tough and the bread soggy. For a crisp crust, do not cover the bread. For a soft crust, cover with a dish towel during cooling. When cool, store in a clean, well-aired breadbox not too near heat.

To avoid mold in hot weather, wrap the bread tightly in wax paper and store in the refrigerator.

Chill bread if you plan to cut it in thin slices.

BRAN BREAD

Follow the recipe for White Bread (p. 349), but use 1 cup bran and 5 cups flour. Omit the sugar and use ¼ cup molasses instead.

DATE *or* RAISIN BREAD

Follow the recipe for White Bread (p. 349), but double the

Making Bread
Kneading the dough
push and pull
Test by
poking
Punch down
Divide into two parts
and shape for pans
or for
French loaves

amount of shortening and sugar. After adding the first 3 cups of flour, add 1½ cups raisins or dates (pitted and cut in small pieces).

CORNELL BREAD (HIGH PROTEIN)

Make White Bread (p. 349), adding with the first 2 cups of flour 6 tablespoons soy flour, 6 tablespoons powdered skim milk and 2 tablespoons toasted wheat germ. (These ingredients will replace 1 cup of flour.) Continue the recipe as for ordinary White Bread.

RYE BREAD

Follow the recipe for White Bread (p. 349), but use brown sugar in place of white and 3 cups sifted rye flour in place of part of the white flour. Rye bread takes longer to rise than white bread and need not quite double in bulk.

German Rye Bread. Use 2 cups sour milk in place of milk and water. Add 2 tablespoons caraway seeds after first rising. Bake 2 hours at 300° to make the characteristic firm texture.

WHOLE-WHEAT BREAD

Whole-wheat flour makes bread somewhat heavy. If you prefer a lighter bread, use 4 cups all-purpose flour and 2 cups whole-wheat flour. See also the recipe for Cornell Bread (above).

Put in a mixing bowl
½ cup lukewarm water
1 package yeast
Let stand 5 minutes. Stir. Put in a separate bowl
1 cup milk
½ cup boiling water
¼ cup sugar *or* molasses
2 teaspoons salt
Mix well, cool to lukewarm and add to the yeast mixture. Stir in
3 cups all-purpose flour
Beat thoroughly. Add
3 cups whole-wheat flour
Stir with a heavy spoon or add a little more flour and knead. When smooth, let rise until double in bulk (about 1 hour). Shape into two loaves. Place in greased tins and let rise again to almost double in size (about 50 minutes). Bake about 50 minutes at 375°. *Makes 2 loaves or 1 loaf and 1 to 2 dozen rolls.*

Colonial Bread. To make this attractive tea loaf, knead into half the dough (after the first rinsing) ½ cup finely cut candied orange peel and ½ cup pecan meats broken in pieces. Shape into 2 or 3 small loaves. Let rise and bake (30 to 40 minutes).

OATMEAL BREAD

Put in a large mixing bowl
2 cups boiling water
1 cup rolled oats, regular *or* quick
Stir thoroughly. Let stand 1 hour. Add
½ cup molasses
2 teaspoons salt
1 tablespoon butter
Put in a small bowl
½ cup lukewarm water
1 package yeast
When dissolved, add to the oatmeal. Stir in
4½ cups flour
Beat thoroughly and let rise until double in bulk. Add enough more flour to make the dough just firm enough to knead. Shape into loaves and put into buttered pans. Let rise until almost double. Bake about 50 minutes at 350°. *Makes 2 loaves.*

Prune Oatmeal Bread. After the first rising, add ½ cup chopped nuts and 1 cup prunes cut in pieces.

Anadama Bread. Use ½ cup corn meal in place of the cup of oatmeal.

FRENCH BREAD

These long thin loaves with chewy crisp crusts are perfect for French or Italian style meals. If you like, shape part of the dough into small rolls. This dough is also good for English muffins or pizza.

Put in a large mixing bowl
1 cup lukewarm water
1 package yeast
Let stand 5 minutes. Add
1 tablespoon sugar
1½ teaspoons salt
2 tablespoons shortening
Stir well. Add
2 cups all-purpose *or* bread flour
Beat thoroughly with a rotary beater or an electric mixer. Add
1 cup flour (or enough to make a stiff dough)
Sprinkle a board with flour. Put the dough on it and let rest 10 minutes. Knead well, let rise, punch down and let rise again (p. 338).

Turn the dough out on a floured surface and divide into two or three parts. Let rest 10 minutes. Flatten each part with a rolling pin to about ¼ inch in thickness. Roll up each sheet of dough tightly to make a long slender loaf. Press firmly along the rolled edges to seal. Sprinkle cooky sheets with
Corn meal
Put the loaves on the sheets, leaving enough space between them so that they will be crusty on all sides. Cut diagonal gashes in the loaves about ½ inch deep. Beat together
1 egg white
1 tablespoon water
1 teaspoon salt
Brush over the top of the loaves. Sprinkle with
Sesame *or* poppyseed, if liked
Let rise uncovered until double in bulk (about 1 hour).

Put a large pan of boiling water in the bottom of the oven with the pans of bread on a rack above. Bake at 425° for 10 minutes. Brush again with the egg white mixture. Reduce the heat to 375° and bake until the bread sounds hollow when you tap it (about 25 minutes). Cool on a rack. *Makes 2 or 3 loaves.*

HOT FRENCH *or* ITALIAN BREAD

Cut a loaf of French or Italian bread or crusty hard rolls diagonally into thick or thin slices, but without cutting all the way through. Spread creamed butter between the slices. Wrap in aluminum foil. Heat in a 400° oven. Serve very hot.

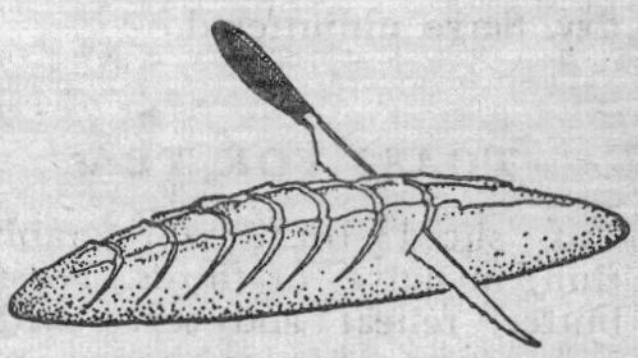

Garlic Bread. Peel and slice a clove of garlic and put it in a bowl with ¼ cup butter. Cover and let stand ½ hour before spreading.

Cheese Bread. Spread with soft cheese instead of butter or with butter creamed with grated Cheddar cheese.

Herb Bread. Spread with Herb Butter (p. 103).

Saffron Bread. Spread with butter creamed with saffron to taste. Especially good with Bouillabaisse.

TOAST

Which does your family prefer? Thick slices of fresh bread, toasted quickly so that it is crisp on the outside but soft inside, or thin slices browned slowly so that the toast is crisp all the way through?

To make toast at the table or a few pieces at a time, an electric toaster is ideal.

To make toast in quantity, put the slices of bread on a cooky sheet and toast them in the broiler. Butter and set in the oven a moment to reheat.

MELBA TOAST

The bread for Melba toast must be fine-grained so that you can cut it in very thin even slices. Chilled bread 2 or 3 days old will cut more easily than fresh bread. Put the slices on a cooky sheet and bake at 250° until delicately brown and completely dry. Serve unbuttered.

TOAST FOR TEA

Cut sliced bread (preferably thin) in halves or thirds. Toast, butter, reheat and serve with jam, marmalade or honey, or make one of the special toasts listed below. If you make toast in an electric toaster, cut the slices in pieces after toasting.

Butterscotch *or* Maple Toast. Sprinkle buttered toast with brown sugar or soft maple sugar. Set in the oven until the sugar melts.

Cinnamon Toast. Toast on one side. Butter the untoasted side and sprinkle with cinnamon sugar (packaged or ¼ cup sugar mixed with 1 teaspoon cinnamon). Toast, buttered side up, until the sugar melts. For a party, prepare early in the day and do the final toasting at teatime.

Orange Toast. Follow directions for making cinnamon toast, but instead of cinnamon sugar, sprinkle with ½ cup sugar mixed with ¼ cup grated orange rind and 2 tablespoons orange juice.

HERBED MELBA RYE

For cocktails or salad. They keep fresh for days and reheat successfully.

Cut in thin slices
1 loaf party rye
Spread on cooky sheets in single layers and bake at 250° until thoroughly crisp and dry (about 1 hour). Melt
½ cup butter
Add to it
1 teaspoon dried marjoram *or* 2 teaspoons chopped fresh herbs
2 teaspoons lemon juice
Brush over the toast. Return to the oven for 10 minutes.

TOASTED ENGLISH MUFFINS

Pull English muffins (packaged or homemade) apart with a fork or your fingers so that the surface is rough. Spread generously with butter. Toast quickly in the broiler, buttered side only. Serve hot with jam, marmalade or honey.

English Muffins with Cheese. Before toasting, sprinkle with grated cheese, or put a thin round slice of soft cheese on each.

Quick Pizzas. Dot hot toasted muffins with bits of fresh or canned tomato and very thin slices of onion. Sprinkle with salt and pepper and a pinch of oregano. Put a slice of Mozzarella cheese on top. Set under the broiler until the cheese melts.

BUTTER TOASTIES

An easy and delectable bread for dinner, tea or lunch.

Cut firm bread in slices 2 inches thick. Remove the crusts and cut each slice in halves or thirds. Dip in melted butter. Bake at 400° until well browned, turning from time to time to brown evenly.

Butterscotch *or* Cinnamon Toasties. Before browning, sprinkle with brown sugar or cinnamon sugar (packaged, or 1/4 cup sugar mixed with 1 teaspoon cinnamon).

Seed Toasties. Before browning, sprinkle lightly with celery seed, poppyseed or sesame.

Tea Toasties. Cut 1-inch slices of bread in cubes. Continue as above, but bake at 325°.

CROUSTADES

Cut the crusts from slices of bread. Butter the bread and fit into muffin tins. Bake at 325° until brown. Use in place of patty shells for creamed chicken or other creamed dishes.

MILK TOAST

Prepare
Hot milk *or* Thin Cream Sauce (p. 94)
Dip in it
4 to 6 slices toast
Place the toast on plates or a serving dish and pour the rest of the sauce over it. Sprinkle with
Chopped parsley, ham *or* hard-cooked egg

FRENCH TOAST

As a heartier dish for luncheon or supper, omit the sugar and top with creamed eggs, chicken, tuna, dried beef or mushrooms.

Mix
1 egg, slightly beaten
Few grains salt
1 teaspoon sugar
3 tablespoons milk
Dip in it, turning to coat each side
4 slices bread (not too soft)
Heat a griddle or heavy frying pan. Butter it well and brown the dipped bread on each side. Serve with maple syrup, jam or marmalade, or sprinkle with cinnamon sugar (1/4 cup sugar mixed with 1 teaspoon cinnamon).

Sandwiches

A perfect sandwich is more than a filling and two slices of bread. The bread must be neatly sliced and evenly spread, the filling appropriate to the occasion and well seasoned, and the finished sandwich properly stored until serving time so that it looks its appetizing best. Then serve it with satisfaction as a picnic standby, a sturdy lunch or an appealing accompaniment to a party beverage.

Sandwich breads should be firm-textured to cut evenly. White, whole wheat, rye, nut, Boston brown and pumpernickel are all suitable. The bread should not be too fresh—24 hours old is best. Chill it in the refrigerator several hours so that it will be easier to slice. Most ready-sliced bread is too thick for any but lunchbox or picnic sandwiches, but there is a gadget for cutting slices in half. A long sharp French knife cuts smooth slices. A loaf weighing 1¼ pounds cuts into 16 to 24 slices, a 2-pound loaf into 45 to 48.

Butter for sandwiches should be soft enough to spread easily. Let it stand at room temperature. If you are making a large number of sandwiches, beat the butter with a spoon or an electric beater until it is soft and fluffy. Then beat in ½ cup milk for each pound of butter. Allow about 4 tablespoons butter for 16 whole slices of bread.

Storing sandwiches. Wrap in tightly closed cellophane bags or in wax paper or in aluminum foil. If you are preparing party sandwiches in advance, arrange them on plates, cover with wax paper, then with a slightly dampened cloth, and store in the refrigerator or other cool place.

Storing sandwiches in the freezer. Wrap in freezer paper. Thaw before serving. They will keep at least 3 months.

MAKING SANDWICHES

Make the sandwiches just before you serve them if the filling is a very moist one; otherwise it may soak into the bread.

Prepare the filling (p. 358). Cream the butter. Slice the bread. Cut off the crusts or not, as you prefer. Spread the slices with butter or mayonnaise. If you are using a smooth filling like cream cheese, butter only one slice for each sandwich.

Spread half the slices with the filling, spreading it evenly to the edges and corners. For tea sandwiches, have the layer of filling thin, so that it will not press out. For heartier sandwiches, have the layer a generous one. Cover with the other slices and press firmly together.

Making sandwiches in quantity. Arrange slices of bread in rows on a large table. Distribute dabs of butter on the slices in alternate rows. Then spread all those slices evenly. Distribute and spread the filling in the same way on the bread in the other rows. Fold together.

If sandwiches are being made hours in advance of serving or to put in the freezer, butter all the slices of bread, so that the filling will not soak into the bread.

PARTY SANDWICHES

Make full-size sandwiches. Cut off the crusts with a long sharp knife. Cut in any of the ways shown below. Or cut sliced bread in rounds and make into sandwiches. (Dry the scraps of bread in a slow oven, roll and save them to use as bread crumbs.)

Open sandwiches. See also Canapés (p. 44). Cut the bread in any shape you choose. Spread with creamed butter, then with filling. Decorate with nut meats, chopped nuts, bit of cherry or a leaf of watercress or parsley, or a slice of stuffed olive.

Flower sandwiches. Butter rounds or oblongs, and on each make a flower design, using pieces of pimiento or a whole shrimp with foliage of watercress or green pepper cut in thin strips.

RIBBON SANDWICHES

Put three or more slices of bread together with creamed seasoned or tinted butter or other soft filling. Have the bread ¼ inch thick. Wrap tightly in a damp cloth and press under a weight. Cut in ¼-inch slices just before serving. Use all white bread or alternate slices of white and dark bread.

Chicken and Ham Ribbon Sandwiches. Use chopped ham highly seasoned and moistened with cream, chopped cooked chicken or turkey moistened with mayonnaise, and chopped nut meats moistened with mayonnaise.

Pepper Ribbon Sandwiches. Chop red and green peppers separately very fine. Wring in a piece of cheesecloth. Moisten with mayonnaise. Use in alternate layers.

Tongue and Gruyère Ribbon Sandwiches. Use brown and white bread alternately. Make alternate layers of cold boiled tongue and Gruyère cheese.

PINWHEEL SANDWICHES

Cut a lengthwise slice from a loaf of bread. Spread with creamed butter and filling. Roll up like a jelly roll. Wrap tightly in a dry towel, then in a slightly moist one, and put in a cold place. When ready to serve, cut in thin slices.

ROLLED SANDWICHES

Cut the crusts from thin slices of very fresh fine-grained bread. Spread with creamed butter or other filling, such as seasoned cream cheese or mushroom filling. Roll, fasten with toothpicks and chill.

When ready to serve, remove the toothpicks. Tuck a sprig of parsley, mint or watercress in the ends of the sandwiches as a garnish.

Asparagus Rolls. Spread slices of bread with mayonnaise or with butter seasoned with lemon juice. Wrap tightly around small asparagus tips, letting the tip end show.

Watercress Rolls. Fill with sprays of watercress, letting a few small perfect leaves show at each end.

MOSAIC SANDWICHES (CHECKERBOARD)

Cut 3 slices each of white and whole-wheat bread ½ inch thick. Spread a slice of white bread with creamed butter and place a slice of whole wheat on it; spread this with creamed butter and place on it a slice of white bread; repeat this process, beginning with a slice of whole wheat.

Put both piles in a cool place under a light weight. When the butter has become firm, trim each pile evenly, and cut each pile in 3 half-inch lengthwise slices. Spread these with butter

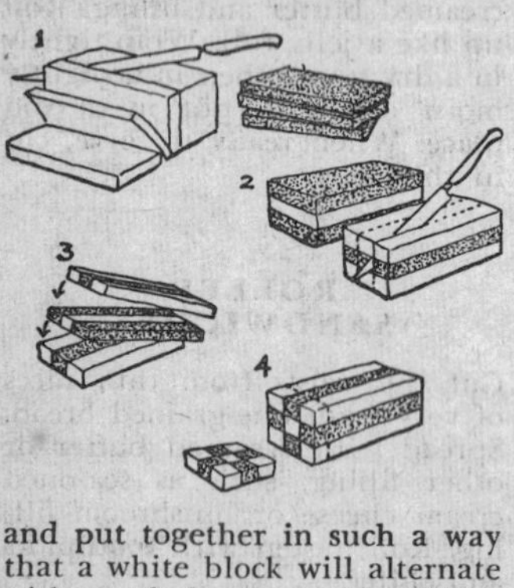

and put together in such a way that a white block will alternate with a whole-wheat one. Wrap firmly in wax paper or foil. Chill under a light weight. When the butter is perfectly hard, cut in thin slices.

SIMPLE SANDWICH FILLINGS

Creamed butter, plain or seasoned with lemon juice, anchovy sauce, honey, grated horseradish, Roquefort cheese crumbs, chopped parsley, chives or watercress.

Peanut butter, plain or moistened with salad dressing. Sprinkle lightly with sugar or spread with jam.

Jelly or jam, plain or with chopped nuts.

Orange marmalade, especially good with nut bread.

HEARTY SANDWICH FILLINGS

Hearty sandwiches are good luncheon or supper fare. See also the suggestions for Cheese Sandwiches (p. 359), Fish Sandwiches (p. 359) and Hot Sandwiches (p. 361).

Eggs, hard-cooked. Chop fine and mix with mayonnaise, cream dressing or melted butter. Add chopped pickles, olives or chives. Season to taste with salt and pepper, anchovy paste or chutney.

Peanut butter. Sprinkle generously with chopped sweet pickle or crumbled crisp bacon.

Chicken or turkey. Cut cooked chicken or turkey in neat slices. Sprinkle with salt and pepper. Add a leaf of lettuce or a sprig of watercress.

Chicken salad. Chop cooked chicken and moisten with mayonnaise. Add crumbled crisp bacon or chopped celery.

Ham, beef, lamb or other cooked meat. Slice or chop and moisten with Tartare Sauce (p. 103).

Ham and cheese. Top a slice of ham with a slice of cheese. Dot with prepared mustard, if you like.

Ham salad. Mix chopped ham and chopped hard-cooked egg and moisten with mayonnaise or cream dressing. Add finely chopped green or red pepper or prepared mustard.

Corned beef or tongue. Cut thin. Spread with mustard, if you like. Rye bread is particularly good.

CHEESE SANDWICH FILLINGS

Cream cheese. Season. Moisten with mayonnaise, French dressing or cream, or mix with any of the following:

Honey and grated orange rind. Use 1 tablespoon of each to a small package of cream cheese.

Black walnut meats, coarsely cut, coconut, chutney or Deviled Almonds (p. 86).

Chicken or ham, chopped fine.

Chopped olives, ripe or stuffed, or nut meats or a combination of both.

Canton ginger, chopped.

Crushed pineapple and chopped pecan nut meats.

Shrimp, mashed with a fork.

Watercress, chopped or in sprays.

Strawberry jam spread on the cheese.

Guava jelly spread on the cheese.

Pimiento and green pepper, cut fine, with a few drops onion juice added.

Gruyère cheese. Grate, mix with chopped walnut meats, and season with salt and cayenne.

Swiss cheese. Slice and dot with prepared mustard. Use rye bread.

Cheese and anchovy. Cream 2 tablespoons butter, add 1/4 cup grated mild cheese and 1 teaspoon vinegar. Season with salt, paprika, mustard and anchovy sauce.

FISH SANDWICH FILLINGS

Lobster. Chop and season with salad dressing or cayenne, mustard and lemon juice. Use on lettuce if desired. As a variation, add an equal quantity of chopped hard-cooked egg.

Salmon (cooked or canned). Flake and mix with chopped cucumber or pickle, or both, and mayonnaise.

Sardines. Skin, bone and mash to a paste. Mix with chopped hard-cooked egg. Season with salt, cayenne and a few drops lemon juice. Moisten with olive oil or melted butter.

Shrimp. Mash with a fork and season to taste with French dressing or mayonnaise or both.

Tuna (or any cooked flaked white fish). Flake and mix with finely cut celery, pickle or cucumber. Moisten with mayonnaise.

FRUIT SANDWICH FILLINGS

Dates. Pit and chop. Moisten with orange juice.

Prunes. Pit and chop. Add chopped walnuts. Moisten with corn syrup and season to taste with salt, paprika and lemon juice.

Strawberries. Slice thin and sprinkle lightly with sugar.

VEGETABLE SANDWICH FILLINGS

Carrot. Grate raw carrot and mix with mayonnaise. Spread on a leaf of lettuce or shredded lettuce.

Cucumber. Chop and moisten with mayonnaise, or cut in thin rounds and sprinkle with salt.

Lettuce. Cut in strips with scissors. Season with a small amount of mayonnaise.

Olive, ripe, or stuffed green. Chop and mix with mayonnaise.

Tomato. Slice, drain and sprinkle with salt or dip in French dressing. Dot with mayonnaise (open or closed sandwich).

Watercress. Sprinkle with salt, or chop and mix with mayonnaise.

ALMOND-CHICKEN SANDWICH FILLING

Mix 1 cup chopped cooked chicken, 1/4 cup chopped blanched almonds and 1/2 cup finely chopped celery. Moisten with mayonnaise and season to taste with lemon juice, salt and paprika.

CHICKEN-HAM SANDWICH FILLING

Cream
1/3 cup butter
Mix with
1/2 cup finely chopped cooked chicken
1/2 cup finely chopped cooked ham
Salt and paprika to taste

LIVER SAUSAGE SANDWICH FILLING

Remove the skin from
1/2 pound liver sausage
Add to the meat
1 small cream cheese (3 ounces)
3 hard-cooked eggs, chopped
3 tablespoons mayonnaise
1/2 teaspoon chopped chives
Salt and pepper
Cream thoroughly. Add more mayonnaise, if needed, to spread easily.

SHRIMP AND CHICKEN LIVER SANDWICH FILLING

Mix and put through food chopper
1/2 cup cooked or canned shrimp
1/2 cup cooked chicken livers
1/2 red pepper, seeded
1/2 large sweet onion
Season with
Salt
Moisten with
Mayonnaise

SPANISH SANDWICH FILLING

Chop very fine or pound in a mortar
2 anchovies
2 pickles
1 sprig parsley
3 tablespoons capers
1 teaspoon prepared mustard
2 tablespoons salad oil
2 tablespoons vinegar
Add
2 hard-cooked eggs, chopped fine
Mix and season to taste with
Salt and paprika

GINGER PECAN SANDWICH FILLING

These are special for small tea party sandwiches.

Mix together

¼ cup chopped Canton ginger
¼ cup chopped pecan nut meats
2 tablespoons orange pulp, cut fine
1 tablespoon ginger syrup
1 teaspoon vinegar
Few grains salt

HOT SANDWICHES

For luncheon or supper. Hot roast beef sandwiches, covered with gravy, Hamburgers (p. 362), Toasted Cheese Sandwiches (p. 362), Club Sandwiches (p. 362), Chicken Sandwiches (p. 358) are all popular as main dishes for luncheon or supper. These will suggest other suitable combinations.

For a tea party. Make small plain or rolled sandwiches on unbuttered bread. Brush outside with melted butter when ready to serve and toast the sandwiches on a cooky sheet in the broiler. Toast a few at a time so that you can serve them piping hot.

The filling may be orange marmalade, sliced cheese or chopped chicken, or chopped sautéed mushrooms moistened with cream. See also Baking Powder Biscuit Sandwiches (below) and Waffle Sandwiches (below).

For a cocktail party. Make sandwiches as for a tea party (above) but do not use sweet fillings. See also Baking Powder Biscuit Sandwiches (below) and Waffle Sandwiches (below).

BAKING POWDER BISCUIT SANDWICHES

Make tiny Baking Powder Biscuits, using a packaged mix or following the recipe on page 326. Split, butter and put together with deviled ham spread, shaved maple sugar, halved and sugared strawberries, jam, thin slices of cheese or chopped chicken moistened with hot gravy or cream sauce.

WAFFLE SANDWICHES

Make small sandwiches with a filling of orange marmalade or a bit of cheese dotted with mustard or a few drops of Worcestershire. Keep the filling away from the edges. Spread the outside of the sandwiches lightly with butter and toast in a waffle iron.

TOASTED SANDWICHES

Make sandwiches without buttering the bread. Spread one side of each sandwich lightly with soft butter. Toast in the broiler, buttered side toward the heat. Turn the sandwich over and spread the other side with butter. Toast. Serve piping hot.

Good fillings for toasted sandwiches are peanut butter, marmalade, chopped ham, sliced tomato or chopped cooked meat, fish or chicken mixed with mayonnaise and seasoned to taste. French Toast Sandwiches (below) are good with any of these fillings, too.

FRENCH TOAST SANDWICHES

Make sandwiches with filling of cheese, sliced chicken or chopped chicken or ham. Press the slices firmly together. Beat 1 egg slightly, add ¼ cup milk and dip the sandwiches in the mixture. Sauté in butter. Serve with a garnish of crisp bacon.

TOASTED CHEESE SANDWICHES

Use 2 slices of bread for each sandwich. Lay thin slices of cheese on half the slices of bread. Arrange all the slices in the broiler 2 inches from the heat.

Toast until the cheese begins to melt and the plain bread to brown. Cover the cheese with the plain bread, toasted side down. Spread tops sparingly with soft butter and toast until delicately brown. Turn over with a spatula, butter again and toast. Cut in half, diagonally, and serve very hot.

Open Toasted Cheese Sandwiches. Toast the bread on one side. Put sliced cheese on the untoasted side, sprinkle with paprika and, if desired, with bits of uncooked bacon and rings of sweet onion. Toast in the broiler until the cheese melts.

CLUB SANDWICHES

Club sandwiches are hearty ones, usually two- or three-deckers, made with buttered toast, plenty of sliced chicken or other meat, lettuce, sliced tomato and mayonnaise. Top with a strip or two of crisp bacon, if you like.

If you are planning to serve a club sandwich on a plate with a fork, cut the toast diagonally in quarters so that the sandwich will be easier to manage.

BLT Sandwiches. Put sliced tomato, lettuce, a dab of mayonnaise and crisp strips of bacon between two slices of buttered toast.

OPEN CHEESE AND BACON SANDWICH

Combine and mix well

3 eggs, beaten until light
¾ pound soft cheese, grated or put through food chopper
1½ teaspoons Worcestershire
¾ teaspoon salt
½ teaspoon paprika
Few grains cayenne

Spread on

8 slices bread, ⅓ inch thick

Cut into tiny squares

¾ pound bacon

Sprinkle over the cheese. Bake 8 to 10 minutes in 400° oven.

WESTERN SANDWICH

In a small frying pan, cook slowly together for 5 minutes

1 teaspoon butter
1 tablespoon minced onion

Beat until just blended

1 egg
1 tablespoon water

Add

1 tablespoon minced ham (or more)

Pour into the pan with the onion and cook until lightly browned on the bottom. Turn and cook a moment on the other side. Put between halves of a toasted bun or slices of buttered bread.

Eastern Sandwich. Make in the same way, but omit the onion.

HAMBURGER BUNS

Split buns and toast. Shape hamburgers ½ inch thick and the size of the buns. Cook the hamburgers 4 minutes on one side, put on half of the split buns, cooked side down. Sprinkle with salt and pepper. Broil until the meat is browned. Top with the other bun halves.

For a more piquant flavor, dot the hamburgers with prepared mustard, chili sauce or both.

Cheeseburger. After putting the hamburger on the bun, top with a slice of cheese. Broil until the cheese melts.

Fruits and Fruit Desserts

Fruit is a piquant addition to any meal of the day—refreshing at breakfast, zestful as an accompaniment to the main dish at lunch or dinner, welcome as dessert, especially after a hearty meal, and good as a snack any time. Fruits are low in calories compared with puddings and pies, and are rewardingly high in important food values such as vitamin C and iron.

In this section are suggestions for fruit cups and compotes as well as information about selecting, storing and preparing fruit. Consult the index for other fruit recipes. Remember that many variations are possible, such as combining different fruits, sweetening fruits with sugar, maple syrup or honey and adding zest with a bit of lemon juice, brandy or rum.

FRESH FRUITS

If you buy more than enough fruit to use immediately, store it in a cool place, preferably spread out so that the pieces do not touch. For the finest flavor, chill just before serving.

FROZEN FRUITS AND FRUIT JUICES

These are often of better flavor than out-of-season fresh fruits Use them promptly after defrosting. Shake frozen juices in a closed jar to blend—aerating reduces the vitamin C content.

CANNED FRUITS AND FRUIT JUICES

Read the labels to compare can sizes and quality as well as prices. Sliced fruit is cheaper than whole fruit of the same quality. Buy special values in quantity if you have storage space.

DRIED FRUITS

Small fruits are less expensive than large ones but equally good. Buy unsulphured fruit whenever possible. Packaged dried fruits do not need soaking before cooking. To cook very quickly, use a pressure saucepan (8 to 10 minutes).

FRESH FRUIT CUP

There is no finer dessert than a beautiful bowl of fresh fruits, carefully prepared and combined.

Chill the fruit. If you use bananas, add them last, as they darken after peeling. Sprinkle cut peaches with lemon juice to prevent darkening.

Prepare ½ cup or more for each serving. Heap in a glass, silver or pottery bowl. Sprinkle lightly with salt, then with sugar. There are many ways to flavor the mixture—tuck in a few mint leaves or sprinkle with rum, sherry, lemon juice or brandy. Cover closely and chill again to blend the flavors. Taste the juice and add more salt, sugar or lemon juice if it is needed. If you use mint, remove the limp leaves before serving and add fresh ones.

Serve from the bowl with crunchy nut wafers or wedges of sponge or angel cake.

Suggested Combinations

- Grapefruit and orange sections, pears and cherries or grapes
- Pineapple (cubed) and strawberries
- Peaches, pears and raspberries
- Watermelon, cantaloupe and honeydew (cut in balls with a vegetable cutter)
- Raspberries and currants

YOGURT FRUIT CUP

Put fruit cup, fresh fruit cut in pieces, canned fruit or berries in old-fashioned glasses or small deep bowls. Cover with yogurt. If you like, sprinkle with light brown sugar.

FRUIT COCKTAIL

Arrange chilled mixed fruit in sherbet glasses. Top with a sprig of mint, a perfect cherry or strawberry, a tiny scoop of orange or lemon ice or a spoonful of ginger ale frozen in the refrigerator tray. Sprinkle with chopped ginger or a few pine nuts.

Bouquet Cocktail. Make a cut through the center of a lace-paper doily and paste the doily around a sherbet glass to represent the frill on an old-fashioned bouquet. Fill with any fruit cocktail.

COTTAGE CHEESE FRUIT BOWL

Circle a mound of cottage cheese with fresh, frozen or canned fruit such as peaches, plums, apricots or pears. As an extra fillip, serve little bowls of powdered coffee, grated chocolate, granulated sugar and cinnamon to be sprinkled over the fruit.

MACÉDOINE OF FRUIT

Choose fruit thoughtfully for contrast in color, shape and texture. Fruits particularly good are avocado in slices or cubes, orange or grapefruit sections, melon balls, seeded white grapes, cherries (canned or fresh), strawberries, raspberries, wedges of fresh pineapple, sliced pears, peaches and nectarines.

Prepare and arrange on a large flat serving dish in an attractive pattern. Squeeze lemon juice over the fruit to keep it from darkening. Sprinkle sparingly with powdered sugar and kirsch or Cointreau. Chill thoroughly.

SHERRIED FROZEN FRUIT

For a refreshing summer dessert, thaw (enough to separate the fruit) a package of frozen raspberries or peaches. The fruit should still be somewhat icy when it is served. Sprinkle with ¼ cup sherry or vermouth. *Serves 3 or 4.*

HOT FRUIT COMPOTE

Beautiful and satisfying as a winter dessert following a hearty roast. Easy to prepare in quantity for a big party.

Drain the juice from

1 can pears
1 can Bing cherries
1 can whole apricots

To the juice add

1 tablespoon slivered orange peel

Simmer 30 minutes. Add the fruit. Heat. Stir in

Brandy, rum *or* vanilla to taste

Serve plain or with

Sweet *or* sour cream

Serves 6 to 8.

To thicken the juice slightly, stir into it packaged vanilla pudding mix. One package is enough to thicken 4 cups of juice.

Other combinations

- Peaches, raisins, plums and slivered almonds
- Peaches, pears, apricots and marrons
- Plums, apricots and cherries
- Pineapple, orange sections and black cherries
- Prunes and apricots
- Cooked apple slices, raisins and walnut halves

BAKED FRUIT COMPOTE

Arrange layers of canned fruit (such as sour cherries, greengage plums, sweet black cherries and peaches) in a deep baking dish. Sprinkle each layer sparingly with brown sugar.

Bake 30 minutes at 350°. Arrange several thin slices of lemon over the fruit and bake 10 minutes longer. If the fruit is very juicy, spoon out some of the juice after the first 10 minutes of baking. Serve warm or cold.

APPLES

Improved varieties of apples are constantly being developed and some of the fine old ones are no longer available. Learn to know and appreciate your local varieties and use each in the most appropriate way. Sweet bland apples do not make good applesauce or pie. Some wonderful early fall apples do not keep well in storage. When stored, apples begin to lose some of their fine flavor. Add zest to apple dishes with a touch of nutmeg, cinnamon or allspice. Dried apples, canned apples and canned applesauce are often a convenience.

BAKED APPLES

Select well-flavored apples. Core. Put in a baking dish. In each apple put 1 tablespoon sugar and a dash of cinnamon or nutmeg. Cover the bottom of the baking dish with boiling water. Bake at 400° until soft (30 minutes or more). Several times during the baking, spoon the pan juices over the apples.

If you prefer to pare apples before baking, core before paring, so that fruit will keep in shape. Or make 2 circular cuts through skin, leaving a ¾-inch band around apple midway between stem and blossom ends.

Apples Baked in Foil. For each apple, cut a square of foil large enough to wrap it completely. Prepare apples for baking (above). Put each apple on a piece of foil. Fold the foil up around it, put in 2 tablespoons hot water and close the foil tightly around the apple. Bake at 400° until soft (30 minutes or more).

APPLE *or* PEACH MERINGUE

Pile Meringue (p. 441) on Baked Apples (p. 365) or canned peaches. Brown in 425° oven. Cool. Serve with Soft Custard (p. 384).

CRUSTY BAKED APPLES

Core and pare halfway down
6 tart apples
Put in a baking dish, pared side up. Melt
3 tablespoons butter
Stir in
2 tablespoons flour
Mix well. Add
½ cup brown sugar
½ teaspoon vanilla
Spread over the apples. Bake at 425° until the crust is set. Lower the temperature to 350°. Bake until the apples are tender (about 30 minutes).

GLAZED BAKED APPLES

Good as a dessert or as a relish with pork or ham.

Core apples. Pare one-third of the way down. Put close together in a saucepan, peeled side up. Add water ½ inch deep. Cover and cook slowly until tender when pierced with a toothpick. Put in a baking dish, peeled side up. Sprinkle with sugar (½ cup or more for 4 apples). Bake at 425° until the sugar dissolves and the tops are crisp and delicately brown. Baste frequently with the water in which the apples were cooked.

CINNAMON APPLES

Core and pare tart apples. Stick each with 2 or 3 cloves. For 6 apples, cook together for 5 minutes 1 cup sugar, 2 tablespoons red cinnamon drops and 1½ cups water. Add apples, simmer until tender but not mushy. Baste often with syrup in pan. Serve as a relish with pork, or chilled on lettuce, or as dessert.

Apple Porcupine. Omit the cinnamon drops and cloves. Drain and cool. Fill with jelly, marmalade or preserved fruit. Stick with bits of sliced almonds. Serve with whipped cream as dessert.

APPLE SAVORIES

Slice bright red apples but do not pare. Spread with cream cheese or Camembert and serve after the dessert course at dinner or as an evening snack.

APPLESAUCE

Wash and quarter apples but do not pare or core. Cook slowly until soft with just enough water to keep from burning. Or cook in a pressure saucepan 5 minutes with ¼ cup water. Put through a food mill or coarse strainer. Add a sprinkling of salt. Add sugar to taste. Stir until the sugar melts completely. Some cooks stir in a bit of butter. Add spice and lemon juice if apples need more flavor.

If you like applesauce less smooth, pare and core the apples before cooking and beat only slightly with a fork when they are done.

STEWED APPLES

Quarter, core and pare
8 apples

Cook for 5 minutes

1 cup sugar
1 cup water
Few shavings of lemon rind

Remove the lemon rind. Cook the apples in the syrup, a few at a time, until tender enough to pierce with a toothpick. Strain the syrup over the cooked apples. Serve as dessert or as a compote with roast duck or pork.

BRANDIED APPLES

Core tart apples. Cut in ½-inch slices. Sprinkle generously with brandy or rum. Cover and let stand at least 4 hours. Drain. Dip in flour. Melt butter in a skillet or a chafing dish. Add the apple slices and cook until tender and brown on both sides.

Serve as a relish with pork, duck, chicken or turkey, or as a hot dessert with powdered sugar and sour cream.

APPLE FRITTERS

See page 409, Fruit Fritters.

APRICOTS

Ripe apricots are plump and firm and golden yellow.

Serve whole or peel and slice and serve with cream and sugar. Add to fruit cups and salads.

To peel apricots. Dip quickly in boiling water, then in cold water. Slip off the skins with your fingers.

COOKED DRIED APRICOTS

Cook 3 minutes in a pressure cooker with ¼ cup water or cover with boiling water, cover the pan, simmer until the fruit is just tender (12 to 20 minutes). Add sugar to taste.

For excellent flavor, cook a sliced lime with the apricots (1 pound).

Apricots in Sour Cream. Drain cooked or canned apricots. Fold into sour cream. Chill. Sprinkle with brown sugar or chopped nut meats.

Apricot Charlotte. Mash cooked apricots. Fold into whipped cream. Spoon into serving dishes and sprinkle crushed peanut brittle over the top.

AVOCADOS (ALLIGATOR PEARS)

Choose fruit that is beginning to soften. Shake—the stone will rattle slightly if the fruit is ripe. The flesh should be evenly green with no dark soft spots. Consult the index for recipes using avocados in salads and spreads.

To serve avocado as a first course, cut in half, remove the seed, but do not pare. Sprinkle with lemon juice and a few grains of salt. Fill the center with French dressing or put 1 tablespoon rum and a sprinkling of powdered sugar into each one. *Serve a half avocado to each person.*

BANANAS

For immediate use, select yellow fruit flecked with brown. If bananas are green, let them ripen thoroughly before using. Bananas that are slightly green at the ends are best for cooking. Do not store in the refrigerator.

Serve bananas whole, sliced (with orange juice or cream and sugar) or cut in half lengthwise, and sprinkled with lemon juice and sugar.

SAUTÉED BANANAS

Peel bananas, cut in half lengthwise, and again cut in half crosswise. Sprinkle with flour. Sauté in butter until delicately brown. Drain. Sprinkle with powdered sugar. Serve with curry or chicken, or as dessert.

Bananas au Rhum. Sprinkle sautéed bananas with sugar and pour warm rum over them (¼ cup for 3 bananas). Light with a match and baste with the flaming syrup. Serve as dessert.

BAKED BANANAS

Peel bananas. Leave whole or cut in halves or quarters. Arrange on a buttered glass or pottery baking dish. Sprinkle with brown sugar and a few gratings of lemon peel. Dot with butter. Bake at 350° (15 to 20 minutes).

If you like, sprinkle with orange juice, sherry or rum. Serve with ham or chicken or as a dessert.

Bananas Berkeley. Pour Melba Sauce (p. 433) over cooled baked bananas. Garnish with whipped cream.

BLUEBERRIES AND HUCKLEBERRIES

Blueberries are bright blue with a slightly frosted look. Huckleberries are larger, darker and have more seeds. Cultivated berries are larger than wild ones but wild ones have the finer flavor. Frozen and canned blueberries are convenient for pies and puddings.

Remove bits of leaf and stem. Wash carefully. Serve with sugar and cream or milk. Delicious with sour cream and powdered sugar mixed with ginger.

Stewed Blueberries *or* Huckleberries. Cook until soft with just enough water to keep them from burning. Sweeten to taste. Serve with cream or not.

CANTALOUPE (MUSKMELON)

Ripe cantaloupe are fragrant and feel slightly soft when pressed with your thumb. There are many delicious varieties.

To preserve the finest flavor, do not chill. Cut in half or in wedges. Remove the seeds. Serve with salt and quartered lemon or lime.

Raspberry Stuffed Cantaloupe. Heap fresh or partially thawed frozen raspberries in the hollow. Sprinkle fresh berries lightly with sugar.

Cantaloupe Ring. Cut in 1-inch slices. Carefully cut off the peel. Put a slice on each plate. Fill with any fruit cup mixture, with melon balls or with vanilla ice cream.

MELONS FRASCATI

Fruit cup with a Baked Alaska topping.

Cut small ripe cantaloupe in halves and remove the seeds. Fill with any fruit cup mixture—raspberries and nectarines are particularly delicious. Sprinkle with sugar and, if you like, a little rum, sherry or Cointreau. Cover with wax paper and chill at least 1 hour.

Cover with a 2-inch layer of Meringue (p. 441), spooned on

lightly. Bake at 400° until delicately browned (about 5 minutes). Serve at once or chill until ready to serve.

CHERRIES

To serve fresh, select sweet cherries that are ripe but not oversoft. Wash and shake dry in a colander. Do not remove the stems. Chill. Serve heaped in a bowl or on a bed of grape leaves in a flat basket.

STEWED CHERRIES

Wash sweet or sour cherries. Remove stems, and pit or prick well. To pit, use a cherry pitter or the curved end of a paper clip. Cook with a small amount of boiling water until nearly tender. Add sugar to taste and cook 3 minutes longer.

Serve as a relish with meat or as dessert. For a richer dessert, serve with sour cream.

BLACK CHERRIES JUBILEE

Drain stewed or canned black cherries, reserving the juice. For 2 cups of cherries, mix 1 tablespoon sugar and 1 tablespoon cornstarch and add 1 cup of the juice, a little at a time. Cook gently 3 minutes, stirring constantly. Add the cherries. Warm ½ cup brandy, pour it over the cherries, and light with a match. Spoon the juices in the pan over the cherries and serve flaming.

For a dramatic effect, prepare in a chafing dish at the table. Superb over vanilla ice cream or orange sherbet. *Serves 6.*

CURRANTS

Currants are used principally for jelly and jam, but they are delicious eaten fresh, especially mixed with raspberries.

Wash. Remove the stems. Sprinkle thickly with granulated sugar.

DATES

Pitted dates are usually packaged.

Consult the index for recipes using dates. Also, cut them small and add to fruit cups and salads, or put a stuffed date on each salad plate.

FRESH FIGS

Store in the refrigerator. Pare off the outer skin with a sharp knife. Cut in slices and serve with cream. Fully ripe figs need no sugar.

STEWED DRIED FIGS

Canned figs are available, ready to eat.

Put in a saucepan

1 pound dried figs
Cold water to cover
1 tablespoon lemon juice

Cover. Simmer until the figs are tender. Take out the figs. Add to the juice

½ cup sugar

Cook until thick. Flavor to taste with

Sherry, vanilla *or* **more lemon juice**

Pour over the figs. Cool. Serve with cream. *Serves 6.*

GRAPES

Wash the bunches in cold water. Drain. Pick off and discard imperfect grapes. Chill. Garnish with grape leaves, if convenient.

Grapes for Salad. Peel (or not, as you like) Malaga (greenish) or Tokay (red) grapes. Cut in half and remove the seeds. Seedless grapes (fresh or canned) are used whole.

Frosted Grapes. *Glitter for the Christmas fruit bowl.* Beat an egg white until frothy. Sprinkle it over a bunch of perfect Malaga grapes. Dust with granulated sugar. Let stand until dry.

GRAPE JUICE FRAPPE

Whirl in an electric blender

1 can frozen grape juice
3 cans crushed ice

Serve in fruit juice glasses as a first course or as party refreshment. *Serves 4.*

Orange Juice Frappe. Substitute frozen orange juice for grape juice.

GRAPEFRUIT

Select firm, smooth-skinned fruit, heavy for its size. Color is unimportant—greenish ones may be of excellent flavor.

Wipe and cut in half crosswise. With a small sharp-pointed knife (special curved ones are made for the purpose), cut the pulp away from the membrane in

each section. Cut out the membrane at the core with scissors or with a grapefruit corer, or cut the membrane between the sections to remove it entirely. Sweeten or not, as desired. Serve very cold.

To serve grapefruit as a first course, you may like to add (for each portion) 1 tablespoon sherry or rum or ½ tablespoon apricot brandy or sloe gin.

Baked or Broiled Grapefruit. Sprinkle each half with 1 tablespoon brown sugar. Dot with butter. Add, if you like, 1 tablespoon sherry or 1 teaspoon brandy. Bake at 450° or in the broiler until the sugar melts and the surface is slightly browned. Serve as first course or dessert.

GRAPEFRUIT *or* ORANGE SECTIONS

Put the fruit on a cutting board. Hold it firmly with your left hand and pare off the skin wtih a long, very sharp knife. Cut away the white layer beneath the skin as you pare. Remove the pulp by sections, cutting it away from the membrane, first on one side of a section, then the other. Cut off any white bits that remain, so that you have perfect sections of fruit.

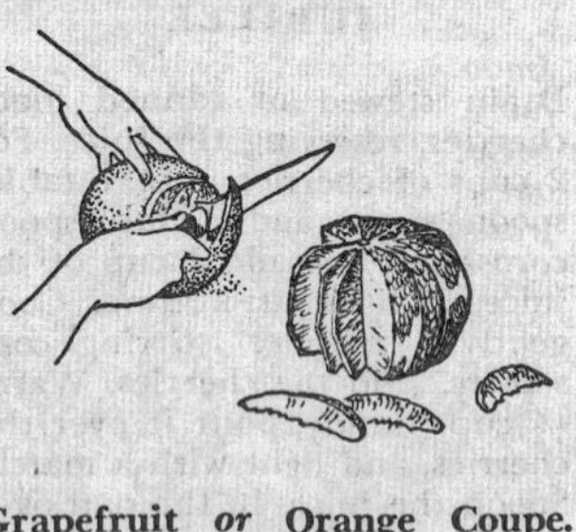

Grapefruit *or* Orange Coupe. Cut sections in pieces, sprinkle with sugar, and chill. Serve in sherbet glasses with a cherry or a sprig of mint on top. For a more pungent mint flavor, sprinkle with crême de menthe or put a few sprigs with the fruit as it chills and remove them when the fruit is put in the glasses.

Rector Grapefruit Cup. Fill 4 sherbet glasses with grapefruit sections. Mix ½ cup powdered sugar, 2 teaspoons curaçao, 1 teaspoon lemon juice, 1 teaspoon kirsch and ⅛ teaspoon salt. Sprinkle over the fruit.

GRAPEFRUIT *or* ORANGE BASKETS

Cut the fruit in half. Remove the pulp and scrape out the white membrane and the core. Scallop the edge with scissors or a special knife. Fill with Fruit Cup (p. 363), sherbet (p. 413) or fruit jelly (p. 383). Grapefruit halves may be used like individual casseroles, filled with creamed chicken or tuna.

KUMQUATS

Eat, skin and all. Sliced kumquats are a pretty garnish on a fruit cup or salad.

LEMONS AND LIMES

Smooth-skinned, heavy fruit is juicy. Dark-green limes have better flavor than pale yellow ones. Concentrated canned or frozen juice is a convenience.

Lemons as garnish, page 86. Consult the index for recipes using lemons or limes, such as lemonade and desserts.

MANGOES

Similar to cantaloupe but with a distinctive, aromatic flavor.

Cut in half lengthwise and eat with a spoon.

MELONS

All the varieties of melon are delicious—cantaloupe (p. 368) and muskmelon, pale green Persian, honeydew, casaba and the rest. Often you can tell by a melon's fragrance that it is ripe, or you can hear the seeds rattle when you shake it.

Cut small melons in half, larger ones in sections. Discard the seeds and the stringy part. Do not chill or put ice inside as it changes the delicate flavor. Serve with salt or powdered sugar. With Persian, honeydew or casaba melons, you will like lemon or lime wedges to squeeze over the fruit. Or mix powdered sugar with a little ginger and put it in a shaker or a small bowl to sprinkle over the melon. Mint leaves are a pleasant garnish for melons.

Melon Suprême. Cut melons in balls with a ball cutter. Combine more than one kind of melon or use just one. Sprinkle with sugar and rum or maraschino. Serve in chilled sherbet glasses.

NECTARINES

Nectarines have a flavor similar to peaches but a smooth skin, like plums. Select unblemished fruit, ripe or nearly ripe. Green fruit will shrivel and not ripen. Eat without peeling, or peel, cut in pieces, and add to fruit cup.

ORANGES

Select fruit that is heavy for its size and free from soft or spongy spots. Scars, scratches or greenish areas do not affect the flavor. Navel oranges have a bright color. Florida oranges are naturally a pale or greenish yellow.

Their brilliant color is usually a dye.

Buy oranges by the pound, dozen, crate or half crate. If you buy them in quantity store them at 40° to 60°, sort over regularly, and remove any that develop soft spots. Small oranges are often an economical buy.

Wash. Serve whole or cut in half to eat with a spoon. Or prepare sections (p. 370) and serve with powdered sugar. Or peel and slice.

Special recipes using oranges follow. Consult the index for other recipes using oranges.

ORANGE JUICE

Select thin-skinned oranges, heavy for their size. Cut in half or, if oranges are very small, cut a slice from the top. Squeeze out the juice. Strain or not. If kept in the refrigerator, cover tightly. Garnish, if desired, with sprig of fresh mint. If the juice is very sweet, add a little lemon or grapefruit juice. Frozen concentrated juice is convenient as an ingredient as well as a breakfast beverage.

ORANGES AMANDINE

Sprinkle orange sections or sliced oranges with shredded toasted almonds and grated maple sugar. Serve icy cold.

AMBROSIA

Mix sliced oranges or orange sections with sliced bananas. Chill and sprinkle with shredded coconut.

ORANGE MINT CUP

Cut in halves
4 large oranges
Remove the pulp with a spoon.
Add
2 tablespoons powdered sugar
2 tablespoons finely chopped mint
1 tablespoon lemon juice
1 tablespoon sherry
Chill. Pour off some of the juice if the oranges are very juicy. Serve in sherbet glasses. Garnish with
Sprigs of mint
Serves 4.

GUATEMALA ORANGE CUP

Do not make this fruit cup too sweet. It is to be served as a refreshing first course.

Remove pulp as for Orange Mint Cup (above) from
4 large oranges
Add
2 tablespoons chopped parsley
1 tablespoon chopped chives
1 tablespoon pimiento, cut small
Add
Sugar and salt to taste
Serves 4.

GLAZED ORANGES

Cook small seedless oranges in syrup to cover (1 cup sugar to 1 cup water) until they are tender when you prick them with a toothpick. Cool in the syrup, adding rum, brandy or Cointreau to taste, if you like. Drain and serve with sour cream and cinnamon sugar. Or roll the drained oranges in cinnamon sugar.

BAKED ORANGES

Wash seedless oranges, cover with boiling water, and cook until the skin is tender when pricked with a toothpick. Drain, cut in half and remove the cores. Put in a baking dish. Fill the centers with sugar and sprinkle sugar over the top. Add 1 tablespoon brandy to each and dot with butter. Heat in the broiler until the sugar melts and browns delicately.

Serve warm with turkey or, as a dessert, with cream, Zabaglione (p. 386) or Hot Orange Sauce (p. 432), flavored with brandy.

ORANGE FRITTERS

See page 409, Fruit Fritters.

PAPAYA (PAWPAW)

Papaya is similar to muskmelon. Its flavor is at its best when the fruit is fully ripe (soft enough to dent with a slight pressure of your thumb).

Chill thoroughly and cut in wedges or quarters. Remove most of seeds (the seeds are edible).

Serve with lemon or lime sections or with salt or sugar. Or use in a fruit cup with lime or lemon juice or combined with pineapple or orange sections.

PEACHES

Select firm ripe peaches, free of bruises. Golden-yellow peaches are delicious and so are the juicy white ones.

Wash and dry. Serve whole or peeled and sliced. Serve sliced peaches immediately, or sprinkle sparingly with lemon juice to prevent darkening.

PEACHES RIVIERA

Peel peaches. Leave whole and pour over them sieved strawberries or raspberries (or a mixture of both), sweetened to taste and flavored with lemon juice and Cointreau.

BAKED PEACHES

Peel, cut in half and remove stones. Place in a shallow baking dish, cut side up. Fill each cavity with chopped nuts, fruits or macaroon crumbs, or 1 teaspoon sugar, ½ teaspoon butter, few drops lemon juice and a slight grating of nutmeg. Bake 20 minutes at 350°. Sprinkle a little sherry or brandy over the peaches for a particularly delicious flavor. Serve warm with Hard Sauce (p. 434), or chilled with whipped cream or sour cream.

BAKED PEACHES FLAMBÉ

Arrange canned peach halves in a shallow baking dish, cut side up. Pour a little of the syrup over the peaches. Sprinkle generously with maple syrup. Bake ½ hour at 350°. Just before serving, pour heated brandy or brandy and kirsch over the peaches and light with a match.

Serve with Foamy Sauce (p. 434) or Floradora Sauce (p. 435), reducing the sugar to ¼ cup.

PEARS

Summer pears do not keep well, so buy in small quantities. Ripen hard winter pears at room temperature. Pears are always picked green; otherwise they will be dark at the core.

SAUTÉED PEARS WITH CHOCOLATE SAUCE

Pare 4 Bartlett pears, cut in fourths lengthwise, and sauté in butter until browned. Canned pears drained from syrup may be used in place of fresh fruit.

Serve warm with Creamy Chocolate Sauce (p. 430).

STEWED *or* BAKED PEARS

Peel firm pears. Quarter large ones but leave small Seckel pears whole. Cook ½ cup sugar with ½ cup water 5 minutes (with a piece of lemon rind or stick cinnamon, if you like). Add the pears. Cook slowly, covered, on top of the stove or bake in a casserole or bean pot at 300° until tender but still firm.

Serve warm or cold with cream.

Pears with Cointreau. Cook whole pears. Cook the syrup until as thick as honey, add 1 tablespoon Cointreau, and pour over the pears. Chill. Flavor with vanilla in place of Cointreau if you prefer. Serve with cream.

Pears in Port Wine. Cover cooked pears with port wine. Cover and let stand at least 1 hour.

PERSIMMONS

Select this decorative fruit when soft but still firm. Chill thoroughly. Cut in half. Eat with a fork and spoon. Use bits of persimmon as garnish on fruit salads.

Oriental and American Wild Varieties

PINEAPPLE

The center spines of a ripe pineapple pull out easily. A medium-sized pineapple weighs 2 pounds and yields 2½ to 3 cups of diced fruit (4 to 6 servings).

Unless the pineapple is very ripe, sprinkle it with sugar after cutting or shredding, and let it stand in the refrigerator at least 1 hour.

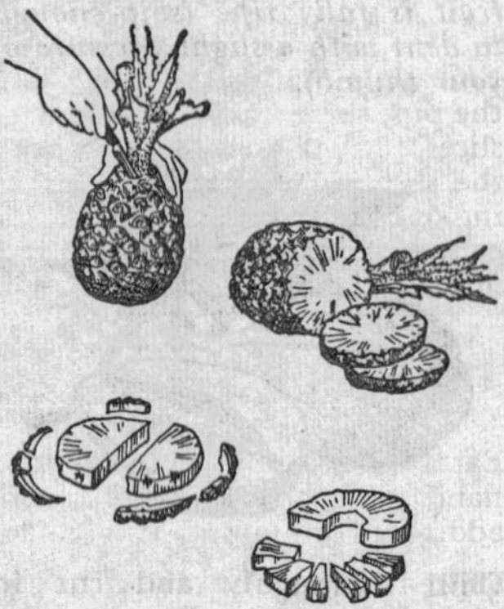

To cut pineapple. Cut off the sharp tips of the leaves. There are many ways to cut pineapple. One easy way is to cut out the crown with a sharp pointed knife, then cut crosswise in ¾-inch slices with a long sharp knife, cut off the rind, cut out the "eyes," cut in half and remove the core. Then cut as you like.

To shred pineapple. Hold upright, pare with a long sharp knife, dig out the "eyes," then tear out the pulp in bits with a fork.

Pineapple in Wine. Shred or cut in chunks. Sprinkle with sugar and cover with white wine or Madeira. Cover and chill at least 1 hour.

PINEAPPLE IN THE SHELL

Without paring, cut the pineapple in halves or quarters, lengthwise, leaving on the top leaves. Cut out the core and carefully cut the flesh away from the rind in one piece. Slice or cut in wedges. Refill the shell. Sprinkle with sugar or kirsch. Serve plain or garnish with cherries, whole strawberries or sprigs of mint.

Pineapple with Avocado. Slice the pineapple and alternate with slices of avocado when you refill the sections. Pour French dressing over the fruit. Serve as a first course or as salad and dessert in one. *A small pineapple serves 4.*

PLUMS

Eat fresh plums whole in your hand or peel, cut in bits, and add to a fruit cup or fruit salad.

Stewed Plums. Cover with just enough water to keep from burning. Cook gently until soft (about 10 minutes). Sweeten to taste and serve in sauce dishes with a little of the juice poured over them.

Brandied Plums. Flavor stewed plums to taste with brandy and serve on vanilla ice cream.

POMEGRANATES

Use this brilliant-colored fruit in a holiday centerpiece. To serve, cut in half and serve with a spoon. Use the tart-flavored seeds to accent a fruit salad.

STEWED PRUNES

Large prunes are more expensive than small ones, but the flavor is the same. Packaged prunes do not need soaking. Follow the directions on the package. Cover bulk prunes with hot water (2 cups to ½ pound), let stand 2 hours and cook slowly in the same water until plump and tender.

To vary the flavor, add a few drops of lemon juice, 1 or 2 slices of lemon or the juice and skin of ¼ orange. Sweeten, if you like.

REFRIGERATOR PRUNES

Put prunes in a fruit jar. Add enough water to cover. Screw on the top. Store in the refrigerator 4 days or more. The prunes will be plump and delicious but with a different flavor and texture from cooked prunes.

BAKED QUINCES

Wipe, quarter, core and pare. Put in a casserole, sprinkle with sugar (2 tablespoons to each quince) and add water ½ inch deep. For an interesting flavor, add 1 sliced orange (for 4 or more quinces). Bake at 300°

until tender and deep red (about 2 hours). Serve cold.

RASPBERRIES

One pint serves 3. Ripe raspberries are very delicate. Look them over and remove all imperfect berries. Then dip them, a few at a time, in and out of cold water, holding them carefully in your hand or in a single layer in a coarse strainer. Drain well on a paper towel.

Serve with powdered sugar and cream. For the finest flavor, serve as soon after picking as possible.

STEWED RHUBARB

One pound makes about 2 cups, cooked. Hothouse rhubarb is pink, with light green leaves. Rhubarb grown out of doors is darker and needs longer cooking. Select firm young stalks with fresh-looking leaves.

Cut off the leaves and the stem ends. Wash. If the rhubarb is young and the skin is tender, do not peel. Cut in 1-inch pieces. Sprinkle generously with sugar and, if you like, a few gratings of orange or lemon peel. Add just enough water to prevent burning. Cover and cook gently until just barely tender (7 to 20 minutes). Taste and add more sugar if necessary.

Baked Rhubarb. Prepare 1 pound of rhubarb. Add ½ cup sugar. Put in a casserole, sprinkle with salt, cover and bake at 325° until tender. If baked slowly for a long time, rhubarb has a rich red color. Taste and add more sugar if needed. Cook in a double boiler, if more convenient.

Rhubarb in Syrup. Prepare 1 pound very tender rhubarb. Put ¾ cup sugar and ¾ cup water in a saucepan. Bring to the boiling point and add the rhubarb. Stir to mix well. Again bring to the boiling point. Cover and let stand until cool.

RHUBARB COMPOTE

Add sliced strawberries or pineapple bits to cooked rhubarb. Sprinkle with grated orange or lemon rind and a slight dusting of ginger.

STRAWBERRIES

One quart serves 4 to 6. Small, early berries often have fine flavor. Learn the best local varieties and ask for them by name.

Discard imperfect berries. Place perfect berries in a colander and pour cold water over them. Drain thoroughly and remove the hulls. Serve with powdered sugar and sweet or sour cream. If the berries are not very sweet, sprinkle with sugar and let stand ½ hour before serving. Large perfect berries are delicious served unhulled, ready to dip in powdered sugar.

Strawberries and Bananas. Cut berries in half. Mix with bananas cut in pieces about the same size.

Strawberries in Whipped Cream. Cut 1 quart berries in half and sprinkle with sugar. Whip ½ pint heavy cream until stiff, sweeten with sugar, and flavor with vanilla, brandy, Cointreau or sherry. Fold in the berries. *Serves 5 or 6.*

Strawberries in Claret. Pour ¼ cup claret over 1 quart berries. Sprinkle with sugar to taste. *Serves 4.*

Lenox Strawberries. Mix ½ cup orange juice, ½ cup sugar and

1 teaspoon curaçao. Pour over 1 quart berries, hulled. Serve with whipped cream.

STRAWBERRIES ROMANOFF

Wash, drain and hull
2 quarts strawberries
Beat with a fork to soften slightly
1 pint vanilla ice cream
Fold in
½ pint heavy cream, whipped
Stir in gently
Juice of 1 lemon
¼ cup rum *or* Cointreau
Taste, and add if needed
Confectioners' sugar
Fold in the berries and serve immediately. *Serves 8.*

STRAWBERRIES IN SHERRY CREAM

A superb dessert, fit for a gala dinner.

Put in a double boiler top
5 egg yolks
Beat with an electric or hand beater until thick and lemon-colored. Beat in
1 cup sugar
1 cup sherry
Cook and stir over hot water until thick. Cool. Shortly before serving time, fold in
½ pint heavy cream, whipped
3 pints strawberries, washed and hulled
Serves 6 to 8.

STRAWBERRIES FLAMBÉ

A handsome party dessert to prepare at the table in a chafing dish.

Wash, hull and dry
1 quart strawberries
Put in a pan
1 lemon peel, cut in pieces
Juice and peel of 2 oranges
8 lumps sugar
Cook slowly 5 minutes, pressing the peel with a spoon to get all the flavor possible. Take out the peel and discard it. Add the berries. Spoon the hot syrup gently over the berries until they are well coated. Add
½ cup brandy
Light with a match. Serve over
1½ quarts vanilla ice cream
Serves 8.

TANGERINES

Wipe fruit. Serve whole or pull off loose skin, separate sections, and remove all white stringlike parts. Serve around simple desserts or cut in pieces, remove the seeds, and add to a fruit cup or fruit salad.

WATERMELON

Buy a whole watermelon or a part of one, by the pound. Chill thoroughly. Cut in wedges or slices and serve with salt or powdered sugar.

WATERMELON COCKTAIL

Cut the ripe deep pink part in ¾-inch cubes or balls. Sprinkle with lemon juice and sugar, put in a jar, and let stand in the refrigerator several hours. Serve in sherbet glasses or on green leaves.

Watermelon with Sherry Dressing. In place of lemon juice and sugar, mix ½ cup sugar, ½ cup sherry, 2 tablespoons sloe gin (if desired) and a few grains of salt. Let stand until the sugar is dissolved. *Serves 6.*

APPLE SNOW

Best when prepared within half an hour of serving.

Beat until stiff
2 egg whites
Beat in slowly
Applesauce (very cold)
adding as much as will keep the whip stiff enough to pile in a bowl or individual dishes. Serve very cold with
Soft Custard (p. 384), made with brown sugar
Serves 4.

BANANA WHIP

Peel and scrape
3 bananas
Force through a sieve. Add
¾ cup sugar
¼ cup lemon juice
Cook just to the boiling point. Chill. Fold into
½ pint heavy cream, whipped
Spoon into dessert glasses. Sprinkle with
Chopped salted peanuts
Serves 4.

RASPBERRY *or* STRAWBERRY WHIP

Beat until stiff with a wire whisk or an electric beater
1¼ cups berries, cut in half
1 cup powdered sugar
1 egg white
Serve on pieces of sponge cake or angel food or pile in a bowl and serve with Soft Custard (p. 384). *Serves 4.*

MARMALADE SOUFFLÉ

For an extra touch, sprinkle each serving with coarsely chopped toasted almonds.

Beat until stiff but not dry
3 egg whites
Beat in gradually
3 tablespoons sugar
Fold in
3 tablespoons orange marmalade
¼ teaspoon orange extract
Grated rind of 1 orange
Spoon into a buttered double boiler top. Cook 1 hour over boiling water. Serve with
Zabaglione (p. 386) *or* Floradora Sauce (p. 435), made with 3 egg yolks
Serves 4 or 5.

PRUNE *or* APRICOT WHIP

Rub cooked or canned fruit through a strainer or use canned strained fruit to make
¾ cup prune *or* apricot pulp
Add
Sugar to taste
Cook until as thick as marmalade. Add
1 tablespoon lemon juice
⅛ teaspoon salt
Cool. Beat until stiff
3 egg whites
Fold the fruit carefully into the egg whites. Spoon into a straight-sided unbuttered baking dish. Set in a pan of hot water. Bake at 300° until firm when pressed lightly with a finger (about 45 minutes). Serve with
Soft Custard (p. 384), Sabayon Sauce (p. 434) *or* whipped cream
Serves 4.

To cook in a double boiler. Spoon into the top of a large double boiler and cook over hot water until firm (about 45 minutes).

Quick Prune Whip. Sweeten canned prune pulp (baby food) to taste. Fold into stiffly beaten egg white. Spoon into dessert glasses. Serve with whipped cream or custard or top with chopped nuts.

NORWEGIAN PRUNE PUDDING

Put in a double boiler top
1 cup prune pulp (see Prune Whip)
½ cup prune juice

¾ cup sugar, brown *or* white
⅛ teaspoon salt
¼ teaspoon cinnamon
1 cup boiling water

Simmer 5 minutes over low heat. Mix until smooth

4 tablespoons cornstarch
⅓ cup cold water

Add to the prune mixture. Cook and stir until thick. Set over hot water and cook 10 minutes longer. Add

2 tablespoons lemon juice (or to taste)

Chill. Serve with cream. *Serves 4 to 6.*

Nut Prune Soufflé. Fold into the finished pudding 2 egg whites, beaten stiff, and ½ cup walnut meats, broken in pieces.

CRÈME AUX FRUITS

Mix

1 envelope gelatine (1 tablespoon)
½ cup sugar
Few grains salt

Add

½ cup milk

Cook and stir over low heat until the gelatine dissolves. Chill until as thick as unbeaten egg white. Add

2 egg whites

Beat until almost stiff. Stir in

½ cup cooked prunes, cut small
½ cup chopped figs

Fold in

½ pint heavy cream, whipped

Mold. *Serves 6 to 8.*

BROWN BETTY

For a rich nutlike flavor (good for you, too) use half bread crumbs and half toasted wheat germ. Corn flakes are good, too, in place of crumbs.

Mix lightly with a fork

2 cups bread crumbs
¼ cup melted butter

Prepare

4 cups sliced tart apples (peeled)

Mix

½ cup sugar, brown *or* white
¼ teaspoon grated nutmeg *or* 1 teaspoon cinnamon
Grated rind and juice of ½ lemon

Butter a baking dish. Put a layer of crumbs in it. Spread half the apples over the crumbs, then half the sugar mixture. Repeat and cover with the rest of the crumbs. Add

½ cup hot water

Bake 40 minutes at 350°. Cover at first so that the crumbs will not brown too quickly. Serve with

Cream *or* Maryland Sauce (p. 435)

Serves 6.

Apricot Brown Betty. Use 2 cups stewed and drained apricots in place of apples. Use apricot juice in place of lemon juice and water.

Peach Brown Betty. Use equal quantities sliced peaches and bread crumbs. Omit lemon and nutmeg. Syrup from canned peaches may be used in place of water (omitting sugar).

Rhubarb Brown Betty. Use equal quantities cooked rhubarb and bread crumbs. Season to taste. Omit water.

APPLE CRISP (APPLE CANDY PIE)

Instead of ¾ cup flour, you may use ¼ cup powdered skim milk, ¼ cup rolled oats and 6 tablespoons flour. An easy way to add extra protein.

Butter a deep baking dish. Put in it

4 cups sliced tart apples (peeled)
½ cup water (less for juicy apples)

Mix with a fork

¾ cup flour
1 cup white *or* brown sugar
1 teaspoon cinnamon

½ cup butter
¼ teaspoon salt

Spread over the apples. Bake at 350° until the apples are tender and the crust brown (about 30 minutes). Serve with

Cream *or* whipped cream

Serves 6 to 8.

Corn Flake Apple Crisp. Use 1 cup crushed corn flakes in place of flour. Melt the butter and stir it in.

Peach Crumble Pie. Slice peaches into a shallow baking dish. Sprinkle with the crumb mixture and bake as above.

CAPE COD APPLE PUDDING

Put in a deep pan

3 cups sliced tart apples (peeled)
¾ cup sugar
¼ teaspoon salt
½ teaspoon nutmeg *or* cinnamon (or both)

Cook until the apples are tender, adding a little water, if necessary, to keep the apples from burning. Roll out to fit the top of the pan

Baking Powder Biscuit dough, homemade (p. 326) or a mix

Spread over the apples. Cover tightly. Cook 15 minutes over moderate heat. Turn out and serve with

Cream

Serves 6.

DUTCH APPLE PUDDING

In the fall, use tart crisp "pie" apples. Later, if apples lack flavor, add nutmeg or cinnamon or grated lemon rind.

Set the oven at 350°. Butter a 9-inch pie pan. Pare, core and dice

2 large apples (about 1 cup)

Beat

1 egg

Beat in

1 cup sugar

Add the apples and

2 tablespoons flour
1 teaspoon baking powder
¼ teaspoon salt
½ cup chopped nut meats

Spread in the pan and bake until brown and crusty (about 25 minutes). Serve in wedges, warm or cold. *Serves 6.*

For a richer dessert, serve with sour cream, whipped cream or ice cream.

APPLE COBBLER

Good with canned fruit, too.

Prepare

2 cups sliced pared apples

Add

Few grains salt
Sugar to taste
1 egg, well beaten, *or* 1 tablespoon quick tapioca *or* flour

Spread in a buttered baking dish and dot with butter. Spread over the top

Shortcake (p. 381) *or* Cottage Pudding (p. 394) batter

Bake at 425° about 30 minutes. Serve with

Whipped cream, Vanilla Sauce (p. 432) *or* Foamy Sauce (p. 434)

Serves 6.

Berry Cobbler. Use blackberries, loganberries or blueberries.

Peach Cobbler. Use peaches. Put in a peach pit or two for extra good flavor.

Sour Cherry Cobbler. Pit the cherries. Cook 5 minutes in just enough water to keep them from burning. Sweeten to taste.

APPLE PAN DOWDY

Set the oven at 350°. Butter a 1½-quart baking dish. Put in it

3 cups sliced tart apples (peeled)

Sprinkle with

½ cup molasses *or* brown sugar
¼ teaspoon nutmeg
¼ teaspoon cinnamon
¼ teaspoon salt

Bake until the apples are soft. Meanwhile prepare

Cottage Pudding batter (p. 394)

Spread it over the apples. Continue baking until the top is brown and crusty (about 25 minutes). Serve from the dish or turn out with the apples on top. Serve with

Hard Sauce (p. 434) *or* whipped cream

Serves 6.

Cherry, Rhubarb *or* Blueberry Pan Dowdy. Stew the fruit, sweeten to taste and pour into the baking dish. Heat, if necessary, and pour the batter over it. Bake as above.

CAPE COD BLUEBERRY GRUNT

An old-fashioned treat.

Cook until soft

2 cups blueberries
½ cup water
⅛ teaspoon allspice

Sweeten to taste. Put in a deep baking dish. Put over the top

Baking Powder Biscuit dough (p. 326) or unbaked biscuits

Set the dish in a pan of boiling water. Cover. Cook 1 hour, keeping the water boiling constantly. Add more water as needed to keep it within 1 inch of the top of the dish. Serve from the dish with

Heavy cream

Serves 4.

MAINE BLUEBERRY PUDDING

Wild berries have the finest flavor. If you use cultivated berries add lemon juice to taste.

Cook 10 minutes

3 cups blueberries
¾ cup sugar
½ cup water

Butter

6 slices bread

Sprinkle with

Cinnamon

Put the bread and the berries in a loaf pan in layers. Chill in the refrigerator several hours. Slice and serve with

Heavy cream

Serves 6.

SHORTCAKE

Old-fashioned shortcake is always made with biscuit dough, not cake, and is served with unsweetened heavy cream, unwhipped. This type of shortcake is perfect for a leisurely Sunday morning breakfast as well as for dessert.

Set the oven at 425°. Butter a 9-inch round cake pan. Sift together.

2 cups flour
4 teaspoons tartrate *or* phosphate baking powder *or* 2 teaspoons combination type
½ teaspoon salt
1 tablespoon sugar
Few grains nutmeg

With a blending fork or fingers, work in

4 tablespoons butter

Stir in, little by little

Milk (about ¾ cup)

until the dough holds together but is still soft. Turn out on a floured board and divide in two parts. Pat or roll out into 9-inch rounds. Put one round in the pan. Spread lightly with

2 tablespoons melted butter

Place the other half on top. Bake 12 minutes. Split carefully with a fork. Spread with

2 tablespoons butter (or more)

Put between the layers and on top

Prepared fruit (p. 382)

Serve warm with

Heavy cream, whipped or not

Serves 6.

To make individual shortcakes, cut the dough with a large biscuit cutter.

Fruit for shortcake. Strawberries and raspberries are the favorites. Allow 1 quart for 6 servings. Crush slightly. Sweeten to taste and warm slightly. Save a few perfect berries to garnish the top. Other fruits to use are warm applesauce, sliced and sugared bananas, warm stewed blueberries, sliced and sweetened peaches or apricots.

Rich Shortcake. Increase the sugar to ⅓ cup and the butter to ⅓ cup. Add a well-beaten egg before stirring in the milk. You will need only about ⅓ cup milk.

BLACKBERRY ROLYPOLY

Set the oven at 425°. Butter a pan 8 by 12 inches.

Prepare
Shortcake dough (p. 381)
Roll into an oblong ½ inch thick. Brush with
2 tablespoons melted butter
Mix
6 cups blackberries *or* blueberries
1 cup sugar
½ teaspoon salt
Sprinkle half the fruit mixture over the dough. Roll up like a jelly roll. Put in the pan with the fold on the bottom. Put the rest of the fruit around the roll. Bake about 30 minutes. Cut in slices and serve with
Whipped cream *or* Lemon Sauce (p. 432).
Serves 6 to 8.

Blueberry Rolypoly. Use blueberries in place of blackberries.

APPLE, PEACH *or* APRICOT DUMPLINGS

Roll or pat Baking Powder Biscuit (p. 326) or Shortcake dough (p. 381) ¼ inch thick. Cut in 4-inch squares. Place whole fruit, pared and cored or pitted, on the squares. Fill the fruit with sugar mixed with cinnamon or nutmeg. Sprinkle with grated cheese or dot with butter. Draw the corners of the dough together on top of the fruit. Pinch the edges together. Prick with a fork.

Bake 30 minutes at 350°. Serve with Hard Sauce (p. 434), Foamy Sauce (p. 434) or Lemon Sauce (p. 432).

DUTCH APPLE KUCHEN

Spread Shortcake (p. 381) or Lightning Cake (p. 496) dough ¾ inch thick in buttered round or oblong pan. Pare 5 tart apples, core, cut in eighths and press sharp edges of apples into dough in parallel rows. Sprinkle with ½ cup sugar mixed with ½ teaspoon cinnamon, also 2 tablespoons currants or seedless raisins, if liked.

Bake at 350° until apples are tender (about 25 minutes). Serve with Hard Sauce (p. 434), Soft Custard (p. 384), Lemon Sauce (p. 432) or whipped cream.
Serves 6 to 8.

Plum, Peach *or* Apricot Kuchen. Use stoned plums, peaches or apricots in place of apples.

APPLE or PLUM CAKE

Line a shallow oblong pan with Galette Pastry (p. 440), having the rim about ¾ inch high. Fill with stewed and strained apples or plums, sweetened to taste. Bake at 400° (about 25 minutes).

LEMON JELLY

Put in a bowl
½ cup cold water

1 envelope gelatine
(1 tablespoon)

Add

½ cup sugar
Few grains salt
1 cup boiling water

Stir until the sugar dissolves. Add

½ cup lemon juice

Pour in molds or sherbet glasses. *Serves 4.*

Grapefruit Jelly. Use only ¾ cup boiling water. In place of lemon juice, use ¾ cup grapefruit juice.

Orange Jelly. Use only ½ cup boiling water. Instead of lemon juice, use 1 cup orange juice, fresh or made from a frozen concentrate. If the orange juice is very sweet, use less sugar and replace part of the orange juice with lemon juice.

APRICOT AND WINE JELLY

Mix

2 envelopes gelatine
(2 tablespoons)
1 cup sugar

Add

1½ cups boiling water

Stir until the gelatine dissolves. Add

1 cup apricot juice
1 tablespoon lemon juice
1 cup sherry *or* port

Put, cut side up, in 8 individual molds

Canned apricot halves

Fill the molds with the jelly mixture. Chill. *Serves 8.*

JELLIED FRUIT

Brush a mold lightly with salad oil. Chill Lemon (p. 382) or Orange (above) or Wine (p. 397) Jelly until it is as thick as unbeaten egg white. Add the prepared fruit (below) and pour into the mold.

To prepare the fruit. Prepare 1 to 2 cups of fruit for each 2 cups of jelly. Appropriate fruits are sliced bananas, whole strawberries, raspberries and pitted cherries, grapefruit and orange sections, peeled and seeded grapes, peeled and diced apples, peaches and pears and drained canned fruit of all kinds. Do not use fresh pineapple—it will prevent the jelly from stiffening.

To unmold. Dip the mold in warm water to the depth of the gelatine. Loosen around the edge with the tip of a knife. Put the serving dish, bottom up, on top of the mold. Quickly turn upside down.

Shake lightly to loosen the jelly. If the jelly sticks, wipe the mold with a cloth wrung out of hot water.

To serve. Surround with more fruit or top with whipped cream.

Custards, Puddings and Other Desserts

In spite of modern efforts to reduce calories, most families enjoy a sweet at the close of the meal. The choice is wide, so that a delicate pudding can follow a hearty main course or a rich dessert can eke out a lighter meal. Desserts may be made the vehicle for added protein and vitamins—add powdered skim milk, toasted wheat germ and brewer's yeast to basic recipes whenever you can.

SOFT CUSTARD

Satin-smooth soft custard is the basis for a whole group of beguiling desserts. A jar of custard in the refrigerator is a joy if you need to concoct a dessert in a hurry. To be sure of perfect custard, clip a candy thermometer to the side of the pan and cook the custard to 175°.

Beat enough to blend evenly
6 yolks *or* 3 eggs
Add
¼ cup white *or* brown sugar
⅛ teaspoon salt
2 cups scalded milk
Cook and stir over very low heat or in a double boiler over hot but not boiling water until the custard coats a spoon (about 7 minutes). Chill. Flavor with
½ teaspoon vanilla *or* sherry to taste

If the custard curdles (because the water boiled or the custard was overcooked), beat with an egg beater. It will be thinner than it should be, but smooth.

Custard Sauce. Use only 3 egg yolks or 1 egg and 1 yolk.

Coconut Custard. Pour the cooked custard into a baking dish. Beat 3 egg whites until stiff, fold in ½ cup sugar and ¾ cup shredded coconut and spread over the custard. Brown delicately in a 450° oven (about 5 minutes).

Chocolate Pôts de Crème. Scald with the milk 2 ounces unsweetened chocolate. Pour the finished custard into small pottery bowls. Let stand until firm. When ready to serve, pour a thin layer of heavy cream over the pudding.

Floating Island. Top chilled custard with whipped cream or spoonfuls of Meringue (p. 441) poached in hot milk. Decorate with shaved sweet chocolate, a bit of bright jelly, slivered toasted almonds or a dribble of Caramel (p. 510).

Chocolate Floating Island. Beat 1 egg white until stiff, beat in 2 tablespoons confectioners' sugar and dry Dutch-type cocoa to taste. Add a few drops vanilla. Put spoonfuls on chilled custard.

TIPSY PUDDING

Put in a bowl

½ cup sherry

Dip in it

¼ pound lady fingers *or* cubes of dry unfrosted cake

Put in a serving bowl. Cover with

Soft Custard (p. 384)

Chill. Garnish with

Whipped cream, macaroon crumbs *or* chopped nut meats

Serves 4 to 6.

English Trifle. Spread over the lady fingers 1 cup sliced fruit such as fresh or canned peaches, pears, bananas or orange sections. For a particularly delicious trifle, spread canned nesselrode sauce over the lady fingers. You will need only about ½ cup since the sauce is rich with marrons and brandied fruits.

PRESSURE-COOKED CUSTARDS

To give these miraculous custards an oven-baked look, sprinkle with brown sugar and glaze under the broiler.

Beat until evenly blended

2 eggs

Beat in

2 tablespoons sugar

Add slowly, beating with a fork

1½ cups scalded milk

Add

1 teaspoon vanilla
⅛ teaspoon salt

Butter 4 glass or aluminum custard cups. Fill. Cover with foil or wax paper held firmly with rubber bands. Set on a rack in a pressure cooker. Pour around them ½ cup boiling water. Adjust the cover and cook 45 seconds at 15 pounds pressure, or follow the directions with your cooker. *Makes 4 small custards.*

Skillet Custard. Put a double thickness of paper towels in a deep heavy frying pan which has a tight-fitting cover. Pour in cold water ¾ inch deep. Put in the custards. Cover. Set over the heat and bring to the boiling point. Turn off the heat and steam until set (15 to 20 minutes).

BAKED CUSTARD

Custards are delicious warm or chilled and served with fresh fruit or cream.

Beat just enough to blend evenly

3 eggs *or* 6 egg yolks

Stir in

½ cup sugar
¼ teaspoon salt

Add slowly, beating with a fork

3 cups scalded milk
1 teaspoon vanilla

Pour into buttered custard cups. Sprinkle with

Nutmeg

Set in a shallow pan on a paper towel. Pour into the pan hot water about 1 inch deep. Bake at 350° about 45 minutes or about 20 minutes at 400°. Test by inserting a silver knife into the custard near the edge: if it comes out clean, the custard will be firm when it cools. *Makes 6 small custards.*

To make custard in one large dish, use 4 eggs so that it will be firm enough to turn out onto a serving dish without cracking. Use brown or maple sugar for a delicious variation.

Baked Coconut Custard. Add ½ cup shredded coconut. Omit the nutmeg.

Coffee Custard. Add instant coffee and vanilla or rum to taste. Omit nutmeg.

Queen Anne Custard. Use 1 egg and 4 yolks. Spread the finished custard with tart jelly or sprinkle with 3 tablespoons curaçao. Chill. Cover with Meringue (p. 441) made of 4 whites and 4 tablespoons sugar. Sprinkle with grated orange peel. Bake 5 minutes at 425°. *Serves 6.*

CARAMEL CUSTARD

For custard and sauce in one, caramelize $1\frac{1}{2}$ cups of sugar and pour half into the cups, adding the rest to the milk.

Scald
3 cups milk
While it is heating, melt in a small heavy pan over low heat
¾ cup sugar
Stir slowly into the hot milk and continue stirring until the sugar melts. Pour slowly over
6 egg yolks *or* 3 eggs, beaten
Add
¼ teaspoon salt
1 teaspoon vanilla
Bake (see Baked Custard, p. 385). Serve with
Caramel Sauce (p. 430)
Serves 6.

ZABAGLIONE

Marsala is traditional for this famous Italian dessert.

Beat until thick and lemon-colored
4 egg yolks
2 tablespoons powdered sugar
Put in a heavy round-bottomed bowl. Set over hot (not boiling) water. Beat constantly with electric or rotary hand beater, adding little by little
2 tablespoons Marsala, port, Tokay *or* sherry
Beat until mixture begins to hold its shape but is still smooth. Pile immediately into heated thick cups or sherbet glasses. (If crust has formed from overcooking, do not scrape bowl.) Serve warm or very cold with simple wafers. *Serves 2 or 3.*

Zabaglione with Pears. Pour Zabaglione over drained canned or stewed pears in a shallow dish. Serve ice-cold.

Coffee Rum Zabaglione. In place of wine, use ¼ cup strong cold coffee and 2 teaspoons rum.

Coffee Zabaglione Frappé and Zabaglione Frappé. See pages 424 and 427.

CRÈME BRÛLÉE

Heavy cream is used in the classic recipe, but half evaporated milk is successful and not as rich. With a French salamander, you can prepare Crème Brûlée in your best china bowl; but if you glaze it under the broiler, use a heatproof dish.

Scald in a double boiler
1 pint heavy cream
Beat until smooth
4 eggs *or* 8 yolks
¼ cup brown sugar
¼ teaspoon salt
Add the cream clowly. Put back in the double boiler and cook 5 minutes or until the custard coats a metal spoon, beating constantly with an electric or hand rotary beater. Do not overcook. Pour into a serving bowl or heatproof dish in a layer not more than 2 inches deep. Chill. Sift over the top
¼ cup brown sugar
Glaze. Chill at least 4 hours so that the glaze will be crackly. *Serves 6.*

Baked Crème Brûlée. After adding the cream, bake in a shallow heatproof dish. Not quite as delicate, but easier.

To glaze with a salamander. Heat the salamander thoroughly

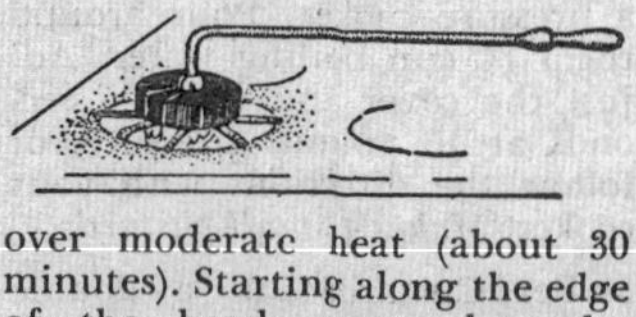

over moderate heat (about 30 minutes). Starting along the edge of the bowl, move the salamander around just above the surface until the sugar browns and melts into a thin even glaze. Reheat the salamander as necessary.

To glaze under the broiler. Pour the cooked crème into a shallow heatproof dish. Set under the broiler in a cold oven. Turn on the heat and brown, moving the dish to make an even glaze.

PUERTO RICO COCONUT CREAM

Its Puerto Rico name, "bien me sabe," means "It tastes good to me."

Drain the milk from

1 coconut

Set it aside. Grate the meat. Heat the coconut meat and milk in a double boiler ½ hour. Squeeze through a piece of linen. You should have about 1 cupful. Beat until thick.

4 egg yolks

Beat in the coconut cream. Put in a small pan

¾ cup sugar
¼ cup water

Boil 5 minutes and add slowly to the coconut mixture. Cook over hot water until thickened, stirring with a wooden spoon. Flavor with

Vanilla *or* rum, to taste

Cool and serve over

Sponge cake squares

Serves 6 to 8.

CORNSTARCH PUDDING (BLANC MANGE)

Simple packaged pudding mixes are similar to this recipe. Any variations suggested here may be used with them.

Scald in a double boiler

2 cups milk

Mix

3 tablespoons cornstarch
⅓ cup sugar
¼ teaspoon salt

Add and stir until smooth

¼ cup cold milk

Add to the scalded milk. Cook 15 minutes over hot water, stirring constantly until the pudding thickens, afterward occasionally. Cool slightly and add

1 teaspoon vanilla

Chill. *Serves 4.*

To vary. Add ½ cup shredded or grated coconut to the scalded milk, or add ¾ cup broken nut meats or crushed pineapple to the finished pudding.

For a more delicate pudding, beat 2 egg whites until stiff and fold them into the finished pudding.

Butterscotch Pudding. Omit the white sugar. Melt 1 tablespoon butter, add 1 cup brown sugar, cook and stir until the sugar melts. Add slowly to the hot scalded milk and stir until well blended. Mix the cornstarch and salt with the cold milk and continue as above.

Chocolate Pudding. Scald the milk with 2 ounces unsweetened chocolate. Beat until smooth. Serve with cream, plain or whipped, or fold in ½ cup heavy cream, whipped.

SPANISH CREAM

For a gala dessert, flavor with sherry or brandy. Garnish with alternate spoonfuls of whipped cream and orange marmalade, Bar-le-Duc currants or marrons, or with canned fruit.

Mix in a saucepan

1 envelope gelatine (1 tablespoon)
Few grains salt
2 tablespoons sugar

Beat together and pour over the gelatine

2 egg yolks, slightly beaten
1 cup milk

Cook and stir over low heat

until the gelatine dissolves (about 5 minutes). Add

1 cup milk
½ teaspoon vanilla

Chill until slightly firm. Beat until they stand in soft peaks

2 egg whites

Beat in, a tablespoon at a time

¼ cup sugar

Fold into the gelatine mixture. Pour into a bowl or into a mold dipped in cold water. As the cream cools, it divides prettily with a foamy top over a layer of smooth custard. *Serves 4.*

Chocolate Spanish Cream. Scald the milk with 1 ounce unsweetened chocolate. Beat until smooth. Sweeten the finished pudding to taste.

Coffee Spanish Cream. Flavor with instant coffee. Add sugar as needed.

Macaroon Spanish Cream. Before adding the egg whites, pour the pudding into a bowl set in ice water and add ½ cup dry macaroon crumbs. Stir until slightly thickened. Fold in the whites, mold, and chill. Change the flavoring by substituting almond flavoring for vanilla or by adding brandy to taste.

BAVARIAN CREAM

Very impressive made in a mold lined with lady fingers or strips of sponge cake.

Mix in a saucepan

1 envelope gelatine (1 tablespoon)
Few grains salt
¼ cup sugar

Beat together until well blended

2 egg yolks
1¼ cups milk

Add to the gelatine. Cook and stir over low heat until the gelatine dissolves (about 5 minutes). Add

½ teaspoon vanilla

Chill until the mixture begins to stiffen. Beat until in soft peaks

2 egg whites

Beat in, a little at a time

¼ cup sugar

Fold into the gelatine mixture. Beat until stiff

½ pint heavy cream

Fold into the gelatine mixture until smooth. Mold in individual molds or one large mold. Garnish or flavor as suggested for Spanish Cream. *Serves 6.*

TAPIOCA CREAM

Tapioca stiffens as it cools; it should be soft when you finish cooking it.

Break into a saucepan

1 egg

Beat with a fork, just enough to blend the yolk and white. Add

2 tablespoons tapioca
¼ cup white *or* brown sugar
¼ teaspoon salt
2 cups milk

Cook and stir over moderate heat until the pudding boils. Let stand 15 minutes. Stir in

½ teaspoon vanilla

As a garnish, top each serving with

Whipped cream *or* a dab of jelly

Serves 4.

For a fluffier pudding, separate the egg. Cook the yolk with the pudding. Beat the white until stiff, beat in 1 tablespoon sugar. Fold into the finished pudding.

Chocolate Tapioca. Add ¼ cup cocoa and 1 tablespoon butter.

Coconut Tapioca. Add ¼ cup shredded coconut.

Coffee Tapioca. Add 2 teaspoons instant coffee.

Baked Tapioca Custard. Add 1 tablespoon butter. Instead of cooking over direct heat, pour into a buttered baking dish and bake 45 minutes at 325°.

BUTTERSCOTCH TAPIOCA

Melt in a small heavy pan
1 tablespoon butter
Add
1 cup brown sugar
Cook and stir over low heat until the sugar melts. Break into a saucepan
1 egg
Beat with a fork just enough to blend the yolk and white. Add
2 tablespoons quick tapioca
2 cups milk
¼ teaspoon salt
Cook and stir over moderate heat until the pudding boils. Add the melted sugar slowly and stir until it dissolves evenly. Cool slightly and add
1 teaspoon vanilla
Serves 4.

Peanut Butterscotch Tapioca. Omit the salt. Stir into the finished pudding ½ cup chopped, salted peanuts.

Date Butterscotch Tapioca. Stir into the finished pudding ½ cup chopped dates.

NEWTON TAPIOCA

Put in a bowl
¼ cup corn meal
Scald in a double boiler
1 quart milk
Pour it over the corn meal. Add
½ cup quick tapioca
¾ cup molasses
3 tablespoons butter
1½ teaspoons salt
Pour back into the double boiler and cook 20 minutes. Pour into a buttered baking dish. Without stirring, pour over the pudding
1 cup cold milk
Bake 1¼ hours. Start the oven at 450°. When the pudding begins to separate like Indian pudding, reduce the heat to 350°. *Serves 6 to 8.*

APPLE TAPIOCA

Set the oven at 350°. Put in a baking dish
3 cups sliced tart apples (peeled)
Mix
½ cup white *or* brown sugar
½ teaspoon cinnamon
Sprinkle over the apples. Bake 15 minutes. Meanwhile, put in a saucepan
2 cups boiling water
⅓ cup quick tapioca
⅛ teaspoon salt
¼ cup sugar
Cook and stir over moderate heat until the tapioca is transparent (5 to 10 minutes). Pour over the apples. Continue baking until the apples are tender. Serve warm or cold with
Heavy cream, whipped or not
Serves 4 to 6.

Peach Tapioca. Drain canned peaches, reserving the juice. Slice the peaches into a baking dish. Sprinkle with powdered sugar (¼ cup for 2 cups fruit). Let stand 1 hour. Heat the peach juice and enough water to make 2 cups, add the tapioca, and cook as above. Pour over the peaches and bake ½ hour at 350°.

RICE DESSERT

Serve hot cooked rice with Chocolate (p. 430) or Butterscotch Sauce (p. 429) or with cream and brown sugar, grated maple sugar or confectioners' sugar mixed with a little cinnamon.

RICE CUSTARD

Add ½ cup raisins, if you like.

Heat in a double boiler
2 cups milk
1 cup cooked rice
Beat until smooth
2 egg yolks

½ cup sugar
¼ teaspoon salt

Add the milk and rice slowly. Pour back into the double boiler and cook until thick. Fold in

2 egg whites, beaten stiff

Add

½ teaspoon vanilla *or* lemon juice to taste

Serve warm or cold. *Serves 4 to 6.*

Rice Meringue. Set the oven at 425°. Without adding the egg whites, pour the cooked pudding into a baking dish. Beat the whites with 2 tablespoons powdered sugar and ½ teaspoon lemon juice and spoon over the top. Bake until delicately brown (about 5 minutes). Meringue is at its best if served within an hour of baking. The pudding can be prepared ahead of time and the meringue added later.

OLD-FASHIONED RICE PUDDING

Very soft and creamy. For a firm pudding, use ½ cup of rice. Brown rice gives a delicious flavor. For a richer pudding, stir in 1 or 2 well-beaten eggs 30 minutes before the pudding is done.

Put in a casserole

4 cups milk
⅔ cup sugar
¼ cup uncooked rice
½ teaspoon salt
1 teaspoon vanilla *or* a dash of nutmeg *or* the grated rind of ½ lemon

Bake, uncovered, 3 hours at 300°. During the first hour, stir three times with a fork so that the rice will not settle. After the first hour, stir in

½ cup raisins, dates *or* figs, cut small

Poor Man's Pudding. In place of sugar, use ⅓ cup molasses. Flavor with ½ teaspoon cinnamon. At the last stirring, add 1 tablespoon butter.

LEMON CREAM RICE

For a richer pudding, stir 1 tablespoon butter into the rice mixture and use 4 eggs instead of 2.

Put in a double boiler top

3 cups milk
½ cup rice

Cook over hot water until the rice is soft (about 30 minutes). Add

½ cup sugar
Grated rind of ½ lemon
1½ tablespoons lemon juice
¾ teaspoon salt
2 egg yolks, slightly beaten

Cook until thickened, stirring gently. Spoon into a buttered baking dish. Cool. Beat until in soft peaks

2 egg whites

Beat in

2 tablespoons confectioners' sugar
½ teaspoon lemon juice

Spoon over the pudding. Bake at 425° long enough to brown the meringue (about 5 minutes). *Serves 6.*

RICE CREAM

Heat in a double boiler

2 cups milk

Add

3 tablespoons uncooked rice

Cook until the rice is tender (about 30 minutes). Mix

1 envelope gelatine (1 tablespoon)
1 tablespoon sugar
¼ teaspoon salt

Add to the rice. Mix thoroughly. Cool. Fold in

½ pint heavy cream, whipped
1 teaspoon vanilla

Mold or spoon into dessert dishes. Serve with any sauce suitable for ice cream or pour maple syrup over the pudding and sprinkle with chopped nuts. *Serves 6.*

Pineapple Rice. Before molding, fold in 1 cup well-drained crushed pineapple.

BREAD PUDDING

So many combinations make an excellent bread pudding that a recipe is only a general guide. If you prefer a sweeter pudding, add more sugar. Season discreetly with any spice. To make a firmer pudding, use less milk, even as little as 2 cups. To make a fluffier pudding, separate the eggs and add the whites last, beaten stiff. For a richer pudding, add 1 cup orange marmalade, chopped raisins, dates or figs, or add ½ cup chopped nut meats.

Butter a baking dish. Put in it

2 cups dry bread crumbs
4 tablespoons butter
1 quart hot milk

Cool. Set the oven at 325°. Add to the crumbs and milk

½ cup sugar
2 eggs, slightly beaten
½ teaspoon salt
1 teaspoon vanilla

Stir to blend. Bake 1 hour. Serve with plain or whipped cream, Melba Sauce (p. 433), Yellow Sauce (p. 435) or Hard Sauce (p. 434). *Serves 6.*

Butterscotch Bread Pudding. In place of white sugar, use 1 cup brown sugar. Cook the sugar with the butter until it melts to a syrup. Add to the crumbs.

Coconut Bread Pudding. Use 1½ cups bread crumbs and ½ cup shredded or grated coconut.

Coffee Bread Pudding. Mix 2 teaspoons instant coffee with the sugar.

MERINGUE BREAD PUDDING

Make any Bread Pudding, using 4 egg yolks instead of 2 whole eggs. Spread the baked pudding with a thin layer of jam or jelly and top with Meringue (p. 441) made of the 4 egg whites. Bake at 425° until delicately brown (about 5 minutes).

Lemon Meringue Bread Pudding. Add grated rind of 1 lemon to pudding. Pour over the hot baked pudding the juice of 1½ lemons mixed with ½ cup sugar. Top with meringue as above.

COLD CHOCOLATE BREAD PUDDING

Put in a double boiler top

1½ cups milk
1 cup sugar
1 cup soft stale bread crumbs
1½ ounces chocolate

Cook over hot water until smooth. Stir in

2 tablespoons butter

Beat until light

2 eggs

Add

¼ teaspoon salt
½ teaspoon vanilla
½ cup milk

Stir into the chocolate mixture. Cook until thick. Pour into a serving dish or, for a firmer pudding, into a buttered baking dish and bake 20 minutes at 350°. Chill. Serve with

Whipped cream

Serves 4 to 6.

Chocolate Nut Bread Pudding. Before spooning into the dish, stir in ½ cup chopped walnut meats.

BREAD AND BUTTER PUDDING

To vary this good old-fashioned pudding, sprinkle between the layers ¾ cup raisins or ½ cup shredded coconut.

Put in a buttered baking dish, buttered side down

4 slices buttered bread

Mix

2 eggs, slightly beaten
⅓ cup sugar

¼ teaspoon salt
3 cups milk

Pour over the bread. Let stand 30 minutes. Bake 1 hour at 325°, covering the first half hour of baking. The top of the pudding should be well browned. Serve warm with Hard Sauce (p. 434) or Creamy Hard Sauce (p. 434). *Serves 4 to 6.*

Bread and Butter Apple Pudding. Put a layer of applesauce in a shallow baking dish. Remove the crusts from sliced dry bread. Butter the bread, cut in triangles and put over the applesauce, close together. Sprinkle generously with sugar and a few drops of vanilla or a shake or two of cinnamon. Bake at 350° about 30 minutes or until the top is brown. Serve with cream, plain or whipped.

LEMON BREAD PUDDING

Remove the crusts from
8 slices firm bread

Spread with Lemon Cream (below) and put in a buttered baking dish. Mix
2 eggs, slightly beaten
1 cup milk
3 tablespoons sugar
⅛ teaspoon salt
Grated rind 1 lemon

Pour over the bread. Cover. Set in a pan of hot water. Bake 1 hour at 350°. *Serves 6.*

Lemon Cream. Put in a saucepan 3 tablespoons lemon juice, grated rind of 1 lemon and ¼ cup butter. Cook 2 minutes. Add 1 cup sugar and 3 eggs, slightly beaten. Cook and stir over low heat until thick. Cool.

INDIAN PUDDING

Corn meal cooked very slowly with milk, molasses and spice is the classic New England Indian Pudding. It should be soft and should separate or whey somewhat. It is important to use the best dark molasses for the finest flavor. Let a true Indian Pudding stand one half hour after baking so that it will be slightly firmer.

Scald in a double boiler
2 cups milk

Mix until smooth
¼ cup yellow corn meal
¼ cup cold milk

Stir into the hot milk. Cook over hot water 20 minutes, stirring frequently. Add
½ cup dark molasses
1 teaspoon salt
¼ cup sugar
1 teaspoon cinnamon
4 tablespoons butter

Stir and pour into a buttered pudding dish. Pour over the top
1¾ cups cold milk

Bake 3 hours at 250°. Serve with heavy cream or vanilla ice cream. *Serves 4 to 6.*

As a variation, add ½ cup raisins or coconut after the first hour of baking. Use ginger in place of cinnamon, if you like.

CLUB INDIAN PUDDING

Similar to traditional Indian Pudding, but firmer and baked in a shorter time.

Scald in a double boiler
1 quart milk

Stir in slowly
5 tablespoons corn meal

Cook over hot water 20 minutes. Add
2 tablespoons butter
1 cup molasses
1 teaspoon salt
1 teaspoon cinnamon
2 eggs, well beaten

Spoon into a buttered baking dish. Pour over it
1 cup cold milk

Bake 1 hour at 350°. *Serves 8.*

To vary the seasoning, use ¾ teaspoon cinnamon and ¼ teaspoon ginger or nutmeg.

Apple Indian Pudding. Put 1 cup thinly sliced peeled apples into the baking dish.

HASTY PUDDING

Just corn meal mush, but very good.

Put in a double boiler top
2 cups boiling water
Stir in
⅓ cup corn meal
½ teaspoon salt
Cook over hot water until thick (about 1 hour), stirring occasionally. Or cook 20 minutes in a pressure cooker. Serve with butter and finely shaved maple sugar.

BAKED CARROT PUDDING

Mix
½ cup shortening
½ cup brown sugar
1 egg, slightly beaten
1 cup grated raw carrots
2 teaspoons chopped candied lemon peel
½ cup seedless raisins
1 cup currants
Sift together
1¼ cups flour (preferably pastry)
1 teaspoon baking powder
½ teaspoon salt
½ teaspoon nutmeg
½ teaspoon cinnamon
½ teaspoon baking soda
Stir into the first mixture. Put in a buttered casserole or 6 to 8 individual molds. Bake, uncovered, at 350° until firm (1 to 1¼ hours for the casserole or about 45 minutes in the small molds). Serve with
Creamy Hard Sauce (p. 434)
Serves 6 to 8.

HONEYCOMB PUDDING

For a richer pudding, add nut meats, raisins or dates.

Set the oven at 350°. Butter a 2-quart baking dish. Mix
1 cup sugar
1 cup flour
½ teaspoon baking soda
Add
1 cup molasses
½ cup butter, melted in 1 cup lukewarm milk
Beat thoroughly. Stir in
4 eggs, well beaten
Pour into a baking dish. Bake until firm (about 45 minutes). Serve with
Thin Lemon Sauce (p. 433) *or*
Floradora Sauce (p. 435) *or*
whipped cream
Serves 6.

BAKED LEMON PUDDING

The top is cakelike. The soft lemon custard beneath provides the sauce. For a richer dessert, spread the chilled pudding with a thin layer of unsweetened whipped cream.

Set the oven at 350°. Butter a 2-quart baking dish.

Sift together
1 cup sugar
½ cup flour
½ teaspoon baking powder
¼ teaspoon salt
Separate
3 eggs
Beat the whites until stiff. Beat in, a spoonful at a time
½ cup sugar
Set aside. Without washing the beater, beat the yolks until light. Add
2 teaspoons grated lemon rind
¼ cup lemon juice
2 tablespoons melted butter
1½ cups milk
Stir into the flour mixture. Beat until smooth. Add the beaten whites and fold gently until no white flecks show. Pour into the

baking dish. Set in a pan of hot water ½ inch deep. Bake 45 minutes. Chill at least 1 hour. *Serves 6.*

LEMON SPONGE PUDDING

Also attractive in a baked pie shell.

Separate

4 eggs

Beat the whites until stiff with

¼ cup sugar

Set aside. Without washing the beater, beat the yolks until thick with

½ cup sugar
⅛ teaspoon salt

Add

Grated rind and juice of 2 lemons

Stir and cook over hot water until thick. Fold in the whites. Pour into a buttered baking dish. Brown lightly in a 375° oven. *Serves 4 to 6.*

COTTAGE PUDDING

Any simple cake—baker's, from a mix or homemade—may be the basis for cottage pudding. For a richer dessert, top with whipped cream.

Set the oven at 400°. Butter a shallow cake pan, 8 by 8 inches, a small angel cake pan or cupcake tins.

Sift together

1½ cups flour
2 teaspoons baking powder
½ teaspoon salt
½ cup sugar

Mix

1 egg, well beaten
½ cup milk
½ cup butter, melted

Stir gently into the flour mixture. Pour into the pan. Bake until brown and crusty (20 to 25 minutes). Serve warm with

Vanilla Sauce (p. 432), Lemon Sauce (p. 432), Orange Sauce (p. 433), Melba Sauce (p. 433) *or* Hard Sauce (p. 434), *or* with crushed and sweetened strawberries, sliced peaches *or* stewed blueberries

Serves 6.

Chocolate Chip Cottage Pudding. Add 1 package chocolate bits to the batter. Serve with Vanilla Sauce.

CHOCOLATE COTTAGE PUDDING

Bake Chocolate Cake (p. 501) or a mix in an angel cake pan. Remove from the pan, cool, and fill the center with sweetened and flavored whipped cream. Pour thin Chocolate Sauce (p. 430) around the cake. Or bake the cake in a shallow pan and cut in squares. Delicious either warm or cold.

UPSIDE-DOWN CAKE

Melt in a heavy frying pan or a cake pan

¼ cup butter

Add and spread evenly

1 cup brown sugar

If desired, sprinkle with

Pecan nut meats

Put in the pan, close together

Peach halves *or* drained canned sliced pineapple

Cover with

Cottage Pudding batter (above)

Bake at 400° until the top is brown and crusty (about 35 minutes). Turn out on a serving dish, fruit side up. Garnish with whipped cream. *Serves 6.*

ICEBOX PUDDING (ICEBOX CAKE)

Prepare a filling (p. 395). Line a mold or a large bowl with

Lady fingers (about 30) *or* strips of sponge, angel *or* pound cake

Pour in the filling. Or put the cake and the filling in the bowl in layers. Chill 12 hours or longer. Turn out onto a serving dish and cover with

Whipped cream

Serves 6.

Butter Filling. Cream ½ cup unsalted or washed butter. Beat in 1 cup powdered sugar until fluffy. Beat in 4 egg yolks, one at a time. Flavor with vanilla or rum and fold in 4 egg whites beaten stiff.

Chocolate Filling. Add to filling 1 ounce unsweetened chocolate, melted with 1 tablespoon water or coffee and cooled to lukewarm.

Coffee Filling. Soak lady fingers or cake in coffee and cream (2 tablespoons cream to 1 cup coffee). Flavor the filling with instant coffee to taste. Add 1 cup toasted and chopped almonds to the filling if you like.

Lemon Filling. Add juice and grated rind of 1 lemon to the filling before folding in the whites.

Macaroon Filling. Add ½ cup macaroon crumbs (dried, rolled and sifted) to the filling.

CHOCOLATE ICEBOX CAKE

Very rich and delicious. Prepare French Chocolate Mousse (below) this way, too.

Put in a cup

½ cup cold water
1 envelope gelatine (1 tablespoon)

Melt over hot water

2 ounces unsweetened chocolate
¾ cup hot water *or* coffee

Stir in the soaked gelatine. Separate

3 eggs

Beat the whites until stiff. Beat in, a tablespoon at a time

⅓ cup sugar

Without washing the beater, beat the yolks until thick and add to the chocolate mixture. Pour over the whites and fold lightly together until well blended. Add

1 small sponge, angel *or* pound cake, cut in ½-inch cubes

Mix gently until well blended. Spoon into a mold. Chill, turn out on a serving dish and cover with

Whipped cream

Serves 6.

FRENCH CHOCOLATE MOUSSE

This is the classic French pôt de crème. Serve it in small covered cups made for the purpose or in custard cups.

Put in a pan

1 package semi-sweet chocolate
2 tablespoons water

Stir over hot water until melted. Separate

4 eggs

Beat the whites until stiff and set aside. Beat the yolks until thick and lemon-colored. Beat in the chocolate and

1 teaspoon vanilla, rum *or* brandy (or more, to taste)

Fold in the whites. Spoon into pôt de crème cups or sherry or cocktail glasses. Chill (12 hours or more, if convenient). Top with chopped nuts, if you like, though this is contrary to the French way. *Serves 4 to 6.*

For an even richer version, add ¼ cup powdered sugar to the melted chocolate, then ¼ pound unsalted butter, bit by bit. Use 6 eggs. *Serves 6 to 8.*

To use as a filling for Icebox Cake (above). Whip ½ cup heavy cream and fold it in.

CHARLOTTE RUSSE

Mix in a saucepan

⅓ cup sugar

1 tablespoon gelatine
½ cup milk
Cook and stir over low heat until the gelatine dissolves. Add
1½ teaspoons vanilla
Chill until almost firm. Beat until fluffy. Whip until stiff
½ pint heavy cream
Beat one-third of the cream into the charlotte. Fold in the rest. Spoon into individual molds or one large mold. Chill. Turn out and garnish with
Lady fingers
Whipped cream
Serves 4 to 6.

Other ways to serve Charlotte Russe. Line a large mold with slices of jelly roll. Or fill Mary Ann cakes (baker's or sponge cake baked in Mary Ann pans) with charlotte and decorate with whole strawberries and a border of whipped cream. Or chill in sherbet glasses and put a spoonful of cold Butterscotch Sauce (p. 429) on each. Add a few shavings of toasted almonds, if you like.

Caramel Charlotte. Caramelize all the sugar and add it slowly to the scalded milk. Stir until dissolved before adding the gelatine. Add confectioners' sugar to taste.

Burnt Almond Charlotte. Make Caramel Charlotte, adding ½ cup finely chopped blanched toasted almonds.

Chocolate Charlotte. Melt 1 ounce unsweetened chocolate over hot water, add 3 tablespoons hot water and ⅓ cup powdered sugar. Add to the gelatine mixture while hot. Sprinkle with slivers of milk chocolate and garnish with whipped cream around base of the mold.

Chocolate Rum Charlotte. Flavor with 3 tablespoons rum before adding the cream. Before molding, fold in 1 ounce unsweetened chocolate, grated.

Coffee Charlotte. Flavor with instant coffee or use strong hot coffee in place of scalded milk.

Marron Charlotte. Add to Caramel Charlotte ½ cup marrons, broken in pieces. Garnish with whipped cream and marrons. Pour over marron syrup (from the jar or can) flavored with sherry or rum.

Peanut Charlotte. Scald 3 tablespoons peanut butter with the milk. Sprinkle with chopped peanuts.

QUICK CHARLOTTE RUSSE

Beat until stiff
1 egg white
Fold in
¼ cup powdered sugar
½ cup heavy cream, whipped
Flavor to taste with
Vanilla, instant coffee, brandy *or* sherry
Line dessert glasses with
Lady fingers *or* thin strips of sponge cake
Fill with the charlotte. Put a bit of preserved fruit in each glass or sprinkle with chopped nuts. Chill. *Serves 4.*

Nut Brittle Whip. Omit the sugar. Add pounded peanut brittle or other brittle to taste.

MAPLE CHARLOTTE

Chopped pecans add a wonderful touch.

Put in a saucepan
1 cup maple syrup
1 envelope gelatine (1 tablespoon)
Stir over moderate heat until the gelatine dissolves. Chill until slightly thick. Fold in
1 pint heavy cream, whipped
Line a mold or paper cups with
Lady fingers
Fill with charlotte and chill. *Serves 6 to 8.*

ORANGE CHARLOTTE

Mix in a small saucepan
1 envelope gelatine (1 tablespoon)
1 cup sugar
⅔ cup water
Cook and stir over low heat until the gelatine dissolves. Cool. Add
3 tablespoons lemon juice
1 cup orange juice and pulp *or* 1 small can frozen orange juice
Chill until as thick as unbeaten egg white. Beat until frothy. Fold in
3 egg whites, beaten stiff
½ pint cream, whipped
Line a mold with sections of orange. Pour in the charlotte. Chill. *Serves 6.*

SNOW PUDDING

Mix
1 envelope gelatine (1 tablespoon)
1 cup sugar
¼ teaspoon salt
Add
1½ cups boiling water
Stir until the gelatine dissolves. Add
¼ cup lemon juice
Chill until as thick as unbeaten egg white. Add
3 egg whites
Beat until thick enough to hold its shape. Mold. Chill until firm. Serve with
Soft Custard (p. 384) *or* crushed fruit
Serves 6.

Macaroon Squares. Flavor with 1½ teaspoons vanilla instead of lemon juice. Before it is stiff enough to mold, pour it into a shallow pan which has been dipped in cold water. Chill. Cut in 3-inch squares and dip them gently in dried macaroon crumbs. Serve with Sabayon Sauce (p. 434) or whipped cream flavored with lemon juice.

WINE JELLY

A dessert or a delicious accompaniment for cold turkey or chicken.

Mix
2 envelopes gelatine (2 tablespoons)
1 cup sugar
Add
2 cups boiling water
Stir until the gelatine dissolves. Add
⅓ cup orange juice
3 tablespoons lemon juice
1 cup sherry *or* Madeira *or* ¼ cup brandy and ⅓ cup kirsch
Mold and chill. *Serves 6 to 8 as a dessert, 12 as an accompaniment.*

COFFEE JELLY

Mix
1 envelope gelatine (1 tablespoon)
¼ cup sugar
Add
2 cups strong hot coffee
Stir until the gelatine dissolves. Mold and chill. *Serves 4.*

Sherry Coffee Jelly. Use only 1½ cups coffee. When the gelatine has dissolved, add ½ cup sherry.

Brandy Coffee Jelly. Use only 1¾ cups coffee. When the gelatine has dissolved, add ¼ cup brandy.

COFFEE SPONGE

Mix
1 envelope gelatine (1 tablespoon)
⅓ cup sugar
Add
1 cup strong hot coffee
Stir until the gelatine dissolves. Chill until as thick as unbeaten egg white. Add
1 egg white
Beat until thick enough to hold its shape. Mold. Serve with
Whipped cream
Serves 3 or 4.

COFFEE MALLOW

Put in a double boiler

½ cup hot coffee
¼ pound marshmallows, tiny ones or large ones cut in quarters with wet scissors

Cook over hot water until the marshmallows melt. Cool. When slightly thickened, fold in

½ pint heavy cream, whipped

Add

Vanilla *or* brandy to taste

Pour into dessert glasses. Chill. *Serves 6.*

STRAWBERRY *or* PINEAPPLE MALLOW

Whip until stiff

½ pint heavy cream

Fold in

½ pound marshmallows (tiny ones or large ones cut in quarters with wet scissors)

Add

Few grains salt
1 cup pineapple chunks *or* frozen or sliced fresh strawberries

Flavor with

Vanilla, sherry *or* rum

Spoon into dessert glasses. Chill at least 1 hour. *Serves 4 to 6.*

MARSHMALLOW PUDDING À LA STANLEY

Other fruits may be used in place of cherries—seeded white grapes, halved strawberries or small chunks of pineapple.

Mix

½ pound marshmallows (small ones or large ones cut in quarters with wet scissors)
½ cup nut meats, broken in pieces
¼ cup maraschino cherries, cut small
1 tablespoon juice from the cherry jar

Whip

½ pint heavy cream

Add

2 tablespoons confectioners' sugar
Vanilla, sherry *or* rum to taste

Fold in the marshmallow mixture. Mold and let stand until firm (about 2 hours). *Serves 6.*

FRENCH SOUFFLÉ

Serve a soufflé the moment it is baked. A soufflé sturdy enough to stand without falling is not delicate enough to be perfect. However, most of the preparation can be done well in advance—all but folding in the beaten egg whites and flavoring just before baking.

Beat until thick and lemon-colored

4 egg yolks
¼ cup sugar

Melt

3 tablespoons butter

Stir in

3 tablespoons flour
¼ teaspoon salt

Add gradually, stirring constantly

1 cup milk

Bring to the boiling point and pour over the egg yolks. Stir well. Cool. When it is time to bake the soufflé, set the oven at 325° or 375° (p. 399). Beat until stiff

4 egg whites (or 5 for a fluffier soufflé)

Beat in, a tablespoon at a time

¼ cup sugar

Stir a tablespoon of the beaten whites into the cooled mixture. Carefully fold in the rest. Add

1 teaspoon vanilla *or* ¼ cup sherry and 1 tablespoon brandy

Pour into an unbuttered straight-sided baking dish, preferably pottery. Fill two-thirds full or, a truly impressive effect, use a smaller dish and tie firmly around it a collar of well-buttered heavy wax paper within which the soufflé can rise. The collar should come 2 or 3 inches above the rim of the dish. Another idea is to make a deep cut all around the soufflé mixture an inch from the edge; the center will rise higher as the soufflé bakes.

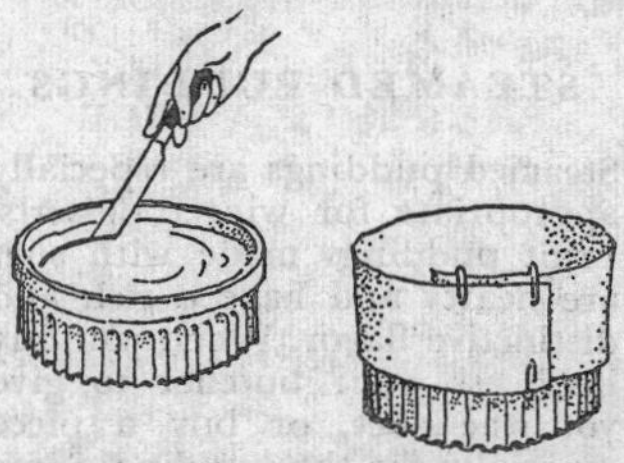

To make a soufflé with a crusty top and a center soft enough to serve as a sauce, bake 20 minutes at 375°.

To make an even, fairly firm soufflé, bake 30 to 40 minutes at 325°. *Serves 6.*

FRENCH SOUFFLÉ VARIATIONS

Apricot *or* Peach Soufflé. Drain (reserve syrup) canned apricots or peaches. Cut fruit into quarters to make 2 cups. Put close together in a baking dish. Pour French Soufflé mixture over the fruit. Bake. Serve with fruit syrup and whipped cream or vanilla ice cream.

Coffee Soufflé. Flavor to taste with instant coffee or use ¾ cup strong coffee and ¼ cup cream in place of milk. Serve with cream or Coffee Cream Sauce (p. 431).

Hazelnut Soufflé. Chop 1 cup toasted hazelnuts. Pour the milk over them and heat to just below the boiling point.

Orange Soufflé. Before adding the egg whites, stir in ½ cup tart orange marmalade and 2 teaspoons grated orange rind.

Soufflé Grand Marnier. Soak 6 lady fingers or 2-inch squares of dry sponge cake in Grand Marnier or Cointreau 1 hour and arrange in a baking dish. Pour soufflé mixture over the cake and bake.

CHOCOLATE SOUFFLÉ

Melt over hot water
1½ ounces unsweetened chocolate
Add
2 tablespoons sugar
2 tablespoons hot water
Stir until smooth. Melt
2 tablespoons butter
Stir in
2 tablespoons flour
¼ teaspoon salt
Blend well. Add gradually
¾ cup milk
Stir and cook to the boiling point. Add to the chocolate mixture. Pour over
3 egg yolks, beaten until thick
Beat well and set aside to cool. When it is time to bake the soufflé, set the oven (see above). Beat until stiff
3 egg whites
Beat in, a spoonful at a time
3 tablespoons sugar
Add
½ teaspoon vanilla
Fold into the soufflé mixture. Bake. Serve with
Cream, plain or whipped
Serves 4 or 5.

FRUIT SOUFFLÉ

Rub peaches, apricots or quinces (if you use canned fruit, drain off the syrup) through a sieve to make
¾ cup fruit pulp
Heat. Add
1 tablespoon lemon juice
Few grains salt
Sugar to taste
Add, hot, to
3 egg whites, beaten stiff
Continue beating until evenly

blended. Butter 4 or 5 individual molds. Sprinkle sugar over the butter and fill three-quarters full with the soufflé mixture. Bake at 325° until firm (20 to 25 minutes). Serve with

Sabayon Sauce (p. 434)

Serves 4 or 5.

LEMON SOUFFLÉ

Set the oven at 325°. Separate

4 eggs

Beat the whites until stiff. Add by tablespoonfuls

⅓ cup sugar

Without washing the beater, beat the yolks until thick and lemon-colored. Beat in

⅓ cup sugar

Add

Grated rind and juice of 1 lemon

Fold in the whites and pour into an unbuttered baking dish. Bake 40 minutes. Serve warm. *Serves 4.*

SOUFFLÉ AU RHUM

Soufflé au rhum should be very soft inside. For a gala touch, pour heated rum around the soufflé on the serving dish and light it with a match just before serving.

Beat until stiff

4 egg whites

Beat in gradually

2 tablespoons confectioners' sugar

Without washing the beater, beat until thick and lemon-colored

2 egg yolks
2 tablespoons confectioners' sugar
Few grains salt
1 tablespoon rum

Fold in the whites. Heat a 6-inch omelet pan. Butter it and pour in half the mixture. Brown on one side, turn with a spatula, brown on the other side, fold and turn out onto a heated serving dish. Sprinkle with

Powdered sugar

Cook the rest the same way. *Serves 4.*

STEAMED PUDDINGS

Steamed puddings are especially appropriate for winter desserts. Fruit puddings made with suet are hearty and have a rich and distinctive flavor. When you buy beef, ask your butcher to give you the suet, or buy a piece especially for the pudding. Some steamed puddings are light and delicate, such as Chocolate Pudding, Orange Puff and Snow Balls (p. 401).

Butter pudding molds, large or individual size, or use any small tins or custard cups. Fill not more than two-thirds full to allow for expansion. Put on covers or cover tightly with aluminum foil.

Place a rack in a deep kettle. Set the filled molds on the rack. Add boiling water until it comes halfway up around the molds. Cover tightly. Adjust the heat to keep the water boiling throughout the steaming, adding more as it boils away. Steam the length of time required by the recipe. **Pressure-cooker** steaming is quick and satisfactory. Pressure cookers vary slightly, so follow the directions which come with the cooker.

Set the molds in cold water for a few seconds. Uncover and turn out. If you like fruit puddings less moist, set in the oven for a few minutes to dry out. Cut large puddings with a very sharp knife. Serve with sauce as suggested with the recipe, but see also the many other sauces, pages 429–436.

BLACK PUDDING

Sift together

2 cups flour
½ teaspoon salt
½ teaspoon baking soda

Add

1 egg, slightly beaten
1 cup molasses
1 cup boiling water

Stir to blend evenly. Steam 1 hour (p. 400). Serve with

Floradora Sauce (p. 435)

Serves 6.

ORANGE PUFF

Melt

3 tablespoons butter

Stir in

¼ cup flour

Blend well. Add gradually

1 cup milk

Bring to the boiling point, stirring constantly, and remove from the heat. Separate

4 eggs

Beat the whites until stiff. Beat in

4 tablespoons sugar

Set aside. Without washing the beater, beat the yolks until thick with

4 tablespoons sugar
1 tablespoon orange juice *or* frozen orange concentrate
1 teaspoon grated orange rind

Add to the hot mixture. Fold in the whites. Steam (p. 400) 35 minutes. Serve with

Orange Sauce (p. 433) *or* Creamy Hard Sauce (p. 434) flavored with orange juice and grated rind

Serves 6.

SNOW BALLS

Cream together

¼ cup butter
½ cup sugar

Add

2 egg whites, beaten stiff
¼ cup milk

Sift together

1 cup flour
1 teaspoon baking powder
¼ teaspoon salt

Stir into the first mixture. Fill buttered custard cups. Steam (p. 400) 20 minutes. Take out of the cups. Roll gently in

Confectioners' sugar

Serve with

Creamy Chocolate Sauce (p. 430) *or* crushed and sweetened fruit

Serves 4 or 5.

STEAMED CHOCOLATE PUDDING

Melt over hot water

1½ ounces unsweetened chocolate
3 tablespoons butter

Stir in

½ cup sugar
1 egg

Beat until smooth. Add

⅓ cup milk
½ teaspoon vanilla

Sift together

1 cup flour
1½ teaspoons baking powder
¼ teaspoon salt

Stir into the first mixture. Steam (p. 400) 45 minutes in small molds or 1½ hours in a large mold. Serve with

Yellow Sauce (p. 435) *or* whipped cream, sweetened and flavored with vanilla *or* rum

Serves 4 or 5.

FIG PUDDING

Rub with fingers or a wooden spoon until creamy

3 ounces suet, chopped

Add

½ pound dried figs, chopped fine

Put in a bowl

2½ cups bread crumbs
½ cup milk

Let stand ½ hour. Add

2 eggs, well beaten
1 cup sugar
½ teaspoon salt

Add the figs and suet. Steam (p. 400) 3 hours. Serve with

Yellow Sauce (p. 435)
Serves 4 or 5.

STEAMED BERRY PUDDING

Cream together
1/3 cup butter
2/3 cup sugar
Add
2 eggs, well beaten
Sift together
2 1/3 cups flour
2 1/2 teaspoons baking powder
1/4 teaspoon salt
Add to the first mixture alternately with
1/3 cup milk
Stir in
1 cup cranberries *or* blueberries
Steam (p. 400) 3 hours. Serve with
Vanilla (p. 432) *or* Lemon Sauce (p. 432) *or* Hard Sauce (p. 434)
Serves 6.

OHIO PUDDING

Sift together
1 cup sugar
1 cup flour
2 teaspoons baking powder
1 teaspoon salt
1 teaspoon baking soda
Add
1 cup finely grated raw potato
1 cup finely grated raw carrot
1 cup currants
1 cup raisins
Mix thoroughly. Steam (p. 400) 2 hours in small molds or 3 hours in a large mold. Serve with
Ohio Sauce (p. 434)
Serves 8.

STEAMED DATE *or* FIG PUDDING

Sift together
1 7/8 cups flour
1/2 teaspoon baking soda
1/2 teaspoon each of salt, clove, allspice and nutmeg
Melt
3 tablespoons butter
Add
1/2 cup molasses
1/2 cup milk
Add the flour mixture and
1/2 pound pitted dates *or* dried figs, cut small
Steam (p. 400) 2 1/2 hours. Serve with
Foamy Sauce (p. 434) *or* Thin Lemon Sauce (p. 433)
Serves 6.

SUET PUDDING

Sift together
3 cups flour
1 teaspoon baking soda
1 1/2 teaspoons salt
1/2 teaspoon ginger
1/2 teaspoon clove
1/2 teaspoon nutmeg
1 teaspoon cinnamon
Add
1 cup finely chopped suet
1 cup molasses
1 cup milk
1 1/2 cups seeded raisins, floured
Steam (p. 400) 3 hours. Serve with
Sterling Sauce (p. 434)
Serves 8 or more.

THANKSGIVING PUDDING

Put in a bowl
2 1/2 cups bread crumbs
3/4 cup milk
Let stand 1/2 hour. Add
4 eggs, well beaten
1 cup brown sugar
1 teaspoon salt
3/4 teaspoon cinnamon
1/2 teaspoon nutmeg
Work with fingers until creamy
1/3 cup chopped suet
Add to the first mixture. Add
1/2 cup chopped walnut meats, floured
1/2 cup seeded raisins, cut small and floured
Sift over the mixture
2 teaspoons baking powder

Beat thoroughly. Steam (p. 400) 3 hours. Serve with

Yellow Sauce (p. 435)

Serves 8.

STERLING FRUIT PUDDING

For a festive look, decorate the mold with citron, sliced and cut in fancy shapes.

Work with fingers or a wooden spoon until creamy

1 cup chopped suet

Add

2⅔ cups dry bread crumbs
1 cup grated raw carrots

Beat until light

4 egg yolks

Beat in

1⅓ cups brown sugar

Add to the first mixture. Add

Grated rind 1 lemon
1 tablespoon vinegar

Mix

2 tablespoons flour
1½ teaspoons salt
1 teaspoon cinnamon
½ teaspoon nutmeg
¼ teaspoon clove
1 cup seeded raisins, cut small
¾ cup currants

Add to the pudding. Fold in

4 egg whites, beaten until stiff

Steam (p. 400) 3½ hours. Serve with

Creamy Hard Sauce (p. 434)

Serves 8 or more.

ENGLISH PLUM PUDDING

Traditional, rich and delicious—the climax of a holiday dinner.

Put in a bowl

1 cup hot milk
1 cup dry bread crumbs

Let stand until cool. Add

½ cup sugar
4 egg yolks, well beaten
½ pound seeded raisins, cut in pieces and floured
¼ pound figs, chopped
2 ounces citron, cut fine

Work with fingers or a wooden spoon until creamy

½ pound suet, chopped

Add to the first mixture. Stir in

¼ cup wine, grape juice *or* currant jelly
1 teaspoon nutmeg
¾ teaspoon cinnamon
¼ teaspoon clove
¼ teaspoon mace
1½ teaspoons salt

Beat until stiff

4 egg whites

Fold in. Steam (p. 400) 6 hours. Serve with both

Hard Sauce (below) and Thin Sauce (below)

Serves 8.

SAUCES FOR ENGLISH PLUM PUDDING

Hard Sauce. Cream ⅓ cup butter. Add gradually 1 cup brown sugar and 2 tablespoons brandy, drop by drop. Force through a pastry bag and a rose tube and garnish with green leaves and candied cherries.

Thin Sauce. Mix ½ cup sugar, ½ tablespoon cornstarch and few grains salt. Stir in gradually 1 cup boiling water and boil 5 minutes. Remove from heat, add 1 tablespoon lemon juice and 2 tablespoons brandy. Tint with red vegetable coloring.

FLAMING CHRISTMAS PUDDING

Steam Sterling Fruit Pudding (above) or English Plum Pudding (above) in a round mold. Put on a serving dish and top with a holly sprig. Pour ¼ cup warmed brandy over it, light with a match, and carry to the table flaming.

CHRISTMAS WREATH

Steam any fruit pudding in a rind mold. Turn out onto a serving dish and decorate with cherries and with leaves cut from candied citron to look like a Christmas wreath.

TORTES

Austrian cooking is famous for tortes, which are rich, often rather heavy cakes. When you invite guests for dessert, torte and coffee make a perfect combination.

To fill the pans. Use pans with removable rims or spring-form tube pans, so that you can remove the baked torte without breaking it. Butter or oil the pan lightly and sprinkle with flour. Spoon in the batter, spreading it evenly.

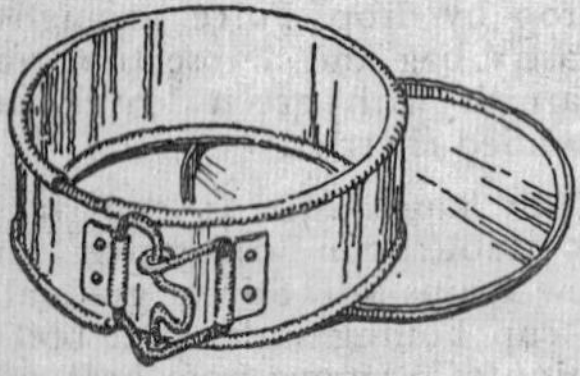

To bake. Preheat the oven to 325°. Bake until the torte shrinks from the pan (about 25 minutes for layers, 40 or more for a large cake).

To serve. Cool. Serve with whipped cream, sweetened and flavored, or put layers together with whipped cream and put whipped cream or an icing on the top. Serve in wedges.

ALMOND *or* PECAN TORTE

Pecans make a moister, richer torte than almonds.

Separate
4 eggs
Beat the whites until stiff. Beat in
¼ cup confectioners' sugar
Set aside. Without washing the beater, beat the yolks until thick and lemon-colored. Beat in
¾ cup confectioners' sugar
Add
½ cup chopped almonds *or* pecans
⅓ cup grated unsweetened chocolate
¾ cup fine cracker crumbs
1 teaspoon baking powder
Fold in the beaten whites. Spoon into a 9-inch pan and bake (above). Cool. Split carefully into 2 layers. Put together with
Whipped cream
Serves 6.

CARROT TORTE

Large dry carrots are best for this pretty and surprisingly delicious dessert.

Separate
4 eggs
Beat the whites until stiff. Beat in
¼ cup sugar
Set aside. Without washing the beater, beat the yolks until thick and lemon-colored. Beat in
¾ cup sugar
Add
1 cup grated raw carrot
Grated rind of 1 lemon
Juice of ½ lemon
½ cup flour
1 teaspoon baking powder
Fold in the beaten whites. Bake (above) in two 8- or 9-inch layer cake pans. Put together with
Whipped cream
Serves 6.

HAZELNUT TORTE

As an added touch, sprinkle chopped hazelnuts over the frosting or whipped cream when the torte is ready to serve.

Separate
4 eggs
Beat the whites until stiff. Beat in
¼ cup sugar

Without washing the beater, beat the yolks until thick and lemon-colored. Beat in

¼ cup sugar

Stir in

⅔ cup ground roasted hazelnuts
2 tablespoons rum
1¾ cups mashed potatoes, packed lightly
1 tablespoon vanilla

Fold in the beaten whites. Bake (p. 404) in an 8-inch spring-form pan. This moist mixture may take as long as 1½ hours. *Serves 8.*

WALNUT TORTE

Butter and flour two 9-inch layer cake tins. Set the oven at 350°.

Separate

5 eggs

Beat the whites until stiff. Beat in gradually

¼ cup sugar

Set aside. Without washing the beater, beat the yolks until thick and lemon-colored. Beat in

¾ cup sugar

Add

2 cups bread crumbs
1 teaspoon baking powder
1 teaspoon vanilla

Fold in the beaten whites. Spread in the tins. Bake 25 minutes. Put between the layers

Nut Filling (below) *or* whipped cream

Cover with

Whipped cream

Serves 6 to 8.

Nut Filling. Put in a saucepan 1 cup milk, 1 tablespoon sugar, 1 teaspoon butter, ½ cup chopped nuts, ½ cup bread crumbs. Cook until thick. Cool. Add 1 teaspoon vanilla.

DATE AND NUT TORTE

If you have any torte left over, cut it in finger-shaped pieces and serve them as date and nut bars.

Mix

1 cup chopped dates
1 teaspoon baking soda
1 cup boiling water

Let stand 1 hour. Set the oven at 325°. Cream

1 tablespoon butter

Add

1 cup sugar
½ teaspoon salt
2 eggs, well beaten
1 cup sifted flour
1 cup nut meats, broken in pieces

Add the dates. Spread in a buttered pan, about 10 by 14 inches. Bake 40 minutes. Cut in squares. Serve with

Whipped cream

Serves 8.

BLITZ TORTE

An impressive party dessert.

Butter two 8- or 9-inch layer cake pans. Line them with wax paper cut to fit the bottom and butter the paper lightly. Set the oven at 250°.

Cream until light and fluffy

½ cup butter

Beat in

½ cup sugar
1 teaspoon vanilla *or* almond flavoring
4 egg yolks (one at a time)

Mix and sift

1 cup flour
1 teaspoon baking powder

Add to the egg mixture alternately with

½ cup milk

Spread in the pans. Beat until stiff

5 egg whites
⅛ teaspoon cream of tartar

Beat in, a little at a time

1 cup confectioners' sugar

Spread evenly over the yolk mixture. Bake 25 minutes. Raise the temperature to 350° and bake 20 minutes longer. Cool. Put the layers together with

Whipped cream

Serves 8.

Almond Blitz Torte. Sprinkle sliced blanched almonds over one cake. Bake. Put the plain layer, meringue side down, on a serving dish, cover with Cream Filling (p. 516), and set the other layer on top.

Strawberry Blitz Torte. Spread the baked torte with 1 cup crushed strawberries, then with whipped cream or sour cream.

BRAZIL NUT CAKE

Set the oven at 350°. Butter a shallow pan, about 10 by 14 inches.

Separate
6 eggs
Beat the whites until they stand in soft peaks. Beat in, gradually
½ cup sugar
Set aside. Without washing the beater, beat the yolks until thick and lemon-colored with
½ cup sugar
¼ teaspoon salt
Fold in the beaten whites and
2 cups ground Brazil nuts
Spread in the pan. Bake about 30 minutes (see Sponge Cake, p. 488). Cut in squares and serve as a dessert, topped with
Whipped cream
Serves 8 or more.

CHOCOLATE ROLL

Butter and flour a jelly roll pan, about 10 by 14 inches. Set the oven at 350°.

Separate
5 eggs
Beat the whites until stiff. Mix and beat in, a little at a time
1 cup confectioners' sugar
3 tablespoons cocoa
Without washing the beater, beat the yolks until thick and fold them in. Spread evenly in the pan. Bake until the cake shrinks from the edges (about 20 minutes). Turn out on a cloth sprinkled with
Confectioners' sugar
Cut off the edges of the cake if they are crisp. Cover the cake with a slightly dampened cloth. Cool. Spread with
½ pint heavy cream, whipped and sweetened, flavored with vanilla *or* rum
Roll firmly and put on a serving dish with the fold underneath. Sprinkle lightly with
Confectioners' sugar
Slice and serve with
Chocolate Sauce (p. 430)
Serves 6 to 8.

Hungarian Chocolate Cake. Cut the cake in four even pieces. Spread three with whipped cream. Stack evenly (no cream on top). Melt 2 ounces unsweetened chocolate in a double boiler, add ½ cup confectioners' sugar and 1 tablespoon hot water. Blend well, add 1 egg, beat until smooth, add 3 tablespoons butter, and spread over the sides and top of the cake.

FUDGE PIE

Make Brownie mixture (p. 476) but omit the nuts. Spread in a well-buttered and floured 7-inch pie tin. Bake 30 minutes at 325°. Cool. Serve in wedges with whipped cream or ice cream.

DENVER CHOCOLATE PUDDING

Sometimes called "Fudge Pudding," this is pudding and sauce in one. Do not overcook it. Serve it the day it is made, while the cakelike top is still somewhat moist. For a richer pudding, add ½ cup chopped nuts.

Sift together
¾ cup sugar
1 cup flour
2 teaspoons baking powder
⅛ teaspoon salt

Melt together over hot water

2 tablespoons butter
1 ounce unsweetened chocolate *or* 3 tablespoons cocoa

Add to the flour mixture. Stir in

½ cup milk
½ teaspoon vanilla

Pour into a buttered baking dish about 9 by 9 inches. Over the top scatter, without mixing

½ cup brown sugar
½ cup white sugar
4 tablespoons cocoa

Pour over the top

1½ cups cold water *or* coffee

Bake 40 minutes at 350°. Let stand at room temperature and serve cool but not chilled. Serve plain or with

Whipped cream *or* ice cream

Serves 6.

NUT ROLL

Butter a jelly roll pan, about 10 by 14 inches. Line with wax paper and butter the paper. Set the oven at 350°.

Separate

6 eggs

Beat the whites until they stand in soft peaks. Beat in

¼ cup sugar

Set aside. Without washing the beater, beat the yolks until thick and lemon-colored. Beat in

½ cup sugar

Mix

1½ cups chopped pecans *or* walnuts
1 teaspoon baking powder
Few grains salt

Stir into the egg yolk mixture. Fold in the beaten whites. Spread evenly in the pan. Bake 20 minutes. Cover with a damp towel and chill. Turn out onto a towel and peel off the paper. Whip

1½ cups heavy cream

Sweeten to taste. Add

Vanilla *or* rum to taste

Spread evenly over the cake. Roll like a jelly roll. Wrap firmly in wax paper and chill. Cut in slices. *Serves 8 or more.*

ANGEL PIE

Butter a 9-inch pie pan. Set the oven at 275°.

Beat until stiff

4 egg whites
¼ teaspoon salt
¼ teaspoon cream of tartar

Beat in, a spoonful at a time

1 cup granulated sugar
½ teaspoon vanilla

Spread in the pan, having the edge higher to make a rim. Bake until dry and firm to the touch but not brown (about 1 hour). Cool. Spread with

½ cup cream, whipped

Let stand several hours or overnight. Cover with

Filling (below)

Spread with

½ cup cream, whipped but not sweetened

Serves 6.

Lemon Filling for Angel Pie. Beat 4 egg yolks until thick with 4 tablespoons sugar and 4 tablespoons lemon juice. Cook over hot water until thick and smooth. Cool.

Strawberry *or* Raspberry Angel Pie. Instead of Lemon Filling, spread a layer of halved strawberries or whole raspberries over the cream. Sprinkle lightly with sugar and cover with a second layer of cream.

COCONUT MACAROON PIE

Butter and flour a 9-inch pie pan. Set the oven at 350°.

Beat until stiff

4 egg whites

Beat in, a spoonful at a time

1 cup sugar
1 teaspoon vanilla

Mix together and fold in

1 cup graham cracker crumbs
1 teaspoon baking powder
¼ teaspoon salt
½ cup shredded coconut
½ cup chopped walnuts

Spread in the pan and bake 30 minutes. Top with

Whipped cream *or* vanilla ice cream

Serves 6.

Chocolate Pecan Pie. Use crumbs of chocolate wafers in place of graham crackers and 1 cup pecan nut meats instead of coconut and walnuts.

CREAM PUFFS (PÂTE À CHOUX)

Cream puff mix is on the market but it is simple to make your own.

Set the oven at 375°. Put in a saucepan

½ cup boiling water
¼ cup butter

Heat until the butter melts. Add, all at once

½ cup all-purpose *or* bread flour

Stir hard until the dough forms a ball in the center of the pan. Remove from the heat and let stand 5 minutes. Add

1 egg

Beat until well blended. Add

1 egg

Beat as before. *The mixture should be very stiff. If it is not, let it stand 10 minutes before shaping.*

Take up by spoonfuls and arrange on a cooky sheet, 2 inches apart. Use a tablespoon for large puffs, a teaspoon for small ones. Bake until there are no beads of moisture on the puffs (about 40 minutes for large puffs). *If the puffs are not baked long enough they will fall and be soft rather than crisp. Test by taking one out of the oven. If it does not flatten down, the puffs are done.*

Cool. Fill with ice cream, whipped cream or any cream filling (p. 516). *Makes 8 large puffs, 18 small or 26 hors d'oeuvre size.*

Éclairs. Shape in finger-shaped oblongs, 1 by 4½ inches. For perfect shaping, use a pastry bag and tube. Bake, split, and fill. Frost with Confectioners' Frosting (p. 512), or add ⅓ cup melted Fondant (p. 530) to the frosting and dip the tops of the éclairs in the hot frosting.

Chocolate Pâte à Choux Rings. Shape in rings, 3½ inches in diameter. Bake, cool, split and fill with whipped cream. Cover with Chocolate Portsmouth Frosting (p. 512) and sprinkle with blanched and shredded almonds.

Gâteau Praline. Butter a ring mold. Fill two-thirds full with the batter. Bake. Split and fill with whipped cream. Spread the top with Caramel (p. 510) and sprinkle with toasted almonds, cut small. *Serves 6.*

Profiteroles. Shape tiny puffs with a teaspoon. Bake 10 minutes at 425°, then reduce the heat to 350° and bake 10 minutes longer. Cool, fill with vanilla ice cream and serve with Creamy Chocolate Sauce (p. 430). Allow 4 to 5 puffs for each serving.

Hors d'Oeuvres Puffs. Shape with a teaspoon or tiny coffee spoon. Bake 10 minutes at 425°. Reduce the heat to 350°. Bake 10 minutes longer. Cool, split and fill with chicken salad or any spread.

QUEEN FRITTERS

Make Cream Puff mixture (above). Drop by spoonfuls into deep cooking fat or oil heated to 375° and fry until delicately brown. The fritters will turn over as one side browns. Drain well on paper towels. Slit and fill with preserve or marmalade or Chocolate Cream Filling (p. 517). Sprinkle with powdered sugar or serve with Vanilla Sauce (p. 432). *Makes 18 fritters.*

Beignets (French Crullers). Drain and sprinkle lightly with confectioners' sugar.

Sfogliatelle. Brush with honey and sprinkle with chopped nuts.

FRITTER BATTER

For a thinner coating, add more milk and omit the baking powder. For a fluffier coating, beat the egg white separately and add it to the batter last.

Sift together
- **1 cup flour**
- **1 teaspoon baking powder**
- **¼ teaspoon salt**

Beat until fluffy
- **2 eggs**

Add
- **2 teaspoons sugar (for sweet fritters)**
- **⅔ cup milk**
- **1 teaspoon salad oil**
- **Dash of lemon juice** *or* **1 teaspoon brandy**

Add the flour and stir only enough to dampen it.

FRUIT FRITTERS

A dash of cinnamon goes well with fritters.

Heat fat (p. 4) to 370°. While it is heating, prepare Fritter Batter (p. 409) and the fruit. Dip pieces of fruit in the batter and lift out with a long-handled fork, letting the batter drain off into the bowl. Lower carefully into the fat and fry until delicately brown (3 to 5 minutes). It is impossible to give the exact amount of flour for perfect fritters. Keep the batter thin for delicacy and crispness. Test one fritter—if the batter does not cling as the fritter fries, add a small amount of flour to the batter and try again. Drain on paper towels. Keep hot until all are done. Sprinkle with
- **Powdered sugar**

Serve hot with meat or chicken, or as a dessert with
- **Thin Lemon Sauce (p. 433), Melba Sauce (p. 433)** *or* **whipped cream**

To prepare fruit for fritters. Peel and core apples and cut in ½-inch slices. Cut bananas in chunks and sprinkle with lemon juice and sugar. Drain canned peaches, apricots, pineapple and other fruit and cut in convenient pieces. Sprinkle lightly with flour.

SWEDISH TIMBALES AND ROSETTE CASES

You will need special irons for making these professional-looking pastries. The deep ones make perfect patty shells for creamed chicken or lobster. The large

Timbale irons come in various shapes

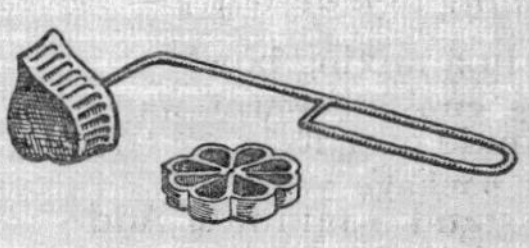

rosettes are delicious with crushed fruit and whipped cream or merely sprinkled with powdered sugar and served with coffee. Use the tiny ones filled with any hors d'oeuvre mixture as a very special cocktail tidbit.

Sift together
- **¾ cup flour**
- **½ teaspoon salt**
- **1 teaspoon sugar**

Stir in
- **¾ cup milk**
- **2 egg yolks, slightly beaten**
- **1 tablespoon salad oil**

Pour into a small deep bowl or cup. Let stand several hours so that the air bubbles will disappear.

Put enough vegetable oil in a small heavy pan to cover the

iron completely. Put the iron into the cold fat and heat to 375°. Lift out the iron, drain it slightly on a paper towel and dip into the batter to about three-quarters its depth. Lift out, lower into the hot oil and fry until delicately brown. The first timbale case may not cling to the iron. Try having the oil a trifle hotter or cooler. You will soon find the perfect temperature. Pry off the timbale case with a fork. Drain, upside down, on a paper towel. Pry the rosettes off the iron with a skewer as soon as they are firm and drop into the oil to finish browning, turning them over to brown evenly. Lift out with a flat wire whisk. *Makes 18 or more.*

BABA CAKES

Delicious with coffee and outstanding as a dessert.

Put in a mixing bowl

½ cup lukewarm water

Sprinkle over it

1 package yeast

Let stand 5 minutes. Add

½ cup flour

Beat well with an egg beater or an electric mixer. Beat in

4 eggs, one at a time
¼ cup sugar
⅛ teaspoon salt
1 cup flour

Cover and let rise until light (about 45 minutes). Beat in, bit by bit

½ cup butter, soft but not melted

Butter deep cupcake tins or special baba tins. Put a tablespoon of batter in each tin. Cover and let stand 10 minutes. Bake at 400° until brown. Finish as suggested below. If you do not need this many for one occasion, put some away in the freezer for another time, or bake part of the batter in a ring mold to serve as a Savarin (below). *Makes 24.*

Babas au Rhum (with Rum Sauce). Boil 1 cup water with 1 cup sugar for 10 minutes. Cool to lukewarm and add ½ cup rum. Dip cooled Baba Cakes in this sauce and pour more sauce around them. As a variation, add ¼ cup raisins (or raisins and currants) to the dough when the butter is added.

Babas with Apricots. Cut a circular piece from the top of each Baba and scoop out a small quantity of the inside. Fill with apricot marmalade. Replace tops. Serve with Thin Lemon Sauce (p. 433).

SAVARIN

Mix Baba Cake dough (above), adding ½ cup flour. Bake about 30 minutes in two ring molds. Turn out onto a serving plate and spoon rum syrup (see Babas au Rhum) generously over the cakes. Fill the center with sliced and sweetened strawberries, a maçédoine of fruit, ice cream or whipped cream, sweetened and flavored with rum. Vary the liquor as you like. Cointreau is delicious with strawberries, and kirsch or brandy with mixed fruit. *One ring serves 6.*

MONT BLANC

A dramatic and very rich dessert called Monte Bianco in Italy. Canned cream of marrons can be found in shops that deal in imported delicacies. Taste, sweeten and flavor.

Shell 1 pound French or Italian chestnuts (p. 13). Cover with milk and cook until soft. Drain, if necessary, and mash with a fork. Sweeten to taste with confectioners' sugar (about 1 cup for 1 pound of nuts) and season with salt and vanilla, kirsch, rum or maraschino. Beat thoroughly. Put through a vegetable mill or ricer. Pile lightly on 3-inch rounds of baked pastry or in a pyramid on a serving dish. Decorate with whipped cream to look like a snow-capped mountain. Or use as a filling between pairs of meringues. *One pound serves 6.*

Frozen Desserts

Ice creams and sherbets are certainly the most universally popular desserts. A crank freezer gives ice cream a velvety texture, but there are many excellent recipes for making frozen desserts in a refrigerator tray.

FREEZER ICE CREAM AND SHERBET

The smoothest ice cream is made in an old-fashioned freezer cranked by hand, slowly at first, then more rapidly as the ice cream stiffens. An electric freezer is almost as good. The 2-quart size is practical for most families. Scald the freezer can each time you use it and rinse it with cold water.

Crush the ice in a canvas bag with a mallet or buy crushed ice. Use coarse rock salt. Measure out the ice and salt beforehand, ready to use, or measure it as you go along (8 parts of ice to 1 of salt). More salt hastens the freezing but the ice cream will be less velvety.

Put the can in the tub and fit the dasher in place in it. Pour the chilled ice cream mixture into the can, filling it no more than two-thirds full (to allow for expansion). Put on the cover and adjust the top and crank. Turn once or twice to be sure all is in place. Fill the tub one-third full of crushed ice. Put in the rest of the ice and salt in layers until slightly above the level of the mixture in the can. Pack the ice down solidly with a wooden spoon. Let stand 5 minutes, then begin turning the crank. When the ice cream is frozen, the crank turns with difficulty (an electric freezer shuts off automatically).

To pack. Drain off the water. Wipe the lid of the can, remove it and lift out the dasher. Pack the ice cream down solidly with a spoon. Cover, putting a cork in the opening unless the freezer has a solid cover to replace the other. Repack, using 4 parts of ice to 1 part of salt. Cover with newspapers or a heavy cloth. Let stand at least ½ hour before serving.

Freezing problems. If a frozen dessert refuses to harden, it may be because the cream is too heavy or there is too much sugar or acid fruit in the mixture. To stiffen, stir in beaten egg whites when the ice cream is frozen to a mush and continue freezing.

SERVING ICE CREAM AND SHERBET

Homemade ice cream. Serve from the can with a large spoon or an ice cream scoop. Or remove the can from the freezer, wipe it carefully, let it stand 1 minute in cool water, remove the cover, run a knife around the edge of the cream and invert it on a serving dish. If the cream does not slip out easily, wipe the can with a cloth wrung out of hot water.

Ice cream molds. Place on the serving dish and add a touch of decoration such as a frill of whipped cream, a sprinkling of chopped toasted nuts or toasted coconut, or bits of glazed fruit or marrons.

Sundaes, Coupes and Special Desserts. See pages 422 ff.

Ices and Sherbets. Serve plain or in a mound surrounded by fruit. Lemon ice is delicious with preserved cherries or orange sections and strips of fresh pineapple. Or top individual servings with whipped cream decorated with chopped pistachios or other nuts. Or pour rum around the sherbet.

Commercial ice cream. Soften bulk ice cream slightly so that you can spoon it into a deep bowl as if it were fresh from a home freezer. Serve in any of the ways suggested on pages 422 ff. **To vary,** soften the ice cream slightly and stir into it added flavoring as suggested below. Pack into a mold or an ice cube tray and set in the freezer compartment to harden.

- Add instant coffee to vanilla, coffee or chocolate ice cream. Add vanilla or brandy to taste.
- Swirl chocolate or butterscotch sauce or peanut butter through vanilla ice cream.
- Add crushed and sweetened raspberries, strawberries or peaches to vanilla ice cream.
- Add chopped toasted nuts or crushed nut brittle to vanilla, chocolate or coffee ice cream.

LEMON ICE

Put in a bowl

2 cups sugar
4 cups boiling water

Stir until dissolved. Cool. Add

¾ cup lemon juice
1 tablespoon grated lemon rind

Freeze in a crank freezer (p. 412) or a refrigerator tray (p. 418). *Makes 3 pints.*

To vary. In place of lemon juice and rind, use any of the following combinations, adding water to make about 4 cups.

Orange Ice. 3 cups orange juice, ¼ cup lemon juice, grated rind of 2 oranges, Sugar Syrup (p. 37) to taste.

Fruit Juice Ice. 1½ cups grapefruit juice, 1½ cups orange juice, ½ cup lemon juice, Sugar Syrup (p. 37) to taste.

Grape Ice. 2 cups grape juice, ⅔ cup orange juice, ¼ cup lemon juice, Sugar Syrup (p. 37) to taste.

Mint Ice. Flavor Lemon Ice with oil of peppermint and color delicately with vegetable coloring.

Raspberry and Currant Ice. ⅔ cup raspberry juice, 1⅓ cups currant juice, 2 cups Sugar Syrup (p. 37).

MILK SHERBET

A smooth creamy sherbet.

Mix

Juice of 3 lemons *or* 2 oranges and 2 lemons
1½ cups sugar
Few grains salt
1 quart milk

Freeze in a crank freezer (p. 412) or a refrigerator tray (p. 418). *Makes 3 pints.*

Cream Sherbet. Use 3 cups milk and 1 cup cream.

ORANGE CREAM SHERBET

Unless oranges are at their best, frozen orange juice may have a better flavor than fresh.

Mix
1¼ cups sugar
1½ cups orange juice
Few grains salt
2 cups milk
½ pint cream
Freeze in a crank freezer (p. 412) or a refrigerator tray (p. 418). *Makes 3 pints.*

PINEAPPLE ICE

If you use fresh fruit, add more sugar to taste.

Boil 5 minutes
2 cups water
1 cup sugar
Add
2 cups crushed *or* shredded pineapple
½ cup lemon juice
Few grains salt
Cool. Freeze in a crank freezer (p. 412) or in a refrigerator tray (p. 418). *Makes 3 pints.*

RASPBERRY *or* STRAWBERRY ICE

Wash, drain and hull
2 quarts berries
Sprinkle with
2 cups sugar
Cover and let stand 2 hours. Mash and squeeze through cheesecloth or a fine sieve. Add
Few grains salt
2 cups water
Lemon juice, to taste
Freeze in a crank freezer (p. 412) or a refrigerator tray (p. 418). *Makes 3 pints.*

FRUIT SHERBET

Put in a small saucepan
1 cup water
¼ cup sugar
1 tablespoon gelatine (1 envelope)
Stir over low heat until the gelatine dissolves. Heat
2 cups puréed fruit, fresh or canned
Stir in the gelatine. Mix well. Add
Few grains salt
Sugar to taste
Lemon juice to taste (2 tablespoons or more)
Freeze in a refrigerator tray (p. 418). *Makes 1 quart.*

To prepare purée. Drain canned fruit or wash and peel fresh fruit and remove the pits or seeds. Put through a coarse sieve, ricer or food mill. To keep peaches from darkening, sprinkle with ACO (a commercial ascorbic) or simmer 5 minutes in thin sugar syrup (¼ cup sugar to 2½ cups water). Drain.

Cream Sherbet. Fold in 1 cup Soft Custard (p. 384) or ½ pint heavy cream, whipped.

CRANBERRY SHERBET

Refreshing as a dessert or as a relish with chicken or turkey.

Beat together
1½ cups cranberry jelly, homemade (p. 87) or canned
Grated rind and juice of 1 lemon
Juice of 1 orange
Freeze to a mush in a refrigerator tray (p. 418). Fold in
2 egg whites, beaten stiff, *or* ½ pint cream, whipped
Finish freezing. *Makes 1 quart.*

LIME SHERBET

Put in a bowl
1 package lime gelatine
1 cup boiling water
Stir until dissolved. Add
½ cup sugar
2 cups milk
1 cup top milk *or* cream
¼ cup lime juice
1 teaspoon grated lime peel
Few grains salt
Mix well. Freeze in a refrigerator tray (p. 418). *Makes 1 quart.*

PINEAPPLE CREAM SHERBET

Boil 5 minutes

½ cup sugar
1 cup water

Cool. Add

1 cup crushed pineapple

Freeze to a mush in a refrigerator tray (p. 418). Fold in

½ pint heavy cream, whipped

Finish freezing. *Makes 1 quart.*

Pineapple Marquise. Use pineapple juice in place of pineapple. Add the juice of ½ lemon. Just before serving, stir in

½ teaspoon vanilla *or*
1 tablespoon rum
½ cup crushed pineapple, sweetened to taste

Garnish with

Candied pineapple *or* chopped pistachios or pecans or both

CARDINAL PUNCH

A Victorian accompaniment for chicken or turkey, but nowadays considered the perfect finale to a rich dinner.

Boil 10 minutes

4 cups water
2 cups sugar

Add

⅔ cup orange juice
⅓ cup lemon juice
¼ cup strong tea (strained)

Cool. Freeze to a mush (p. 418). Add

¼ cup brandy
¼ cup curaçao

Freeze until firm. Serve in tall coupe glasses. *Makes about 2 quarts.*

Roman Punch. Instead of brandy and curaçao, use ½ cup rum.

CLUB PUNCH

Boil 10 minutes

2½ cups sugar
3 cups water

Add

1 cup lemon juice
1 cup orange juice
1 cup pineapple juice

Cut in pieces

1 cup candied fruit (such as a mixture of cherries, pineapple and apricots)

Add

¼ cup rum
¼ cup brandy

Cover and let stand 1 hour. Freeze the first mixture to a mush (p. 418), add the fruit, and freeze until nearly firm. Serve in tall coupe glasses. *Makes 2½ quarts.*

PHILADELPHIA ICE CREAM

The richest mixture of all. Traditionally, it should be made with grated vanilla bean instead of vanilla essence.

Scald

1 quart cream

Add

¾ cup sugar
Few grains salt

Stir until the sugar dissolves. Chill. Add

1½ tablespoons vanilla *or* 1 teaspoon grated vanilla bean

Freeze in a crank freezer (p. 412). *Makes 3 pints.*

CUSTARD ICE CREAM

Scald

1½ cups milk

Mix until smooth

1 tablespoon cornstarch *or* flour
¾ cup sugar
½ cup cold milk

Add the scalded milk slowly and cook and stir over hot water 8 minutes. Add

1 egg *or* 2 egg yolks, slightly beaten

Cook 2 minutes. Cool. Add

1 pint heavy cream
1 tablespoon vanilla
¼ teaspoon salt

Fr[illegible]

FRENCH VANILLA ICE CREAM

Mix

½ cup sugar
⅛ teaspoon salt
4 egg yolks, slightly beaten

Add, stirring constantly

2 cups scalded milk

Cook over hot water until the mixture coats a spoon. Cool, strain and add

½ pint heavy cream
1 tablespoon vanilla

Freeze (p. 412). *Makes 3 pints.*

REFRIGERATOR ICE CREAM

Put in a double boiler top

¼ cup cold water
1 tablespoon gelatine

Let stand 5 minutes. Add

1 cup hot milk *or* cream

Mix

⅜ cup sugar *or* ¼ cup sugar and 3 tablespoons corn syrup
1 teaspoon flour
Few grains salt

Add to the gelatine and milk. Cook and stir over low heat until thick. Cover and cook over hot water 10 minutes. Stir in slowly

1 egg yolk, slightly beaten

Cook 1 minute. Strain into a refrigerator tray and put in the refrigerator until chilled. Spoon into a chilled bowl and beat with an egg beater until very light. Fold in

1 pint heavy cream, whipped
1 egg white, beaten stiff
1 teaspoon vanilla

Pour back into the tray and freeze (p. 418). *Makes about 1 quart.*

ICE CREAM VARIATIONS

Vary any of the basic ice cream recipes in the ways suggested below.

Bisque Ice Cream. Add to the mixture one cup finely chopped nut meats. Toasted (not salted) almonds and hazelnuts are especially good.

Burnt Almond Ice Cream. Add 1 cup finely chopped blanched and toasted almonds to Caramel Ice Cream mixture.

Butterscotch Ice Cream. Cook sugar with 2 tablespoons butter until melted and well browned. Dissolve in hot milk or cream.

Caramel Ice Cream. Caramelize half the sugar (p. 15). Add it slowly to hot mixture.

Chocolate Ice Cream. Make Custard Ice Cream (p. 415), melting 2 squares chocolate with the milk as it is scalded. Increase sugar to 1¼ cups.

Coffee Ice Cream. Flavor to taste with instant coffee and brandy or vanilla.

Frozen Tom and Jerry. Freeze French Vanilla Ice Cream (above) to a mush. Add 2 tablespoons rum and 1 tablespoon brandy and finish freezing. Serve in frappé glasses.

Ginger Ice Cream. Add ½ cup Canton ginger cut in small pieces and 3 tablespoons ginger syrup. Add 2 tablespoons sherry, if desired.

Grape-Nut Ice Cream. Add 1 cup Grape-Nuts. Flavor with almond extract.

Macaroon Ice Cream. Add 1 cup macaroon crumbs (8 dry macaroons pounded). Reduce sugar to ½ cup. Flavor with sherry, if liked.

Maple Ice Cream. Use maple syrup or maple sugar in place of sugar. If desired, add 1 cup nut meats, cut in pieces or chopped, stirring them into cream when nearly frozen.

Marron Ice Cream. Add 1 cup canned marrons, forced through a sieve. Reduce sugar by one half. Flavor to taste with sherry.

Mint Ice Cream. Flavor with oil of peppermint. Color delicately green with vegetable coloring. Serve with Chocolate Sauce (p. 430).

Peanut Brittle Ice Cream. Omit sugar. Pound ½ pound peanut brittle, roll and sift. Add to mixture. Add sugar to taste.

Peppermint Candy Ice Cream. Omit sugar. Crush ½ pound peppermint stick candy and add to hot milk or cream.

Pistachio Ice Cream. Add 1 teaspoon almond extract and ½ cup pistachio nuts, chopped fine. Color green.

Praline Ice Cream. Add 1 cup almonds, blanched, toasted, and finely chopped. Caramelize half the sugar and add slowly to scalded milk or cream. Or add 1 cup Praline Powder (p. 14), made with pecans.

CHOCOLATE ICE CREAM

Smoother than some because sweet chocolate blends evenly with the ice cream during the freezing.

Cook until thick and smooth
- **½ pound sweet chocolate**
- **2 cups cold milk**

Beat well
- **3 eggs**
- **1 cup sugar**

Add
- **1 pint thin cream**
- **1 tablespoon vanilla**
- **⅛ teaspoon salt**

Add the chocolate mixture, stir well and strain. Freeze in a crank freezer (p. 412). *Makes 3 pints.*

GRAPE ICE CREAM

Mix
- **1 pint cream**
- **1¼ cups grape juice**
- **⅓ cup sugar**
- **Lemon *or* lime juice to taste**

Freeze (p. 412). *Makes 1 quart.*

FROZEN PUDDING

Prepare (using mixed candied fruits or candied pineapple with a small amount of preserved ginger)
- **⅔ cup fruit, cut small**

Freeze to a mush
- **Custard Ice Cream (p. 415)**

Add the fruit and
- **½ cup chopped almonds**
- **3 tablespoons brandy *or* sherry**

Freeze until firm. *Makes about 3 pints.*

Frozen Plum Pudding. Make the ice cream with 4 egg yolks, omitting the flour. In place of fruit and nuts, add ⅓ cup sultana raisins and ½ cup dry macaroon crumbs.

Nesselrode Pudding. In place of fruit and nuts, add 1 cup preserved marrons, forced through a sieve. Flavor with maraschino. **To vary,** add bits of candied fruit.

FRESH FRUIT ICE CREAM

Mix
- **2 cups thin cream**
- **2 cups prepared fruit (pp. 417–418)**
- **¼ teaspoon salt**
- **Sugar to taste**

Freeze until firm (p. 412). *Makes about 1½ quarts.*

Banana Ice Cream. Put 2 ripe bananas through a sieve and sprinkle with lemon juice.

Blueberry Ice Cream. Stew 1 quart blueberries until soft. Add 1 cup sugar, mash, strain and cool.

Peach Ice Cream. Pare, slice and crush fruit to make 2 cups. Sprinkle with ½ cup sugar. Add lemon juice or almond flavoring if the peaches are too bland.

Raspberry *or* **Strawberry Ice Cream.** Mash 1 quart berries, sprinkle with ½ cup sugar, cover and let stand at least 20 minutes. Strain to remove the seeds.

ORANGE ICE CREAM

Orange juice, sweetened to taste and combined with an equal amount of thin cream, is the simplest recipe, but a custard base makes a smoother ice cream.

Boil 5 minutes
- **2 cups sugar**
- **1 cup water**

Add
- **2 cups orange juice**

Scald
- **½ pint thin cream**

Add
- **2 egg yolks**

Cook and stir over hot water or very low heat until thick. Cool. Add the first mixture. Fold in
- **½ pint heavy cream, beaten stiff**

Freeze (p. 412). When nearly firm, stir in
- **¼ cup candied orange peel, cut in thin slivers**

Makes 2 quarts.

MOUSSES AND PARFAITS

Mousses and parfaits are frozen without stirring. See also Parfaits (Coupes) on page 423.

To freeze in the refrigerator. Set the temperature according to the manufacturer's directions. Remove the bars from the ice cube tray and pour in the prepared mixture. Cover with foil or wax paper. If you have a little too much for one tray and not enough for two, fill small paper soufflé cups and freeze them in another tray. When the mousse is frozen hard, return the temperature to normal.

To freeze in ice and salt. Fill molds to overflowing with the mixture and cover with buttered paper, then with tight covers. It is important to keep the salt water out of the mold, so bind on the cover with a strip of cloth (finger bandage is practical) which has been dipped in melted fat, not oil. Cover individual molds with a double thickness of wax paper held with elastic bands. Pack the molds in equal amounts of crushed ice and salt in the freezer tub or a large kettle. Be sure the ice and salt are *under, around* and *over* the molds. Pour off salt water as it forms so that it will not get into the molds.

Leave small molds 2 hours, large ones 3 to 4 hours. Take out the mold and wipe with a cloth wrung out of hot water, and remove the strip of cloth and the cover. Invert on the serving dish.

VANILLA MOUSSE I

Vary the flavoring as suggested on pages 416–417.

Beat until stiff
- **2 egg whites**

Beat in gradually
- **¼ cup powdered sugar**

Whip until thick but not stiff
- **1 pint heavy cream**
- **¼ cup powdered sugar**
- **1 teaspoon vanilla**

Fold in the egg whites. Freeze (above). *Makes 1 quart.*

To make with whole eggs. Beat 2 egg yolks with half the sugar and the vanilla. Fold in the whites and the cream. Add sugar to taste. One cup cream may be omitted, in which case reduce the sugar to ⅓ cup.

Biscuit Tortoni I. Flavor with sherry. Add ½ cup dried macaroons, finely crushed. Pack in a mold or in paper cups, sprinkle with powdered macaroons and set in a refrigerator tray to freeze.

Chantilly Mousse. Add 1 cup meringues, broken in pieces.

Chestnut Mousse. Add ½ cup marrons, broken in pieces.

Apricot Mousse. Press stewed apricots through a sieve. Spread a layer in a refrigerator tray and cover with the mousse. Freeze (p. 418). Cut in cubes and pile in dessert glasses.

Coffee Mousse. Add 2 tablespoons instant coffee dissolved in ¼ cup water.

Orange Mousse. Melt 1 can frozen orange concentrate and stir it into the mousse.

VANILLA MOUSSE II

Less expensive than the classic recipe and lower in calories, too. Vary the flavoring (pp. 416–417).

Heat until thoroughly blended
¾ cup condensed milk
½ cup water
Chill. Add
1½ teaspoons vanilla
Fold in
½ pint heavy cream, whipped
Freeze in a refrigerator tray (p. 418). *Makes 1½ pints.*

Peach Mousse. Add 1 cup crushed peaches to the chilled condensed milk and water. Sweeten to taste before folding in the cream.

MARSHMALLOW MOUSSE

Cut in pieces with wet scissors (or use small marshmallows)
20 marshmallows
Pour over them
1 cup fruit juice
Cook in a double boiler until the marshmallows melt. Cool. Add
Juice of ½ lemon
Fold in
½ pint heavy cream, beaten stiff
Freeze in a refrigerator tray at the regular temperature. *Makes 1 quart.*

Coffee Marshmallow Mousse. Use coffee in place of fruit juices. Flavor with vanilla, sherry or brandy to taste.

BISCUIT TORTONI II

See also the variation following Vanilla Mousse (p. 419).

Roll dry macaroons to make
1 cup macaroon crumbs
Cover with
1 pint thin cream
Soak 1 hour. Add
½ cup sugar
⅓ cup sherry
Freeze to a mush in a refrigerator tray (p. 418). Fold in
1 pint heavy cream, beaten stiff
Pack in fluted paper cups. Sprinkle over the tops
Dried macaroon crumbs
Set in the freezer compartment and freeze until firm. *Makes 3 pints.*

Coffee Tortoni. In place of sherry, flavor with 1 teaspoon vanilla and 2 tablespoons instant coffee, dissolved in ⅛ cup water. Chopped toasted almonds are delicious instead of macaroons. You will need about ½ cup.

CHOCOLATE MOUSSE

Cook over low heat or in a double boiler, stirring frequently
1 cup milk
2 ounces unsweetened chocolate
¼ cup sugar
1 teaspoon gelatine
Beat until smooth and well blended. Chill until thick. Add
1 teaspoon vanilla

Beat until light. Fold in

1 pint heavy cream, whipped

Freeze in a refrigerator tray (p. 418). *Makes 1 quart.*

COFFEE MOUSSE

See also Marshmallow Mousse (p. 419) and Vanilla Mousse (p. 418).

Put in a small saucepan

1 cup strong coffee
¾ cup sugar
Few grains salt
1 teaspoon gelatine

Cook and stir over low heat until the gelatine and sugar dissolve. Stir well and pour into a refrigerator tray. Chill until thickened. Fold in

1 pint heavy cream, beaten stiff

Freeze until firm. *Makes 1 quart.*

Coffee Coconut Mousse. Melt 1 tablespoon butter. Stir in 1 cup flaked coconut and cook until lightly browned. Fold into the mousse with the cream.

FRUIT MOUSSE

Raspberries, strawberries and peaches are especially delicious, but other fruits are good, too. If the fruit is bland, add lemon juice to taste. Almond extract intensifies the flavor of peaches.

Prepare, by rubbing fruit through a sieve

1 cup fruit pulp and juice

Add

Few grains salt
Sugar to taste

Put in a small saucepan

½ cup water
¼ cup sugar
1 teaspoon gelatine

Cook and stir until the sugar and gelatine melt. Add to the fruit. Pour into a refrigerator tray or a bowl. Chill until thickened. Beat until very light. Fold in

1 pint heavy cream, whipped

Freeze in a refrigerator tray or in salt and ice (p. 418). *Makes 1 quart.*

PINEAPPLE MOUSSE

Put in a small saucepan

1¼ cups syrup from canned pineapple
½ cup sugar
1 teaspoon gelatine
Few grains salt

Cook and stir over low heat until the gelatine and sugar dissolve. Add

2 tablespoons lemon juice

Chill until thickened. Beat until stiff. Fold in

1 pint heavy cream, whipped

Freeze until firm in a refrigerator tray (p. 418). *Makes 1 quart.*

FROZEN APPLE CREAM

For a richer dessert, fold in toasted flaked coconut or chopped nuts.

Mix in a refrigerator tray

1 cup applesauce
Few grains cinnamon
Few grains nutmeg
1 teaspoon melted butter
2 teaspoons lemon juice

Chill. Fold in

½ pint heavy cream, whipped

Freeze in the tray until firm (2 to 4 hours). *Makes 1½ pints.*

ANGEL PARFAIT

Boil until the syrup spins a thread (about 5 minutes)

1 cup sugar
½ cup water

Beating constantly, pour slowly on

3 egg whites, beaten stiff

Beat until cool. Fold in

1 pint heavy cream, whipped
2 teaspoons vanilla

Spoon into a bombe mold lined with ice cream (p. 425) or serve in a refrigerator tray. Serve in dessert glasses, garnished with whipped cream, chopped nuts or fruit. *Makes about 1 quart.*

Vary as suggested on pages 416–417.

Pistachio Parfait. Color delicate green. Add 1 teaspoon almond extract and ½ cup chopped pistachios.

STRAWBERRY PARFAIT

Wash, hull and mash
1 quart strawberries
Sprinkle with
1 cup sugar
Let stand several hours. Strain through a fine sieve. Pour into a refrigerator tray. Freeze until slightly icy. Boil until the syrup spins a thread (about 5 minutes)
1 cup sugar
½ cup water
Beating constantly, pour slowly over
3 egg whites, beaten stiff
Beat until cool. Fold in
1 pint heavy cream, whipped
Fold into the strawberries and freeze until firm. *Makes 3 pints.*

FROZEN ORANGE WHIP

Boil until the syrup spins a thread (about 5 minutes)
1 cup sugar
⅔ cup water
Add
Grated rind of 2 oranges
¼ cup orange juice
Cover and keep warm 1 hour. Cool. Add gradually to
1 pint heavy cream, whipped
Cut in half and remove the pulp of
2 oranges
Cut the pulp in small pieces. Pour the orange syrup into a refrigerator tray. Put in alternate layers of the cream mixture and the bits of orange until the tray is full. Freeze until firm. *Makes 1 quart.*

PEANUT COCONUT MOLD

Blend thoroughly
½ cup peanut butter
1 can condensed milk
2 tablespoons lemon juice
1 can flaked coconut
Soften slightly
1 quart vanilla ice cream
Spoon into refrigerator trays or a mold in layers, spreading each layer with some of the peanut mixture. Cover. Set in the freezer compartment until firm. *Makes about 1½ quarts.*

MAPLE MOUSSE

Extravagant, high-caloried but a superb indulgence once in a while.

Beat slightly
4 eggs *or* 6 egg yolks
Add, little by little
⅔ cup hot maple syrup
Stir and cook in a double boiler until thick. Cool. Fold in
1 pint heavy cream, whipped
Freeze (p. 418). Serve in parfait glasses. Sprinkle with
Pecan nut meats
Makes 1 quart or 8 small servings.

MARRON PARFAIT

Prepare
1 cup preserved marrons, cut in small pieces
Add
1 tablespoon vanilla
Boil 5 minutes
⅔ cup sugar
¼ cup water
Beating constantly, pour gradually over
6 egg yolks, beaten thick
Cook over hot water, stirring constantly, until thick. Beat until cold. Add the marrons. Fold in
1 pint heavy cream, whipped
Freeze (p. 418). *Makes 1 quart or 8 small servings.*

To vary, use chopped nut meats or dry macaroon crumbs in place of marrons.

MANHATTAN PUDDING

Mix
- **1½ cups orange juice**
- **¼ cup lemon juice**

Sweeten to taste with
- **Sugar**

Pour into a refrigerator tray or a 1-quart brick mold. Whip
- **½ pint heavy cream**
- **¼ cup powdered sugar**
- **1 teaspoon vanilla**

Add
- **⅔ cup chopped walnut meats *or* macaroon crumbs**

Pour over the first mixture. Freeze (p. 418) until just firm enough to cut in slices. The orange layer should not be icy. *Makes 1 quart.*

Standish Pudding. Prepare strawberries as for Strawberry Parfait (p. 421). Add lemon juice to taste and enough water to make 2 cups. Use in place of fruit juices.

FROZEN LIME PIE

Beat until thick
- **2 eggs**

Beat in
- **½ cup sugar**

Add
- **½ cup light corn syrup**
- **1 pint heavy cream**
- **¼ cup lime juice**
- **1 teaspoon grated lime peel**

Freeze in a refrigerator tray (p. 418). Beat until fluffy. Mix
- **1 cup graham cracker crumbs**
- **½ cup butter, melted**
- **½ cup sugar**

Line a refrigerator tray or a pie pan with wax paper. Spread with half the crumb mixture, pour in the beaten lime mixture, and cover with the remaining crumbs. Freeze (p. 418). *Serves 6 to 8.*

SUNDAES

Serve the sauce separately or pour a little over each serving of ice cream, adding, if you like, a bit of decoration such as a few nut meats, toasted coconut, a cherry or a dab of whipped cream.

Butterscotch Sundae. Vanilla or chocolate ice cream with hot Butterscotch Sauce (p. 429). Garnish with a few whole toasted almonds.

Chocolate Sundae. Vanilla, peppermint, orange or coffee ice cream with Chocolate Sauce (p. 430).

Coffee Sundae. Vanilla or chocolate ice cream with strong hot coffee poured over it. Whipped cream, too, if you like, and a maraschino cherry.

Fruit Sundae. Vanilla ice cream with crushed and sweetened peaches, raspberries or strawberries.

Ginger Sundae. Mix 1 cup sugar, ½ cup water and 3 tablespoons chopped crystallized ginger. Boil 10 minutes, cool and serve over vanilla ice cream.

Maple Sundae. Vanilla ice cream with warm maple syrup, flavored, if you like, with rum.

Marshmallow and Marshmallow Mint Sundae. See page 431.

Brandied Peach Sundae. Fill half a brandied peach with toasted almonds and put a scoop of vanilla ice cream on top.

Nut Sundae. Chopped salted nuts on vanilla, coffee, butterscotch or chocolate ice cream. Peanuts are especially good on chocolate ice cream.

HOLIDAY SUNDAE

For Christmas or Thanksgiving.

Mix
1 cup dates, cut small
½ pint jar maraschino cherries
½ pint jar green figs, cut small
Syrup from the jars
Let stand over night or for several hours. Add
¼ pound toasted almond halves
Few grains salt
Boil 5 minutes
½ cup sugar
½ cup water
Add the fruit and
Brandy *or* rum to taste
Spoon over servings of
Vanilla ice cream (2 quarts)
or soften the ice cream, stir in the sauce and repack until firm. *Serves 12.*

PEPPERMINT SUNDAE

Mix in a saucepan
½ cup crushed peppermint stick candy
½ cup sugar
1 cup water
¼ cup light corn syrup
Simmer until the candy dissolves. Mix until smooth
1 tablespoon cornstarch
2 tablespoons water
Stir into the peppermint syrup. Cook and stir until thick. Tint with
Green food coloring
Cool and pour over servings of
Chocolate or vanilla ice cream (1 quart)
Serves 6.

PINEAPPLE MINT SUNDAE

Mix
1 small can crushed pineapple
1 cup sugar
¾ cup water
Simmer 10 minutes. Cool, tint with
Green food coloring
Add
3 drops oil of peppermint
Spoon over servings of
Vanilla ice cream (1 quart)
Serves 6.

COUPES AND PARFAITS

For a party dessert, use tall parfait glasses.

Put a scoop of ice cream in each glass and pour over the ice cream a spoonful of sauce or crushed sweetened fruit. Garnish further, if you like, with whipped cream, marshmallow cream, candied fruit, chopped nuts, crushed nut brittle, marrons, candied orange peel or toasted coconut. Use any of the combinations suggested for sundaes (p. 422) or these special ones.

Orange Coupe. Spoon orange ice into hollowed-out orange halves. Pour 1 teaspoon curaçao over the ice and decorate with sprig of mint or other green leaves. Or stir a little curaçao into vanilla ice cream and serve topped with shaved toasted hazelnuts.

Orange Pistachio Cream. Garnish orange ice or orange ice cream with whipped cream and chopped pistachio nuts.

Chocolate Mint Coupe. Alternate layers of chocolate ice cream and mint ice cream. Garnish with squares of glacé mint or a sprig of fresh mint. Or use chocolate ice cream, garnished with whipped cream flavored with oil of peppermint and colored green. Or chocolate ice cream with Marshmallow Mint Sauce (p. 431).

Ice à la Margot. Flavor sweetened whipped cream with pistachio and tint pale green.

Spoon over vanilla ice cream. Garnish with pistachio nuts or Malaga grapes, peeled, seeded and halved.

Coupe St. Jacques. Put fruit cocktail in a parfait glass. Spoon lemon ice on top. Pear, grapefruit, orange and Malaga grapes or strawberries make a delicious combination.

SORBET À LA BRUXELLES

Crush raspberries or strawberries. Put through a strainer to remove the seeds. Sweeten to taste and flavor with brandy or kirsch. Stir into slightly softened vanilla ice cream and serve in goblets. This dessert should not be firm.

COFFEE ZABAGLIONE FRAPPÉ

Spoon hot Zabaglione (p. 386) over coffee ice cream. A 4-egg-yolk Zabaglione will be enough for 4 to 6 servings.

CORDIAL PARFAITS

All the cordials make interesting parfaits. Put the ice cream in a parfait glass or dessert dish. Pour the liqueur over it and embellish it further, if you like, with whipped cream. Some successful combinations are:

- Coffee ice cream with crème de cacao
- Orange or chocolate ice cream with curaçao or Cointreau
- Chocolate ice cream with crème de menthe
- Peach ice cream with brandy or Benedictine
- Vanilla ice cream with crushed fruit or fruit cup and Cointreau or Cherry Heering

ICEBERGS

Mix finely chopped almonds, hazelnuts, pecans and walnuts in equal proportions. Sprinkle over scoops of mint ice.

PEACH *or* PEAR MELBA

Put a scoop of vanilla ice cream on a peach or pear half. Pour Melba Sauce around the fruit. Use canned fruit or cook fresh fruit 5 minutes in sugar syrup.

Melba Sauce. Crush 1 cup canned, frozen or fresh raspberries. Strain to remove the seeds. Add 1/4 cup sugar and cook slowly 10 minutes. See also page 433 for a thickened Melba sauce.

BLACK CHERRIES JUBILEE

See page 369.

STRAWBERRIES FLAMBÉ

See page 377.

STRAWBERRIES ROMANOFF

See page 377.

FROZEN ÉCLAIRS *or* CREAM PUFFS

Fill éclairs or cream puffs (p. 408) with vanilla ice cream. Serve with Chocolate Sauce (p. 430) or Butterscotch Sauce (p. 429).

PROFITEROLES AU CHOCOLAT

See page 408.

MERINGUE GLACÉ

Press two meringues around a scoop of ice cream. Serve with whipped cream, a sauce or crushed fruit.

ICE CREAM CROQUETTES

Shape firm ice cream with an ice cream scoop. Roll in finely chopped toasted almonds or macaroon crumbs.

ICE CREAM FLOWERPOTS

Fill colored pottery custard cups with ice cream. Smooth the tops and sprinkle with grated sweet chocolate. Wrap the stems of flowers in wax paper and set in pots as if they were growing.

ICE CREAM ROLL

Make Chocolate Roll (p. 406). Spread with ice cream instead of whipped cream. The ice cream must be somewhat soft.

PEANUT BALLS

Shape firm ice cream with a scoop. Roll in chopped peanuts and serve with hot Chocolate Sauce (p. 430).

BOMBES AND MOLDS

Chill a brick or melon mold or a refrigerator tray. Put in homemade or commercial ice cream in layers or line with one flavor (using a spoon to smooth it in) and fill the center with another or with a special mixture such as whipped cream, any mousse (p. 418), Charlotte Russe (p. 395), Angel Parfait (p. 420), Italian Meringue or Butterscotch Parfait (p. 426). Fill to overflowing. Put on the cover and press it down. Pack in salt and ice, using four parts ice to one of salt, if the center is unfrozen, or equal parts ice and salt if both are frozen. If you are using a refrigerator tray, set the temperature low enough for freezing until the cream is firm.

There are many delicious combinations but here are a few suggestions.

For the outer layer: Vanilla Ice Cream (pp. 416 ff.). *For the center:* Butterscotch Parfait (p. 426) *or* Frozen Tom and Jerry (p. 416) *or* Coffee Mousse (p. 420).

For the outer layer: Chocolate Ice Cream (p. 417). *For the center:* Mint, Peppermint, Pistachio or Coffee Ice Cream (p. 416) *or* Chantilly Mousse (p. 419) *or* Orange Ice or Ice Cream (pp. 413, 418)

For the outer layer: Coffee Ice Cream (p. 416). *For the center:* Burnt Almond or other nut ice cream (p. 416) *or* Italian Meringue (below) *or* Marron Parfait (p. 421)

For the outer layer: Orange Ice (p. 413). *For the center:* Macaroon Ice Cream (p. 416) *or* Orange Ice Cream (p. 418)

ITALIAN MERINGUE

Beat until stiff

3 egg whites

Boil 5 minutes

½ cup sugar
¼ cup water

Pour over the egg whites, beating constantly. Place in a pan of ice water and beat until cold. Fold in

1 cup heavy cream, whipped

Add

1 teaspoon vanilla
Few grains salt

Enough for the center of a 2-quart mold (p. 425).

BUTTERSCOTCH PARFAIT

Put in a saucepan

⅓ cup brown sugar
1 tablespoon butter

Cook until melted. Add

¼ cup boiling water

Stir and cook until blended. Pour slowly over

2 egg yolks, well beaten

Cook over hot water until fluffy, beating constantly. Chill. Fold in

½ pint heavy cream, whipped

Add

Few grains salt
1½ teaspoons vanilla

Use as the center for a bombe (p. 425) or freeze in a refrigerator tray and serve in parfait glasses with a topping of chopped nuts. *Enough for the center of a 2-quart mold or 4 small servings.*

NEW YEAR'S BOMBE

Put in a small saucepan

½ cup water
¼ cup sugar
1 tablespoon gelatine (1 envelope)

Cook and stir over low heat until the gelatine dissolves. Cool slightly and stir gently into

1 pint heavy cream, whipped

Fold in

1 cup crushed nut brittle (homemade, p. 14)
⅓ cup chopped toasted almonds
1 teaspoon vanilla
⅛ teaspoon salt

Line a 2-quart mold with

1 quart French vanilla ice cream

Fill the center with the prepared cream. Put on the cover and freeze (p. 425). *Serves 12.*

STRAWBERRY BOMBE

Prepare

1 cup sieved strawberries

Stir gently into

1 cup heavy cream, whipped

Add

1 tablespoon kirsch
2 teaspoons vanilla
¾ cup powdered sugar

Line a 2-quart mold with

1 quart strawberry ice

Fill with the prepared cream, cover and freeze (p. 425). Garnish with

Whipped cream
Whole perfect strawberries

Serves 10.

SULTANA ROLL

Line round molds or tin boxes with pistachio ice cream. Sprinkle with sultana raisins which have been soaked 1 hour in brandy. Fill the centers with vanilla ice cream or whipped cream. Cover with pistachio ice cream. Pack (p. 425). Serve with Melba Sauce (p. 433) or Claret Sauce.

Claret Sauce. Boil 1 cup sugar and ¼ cup water 8 minutes. Cool slightly and add ⅓ cup claret.

SPUMONE

Line a melon mold with lemon ice or French vanilla ice cream. Fill with bisque ice cream and chocolate mousse, one layer of each. Freeze.

NEAPOLITAN ICE CREAM

Pack two or three flavors of slightly softened ice cream in

layers in a brick mold. One layer is usually lemon or orange ice. Freeze until firm.

CASSATA À LA SICILIANA

Pack a brick mold with layers of slightly softened pistachio and vanilla ice cream and raspberry ice. Freeze until firm.

Cassata Flambé. Heat cognac, light with a match and pour, flaming, over slices of cassata.

ZABAGLIONE FRAPPÉ

Mix
- **1 envelope gelatine (1 tablespoon)**
- **½ cup cold water**

Make double recipe of
- **Zabaglione (p. 386)**

Stir in the gelatine. Beat thoroughly. Pour into a bowl or paper soufflé cups. Place in the refrigerator freezing compartment. Chill until firm. *Serves 4 to 6.*

Vary by adding cognac and maraschino and toasted almonds, bits of brandied fruit or macaroon crumbs.

BAKED ALASKA

Always an impressive dessert but not difficult to prepare. With ice cream frozen firm, you can prepare it before dinner and set it in the refrigerator ready to be put in the oven to brown while the table is being cleared for dessert. As added decoration, you may like to sprinkle chopped toasted filberts or almonds on the meringue before baking. Do not double the amount of meringue when you make a 2-quart Alaska—one based on 6 whites will be enough.

Beat until stiff
- **4 egg whites**
- **⅛ teaspoon cream of tartar**

Beat in gradually
- **½ cup sugar**

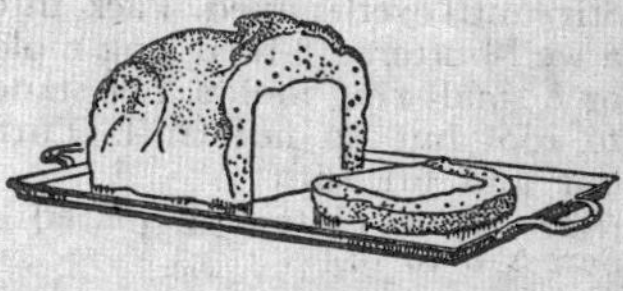

Continue beating until very stiff. Put several thicknesses of brown paper on a small board that will fit in your oven. Set on the paper
- **1 quart ice cream, frozen hard**

Cover completely with the meringue. When ready to serve, set in a 450° oven and brown lightly (about 5 minutes). *Serves 6 to 8.*

Baked Alaska on Sponge Cake. Put a ½-inch layer of sponge cake on the paper. Place the ice cream on the cake, leaving a ½-inch rim of the cake all round. The cake insulates, too.

Baked Alaska en Surprise. Before spreading the ice cream with meringue, make a hollow in it and fill with crushed sweetened fruit or marrons.

Frozen Meringue Pies. Fill baked pie shells or tarts with ice cream and continue as above.

Grapefruit Surprise. Cut grapefruit in half, remove the fruit pulp and cut away the white part to make a clean bowl. Put in each a layer of grapefruit sections or a combination of fruits and cover with vanilla ice cream or lemon ice. Top with meringue and finish like Baked Alaska (above).

BUTTERSCOTCH ICE CREAM RING

Cook to the soft ball stage (238°)
- **1 cup brown sugar**
- **1½ tablespoons light corn syrup**

⅓ cup milk
3 tablespoons butter
Butter a mixing bowl. Pour in the syrup. Add
4 cups corn flakes
Stir until well mixed. Pack into a well-buttered 8-inch ring mold or 8 small ring molds. Let stand to cool but do not chill. Turn out and fill with
Ice cream (1 to 1½ quarts)
Serves 6 to 8.

FROZEN RUM CAKE

Put a thin layer of sponge cake in a refrigerator tray. Sprinkle generously with rum. Cover with a layer of vanilla, coffee or chocolate ice cream. Put another layer of cake on top and sprinkle it with rum. Leave in the refrigerator to become firm. Cut in slices to serve. Serve with Rum Sauce (p. 410).

For variety, spread on the top layer chopped nut brittle or macaroon crumbs soaked in rum.

GÂTEAU RICHE

Prepare Swedish Almond Wafer mixture (p. 469). Bake by tablespoonfuls on 8- or 9-inch inverted layer cake tins, buttered and floured. Bake two at a time (this amount makes 8 large circles). The batter will spread to cover the tin as it bakes.

Put together in pairs with somewhat soft vanilla ice cream. Serve in wedges with hot Chocolate Sauce (p. 430). The pieces will have uneven edges, since the thin, brittle wafers will crack as you cut them. *Makes 8 or more servings, according to the amount of ice cream used.*

Dessert Sauces

Some desserts require a particular sauce to complete the blending of flavor and texture necessary to perfection and, when this is so, the recipe refers to the special sauce required. Often you can concoct a delicious dessert out of leftover cake or pudding by adding an interesting sauce, such as Coffee Custard Sauce (p. 430) or Maple Cream Sauce (431).

AMOUNT TO MAKE

One cup of sauce serves 6 or 8, but of course this is a matter of individual taste. If the sauce is passed, you may need more than if you arrange each serving yourself. Leftover sauce can often be eked out for another day's dessert by adding water or cream, reheating, and then tasting to see if more flavoring is needed.

BUTTERSCOTCH SAUCE

Cook 10 minutes

½ cup brown sugar
½ cup light corn syrup

Add

½ teaspoon salt
2 tablespoons butter
1 teaspoon vanilla

Stir well.

Cream Butterscotch Sauce. Add ½ cup thin cream to the sugar and syrup. Cook 30 minutes in a double boiler, stirring occasionally. Add the salt, butter and vanilla. Serve warm or cold. **For a thinner sauce, add more cream.**

RICH BUTTERSCOTCH SAUCE

Mix in a double boiler top

½ cup butter
2⅔ cups light brown sugar (1 pound)
1 tablespoon lemon juice *or*
½ teaspoon vinegar
½ cup heavy cream
Few grains salt

Cook over simmering water 1 hour, stirring occasionally. *Makes 1 pint (enough for about 2 quarts of ice cream).*

HENRI'S BUTTERSCOTCH SAUCE

A de luxe sauce, almost transparent. Store it in a covered jar in the refrigerator.

Cook to 246° (firm-ball stage)

1½ cups sugar
1¼ cups corn syrup
¼ teaspoon salt
¼ pound butter
½ pint cream

Remove from the heat. Add

½ pint cream

Cook to 224° (just barely thick).

Add

1 teaspoon vanilla

Cool. *Makes about 1 quart.*

CARAMEL SAUCE

Put in a small heavy pan

1 cup sugar

Heat over low heat, stirring constantly, until the sugar melts and is slightly brown. Add slowly

1 cup boiling water

Boil 6 minutes. Cool.

To make slightly less sweet, use ¾ cup water and ¼ cup coffee in place of 1 cup water.

CHOCOLATE SAUCE

Put in a small heavy saucepan

2 tablespoons butter
2 ounces unsweetened chocolate

Stir over low heat until the chocolate melts. Add

1 cup sugar
Few grains salt
½ cup water

Cook, stirring constantly, until the sauce is as thick as you like it. Flavor to taste with

Vanilla, vanilla and brandy, *or* peppermint

QUICK CHOCOLATE SAUCE

Melt over hot water

2 ounces unsweetened chocolate

Add

¼ teaspoon salt
1½ cups condensed milk (1 can) *or* 1 cup light corn syrup

Stir until thick. Add

1 teaspoon vanilla

Add until as thin as you like

Boiling water (½ to 1 cup)

CREAMY CHOCOLATE SAUCE

Creamy even when reheated.

Put in a saucepan

1½ cups milk
2 ounces unsweetened chocolate

Heat until the chocolate melts. Beat with a rotary beater until smooth. Mix

½ cup sugar
1 tablespoon flour
Few grains salt

Stir slowly into the chocolate mixture. Cook and stir 5 minutes. Add

2 tablespoons butter
½ teaspoon vanilla

For Profiteroles or Cottage Pudding.

CHOCOLATE CREAM SAUCE

Melt in a double boiler

1 package semi-sweet chocolate (7 ounces)

Add

1 tablespoon corn syrup

Stir until smooth. Add

⅓ cup cream
Few grains salt
Vanilla *or* peppermint essence to taste

Blend well.

FUDGE SAUCE

Mix in a double boiler top

1 cup cocoa *or* 2 ounces unsweetened chocolate
¾ cup sugar
½ teaspoon salt
1 tablespoon cornstarch

Add

½ cup light corn syrup
½ cup milk

Cook 15 minutes over hot water, stirring until thickened. Add

2 tablespoons butter

Cool. Add

2 teaspoons vanilla, sherry *or* brandy

For ice cream.

Quick Fudge Sauce. Cook fudge mix to the soft ball stage.

COFFEE CUSTARD SAUCE

Beat slightly in a double boiler top

3 egg yolks

Stir in

4 tablespoons sugar
⅛ teaspoon salt

Add gradually

1 cup hot coffee

Cook over hot water until thick, stirring occasionally. Cool. Fold in

⅓ cup heavy cream, whipped

For ice cream, puddings or cream puffs.

COFFEE CREAM SAUCE

Beat until thick

2 egg yolks

Cook to 234° (thread stage)

1 cup sugar
⅓ cup strong coffee

Pour over the yolks, beating constantly. Add

Few grains salt

Chill. Just before serving, whip

½ pint heavy cream

Fold in the coffee mixture. Add

½ teaspoon vanilla or brandy

Serve on any chocolate pudding or on squares of cake. Particularly delicious on steamed chocolate pudding.

HONEY SAUCE

Mix in a small saucepan

2 tablespoons melted butter
2 teaspoons cornstarch

Stir until smooth. Add

½ cup honey

Cook 5 minutes.

HONEY CREAM SAUCE

Beat until thick

½ cup heavy cream

Beat in

½ cup strained honey
1 teaspoon lemon juice

MARSHMALLOW SAUCE

Cut in pieces with wet scissors (or use very small marshmallows)

¼ pound marshmallows

Melt in a double boiler. Mix

1 cup confectioners' sugar
¼ cup boiling water

Add to the marshmallows. Stir until thoroughly blended.

MARSHMALLOW MINT SAUCE

Boil 5 minutes

½ cup sugar
¼ cup water

Add

1 cup tiny marshmallows or large ones, cut in pieces

Stir well. Pour slowly over

1 egg white, beaten stiff

Beat until well blended. Add

1 drop oil of peppermint

Tint with

Green food coloring

For chocolate pudding or ice cream.

MAPLE SYRUP

Delicious not only on pancakes and waffles but as a sauce on vanilla ice cream. Warm it slightly, and sprinkle a few nuts on top.

Rum Maple Sauce. Add rum to taste.

MAPLE CREAM SAUCE

Boil to the soft ball stage (232°)

1 cup maple sugar *or* syrup
½ cup cream

Beat 1 minute. Add

1 teaspoon vanilla

Maple Cream Sauce with Nuts. Add ½ cup chopped pecans.

MOCK MAPLE SYRUP

Boil until sugar dissolves (1 minute)

1 cup light brown sugar
⅓ cup water

Add

Few grains salt
1 teaspoon vanilla

Serve hot or cold. *For pancakes and puddings.*

CAMBRIDGE SAUCE

Cream

⅓ cup butter

Beat in gradually

1 cup powdered sugar

Mix until smooth

2 teaspoons flour
1½ tablespoons cold water

Add to

½ cup boiling water

Boil 5 minutes. Cool. Just before serving, combine the two mixtures. Add

1 teaspoon vanilla

For steamed puddings or Cottage Pudding.

Yankee Sauce. Add 1 teaspoon vinegar.

MOLASSES SAUCE

Boil 5 minutes

1 cup molasses
1½ tablespoons butter

Remove from the heat. Add

2 tablespoons lemon juice *or* 1 tablespoon vinegar

VANILLA SAUCE

The standard old-fashioned sauce for Cottage Pudding (p. 394).

Mix in a small saucepan

½ cup sugar
1 tablespoon cornstarch

Add, stirring constantly

1 cup boiling water

Boil 5 minutes. Remove from the heat. Stir in

2 tablespoons butter
1 teaspoon vanilla
Few gratings nutmeg
Few grains salt

Lemon Sauce. Omit the vanilla. Add 1½ tablespoons lemon juice.

Hot Orange Sauce. Use orange juice in place of water.

Maraschino Sauce. Use 2 tablespoons cornstarch. Add ¼ cup maraschino cherries, cut in halves, and ½ cup maraschino syrup.

ROXBURY SAUCE

Beat until thick and lemon-colored

1 egg yolk

Beat in gradually

¾ cup powdered sugar

Mix in a double boiler top

¼ cup powdered sugar
1 teaspoon cornstarch
⅛ teaspoon salt

Add gradually

½ cup scalded milk

Cook over hot water 10 minutes, stirring constantly until thick. Add the egg mixture and

½ teaspoon vanilla
1 tablespoon lemon juice
1 teaspoon grated lemon rind

Fold in

1 egg white, beaten stiff

For steamed puddings.

MONROE SAUCE

Boil 12 minutes

2 cups brown sugar
1 cup boiling water

Mix until smooth

2 teaspoons cornstarch
¼ cup cold water

Add gradually to the syrup. Simmer 40 minutes, stirring occasionally. Just before serving, add

4 tablespoons butter
1 teaspoon vanilla
Slight grating of nutmeg
Few grains salt

For steamed puddings.

FRUIT SAUCES

Crush peaches, raspberries or strawberries. Sweeten to taste. Serve over ice cream or simple puddings.

CURRANT JELLY SAUCE

Beat slightly with a fork

½ cup currant jelly

Add

2 tablespoons hot water

2 teaspoons lemon juice
Few grains salt
For a smooth sauce, heat until the jelly melts.

FRUIT JUICE SAUCE

If the fruit juice is very sweet, use less sugar.

Mix in a saucepan
1 cup sugar
1 tablespoon cornstarch
Few grains salt
Add slowly
½ cup boiling water
Boil 5 minutes. Cool and add
1 cup fruit juice, fresh or canned
2 tablespoons lemon juice

THIN LEMON SAUCE

Put in a small saucepan
¾ cup sugar
2 tablespoons light corn syrup
¼ cup water
Boil 5 minutes without stirring. Remove from the heat. Add
2 teaspoons butter
1 tablespoon lemon juice

MELBA SAUCE

Crush
2 cups fresh raspberries or 1 package frozen raspberries
Strain to remove the seeds. Add
½ cup currant jelly
Bring to the boiling point. Add
Sugar to taste
Mix until smooth
1 teaspoon cornstarch *or* arrowroot
1 tablespoon cold water
Add to the berries. Cook and stir until thick. Strain and cool. *For fruit, puddings and ice cream.*

ORANGE SAUCE

Beat until stiff
3 egg whites
Beat in gradually
1 cup powdered sugar
Blend in
Juice and rind of 2 oranges
Juice of 1 lemon

ORANGE CUSTARD SAUCE

Mix in a saucepan
Grated rind of ½ lemon
Juice of ½ lemon
½ cup orange juice
⅓ cup sugar
Few grains salt
2 egg yolks, slightly beaten
Cook and stir over low heat until thick. Add gradually, beating constantly, to
2 egg whites, beaten stiff
Cool. Add
1 teaspoon vanilla
For cottage pudding, fruit or sponge cake.

ORANGE CREAM SAUCE

Put in a double boiler top
1 egg
Grated rind of 1 orange
2 tablespoons orange juice
¾ cup sugar
3 tablespoons flour
Stir thoroughly. Cook and stir over hot water until thick. Cool. Fold in
1 cup heavy cream, whipped
For sponge cake squares or any simple pudding.

STRAWBERRY SAUCE

Mash berries, sprinkle with sugar and let stand 1 hour. Taste and add more sugar, if necessary. See also Strawberry Whip (p. 378).

STRAWBERRY CREAM SAUCE

Beat until stiff
1 egg white
Without washing the beater, beat

1 egg yolk

Stir gently together. Add

1 cup powdered sugar
1 cup mashed strawberries
½ cup heavy cream
¼ cup milk

Beat just enough to blend well. *For cottage pudding or squares of sponge cake.*

HARD SAUCE

For a perfect sauce, beat long enough to make it fluffy and smooth.

Let stand at room temperature until soft but not melted

⅓ cup butter

Cream thoroughly. Beat in gradually

1 cup confectioners' sugar (sifted)

Beat until light as whipped cream. Beat in, drop by drop

½ teaspoon vanilla

If the sauce separates, add a teaspoon of boiling water, drop by drop. If you use an electric mixer, scrape down the sides of the bowl from time to time. Chill or serve at room temperature. *For steamed puddings.*

For a richer sauce, beat in ¼ cup heavy cream (lukewarm).

Brandy *or* Wine Hard Sauce. Flavor with 1 teaspoon brandy or 1 to 3 tablespoons sherry or Madeira.

Creamy Hard Sauce. Add 3 tablespoons warm milk, drop by drop.

Lemon Hard Sauce. Add ⅓ teaspoon lemon extract or 1 teaspoon lemon juice and 1 tablespoon grated rind.

Mocha Hard Sauce. Flavor with 2 tablespoons strong coffee and 2 teaspoons dry cocoa. Add cream.

Orange Hard Sauce. Flavor with 2 tablespoons orange juice and add 2 tablespoons grated orange rind.

Raspberry Hard Sauce. Beat in 2 or 3 tablespoons strained raspberry juice, fresh or canned (p. 553), adding it drop by drop to prevent separating.

Strawberry Hard Sauce. Wash, hull and drain ⅔ cup strawberries. Beat in one at a time. If desired, beat 1 egg white into sugar and butter mixture before adding berries.

STERLING SAUCE

The brown sugar version of hard sauce.

Follow the recipe for Hard Sauce (above) but use ⅔ cup light brown sugar in place of white sugar. Add 2 tablespoons heavy cream, drop by drop. Flavor with 1½ tablespoons sherry and 2 teaspoons brandy, added drop by drop.

Ohio Sauce. Add 2 tablespoons chopped nut meats and 2 tablespoons chopped dates. Flavor with lemon extract.

FOAMY SAUCE

Cream

½ cup butter

Beat in gradually

1 cup powdered sugar
1 egg or 2 egg yolks, well beaten
Few grains salt

Set over hot water and beat until smooth and light (about 7 minutes). Flavor with

Vanilla, sherry *or* brandy

For steamed puddings.

Foamy Sauce with Cream. Fold in ½ cup cream, whipped until stiff.

SABAYON SAUCE

Zabaglione (p. 386) is a wonderful sauce, too.

Mix in a double boiler top

Grated rind and juice of ½ lemon

½ cup orange juice *or* white wine *or* ¼ cup sherry

⅓ cup sugar

2 egg yolks

Set over hot water and beat with a whisk until thick. Cut and fold into

2 egg whites, beaten until stiff

Delicious over fresh fruit or a hot fruit compote.

CREAM SABAYON SAUCE

Heat in a double boiler top

½ cup milk

½ cup cream

Beat together until thick

2 egg yolks

2 tablespoons sugar

Pour the hot milk and cream over the egg yolks, beating constantly. Pour back into the double boiler top and cook over hot water, beating constantly with a whisk until thick. Add

2 tablespoons sherry

½ teaspoon vanilla

Few grains salt

Cut and fold into

2 egg whites, beaten stiff

For fresh fruit or fruit pudding.

HOT BRANDY SAUCE

Cream together

¼ cup butter

1 cup powdered sugar

Add

2 egg yolks, well beaten

½ cup cream

Cook over hot water until the mixture coats a spoon, stirring occasionally. Pour slowly over

2 egg whites, beaten stiff

Add

2 tablespoons brandy

For holiday steamed puddings.

MARYLAND SAUCE

Cream together

½ cup butter

1 cup sugar

Beat in gradually

4 egg yolks, well beaten

6 tablespoons hot water

3 tablespoons brandy

Put in a bowl and spoon over the top

4 egg whites, beaten stiff

Mix while serving. *For holiday steamed puddings.*

YELLOW SAUCE

Beat until stiff

2 egg whites

Beat in gradually

½ cup confectioners' sugar

Without washing the beater, beat until thick

2 egg yolks

¼ cup confectioners' sugar

Combine. Flavor with

1 teaspoon vanilla *or* ½ teaspoon vanilla and 1 teaspoon brandy

Floradora Sauce. Fold in ¾ cup heavy cream, whipped. Flavor with rum or sherry to taste.

SEA FOAM SAUCE

Cream

2 tablespoons butter

2 tablespoons flour

½ cup sugar

Beat together

1 egg yolk

½ cup water

Add to the butter mixture. Cook over low heat or in a double boiler until thick, stirring constantly. Cool. Just before serving, stir in lightly

1 teaspoon vanilla

1 egg white, beaten stiff

WHIPPED CREAM FOR DESSERTS

Whip cream, adding confectioners' sugar to taste as the cream begins to thicken. For ½ pint of cream the average amount to use is 1 tablespoon, but to serve with a very sweet dessert unsweetened cream is delicious. Add a few grains of salt and vanilla to taste. Whip until fluffy but not stiff. For details about whipping cream see page 12.

Frozen Whipped Cream. Pack in a refrigerator drawer and chill until firm. Serve in cubes. Particularly good on warm apple or blueberry pie.

Molasses *or* Honey Cream. Sweeten with molasses or honey instead of sugar. *For spice or fruit puddings.*

WHIPPED DRY MILK

A light fluffy topping which can substitute for whipped cream. High in protein and low in fat.

Mix and whip until light
- **½ cup powdered skim milk**
- **½ cup water**
- **1 tablespoon lemon juice**

Add, to taste
- **Powdered sugar**
- **Vanilla**

MOCK DEVONSHIRE CREAM

Mash until soft
- **1 package cream cheese (3 ounces)**

Beat in
- **½ cup heavy cream**

Beat until smooth. Serve with hot scones and raspberry jam or on fresh or stewed fruit.

Pastry, Pies and Small Pastries

Perfect pastry is a triumph. Made by the standard method, it is superbly flaky, but Hot Water Pastry (p. 440), Stirred Pastry (p. 441) and No-Roll Pastry (p. 441) are easier for the beginner to make and are tender and delicious. Packaged mixes are welcome timesavers. Puff Paste (p. 453), the queen of pastries, is used for patty shells and small pastries. It is satisfying to have a ball of pastry in the refrigerator, ready for hurry-up desserts, cocktail snacks and meat or chicken pies.

PASTRY INGREDIENTS

Flour. Pastry flour makes the most tender pastry. If you use all-purpose flour, reduce the amount in the recipe by 2 tablespoons in each cup. Puff Paste requires all-purpose or bread flour because there is so much shortening in the recipe that a delicate flour would make the pastry crumble.

Shortening. Vegetable oils and shortenings, lard and butter are commonly used in pastry making. Half butter and half lard makes pastry of excellent flavor.

Liquid. Ice water keeps the shortening from melting while the pastry is being blended. Too much water makes pastry tough.

PIE MAKING

See also the directions for making Stirred Pastry (p. 441) and No-Roll Pastry (p. 441).

To roll pastry. Dust a canvas pastry cloth or a board very lightly with flour. Too much flour makes pastry tough. Well-chilled pastry dough needs very little to keep it from sticking. Set the ball of chilled dough on the cloth. Tap it with a few light strokes of the rolling pin to flatten it but do not press it hard. Roll with quick light strokes, working outward from

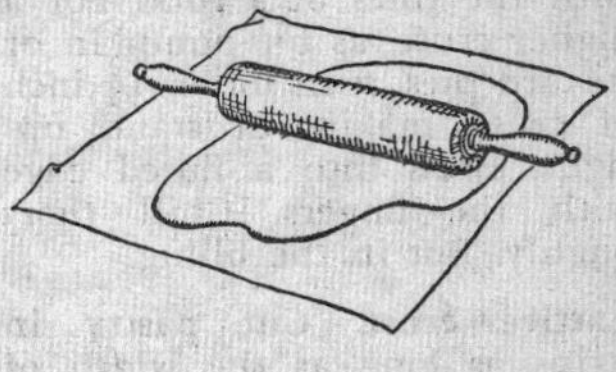

the center. Lift the pastry occasionally with a broad spatula and dust under it with just enough flour to keep it from sticking. Roll as evenly as possible so that the baked pastry will be the same thickness throughout.

Two-crust pie. Divide the pastry in two parts, one slightly larger. Put the smaller one in the refrigerator. Roll the larger piece into a circle about 1/8 inch thick and an inch larger than the pie pan. Fold double and lift gently into the pan. Unfold and fit lightly in place. Do not stretch. Trim the edge evenly with scissors or a sharp knife, allowing about 1/2 inch extra all around.

Put in a generous amount of filling. Heap fresh fruit high in the center because it will cook down while baking. Roll out the other piece of pastry the same way. Fold double and cut several slits or a fancy design near the center to let out steam during the baking. Or prick well with a fork after you have set it on the pie. Brush the edge of the undercrust with water, fit the top crust over the filling, and press the edge of the top crust lightly over the undercrust. Trim the edges evenly and crimp with the fingers or the tines of a fork. Bind the edge of juicy fruit pies with pie tape, removing it after the pie is baked.

One-crust pie. Line a pie pan as for a two-crust pie. Press the pastry to the edge of the pan with the tines of a fork. For a higher crust, as for pumpkin or custard pies, turn under 1/2 inch of crust, making it stand upright. Press into a fluted edge with the fingers. Chill thoroughly. Put in the filling.

Lattice crust. Cut pastry in strips as long as the width of the pie and about 3/4 inch wide. Weave them directly onto the top of the pie or weave them onto wax paper, chill, and transfer to the pie. Trim off the ends. Finish the edge with the tines of a fork or crimp with the fingers. Another way to make a lattice top is to twist the strips, lay half of them in rows across the pie and the rest across them to make a diamond pattern without actually weaving them.

Baking pies. Bake fruit pies at 450° until the fruit is tender when you test it with a fork (about 40 minutes). If the upper crust begins to brown too quickly, cover it with a piece of brown paper. Bake deep-dish pies at 350°. See also individual recipes.

To glaze pies. Dot the upper crust of the pie with butter just before baking, or brush with ice water, top milk or cream 10 minutes before the pie is done.

To keep the juices from dripping in the oven, put a piece of aluminum foil under the pie pan and fold the edges up.

Baked Pie Shell. Line a pan with pastry as for a one-crust pie. Set another pan inside to hold it in shape or prick it well all over. Bake at 450° until well browned (about 12 minutes).

PLAIN PASTRY (STANDARD)

Save the scraps of pastry for Cheese Straws (p. 334), or Petites Galettes (p. 456) or cut with a cooky cutter, bake and spread with jelly or jam.

Measure accurately until you can judge by the "feel." Work very quickly and with a light touch. Beginning cooks can be too conscientious about pastry making and blend it so thoroughly that the layers of shortening and flour cannot separate into tender sheets.

Sift into a mixing bowl

- **2 cups pastry flour** *or* **1 3/4 cups all-purpose flour**
- **1 teaspoon salt**

Pie Crusts
Lining the Pie Plate or Tin.
Filling and
Applying the Top Crust
Two Methods for Making a Single Crust
Three Methods for Making a Lattice Top Crust
Two Methods for Making a Baked Shell
Making Patty Shells

Add

⅔ cup vegetable shortening *or* lard *or* ⅓ cup lard and ⅓ cup butter

Mix with a pastry blender, a blending fork or two knives (one held in each hand) until the mixture is in even bits about the size of peas. (*Old-fashioned cooks use their fingers and work very quickly so that the shortening does not soften.*) Put in a cup

⅓ cup ice water

Sprinkle it over the flour by tablespoonfuls, stirring it in with a fork until just enough has been added so that you can pat the dough lightly into a ball. Flours vary, so you may not need all the water. Handle the dough as little as possible and do not knead it. Wrap in wax paper or foil and chill. Roll out, fill and bake (p. 437). *Makes a 9-inch two-crust pie or a 1-crust pie and some tarts.*

Cheese Pastry. Add 5 tablespoons grated cheese, cutting it in with shortening. *For fruit pies.*

Nut Pastry. Substitute ½ cup finely ground nut meats for ½ cup of the flour. *For cream pies.*

Coffee Pastry. Add 1 tablespoon instant coffee. *For cream pies.*

Whole-Wheat Pastry. Replace ⅓ cup of the flour with ⅓ cup whole-wheat flour. *For pumpkin, apple or meat pies.*

Sesame Pastry. Add ¼ cup sesame seeds. *For cream pies.*

CATHERINE'S PASTRY

Almost as flaky as Puff Paste (p. 453). Particularly good for Cream Pie (p. 448).

Sift into a bowl

2 cups sifted pastry flour
1 teaspoon salt
½ teaspoon baking powder

Add, following directions for Plain Pastry (p. 438)

⅓ cup lard
⅓ cup ice water

Have ready

⅓ cup butter

Roll out the pastry. Dot with a third of the butter, roll up like a jelly roll, pat and again roll out. Repeat twice. Chill. Roll out, fill and bake (p. 437). *For a 9-inch pie.*

GALETTE PASTRY

Sweeter and richer than plain pastry but less flaky. Especially for open fruit pies of the European type.

Sift into a bowl

1 cup pastry or all-purpose flour
½ teaspoon salt
1 tablespoon sugar

Blend in as for Plain Pastry (p. 438)

6 tablespoons butter

Beat together and stir in

1 egg yolk
1 tablespoon water
1½ tablespoons lemon juice *or* rum

Pat together and chill. Roll ¼ inch thick and fit into a pie pan or a flan ring. Fill and bake (p. 438).

HOT WATER PASTRY

A quick and easy method. The pastry is less flaky than pastry made by the standard method (p. 438) but it is crisp and tender.

Put in a bowl

½ cup shortening (lard is best)
¼ cup boiling water

Stir until the shortening melts. Add

1½ cups sifted pastry or cake flour
¼ teaspoon salt
¼ teaspoon baking powder

Stir with a knife until well blended. Pat into a ball, wrap in wax paper and chill. Roll out, fill and bake (p. 437). *For an 8-inch pie.*

STIRRED PASTRY

Sift into a bowl

2 cups pastry or all-purpose flour
1½ teaspoons salt
1½ teaspoons sugar

Put in a cup and stir with a fork

½ cup salad oil (corn, cottonseed, peanut or soy)
¼ cup milk

Pour over the flour and stir until no dry flour shows. Pat into two balls for two crusts or into one for a large 10-inch crust. Place a ball on a sheet of wax paper, flatten with your palm, cover with another sheet of wax paper and roll out with a rolling pin. Peel off the top paper and ease the crust into the pie tin. Peel off the other paper. If the paper sticks, set the pastry in the refrigerator for a few minutes. Trim the edge. Fill and bake according to any recipe.

To make a pastry shell, prick the crust all over with a fork. Bake about 12 minutes at 425°.

NO-ROLL PASTRY

Sift directly into a 9-inch pie pan

1½ cups pastry *or* all-purpose flour
1 teaspoon salt
1½ teaspoons sugar

Mix in a cup

½ cup vegetable cooking oil
2 tablespoons milk

Pour over the flour and mix with a fork until no dry flour shows. Press with your fingers to line the pan and the sides as evenly as possible. Fill and bake accordingly to the recipe for any one-crust pie.

To make a baked shell, prick all over with a fork. Bake 15 minutes at 425°.

CRUMB PIE SHELL

Prepare

1½ cups finely rolled crumbs (graham cracker, ginger snap, rusk or zweibach)

Add

½ cup sugar (or less)
½ cup melted butter *or* margarine

Mix well. If you will need crumbs for the top of the pie, set ½ cup aside and line a 9-inch pie pan with the rest, patting firmly with your fingers or the back of a spoon. Chill until firm in the refrigerator or bake 8 minutes at 375° and chill.

Use for chiffon pies (p. 449) or for any cream pie or fruit pie.

Chocolate Crumb Shell. Make the crumbs of chocolate wafers. Add no sugar.

COCONUT MACAROON SHELL

Beat until stiff

1 egg white

Beat in gradually

2 tablespoons sugar
1 tablespoon light corn syrup
½ teaspoon vanilla

Add

2 cups shredded coconut, chopped fine

Line a pie pan as directed for a Crumb Pie Shell (above). Bake 15 minutes at 350°. Chill and fill with any fruit or cream filling.

MERINGUE FOR PIES AND DESSERTS

At its best when put on the pie shortly before serving. If it must be baked ahead of time, set the pie in the refrigerator until serving time.

Put in a bowl

2 egg whites

Beat with a whisk or an egg beater until in soft peaks when you lift out the beater. Beat in gradually

4 tablespoons sugar
1 teaspoon lemon juice *or* ¼ teaspoon vanilla
Few grains salt

Spoon evenly over the pie but do not make it too smooth. Spread well to the edge. For a different effect, spread part of the mixture and put the rest through a pastry bag and tube to make a pattern. Bake 4½ minutes at 425.°

If a meringue "weeps," too much sugar was used or the sugar was too coarse.

If a meringue shrinks or is tough, the oven was too slow.

To cut a meringue pie easily, dip the knife in hot water.

For individual desserts, bake the meringue in muffin tins half full of hot water. Lift onto the desserts with a spatula.

FRUIT PIE (GENERAL RECIPE)

For almost any fruit or a combination of fruits. See also recipes for individual fruits.

Prepare

2½ cups fresh fruit (without skins or pits)

(Sprinkle hard fruits such as pears with sugar and cook gently until just tender.) Line a 9-inch pie plate with

Plain Pastry (p. 438)

Fill with the fruit. Mix and sprinkle over the fruit

½ cup sugar
⅛ teaspoon salt
2 tablespoons flour *or* tapioca

Season with

Cinnamon, allspice *or* ginger

Put on a top crust or a lattice top and bake (p. 438). Serve warm or cold.

To make with a crumb crust. Reserve ½ cup crumbs when making Crumb Pie Shell (p. 441). Fill the shell with sweetened fresh or cooked fruit, cover with Meringue (p. 441), sprinkle with reserved crumbs and bake 5 minutes at 450°.

Apricot Pie. Mash cooked or canned apricots to make 3 cups. Sweeten to taste.

Blackberry Pie. Cook 2½ cups berries with just enough water to keep from burning. Sweeten to taste. Add ⅛ teaspoon salt.

Cranberry Pie. Mix 2 cups berries, ¾ cup sugar, ½ cup water and 1½ tablespoons flour. Cook 10 minutes. Cool.

Cranberry and Raisin Pie. Add ½ cup seeded raisins to cranberry filling.

Date Pie. Cook 2 cups pitted dates with 1 cup water until thick. Add 2 tablespoons orange juice. Cool. Serve with whipped cream or sour cream.

Peach Pie. Cooked dried peaches or canned peaches make a delicious pie. Mash and sweeten to taste.

GALETTE (FRENCH FRUIT PIE)

Line a 9-inch layer cake tin (square or round) with Galette Pastry (p. 440). Fill with cut fresh fruit, such as plums, apricots, peaches or apples. Sprinkle generously with brown or white sugar. Unless the fruit is tart, squeeze a little lemon juice over it. Bake at 425° until the fruit is tender (25 minutes or more). Cool. *Serves 6 or 8.*

To glaze. Melt currant jelly and pour over the finished pie.

APPLE PIE

Apple pie mixes may please your family better if you add an extra apple or two and more spice. When apples are at the peak of their flavor they need very little seasoning—perhaps only a whiff of cinnamon—but if they are somewhat bland, add lemon juice, grated lemon rind and more spices.

Pare, core and slice

6 to 8 tart apples (about 3 cups)

Line a 9-inch pie pan with

Plain Pastry (p. 438)

Fill evenly with the apples, piling them higher in the center. Mix and sprinkle over the apples

Brown *or* white sugar (½ to ¾ cup, according to the apples)
¼ teaspoon salt
½ teaspoon cinnamon
¼ teaspoon nutmeg

If the apples are very juicy, add

1 tablespoon flour

Dot with

1 tablespoon butter

Cover with the upper crust and bake (p. 438). Serve warm or cold with sharp cheese, with ice cream (à la mode) or with Frozen Whipped Cream (p. 436). *Serves 6.*

Deep Dish Apple Pie. Pack sliced apples closely in a buttered baking dish. Season as above. Put on a top crust only. Bake at 350° until the apples are tender and the crust is brown (about 50 to 60 minutes). Serve warm with cheese, cream, whipped cream (plain or frozen), ice cream or Molasses Sauce (p. 432).

APPLE GRAHAM CRACKER PIE

Cut in eighths

6 tart apples

Add

1½ cups sugar
¼ cup water

Cook slowly until the apples are tender. Add

1 tablespoon lemon juice

Mix

24 graham crackers, crushed fine
2 tablespoons sugar
¼ pound butter, melted
1 teaspoon cinnamon
¼ teaspoon nutmeg

Pat into a 9-inch pie plate. Fill with the apple mixture. Dot with crumbs. Bake 1 hour at 300°. Cool, and serve with or without whipped cream.

APPLE-CRANBERRY-RAISIN PIE

Line a 9-inch pie pan with

Plain Pastry (p. 438)

Core, peel and slice into the pan

4 large tart apples

Scatter over the apples

1 cup cranberries
½ cup raisins

Mix and sprinkle over the fruit

½ cup sugar
¼ teaspoon salt
2 tablespoons flour

Dot with

2 tablespoons butter
Grated lemon rind

Put on top crust and bake (p. 438). *Serves 6.*

BANANA CREAM PIE

Prepare a Baked Pie Shell (p. 438). Fill with sliced bananas. Cover with cold Soft Custard (p. 384) or butterscotch pudding made with a mix. Chill. Cover with whipped cream, shredded or grated coconut or chopped peanuts.

BANANA CUSTARD PIE

As a timesaver use a pudding mix, but flavor it sharply with lemon juice.

Mix in a double boiler top
⅓ cup sugar
1 tablespoon flour
⅛ teaspoon salt
Add
2 egg yolks, slightly beaten
Stir in gradually
1 cup scalded milk
Cook 15 minutes over hot water, stirri g constantly until thick, and afterward occasionally. Chill and add
¼ cup thin cream *or* top milk
1 tablespoon lemon juice
1 large banana, cut in thin slices
Just before serving, spoon into a
9-inch Baked Pie Shell (p. 438)
Cover with
Meringue (p. 441)
Bake. *Serves 6.*

BLUEBERRY PIE

Wild blueberries have the finest flavor—tart and fresh.

Prepare
3 cups berries, fresh or frozen
(Fresh berries need to be picked over; discard the stems and leaves. Wash and drain well.)
Add
2 tablespoons flour
¾ cup sugar
⅛ teaspoon salt
Mix thoroughly. Line a 9-inch pie pan with
Plain Pastry (p. 438)
Fill with the berries. Except for wild berries, sprinkle over them
1 tablespoon lemon juice
Dot with
1 tablespoon butter
Put on the top crust, prick well and bake (p. 437). *Serves 6.*

FAVORITE BLUEBERRY PIE

The uncooked berries give this pie its distinctive flavor.

Prepare
9-inch Baked Pie Shell (p. 438)
Wash and drain thoroughly
1 quart blueberries
Mix together in a saucepan
1 cup sugar
3 tablespoons cornstarch
⅛ teaspoon salt
1 cup water
1 cup berries
Cook and stir over low heat or over hot water until thick. Add the rest of the berries and
1 tablespoon butter
Mix well and cool. Just before serving, pour into the pie shell. Pour over the top
1 cup heavy cream, whipped and sweetened
Serves 6.

OLD-FASHIONED CHERRY PIE

Cherry pie should be juicy. Bind the edge with pie tape or a strip of foil to keep the juice in the pie. Remove the tape when you serve the pie. Frozen cherries are excellent for pie.

Pit
1 quart cherries (preferably sour)
Line a 9-inch pie pan with
Plain Pastry (p. 438)
Fill with the cherries. Sprinkle over them
⅛ teaspoon salt
1 cup sugar (¾ for sweet cherries)
1 tablespoon flour
Put on the top crust or a lattice crust and bake (p. 438). *Serves 6.*

SWEET CHERRY PIE

Line a 9-inch pie pan with
Plain Pastry (p. 438)
Fill with
3 cups canned cherries, pitted
Mix
¼ cup cherry juice
2 tablespoons sugar (or to taste)
2½ tablespoons quick tapioca (or 1½ for a softer filling)
Pour over the cherries. Dot with
1 teaspoon butter

Put on the top crust or a lattice top and bake (p. 438). *Serves 6.*

GLACÉ CHERRY PIE

Prepare a

9-inch Baked Pie Shell (p. 438)

Drain, reserving the juice

1 large can Bing cherries, pitted

Put the cherries in the shell. Measure the juice and add water if necessary to make 1 cup. Add

Salt and sugar to taste

Put in a small saucepan. Add

1 teaspoon gelatine

Cook and stir until the gelatine dissolves. Pour over the cherries. Chill. Cover with

1 cup heavy cream, whipped and sweetened

Serves 6.

GLACÉ PEACH *or* STRAWBERRY PIE

Prepare a

9-inch Baked Pie Shell (p. 438)

Mix in a saucepan

1 cup sugar
3 tablespoons cornstarch
¼ teaspoon salt
¾ cup fruit juice *or* water
1 teaspoon lemon juice

Stir and cook over low heat until thick. Then cook in double boiler 20 minutes. Fill the pie shell with

Hulled strawberries *or* sliced peaches (about 3 cups)

Cover with the cornstarch mixture. Chill. Spread with

1 cup heavy cream, whipped and sweetened

Serves 6.

PEACH PIE

Follow the recipe for Apple Pie (p. 443), using peeled sliced peaches in place of apples. If the peaches are very sweet, use only ½ cup sugar. See also Galette (p. 442). Or prepare a Baked Pie Shell (p. 438), Crumb Pie Shell (p. 441) or Coconut Macaroon Shell (p. 441) and fill with sweetened sliced peaches.

PINEAPPLE PIE

Prepare a

9-inch Baked Pie Shell (p. 438)

Heat in a double boiler top

2 cups crushed or shredded pineapple

Mix

2 tablespoons cornstarch
½ cup sugar (2 tablespoons for canned pineapple)
¼ teaspoon salt

Add to the pineapple. Cook 20 minutes over hot water, stirring constantly until thick. Cool. Add

1 tablespoon butter
1 tablespoon lemon juice
1 tablespoon grated lemon rind

Fill the pie shell. Cover with

Meringue (p. 441)

Bake until delicately brown. *Serves 6.*

PRUNE PIE

Cook, pit and cut in quarters

1 pound dried prunes

Add

½ cup sugar
1 tablespoon lemon juice

Drain off the juice and cook until it is reduced to 2 tablespoonfuls. Line a 9-inch pie pan with

Plain Pastry (p. 438)

Fill with the prunes and pour over the juice. Dot with

1½ tablespoons butter

Sprinkle with

1 tablespoon flour

Put on the top crust and bake (p. 437). *Serves 6.*

RAISIN PIE

Put in a bowl

¾ cup raisins
2 cups water

Let stand 2 hours. Mix

1½ cups sugar
¼ cup flour
1 egg, well beaten
3 tablespoons lemon juice
3 tablespoons grated lemon rind
⅛ teaspoon salt

Add the raisins and the liquid. Cook over hot water or over low heat until thickened (about 15 minutes), stirring occasionally. Cool. Line a 9-inch pie pan with

Plain Pastry (p. 438)

Fill with the raisin mixture. Make a lattice top and bake (p. 438). *Serves 6.*

RHUBARB PIE

For a softer filling, omit the egg.

Cut in pieces and measure

3 cups rhubarb

Mix

1 cup sugar
2 tablespoons flour
1 egg

Add to the rhubarb. Line a 9-inch pie pan with

Plain Pastry (p. 438)

Spoon in the filling. Put on the top crust or a lattice top. Bake (p. 438). *Serves 6.*

Rhubarb and Raisin Pie. Before putting on the top crust, sprinkle ½ cup raisins over the rhubarb.

LEMON MERINGUE PIE

The classic recipe, but there are excellent variations. Some like it very tart, others sweeter. Some like it stiff enough to cut in neat pieces, others prefer it soft and creamy. Try it various ways until you have the version you like best. For a softer filling, reduce the flour and cornstarch or use fewer egg yolks. But always have a high fluffy meringue made of 4 whites.

Mix in a double boiler top

4 tablespoons cornstarch
4 tablespoons flour
½ teaspoon salt
1½ cups sugar

Add

1½ cups boiling water

Cook and stir over direct heat until the mixture boils. Set over hot water, cover, and cook 20 minutes. Add

1 tablespoon butter
Few gratings lemon rind
⅓ cup lemon juice
4 egg yolks

Cook and stir until thick. Cool. Prepare and cool

9-inch Baked Pie Shell (p. 438)

Using 4 egg whites, make

Meringue (p. 441)

Fold 2 tablespoons into the filling and pile into the shell. Spoon the rest on top. Bake at 425° until delicately brown (5 minutes). *Serves 6.*

Lemon Meringue Tarts. Make large Tart Shells (p. 455) instead of a pie shell. Especially attractive and easy to serve if the filling is soft.

LEMON CRUMB PIE

Prepare, reserving ¼ cup of the crumbs for the top

9-inch Crumb Pie Shell (p. 441)

Set the oven at 325°. Separate

3 eggs

Beat the yolks until thick. Stir in

Grated rind and juice of 1½ lemons
1 can condensed milk
⅛ teaspoon salt

Beat the whites until stiff and fold them in. Pour into the crumb shell. Sprinkle the reserved crumbs over the top. Bake 40 minutes. *Serves 6.*

Lime Crumb Pie. In place of lemon juice and rind, use the grated rind and juice of 4 limes or ½ cup frozen or fresh lime juice.

ORANGE PIE

Prepare a
9-inch Baked Pie Shell (p. 438)
Separate
3 eggs
Beat the yolks until thick. Stir in
½ cup sugar
3 tablespoons flour
1 cup orange juice
Juice of 1 lemon
Cook and stir over hot water until thick (about 10 minutes). Pour into the pie shell. With the 3 egg whites, make
Meringue (p. 441)
Bake. *Serves 6.*

PECAN PIE

Serve this very rich pie in small wedges.

Set the oven at 450°. Line a 9-inch pie pan with
Plain Pastry (p. 438)
Mix and pour into the pan
3 eggs, slightly beaten
½ cup brown or white sugar
¼ teaspoon salt
1 cup light corn syrup
½ teaspoon vanilla
1 cup pecans, broken in pieces
Bake 10 minutes. Reduce the heat to 350° and bake 35 minutes longer. Chill. When ready to serve, spread over the top
½ cup heavy cream, whipped
Garnish with
Pecan halves
Serves 8.

SOUTHERN NUT PIE

Line a 9-inch pie pan with
Plain Pastry (p. 438)
Chill. Set the oven at 450°. Cream together
¼ cup butter
¾ cup sugar
1 teaspoon vanilla
Add
2 tablespoons flour
½ teaspoon salt
Mix well. Beat in, one at a time
3 eggs
Stir in
1 cup dark corn syrup
¾ cup evaporated milk
1 cup chopped pecans *or* walnuts
Mix well. Pour into the pie pan. Bake 10 minutes. Reduce the heat to 325° and bake until firm (about 50 minutes). *Serves 8.*

CORNISH TREACLE TART

A traditional English delicacy. Find the golden syrup in stores selling imported delicacies.

Set the oven at 400°. Line an 8-inch pie pan with
Catherine's Pastry (p. 440)
reserving enough for a lattice top. Mix
¾ cup golden syrup
4 tablespoons fresh white bread crumbs
2 teaspoons lemon juice
2 teaspoons grated lemon rind
Fill the pie shell (it will not be quite full), and cover with the lattice. Bake until brown (about 35 minutes). *Serves 4 to 6.*

NORFOLK TREACLE TART

Another English delicacy.

Set the oven at 350°. Line an 8-inch pie pan with
Galette Pastry (p. 440)
Warm in a saucepan
6 tablespoons golden syrup
Stir in, bit by bit
3 tablespoons butter
When the butter is melted, add
3 tablespoons cream
1 egg and 1 yolk, beaten
1 teaspoon grated lemon rind
Fill the pastry shell. Bake until the shell is brown and the filling is set (about 25 to 30 minutes). After the first 10 minutes, prick the tart gently with a skewer so that the pastry will not puff up

too much in the bottom of the plate. *Serves 4 to 6.*

CREAM PIE

Prepare a Baked Pie Shell (p. 438) or a Crumb Pie Shell (p. 441). Make a Cream Pie Filling (below) or a filling from a mix and pour into the baked shell. Or bake two or three 9-inch circles of pastry (Catherine's Pastry, p. 440, is especially good), put them together with the filling, and sprinkle powdered sugar over the top.

Meringue Cream Pie. With the reserved whites, make **Meringue** (p. 441), spread over the top, and bake 4½ minutes at 425°.

CREAM PIE FILLING

Mix in a double boiler top
 1 cup sugar
 ½ cup flour
 ¼ teaspoon salt
Stir in
 3 cups milk
Cook 15 minutes over hot water, stirring constantly until thick. Add
 3 egg yolks, slightly beaten
Cook 3 minutes. Add
 2 tablespoons butter
Cool. Add
 1 teaspoon vanilla

Butterscotch Cream Pie. Use brown sugar in place of white. Cook the sugar over low heat with 6 tablespoons butter until it melts to a golden brown syrup. Add to 2½ cups of scalded milk. Add ½ cup cold milk to the flour, stir into the hot mixture and continue as above.

Chocolate Cream Pie. Scald the milk with 2 ounces unsweetened chocolate (3 if you like a more pronounced chocolate flavor). Beat until smooth before adding the flour mixture.

Coconut Cream Pie. Add ½ cup coconut. Sprinkle the top of the finished pie with coconut, plain or toasted.

Frangipan Pie. Add 6 tablespoons dried and rolled macaroon crumbs and ½ teaspoon lemon extract.

DEVONSHIRE CREAM PIE

Cut out three 9-inch circles of Plain Pastry (p. 438). Cut the center from one, leaving a 1½-inch ring. Bake. Put the 2 circles together with Cream Pie Filling (above). Place the ring on top. Fill with fresh strawberries or other fruit, sweetened to taste. Garnish with whipped cream or glaze with melted currant jelly poured over the fruit.

CUSTARD PIE

Baked this way, the crust is crisp and dry. Easier to do than it sounds.

Set the oven at 375°. Butter a 9-inch pie pan.
Beat until well blended
 4 eggs
Stir in
 ½ cup sugar
 ¼ teaspoon salt
 3 cups milk, scalded
 1 teaspoon vanilla
Pour into the pan. Set in a larger pan and pour hot water into the outer pan ½ inch deep. Bake until firm (about 45 minutes). Cool on a wire cake rack. Prepare a
 9-inch Baked Pie Shell (p. 438)
Half an hour before serving, loosen the edge of the custard with a sharp knife. Shake gently to loosen the bottom. Hold over the pie shell with both hands, tilt, and ease the filling gently into the shell. Sprinkle with
 Nutmeg
Serves 6.

To bake by the old-fashioned method, line the pie pan with pastry, brush with slightly beaten egg white, put in the filling and bake 10 minutes at 450°. Then reduce the heat to 300° and bake until firm (45 to 50 minutes).

Caramel Custard Pie. Caramelize the sugar (p. 14) and stir it into the hot milk. Continue stirring until the sugar melts.

Coconut Custard Pie. Add ½ cup grated coconut to the custard.

CHIFFON PIE

For a richer pie, fold in ½ cup heavy cream, whipped.

Prepare a
- **9-inch Baked Pie Shell (p. 438) or Crumb Shell (p. 441)**

Separate
- **4 eggs**

Put in a heavy saucepan
- **1½ cups milk**
- **1 envelope gelatine (1 tablespoon)**
- **½ cup sugar**
- **¼ teaspoon salt**

Add the egg yolks and beat with a rotary egg beater to blend thoroughly. Cook and stir over low heat until as thick as custard. Add the flavoring (below). Chill until slightly thickened.

Beat the egg whites until they stand in soft peaks when you lift out the beater. Fold into the gelatine mixture. Spoon into the pie shell. Chill. *Serves 6.*

Chocolate Chiffon Pie. Add to the hot custard 6 tablespoons cocoa or 2 ounces melted chocolate. Flavor with rum, brandy or vanilla. Particularly good in Chocolate Crumb Shell (p. 441). Sprinkle with chocolate shot.

Chocolate Chip Chiffon Pie. Stir into the hot custard 1 cup chocolate chips.

Coffee Chiffon Pie. Instead of milk, use strong coffee or flavor the custard with instant coffee. Add a tablespoon of lemon juice and sugar to taste. Spread the finished pie with a thin layer of unsweetened whipped cream.

Eggnog Chiffon Pie. Add 3 tablespoons rum. Cover the finished pie with a thin layer of unsweetened whipped cream. Sprinkle with nutmeg.

Chiffon Candy Pie. Stir crushed peppermint stick candy, butter crunch or nut brittle into the hot custard.

BLACK BOTTOM PIE

Follow the recipe for Chiffon Pie (above) but after making the custard, divide it in half. To one part add 1½ ounces unsweetened chocolate, melted, and ½ teaspoon vanilla. To the other part add 1 tablespoon rum. Add half the beaten egg whites to each. Cool. When the mixtures begin to thicken, pour the chocolate part into the pie shell and cover with the rum-flavored custard. Top with a thin layer of sweetened whipped cream. Sprinkle with thin shavings of chocolate.

COCONUT ALMOND PIE

Follow the recipe for Chiffon Pie (above), adding to the filling ½ teaspoon almond extract and ½ cup shredded coconut. Pour into the pie shell and pat into the surface ¼ cup chopped toasted almonds mixed with ¼ cup chopped shredded coconut.

LEMON CHIFFON PIE

Prepare a
- **9-inch Baked Pie Shell (p. 438) or Crumb Crust (p. 442)**

Separate
4 eggs
Put in a small heavy saucepan
1 envelope gelatine (1 tablespoon)
½ cup sugar
⅛ teaspoon salt
¼ cup water
½ cup lemon juice
Add the egg yolks and beat with a rotary egg beater until well blended. Cook and stir over low heat until the gelatine dissolves (about 5 minutes). Stir in
1 teaspoon grated lemon rind
Chill until the mixture begins to thicken. Beat the egg whites until foamy. Beat in gradually
½ cup sugar
Beat until stiff. Fold in the gelatine mixture. Spoon into the pie shell. Chill. *Serves 6.*

Lime Chiffon Pie. Use lime juice and grated lime rind.

Orange Chiffon Pie. Use 2 tablespoons lemon juice and ½ cup orange juice. Use orange rind in place of lemon.

STRAWBERRY CHIFFON PIE

For a richer pie, fold in ½ cup heavy cream, whipped, or spread the finished pie with sweetened whipped cream.

Prepare a
9-inch Baked Pie Shell (p. 438) or Crumb Shell (p. 441)
Wash and hull
1½ cups strawberries
Save a few perfect berries to garnish the finished pie. Slice the rest and cover with
½ cup sugar
Let stand ½ hour. Mix in a saucepan
1 envelope gelatine (1 tablespoon)
¼ cup sugar
¾ cup water
1 tablespoon lemon juice
⅛ teaspoon salt
Cook and stir over low heat until the gelatine dissolves. Add to the berries, stir well, and chill until the mixture begins to thicken. Beat until stiff and fold in
2 egg whites
Pour into the pie shell. Garnish with berries. Chill. *Serves 6.*

Raspberry Chiffon Pie. Use black or red raspberries in place of strawberries. Taste and add more sugar, if needed.

CHEESE PIE (CHEESE CAKE)

One of the best of the many good versions of this popular dessert.

Mix
1 cup zweibach crumbs
¼ cup melted butter
¼ cup sugar
¼ teaspoon cinnamon
¼ teaspoon nutmeg
Pat over the bottom of a 9-inch spring pan and up about 1 inch on the sides. Set the oven at 325°. Separate
4 eggs
Beat the whites until stiff with
¼ cup sugar
Set aside. Without washing the beater, beat the yolks until thick. Add
1 cup sour cream
1 teaspoon vanilla
Beat in
¾ cup sugar
2 tablespoons flour
¼ teaspoon salt
Stir in, bit by bit
1 pound soft cream cheese
Beat until smooth. Fold in the whites. Spoon into the pan. Bake until firm to the touch (about 1 hour). Cool, then chill in the refrigerator. Turn out onto a serving plate. Serve in wedges, plain or with crushed sugared strawberries, raspberries or sliced peaches. *Serves 8.*

Cheese Pie Royale. Do not add the sour cream and vanilla to the mixture. Bake the pie at 375° for 20 minutes and cool. Stir the vanilla and 2 tablespoons sugar into the sour cream and pour it over the pie. Sprinkle with cinnamon and bake 5 minutes at 400°. Cool.

COTTAGE CHEESE PIE

Set aside ½ cup of the buttered crumbs while making a

Crumb Shell (p. 441)

Set the oven at 350°. Press through a fine sieve

1 pound dry cottage cheese

Add

⅓ cup sugar
½ teaspoon salt
½ cup light cream *or* top milk
3 eggs, well beaten
2 tablespoons melted butter
Grated rind and juice of 1 lemon

Pour into the crumb shell. Bake until firm (about 1 hour). *Serves 6.*

Raisin Cottage Cheese Pie. Add ½ cup raisins.

STRAWBERRY CHEESE PIE

Spread a Baked Shell (p. 438) with cream cheese softened with sour cream. Cover evenly with perfect strawberries. Melt a small glass of currant jelly, cool until almost firm and spoon over the berries. Chill.

PUMPKIN PIE

For a spicier filling, add ¼ teaspoon clove or nutmeg.

Use canned pumpkin or cut raw pumpkin in pieces, peel, steam, drain, mash and put through a strainer. Mix

1½ cups cooked or canned pumpkin
⅔ cup brown sugar
1 teaspoon cinnamon
½ teaspoon ginger
½ teaspoon salt
2 eggs, slightly beaten
1½ cups milk
½ cup cream or evaporated milk

Cook the filling in a double boiler until thick, cool slightly and pour into a

9-inch Baked Pie Shell (p. 438)

Pumpkin Pie with Whipped Cream. Spread the pie with whipped cream, sweetened slightly and flavored with vanilla or brandy.

Pecan Pumpkin Pie. Flavor the filling with brandy. Decorate the top of the pie with pecan halves. Sprinkle with ½ cup Caramel Syrup (p. 14) to glaze the nuts.

Pumpkin Pie with Ginger Meringue. Make Meringue (p. 441). Fold into it 2 tablespoons chopped preserved ginger. Spread on the pie and bake.

SQUASH PIE

When you have squash as a vegetable, cook enough for a pie, too.

Mix

3½ cups cooked mashed winter squash
½ cup sugar
1 teaspoon salt
½ teaspoon cinnamon
½ teaspoon ginger
½ teaspoon nutmeg
1 egg
1¾ cups milk

Line a 9-inch pie pan with

Plain Pastry (p. 438)

Bake like Custard Pie (p. 448), using either method. *Serves 6.*

RICH SQUASH PIE

Mix

1 cup steamed strained winter squash

1 cup heavy cream
1 cup sugar
3 eggs, slightly beaten
¼ cup brandy
1 teaspoon cinnamon
1 teaspoon nutmeg
½ teaspoon ginger
½ teaspoon salt
¼ teaspoon mace

Line a 9-inch pie pan with
Plain Pastry (p. 438)
Bake like Custard Pie (p. 438), using either method. *Serves 6.*

SWEET POTATO PIE

Set the oven at 450°. Line a 9-inch pie pan with
Plain Pastry (p. 438)
Mix
1½ cups mashed boiled sweet potatoes
1 egg, well beaten
1 cup milk
1 teaspoon vanilla *or* 1 tablespoon rum
Sugar, salt and spices to taste
2 tablespoons melted butter

Spoon into the pie shell and bake until brown (about 30 minutes). *Serves 6.*

Sweet Potato Pudding. Pile into a buttered baking dish instead of a pie shell. Bake as above.

MINCE PIE

Commercial mincemeat is improved by adding to it a few raisins, some chopped fresh apple, a dab of butter and brandy to taste. Add to any mincemeat chopped cooked meat, bits of jelly, ground orange or lemon peel and extra liquor.

Set the oven at 450°. Line a 9-inch pie pan with
Plain Pastry (p. 438)
Fill to the level of the edge of the pan with
Homemade or commercial mincemeat (about 2 cups)
Put on a top crust or cover with a lattice top (p. 438). Bake 10 minutes, then reduce the heat to 350° and bake until the top is evenly brown (about 30 minutes). Serve warm. Reheat if necessary. *Serves 6.*

For a gala effect, sprinkle the pie with warmed brandy, light with a match and serve flaming.

MINCEMEAT

With this basic recipe as a guide, many variations are possible. Use leftover cooked meat, ground orange or lemon peel, bits of jelly, fruit juice and any inexpensive wine or liquor.

Put into a large kettle
4 pounds lean chopped beef
2 pounds chopped beef suet
3 pounds brown sugar
2 cups molasses
2 quarts cider
3 pounds currants
4 pounds seeded raisins
½ pound citron, chopped

Cook slowly, stirring occasionally, until the sugar and citron melt. Meanwhile, prepare
2 quarts peeled sliced apples
Add to the mincemeat and cook until the apples are tender. Add
1 quart brandy
1 tablespoon cinnamon
1 tablespoon mace
1 tablespoon powdered clove
1 teaspoon nutmeg
1 teaspoon allspice
2 teaspoons salt (or to taste)

Pour into jars, seal and store. *Makes 20 pints.*

CALIFORNIA MINCEMEAT

Quick and delicious.

Put through the food chopper, using the coarse blade
1 cup seeded raisins
3 tart apples, cored
½ orange
¼ lemon

Add
½ cup cider

Heat to the boiling point. Simmer 10 minutes. Add

1 cup brown sugar
½ teaspoon salt
½ teaspoon cinnamon
½ teaspoon nutmeg
½ teaspoon powdered clove

Simmer 15 minutes longer. *For one pie.*

QUICK MINCEMEAT

Mix in a deep saucepan

1 cup chopped tart apple
½ cup seeded raisins
½ cup currants
¼ cup chopped suet *or* butter
1 tablespoon molasses
1 cup brown sugar
1 teaspoon cinnamon
½ teaspoon powdered cloves
¼ teaspoon nutmeg
1 teaspoon salt
½ cup canned consommé *or* Brown Stock (p. 60)

Simmer 1 hour. Add

1 cup chopped cooked meat
2 tablespoons fruit jelly (any kind)
¼ cup brandy

Simmer 15 minutes. *For one pie.*

GREEN TOMATO MINCEMEAT

Put in a deep kettle

6 cups chopped apples
6 cups chopped green tomatoes
4 cups brown sugar
1⅓ cups vinegar
3 cups raisins
1 tablespoon cinnamon
1 teaspoon powdered cloves
¾ teaspoon allspice
¾ teaspoon mace
¾ teaspoon pepper
2 teaspoons salt

Bring slowly to the boiling point. Simmer 3 hours. Add

¾ cup butter

Pour into 6 one-pint jars, seal and store. *For 6 pies.*

PUFF PASTE

The classic recipe requires washing the butter (p. 8) and patting it into a thin square about 5 by 5 inches. However, the following method is so simple that it will stimulate you to make this delectable flaky pastry often. If you need more than this amount, make it in two batches for easier handling.

Cut in 3 slices

1 stick of butter (¼ pound), preferably unsalted

Put on a piece of foil and chill. Put in a bowl

¾ cup sifted all-purpose *or* bread flour
¼ teaspoon salt

Sprinkle over the flour

¼ cup ice water

Blend with a fork, adding an extra tablespoon of water if necessary so that you can pat the dough into a ball. Put on a lightly floured board, cover with the bowl and let "rest" 5 minutes.

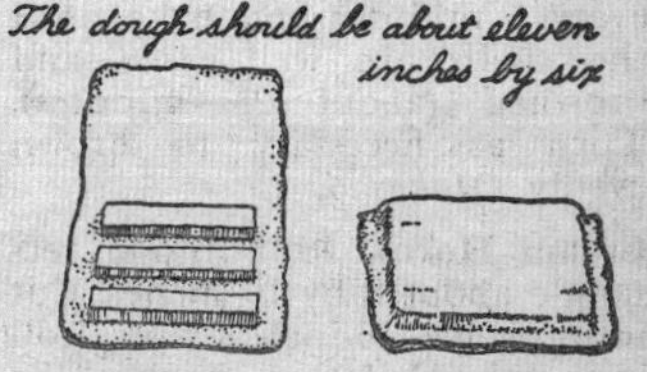

Knead until smooth and elastic (about 5 minutes). Roll out to make a neat oblong about 11 by 6 inches. Place the pieces of butter on the dough as in the illustration. Fold the dough to cover the butter. Press the edges firmly. Wrap in foil and chill in the refrigerator at least 30 minutes.

Unwrap the dough and put on the pastry board with the fold to your left. Tap with the rolling pin to flatten the dough and roll it into an oblong 18 by 6 inches, keeping it of even thickness and rolling with long light strokes. Lift the dough occasionally and dust the board lightly with flour. Fold into three layers, turn it clockwise so that the fold is not facing you, and roll out as before. This completes two "turns." Repeat until you have made six turns. Unless you are working in a very cold room, wrap the dough in foil and chill it after each two turns. Shape, chill and bake according to the recipe.

Patty Shells. Roll into an oblong about 18 by 6 inches. Cut out 12 rounds with a 3-inch cutter. Remove the centers from half the rounds with a smaller cutter to make rims and tops. Put the plain rounds on a cooky sheet covered with two thicknesses of brown paper. Moisten the edges of the large rounds and set the rings on them. Press gently. Chill at least 20 minutes. Heat the oven to 500°. Put in the pastry. Reduce the heat 50° every 5 minutes and bake until the shells are well risen and browned (about 25 minutes). Turn as necessary to brown evenly. *Makes 6.*

Cream Horns. Roll into a rectangle about 8 by 10 inches. Cut into twelve 10-inch strips. Roll over special forms, having the edges overlap. Chill 20 minutes. Bake at 450° until well puffed and slightly brown. Brush with

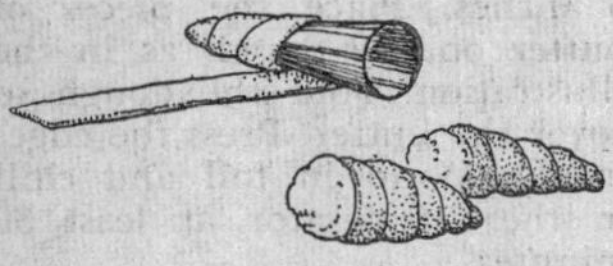

slightly beaten egg white diluted with 1 teaspoon water. Reduce the heat to 350° and bake until glazed and brown. Slip from the forms and cool. Fill with whipped cream or Cream Filling (p. 516). *Makes 12.*

Napoleons. Roll into a rectangle 6 by 15 inches. Cut into six pieces 6 by 2½ inches. Put on a baking sheet covered with two layers of brown paper. Prick well. Bake 10 minutes at 450°. Reduce the heat to 350°. Bake

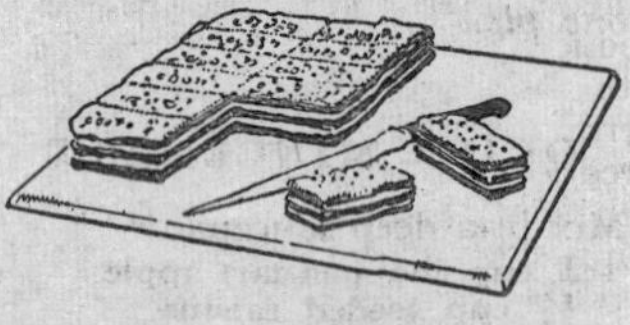

until well puffed and brown (about 15 minutes longer). Cool. Put together in pairs or in three layers with whipped cream or Cream Filling (p. 516). Sprinkle with confectioners' sugar or spread with Confectioners' Frosting (p. 512). Cut in half with a saw-toothed knife.

Palm Leaves. Sprinkle the cloth or board with granulated sugar. Roll the pastry ¼ inch thick. Turn over and roll into an oblong 6 by 18 inches. Fold each end toward the center, making three layers on each side. Fold double, making six layers. Cut in ¼ inch slices. Pinch the

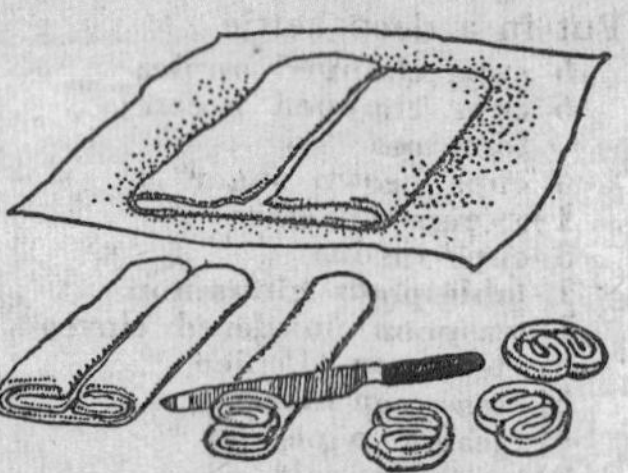

centers slightly together. Place, cut side down, on a cooky sheet covered with brown paper. Chill 10 minutes. Bake 4 minutes at 450°. Turn over and bake until crisp and brown (5 minutes or more).

Florentine Meringue. Roll into an oblong about 6 by 18 inches. Cut off ½-inch strips from the ends and sides. Place the oblong on a cooky sheet. Wet the edges with cold water. Press the strips around the edge to make a rim. Prick in several places with a fork. Bake at 450° until well puffed and lightly browned (about 10 minutes). Cool. Spread with any tart jam. Cover with Meringue (p. 441). Sprinkle with shredded toasted almonds. Dust with powdered sugar. Bake 5 minutes at 425°.

TARTS

Roll out Plain Pastry, Hot Water Pastry, Stir and Roll Pastry (pp. 438–441) or pastry from a mix. Cut out with a cooky cutter or a pastry wheel or shape in any of the ways described below. Bake at 450° until delicately brown (5 to 15 minutes). Fill with jam, jelly, marmalade or any cake filling (pp. 515–518).

Rounds. Cut with a large or small cooky cutter. Cut the centers out of half of them with a smaller cutter to make rims. Brush the plain rounds with cold water. Set the rims in place and press gently.

Squares. Cut out 2½-inch squares. Wet the corners and fold toward the center.

Deep Tart Shells. Cut in rounds large enough to cover inverted muffin pans. Press gently onto the pans. Prick all over with a fork. Cool slightly before easing from the pans. Or line the pans with pastry, press gently so there will be no air under the pastry and prick well.

FRUIT TARTS

Make Deep Tart Shells (above) in cupcake tins or special tart pans. Fill with sweetened fresh fruit or drained canned fruit. Top with Meringue (p. 441) or whipped cream or garnish with chopped nuts or jelly.

To glaze (Glacé Fruit Tarts). Cook and stir ¾ cup water or fruit juice with 2 tablespoons sugar until thick. Cook 20 minutes longer over hot water, stirring occasionally. Pour over the fruit. Or pour melted currant jelly over the fruit.

Glacé Strawberry Tarts. Bake tart shells in tiny cupcake tins. Put a single perfect strawberry in each. Glaze (see above).

LEMON TARTS

Bake Tart Shells (above). Fill with Lemon Pie (p. 446) filling. Top with Meringue and bake. Or make tiny tart shells and fill with Lemon Cheese (below).

LEMON CHEESE FOR TARTS (LEMON CURD)

Also delicious spread between lady fingers or slices of sponge cake.

Put in a double boiler top

- **¼ pound butter**
- **1½ cups sugar**
- **2 lemon rinds, grated**
- **Juice of 3 lemons**
- **6 eggs, slightly beaten**

Stir well. Cook over hot water until thick, stirring occasionally. Store in the refrigerator.

PECAN TARTS

Tiny ones are delicious sweets for a tea party. Serve larger ones as dessert.

Line muffin pans with Plain Pastry (p. 438). Fill with Pecan Pie (p. 447) filling. Bake at 450° until the filling is firm (15 to 30 minutes). Top with whipped cream.

COCONUT TARTS

If you need only 12 tarts, set aside half the mixture, add ½ cup flour to it and make into cookies, baking them like Sugar Cookies (p. 462).

Cream together

¼ cup butter
1¼ cups sugar

Add and beat until light

1 egg

Stir in

⅓ cup milk
1 cup moist coconut

Line deep cupcake tins with

Plain Pastry (p. 438)

Fill about a third full of the mixture. Bake 15 minutes at 350°. Makes 24 tarts or 12 tarts and 24 small cookies.

BANBURY TARTS

Prepare

Plain Pastry (p. 438)

Roll ⅛ inch thick and cut in pieces 3 by 3½ inches. Mix

1 cup seeded raisins, chopped
1 cup sugar
1 egg, slightly beaten
1 tablespoon cracker crumbs
Juice and grated rind 1 lemon

Put 2 teaspoons on each pastry strip. Moisten the edges with cold water, fold over and press the edges together with a 3-tined fork dipped in flour. Prick the tops well. Bake 20 minutes at 350°. *Makes 12 tarts.*

Cheese Banbury Tarts. Place a thin square of cheese on the filling before folding. Start baking at 450°. After 5 minutes, reduce the heat to 350°.

PATTY'S RAISIN TARTS

Serve these thin tarts like cookies.

Roll very thin

Plain Pastry (p. 438)

Cut out 3-inch rounds (at least 60). Mix

¾ cup chopped seeded raisins
2 tablespoons chopped citron
3 tablespoons honey
2 tablespoons melted butter
1 tablespoon grated orange peel
¼ cup brown sugar

Put teaspoonfuls on half the pastry circles. Moisten the edges with

Milk

Cover with the other circles. Roll flat and prick the tops with a fork. Bake 15 minutes at 450°. *Makes 30 or more.*

SWEDISH ALMOND TARTS

Line 12 muffin tins with

Galette Pastry (p. 440)

Mix and divide in the tins

½ pound almond paste
1 egg white

Put 2 strips of pastry over the top of each tart. Bake 25 minutes at 425°. Cool. *Makes 12.*

STRAWBERRY ALMOND TARTS

Line 8 muffin tins with

Plain Pastry (p. 438)

Put in each

1 teaspoon strawberry jam

Cream together

¼ cup butter
⅔ cup sugar

Stir in

⅛ teaspoon salt
2 eggs, well beaten
1 tablespoon flour
1 teaspoon almond extract

Fill the tarts two-thirds full. Bake at 425° until golden-brown (about 13 minutes). Garnish if you like with

Whipped cream and chopped toasted almonds

Serve warm or cold. *Makes 8.*

PETITES GALETTES

Cut out rounds of Plain (p. 438) or Galette Pastry (p. 440) with a small cooky cutter. Brush with egg white. Sprinkle with cinnamon and sugar. Bake at 450° until delicately brown. Serve plain or spread with jelly or jam.

LEMON *or* ORANGE STICKS

Bake pastry oblongs at 450° until pale brown. Put together with Lemon or Orange Filling (p. 517).

NUT PASTRY STICKS

Cut pastry in strips 5 inches by 1 inch. Bake at 450° until pale brown. Cool slightly. Brush with egg white slightly beaten and diluted with 1 teaspoon cold water. Sprinkle generously with chopped pecans and press lightly with fingers. Return to the oven and bake 2 minutes.

ORANGE PASTRIES

Roll Puff Paste (p. 453) ¼ inch thick. Cut out 2½-inch rounds. Bake at 450° until pale brown. Split. Fill with orange marmalade, cover the tops with Orange Frosting (p. 515) and sprinkle a border of chopped candied orange peel around the edge.

COCONUT TEA CAKES

Bake pastry rounds until nearly done. Cool slightly, brush with beaten egg white, sprinkle with shredded coconut and finish baking.

SWEDISH TEA CIRCLES

Roll Plain (p. 438) or Puff Pastry (p. 453) ⅓ inch thick. Spread generously with chopped blanched almonds, mixed with sugar, using half as much sugar as nut meats. Pat and roll ⅛ inch thick and shape with a small round cutter dipped in flour. Bake at 450°.

NUT PASTRY ROLLS

Cut pastry in strips 5 by 3 inches. Spread with a thin layer of tart jelly, beaten with a fork. Sprinkle with chopped pecan meats. Roll like jelly roll. Place rolls on a cooky sheet, with edges on bottom so that rolls will stay firm. Bake about 8 minutes at 450°.

BOUCHÉES

Make very small Tart Shells or Cream Puff Shells (p. 408). Fill with Cream (p. 516) or Lemon Filling (p. 517), or use as cocktail tidbits with lobster or chicken salad as filling.

COCKTAIL PASTRIES

Roll out pastry. Sprinkle with grated cheese and paprika or spread lightly with anchovy paste or finely chopped ham or ham spread mixed with melted butter. Cover with a sheet of wax paper and roll lightly to press the cheese or the spread into the pastry. Remove the paper. Cut in oblongs or fancy shapes. Bake at 450° until pale brown.

COCKTAIL PINWHEELS

Roll pastry ⅛ inch thick into an oblong. Spread with prepared mixture. Roll up firmly, beginning with the long side. Cut in pieces ⅓ inch thick. Bake at

425° about 15 minutes and serve hot.

Anchovy Tuna Filling. Mix 1 can tuna (not drained) with 3 chopped anchovies, 1 tablespoon lemon juice, 2 tablespoons tomato paste and 1/4 teaspoon Tabasco.

Bleu Cheese Filling. Mix bleu cheese and cream cheese and moisten with cream.

Mushroom Filling. Sauté finely chopped mushrooms in butter. Season to taste.

Deviled Ham Filling. Add finely chopped pickle if liked.

CONDÉS

Roll 1/4 inch thick
Plain (p. 438) *or* Puff Pastry (p. 453)
Cut in strips 3 1/2 by 1 1/2 inches.
Beat until stiff
2 egg whites
Beat in gradually
3/4 cup powdered sugar
Stir in
2/3 cup chopped blanched almonds
Spread on the pastries, leaving a space around the edges. Sprinkle with powdered sugar. Bake 15 minutes at 350°. *Makes 30 or more.*

BENNE PASTRIES

If brown sesame seed is not available, put white sesame in a small heavy skillet and cook and stir over low heat until it browns a little.

Prepare
Half the recipe for Plain Pastry (p. 438) *or* the same amount of pastry mix
Mix into it
1/2 cup sesame seed
Few drops Worcestershire

Roll 1/4 inch thick. Cut out with a tiny biscuit cutter. Bake at 400° until lightly browned (about 8 minutes). Serve with cocktails or salads. *Makes 60.*

TURNOVERS

Cut out pastry squares or rounds. Put a spoonful of filling in the middle of one side. Wet the edge with cold water, fold over and press lightly together. Prick the tops well. Bake at 450° until brown (about 15 minutes).

Fruit Turnovers. Make 4-inch squares. Fill with applesauce, mincemeat, jam or jelly or with fruit prepared as for any fruit pie. Apple and peach turnovers are very popular.

Tea Party Turnovers. Make tiny turnovers with any filling. Serve hot.

Rissoles (Luncheon Turnovers). Chop cooked meat, moisten slightly with gravy, season highly and fill turnovers. Bake and serve hot with gravy. Chopped ham combined with chopped chicken is particularly good, but there are countless possibilities.

Cocktail Turnovers. Fill tiny turnovers with a bit of cheese or any savory mixture. Serve hot. See also Cheese Brambles (p. 459).

Piroshski. *Traditionally made of Puff Paste.* Fill with a mixture of ham, chives, onion, parsley and hard-cooked egg (all chopped), moistened with sour cream and seasoned with salt and cayenne. Another good filling is sautéed mushrooms, chopped green onions and hard-cooked egg (all chopped). Serve hot with sour cream to spoon over them.

CREAM CHEESE TURNOVERS

Cream until smooth

1/3 cup butter
2 small packages cream cheese (6 ounces)

Blend in

1 cup sifted pastry *or* cake flour
1/4 teaspoon salt

Chill. Roll 1/8 inch thick. Cut in 2-inch rounds or squares. Put on each a dab of

Tart jelly *or* jam

Fold double. Bake at 450° until brown (about 10 minutes). *Makes 30 or more.*

Cheese Brambles. Add to the pastry a dash of cayenne and a few drops of Worcestershire. Put a 1/2-inch piece of sharp cheese on each. Chill until ready to bake. Serve hot with soups, salads or drinks.

MINIATURE CHEESE CAKES

Cream together until smooth

1 small package cream cheese
1/4 pound butter

Blend in

1 cup flour

Divide in 24 small balls. Put one in each of 24 small muffin tins. Press against the sides with your fingers to line each tin evenly. Spoon filling (below) into each. Bake 20 minutes at 350°. Cool. Spread each with

Sour cream

Top with a bit of

Raspberry *or* cherry jam

Makes 24.

Cheese Cake Filling. Crush 2 small packages cream cheese. Beat in 2 tablespoons sugar, 1 teaspoon vanilla and 1 egg.

Cookies

Cookies are particularly practical for a small family. Make a variety of cookies from one batch of cooky dough by dividing it in several parts and flavoring or decorating each part differently. Use the same dough for drop cookies and rolled cookies by baking some as drop cookies, then adding more flour to the rest, chilling and making into rolled cookies.

Cookies are ideal sweets for children, easy to handle and pack into lunchboxes. The nutrition-wise mother can easily tuck into the cooky batter many extras which promote a child's health and growth, such as whole-wheat flour, oatmeal, soy flour, powdered dry milk, toasted wheat germ and brewer's yeast. Raisins and nuts, brown sugar and molasses are rich in nutritional values, too.

MAKING COOKIES

Cookies are easier to make than most cakes. Most cookies are successful thick or thin, crisp or chewy. **Pastry flour** makes cooky dough that spreads out during the baking to make thin delicate cookies. **All-purpose flour** makes firm cookies which hold their shape while baking. The amount of flour suggested in each recipe is approximate. Bake a sample cooky, then add more flour to the dough if you prefer thicker cookies. But do not add too much or the cookies will be hard and tough.

PREPARING COOKY PANS

Select cooky sheets the correct size for your oven. They should be small enough to allow good heat circulation around them. Cookies bake best on heavy cooky sheets.

To grease pans (unnecessary for most cookies if you bake them on a heavy pan). Crush a piece of wax paper. Dip it in soft or melted butter or vegetable shortening. Rub lightly over the pan. If the cooky mixture is very thin, dust the pan with flour and shake off any that does not cling to the butter. It will be easier to remove the baked cookies from the pan.

SHAPING COOKIES

A cupful of cooky dough will make as many as 3 or 4 dozen thin small cookies or half that number if you make large thick cookies. The number suggested with each recipe is based on the way that particular recipe is usually made, but vary it as you prefer.

Drop Cookies. Take up even teaspoonfuls of cooky dough and push them off onto the cooky sheet. Leave space between the cookies for them to spread. A very thin mixture will need 2 inches between the cookies. If the mixture is firm you may prefer to press each cooky flat with a floured fork or the bottom of a glass or spread it with a knife dipped in cold water. Or shape with your fingers into even balls.

Rolled Cookies. Put the dough in a covered bowl or wrap firmly in wax paper. Chill. Dust the board lightly with flour or powdered sugar. Put no more than a cupful of dough on the board at a time. Keep the rest cold. Pat and roll to about 1/8 inch thick. Cut out cookies with a floured cutter. Put on an unbuttered cooky sheet, close together. Lay the scraps of dough on top of each other, roll and cut out or pat together and shape with your fingers into balls and flatten with a floured fork. **To simplify the shaping,** roll the dough into an oblong and cut with a long knife into squares or diamonds.

Refrigerator Cookies. Pack the dough in special molds or shape firmly into rolls about 2 inches in diameter. Wrap in wax paper, twisting the ends to close. Chill thoroughly. With a long sharp knife, cut in slices 1/8 to 1/2 inch thick, as you prefer. Bake on unbuttered pans.

Cooky Bars. Butter a pan with a 2-inch rim. Spoon in the dough and spread it evenly. Cut the cookies in bars or squares after they are baked.

MAKING COOKIES IN QUANTITY

Assembly-line technique.

Put a sheet of aluminum foil on a cooky sheet. Put cookies on it and put it in the oven to bake. Fill another sheet of foil with cookies. When the first batch is done, slide the sheet of baked cookies onto a wire cake cooler and replace it with the second one. With two cooky sheets and four pieces of foil, quantity baking can be very quick. The cookies slide off the foil very easily and there are no pans to wash.

BAKING COOKIES

Instead of baking all the cookies at one time, store the dough in the refrigerator or freezer, tightly covered, and bake fresh cookies as you need them. There is a special recipe for Refrigerator Cookies (p. 464), but any cooky dough is successfully stored which has at least 1/4 cup of shortening to each cup of flour. A dough with less shortening will crumble and dry out.

Bake most cookies at 375°. Bake molasses cookies or cookies rich with fruit or nuts at 325°. Watch carefully during baking so that the cookies will bake evenly. If some bake more quickly than others, take them from the pan with a spatula and continue baking the rest. Bake very thin cookies 5 to 7 minutes. Thick cookies and bars take longer. A slight variation in baking time does no harm, which is one reason why cookies are easier to make than cake. Most cookies are equally delicious whether they are slightly soft or are baked longer and become more crisp. As a general rule, bake cookies until they are delicately brown, with a dry glossy surface and firm edges. Dark-colored cookies (ginger and chocolate) are sufficiently baked when the surface is dry and the edge firm. If cooky dough is spread in a pan to be cut after baking, it is baked enough when it begins to shrink from the edges and when the top springs back when you press it.

TAKING COOKIES FROM PANS

Lift baked cookies from the pan with a thin spatula. Let very delicate cookies cool slightly to stiffen so that you can lift them without breaking them. If they become too stiff, hold the pan

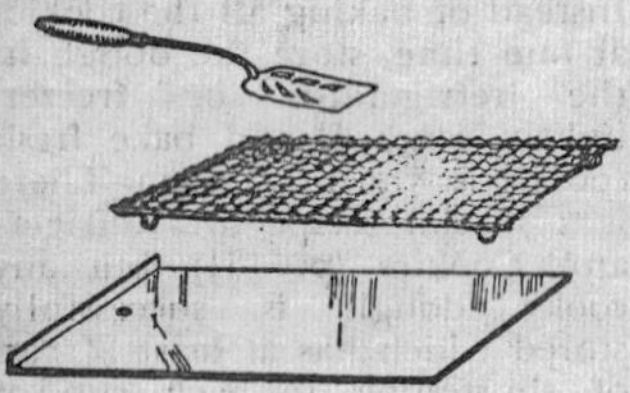

over moderate heat to soften the cookies again. Cut bar cookies according to the recipe. Some need to become firm before cutting while others cut more easily when warm. Place the cookies on a wire cake cooler in a single layer, not touching.

STORING COOKIES

Cool thoroughly. Pack in a tightly covered jar or metal box, or wrap in freezer paper and store in a freezer. If the cookies are very delicate, put sheets of wax paper between the layers. **To keep soft cookies from drying out,** put a slice of bread or a cut section of apple into the jar with them.

DECORATING COOKIES

Sprinkle unbaked cookies with sugar, plain or colored, or press lightly on each cooky a few nut meats, raisins or bits of citron, coconut, angelica, or dates, figs, candied fruit or fruit peel. For special occasions, decorate baked cookies with frosting put through a pastry bag and tube to make jack-o'-lantern faces, hearts, pairs of initials or other appropriate designs.

CHRISTMAS COOKIES

Weeks ahead, make any cookies made with honey or fruit. Make thin ginger cookies and other rolled cookies a week or two in advance. In the last few days before Christmas, make meringue-type cookies, macaroons and butter cookies. Make Orange Cookies (p. 463) to use leftover yolks.

OLD-FASHIONED SUGAR COOKIES

Plain sugar cookies need the distinctive flavor of butter, but you may use a substitute successfully for the variations. For richer cookies, use more butter (up to 1 cup). To deepen the color, add an extra egg yolk. To emphasize the butter flavor, brush the baked cookies lightly with melted butter while they are still warm.

Cream until light and fluffy
- **½ cup butter**

Beat in
- **¾ cup sugar**

Add
- **1 egg *or* 2 egg yolks**
- **½ teaspoon vanilla**

Beat thoroughly. Add
- **1 tablespoon cream *or* milk**

Sift together and stir in
- **1¼ cups flour**
- **¼ teaspoon salt**
- **¼ teaspoon baking powder**

Mix well and arrange by teaspoonfuls on a buttered cooky

sheet, 1 inch apart. Bake about 8 minutes at 375°. *Makes 50 to 60.*

Rolled Sugar Cookies. Add just enough flour to make the dough stiff enough to roll out—about 1/4 cup. Be careful not to add too much flour or the cookies will be hard and tough. Chill 1 hour or more. Roll 1/4 inch thick and cut out (p. 461).

Sugar Cooky Shells. Cut out in 4-inch rounds. Press on the outside of scallop shells or fluted tins. Bake. Serve filled with ice cream or fruit.

SUGAR COOKY VARIATIONS

Almond Cookies. Add 1/3 cup almonds, blanched and finely chopped, 1/2 teaspoon each of cinnamon, clove and nutmeg, and the grated rind of 1/2 lemon.

Butterscotch Cookies. Use brown sugar in place of white. Melt butter, add sugar and heat slowly until well blended. If desired, add 1/4 cup chopped nut meats (black walnuts are especially good).

Chocolate Cookies. Before adding flour, add 1/3 cup dry cocoa or 2 ounces unsweetened melted chocolate. Bake at 325°. Frost with Chocolate Frosting (p. 512) if desired.

Coconut Cookies. Add 1/2 cup shredded coconut chopped fine.

Date Cookies. Add 1/2 cup dates, cut fine with wet scissors.

Lemon Sugar Cookies. Omit vanilla. Add 1/2 teaspoon lemon extract and 2 teaspoons grated lemon rind.

Maple Cookies. Use maple sugar, crushed fine, in place of white.

Marmalade Cookies. Reduce sugar to 2/3 cup. Add 6 teaspoons marmalade.

Nut Cookies. Add 1/2 cup chopped nut meats.

Orange Cookies. Use orange juice in place of milk. Add grated rind of 1/2 orange. To heighten the color, use 2 to 4 egg yolks in place of whole egg.

Raisin Cookies. Add 1/2 cup chopped seeded raisins.

Seedcakes. Add 1 1/2 tablespoons caraway seeds.

Spiced Sugar Cookies. Add 1/4 teaspoon nutmeg or cinnamon.

MERINGUE LAYER COOKIES

Spread Sugar Cooky mixture evenly in a buttered pan about 9 by 9 inches. Beat 1 egg white, add 1 cup brown sugar, a few grains of salt and 1/2 teaspoon vanilla. Spread over the cooky mixture. Sprinkle with 1 cup chopped nut meats and press lightly. Bake 30 minutes at 325°. Cut in squares or strips.

Jelly Layer Cookies. Spread a thin layer of tart jam or jelly over the cooky mixture. Beat 1 egg white stiff, add 5 tablespoons sugar, 1 teaspoon cinnamon and 6 tablespoons chopped walnut meats and spread over the jelly. Bake and cut as above.

FILLED COOKIES (JUMBLES)

Cut out Rolled Sugar Cookies (above) 3 inches or more in diameter. On centers of half the cut-out pieces, put a teaspoon of filling or bits of jam, jelly or mincemeat. Cover with the other cookies. (Some old-fashioned cooks make three small openings in the top cookies with a thimble, using it like a tiny cooky cutter.) Press the edges together and prick with fork.

Bake at 325° until delicately brown (about 12 minutes).

Fruit and Nut Filling. Mix ½ cup chopped seeded raisins, ½ cup dates, cut fine, ¼ cup chopped walnuts, ½ cup water and ½ cup sugar mixed with 1 teaspoon flour. Cook slowly until thick.

Date *or* Fig Filling. Mix 1 cup chopped dates or figs, ⅓ cup sugar, ⅓ cup boiling water, 1½ teaspoons lemon juice, ½ tablespoon butter. Cook slowly until thick.

SAND TARTS

Cut out Rolled Sugar Cookies (p. 463) with a doughnut cutter. Brush with egg white and sprinkle with 1 tablespoon sugar mixed with ¼ teaspoon cinnamon. Split blanched almonds and arrange 3 halves on each cooky.

RICH COOKIES

Cream until light and fluffy
- **1 cup butter**
- **1 teaspoon vanilla**

Beat in gradually
- **⅔ cup sugar**
- **2 eggs, well beaten**

Stir in
- **1½ cups flour (pastry flour for very delicate cookies)**

Arrange by teaspoonfuls on a cooky sheet. Spread thin with a knife dipped in cold water. On each cooky place
- **Raisins, nut meats *or* bits of citron**

Bake like Sugar Cookies (p. 462). *Makes 60.*

SOUR CREAM COOKIES

Beat thoroughly
- **2 eggs**

Add
- **1 cup sugar**
- **½ cup sour cream**
- **⅓ cup butter, melted**

Mix well. Sift together
- **2 cups flour**
- **½ teaspoon baking soda**
- **¼ teaspoon nutmeg**

Add to the first mixture. Bake like Sugar Cookies (p. 462). *Makes 60.*

REFRIGERATOR COOKIES

Cream thoroughly
- **½ cup butter**
- **1 teaspoon vanilla**

Beat in
- **⅔ cup brown sugar**
- **⅓ cup white sugar**
- **1 egg, slightly beaten**

Sift together
- **1½ cups flour (preferably pastry)**
- **¼ teaspoon cream of tartar**
- **¼ teaspoon salt**

Add to the first mixture. Shape in a roll or several small rolls. Wrap lightly in wax paper. Store in the refrigerator. Slice with a very sharp, long thin knife. Bake at 400° about 8 minutes or at 250° about 15 minutes. Both ways are delicious. *Makes 60.*

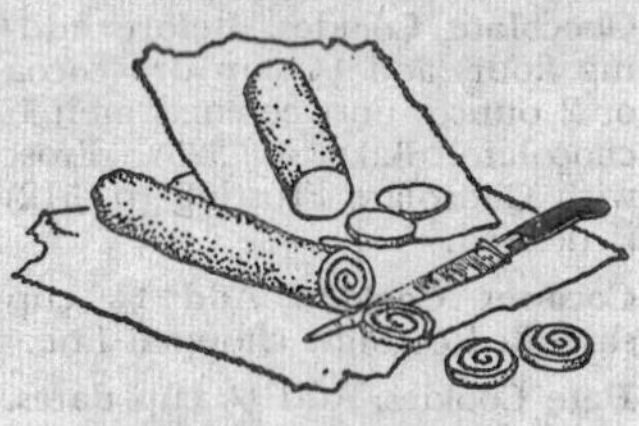

To vary the flavoring, add ⅓ teaspoon cinnamon or nutmeg or 2 ounces chocolate, melted. Or add a package of chocolate bits or ½ cup broken or chopped nut meats, whole blanched almonds, raisins or coconut.

Pinwheel Cookies. Divide the mixture in two equal parts. Melt 1 ounce unsweetened chocolate, cool slightly, add to one part and mix well. Chill. Roll each part separately into equal oblongs 1/8 inch thick. Place one on top of the other and roll up like jelly roll. Chill, slice and bake as on page 464.

Pecan Cookies. Add 1/2 cup chopped pecans.

COOKY-PRESS COOKIES

Some of the best mixtures for cooky-press cookies are Norwegian Butter Cookies (below), Refrigerator Cookies (p. 464) and Peanut Butter Cookies (p. 469), made with 1 1/2 cups flour.

Pack the mixture into a press and push out onto an unbuttered cooky sheet. Bake about 10 minutes at 375°.

NORWEGIAN BUTTER COOKIES

Cream thoroughly
1/2 cup butter
Add
2 hard-cooked egg yolks, pressed through a sieve
Beat in
1/4 cup sugar
Add and mix well
1 cup flour
1/2 teaspoon lemon *or* vanilla extract
Put through a cooky press and bake (p. 464). *Makes 40.*

CHOCOLATE COOKY-PRESS COOKIES

Cream thoroughly
3/4 cup shortening
Add gradually, creaming well
1 cup sugar
Beat until fluffy. Add
1 egg, well beaten
1/2 teaspoon vanilla
1/4 teaspoon salt
2 ounces unsweetened chocolate, melted
Beat well. Stir in gently
2 cups pastry *or* cake flour
Mix, shape and bake (p. 464). *Makes 60.*

SCOTCH SHORTBREADS

Shortbreads have a distinctive texture—sandy and somewhat crumbly.

Cream thoroughly
1 cup butter
Add gradually, while beating
1/2 cup confectioners' *or* light brown sugar
Sift together
2 cups flour
1/4 teaspoon salt
1/4 teaspoon baking powder
Add to the mixture. Mix well and roll out 1/4 inch thick. Cut in squares or rounds. Prick with a fork. Bake at 350° until delicately brown (20 to 25 minutes). *Makes 24 or more.*

Royal Fans. Cut in rounds (2 to 5 inches). Cut in quarters and mark with the back of a knife like a fan. Brush with egg yolk diluted with water. Bake.

Piñon Cookies. Cut out. Cover thickly with pine nuts, pressing them firmly into the cookies. Bake.

MILDRED'S SAND TARTS

A famous Virginia recipe similar to a very rich shortbread.

Cream until light and fluffy
1 1/4 pounds butter (*or* part margarine)
Beat in
2 pounds dark brown sugar
Beat well (setting 1 white aside for the top)
3 eggs
Add to the butter-sugar mixture. Add
2 teaspoons vanilla
2 pounds flour

Beat to blend thoroughly. Pat evenly into a lightly buttered jelly roll pan. The dough should be about 1 inch thick. If your pan is too small, put the extra in a cake pan. Beat the egg white slightly and brush it over the top of the dough. Sprinkle lightly with

Cinnamon sugar

Press evenly into the dough

½ pound blanched almonds, separated in halves

Bake at 325° until delicately brown and firm to the touch (about 20 minutes). Cut in squares. *Makes about 60.*

LEMON BUTTER COOKIES

Cream thoroughly

1 cup butter

Add gradually, creaming well

1 cup brown sugar

Add

2 eggs, well beaten
Grated rind of 1 lemon
Juice of ½ lemon
1 teaspoon cinnamon
¼ teaspoon powdered clove
¼ teaspoon salt

Mix well. Blend in

2 cups flour

Add more flour, if necessary, to make the dough thick enough to roll out. Chill. Roll ⅛ inch thick, cut out and bake until delicately brown at 350° (about 10 minutes). *Makes 60.*

BUTTER STARS

Cream thoroughly

1 cup butter *or* margarine

Add

1 egg yolk
6 tablespoons powdered sugar
3 cups flour
1 tablespoon sherry *or* brandy

Mix thoroughly. Chill. Roll ½ inch thick. Cut out with a star cutter. Beat until stiff

1 egg white

Fold in

½ cup sugar

Put a spoonful on each cooky. Prepare

⅓ cup chopped almonds

Sprinkle ½ teaspoon on each cooky. Bake 30 minutes at 325°. *Makes 36.*

JUBILEES

Cream thoroughly

½ cup butter

Add, gradually, creaming well

1 cup sugar

Beat until light and fluffy. Beat together

2 eggs
1 teaspoon vanilla
1 teaspoon baking powder

Add to the butter mixture. Sift

1½ cups flour
¼ teaspoon soda
½ teaspoon salt

Stir in. Blend until evenly mixed. Let stand until firm enough to handle. Shape with fingers into 1-inch balls. Roll in

Flaked cereal (corn *or* rice)

Put on a cooky sheet 1½ inches apart. Poke a hole in each with your finger or the handle of a small wooden spoon. Fill with

Jam *or* jelly

Bake at 350° until firm (about 20 minutes). *Makes about 40.*

COFFEE COOKIES

Also delicious without the nuts.

Butter a cooky sheet. Set the oven at 350°. Cream together until very light

½ cup shortening
⅔ cup sugar
2 tablespoons instant coffee

Add

1 egg, slightly beaten
¾ cup flour
¼ teaspoon salt
½ teaspoon vanilla
½ cup chopped nuts

Mix well. Put on the cooky sheet by teaspoonfuls. Bake until the edges are firm and the tops dry (about 12 minutes). Remove from the tin immediately. *Makes 36.*

MOLASSES COOKIES

Cream together

¼ cup shortening
¼ cup butter
⅓ cup brown sugar

Add

1 egg, slightly beaten
½ cup molasses
¼ cup milk, coffee *or* water

Sift together and add

2 cups flour
½ teaspoon salt
½ teaspoon ginger *or* cloves
½ teaspoon cinnamon
1 teaspoon baking soda

Beat well and add more flour if needed. For crisp cookies, keep the mixture as thin as possible. For thick soft cookies, add more flour but avoid using too much, which will make the cookies hard and dry. Flour vary, so test the mixture by baking a sample cooky. Put spoonfuls on cooky sheet. Bake at 375° about 10 minutes. *Makes 30 to 60.*

To vary, add ¼ teaspoon each of nutmeg, cloves and allspice. Or add ½ cup floured raisins.

Molasses Crinkles. Omit the coffee, milk or water. Add enough flour to shape with the fingers. Measure by teaspoonfuls and roll into balls. Dip the tops in granulated sugar. Put on a cooky sheet. Sprinkle 2 or 3 drops of water on each. Bake.

Molasses Bars. Spread in two square cake tins, 9 by 9 inches. Bake about 12 minutes. While hot, sprinkle with sugar. Cut in squares or bars.

Rolled Molasses Cookies. Add enough more flour (about ½ cup) to make the mixture just stiff enough to handle. Chill. Roll (p. 461) and cut out or shape and cut like Refrigerator Cookies (p. 464).

CALIFORNIA MOLASSES COOKIES

Delicious high-energy cookies—crisp at first, then chewy as they ripen. Vary them by adding 1 cup shredded coconut or raisins or ½ cup chopped nut meats.

Set the oven at 350°. Grease cooky sheets very lightly.

Cream together

½ cup shortening
⅓ cup sugar

Add and mix well

1 egg
½ cup dark molasses
¼ cup milk

Sift together and add

½ cup sifted whole-wheat pastry flour
½ cup soy flour
½ cup powdered milk
4 teaspoons baking powder (or 2 teaspoons double-acting type)
½ teaspoon each of cinnamon, ginger, nutmeg and cloves

Add

½ cup toasted wheat germ *or* wheat germ flour

Stir only enough to blend. Drop by teaspoonfuls on cooky sheet. Bake until firm (12 to 15 minutes). Makes about 48 3-inch cookies.

GINGER SNAPS

Old-fashioned ginger snaps keep so well that you will want to make them in quantity. Follow the "assembly line" technique on page 461 to do them in a hurry.

Heat to the boiling point

1 cup molasses

Pour it over

½ cup shortening

Sift together and stir in

3¼ cups flour
½ teaspoon baking soda
1 tablespoon ginger
1½ teaspoons salt

Shape one-fourth of the mixture at a time, keeping the rest of the dough in the refrigerator until you are ready to cut it out. Roll as thin as possible and cut with a small round cutter. Bake at 350° until crisp and dry (8 to 10 minutes). *Makes 100 or more.*

SPICE COOKIES

Heat to the boiling point

½ cup molasses

Add

¼ cup sugar
3 tablespoons butter *or* other shortening
1 tablespoon milk

Sift together and add

2 cups flour
½ teaspoon each of baking soda, salt, nutmeg, cinnamon, powdered clove and ginger

Follow directions for making Sugar Cookies (p. 462). *Makes 60.*

Gingerbread Men. Cut out with a special cutter or a very sharp knife. Bake. Frost with Confectioners' Frosting (p. 512) and decorate with candies, raisins or bits of citron.

CORNELL SPICE COOKIES

Add wheat germ and brewer's yeast to other cookies as well, to make them richer in protein and vitamins.

Heat to the boiling point

½ cup molasses

Add

¼ cup light brown sugar
½ cup butter, margarine *or* chicken fat

Mix

1½ cups flour
½ cup toasted wheat germ
⅛ teaspoon salt
1 tablespoon brewer's yeast
1½ teaspoons ginger
½ teaspoon cinnamon
1½ teaspoons baking soda

Stir into the first mixture. Shape like Drop Cookies (p. 461) or Refrigerator Cookies (p. 464). Bake at 350° until firm (8 to 10 minutes). *Makes 50 or more.*

CRUNCHY GINGER COOKIES

Set the oven at 350°. Cream

½ cup shortening

Add

1 egg, well beaten
½ cup molasses
½ cup grape-nuts *or* toasted wheat germ

Let stand 10 minutes. Beat in

½ cup sugar
½ teaspoon vanilla

Sift together

1½ cups flour
1 teaspoon baking soda
½ teaspoon salt
2 teaspoons ginger

Add to the batter. Bake like Sugar Cookies (p. 462). *Makes about 50.*

CHOCOLATE CHIP COOKIES

Set the oven at 375°. Cream

½ cup butter

Beat in until light and smooth

⅜ cup brown sugar
⅜ cup white sugar

Add

1 egg, slightly beaten
½ teaspoon salt
½ teaspoon baking soda in 1 tablespoon hot water
1⅛ cups flour
½ cup chopped nut meats
1 teaspoon vanilla
1 package chocolate bits (6 ounces) *or* a 6-ounce semi-sweet chocolate bar *or* nut bar, cut small

Mix well. Bake like Sugar Cookies (p. 462). *Makes about 40.*

Chocolate Oatmeal Cookies. Use oatmeal in place of nuts.

Date and Nut Cookies. Instead of chocolate chips, use ½ cup chopped dates. See also cookies made of the mixture for Date and Nut Bars (p. 474).

CHOCOLATE WALNUT WAFERS

Set the oven at 350°. Melt

2 ounces unsweetened chocolate

Cream until light and fluffy

½ cup butter

Beat in

1 cup sugar
2 eggs, well beaten

Stir in the chocolate. Add

1 cup chopped walnut meats
¼ teaspoon salt
¼ teaspoon vanilla
⅔ cup flour (preferably pastry)

Mix well. Arrange by teaspoonfuls on cooky sheets. Bake 10 minutes. *Makes 36.*

PEANUT BUTTER COOKIES

Set the oven at 350°. Cream together

½ cup butter *or* margarine
½ cup peanut butter

Beat in

½ cup white sugar
½ cup brown sugar

Stir in

1 egg
½ teaspoon vanilla
½ teaspoon salt
½ teaspoon baking soda
1 cup flour (preferably pastry)

Arrange by teaspoonfuls on cooky sheets. Press flat with a floured spoon or mark with a floured fork. Bake until firm (about 10 minutes). *Makes 60.*

BRANDY WAFERS

The only tricky part of making these delicate wafers is removing them from the pan. They must be firm enough to lift but not so stiff that they crumble.

Set the oven at 300°. Heat to the boiling point

½ cup molasses

Add

½ cup butter

Sift

1 cup flour
⅔ cup sugar
1 teaspoon ginger

Stir slowly into the molasses and butter. Arrange by teaspoonfuls on heavy cooky sheets or the back of a shallow baking pan. Bake until dry on top (about 15 minutes). Let stand about 3 minutes before removing from the pans. *Makes about 60.*

To shape in tubes. Roll the baked wafers over the handle of a wooden spoon while they are still warm.

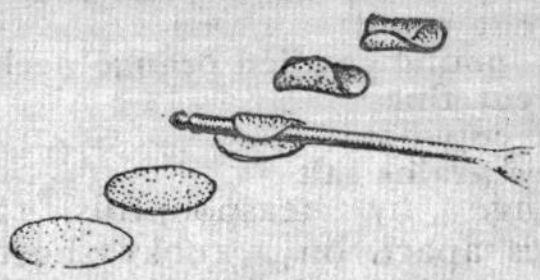

SWEDISH ALMOND WAFERS

Serve these delicate wafers plain or put them together in pairs with Paris Cream (p. 478). See also the recipe for Gâteau Riche (p. 428).

Set the oven at 350°. Mix in a small heavy saucepan

¾ cup finely ground almonds (unblanched)
½ cup butter
½ cup sugar
1 tablespoon flour
2 tablespoons top milk *or* cream

Cook and stir over moderate heat until the butter melts. Arrange by teaspoonfuls, 3 inches apart, on a heavy cooky sheet or on a sheet of foil on a cooky sheet. Bake until delicately brown around the edges but still bubbling slightly in the center (about 7 minutes). Cool until the edge is firm enough so that you can lift the cookies with a long, thin, sharp knife or a spatula.

Repeat until all are baked. *Makes 36.*

Hazelnut Wafers. Use unblanched hazelnuts in place of almonds.

FLORENTINES

In Austria and Germany there are many variations of this recipe, but this is nearest to the particularly delectable Salzburg version.

Set the oven at 350°. Mix

½ cup cream
½ cup sugar
1 cup almonds *or* hazelnuts, cut small
¼ pound candied orange peel, cut fine
¼ cup flour
Few grains salt

Arrange by teaspoonfuls, 2 inches apart, on a cooky sheet. Flatten with a knife dipped in cold water. Bake until brown around the edges (about 10 minutes). Cool, flat side up, on a wire cake cooler. Melt over hot water

8-ounce bar semi-sweet chocolate

Stir until smooth and spread on the cookies on the flat side. *Makes 24.*

NUT COOKIES

Set the oven at 350°. Beat until thick and lemon-colored

2 egg yolks

Beat in gradually

1 cup brown sugar

Add

1 cup chopped nut meats
Few grains salt

Fold in

2 egg whites, beaten stiff

Stir in

6 tablespoons flour

Place teaspoonfuls on cooky sheets and flatten with a knife. Bake until firm (5 to 8 minutes). *Makes 50.*

VIENNESE CRESCENTS

Delicious any time of year, but traditional for Christmas.

Set the oven at 300°. Cream thoroughly

1 cup butter

Add

¼ cup sugar
2 cups flour
1 cup ground almonds (unblanched)
1 teaspoon vanilla

Mix well. Shape with fingers in crescents about 3 inches by 1 inch and ½ inch thick. Roll in

Confectioners' sugar

Place on cooky sheets. Bake 35 minutes. Cool. Roll in sugar again. *Makes 36.*

Pecan Delights. Increase sugar to ½ cup and use 2 cups chopped pecans in place of almonds. Add 3 teaspoons water. Shape like dates.

Spitzbuben. Increase sugar to 1 cup. Pat out with hands on floured board. Cover with wax paper and roll ⅛ inch thick. Cut out with small biscuit cutter. Bake. Put together with currant jelly.

Nut Balls. Use almonds, hazelnuts, pecans, walnuts or black walnuts. Use 1½ cups flour. Shape in balls the size of large marbles.

SWEDISH NUT WAFERS

Prepare

⅓ cup chopped nut meats

Cream

4 tablespoons butter

Beat in

¾ cup sugar

Add

1 egg, well beaten
2 tablespoons milk
1 teaspoon vanilla

Sift and stir in

1⅓ cups flour
1 teaspoon baking powder
½ teaspoon salt

Spread evenly with a knife on the bottom of a lightly buttered inverted loaf pan. One tablespoon will cover a pan 7 by 3 inches. Sprinkle with nut meats. Press them gently into the cooky dough. Mark in strips 1 inch wide. Bake until delicately brown (about 12 minutes).

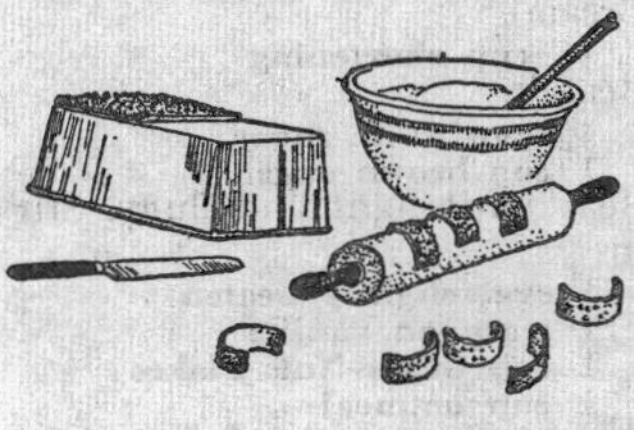

Cut the strips apart and lay immediately over a rolling pin to shape. Repeat until all the dough is used, baking a few at a time so that the wafers will be soft enough to shape. If they stiffen too much to shape, put them in the oven a moment to reheat and soften. *Makes 120.*

CHARLESTON BENNE WAFERS

True benne is wild sesame seed.

Set the oven at 350°. Put in a small heavy pan

½ cup sesame seeds

Stir over moderate heat until slightly brown. Remove from the heat. Add

1 tablespoon butter
1 cup brown sugar
3 tablespoons flour
1 egg, beaten
1 teaspoon vanilla
¼ teaspoon salt

Arrange by teaspoonfuls on well-buttered cooky sheets. Bake until firm (5 to 8 minutes). Remove carefully while still warm. *Makes 30.*

CAPE COD OATMEAL COOKIES

Set the oven at 350°. Sift together

1½ cups flour
½ teaspoon baking soda
1 teaspoon cinnamon
½ teaspoon salt

Stir in

1 egg, well beaten
1 cup sugar
½ cup melted butter
½ cup melted lard
1 tablespoon molasses
¼ cup milk
1¾ cups oatmeal
1 cup seeded raisins *or* nut meats, cut fine, *or* ½ cup of each

Arrange by teaspoonfuls on buttered cooky sheets. Bake until the edges are brown (about 12 minutes). *Makes 75.*

For thicker cookies, increase the oatmeal to 2 cups and the flour to 1¾ cups.

CORNELL OATMEAL COOKIES

High-protein and excellent for the school lunchbox or after-school snacks.

Set the oven at 375°. Cream together

¾ cup soft shortening
1 cup brown sugar

Beat in

2 eggs
⅓ cup milk, sweet *or* sour

Sift together

¾ cup flour
4 tablespoons soy flour
2 tablespoons brewer's yeast
1 teaspoon baking powder
½ teaspoon salt
1 teaspoon cinnamon
¼ teaspoon nutmeg
⅛ teaspoon powdered cloves

Add to the first mixture. Add

1 cup raisins
¼ cup toasted wheat germ
2¾ cups oatmeal

Mix well. Arrange by teaspoonfuls on buttered cooky sheets. Bake until lightly browned (about 10 minutes). *Makes about 50.*

DATE OATMEAL COOKIES

Cook slowly until thick and smooth

1 cup pitted dates
½ cup sugar
½ cup water

Cream together

½ cup shortening
½ cup brown sugar

Sift together and add

1½ cups flour
¼ teaspoon baking soda
½ teaspoon salt

Add

1¼ cups oatmeal

Mix well and add enough water to make the dough firm enough to roll. Roll ⅛ inch thick. Cut in 2-inch rounds. Put together in pairs with the date mixture as filling. Press the edges firmly together. Bake at 350° until browned (about 15 minutes). *Makes 24.*

LACE COOKIES

These cookies spread to make very thin wafers, almost transparent. Make large ones and use them for a dessert like Gâteau Riche (p. 428).

Set the oven at 375°. Mix in a bowl

2¼ cups oatmeal
2¼ cups light brown sugar
3 tablespoons flour
1 teaspoon salt

Stir in

1 cup butter *or* margarine, melted

Add

1 egg, slightly beaten
1 teaspoon vanilla

Blend well. Arrange by teaspoonfuls, at least 2 inches apart, on heavy cooky sheets or on foil (p. 461). Bake until lightly browned (about 7 minutes). As soon as firm enough, remove from the cooky sheets. *Makes about 90.*

AUNT AMY'S COOKIES

Sift together

1 cup flour (preferably pastry)
½ teaspoon baking soda
¼ teaspoon baking powder
½ teaspoon salt

Cream

½ cup shortening

Beat in

½ cup white sugar
1 cup brown sugar

Beat until light and fluffy. Stir in

1 egg, slightly beaten
1 teaspoon vanilla
1 cup Grape-Nuts Flakes
1 cup oatmeal

Arrange by teaspoonfuls on buttered cooky sheets. Flatten with a knife or fork dipped in cold water. For very delicate cookies, flatten until almost paper-thin. Bake at 350° until delicately brown (8 to 10 minutes). Take from the cooky sheet while still warm. *Makes 60.*

For a delicately spicy flavor, sift ½ teaspoon cinnamon with the flour.

CHOCOLATE OATMEAL COOKIES

Sift together

1 cup flour (preferably pastry)
1 teaspoon baking powder
½ teaspoon salt

Cream together

½ cup shortening
1 cup sugar

Beat in

1 egg
2 ounces chocolate, melted
1 teaspoon vanilla
1 teaspoon almond flavoring

Stir in the flour and

1 cup oatmeal

Bake like Aunt Amy's Cookies (above). *Makes 40.*

To vary. Add ⅔ cup shredded coconut. *Makes 60.*

GRAPE-NUTS COOKIES

Sift together

⅔ cup flour (preferably pastry)
1 teaspoon baking powder
½ teaspoon salt

Cream together

½ cup shortening
½ cup white sugar
¼ cup brown sugar

Beat in

1 egg
1 teaspoon vanilla
¼ teaspoon almond extract

Stir in the flour. Add

1½ cups Grape-Nuts
¾ cup coconut

Bake like Aunt Amy's Cookies (p. 472). *Makes 60.*

SCOTTISH FANCIES

Beat until light

1 egg

Beat in

½ cup sugar

Stir in

2 teaspoons melted butter
1 cup oatmeal
¼ teaspoon salt

Arrange by teaspoonfuls 1½ inches apart on well-buttered cooky sheets. Spread into rounds with a knife dipped in cold water. Bake at 325° until delicately brown (about 10 minutes). *Makes 36.*

To shape in tubes, see page 469.

APPLESAUCE COOKIES

Butter cooky sheets. Set the oven at 425°. Sift together

2 cups flour
1 teaspoon baking soda
½ teaspoon salt
1 teaspoon cinnamon
1 teaspoon nutmeg
½ teaspoon powdered cloves

Cream together until light

½ cup butter *or* margarine
½ cup brown sugar
½ cup white sugar

Stir in

1 egg
1 cup smooth applesauce

Add the flour mixture. Add

1 cup seeded or chopped raisins
½ cup chopped nut meats

Arrange by spoonfuls on cooky sheets. Bake until lightly browned (8 to 10 minutes). *Makes 40 or more.*

Applesauce Bars. Spread in a pan about 9 by 15 inches, lined with foil. Bake at 350° until browned (30 to 40 minutes). While warm, spread with confectioners' sugar moistened with hot milk. Cool and cut in bars.

MINCEMEAT COOKIES

Cream

1 cup shortening

Beat in

½ teaspoon vanilla
1 cup honey
3 eggs, well beaten

Sift together and add

3¼ cups flour
1 teaspoon salt
1 teaspoon baking soda

Stir in

1 cup chopped nut meats
1 package mincemeat *or* 1½ cups homemade mincemeat, drained if necessary

Arrange by teaspoonfuls on buttered cooky sheets. Bake at 350° until light brown (about 15 minutes). *Makes 75.*

BOSTON COOKIES

Set the oven at 350°. Sift together

1 cup flour
¼ teaspoon baking soda
Few grains salt
½ teaspoon cinnamon

Cream together

4 tablespoons butter
½ cup sugar

Add

1 egg, well beaten

Mix well. Stir in half the flour.

Add

⅓ cup chopped nut meats
⅓ cup seeded raisins, chopped

Add the rest of the flour. Arrange by spoonfuls 1 inch apart on buttered cooky sheets. Bake until delicately brown (about 12 minutes). *Makes 36.*

DATE PINWHEELS

Cream

1 cup shortening

Beat in gradually

2 cups light brown sugar

Stir in

3 eggs, well beaten

Sift together

4 cups flour
½ teaspoon salt
½ teaspoon baking soda

Add to the first mixture. Mix well. Chill. Divide in two or three parts. Roll in oblongs ¼ inch thick. Spread with date filling (below) and roll up. Wrap in wax paper or foil and chill overnight. Cut in ½-inch slices, arrange on cooky sheets, and bake at 400° until firm (about 10 minutes). *Makes 60 or more.*

Date Pinwheel Filling. Mix 2¼ cups chopped dates with 1 cup sugar and 1 cup water. Cook 10 minutes or until thick and add 1 cup chopped nuts.

DATE AND NUT BARS

Butter a pan about 14 by 8 inches. Set the oven at 350°. Beat until foamy

3 eggs

Beat in gradually

1 cup sugar

Sift together

1 cup flour
½ teaspoon baking powder
Few grains salt

Add

1 cup dates, cut fine
1 cup chopped nut meats

Stir into the egg mixture. Spread in the pan and bake until firm and delicately brown (about 30 minutes). Cut in finger-shaped pieces and roll while still warm in

Powdered sugar

Makes 40.

Honey Date Bars. Use honey in place of sugar. Increase the flour to 1¼ cups and the baking powder to 1 teaspoon.

Date and Nut Cookies. Arrange by teaspoonfuls on buttered cooky sheets. Bake until delicately brown (about 12 minutes).

DATE LEBKUCHEN

Moist and delicious for weeks after baking.

Grate the peel and extract the juice of

1 lemon
1 orange

Add

1 pound dates, cut small

Cover and let stand at least 12 hours. Butter a pan about 12 by 15 inches. Set the oven at 375°. Beat until light

4 eggs

Beat in gradually

1 pound brown sugar

Sift together and add

2 cups flour
¼ teaspoon salt
1 teaspoon instant coffee
2 teaspoons baking powder
2 teaspoons cinnamon

Stir in the date mixture and

1 cup chopped nut meats

Spread in the pan. Bake 30 minutes. Cool in the pan. Put in a bowl

½ cup orange juice

Add gradually until thick enough to spread

Confectioners' sugar

Stir in

1 teaspoon melted butter

Spread over the lebkuchen. Cut in 1½-inch squares. *Makes 80.*

LINZER SCHNITTEN

Beat until light

2 eggs

Beat in gradually

1½ cups sugar

Melt and add

¾ cup butter

Sift together and add

3½ cups flour
1 teaspoon baking powder
2 teaspoons cinnamon
1 teaspoon powdered cloves
¼ teaspoon salt

Grate and add

Rind of 1 lemon

Turn out on a floured board and knead until smooth and no longer sticky. Let stand at least 1 hour. Roll ½ inch thick. Cut in strips 1½ by 10 inches. Mark a groove down the center of each strip with the handle of a wooden spoon. Fill the grooves with jelly. Put on a cooky sheet and bake at 375° until light brown (about 15 minutes). Beat together

1 egg
¾ cup sugar

Brush over the baked strips while they are still hot and cut immediately into diagonal pieces. *Makes 40 or more.*

WALNUT MERINGUE BARS

Butter a shallow pan about 8 by 12 inches. Set the oven at 300°.

Cream together

½ cup butter
1 cup light brown sugar

Add

½ teaspoon salt
1 teaspoon vanilla

Beat in

2 egg yolks

Sift together and stir in

1¼ cups flour
1½ teaspoons baking powder

Stir until blended. Spread evenly in the pan. Beat until stiff

2 egg whites

Beat in

1 cup light brown sugar

Add

1 cup chopped walnut meats
1 teaspoon vanilla

Spread over the cooky mixture. Bake 35 minutes. Cool. Cut in squares with a very sharp knife. Lift out carefully with a spatula. *Makes 50.*

COCONUT SQUARES

Butter a pan 8 or 9 inches square. Set the oven at 350°.

Beat until foamy

2 eggs

Beat in

2 cups brown sugar
⅛ teaspoon salt
½ teaspoon vanilla

Stir in

2 cups shredded coconut
¼ cup broken walnut meats

Sift over the batter

6 tablespoons flour

Stir lightly and spoon into the pan. Bake 30 minutes. Cut in squares while warm. Cool and remove from the pan. *Makes 16.*

JAM BARS

Butter a shallow pan 8 or 9 inches square. Set the oven at 400°.

Cream together

½ cup shortening
½ cup sugar
½ teaspoon vanilla
½ teaspoon almond flavoring

Stir in

1 egg

Sift together and add

1½ cups flour
1 teaspoon baking powder
½ teaspoon cinnamon
¼ teaspoon powdered cloves
½ teaspoon salt

Mix well and spread half in the pan. Cover with a layer of

Raspberry jam, tart jelly, marmalade *or* Lemon Curd (p. 455)

Pat the rest of the dough on top. Bake 25 minutes. Cool. Cut in bars. *Makes about 20.*

BROWNIES

Everyone seems to have an idea about how to bake brownies—at

300°, 325°, 350° or even 425°. All are good. The thing to be careful about is to avoid overbaking — brownies should be moist and chewy.

Butter a shallow pan 9 by 9 inches. Line the bottom with wax paper cut to fit. Butter the paper. Set the oven at 325°.

Put in a double boiler top or a saucepan large enough to use as the mixing bowl

2 ounces unsweetened chocolate
¼ cup butter *or* margarine

Stir over hot water or low heat until melted. Remove from the heat. Stir in

1 cup sugar
2 eggs, unbeaten
⅛ teaspoon salt
½ cup pastry *or* all-purpose flour
½ cup walnut meats, cut in pieces
1 teaspoon vanilla

Spread in the pan. Bake until dry on top and almost firm to the touch (30 to 35 minutes). Turn upside down on a cake cooler. Cool. Peel off the paper. Cut in squares. *Makes 16.*

Sultana Sticks. Add ¼ cup raisins to the mixture. Cut in fingers.

Chocolate Orange Squares. Add ½ cup slivered orange peel (candied or fresh) to the mixture.

Harvard Brownies. *Especially rich and chewy.* Use only one egg. Bake in an 8- by 8-inch pan at 300° about 35 minutes.

FROSTED COCONUT BARS

Line an 8- by 8-inch pan with wax paper. Set the oven at 350°.

Blend thoroughly

½ cup butter
2 tablespoons confectioners' sugar
1 cup cake flour

Spread evenly in the pan. Bake 15 minutes. Beat together until thick

2 eggs
1¼ cups brown sugar
1 teaspoon vanilla

Sift together and add

2 tablespoons flour
¼ teaspoon salt
1½ teaspoons baking powder

Stir in

1 cup broken nut meats
1 cup moist shredded coconut

Spread over the first mixture and bake 30 minutes longer. Cool in the pan. Frost (below). Cut in bars. *Makes 16.*

Frosting. Beat together 1½ cups confectioners' sugar, 2 tablespoons melted butter, 2 tablespoons orange juice and 1 tablespoon lemon juice.

HAZELNUT STRIPS

Beat until stiff

1 egg white

Beat in gradually

1 cup confectioners' sugar
1 cup hazelnuts, ground fine

Pat out on a lightly floured board into an oblong ¼ inch thick. Beat together

1 egg yolk
6 tablespoons confectioners' sugar
½ teaspoon vanilla

Spread over the first mixture. Let stand 30 minutes to dry. Cut in finger-shaped strips with a knife dipped in hot water. Place on a buttered and floured cooky sheet. Let stand 10 minutes. Bake at 300° until delicately brown (about 15 minutes). Cool and lift from the pan. *Makes 18 or more.*

GUMDROP SQUARES

Butter a pan about 10 by 14 inches. Set the oven at 325°.

Mix and set aside

1 cup tiny gumdrops, sliced

¼ cup flour
Beat together until light
4 eggs
1 tablespoon cold water
Beat in gradually
2 cups light brown sugar
Sift together and add
1¾ cups flour
¼ teaspoon salt
1 teaspoon cinnamon
Stir in the gumdrops and
½ cup chopped pecan meats
Spread in the pan. Bake 30 minutes. Cut in 2-inch squares. Roll in
Powdered sugar
Makes 36.

HERMITS

Butter a pan about 7 by 14 inches. For thinner hermits, use a larger pan. Set the oven at 350°.

Mix
¼ cup raisins, cut fine
¼ cup currants
3 tablespoons citron *or* candied orange peel, cut small
¼ cup chopped nut meats
¼ cup flour
Cream together
4 tablespoons butter
½ cup sugar
Add
½ teaspoon salt
2 eggs, well beaten
½ cup molasses
Beat well. Sift together and add
1¾ cups flour
1 teaspoon baking soda
½ teaspoon cream of tartar
1 teaspoon cinnamon
½ teaspoon powdered cloves
¼ teaspoon mace
¼ teaspoon nutmeg
Beat well and stir in the floured fruit and nuts. Spread in the pan. Bake until the top is firm (15 minutes or more). Cut in squares or bars while warm. *Makes 36.*

Concord Hermits. Use 1 cup brown sugar in place of white sugar and molasses. Add ½ cup coffee, sour cream or sour milk.

BUTTERSCOTCH BROWNIES

Butter a shallow pan about 8 by 8 inches. Set the oven at 350°.

Mix
¼ cup melted butter
1 cup dark brown sugar
1 egg
¼ teaspoon salt
¾ cup flour
1 teaspoon baking powder
½ teaspoon vanilla
½ cup nut meats, broken in pieces
Spread in the pan. Bake 25 minutes. Cut in squares or strips while warm. *Makes 16 or more.*

CHEWY NOELS

Set the oven at 350°. Melt in a 9- by 9-inch pan
2 tablespoons butter
Beat slightly
2 eggs
1 teaspoon vanilla
Mix and add to the eggs
1 cup dark brown sugar
5 tablespoons flour
⅛ teaspoon baking soda
¼ teaspoon salt
1 cup nut meats, broken in pieces
Mix well. Pour into the pan. Bake until firm to the touch (about 25 minutes). Turn out onto wax paper, buttered side up. Dust lightly with
Powdered sugar
Cut in squares or bars. *Makes 25 or more.*

PECAN SQUARES

Butter a cooky sheet. Set the oven at 375°.

Cream together
½ cup butter
1 cup sugar
Beat in
1 egg yolk
1 teaspoon vanilla
Stir in
2 cups flour

Blend well. Pat evenly on the cooky sheet. Beat slightly and brush over the cooky dough

1 egg white

Scatter evenly over the top

1 cup chopped pecans

Press in slightly. Bake until golden-brown (10 to 20 minutes). Cut in squares. *Makes about 36.*

PARIS CAKES

Butter a pan about 8 by 14 inches. Line it with wax paper. Set the oven at 350°.

Melt over hot water

2 ounces unsweetened chocolate

Stir in

½ cup butter *or* margarine

When the butter is melted, stir in

2 egg yolks
½ cup sugar
1 teaspoon vanilla
¾ cup flour
¼ teaspoon salt

Fold in

2 egg whites, beaten stiff

Spread in the pan. Bake 25 minutes. Spread with

Paris Cream (below)

Pat evenly over the top

1 cup nut meats, cut small

Cut in 1½-inch squares. *Makes 50.*

Paris Cream. Put ½ pint heavy cream in a small heavy saucepan. Add 4 ounces unsweetened chocolate, 4 tablespoons sugar and a few grains of salt. Heat slowly to the boiling point. Boil 2 minutes, stirring constantly. Cool to lukewarm and beat until smooth.

MERINGUES (KISSES)

Egg whites beat best if they are at room temperature, not icy cold. For very dry meringues, the baking must be so slow that the meringues color only slightly as they bake. Some meringue-type cookies are baked in a hotter oven to make them chewy. Packaged meringue mix is a convenience, but you may find it too sweet for your taste.

Cover a cooky sheet with unglazed paper. Set the oven at 250°. Beat until very stiff and dry

2 egg whites

Beat in, a spoonful at a time

6 tablespoons sugar

Continue beating until the mixture holds its shape when you lift a spoonful. Add

1 teaspoon vanilla

Fold in carefully

2 tablespoons sugar

Shape on the cooky sheet with a pastry bag and tube or with a spoon. Bake 50 minutes. Remove from the paper. If the meringues stick, wipe the back of the paper with a damp cloth. *Makes 6 large or about 18 small meringues.*

Meringue Shells. Arrange by spoonfuls or shape in 3-inch rings. Bake. Crush the center. Put together in pairs with whipped cream or ice cream. Serve with crushed strawberries, chocolate or other sauce. Filled with ice cream, these are called **Meringues Glacées.**

Nut Meringues. Add ½ cup or more chopped nut meats (almonds, hazelnuts, walnuts, peanuts or hickory nuts). Shape. Sprinkle with nut meats and bake.

Date and Nut Meringues. Fold in ½ cup chopped nut meats and ¼ pound dates, cut fine. Pecans are especially good. Bake 25 minutes at 350°. *Makes 40 small meringues.*

Creole Kisses. Add finely pounded Nut Brittle (p. 523) made with almonds. Shape. Sprinkle with shredded almonds and sift sugar over them. Bake 25 minutes at 300°.

FRENCH MERINGUES

For very chewy meringues.

Boil to the firm ball stage (242°)
2 cups sugar
1 cup water
Meanwhile, beat until stiff
5 egg whites
Add the hot syrup gradually, beating constantly. Set the bowl in a pan of ice water. Add
1 teaspoon vanilla
Fold over and over with a mixing spoon for 5 minutes. Cover. Let stand 15 minutes. Shape (see p. 478) on buttered cooky sheets dusted with cornstarch. Bake 30 minutes at 300°. *Makes about 12.*

PECAN KISSES

Do not attempt these delectable tidbits on a damp day. They should be very chewy but firm.

Butter and flour two cooky sheets. Set the oven at 325°. Beat until very stiff
1 egg white
Add gradually, beating constantly
1 cup light brown sugar
Add
¼ teaspoon salt
½ teaspoon vanilla
Fold in
1 cup pecan meats, chopped fine
Put teaspoonfuls on the cooky sheets. Bake until dry on top (8 to 12 minutes); they will be firmer when cold. *Makes 24.*

Pecan Berkeleys. Use dark brown sugar, 1 teaspoon vanilla and 2 cups unchopped pecan halves. Bake at 300°.

CHOCOLATE NUT MERINGUES

Melt and set aside to cool slightly
2 ounces unsweetened chocolate
Blanch and chop
⅔ cup almonds
Butter 2 cooky sheets. Set the oven at 300°. Beat until very stiff
2 egg whites
Add gradually, beating constantly
⅞ cup powdered sugar
Carefully fold in the chocolate and ½ cup of the nut meats. Put on the cooky sheets by teaspoonfuls. Sprinkle with the rest of the nut meats. Bake 40 minutes. *Makes 40.*

WASPS' NESTS

Traditional Christmas cookies, but wonderful any time of year.

Butter and flour cooky sheets. Set the oven at 300°.

Shred lengthwise
½ pound blanched almonds
Cook together until the syrup spins a thread (240°)
½ cup sugar
¼ cup water
Stir in the almonds. Grate or chop fine
1 package semi-sweet chocolate
Beat until very stiff
3 egg whites
Add by spoonfuls, beating constantly
2 cups confectioners' sugar
Add the chocolate and the almond mixture. Put half-teaspoonfuls of the dough on the cooky sheets. Bake until dry (about 25 minutes). Let stand 10 minutes and remove from the pan. *Makes 100.*

CHOCOLATE MERINGUE COOKIES

Set the oven at 300°. Melt over hot water
1 ounce chocolate
Stir in
⅔ cup confectioners' sugar
1 egg white
1 teaspoon vanilla

Mix until smooth. Add until thick enough to roll out

Confectioners' sugar (about 1 cup)

Sprinkle a board with

Granulated sugar

Roll the mixture 1/4 inch thick. Sprinkle with more granulated sugar. Cut out with a small biscuit cutter. Bake on a cooky sheet until dry (about 30 minutes). *Makes 18.*

VIENNESE WAFERS

Butter and flour a cooky sheet. Set the oven at 350°.

Mix in a bowl

1 egg white
1/2 teaspoon vanilla
1/2 teaspoon lemon juice

Mix and stir in

1/4 cup powdered sugar
1/4 cup finely chopped almonds *or* filberts

Put on the cooky sheet by small teaspoonfuls. Bake until dry (about 12 minutes). Frost, if you like, with

Confectioners' Frosting (p. 512)

Makes 18.

CINNAMON STARS

Set the oven at 300°. Butter 2 cooky sheets lightly.

Beat to a stiff froth

3 egg whites

Mix

1 cup granulated sugar
1 tablespoon flour
1 1/2 teaspoons cinnamon
1 1/3 cups chopped unblanched almonds
Grated rind of 1/2 lemon

Fold into the egg whites. Put a sheet of wax paper on a board. Sprinkle with

1/4 cup confectioners' sugar sifted with 1/4 cup flour

Put the dough on it and cover with another sheet of wax paper. Pat and roll out 1/4 inch thick. Shape with a star cutter. Put on the cooky sheets. Bake 20 minutes. Spread with

Confectioners' Frosting (p. 512)

Makes 36.

CHOCOLATE COCONUT KISSES

Butter cooky sheets lightly. Set the oven at 350°.

Sift together

1 1/2 cups confectioners' sugar
1 tablespoon flour

Beat until they stand in soft peaks

3 egg whites

Beat in the sugar mixture, 2 tablespoonfuls at a time. Add

1 teaspoon vanilla

Fold in

1/2 cup shredded coconut
1 package chocolate bits (6 ounces)

Arrange by teaspoonfuls on the cooky sheets. Bake until dry (12 to 15 minutes). Cool slightly and remove from the pans. *Makes about 50.*

PEANUT MACAROONS

Butter a cooky sheet. Set the oven at 300°.

Prepare

5 tablespoons chopped skinned peanuts

Beat until stiff

1 egg white

Add gradually, beating constantly

1/4 cup sugar

Add the peanuts. Stir in

1 teaspoon vanilla

Put on the cooky sheet by teaspoonfuls, 1 1/2 inches apart. Garnish each with half a peanut. Bake until dry (12 to 15 minutes). *Makes 16.*

CORN FLAKE MACAROONS

Butter a cooky sheet. Set the oven at 350°.

Beat until stiff
1 egg white
Stir in
½ cup sugar
½ cup shredded coconut
1 cup corn flakes
¼ teaspoon almond extract
¼ teaspoon vanilla
Few grains salt
Put on the cooky sheet by teaspoonfuls. Bake 20 minutes. *Makes 18.*

Chocolate Chip Macaroons. Use only ¼ cup sugar. Instead of coconut, use ⅓ cup semi-sweet chocolate, cut in small pieces.

CINNAMON FINGERS

Butter a cooky sheet. Set the oven at 400°.

Mix
1 can condensed milk
1 teaspoon cinnamon
Few grains salt
½ teaspoon vanilla
Dip in the mixture
Sliced bread, cut in fingers
Put on the cooky sheet. Bake until brown, turning once. Dry on a cake cooler.

RUM BALLS

No baking to make these. Store at least a week to develop the best flavor.

Prepare
2 cups vanilla wafer crumbs, rolled fine
Add
1 cup finely chopped coconut *or* pecan meats
1 cup confectioners' sugar
2 tablespoons cocoa
2 tablespoons white corn syrup
⅓ cup rum, brandy *or* Cointreau
Mix well. Shape by teaspoonfuls into firm balls. Roll in
Confectioners' sugar, instant coffee *or* dry cocoa
Store tightly covered. *Makes 50.*

CHOCOLATE COCONUT COOKIES

Butter a cooky sheet. Set the oven at 350°.

Heat until the chocolate melts
1 can sweetened condensed milk
3 ounces unsweetened chocolate
Add
2 cups shredded coconut
1 cup pecan meats, in pieces
1 teaspoon vanilla
Put on the cooky sheet by teaspoonfuls. Bake 10 minutes. *Makes about 40.*

PEANUT BUTTER CHEWIES

Butter a cooky sheet. Set the oven at 375°.

Mix
1 can sweetened condensed milk
½ cup peanut butter
½ teaspoon lemon juice
¼ teaspoon salt
1 cup chopped peanuts
1 teaspoon vanilla
Put on the cooky sheet by teaspoonfuls. Bake 12 minutes. *Makes about 40.*

To vary. Instead of peanuts, use 2 cups raisins, coconut, chopped dates, bran flakes or corn flakes.

PRUNE MACAROONS

Butter 2 cooky sheets. Set the oven at 350°.

Mix
½ can sweetened condensed milk
1 cup shredded coconut
¼ teaspoon salt
1 cup prunes, cut small
2 cups corn flakes
½ teaspoon vanilla
Shape in small balls with your fingers. Place on the cooky sheets. Bake 10 minutes. *Makes about 60.*

MACAROONS

True macaroons are made of egg whites, sugar and almond paste. But the name has come to be applied to many chewy cookies of similar texture. Packaged macaroon mix is available.

Mix thoroughly with your hands

½ pound almond paste (homemade or packaged)

Add, little by little

1 cup sugar
3 egg whites, unbeaten

Blend thoroughly and sift in

⅓ cup powdered sugar
2 tablespoons pastry *or* cake flour
⅛ teaspoon salt

Cover cooky sheets with unglazed paper. Put teaspoonfuls of the mixture on the paper or shape with a pastry bag and tube. Flatten with fingers dipped in cold water. Cover and let stand 2 hours or more. Bake 30 minutes at 300°. Put the paper on a damp cloth and remove the macaroons. *Makes about 30.*

To vary, add finely chopped candied cherries to the mixture or decorate tops before baking with chopped almonds, pignolias, walnut meats, raisins or bits of cherry.

Almond Macaroons. Sprinkle before baking with almonds, blanched and shredded or chopped.

Chocolate Fingers. Shape in fingers. Put together in pairs with Chocolate Filling (p. 517). Dip the ends in sugar syrup, then in chocolate shot.

CRESCENTS

Mix with your hands

½ pound almond paste
½ cup confectioners' sugar
1 egg white

Shape in a long roll. Cut in ¾-inch pieces. Roll each piece in

Chopped blanched almonds

Shape in crescents. Put on a lightly buttered cooky sheet. Let stand 20 minutes. Bake 20 minutes at 300°. Cool. Frost with

Confectioners' Frosting (p. 512), flavored with lemon juice (enough to make the frosting very tart)

Have the frosting thin enough to spread on the crescents with a pastry brush. *Makes about 30.*

MARGUERITES

Butter tiny cupcake tins. Set the oven at 350°.

Mix thoroughly

2 eggs, slightly beaten
1 cup light brown sugar
½ cup flour
¼ teaspoon baking powder
½ teaspoon salt
1 cup pecan meats, cut small

Fill the tins two-thirds full. Place on each

Pecan meats

Bake until the cakes shrink slightly from the pans (8 to 15 minutes). *Makes 24 2-inch cakes.*

Marguerite Bars. Spread the mixture in a buttered pan 8 by 8 inches, bake, cool and cut in squares or bars.

MOLASSES MARGUERITES

Mix

1 egg
⅓ cup butter
⅓ cup powdered sugar
⅓ cup molasses
⅞ cup flour
1 cup pecan meats, cut small

Bake as Marguerites (above). *Makes 24.*

LADY FINGERS

Butter lady finger tins or cover cooky sheets with unglazed paper. Set the oven at 350°.

Beat until in soft peaks

3 egg whites

Add gradually, beating constantly

1/3 cup powdered sugar

Without washing the beater, beat until thick and lemon-colored

2 egg yolks
1/2 teaspoon vanilla
1/8 teaspoon salt

Fold in

1/3 cup sifted flour

Fold in the egg whites. Spoon into the tins or shape with a pastry bag and plain tube onto the paper. Bake about 12 minutes. Use a long sharp knife to remove easily from the paper. *Makes about 30.*

Sponge Drops. Put teaspoonfuls on the cooky sheets and bake as above. Put together in pairs with Paris Cream (p. 478) or whipped cream.

CALIFORNIA TEA CAKES

Put homemade (p. 482) or baker's lady fingers together, sandwich fashion, with a filling of mashed cream cheese and chopped candied ginger.

LEMON QUEENS

Butter and flour 18 or more small cupcake tins. Set the oven at 350°.

Cream together

1/4 cup butter
1/2 cup sugar

Stir in

Grated rind of 1/2 lemon
1 teaspoon lemon juice
2 egg yolks, beaten until thick

Sift together and add

5/8 cup flour
1/4 teaspoon salt
1/8 teaspoon baking soda

Beat well and fold in

2 egg whites, beaten stiff

Spoon into the tins, having them two-thirds full. Bake until the cakes shrink slightly from the pans. *Makes 18 or more.*

PEANUT BUTTER CUPCAKES

At their best when freshly baked.

Put paper baking cups in muffin tins (16 or more, according to size). Set the oven at 375°. Cream together until smooth

1/4 cup peanut butter
1/4 cup butter

Beat in

3/4 cup brown sugar
1 egg
1/4 teaspoon salt
1/2 teaspoon vanilla

Sift together

1 cup pastry flour *or* 3/4 cup all-purpose flour
1 1/4 teaspoons baking powder

Add in small amounts, alternating with

3/8 cup milk

Fill the paper cups half full. Bake about 20 minutes. Frost with

Portsmouth Frosting (p. 512)

Makes 16 or more.

BOSTON CUPCAKES

See also page 488 for other suggestions.

Set the oven at 375°. Butter a set of cupcake tins.

Cream together until light and fluffy

1/3 cup butter
1 cup sugar

Stir in

2 eggs, well beaten

Sift together

1 3/8 cups pastry *or* cake flour
2 teaspoons baking powder
1/4 teaspoon mace
1/4 teaspoon salt

Add to th first mixture alternately with

1/2 cup milk

Spoon into the pans. Bake about 20 minutes. *Makes 12.*

Cakes

Cake recipes are often treasured family heirlooms, and many of Fannie Farmer's recipes have been in use in the same family for over sixty years. Some new and simple recipes have been added which are almost as easy as the popular packaged cake mixes.

SUCCESS IN CAKE MAKING

A perfect cake is light, fine and even-textured, with a tender, slightly moist surface. The top should be smooth and flat or only slightly rounded. A cake should have a "velvety" crumb when you taste it. Sponge cake should appear slightly "pebbled" on the surface.

Measure carefully. Too much shortening, sugar or baking powder may cause the cake to fall, to run over the top of the pan, or to be too crumbly to handle. Too much flour or too little liquid will make it humped and uneven, tough or dry.

Mix or beat only as much as needed. Inexperienced cooks often overbeat and so break down the air bubbles after they are formed. This makes a cake heavy, dry and uneven.

Bake at the correct temperature for the required time in an uncrowded oven. If the oven is too hot, the cake will be too small, cracked and heavy. If it is too cool, the cake may run over the top of the pan, stick to the pan, or be coarse or soggy. Not enough baking may cause the cake to fall or break as it comes from the pan. Baking too long makes a cake dry and hard.

INGREDIENTS

Flour. There are many types of flour and it is important to know how they differ in order to work with any of them successfully. **Cake flour** is very fine and light. **Pastry flour** makes a very tender cake, slightly less dry than one made with cake flour. **All-purpose and bread flours** absorb more liquid, so it is often wise to cut down the amount of flour by 2 tablespoons to the cup unless the recipe definitely calls for them. If you use all-purpose or bread flour, be particularly careful not to overbeat, as that develops the gluten in these hard wheat flours and will make the cake stretchy and tough.

Sift flour before measuring. Otherwise it may be so packed down that you will have too much. Sift onto wax paper to save using an extra bowl. A single-screen sifter is easier to keep clean than one with several screens. An experienced cake baker will set aside one-quarter of the flour and add only as much of it as is needed when the cake batter is mixed. Reducing the flour makes a cake very delicate.

Shortening. For plain cakes, butter or margarine is desirable to give the cake its characteristic flavor. For chocolate or spice cakes use butter or any of the excellent cooking fats or oils. If you use an unsalted fat, add more salt to the ingredients in the proportion of 1 teaspoon to each cup of fat. If you use oil or a solid fat, use one-eighth less than the amount called for in the recipe, since butter is about seven-eighths fat, and hydrogenated fats have air whipped in to make them easier to cream. Have all fats at room temperature so that they will blend easily.

Eggs. Eggs beat to greater volume at room temperature than when cold, but it is easier to separate them when they are cold. If you are using pullet eggs or very large eggs, measure by the cup (p. 7).

Baking powder. Most of the recipes in this book are adapted to all types of baking powder. If a change is needed, a note in the recipe explains.

Flavoring. High-grade extracts are often an economy because they are more concentrated, so that less is needed.

MIXING SPONGE CAKES

Directions for making sponge cake and other cakes without shortening are given with each recipe. Beating the eggs thoroughly is essential if the cake is to be perfect, but overbeating after the flour is added will spoil the light texture.

QUICK-MIX AND CHIFFON CAKES

Neither sponge nor butter cakes, these cakes have some characteristics of each. The result is a fine, light, moist cake, very easy to make. The recipes give details.

MIXING BUTTER CAKES

Preheat the oven if yours requires it so that it will be at the right temperature when the cake batter is ready.

Sift the flour onto a piece of wax paper before measuring. Measure, add baking powder and salt and sift again. Measure the butter into a mixing bowl. Set out the other ingredients. Have everything at room temperature, the butter soft but not melted.

By hand. If you are adding the whites separately, beat them until they stand up in soft peaks, beating in some of the sugar called for in the recipe—1 tablespoon for each egg white. Set aside while you prepare the rest of the batter. The sugar will keep the beaten egg whites stiff. Without washing the beater, beat the egg yolks until thick and lemon-colored.

Cream the butter until it is very soft and fluffy by rubbing it against the side of the bowl with a blending fork or a wooden mixing spoon. Add the flavoring. Beat in the sugar, a little at a time, and continue beating until the mixture is like whipped cream. Beat in whole eggs or egg yolks. Thorough beating up to this stage makes a fine light cake. Stir in the flour mixture by thirds, alternating with the milk. Add some of the flour last. Beat only enough to blend well. Overbeating breaks down the air cells and makes a cake heavy. Fold in the beaten egg whites gently (p. 7) until flecks of white are evenly distributed.

There is a difference in the texture of cake if the eggs are separated or added whole. Adding the beaten whites last makes a light fluffy cake. Adding eggs whole makes a fine-grained cake.

In an electric mixer. Beat the egg whites first with 1 tablespoon sugar for each white, and set aside. Without washing the beater, work the shortening until soft and creamy (about 1 minute at high speed). Add the flavoring. Beat in the rest of the sugar until light and fluffy. Stop the beater once or twice and scrape down the sides of the bowl with a rubber scraper. Add the egg yolks and beat 1 minute at high speed. Scrape down. Add the flour mixture and the milk by hand (see p. 485) or at very slow speed so that you will not overbeat the batter. Fold in the egg whites with a mixing spoon.

MAKING FRUIT CAKES

To prepare fruit. Leave currants and seedless raisins whole. Cut seeded raisins in half with wet scissors. Cut cherries in half. Slice candied pineapple, citron and fruit peels thin. Cut dates and nuts in quarters. Some shops sell fruit prepared for fruit cake, especially at holiday time.

To prepare pans. Use deep loaf pans. Butter the pans lightly and line with aluminum foil. Glass or ovenware casseroles, small or large, are attractive to use, especially if you are planning the fruit cake as a gift. Butter lightly but do not line with foil. After baking, cool, put on covers and set cakes away to ripen.

To decorate. Spread with a thin layer of almond paste, canned or homemade (p. 529), moistened with egg white. When firm, frost and decorate as you like (pp. 509 ff.). For a more elaborate effect, remove from the oven 15 minutes before baking is completed. Brush with slightly beaten egg white and quickly arrange on the cake a pattern of bits of candied fruit and nuts. Return to the oven to finish baking.

To store. Cool baked cakes 30 minutes. Loosen around the edges with a knife and turn out on cake racks. When entirely cold, wrap in heavy wax paper and tie securely. Store in a crock or tin box with a tight cover. If baked in a casserole, store in the casserole. Rich fruit cakes improve in flavor if aged at least two weeks before using. If you like, sprinkle stored fruit cakes very lightly with brandy once a week until used. This helps keep the cake moist and improves the flavor.

CAKE MIX CAKES

Cake mixes are often excellent and give the beginning cook a good place to start. For the experienced cook, they may save a little much needed time. Angel cake mixes avoid the problem of what to do with leftover yolks.

Follow directions on the package exactly for mixing and baking, but vary the flavoring a little to give the cake a homemade taste. Add real vanilla or grated orange rind, or sprinkle the finished cake with rum or brandy.

PREPARING CAKE PANS

Use the appropriate size of pan for the amount of batter so that it will be two-thirds full. If the pan is too large, the cake will be dry and crusty. If it is too small, the batter will run over the top as it rises. If you have too much batter for the pan you are using, put the extra in cupcake tins.

Do not butter pans for sponge or angel cakes. For other cakes, butter the bottom of the pan only. Cakes rise evenly if the sides are not buttered. Use a pastry brush or a crushed piece of wax paper dipped in melted butter. Butter gives a delicious flavor to the crust of the cake and so is recommended, but any good cooking fat will keep the cake from sticking. After spreading the butter, sprinkle lightly with flour, then shake out extra flour. With a very delicate cake batter, the safest way is to grease the pan, then cover the bottom with a piece of wax paper cut to fit, and then grease again.

FILLING CAKE PANS

Spread the batter well into the corners and sides of the pan with the center slightly lower. Fill pans about two-thirds full to allow for rising.

BAKING THE CAKE

Preheat if your oven requires it. Be sure the oven temperature is correct. Check your regulator occasionally with an oven thermometer.

Set the cake as near the center of the oven as possible so that the heat will circulate evenly. Do not overcrowd the oven and do not bake cake while there is much moisture in the oven—custards baking in a pan of water, for example. After 20 minutes, if the cake is baking unevenly because the oven heats unevenly, turn the pan around.

When the time for baking is nearly over, test the cake by pressing lightly with a finger tip: if the cake is done it will spring back. Or test with a wire cake tester, which will come out clean when the cake is done.

If you use the same mixture for loaf cake and for layers, the loaf cake will bake more evenly at a temperature about 25° lower than the layers.

TAKING THE CAKE FROM THE PAN

Sponge cake. Invert on a wire cooler. Let stand until cold. Loosen with a spatula or a knife.

Butter cake. Invert on a cake cooler. Let the cake stand until it begins to shrink from the sides of the pan. Loosen with a spatula if necessary, but gently, so that you will not break the tender crust.

Angel food and chiffon cake. Invert and let stand until cold. If your tube pan does not have rests to raise it above the table, set the tube in a milk bottle so that the cake will hang free while it is cooling.

CAKE MAKING AT HIGH ALTITUDES

At 3500 feet or higher, cakes made without some modifications may be somewhat dry, coarse and crumbly. As the outside air pressure decreases, the amount of leavening within the cake (baking powder or baking soda or both) must also be reduced. Decrease the leavening by one-third at 3500 feet, by one-half at 5000 feet, and by two-thirds above 5000 feet. Beat egg whites less than the recipe suggests—until soft and fluffy but still very moist-looking. Raise the baking temperature by 25°.

For special recipes consult state departments of agriculture or home economics departments.

CUTTING THE CAKE

Cut a round cake in narrow or wide pie-shaped wedges.

Cut a loaf cake in squares or slices, or in diamonds or triangles.

Cut fruit cake in small squares or slices, or serve the loaf whole, cutting off pieces as needed.

Separate sponge cake in pieces with two forks or a special sponge cake divider. Do not cut with a knife.

On page 508 you will find directions for cutting a wedding cake.

USING LEFTOVER CAKE

Cut unfrosted cake in squares, steam over hot water and serve with whipped cream or any pudding sauce.

In whipped cream. Fold cubes or crumbs into whipped cream. Serve with crushed fruit or a sauce.

Chocolate Ice Cream Balls. Roll firm scoops of vanilla ice cream in chocolate cake crumbs and set in the freezer until ready to serve.

Ice Cream on Toasted Cake. Toast half-inch slices of any pound cake. Top with ice cream and serve immediately while the cake is still warm.

Other suggestions:

Tipsy Pudding (p. 385).
English Trifle (p. 385).
Icebox Pudding (p. 394).
Bread Pudding (pp. 391 ff.). Use cake crumbs in place of bread crumbs and decrease the sugar.
Rum Balls (p. 481). Use cake crumbs as part of the crumbs.

CUPCAKES

Use any cake or gingerbread recipe. For a small family, you may like to mix a cake batter and bake part in a small loaf tin, the rest in cupcake tins. Cupcakes bake better with slightly less flour, so use 1 tablespoon less to the cup if you are adapting a recipe to bake as cupcakes. See also Cupcakes (p. 483) and Lemon Queens (p. 483). Bake at 375°. Sprinkle with powdered sugar or cover with butter frosting or boiled icing. Garnish with chopped nuts or half a nut meat, bit of cherry or chocolate shot.

Filled Cupcakes. Cut thin slices off the tops of plain cupcakes. Scoop out some of the center. Fill with jam, marmalade, preserves, whipped cream, Chocolate Filling (p. 512) or other filling. Replace the tops. Frost as desired.

TRUE SPONGE CAKE

True sponge cake has no leavening except the air beaten into the eggs. After adding the flour, blend very gently with a spoon. Overbeating would break down the tiny air bubbles. For further details on beating and folding, see page 484.

Set the oven at 325° if you are using a tube pan or other deep pan, 350° for layer or muffin tins.

Separate
5 eggs
Beat the whites until they stand up in soft peaks. Beat in, a tablespoon at a time

¼ cup sugar
Without washing the beater, beat the yolks with
1 tablespoon lemon juice
until thick and lemon-colored. Beat in gradually
¾ cup sugar
Pour over the beaten whites and fold together gently with a spoon until well blended. Sift together and fold into the egg mixture
1 cup flour
¼ teaspoon salt
Spoon into an unbuttered 9-inch tube pan, two 9-inch layer pans or 12 to 18 muffin tins. Cut through the batter gently several times to break any large air bubbles. Bake a large cake about 1 hour, layers and small cakes about 30 minutes. (To test, press lightly with a finger. If the cake is done it will spring back.) Invert on a wire cake cooler. Let stand until cold. Loosen with a spatula and ease the cake out of the pan.

HOT WATER SPONGE CAKE

Set the oven at 350°. Separate
2 eggs
Sift together
1 cup pastry *or* cake flour
1¼ teaspoons baking powder
Few grains salt
Beat the whites until they stand up in soft peaks. Beat in gradually
¼ cup sugar
Add to the egg yolks
¼ cup hot water
½ teaspoon vanilla
Beat until thick and beat in
½ cup sugar
Pour the yolks over the whites and cut and fold until well blended. Fold in the flour mixture. Spoon into a small unbuttered tube pan or a lightly buttered 9-inch square pan or 12 cupcake tins. Bake 20 to 30 minutes.

(To test, see True Sponge Cake).

CREAM SPONGE CAKE

For layer cakes, jelly rolls or Vienna Cake. A perfect birthday cake because its light texture goes well with a rich frosting. Excellent for cupcakes, too.

Set the oven at 325° for a tube pan, 350° for layers.

Separate
4 eggs
Sift
1 cup pastry *or* cake flour
1¼ teaspoons baking powder
¼ teaspoon salt
Beat the egg whites until they stand up in soft peaks. Beat in
¼ cup sugar
Without washing the beater, beat the egg yolks until thick and lemon-colored. Beat in
1 teaspoon vanilla
1½ tablespoons cold water
1½ tablespoons lemon juice
¾ cup sugar
Pour over the whites and fold together until well blended. Fold in the flour mixture. Pour into two 8-inch layer cake pans or an 8-inch tube pan. Bake 40 to 50 minutes in tube pan, 25 to 30 in layers. (To test, see True Sponge Cake, p. 488.)

Mocha Cake. Add to the batter ½ cup walnut meats broken in pieces. Bake in an 8-inch tube pan about 45 minutes. Cool. Split and fill with French Coffee Cream Filling (p. 518). Cover the top with Confectioners' Frosting (p. 512), flavored with instant coffee.

GENOISE

Half the standard French recipe, but enough for a two-layer cake or two dozen petits fours.

Butter two 8-inch layer cake pans or a pan about 10 by 6 inches. Line the bottom of the pans with wax paper and butter again. Set the oven at 350°.

Melt

2 tablespoons butter

Set aside to cool to lukewarm. Put in a mixing bowl

3 eggs (not icy cold)
½ cup fine granulated sugar
½ teaspoon vanilla

Beat (easiest with an electric beater at high speed) until thick enough to stand in peaks when the beater is lifted out. Set over warm water if the eggs are cold. Using a rubber spatula, fold in gently by spoonfuls

½ cup sifted cake or pastry flour

Sprinkle the melted butter over the batter. Blend gently. Pour into the pans. Bake 35 to 40 minutes. Turn out carefully onto a cooling rack. Peel off the paper. Frost or fill and frost with

Butter Cream (p. 517) *or* a variation

See also Vienna Cake (p. 491).

RUM CAKE

Cut in serving-size sections a 9-inch sponge or angel cake (homemade or not). Press together in original shape. Sprinkle with rum, using about ¼ cup or as much as the cake will absorb. Whip ½ pint cream, sweeten, and flavor as you like or fold into it a jar of nesselrode sauce. Spread evenly over the top and sides of the cake.

JELLY ROLL

Line the bottom of a shallow pan (about 7 by 11 inches) with heavy wax paper. Butter the paper and the sides of the pan. Cover the bottom of the pan with Hot Water Sponge Cake (p. 489) or half the recipe for Cream Sponge Cake (p. 489). (Use the rest for a few cupcakes if you make up the whole amount.) Spread evenly. Bake 12 minutes at 350°. Do not overbake.

Turn out onto a towel sprinkled thickly with confectioners' sugar. Pull off the paper quickly. With a long sharp knife cut off thin strips from the edges of the cake so that it will roll without breaking. Roll the cake in a towel and let stand a few minutes. Unroll and spread with jam or jelly. Roll up firmly and wrap in wax paper until serving time. Sprinkle the top with confectioners' sugar.

Lemon *or* Orange Roll. Spread with Lemon or Orange Filling (p. 517).

Ice Cream Roll. Spread with a thick layer of vanilla ice cream soft enough to spread but not melted. Roll up. Serve with a sauce or not.

Whipped Cream Roll. Spread with whipped cream sweetened and flavored with vanilla, instant coffee, maple syrup or chocolate. Rum goes well with coffee or chocolate. Mix in chopped nuts if you like.

PARTY CAKES

Bake any sponge cake mixture in shallow pans. Cool and cut in rounds with a small cooky cutter. Cut each round in three layers.

Put together with a thin layer of Mocha or Orange Portsmouth or Chocolate Frosting (p. 512). Spread frosting around the sides. Roll the sides in shredded coconut. Ornament the top with frosting put on with a pastry bag and tube. Begin at the center of the top and coil the frosting around until the surface is covered.

VIENNA CAKE

Make Cream Sponge Cake (p. 489), increasing the egg whites to 6. Spoon into a 9-inch tube pan. Bake at 325° about 1 hour. Turn upside down on a wire cooler. When cool, remove from the pan and cut crosswise in four layers of equal thickness.

Make 1½ times the recipe for Butter Cream Filling (p. 517) and flavor one-third of it with 1 ounce chocolate, melted. Put the layers together with plain filling in the center, chocolate part in the others. Cover the top and sides with plain filling. Sprinkle all the frosted surface with crushed nut brittle (almond or peanut).

Another way to make Vienna Cake is to put Caramel Glaze (p. 510) on the top and have no frosting on the top or sides.

DAFFODIL CAKE (MARBLE SPONGE)

Set the oven at 325°. Set out a large tube pan.

Beat until foamy
- **1¼ cups egg whites (about 9)**

Add
- **½ teaspoon salt**
- **1 teaspoon cream of tartar**

Beat until stiff but not dry. Beat in, a little at a time
- **1⅛ cups sugar**

Divide in half. Fold into one part
- **½ cup pastry *or* cake flour, sifted**
- **½ teaspoon vanilla**

Fold into the other part
- **6 egg yolks, well beaten**
- **⅔ cup pastry *or* cake flour, sifted**
- **½ teaspoon orange *or* lemon extract**
- **½ teaspoon salt**

Put by spoonfuls into the pan, alternating yellow and white. Bake 1¼ hours. Turn upside down. Let stand until cold before removing from the pan. Sprinkle with sifted confectioners' sugar.

SUNSHINE CAKE

Set the oven at 350°. Set out a large tube pan but do not butter it.

Beat until they stand up in soft peaks
- **10 egg whites**

Beat in
- **½ cup confectioners' sugar**
- **1 teaspoon cream of tartar**

Beat until thick
- **7 egg yolks**

Add
- **1 cup confectioners' sugar**
- **1 teaspoon lemon *or* almond extract**

Beat well. Pour over the whites and fold together gently until well blended. Sift over the egg mixture
- **1 cup pastry *or* cake flour**
- **¼ teaspoon salt**

Cut and fold together. Pour into the pan. Bake 50 minutes. Invert on a wire cooler and let stand until cold.

CHOCOLATE SPONGE CAKE

Butter a 9-inch tube pan. Set the oven at 350°.

Put in the top of a double boiler
- **1 bar (6 ounces) sweet chocolate**
- **¼ cup water**

Set over hot water until the chocolate is melted. Beat until light and fluffy
- **4 eggs**

Beat in gradually
- **¾ cup sugar**
- **½ teaspoon vanilla**
- **⅛ teaspoon salt**

Add the chocolate mixture. Fold in
- **½ cup flour**

Spoon into the pan. Bake about 45 minutes. Frost with Butter Frosting (p. 516).

ANGEL FOOD CAKE

Make angel fod the day before you plan to serve it. It "ripens" to a finer flavor and texture.

Set the oven at 325°. Dust a 10-inch tube pan with flour but do not butter it.

Beat with a flat wire whisk or a beater until foamy

1 cup egg whites (8 or more)
¼ teaspoon salt

Add

1 teaspoon cream of tartar

Beat until the egg whites stand up in soft peaks. Add

½ teaspoon almond extract
1 teaspoon vanilla

Sift together four times

1¼ cups fine granulated sugar
1 cup cake flour

Fold carefully into the beaten whites, 2 tablespoons at a time, using a whisk or spatula. Fold gently over and over until the mixture is even. Spoon into the pan. Bake 50 minutes, then turn off the heat and leave the cake in the oven 10 minutes longer. Turn the pan upside down (p. 487) and let stand until the cake is cold (at least 1 hour).

Cocoa Angel Cake. Substitute ⅓ cup dry cocoa for ¼ cup flour. Sift with the flour. Omit almond extract. Cover the whole cake with a thin layer of whipped cream.

Angel Food Roll. Make half the recipe. Pour into a shallow pan, 10 by 15 inches, lined with wax paper. Bake 20 minutes at 325°. Fill as suggested for Jelly Roll (p. 490).

MOCK ANGEL CAKE

Much improved in flavor if not served until a day after baking.

Set the oven at 350°. Set out a small tube pan but do not butter it.

Sift together four times

1 cup sugar
1⅓ cups cake flour
3 teaspoons baking powder
¼ teaspoon salt

Stir in, little by little

⅔ cup scalded milk

Add

1 teaspoon vanilla

Beat until stiff

2 egg whites

Fold into the batter. Pour into the pan. Bake 45 minutes.

COCONUT SNOWBALLS

Cut angel food in 3-inch cubes or pull into irregular pieces. Roll in Seven-Minute Frosting (p. 514), then in grated coconut. Place on wax paper to dry.

QUICK-MIX CAKE

The quick-mix method of cake making is easy, requires but one bowl and takes only a few minutes. The proportion of ingredients is different from that in other recipes, so use only recipes that have been tested for this method. The batter will be smooth and thin.

Set the oven at 350° for tube or layer pan, at 325° for loaf pan. Set out a 10-inch tube pan, two 8-inch layer cake pans or a 9- by 5-inch loaf pan. Do not butter the pans.

Sift together into a mixing bowl

2¼ cups cake flour (sifted before measuring)
3 teaspoons baking powder
1 teaspoon salt
1¼ cups sugar

Add

½ cup salad oil (not olive oil)
½ cup milk

Stir until the flour is dampened, then beat 2 minutes. Add

½ cup milk
2 eggs *or* 5 egg yolks
1 teaspoon vanilla *or* 2 teaspoons grated lemon rind

Beat 2 minutes longer. Pour into the pan or pans. Bake about 55 minutes in tube or loaf pan, 30 minutes in layer pans.

QUICK-MIX WHITE CAKE

Set the oven at 350°. Butter a 10-inch tube pan or two 8-inch layer pans.

Sift into a mixing bowl

2 cups cake flour (sifted before measuring)
1 teaspoon salt
1⅓ cups sugar

Add

½ cup salad oil (not olive oil)
⅔ cup milk

Stir until the flour is dampened and beat 1 minute. Stir in

3 teaspoons baking powder

Add

⅓ cup milk
4 egg whites
1 teaspoon vanilla

Beat 2 minutes. Pour into the pans. Bake 25 to 40 minutes.

QUICK-MIX FUDGE CAKE

Set the oven at 350°. Butter a pan 12 by 8 by 2 inches.

Place in a mixing bowl

3 ounces unsweetened chocolate, cut fine

Add

¾ cup boiling water

Stir until the chocolate melts. Cool. Sift into the chocolate mixture

1¾ cups cake flour (sifted before measuring)
1½ cups sugar
¾ teaspoon salt
½ teaspoon baking powder
¾ teaspoon baking soda

Add

½ cup salad oil (not olive oil)

Beat 1 minute by hand or with electric beater at lowest speed. Add

⅓ cup sour milk
1 teaspoon vanilla
2 eggs

Beat 2 minutes, keep the sides of the bowl scraped down at all times. Spoon into the pan and bake 30 to 40 minutes.

QUICK-MIX DATE MIX

Set the oven at 350°. Butter and flour 12 muffin pans or a 9-inch square cake pan.

Put into a mixing bowl

⅓ cup soft butter *or* margarine
1 cup brown sugar
2 eggs
½ cup milk
1¾ cups all-purpose flour
2 teaspoons baking powder
½ teaspoon cinnamon
½ teaspoon grated nutmeg
½ pound dates, cut in pieces

Beat 3 minutes with a wooden spoon. Pour into the pans. Bake 30 to 40 minutes.

CHIFFON CAKE

Set the oven at 325°. Set out a 10-inch tube pan but do not butter it.

Sift into a large mixing bowl

2¼ cups cake flour
3 teaspoons baking powder
1½ cups sugar
1 teaspoon salt

Make a well in the center. Pour in

½ cup salad oil (not olive oil)
5 egg yolks
¾ cup cold water
2 teaspoons vanilla

Beat thoroughly until satin-smooth (2 minutes with an electric beater). Beat until stiff

1 cup egg whites (7 or 8)
½ teaspoon cream of tartar

Pour the first mixture over the egg whites a little at a time, gently folding it in with a spatula or a rubber scraper until evenly blended. Do not beat or stir. Pour into the pan. Bake 50 minutes. Increase the heat to 350° and bake until the top springs back when you dent it with your finger (about 15 minutes). Turn the pan upside down (p. 487). Let stand until cold. Loosen the cake from the sides of the tin with a spatula.

Chocolate Chiffon Cake. Use only 2 cups flour. Sift with it ¼ cup cocoa.

Lemon *or* Orange Chiffon Cake. Omit the vanilla. Add 2 teaspoons grated lemon or orange rind.

Spice Chiffon Cake. Use brown sugar in place of white. Add 1 teaspoon cinnamon and ½ teaspoon each of nutmeg, powdered cloves and allspice.

Chiffon Nut Cake. Just before pouring the batter (or any variation) into the pan, add 1 cup nut meats, chopped fine.

BOSTON FAVORITE CAKE (BUTTER CAKE)

The standard butter cake recipe. For a small family, bake in cupcake tins, frost some and use the others for cottage pudding with a vanilla or lemon sauce. If you use all-purpose flour, reduce the amount by 2 tablespoons and be careful not to overbeat.

Butter a pan 9 by 9 by 2 inches or two 8-inch layer pans or 12 muffin tins. Set the oven at 350° for a square pan, 375° for layers or cupcakes.

Sift together

1¾ cups pastry *or* cake flour
½ teaspoon salt
2 teaspoons baking powder

Cream thoroughly

⅓ cup butter *or* margarine

Add

½ teaspoon vanilla

Beat in gradually

1 cup sugar

Beat until fluffy. Beat in

2 egg yolks

Stir in ½ cup of the flour mixture. Stir in

¼ cup milk

Add another ½ cup of the flour mixture and

¼ cup milk

Add the rest of the flour mixture and beat just enough to blend well. Beat until they stand up in soft peaks

2 egg whites

Fold into the batter. Spoon into the pans. Bake square cake 30 to 45 minutes, layers and cupcakes 20 to 30 minutes.

To make with an electric mixer or beater. Do not separate the eggs. Add to the creamed butter and sugar one at a time, beating well.

Chocolate Chip Cake. Fold in ½ cup chocolate bits or semi-sweet chocolate, cut in pea-size pieces.

Citron *or* Currant Cake. Add 1 cup citron, thinly sliced, or 1 cup currants. To add fruit while fillling the pan see Light Fruit Cake (p. 505).

Coconut Layer Cake. Frost and put the layers together with Seven-Minute Frosting. Sprinkle thickly with freshly grated or canned shredded coconut and pat it in gently.

Date and Nut Cake. Reserve ¼ cup of the flour. Mix into ¼ cup each of dates and nut meats, broken in pieces. Fold gently into the batter.

Honey Cake. Replace all or part of the sugar with honey. Sift ½ teaspoon ginger and ½ teaspoon cinnamon with the flour.

Marble Cake. Add 1 square chocolate, melted, to half the mixture. Fill the pans by spoonfuls, alternating plain and chocolate mixtures.

Priscilla Cake. Increase the sugar to 1⅓ cups and use 3 eggs.

This makes a slightly richer cake.

Spanish Cake. Flavor with ½ teaspoon cinnamon or ¼ teaspoon mace instead of vanilla. Bake in a loaf or in layer cake pans, with Caramel Frosting (p. 515) between the layers and on top.

Walnut Cake. Add ¾ cup walnut meats, broken in pieces. Increase the baking powder to 2¾ teaspoons. Cover with any white frosting, crease in squares, and put half a walnut meat on each square.

BOSTON CREAM PIE

Bake a cake in two 7- or 8-inch layer cake tins, using a cake mix or Boston Favorite Cake (p. 494), One-Egg Cake (below) or Golden Layer Cake (p. 500). Or use a packaged cake. Put the layers together with whipped cream, Cream Filling (p. 516) or Rich Cream Filling (p. 517). Sprinkle the top with confectioners' sugar or spread with Chocolate Frosting (p. 512).

To make a fancy top, lay a lace doily on the cake. Sift confectioners' sugar over it and press down lightly with a spoon. Lift off the doily gently so that the design will not be disturbed. Cut in wedges to serve.

Chocolate Cream Pie (Boston type). Use Chocolate Filling (p. 512) between the layers.

Washington Pie. Use raspberry jam between the layers. Sprinkle the top with confectioners' sugar.

CREAM CAKE

Set the oven at 325°. Butter two 8-inch layer cake pans or a pan about 7 by 10 inches.

Beat together vigorously

2 eggs
⅞ cup sugar
⅔ cup light cream
1 teaspoon vanilla

Mix and sift into a bowl

1⅔ cups pastry *or* cake flour
2½ teaspoons baking powder
½ teaspoon salt

Stir in the egg mixture. Pour into the pan. Bake 30 minutes. Frost as desired.

ONE-EGG CAKE

For a simple loaf cake, cupcakes or Upside-down Cake (p. 394).

Set the oven at 350°. Butter a pan 8 by 8 inches or a set of cupcake tins.

Sift together

1⅓ cups pastry *or* cake flour
2 teaspoons baking powder
¼ teaspoon salt

Cream until light and fluffy

¼ cup butter *or* margarine

Beat in gradually

¾ cup sugar
½ teaspoon vanilla
1 egg, well beaten

Stir in ½ cup of the flour mixture, then

¼ cup milk

Stir in another ½ cup of the flour and another

¼ cup milk

Add the rest of the flour and spoon into the pan. Bake about 25 minutes.

Blueberry Cake. Pour the batter into a pan 8 by 8 inches. Cover with ½ to 1 cup blueberries. Sprinkle with ¼ cup sugar mixed with ½ teaspoon cinnamon, if liked. Bake. Cut in squares. Serve warm.

Coconut Upside-down Cake. In a pan 6 by 10 or 8 by 8 inches, put 6 tablespoons butter, ½ cup brown sugar and 2 tablespoons water. Cook over low heat until melted. Add 1 cup toasted coconut. Pour the cake batter into the pan. Bake 40 to 50 minutes at 350°. Serve with whipped cream topped with a sprinkling of toasted coconut.

Quick Tea Cake. Spread in a buttered and floured shallow pan 8 by 8 inches. Sprinkle with sugar. Bake. Serve warm.

Seed Cake. Add 1½ teaspoons caraway seeds to Quick Tea Cake batter.

LIGHTNING CAKE

This small, delicious and easy cake is excellent either frosted or with a special topping as in the recipe for Lazy Daisy Cake.

Set the oven at 375°. Butter a square pan 8 by 8 by 2 inches.

Beat until thick
- **2 eggs**
- **1 teaspoon vanilla**

Beat in, a little at a time
- **1 cup sugar**

Sift together and stir in
- **1 cup sifted all-purpose flour**
- **1 teaspoon baking powder**
- **¼ teaspoon salt**

Heat until the butter melts
- **½ cup hot milk**
- **1 tablespoon butter**

Stir into the first mixture and beat 1 minute or until smooth. Pour into the pan and bake about 25 minutes.

LAZY DAISY CAKE

Bake Lightning Cake (above) and leave it in the pan. Mix
- **3 tablespoons melted butter**
- **3 tablespoons brown sugar**
- **2 tablespoons cream *or* top milk**
- **½ cup chopped nuts *or* coconut**

Spread over the cake. Put under the broiler and cook until the topping is lightly browned. Watch carefully and turn so that the topping browns evenly.

SPICE CAKE

For a small family bake this recipe in an 8- or 9-inch square tin. Cut in half and serve part as a pudding with a simple sauce and frost the rest for another meal.

Butter and flour two 8- or 9-inch square tins. Set the oven at 375°.

Sift together
- **2 cups flour**
- **1 teaspoon cinnamon**
- **1 teaspoon powdered cloves**
- **½ teaspoon allspice**
- **½ teaspoon salt**
- **1 teaspoon baking soda**
- **2 teaspoons baking powder**

Beat until thick and lemon-colored
- **2 eggs**

Beat in gradually
- **1 cup sugar**
- **2 tablespoons molasses**

Beat well. Add alternately with the flour mixture
- **1 cup sour milk *or* buttermilk**

Stir in lightly
- **⅔ cup melted shortening *or* oil**

Pour into the tins and bake about 25 minutes. Frost with Quick Caramel Frosting (p. 512).

Harvard Cake. In place of white sugar and molasses, use 2 cups brown sugar.

JAM CAKE

Butter and flour two 9-inch layer tins. Set the oven at 375°.

Sift together
- **2 cups flour**
- **1 teaspoon allspice**
- **1 teaspoon cinnamon**
- **1 teaspoon nutmeg**
- **1 teaspoon baking soda**
- **½ teaspoon salt**

Cream until light and fluffy
- **¼ cup butter**
- **1 cup sugar**

Add
- **3 eggs, beaten until light**

Mix

1 cup blackberry, raspberry *or* strawberry jam
¼ cup sour milk

Stir into the batter by thirds, alternating with the flour mixture. Spoon into the tins. Bake about 25 minutes. Frost with Portsmouth Frosting (p. 512).

APPLESAUCE CAKE

Delicious served in finger-shaped pieces or, as a complete dessert, in squares topped with whipped cream or a sauce. If you prefer a spicier cake, add 1 teaspoon ginger or ¼ cup finely cut candied ginger.

Set the oven at 350°. Butter and flour a 9-inch pan, or two 8-inch pans if you prefer thin squares of cake.

Mix thoroughly

1 cup applesauce, sweetened or not
⅞ cup brown sugar
½ cup melted shortening *or* salad oil

Sift into a large bowl

1¾ cups flour
1 teaspoon baking soda
½ teaspoon salt
1 teaspoon cinnamon
½ teaspoon powdered cloves

Add

½ cup raisins
½ cup nut meats, cut in pieces

Add the applesauce mixture. Blend well and spoon into the pan. Bake about 40 minutes.

BANANA CAKE

Set the oven at 350°. Butter a 9-inch square pan.

Cream until light and fluffy

½ cup butter

Beat in gradually

1½ cups sugar

Add

2 eggs, slightly beaten

Beat thoroughly. Add

1 cup mashed bananas
1 teaspoon vanilla *or* lemon extract *or* ½ teaspoon of each

Sift together

2 cups pastry *or* cake flour
½ teaspoon baking soda (1 teaspoon if sour milk or cream is used)
¼ teaspoon salt

Add the flour mixture to the butter mixture alternately with

½ cup milk *or* cream, sweet *or* sour

Spoon into the pan. Bake about 40 minutes. Frost with Cream Cheese Frosting (p. 513), or serve in squares with whipped cream on top.

Banana Coconut Cake. Melt 4 tablespoons butter, stir in 7 tablespoons brown sugar, 1 cup coconut and 1 cup chopped nuts. Spread over the baked cake.

Banana Nut Cake. Add ½ cup chopped nut meats to the mixture. Bake in layer cake tins. Put the layers together with whipped cream. Sprinkle with confectioners' sugar, or put White Mountain Frosting (p. 515) between and on top.

GINGERBREAD

Packaged gingerbread mixes shorten preparation time slightly. Add a little spice and melted butter to improve a mix.

For a spicier gingerbread, add ½ teaspoon cinnamon and ¼ teaspoon each of powdered cloves and nutmeg.

Butter a shallow pan 8 or 9 inches square or 12 muffin tins. Set the oven at 325° for the square pans, 350° for the muffin tins.

Sift together

1½ cups flour
⅓ cup sugar
2 teaspoons baking powder
1 teaspoon ginger
¼ teaspoon salt

Combine

¼ cup butter
½ cup boiling water

When the butter melts, add

½ cup molasses

Stir into the flour mixture and beat just enough to make a smooth batter. Spread in the pans. Bake about 35 minutes in the square pan or 15 minutes in the muffin tins. Serve hot with butter with breakfast, lunch, afternoon tea or coffee. Or as a dessert, serve with applesauce, with cream cheese thinned with cream and beaten until light, or with whipped cream, sweetened or with grated cheese folded into it.

SOUR CREAM GINGERBREAD

Made with butter, this gingerbread stays moist and delicious for days. For a simpler gingerbread, omit the butter.

Butter a shallow pan 8 or 9 inches square. Set the oven at 350°.

Beat

2 eggs

Add

½ cup sour cream
½ cup molasses
½ cup brown sugar

Beat well. Sift together

1½ cups pastry *or* cake flour
1 teaspoon baking soda
1 teaspoon ginger
¼ teaspoon salt

Stir into the first mixture. Add

½ cup melted butter *or* margarine

Beat well and pour into the pan. Bake about 30 minutes.

SOFT MOLASSES GINGERBREAD

Set the oven at 325°. Butter a pan 8 or 9 inches square.

Sift together

2 cups all-purpose flour
1½ teaspoons baking soda
1½ teaspoons ginger
½ teaspoon salt

Heat together

1 cup molasses
⅓ cup butter *or* other shortening

Cool. Add

½ cup sour milk *or* buttermilk
1 egg

Beat thoroughly. Stir into the flour mixture and beat just enough to make a smooth batter. Spoon into the pan and bake about 35 minutes.

Applesauce Gingerbread. Add ½ cup cold applesauce with the molasses.

Raisin *or* Prune Gingerbread. Before stirring in the liquids, add ½ cup raisins or cooked prunes, drained and cut small.

Nut Gingerbread. Before stirring in the liquids, add ½ cup nut meats, broken in pieces.

Cornell Gingerbread (High-Protein). Instead of 1½ cups flour, use 1 cup whole-wheat flour and ¼ cup powdered milk. Before adding the liquid, add ½ cup toasted wheat germ and 2 teaspoons brewer's yeast.

GINGERBREAD UPSIDE-DOWN CAKE

Melt ¼ cup butter in an oblong baking pan or shallow casserole. Add ⅓ cup dark brown sugar and stir until melted. Arrange canned peach or pear halves, cut side down, evenly in the syrup. Cover with any gingerbread batter. Bake. Loosen the edges and turn out onto a serving plate, fruit side up. Serve with plain or whipped cream.

Apple Gingerbread. Peel, core and quarter tart apples to make 2 cups. Cook 10 minutes in syrup (½ cup sugar boiled with ½ cup water). Use in place of peach or pear halves.

FRESH COCONUT CAKE

A large coconut should provide enough liquid for this cake. If it does not, eke it out with milk.

Prepare (p. 13), reserving the coconut milk
1 cup grated fresh coconut
Separate
3 eggs
Beat the whites until they stand in soft peaks. Beat in gradually
½ cup sugar
Without washing the beater, beat the egg yolks until thick. Cream
¾ cup shortening
½ teaspoon vanilla
Beat in gradually
1 cup sugar
Stir in the egg yolks and ¼ cup of the prepared coconut. Beat well. Sift together
2¼ cups pastry flour
2¼ teaspoons baking powder
½ teaspoon salt
Add alternately with 1 cup coconut milk. Fold in the egg whites. Spoon into the pans and bake about 25 minutes. Put the layers together with Seven-Minute Frosting (p. 514) and cover the top and sides with the frosting. Sprinkle the top and sides with the rest of the coconut.

VELVET CAKE

Butter a pan 8 by 10 inches or two 9-inch layer pans. Set the oven at 375°.

Separate
4 eggs
Beat the whites until stiff. Beat in gradually
½ cup sugar
Without washing the beater, beat the yolks until thick with
½ cup cold water
Cream
½ cup butter *or* margarine
Beat in gradually
1 cup sugar
Add the beaten yolks. Sift
1½ cups pastry *or* cake flour
½ cup cornstarch
½ teaspoon salt
4 teaspoons baking powder
Add to the butter mixture. Beat well and fold in the egg whites. Spread in the pan. Bake about 40 minutes.

Almond Velvet Cake. Before baking, cover the top with ⅓ cup shredded almonds. Sprinkle with powdered sugar.

Princeton Orange Cake. Use orange juice in place of cold water and add the grated rind of 1 orange.

Orange Nut Cake. Spread Princeton Orange Cake batter in a loaf pan and sprinkle with ½ cup chopped walnut meats and ¼ cup powdered sugar. Bake and cool. Split in two layers and put together with Orange Filling (p. 517).

BLACK WALNUT TEA CAKE

Set the oven at 375°.

Cream
½ cup butter *or* margarine
Beat in
½ cup brown sugar
¾ cup white corn syrup
2 teaspoons vanilla
Add, one at a time, beating thoroughly
4 eggs
Sift together
2½ cups pastry *or* cake flour
3 teaspons baking powder
¼ teaspoon salt
Add to butter mixture alternately with
½ cup milk
Spread in a buttered shallow pan 9 by 9 inches. Sprinkle with
½ cup chopped black walnuts
½ cup brown sugar
Pat in lightly. Bake about 20 minutes. Serve warm.

GOLD CAKE

Particularly good topped with Coffee Frosting (p. 515) and sprinkled with grated coconut.

Butter and flour two pans 8 by 8 by 2 inches. Set the oven at 350°.

Sift together
- **1¾ cups pastry *or* cake flour**
- **2½ teaspoons baking powder**
- **¼ teaspoon salt**

Cream thoroughly
- **½ cup butter**

Beat in gradually
- **1 cup sugar**

Continue beating until fluffy. Beat until lemon-colored
- **1 egg**
- **5 egg yolks (⅓ cup)**
- **½ teaspoon vanilla**

Stir into the butter and sugar. Stir in the flour mixture alternately with
- **½ cup milk**

Beat just enough to blend. Spoon into the pans and bake 45 minutes.

Lord Baltimore Cake. Bake in three buttered and floured 7-inch layer pans. Put together with Lord Baltimore Filling (p. 516).

GOLDEN LAYER CAKE

Easy to make, not too rich, and excellent as a layer cake with any filling or put together with whipped cream.

Butter two 7- or 8-inch layer cake pans. Set the oven at 375°.

Sift together
- **1½ cups pastry *or* cake flour**
- **3 teaspoons baking powder**
- **¼ teaspoon salt**

Cream thoroughly
- **4 tablespoons butter**
- **¾ cup sugar**
- **1 teaspoon vanilla**

Beat in, one at a time
- **3 egg yolks**

Beat until fluffy. Add alternately with the flour mixture
- **½ cup milk**

Spread in pans and bake about 20 minutes.

ELECTION CAKE

An old-fashioned Connecticut specialty. The leavening is yeast, so allow plenty of time.

Put in a bowl
- **1 cup warm water (not hot)**

Sprinkle over it
- **1 package yeast**

Add
- **1 tablespoon sugar**
- **1 tablespoon salad oil**
- **2½ cups flour**

Beat thoroughly, cover, and let rise overnight or at least 6 hours. Butter 3 small loaf tins. Cream.
- **1 cup butter**

Cream in
- **2 cups dark brown sugar**

Add
- **4 eggs, well beaten**

Stir in
- **1 tablespoon grated lemon rind**
- **1 tablespoon lemon juice**

Sift together
- **1½ cups flour**
- **1½ teaspoons baking soda**
- **½ teaspoon powdered cloves**
- **½ teaspoon mace**
- **½ teaspoon nutmeg**
- **½ teaspoon salt**

Add to the butter mixture. Add
- **2 cups seeded raisins**
- **1 cup whiskey**

Stir into the yeast batter and beat to blend well. Divide the dough in the tins. Cover and let rise 1 hour. Bake 1 hour at 350°.

QUEEN CAKE

Butter a shallow pan 6 by 10 inches, or three 8- or 9-inch cake pans. Set the oven at 350°.

Sift together
- **1⅔ cups pastry *or* cake flour**
- **¼ teaspoon salt**
- **¼ teaspoon baking soda**

Cream until light and fluffy
- **⅔ cup butter**

Beat in the flour mixture. Add

1½ teaspoons lemon juice
Beat until stiff
6 egg whites
Beat in, little by little
1¼ cups confectioners' sugar
Spoon over the batter. Cut and fold until well blended, but do not beat. Spoon into the pan. Bake 50 minutes.

White Fruit Cake. Add ⅔ cup candied cherries, cut in pieces, ⅓ cup almonds, blanched and shredded, ½ cup citron, thinly sliced, and 1 teaspoon almond extract. Bake in a buttered deep cake pan 1 hour at 325°.

SNOW CAKE

Butter two 8- or 9-inch layer pans. Set the oven at 350°.

Beat until stiff
3 egg whites
Beat in gradually
½ cup sugar
Cream until light and fluffy
½ cup butter
Beat in
½ cup sugar
½ teaspoon vanilla *or* ¼ teaspoon almond extract
Sift together
1½ cups pastry *or* cake flour
2 teaspoons baking powder
¼ teaspoon salt
Add to the butter mixture alternately with
½ cup milk
Fold in the beaten egg whites. Spread in the pans and bake about 45 minutes. Put together with Prune Almond Filling (p. 515). Frost the top and sides with Seven-Minute Frosting (p. 514) or White Mountain Cream (p. 515).

White Nut Cake. Add 1 cup nut meats, cut in pieces.

Lady Baltimore Cake. Double the recipe. Bake in three 9-inch tins. Put together with Lady Baltimore Filling (p. 515).

BURNT SUGAR CAKE

Melt ½ cup sugar in a small heavy pan. Cook slowly until almost black. Add ½ cup hot coffee and stir until dissolved. Cool. Follow the recipe for Snow Cake (above) using the prepared syrup in place of milk. Before putting the batter in the baking pan, fold in ½ cup sliced nut meats. Black walnuts are particularly good. Frost with Penuche Frosting (p. 513).

CHOCOLATE CAKE

Use water, coffee or sour milk in place of sweet milk. Water makes an especially tender cake. If you use sour milk, substitute 1 teaspoon baking soda for the baking powder.

Butter a pan 6 by 9 inches or two 9-inch layer cake pans. Set the oven at 350°.

Cream well
½ cup shortening (*or* use ½ cup oil)
Beat in
1½ cups sugar
1 teaspoon vanilla
2 ounces chocolate, melted over hot water
2 eggs, well beaten
Sift together
2 cups pastry *or* cake flour
2 teaspoons baking powder
½ teaspoon salt
Add to the first mixture alternately with
1 cup milk
Spread in the pan and bake about 30 minutes.

Rich Chocolate Pecan Cake. Increase the sugar to 2 cups, the chocolate to 4 ounces and the milk to 1½ cups. Add 1 cup chopped pecans. Bake in a 10-inch tube pan about 50 minutes. Let stand 24 hours before serving. Serve with whipped cream and sprinkle with chopped pecans.

Chocolate Potato Cake. Reduce the flour to 1½ cups. Beat ½ cup hot mashed potatoes into the mixture after adding the eggs.

Chocolate Cream Cake. Put layers together with whipped cream. Sprinkle with powdered sugar. Serve with Chocolate Sauce (p. 430).

Chocolate Spice Cake. Sift 1 teaspoon cinnamon and ½ teaspoon powdered cloves with the flour.

Chocolate Fruit Cake. Add to the batter ⅓ cup each of candied cherries, seeded raisins and walnut meats, cut in pieces. Spoon into a tube pan and bake 50 minutes.

OLLO'S CHOCOLATE CAKE

Butter a pan 8 by 8 inches. Set the oven at 325°.

Beat until light
1 egg
Beat in
1 cup sugar
⅓ cup shortening *or* oil
1 teaspoon vanilla
Put in a 1-cup measure
2 ounces chocolate
Fill the cup with
Hot coffee
Let stand until the chocolate is soft. Pour off the coffee into another cup and add the chocolate to the egg mixture. Sift together
1⅓ cups flour
1 teaspoon baking powder
1 teaspoon baking soda
Add the flour mixture and the coffee alternately to the egg mixture. Bake 25 minutes. Frost with Butter Frosting (p. 516).

CHOCOLATE BUTTERMILK CAKE

Butter and flour a pan 9 by 12 inches. Set the oven at 375°.

Sift together
1⅔ cups flour
1 cup sugar
½ cup cocoa
1 teaspoon baking soda
½ teaspoon salt
Beat in
1 cup buttermilk *or* sour milk
½ cup melted shortening *or* oil
1½ teaspoons vanilla
Stir until smooth. Spread in the pan and bake 30 minutes.

MADELEINE'S CHOCOLATE CAKE

Butter a pan 8 by 8 inches. Set the oven at 350°.

Melt over low heat or in a double boiler
2 ounces chocolate
½ cup shortening
Remove from the heat and add
1 teaspoon vanilla
Sift together
1 cup pastry flour
⅞ cup sugar
1 teaspoon cream of tartar
½ teaspoon baking soda
½ teaspoon salt
Add to the chocolate mixture alternately with
½ cup milk
Beat in, one at a time
2 eggs
Beat well. Spread in the pan and bake about 30 minutes.

DEVIL'S FOOD

Butter and flour a pan 9 by 12 inches or two pans 9 inches square. Set the oven at 350°.

Melt over very low heat or in a double boiler
4 ounces chocolate
Add
⅔ cup light brown sugar
1 cup milk
1 egg yolk, slightly beaten
Stir and cook over hot water until smooth. Beat until stiff
3 egg whites
Beat in gradually
⅓ cup light brown sugar
Cream until light and fluffy
⅓ cup shortening

Add gradually, beating constantly

⅔ cup light brown sugar

Stir in

2 egg yolks, beaten thick

Sift together

2 cups flour
¼ teaspoon salt
1 teaspoon baking soda

Add to the shortening mixture alternately with

1½ cups milk

Add the chocolate mixture. Beat well. Fold in the egg whites. Spoon into the pan. Bake about 35 minutes.

Devil's Food with Walnuts and Citron. Before folding in the whites, add 1 cup citron, cut small, and 1½ cups chopped walnut meats.

RICH DEVIL'S FOOD

Butter a pan 9 inches square. Set the oven at 350°.

Cook until thick in a double boiler

4 tablespoons cocoa
2½ tablespoons sugar
2 tablespoons water

Remove from the heat. Stir in

½ cup milk

Separate

2 eggs

Beat the whites until stiff. Beat in gradually

½ cup sugar

Cream together until light

½ cup shortening
1 teaspoon vanilla
½ cup sugar

Beat the egg yolks, one at a time. Add the cocoa mixture. Sift

1 cup flour
½ teaspoon cream of tartar
½ teaspoon salt

Beat into the batter. Fold in the egg whites. Spoon into the pan. Bake about 35 minutes.

SOUR CREAM CHOCOLATE CAKE

Butter a pan 8 inches square. Set the oven at 350°.

Mix

1 cup thick sour cream
1 cup sugar
1 teaspoon vanilla
1 tablespoon butter, melted

Sift together.

1½ cups cake *or* pastry flour
⅔ cup cocoa
1 teaspoon baking soda
½ teaspoon salt

Add to the first mixture. Beat in, one at a time

3 eggs

Spoon into the pan and bake about 25 minutes.

FUDGE LAYER CAKE

Butter three layer cake pans. Set the oven at 350°.

Cream until light and fluffy

½ cup shortening
1 cup sugar
½ teaspoon vanilla

Cook together until smooth

4 ounces chocolate
3 tablespoons boiling water
⅓ cup sugar

Beat into the creamed mixture. Add, one at a time, beating thoroughly

3 eggs

Sift together

1¾ cups flour
1 teaspoon cream of tartar
½ teaspoon baking soda
½ teaspoon salt

Add to the first mixture alternately with

½ cup milk

Pour into the pans and bake 25 minutes. Put together with Mocha Rum Butter Frosting (p. 516).

GRANDMOTHER'S POUND CAKE

Use an electric mixer for superior cake. Pound cake improves if stored a day or two. Butter is its characteristic flavor, but you may like to add ½ teaspoon mace, 2 tablespoons brandy or orange juice or 1 tablespoon caraway seeds.

Butter and flour a large loaf pan or two small ones. Set the oven at 300°.

Cream until light and fluffy

1 cup butter
1⅔ cups sugar

Beat in, one at a time

5 eggs

When creamy, fold in

2 cups pastry *or* cake flour
¼ teaspoon salt

Spoon into the pan and bake about 1½ hours.

NEWPORT POUND CAKE

Butter and flour a loaf pan. Set the oven at 350°.

Cream until light and fluffy

⅞ cup butter *or* margarine

Add

Few grains salt
1 teaspoon vanilla

Beat in gradually

1½ cups pastry *or* cake flour

Separate

5 eggs

Beat the whites until stiff but not dry. Beat in

¾ cup powdered sugar

Beat the yolks until thick and lemon-colored. Add gradually

¾ cup powdered sugar

Add to the butter mixture and beat well. Fold in the egg whites. Sift over the batter

1 teaspoon baking powder

Beat thoroughly. Pour into the pan and bake about 1 hour.

New York Gingerbread. Omit the vanilla and add 2 tablespoons yellow ginger to the mixture.

Imperial Cake. Cut ½ pound seeded raisins in pieces and dredge lightly with flour. Break ½ cup walnut meats in pieces. Grate the rind of ½ lemon. Prepare the cake batter and add 2 teaspoons lemon juice. Fold in the raisins, nuts and lemon rind, and bake.

MOLASSES POUND CAKE

Butter and flour a loaf pan. Set the oven at 350°.

Cream until light and fluffy

⅔ cup butter
¾ cup sugar

Add

2 eggs, well beaten
⅔ cup milk
⅔ cup molasses

Sift together

2⅛ cups pastry *or* cake flour
¾ teaspoon baking soda
1 teaspoon cinnamon
½ teaspoon allspice
¼ teaspoon ground cloves
¼ teaspoon mace

Add to the first mixture. Stir in

½ cup seeded raisins, cut in pieces and dredged with flour
⅓ cup citron, cut in thin strips and dredged with flour

Spoon into the pan and bake about 40 minutes.

DARK FRUIT CAKE

A moist rich cake which improves with age. Make it in two large loaf pans or in several small ones. Details on making fruit cake (p. 486).

Cover with boiling water and let stand 2 hours

1 pound dried fruits (peaches, pears, prunes and apricots)
1 cup seeded raisins, cut in pieces
¾ cup currants
1 jar (4 ounces) mixed candied fruits and peels
1 jar (4 ounces) candied cherries

Set the oven at 325°. Line the pans with aluminum foil. Sift together

2 cups all-purpose flour
½ teaspoon baking soda
1 tablespoon cinnamon
½ teaspoon each of allspice and mace
¼ teaspoon ground cloves

Beat together

½ cup soft shortening *or* oil

¾ cup brown sugar
½ teaspoon lemon extract
Stir in
2 eggs
½ cup molasses
½ cup milk
Add the flour mixture, fruit and nuts. Spoon into the pans and bake about 1¼ hours.

LIGHT FRUIT CAKE

The pieces of whole fruit make this a particularly handsome cake—a cake with style as well as delicious flavor.

Set the oven at 250°. Line three deep loaf pans with aluminum foil.

Cream
1 cup butter
Beat in
2 cups white sugar
1 teaspoon vanilla
Beat until fluffy. Beat in, one at a time
7 egg yolks
Sift together
3 cups pastry *or* 2¾ cups all-purpose flour
½ teaspoon salt
2 teaspoons baking powder
Add to the butter mixture alternately with
1 cup milk
Fold in
1 pound white raisins
1 pound pecan meats
Fold in
7 egg whites, beaten stiff
Have ready for decorating the layers
1 pound candied cherries, red and green
1 pound candied pineapple fingers
1 pound whole Brazil nut meats
1 pound pitted dates (place a nut in each, and roll in sugar)
Put a thin layer of the cake batter in each pan. Arrange on the batter whole fruit (using one kind of fruit for each layer). Cover with a layer of batter. Repeat until the fruit is used and put a layer of batter on the top. To make loaves even, work with all three pans at the same time. Fill the pans to ¾ inch from the top. Bake 2 hours.

BIRTHDAY FRUIT CAKE

Butter and flour a large angel cake tin. Set the oven at 300°.

Place in bowl and mix well
½ cup seeded raisins, cut in pieces
½ cup walnut meats, cut in pieces
⅓ cup currants
2 tablespoons candied orange peel, cut fine
¼ cup flour
Separate
2 eggs
Beat the whites until stiff. Beat in gradually
¼ cup brown sugar
Cream
½ cup butter *or* other shortening
Beat in
1 cup brown sugar
1 teaspoon orange extract
1 teaspoon vanilla
Beat the egg yolks slightly and stir them in. Sift together
2 cups flour
3 tablespoons baking powder
Add to the creamed mixture alternately with
⅔ cup milk
Fold in the egg whites. Fill the pan, distributing the floured fruit on the layers as for Light Fruit Cake (above). Bake about 1¼ hours. Cover with Royal Frosting (p. 515).

DUNDEE CAKE

A famous old recipe. Serve it with tea, coffee or sherry. To serve in the traditional style, put the whole loaf on a plate and slice it as you serve it.

Line two or three small loaf pans with aluminum foil. Set the oven at 275°.

Cream until light and fluffy

⅞ cup butter

Beat in gradually

⅔ cup sugar

Add, one at a time, beating 5 minutes after adding each

4 eggs

Stir in

⅓ cup almonds, blanched and chopped

Sift together

2½ cups pastry flour *or* 2¼ cups all-purpose flour
1 teaspoon baking powder
½ teaspoon salt

Mix with

1 cup seedless raisins
1⅓ cups currants *or* seeded raisins, cut in pieces

Add to the first mixture

⅓ cup candied orange and lemon peel, cut small
2 tablespoons orange juice

Mix thoroughly. Fill the pans. Cover the tops with blanched almonds, candied cherries and citron. Bake 1¼ hours. As soon as the cakes begin to brown, cover them with a sheet of brown paper.

PECAN WHISKEY CAKE

Butter three small loaf pans. Set the oven at 250°.

Separate

6 eggs

Beat the whites until they stand in soft peaks. Beat in

1 cup sugar

Without washing the beater, beat the yolks until thick. Cream

¾ pound butter

Beat in gradually

1 cup light brown sugar
1 cup white sugar

Add the egg yolks and beat well. Mix

1 cup flour
2 pounds pecan nut meats
1½ pounds white raisins

Sift together

2 cups flour
1 teaspoon baking powder
1 teaspoon nutmeg

Add to the butter mixture. Add

1 cup Bourbon whiskey

Stir in the floured nuts and raisins. Fold in the whites. Fill the pans. Bake 2 hours.

WEDDING FRUIT CAKE

The traditional dark rich fruit cake. Serve either this type or Bride's Cake (p. 507), which is a white cake with a fruit cake layer on top, or serve both. Vary this recipe by adding more fruits, such as 1 pint preserved strawberries or 1 pound candied cherries. Or add 1 pound almonds, blanched and cut fine. If your oven is too small to bake four large loaves at once, add half the soda to half the batter and bake two loaves. When they are done, add the rest of the soda to the remaining batter and bake the other two loaves.

Line four large loaf pans with aluminum foil.

Cream until light and fluffy

1 pound shortening

Beat in, little by little

1 pound brown sugar

Stir in

1 cup molasses
12 egg yolks, well beaten

Sift together

3 cups all-purpose flour
4 teaspoons cinnamon
4 teaspoons allspice
1½ teaspoons mace
2 teaspoons nutmeg

Add to the first mixture. Mix

⅓ cup flour
3 pounds seeded raisins, cut in pieces
2 pounds sultana raisins
1½ pounds candied citron, sliced thin and cut in strips
1 pound currants
¼ cup chopped preserved lemon rind (½ rind)
½ cup chopped preserved orange rind (½ rind)

Add to the batter. Add

1 cup brandy

4 ounces chocolate, melted (optional)

Fold in

12 egg whites, beaten stiff

Just before putting the batter in the pans, add

¼ teaspoon baking soda, dissolved in 1 tablespoon hot water

Fill the pans and cover the tops closely with aluminum foil. Set the oven at 250°. On the oven bottom place several shallow pans filled with hot water to a depth of 1 inch. Set the pans of fruit cake on the shelf above. Bake 3 hours, remove the pans of water and remove the aluminum foil from the tops of the cakes. Bake 1½ hours to dry out the cakes.

WEDDING CAKE (BRIDE'S CAKE)

This recipe serves 30 guests (or more if you cut smaller pieces). For 60 guests, make the recipe twice in two separate batches. Twice the recipe makes a cake with a double 12-inch layer topped by a double 8-inch layer. Do not overcrowd the oven or the cakes will bake unevenly. Put some of the pans of batter in the refrigerator while the others are baking.

Set the oven at 350°. Butter an 8-inch layer cake pan and a 12-inch round pan.

Sift together

3⅜ cups cake *or* pastry flour
5 teaspoons baking powder
2¼ cups sugar
1½ teaspoons salt

Add

¾ cup shortening (soft)
1 cup milk
1½ teaspoons vanilla

Beat with a large spoon until well mixed (or 2½ minutes at medium speed in an electric mixer). Add

½ cup milk
¾ cup egg whites (6 or 7), unbeaten

Beat well. Put about one-third of the batter in the 8-inch layer pan, the rest in the 12-inch pan. Bake the 8-inch layer 30 to 35 minutes, the 12-inch layer 35 to 40 minutes.

FRUIT CAKE LAYER FOR BRIDE'S CAKE

Enough for a small rich layer to top the wedding cake.

Line with foil a deep round pan 5 inches in diameter. Butter well. Set the oven at 250°.

Sift together

¾ cup flour
½ cup sugar
1 teaspoon baking powder
⅛ teaspoon salt

Stir in

¼ cup melted shortening
¼ cup water
2 eggs, well beaten

Mix

⅓ cup each of white raisins, coconut and chopped toasted almonds
¼ cup each of citron, candied orange peel and candied lemon peel, all cut fine
¼ cup candied cherries, halved
¼ cup flour

Add to the cake batter. Fill the pan. Bake 2½ hours.

BUTTER ICING FOR BRIDE'S CAKE

If more convenient, make the icing in smaller batches. Make double this amount for the larger cake.

Cream until light and fluffy

½ cup butter *or* margarine
½ cup vegetable shortening

Blend in gradually

8 cups sifted confectioners' sugar

Beat until smooth. Stir in

½ cup cream
1½ tablespoons vanilla

Mix well.

DECORATING THE WEDDING CAKE

Spread Butter Icing (p. 507) between the layers and over the top and sides. Decoratc with dragées or other ornaments. On the top set silver bells, bride and groom figures or fresh flowers in a small glass covered with icing.

CUTTING THE WEDDING CAKE

As the pieces of cake are cut, arrange them on a large cake tray to be passed to the guests. Sometimes they are packed in tiny boxes for the guests to take home. It is a pleasant custom for the bride to keep the top layer for her first party.

Frostings and Fillings

Sponge cakes and pound cakes are usually served plain or with only a light sprinkling of confectioners' sugar. Homemade frosting gives a simple "store" cake an appetizing look. For a small family, frost part of a cake and serve the rest as a Cottage Pudding, Boston Cream Pie or Washington Pie.

CHOOSING THE FROSTING

Simplest of all is a **sweet topping** baked or broiled on the cake (p. 511).

Confectioners' frostings are easy, too, and the amount can be adapted for smaller or larger cakes. **Cooked frostings** made with egg white are a little fussier to make but worth the trouble if you have time. **Fudge-type frostings** must be carefully made so that they will not be hard and sugary. A candy thermometer insures success. **Rich butter frostings** stay creamy for several days.

FILLING LAYER CAKES

Cool the cake. Brush off any loose crumbs. Put the bottom layer upside down so that a smooth surface is uppermost. Spread with a filling (pp. 515–518) or use part of the frosting as filling.

FROSTING CAKES

Spread uncooked frosting while the cake is still warm but not hot. Cool the cake before spreading with a cooked frosting. If the frosting is very soft, put it on just before serving the cake.

Have the frosting stiff enough to pile on the cake without its sliding off. Try a little on the cake to be sure. If necessary, beat in a little more confectioners' sugar (for uncooked frosting) or put cooked frosting in a double boiler and beat over hot water until thick. If the frosting is too thick, beat in a few drops of hot water.

Spread the frosting over the cake with a spatula or the back of a large spoon. It is prettier if you do not smooth it on too evenly. If you are frosting the sides of the cake, do them first, then put the rest of the frosting on top and swirl it to the edge.

SIMPLE CAKE DECORATING

Scatter any of the following over the frosting or arrange in a pattern. Pat gently into place.

Nut meats, whole or chopped.

Coconut, preferably fresh grated. Toasted (p. 14). Tinted (p. 14).

Chocolate shot, dragées or tiny colored candies

Colored sugar

Candied fruit

Caramel Glaze. Cook 1 cup sugar with ½ cup water and ½ teaspoon cream of tartar to 252° (firm ball stage). Pour evenly over the cake. Crease with an oiled sharp knife to mark the pieces for cutting.

Chocolate Glaze. Melt unsweetened chocolate with butter (1 tablespoon for each ounce). Cool slightly and dribble over white frosting after it has set. To make lines or a crisscross effect, streak the chocolate with a fork.

ELABORATE CAKE DECORATING

Practice making designs on wax paper before attempting a fancy cake.

Prepare Royal (p. 515) or Ornamental Frosting (p. 514) or any Butter Frosting (p. 516). Other frostings become hard and dry after standing. Tint with food coloring.

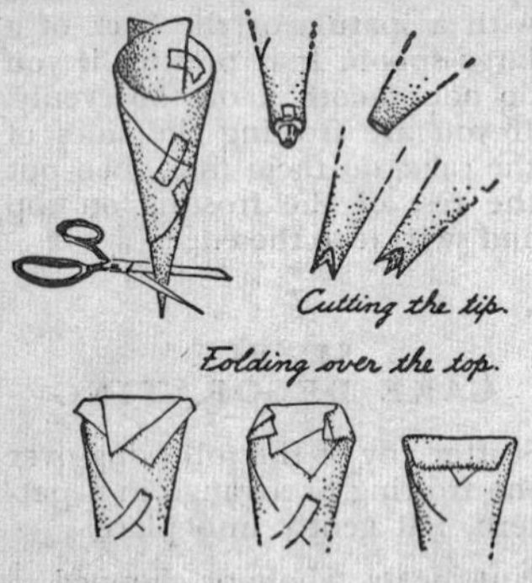

Cake decorating sets include a pastry bag or a metal cylinder with a set of tubes to shape the frosting in various ways. A paper bag is easy to make. If you are using more than one color, make a bag for each.

To make a pastry bag. Fold a sheet of heavy typewriter paper or baker's paper into a tight cornucopia with a sharp point. Fasten firmly with Scotch tape. Pinch the point flat and cut it straight across to make a ribbon design (1), in two points for leaves (2), in three points for stars (3). Or drop fancy metal tubes into the bag.

To fill a pastry bag. Fill not more than one-third full at a time. Bring the top edges together, fold in at the corners, then fold down to the level of the frosting.

To decorate the cake. Put a thin layer of frosting on the cake, let it dry, then cover with a thicker layer. Mark lines on the frosting with a toothpick as a guide to putting on the pattern. Hold the filled pastry bag or cylinder close to the top of the cake. Guide the point with one hand and push the frosting out with the other by folding down the top of the bag or pushing down the cylinder plunger.

FROSTING PETITS FOURS

Party cakes for special festivities.

Bake Cream Sponge Cake (p. 489), Angel Cake (p. 492), Genoise (p. 489) or Newport Pound Cake (p. 504) in shallow pans. Cool and cut in strips 1¼ inches wide, then in rectangles or triangles. Put in rows on a cake cooler with plenty of space between the rows.

Set over a shallow pan. Heat Petits Fours Frosting (p. 514) over hot water until thin enough to pour. If the frosting is too thick, thin it with water. If it is too thin, stir in confectioners' sugar. Pour the frosting over the cakes, moving steadily to the end of the row and back again. Lift the cake cooler gently and move it back and forth to loosen the dripping frosting. Scrape the frosting into the pan to reheat and use for the rest of the cakes. Let the cakes dry. Lift them with a spatula and trim the bottom edges with a sharp knife.

To dip petits fours. Hold each piece of cake on a fork and dip it in the frosting. Set on a cake cooler to dry. The difficulty with this method is that crumbs may fall into the frosting.

To color the frosting. For a series of colors, tint the frosting delicately with food coloring and frost one row of cakes. Reheat the frosting and add more coloring for the next row. Continue until all the cakes are frosted, adding more color each time. The series may be (1) yellow, green and brown (with melted chocolate); (2) white, pink, rose and red; or (3) white, yellow, pale orange and deep orange. If you are frosting a great many cakes, it may be easier to divide the frosting in separate bowls and color each. Cover the bowls with foil to keep the frosting moist.

To decorate petits fours. Put on each cake a nut meat, a bit of candied fruit or a sprinkle of chocolate shot, dragées or tiny colored candies. For more elaborate decorations, see page 510.

BIRTHDAY CAKES

Candles are the traditional decoration—and the simplest. There are many pretty holders or you can concoct your own—of colored paper or frosting. A special cake board—with a row of candle holders around the edge—is attractive. For more elaborate decoration, use a cake decorating set or trim the cake with candy ornaments or with initials or greetings made of candy letters.

For children, frost a simple cake such as Cream Sponge (p. 489). If you have some of the little wooden bird candle holders, you can put a flock of them on the cake with a scattering of tiny candies for them to feed on. For a merry-go-round cake, dip animal crackers in melted dipping chocolate and press them into the sides of the cake or stand them around the top. Put a gay paper awning above, held aloft by peppermint candy sticks or colored straws.

BUTTERSCOTCH NUT FROSTING

Spread this simple mixture over unbaked plain or spice cake in a shallow pan.

Beat until stiff

1 egg white

Beat in gradually

¾ cup brown sugar
⅛ teaspoon salt

Spread on the cake batter. Sprinkle with

¼ cup broken nut meats

Bake on the cake.

Coconut Meringue Frosting. Use ½ cup coconut in place of nuts. Use white sugar. Add 1 tablespoon grated orange rind.

COCONUT CRANBERRY FROSTING

Spread cranberry jelly over a warm, freshly baked cake. Sprinkle with coconut and put under the broiler until the coconut browns delicately.

BROILED COCONUT FROSTING

Mix

1 cup brown sugar
3 tablespoons cream
½ cup coconut
2 tablespoons melted butter

Spread over a warm, freshly baked cake and set under the broiler for a few minutes until delicately brown and bubbly.

CONFECTIONERS' FROSTING

This simple frosting can be delicious if you beat it thoroughly so that it is creamy. A small electric beater helps, but you can use a wooden spoon, too.

Put ¼ cup boiling water in a small bowl. Stir in confectioners' sugar until thick enough to spread. Beat thoroughly. Flavor with vanilla or rum or make one of the variations suggested below.

Lemon *or* Orange Confectioners' Frosting. Use cool lemon or orange juice in place of water.

Coffee Confectioners' Frosting. Add 1 teaspoon instant coffee and 1 teaspoon butter to the water.

Mocha Confectioners' Frosting. Make Coffee Confectioners' Frosting, adding 2 tablespoons cocoa to the sugar.

PORTSMOUTH FROSTING

Melt in a small heavy pan

4 tablespoons butter

Remove from the heat. Add

¼ cup cream

Beat in confectioners' sugar until thick enough to spread. Beat until smooth and flavor with vanilla or rum or make one of the variations suggested below.

Orange Portsmouth Frosting. Use orange juice as the liquid. Stir in an egg yolk for brighter color and smoothness.

Chocolate Portsmouth Frosting. Stir in Dutch-type cocoa to taste or 1 ounce unsweetened chocolate, melted over low heat.

QUICK CARAMEL FROSTING

Melt in a small pan

½ cup butter

Add

½ cup brown sugar

Cook and stir over low heat until the sugar melts. Add

¼ cup milk

Cool. Beat in until thick enough to spread

Confectioners' sugar (about 1¾ cups)
1 teaspoon vanilla

CHOCOLATE FROSTING *or* FILLING

Put in the top of a double boiler

2 ounces unsweetened chocolate

1 tablespoon butter
½ cup milk
Cook until the chocolate melts. Stir well. Let stand until lukewarm. Stir in
2 cups confectioners' sugar
½ teaspoon vanilla
Beat until thick enough to spread.

FUDGE FROSTING

Mix in a saucepan
2 ounces unsweetened chocolate, cut small
1½ cups sugar
7 tablespoons milk
¼ cup butter
1 tablespoon corn syrup
¼ teaspoon salt
Bring to rolling boil, stirring constantly. Boil 1 minute. Cool. Add
1 teaspoon vanilla
Beat until thick.

CREAMY CHOCOLATE FROSTING

Grate into a saucepan
2 ounces unsweetened chocolate
Add
1 cup sugar
3 tablespoons cornstarch
Mix well. Stir in
1 cup boiling water
Cook and stir until thick and smooth. Add
1 tablespoon butter
1 teaspoon vanilla
Few grains salt
Beat thoroughly.

QUICK FUDGE FROSTING I

Melt 1 package (7 or 8 ounces) semi-sweet chocolate with ½ cup butter. Beat until thick.

QUICK FUDGE FROSTING II

Put in a double boiler
2 ounces unsweetened chocolate
1 can condensed milk
Stir until the chocolate is melted. Add
1 teaspoon vanilla
Few grains salt
Add drop by drop, until the frosting is thin enough to spread
Hot water (about 1 tablespoon)

CREAM CHEESE FROSTING

Work until soft
4 tablespoons cream cheese
Add
1 egg white, slightly beaten
1½ cups confectioners' sugar
½ teaspoon vanilla
½ teaspoon salt
Beat thoroughly.

VANILLA FUDGE FROSTING

Melt in a pan
1 teaspoon butter
Add
1½ cups sugar
½ cup milk
½ teaspoon salt
Stir and heat to the boiling point. Boil without stirring to the soft ball stage (234°). Cool and beat until thick enough to spread. Add
½ teaspoon vanilla
If the frosting begins to stiffen too much, heat it over hot water. Spread evenly on the cake with the back of a spoon. Mark as soon as firm.

Chocolate Fudge Frosting. Add 1½ ounces unsweetened chocolate as soon as the boiling point is reached. Flavor with ⅛ teaspoon cinnamon.

PENUCHE FROSTING

For a richer frosting, use heavy cream in place of milk and butter.

Mix in a saucepan

1 cup brown sugar
½ cup white sugar
Few grains salt
⅓ cup milk
2 tablespoons butter
1 tablespoon corn syrup

Bring slowly to the boiling point, stirring constantly. Boil 1 minute. Cool to lukewarm. Add

½ teaspoon vanilla

Beat until thick enough to spread.

SULTANA NUT FROSTING

Cook to the soft ball stage (234°)

2 cups brown sugar
¾ cup heavy cream

Pour onto a marble slab or a large platter. Cool. Work until creamy with a spatula or a large wooden spoon. Add

¼ cup seedless raisins
¼ cup walnut meats, cut small

Spread on the cake.

MAPLE FUDGE FROSTING

Mix in a saucepan

1⅓ cups sugar
⅔ cup grated maple sugar
½ cup butter
⅔ cup cream

Cook (about 13 minutes) to the soft ball stage (234°). Cool. Beat thick enough to spread.

Caramel Fudge Frosting. Use brown sugar in place of maple sugar.

SOUR CREAM RAISIN FROSTING

So rich that you may prefer to use it only as filling, topping the cake with a simple frosting.

Mix in a double boiler top

1 cup sour cream
1 cup sugar
1 cup seeded raisins

Cook over hot water until thick.

FROSTING FOR PETITS FOURS

Put in a saucepan

2 cups sugar
⅛ teaspoon cream of tartar
1 cup hot water

Boil to a thin syrup (226°). Cool to slightly above lukewarm (100°). Add until just thick enough to coat a spoon

Confectioners' sugar (1 cup or more)

Test by pouring a little frosting over a cake (see p. 510).

Ornamental Frosting. Cook the syrup to 240°. Pour gradually over 3 egg whites beaten stiff and continue beating until thick. Color and flavor.

SEVEN-MINUTE FROSTING

Most cooks make "boiled" icing this easy way.

In the top of a double boiler mix

¾ cup sugar
2 tablespoons water
⅛ teaspoon cream of tartar *or* 1 teaspoon light corn syrup
Few grains salt
1 egg white

Beat 1 minute with a rotary beater (hand or electric type). Set over boiling water and beat until stiff enough to stand up in peaks. With an electric beater, the frosting may be stiff enough in 4 minutes. Remove from the heat and continue beating until thick enough to spread. Add

½ teaspoon vanilla

or make one of the variations listed below.

FROSTING VARIATIONS

Use these variations with either Seven-Minute Frosting (above) or White Mountain Cream (p. 515).

Caramel Frosting. Use ½ cup brown sugar and ¼ cup white. Add broken walnut meats and spread.

Coconut Frosting. Add ¼ cup shredded coconut (preferably fresh grated) to the finished frosting. Spread over the cake and sprinkle coconut thickly over the top.

Coffee Frosting. Use ½ cup white sugar and ¼ cup brown. Flavor with instant coffee to taste. Shredded coconut is good with this.

Lemon or Orange Frosting. Use cool lemon or orange juice in place of water. When ready to spread, add ½ teaspoon each of grated orange and lemon peel, or 1 teaspoon candied orange peel.

Marshmallow Frosting. Cut 8 marshmallows in small pieces and add to the finished frosting. Fold over and over until the frosting is stiff enough to hold its shape.

Nut or Fruit Frosting. To the finished frosting, add chopped walnuts, almonds, figs, dates or raisins, separately or in combination.

Peppermint Frosting. Add ¼ teaspoon oil of peppermint and a few drops of green coloring.

Prune Almond Frosting. Stone ½ cup prunes and cut in small pieces. Blanch and cut in pieces ⅓ cup almonds. Add to the finished frosting.

WHITE MOUNTAIN CREAM

The classic "boiled frosting" at its fluffy best made with 2 egg whites

Put in a saucepan

1 cup sugar
⅓ cup water
⅛ teaspoon cream of tartar
Few grains salt

Cook until the syrup spins a 6-inch thread (240°). To keep the syrup from crystallizing, cook it slowly and cover for the first 3 minutes. Beat until stiff

2 egg whites

Pour the syrup slowly over the egg whites, beating constantly. Beat until thick. Add

½ teaspoon vanilla

or make one of the variations suggested on pages 514–515.

ROYAL FROSTING

Another basic frosting to vary in any of the ways suggested on pages 514–515.

Put in a large bowl

1 cup confectioners' sugar
¼ teaspoon cream of tartar
⅓ cup boiling water
1 egg white

Beat with a rotary beater or an electric beater at high speed, until the frosting is thick enough to stand in peaks. This will take 8 minutes or more, but it does the frosting no harm to interrupt the beating from time to time.

HONEY *or* MAPLE FROSTING *or* FILLING

Beat until stiff

1 egg white

Cook to 238°

½ cup honey *or* maple syrup

Pour the honey or syrup slowly over the egg white, beating constantly. Continue beating until thick enough to hold its shape.

LADY BALTIMORE FILLING

Make Seven-Minute Frosting (p. 514). Add to one-half the frosting

1/3 cup chopped pecan nut meats
3 figs, cut in thin strips
1/2 cup seeded raisins, chopped
1/2 teaspoon almond extract

Use as the filling for 1 large cake. Use the rest of the frosting for the top and sides of the cake.

LORD BALTIMORE FILLING

Make Seven-Minute Frosting (p. 514). Add to one-half the frosting

1/2 cup rolled dry macaroons
1/4 cup chopped pecan nut meats
1/4 teaspoon orange extract
1/4 cup chopped blanched almonds
12 candied cherries, cut in quarters
2 teaspoons lemon juice
3 teaspoons sherry

Use as the filling for 1 large cake. Use the rest of the frosting for the sides and top of the cake.

BUTTER FROSTING I

Beat until very creamy

1/4 cup butter (unsalted, for the most delicious flavor)

Stir in

1 egg yolk

Beat in, 2 tablespoons at a time

1 cup confectioners' sugar

Beat hard until light and fluffy. Flavor with vanilla or other flavoring.

For a large cake, double the amount of butter and sugar, but use only 1 egg yolk.

BUTTER FROSTING II

Cream together

4 tablespoons butter
4 tablespoons vegetable shortening

Beat until thick

1 egg yolk

Boil to 240°

1/2 cup sugar
1/4 cup water

Pour slowly over the egg yolk, beating well. Beat in the shortening, bit by bit. Beat well. Flavor to taste.

Chocolate Butter Frosting. Melt 1/2 package (4 ounces) semi-sweet chocolate over hot water with 1 tablespoon coffee or water. Stir until smooth. Cool to lukewarm. Beat into the frosting.

Coffee Butter Frosting. Cream 1 teaspoon instant coffee with the shortening.

Mocha Rum Butter Frosting. Melt 1 ounce unsweetened chocolate with 1 tablespoon strong coffee. Stir in 1 1/2 tablespoons rum. Cool to lukewarm. Beat into the frosting.

FLUFFY BUTTER FROSTING

Cream

1/4 cup butter

Add gradually, beating constantly

1/2 cup confectioners' sugar, sifted

Beat until stiff

2 egg whites

Beat in gradually

1 cup confectioners' sugar, sifted

Combine the mixtures and add enough more sugar to make the frosting thick enough to hold its shape. Flavor like Butter Frosting (above).

CREAM FILLING

Put in a small heavy pan

1/2 cup sugar
3 tablespoons flour *or* 1 tablespoon cornstarch
Few grains salt

Stir in

1 cup milk

Cook and stir over low heat

until the mixture thickens (about 5 minutes). Add

1 egg *or* 2 egg yolks, slightly beaten

Cook and stir 3 minutes longer. Chill and flavor.

Banana Cream Filling. Add 1 cup mashed banana pulp (forced through strainer) and 2 tablespoons lemon juice.

Caramel Cream Filling. Use ½ cup flour. Add ⅓ cup Caramel Syrup (p. 14).

Chocolate Cream Filling. Increase sugar to 1 cup. Scald milk with 2 ounces unsweetened chocolate. Flavor with vanilla.

Coffee Cream Filling. Flavor to taste with instant coffee.

Macaroon Cream Filling (Frangipan). Add 2 tablespoons butter and 4 tablespoons dried and rolled macaroons. Flavor with lemon extract, rum, sherry or brandy.

Mocha Cream Filling. Flavor Chocolate Cream Filling with instant coffee.

Praline Cream Filling. Add ⅔ cup Praline Powder (p. 14).

RICH CREAM FILLING

Make Cream Filling, using only ¾ cup milk. Flavor in any of the ways suggested above. Cool and fold in ¼ cup heavy cream, beaten stiff.

LEMON FILLING

Mix in a small saucepan

1 cup sugar
2½ tablespoons flour

Add

¼ cup lemon juice
Grated rind 2 lemons
1 egg, slightly beaten
1 teaspoon butter

Cook over low heat to the boiling point, stirring constantly. Cool.

LEMON COCONUT CREAM

Mix in a double boiler top

Juice and grated rind 1 lemon
1 cup powdered sugar
2 egg yolks, slightly beaten

Cook over boiling water 10 minutes, stirring constantly. Add

1 cup shredded coconut

ORANGE FILLING

Mix in a double boiler top

¾ cup sugar
4 tablespoons flour
Grated rind 1 orange
⅓ cup orange juice
1 tablespoon lemon juice
2 egg yolks *or* 1 egg, slightly beaten
Few grains salt

Cook over boiling water 15 minutes, stirring constantly. Cool.

BUTTER CREAM FILLING

Mix in a double boiler top

⅓ cup sugar
⅓ cup flour

Add gradually, stirring constantly

2 cups milk

Cook until thick over boiling water, stirring constantly (about 15 minutes). Stir in, bit by bit

1 cup butter

Flavor with

1 teaspoon vanilla *or* other flavoring

BUTTERSCOTCH FILLING

Mix in a small saucepan

½ cup brown sugar
2 tablespoons butter

Cook 2 minutes or until the syrup is brown. Add

½ cup milk

Cook and stir over low heat until well blended. Mix

3 tablespoons flour *or* 1 tablespoon cornstarch

½ teaspoon salt
½ cup milk

Add to the first mixture. Cook 15 minutes over hot water. Add

2 eggs, slightly beaten

Cook and stir 2 minutes. Cool. Add

¼ teaspoon vanilla

CHOCOLATE WHIPPED CREAM FILLING

Melt together

4 ounces unsweetened chocolate
2 tablespoons butter

Cool slightly. Add

½ pint heavy cream
2 cups confectioners' sugar
Few grains salt

Beat until thick and smooth (20 minutes with a hand egg beater, 8 to 10 minutes with an electric beater).

COCOA WHIPPED CREAM FILLING

Mix

½ pint heavy cream
½ cup confectioners' sugar
¼ cup dry cocoa
Few grains salt

Let stand overnight (or for several hours) in the refrigerator. Beat until thick. Flavor with

Vanilla

FRENCH CREAM FILLING

Beat until stiff

½ pint heavy cream

Beat in slowly

¼ cup confectioners' sugar

Fold in

1 egg white, beaten stiff
Few grains salt
½ teaspoon vanilla

French Coffee Filling. Add instant coffee to taste.

French Strawberry Filling. Increase the sugar to ⅓ cup. Fold in ½ cup mashed strawberries.

FRUIT CREAM FILLING

If you are not serving the cake immediately, add ½ teaspoon gelatine soaked in 1 tablespoon cold water and dissolved in 1 tablespoon boiling water. This will keep the filling somewhat firm.

Prepare

⅓ cup figs, cut small
⅓ cup prunes, cut small
¼ cup chopped walnut meats

Beat until stiff

½ pint heavy cream

Beat in slowly

⅓ cup confectioners' sugar
Few grains salt
2 teaspoons lemon juice

Fold in the fruit and nuts.

Syracuse Filling. In place of fruit and nuts, add 6 marshmallows, cut small, 4 macaroons, dried and rolled, 9 candied cherries, cut small, and ½ teaspoon vanilla.

Nuts and Candies

Home-salted nuts and perfect candies are toothsome additions to the cook's repertory. Calorie-wise moderns serve rich sweets with coffee as dessert rather than as extra tidbits. Making a batch of candy may be a party in itself, whether it be fudge, molasses taffy or one of the uncooked fruit sweets. Attractively packed nuts and candies are ideal gifts.

CANDY MAKING

Candies cook best in dry cool weather. In warm sticky weather they may be sugary.

The pan should be large enough so that the candy will not boil over. To help prevent crystallizing, stir with a wooden spoon, not a metal one. Cook to the stage recommended in the recipe, testing with a candy thermometer or in cold water.

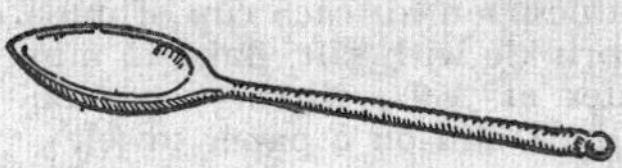

A wooden spoon

Testing with a thermometer. Never put a thermometer directly into the boiling syrup. Heat it first in water brought slowly to the boiling point. This will also test the accuracy of the thermometer, which should register 212° (at or near sea level) when the water boils. Place in the candy kettle and cook the candy to the required temperature (slightly lower at very high altitudes). After use, place the thermometer immediately in very hot water and cool it gradually.

Testing in cold water. Dip about ½ teaspoon of the boiling syrup into a cup of cold water and shape it with your fingers. Use fresh water for each testing. When the candy is nearly ready, take the pan from the heat while you are testing so that cooking will stop. The stages are

Soft ball (234° to 238°). The ball of candy flattens out somewhat.

Medium soft ball (238° to 240°). The ball of candy just barely holds its shape.

Firm ball (244° to 250°). The ball of candy is firm but not hard.

Hard ball (265°). The ball of candy is very firm and hard.

Hard crack (270° to 310°). The ball of candy is brittle when you tap it against the side of the cup. The syrup separates into threads when poured into the cup.

POPCORN

Packaged popcorn is especially selected for popping. Buy only what you need at the time, because corn that has been stored too long may be too dry to pop. Pop only a small amount of corn at a time to allow for expansion (½ cup makes about 1 quart).

Melt a tablespoon of butter or cooking oil in a heavy pan which has a tight cover. Put in the corn, cover and cook over moderate heat, shaking constantly until the popping stops. Uncover and remove any hard kernels which did not pop.

Buttered Popcorn. For 1 quart of popped corn, melt 3 tablespoons butter in a large saucepan, add the corn and stir until the corn is thoroughly coated. Sprinkle with salt.

Sugared Popcorn. For 1 quart of popped corn, melt 2 tablespoons butter in a pan. Add 1½ cups brown sugar and ⅓ cup water. Boil 16 minutes or to 238° (soft ball stage). Pour over the corn. Stir until every kernel is well coated.

POPCORN BALLS

Prepare
  3 quarts popcorn (p. 519)
Cook to 270° (hard crack stage)
  1 cup molasses
  1 cup corn syrup
  1 teaspoon vinegar
Stir in
  3 tablespoons butter
  ½ teaspoon salt
Pour slowly over the popcorn and stir with a wooden spoon to coat each kernel. Butter your hands slightly and shape the corn lightly into 3-inch balls. Set on wax paper to harden. Wrap in wax paper.

SALTED NUTS

At their best served while still warm. Reheat if necessary.

Blanch (p. 13) Brazil nuts and filberts. Blanch almonds or not. Shell peanuts and slip off the skins. Shell pecans and walnuts, keeping the nut meats unbroken if possible.

Spread in a shallow pan. Dot with 1 tablespoon butter for each cup of nuts or sprinkle with olive oil. Brown in a 400° oven, stirring every 5 minutes so the nuts will toast evenly. Do not overcook, because nuts darken as they cool. Pecans are ready as soon as the butter sizzles. Spread on a paper towel to dry. Sprinkle with salt.

Sautéed Nuts. Cook the nut meats, a few at a time, in a small frying pan lightly greased with butter or olive oil. Dry and salt as above.

BRAZIL NUT CHIPS

Perfect with cocktails.

Cover shelled Brazil nuts with cold water. Bring slowly to the boiling point. Simmer 3 minutes. Drain and cool. Cut in thin lengthwise strips. Spread in a shallow pan. Dot with butter (1 tablespoon for each cup of nuts). Sprinkle with salt. Bake 15 minutes at 350°, stirring occasionally. Drain on a paper towel.

SUGARED PECANS *or* ALMONDS

Put in a heavy frying pan
  1 cup sugar
  ½ cup water
Cook 5 minutes. Add
  ½ pound pecan meats *or* blanched almonds
Cook and stir until the syrup begins to look white and slightly sugared. Add
  1 teaspoon vanilla
  ½ teaspoon cinnamon
Set the pan aside 10 minutes. Set on an asbestos pad over low heat. Stir constantly until the

sugar starts to melt. Pour on a cake cooler with a sheet of wax paper under it. Separate the nuts to dry.

Orange Pecans. Omit the cinnamon. Cook 2 tablespoons grated orange rind with the syrup.

SHERRIED WALNUTS

Mix in a bowl
¾ cup brown sugar
2 tablespoons sherry
1 tablespoon light corn syrup
Add
1½ cups walnut meats
Stir until the nuts are well coated. Roll in sugar and put on wax paper to dry.

SPICED NUTS

Mix in a small bowl
¼ cup sugar
1 tablespoon cinnamon
⅛ tablespoon ground cloves
⅛ teaspoon nutmeg
In another bowl, beat slightly
1 egg white
Add, a few at a time
1 cup nut meats (almonds, pecans, walnuts, Brazil nuts)
Rub the nut meats in the egg white with your fingers to coat them thoroughly. Drop into the bowl of sugar and spices and coat each nut completely. Place on a buttered cooky sheet. Bake 30 minutes at 300°.

STUFFED DATES *or* PRUNES

Pit large dates or prunes. If the prunes are very dry, put them in a strainer and set over boiling water until they soften. Cool before stuffing. Stuff with any of the following. Roll the stuffed dates or prunes in granulated sugar or shake (4 to 6 at a time) in a paper bag containing ¼ cup sugar. One teaspoon cinnamon may be mixed with the sugar.

Walnut *or* **pecan meats,** broken in pieces
Salted almonds
Brazil nut meats
Candied ginger, cut fine
Candied pineapple, cut fine
Fondant (pp. 529, 530)
Peanut butter, mixed with orange juice
Marshmallows, quartered and dipped in finely chopped coconut

FRUIT BARS

Put through a food chopper
1 cup figs
1 cup pitted dates
2 cups walnut meats
Mix well. Press firmly into a buttered pan about 9 inches square. Or shape with your fingers in balls. Roll in
Powdered sugar
Makes about 1¼ pounds.

To vary, use half walnut meats and half pecans. Or add the grated rind of 1 orange and 1 tablespoon orange juice, apricot or peach brandy or rum.

RAISIN ROLL

Put through a food chopper
1½ cups raisins
½ cup walnut meats
Mix well. Add
Salt to taste
Shape firmly into a roll about 3 inches thick. Chill and slice.
Makes about ½ pound.

CAROLINA DATE AND NUT CAKES

Actually a confection, but especially good served with coffee as a dessert or as party refreshment.

Put in a saucepan
2 cups sugar
1 cup milk
1 tablespoon butter

Cook to the soft ball stage (238°). Add

1 package (8 ounces) pitted dates, cut small
Few grains salt

Stir 10 minutes over low heat. Add

2 cups chopped nut meats

Cool. Shape in a roll 2 inches thick. Wrap in foil. Chill in the refrigerator. Cut in ¼-inch slices. *Makes about 2 pounds.*

PEACH LEATHER

A specialty from Charleston, South Carolina.

Put through a meat chopper twice, using the finest cutter

2 pounds dried apricots
1 pound dried peaches

Sprinkle a board thickly with

Powdered sugar

Put the fruit mixture on it and pat and roll it until it is ⅛ inch thick. Cut in strips 1¼ by 2 inches. Roll each strip into a tight roll. Store in a tightly closed tin box. *Makes 3 pounds.*

CANDIED ORANGE *or* GRAPEFRUIT PEEL

For a hard, candylike surface, omit the corn syrup. With corn syrup, the peel will be chewy.

Cook to the boiling point

1 cup sugar
¼ cup water
2 tablespoons corn syrup

Add

1 cup prepared peel (below)

Cook slowly until the peel is almost transparent (230° on a candy thermometer). Take up the peel with a skimmer and spread on a plate to cool. Roll in granulated sugar. Spread on wax paper to dry. Store in a glass jar.

To prepare orange peel. Cut the peel in lengthwise sections. Cover with cold water, bring to the boiling point, and cook slowly until soft (about 15 minutes). Drain. Scrape out the white part with a spoon and cut the peel in thin strips with scissors.

To prepare grapefruit peel. Cut the peel in lengthwise sections. Soak overnight in 1 quart cold water with 1 tablespoon salt. Drain, cover with cold water, bring to the boiling point, and boil 20 minutes. Repeat three times and cook in the last water until tender (about 4 hours). Drain and cut in strips ⅛ inch wide.

CHOCOLATE-DIPPED ORANGE PEEL

Dip candied orange peel (unsugared) in melted coating chocolate. Dry on wax paper.

COCONUT CAKES

Cook in a double boiler until the mixture clings to a spoon

2 cups fresh grated coconut
2 tablespoons corn syrup
7 tablespoons sugar

Stir in

1 egg white

Cook until the mixture feels sticky when you try it between your fingers. Spread in a wet pan, cover with dampened paper and chill. Shape in small balls, first dipping your hands in cold water. Heat a cooky sheet slightly, grease with salad oil, and put the coconut cakes on it. Bake 20 minutes at 300°. *Makes 20.*

CHOCOLATE COCONUT CAKES

Melt over hot water

2 ounces unsweetened chocolate

Add

1½ cups condensed milk
1 teaspoon baking powder

Mix well. Stir in

Coconut (about 4 cups or ½ pound)

until the mixture is firm enough to shape by teaspoonfuls on a buttered cooky sheet. Bake at 325° until firm to touch (10 to 15 minutes). *Makes 36.*

GLACÉED NUTS

Have ready

1 pound blanched almonds *or* pecan *or* walnut meats

Put in a saucepan

2 cups sugar
1 cup boiling water
⅛ teaspoon cream of tartar

Cook to the boiling point, washing down the sides of the pan from time to time with a pastry brush dipped in cold water. Boil without stirring until the syrup begins to color (310° on a candy thermometer). Place the pan in a larger pan of cold water to stop the boiling instantly. Remove from the pan of cold water and set in a pan of hot water. Take up the nuts, one at a time, on a skewer and dip in the syrup to coat completely. Drain off the syrup and put on wax paper to dry.

GLACÉED FRUITS

A clear cool day is essential for success in making these epicurean tidbits. Serve them the day they are made, with after-dinner coffee or at an engagement party or a wedding reception.

Prepare white grapes, whole strawberries, sections of mandarins, oranges or kumquats or candied cherries. Take the grapes separately from the clusters, leaving a short stem on each grape. Prepare syrup as for Glacéed Nuts (above). Hold the fruit with pincers and dip one piece at a time in the syrup. Dry on wax paper.

ALMOND BUTTER CRUNCH

Chop fine

½ pound blanched almonds

Spread in a pan and toast lightly in a 350° oven. Put in a saucepan

1 cup butter
1 cup sugar

Cook over low heat until the sugar melts. Add half the nuts. Cook to 310°, stirring occasionally. Pour into a lightly buttered pan about 8 by 8 inches. Cool. Heat over boiling water until nearly melted

1 package semi-sweet chocolate *or* chocolate bits (about 7 or 8 ounces)

Stir until smooth. Spread half of it over the cooled nut mixture. Sprinkle with half the reserved nuts. Cool. Turn the candy upside down on wax paper and spread with melted chocolate and nuts the same way. Cool. Break in irregular pieces. *Makes 1¼ pounds.*

PEANUT BRITTLE

Spread in a pan

1½ cups shelled raw peanuts, skinned or not

Sprinkle with

¼ teaspoon salt

Heat 5 minutes in a 350° oven. Put in a saucepan

1 cup sugar
½ cup corn syrup
½ cup water

Cook, stirring until the syrup begins to boil. Wash down the sides of the pan with a wet pastry brush. Cook to 300° (hard crack stage). Add the nuts and

1½ tablespoons butter
½ teaspoon lemon extract

Pour into a shallow buttered pan. As soon as cool enough to handle, stretch with your fingers to make as thin as possible. Break in irregular pieces. *Makes about 1 pound.*

Nut Brittle. Prepare the same way, using almonds, Brazil nuts or walnuts or a combination of nuts.

MAINE PEANUT BRITTLE

Butter a 9- by 9-inch pan. Spread in it

1 cup chopped roasted peanuts

Put in a small heavy pan

2 cups sugar

Cook over low heat, stirring constantly, until the sugar melts into a thin syrup. Pour it over the nuts. Mark in squares when nearly cold. *Makes 1 pound.*

Nut Bars. Make the brittle with Brazil nuts, walnuts or almonds instead of peanuts.

Charleston Benne Candy. *Benne is wild sesame.* Put 1 cup sesame seed in a heavy skillet and stir over moderate heat until slightly brown. Make the brittle, using the sesame seeds in place of peanuts.

PEANUT MOLASSES CANDY

Melt in a saucepan

3 tablespoons butter

Add

2 cups molasses
⅔ cup sugar

Boil to 256°. Stir in

2 cups salted peanuts (skinned)

Pour into a buttered pan 10 by 18 inches. Cool slightly and mark in squares. *Makes 2 pounds.*

VELVET MOLASSES CANDY

Also called Molasses Taffy. A party in itself for children or for nostalgic oldsters.

Put in a heavy pan

½ cup molasses
1½ cups sugar
½ cup water
1½ tablespoons vinegar

Cook, stirring constantly, to the boiling point. Add

¼ teaspoon cream of tartar

Boil to 256°, stirring constantly during the last part of the cooking. When nearly done, add

4 tablespoons melted butter
⅛ teaspoon baking soda

Pour into a buttered pan. As the candy cools around the sides, fold toward the center. When it is cool enough to handle, pull until porous and light-colored, using your finger tips and thumbs. Shape into a rope. Cut in small pieces with scissors or a sharp knife. Put on wax paper to harden. *Makes about 1 pound.*

To flavor, add to the cooked candy a few drops of oil of peppermint or wintergreen, ½ teaspoon vanilla or lemon extract or ¼ teaspoon powdered cloves or cinnamon.

BUTTERSCOTCH NUT CANDY

Butter a pan about 8 by 14 inches. Sprinkle in it

1 cup chopped nut meats

Put in a heavy saucepan

1 cup sugar
¼ cup molasses
½ cup butter
1 tablespoon vinegar
2 tablespoons boiling water
Few grains salt

Cook to 290° (hard crack). Pour over the nuts. Cool slightly and mark in squares. *Makes about 1 pound.*

TOFFEE

Put in a heavy saucepan

2 cups brown sugar
¼ cup butter
1 tablespoon vinegar
2 tablespoons boiling water
Few grains salt

Cook to 290° (hard crack). Pour into a buttered pan about 8 by 14 inches. Cool slightly and mark in squares. *Makes about 1 pound.*

CHANTILLY CREAM SQUARES

Put in a saucepan

2 cups sugar
¾ cup heavy cream
1 cup milk
2 tablespoons light corn syrup
⅛ teaspoon salt

Cook and stir to 238° (soft ball stage). Add

1 teaspoon vanilla

Beat until creamy. Add

1 cup nut meats, broken in pieces

Pour into a buttered pan about 11 by 7 inches. Cut in squares. *Makes about 1½ pounds.*

CHAMPION NOUGAT

Mix in a bowl

¼ cup sweetened condensed milk
1 teaspoon vanilla *or* brandy
Few grains salt
1 tablespoon brown sugar

Stir in

¾ cup powdered skim milk
¼ cup chopped nut meats

Knead until smooth. Roll between your palms into a rope 1 inch thick. Dust with sugar and cut in 1-inch pieces.

Coffee Nougat. Omit the brown sugar. Add 1 tablespoon instant coffee.

FRENCH NOUGAT

Put in a heavy pan

1 cup confectioners' sugar

Stir over low heat until melted. Add

1 cup finely chopped almonds

Pour onto an oiled marble slab or platter. Fold the nougat as it spreads with a broad-bladed knife, keeping it constantly in motion. As soon as cool enough to handle, divide in four parts and shape in long rolls about ⅓ inch thick. Keep the rolls moving until they are almost cold. When they are cold, hold each roll over the sharp edge of a broad-bladed knife and snap in pieces about 1½ inches long. You will need to have someone hold the knife for you. *Makes 20 pieces.*

To dip in chocolate (p. 531).

AFTER-DINNER MINTS

Mix in a saucepan

2 cups sugar
⅔ cup boiling water
¼ teaspoon cream of tartar
1 teaspoon vinegar

Boil without stirring to 256° (very firm ball). Pour on an oiled marble slab or in a shallow pan. Cool, lift (avoiding a stirring motion) and pull, keeping the grain all one way. During the pulling, sprinkle the candy with a few drops of flavoring, using

Vanilla, orange extract, lemon extract, oil of peppermint, wintergreen, clove *or* cinnamon

Add food coloring at the same time, if you like.

When the candy is too stiff to pull, stretch it into a long rope ½ inch thick, and cut into small pieces with scissors. Drop the pieces into a bowl of powdered sugar and stir until well coated. When dry, store in a glass jar, cover, and keep in a warm place several days before serving.

OLD-FASHIONED PEPPERMINTS

Put in a pan

1½ cups sugar
½ cup boiling water

Stir until the sugar dissolves.

Boil until the syrup spins a thread (256°). Add

6 drops oil of peppermint

Beat until creamy. Drop from the tip of a teaspoon onto wax paper. Reheat the syrup from time to time if it becomes too thick to shape.

Wintergreen Wafers. Flavor with oil of wintergreen instead of peppermint. Tint delicately with food coloring, if you wish.

CHOCOLATE CREAM PEPPERMINTS

Put in a bowl

2 tablespoons top milk, heated

Stir in slowly

1½ cups confectioners' sugar
½ tablespoon melted butter
3 drops oil of peppermint

Work until creamy, using your hands. Shape in balls, flatten and dip (p. 531) in

Melted coating chocolate

CHOCOLATE FUDGE

Perfect fudge is smooth and creamy. Corn syrup insures this, but you can make good fudge without it. To help prevent sugaring, use a wooden spoon for stirring and beating.

Put in a heavy saucepan

2 cups sugar
¾ cup top milk *or* thin cream
2 tablespoons light corn syrup
2 ounces unsweetened chocolate *or* 4 tablespoons cocoa

Set over moderate heat. Stir gently until the chocolate melts, afterward just enough to keep the fudge from burning. Cook to the soft ball stage (234°). Remove from the heat. Add, without stirring it in

2 tablespoons butter

Let stand until almost cold. Add

1 teaspoon vanilla

Beat until the fudge is no longer glossy and is thick and creamy. Pour into a slightly buttered pan about 8 by 14 inches. Mark in squares. *Makes 1½ pounds (about 18 large pieces).*

Sour Cream Fudge. Use sour cream in place of milk and butter.

Nut Fudge. Before pouring into the pan, add ½ to 1 cup broken nut meats.

Marshmallow Fudge. Before pouring into the pan, add 12 marshmallows cut in pieces with wet scissors.

TWENTY-MINUTE FUDGE

Mix

1 egg, well beaten
3 tablespoons cream
1 teaspoon vanilla
¼ teaspoon salt
1 pound confectioners' sugar

Melt together

4 ounces unsweetened chocolate
1 tablespoon butter

Add to the first mixture. Stir in

1 cup chopped walnut meats *or* marshmallows, cut in pieces, *or* some of each

Spread in a buttered pan 8 by 8 inches. Cut in squares. *Makes 1½ pounds.*

MILLION-DOLLAR FUDGE

Put in a bowl

6 ounces semi-sweet chocolate
12 ounces German sweet chocolate
1 cup marshmallow cream

Put in a saucepan

2 cups sugar
1 teaspoon butter
¾ cup evaporated milk

Set over low heat and bring gradually to the boiling point. Boil 6 minutes. Pour over the chocolate mixture. Add

⅛ teaspoon salt
½ teaspoon vanilla

Beat until the chocolate melts.

Stir in

1 cup chopped nut meats

Spread in a lightly buttered pan about 8 by 12 inches. Let stand a few hours before cutting in squares. Store in a tin box. *Makes about 3 pounds.*

PECAN PENUCHE

Put in a saucepan

3 cups light brown sugar
1 cup sour cream
¼ cup dark corn syrup

Cook to the soft ball stage (234°). Add

1 tablespoon butter
1 teaspoon vanilla

Let stand without stirring until the candy cools to 112°. Add

1 cup pecan halves

Stir until stiff enough to drop by teaspoonfuls on wax paper. Let stand a few hours before removing from the paper. Store in layers with wax paper between. *Makes about 2 pounds.*

DIVINITY FUDGE

Put in a saucepan

1½ cups light brown sugar
½ cup water
1 teaspoon vinegar

Cook to the firm ball stage (244°). Meanwhile, beat until stiff but not dry

1 egg white

Pour the syrup slowly over the egg white, beating until creamy. Add

½ cup chopped nuts *or* coconut
½ teaspoon vanilla

Drop by teaspoonfuls on wax paper or spread in a buttered pan about 8 by 8 inches and cut in squares. *Makes 1 pound.*

PEANUT BUTTER FUDGE

Put in a saucepan

2 cups sugar
⅛ teaspoon salt
¾ cup top milk *or* cream
2 tablespoons light corn syrup

Cook to the soft ball stage (234°). Cool to lukewarm. Add

4 tablespoon peanut butter
1 teaspoon vanilla

Beat until creamy. Pour into a lightly buttered pan about 8 by 8 inches and cut in squares. *Makes 1 pound.*

MARSHMALLOW PEANUT FUDGE

Put in a saucepan

2 cups sugar
⅔ cup milk

Cook to the soft ball stage (234°). Add

1 jar marshmallow cream
1 cup peanut butter
1 teaspoon vanilla

Mix well and pour into a buttered pan about 9 by 9 inches. Cool and cut in squares. *Makes about 2 pounds.*

NEW ORLEANS PRALINES

Scandalously rich and delicious.

Put in a saucepan

3 cups sugar
1 cup light cream
Few grains salt

Cook to 234° (soft ball). When nearly ready, melt in a small heavy pan

1 cup dark brown sugar

Add to the syrup. Add

3 cups pecan meats, broken in pieces

Cook 2 minutes. Stir well. Drop by spoonfuls on wax paper or a buttered cooky sheet. *Makes 18.*

MAPLE PRALINES

Pecans, hickory nuts or black walnuts are wonderful in this recipe.

Put in a saucepan

1⅞ cups powdered sugar

1 cup maple sugar
½ cup cream

Boil to the soft ball stage (234°). Let stand until cool. Beat with a wooden spoon until thick. Add

2 cups nut meats, broken in pieces

Drop from the tip of a spoon on wax paper or spread in a buttered pan about 9 by 9 inches and cut in squares. *Makes 1½ pounds.*

NUT BALLS

Good for you because they are high in protein—delicious as well.

Put in a bowl

¼ cup corn syrup
1 teaspoon vanilla
⅛ teaspoon salt

Mix and add

½ cup powdered skim milk
¼ cup chopped nut meats

Stir with a knife until well blended. Pat into a ball and put on a board sprinkled lightly with sugar. Knead until creamy. Let stand until firm enough to shape in 1-inch balls. Roll in

Sugar

Makes ½ pound.

Fruit Balls. Use candied fruit, cut small, in place of nuts.

Peppermint Balls. Flavor with ½ teaspoon peppermint, instead of vanilla. Omit the nuts, using an extra ¼ cup powdered milk istead.

PEANUT BUTTER CHEWIES

Another high-protein candy.

Mix in a bowl

½ cup crunchy peanut butter
2 tablespoons honey
1 teaspoon vanilla

Add

Few grains salt
¾ cup powdered skim milk

Stir with a knife until well blended. Add

Powdered sugar *or* liquid Sucaryl to taste

Shape in 1-inch balls. Roll in

Peanuts, chopped fine, *or* confectioners' sugar

Makes about ½ pound.

CARAMELS

Cream and corn syrup make smooth waxy caramels.

Put in a heavy saucepan

1 cup sugar
⅔ cup corn syrup
½ cup light cream

Stir until the sugar dissolves. Boil, stirring gently, to the soft ball stage (234°). Add

½ cup light cream

Boil as before to 234°. Add

½ cup light cream

Boil again to 234°. Add

1 teaspoon vanilla

If sugary, add more cream and boil again. Pour into a lightly buttered pan so that the mixture is about ¾ inch deep. Let stand 12 hours. Cut in squares. Wrap each square in wax paper.

To vary. Just before pouring into the pan to cool, add broken nut meats, shredded coconut or raisins.

Chocolate Caramels. Add 3 ounces grated unsweetened chocolate with the last ½ cup of cream.

MR. B'S CARAMELS

Set a deep saucepan on the kitchen scales. Weigh into it

10 ounces light corn syrup
4 ounces strained honey
1 pound sugar

Add

¼ teaspoon salt
1 cup heavy cream

Cook to the firm ball stage (244°), stirring constantly. Remove from the heat. Add

1 cup heavy cream

Cook to 236°, stirring constantly. Add

1 tablespoon butter

Cook to 240°, stirring constantly. Remove from the heat. Add

1 teaspoon vanilla

Pour into a buttered pan 8 by 8 by 2 inches. Set in a cold place. When firm, turn out on a board and cut in squares. Wrap in wax paper. *Makes about 2½ pounds.*

Mr. B's Chocolate Caramels. Add 4 ounces unsweetened chocolate to the first mixture. Follow directions as above, but bring to 242° at the final cooking and increase the vanilla to 1½ teaspoons.

ALMOND PASTE

Canned almond paste is a convenience, but it is simple to make.

Grind in a meat chopper, using the finest cutter

1 pound blanched almonds

Run through the chopper three or four times until very fine. Put in a saucepan

1 pound sugar
1 cup water

Cook to 240°. Mix with the chopped almonds. Add

½ cup orange juice

Stir until creamy. Spoon onto a marble slab or a platter dusted with

Confectioners' sugar

Let stand until cool. Pack in airtight containers. Store in a cool dry place at least a week before using. *Makes 2 pounds.*

BLENDER ALMOND PASTE

Put in an electric blender

½ cup orange juice
1 cup blanched almonds
1 cup sugar

Whirl until the nuts are very fine. Add

1 cup blanched almonds

Whirl again until very fine. Store in the refrigerator.

MARZIPAN

Rose water is the traditional flavoring. Buy it at a drugstore.

Mix thoroughly

1 cup Almond Paste (above)
1 cup confectioners' sugar
Few drops rose water *or* orange extract

Put on a marble slab or a chilled platter. Knead 20 minutes. Shape with your fingers into tiny fruits and vegetables. Paint with food coloring or dip in a small bowl of coloring. Tuck in cloves for stems and bits of angelica as leaves. Set on a cake rack to dry. Crystallize (below) for a Christmas glitter.

To crystallize. Cook 5 pounds sugar with 2½ cups water to 223°. Do not stir after the sugar is dissolved. Remove from the heat very gently and let stand undisturbed until perfectly cold. Place marzipan in a pan in a single layer. Cover completely with the syrup, pouring it with as little agitation as possible. Let stand at least 8 hours. Drain in a sieve. Dry on a wire rack.

Marzipan Potatoes. Shape. Roll in a mixture of cocoa or instant coffee and confectioners' sugar. Do not crystallize.

FONDANT

Put in a bowl

1 egg white
1 teaspoon cold water
1 teaspoon vanilla

Stir until well blended. Beat in gradually until very stiff

Sifted confectioners' sugar (about 2 cups)

Knead on a marble slab or a platter until very smooth. Color and flavor as liked. Shape in balls. Roll in

Chopped nuts, shredded coconut, instant coffee, cocoa *or* silver shot

Or dip in chocolate (p. 531).

Fondant Stuffed Dates. See page 521.

COOKED FONDANT

To keep fondant creamy, do not stir it after the sugar dissolves and let it cool before working it.

Put in a smooth saucepan

2 cups sugar
1¼ cups water

Stir over low heat until the sugar dissolves. Add

⅛ teaspoon cream of tartar *or* 2 tablespoons light corn syrup

Cover and boil 3 minutes. Remove the cover, put in a candy thermometer and boil to the soft ball stage (238°). During cooking, crystals will form on the sides of the pan. Wipe them off with a wet pastry brush.

Pour onto a marble slab or a large platter which has been wiped with a damp cloth. Cool until just barely warm. Scrape and turn the fondant toward the center with a spatula until it is white and creamy. Knead with your hands until it is perfectly smooth. Cover with a cloth wrung out of cold water and let stand ½ hour.

Cut in pieces. Store in a glass jar covered with a wet cloth or a glass cover. Let stand three or four days before using. *Makes 1 pound.*

Butter Fondant. Add 2 tablespoons butter and ½ teaspoon vanilla. Knead until creamy.

Coffee Fondant. Add 2 teaspoons instant coffee.

Cream Mints. Melt ¾ cup fondant over hot water, flavor with 1 drop oil of peppermint, wintergreen, clove or orange. Color if liked. If desired, add 2 tablespoons chopped nuts. Drop from the tip of a spoon on wax paper. Dry thoroughly.

Fondant Dipped Walnuts, Pecans *or* Almonds. Melt fondant over low heat. Dip nut meats in it and put on a cake rack to dry.

Maple Fondant. Use half maple sugar and half white sugar.

MARSHMALLOW MINT BONBONS

Cut marshmallows in half crosswise. Flavor with peppermint by putting a toothpick in a bottle of oil of peppermint, then on the cut surface of the marshmallow. Arrange in layers in a box, cover and let stand 12 hours. Dip in fondant flavored with a few drops of oil of peppermint.

BONBONS

Flavor fondant with rum, cocoa, instant coffee or oil of peppermint or wintergreen. Shape in balls. If you like, use pieces of nut meats or candied fruit as centers. Leave on a board covered with wax paper until firm. Dip (see below). Put on wax paper to dry. Decorate top, if desired, with bit of nut meat, candied fruit, coconut or ginger.

To dip in fondant. Melt fondant (above) over hot water, flavor and color with food color. Do not allow fondant to become hot. If too thick, add a few drops of cold water. Drop one center at a time into the melted fondant. Stir with a two-tined fork or a candy dipper until entirely covered, lift up, and put on wax paper. Make a coil over the top of the bonbon with the dipper or fork. Stir the fondant frequently.

CHOCOLATE CREAMS

Dip any fondant or fudge center in chocolate.

To dip in chocolate. Room temperature should be about 65°. Melt coating chocolate (no other type) over hot, not boiling water. Beat gently until the chocolate feels a little cooler than your hand (80° to 85° on candy thermometer). Dip the centers one at a time (see p. 530).

Fruit Jellies and Jams

A well-stocked jelly cupboard is a satisfaction. Homemade jellies and jams add a piquant touch to a simple meal and can make a delicious dessert of a plain homemade or baker's cake. Perfect jellies and jams are ideal gifts for almost anyone.

PREPARING GLASSES FOR JELLIES AND JAMS

Before starting to make jelly or jam, wash the glasses and put them in a kettle of cold water. Heat the water gradually to the boiling point. When the jam or jelly is ready, remove the glasses, drain and place on a tray covered with a cloth wrung out of hot water.

MAKING JELLIES

Prepare fruit in small amounts to keep its fresh flavor. Select perfect fruit. Unless you are planning to add pectin, the fruit should be slightly underripe. Wash the fruit thoroughly, but do not pare any fruit except pineapple because fruit skin is rich in pectin. Cut large fruit in pieces, small fruit like crabapples in half. Remove the cores from quinces but not from other fruits.

Extract the juice. Put the prepared fruit in a flat-bottomed saucepan. Crush soft fruits and berries and add only enough water to keep the fruit from burning. Add just enough water to other fruit to be seen through the top layer. Cover and cook slowly until the juice flows freely (3 minutes for berries, 15 minutes or more for hard fruits). Strain through a damp jelly bag or several layers of dampened cheesecloth. For crystal-clear jelly, do not squeeze or press the bag.

For a greater yield, squeeze or press the juice through the bag, then strain again without pressing. **To extract the juice in a pressure saucepan,** crush the fruit and add ¼ cup water for each 2 pounds. Put on the cover and bring the pressure to 15 pounds. Remove from the heat and let the pressure drop to normal. Strain through a fine sieve. This is the easiest method of all for juicy berries and grapes.

Add the sugar. Measure no more than 4 cups of juice into a deep saucepan and boil 5 minutes (20 minutes for quince juice). Fruits vary in the amount of sugar needed, but as a general rule, add ¾ cup of sugar for each cup of fruit juice. With too little or too much sugar, fruit will not jell.

To test fruit juice for the precise amount of sugar needed, use a jellmeter or pour 3 tablespoons denatured alcohol into a glass, add 1 tablespoon fruit juice, shake gently and let stand 1 minute. If solid jelly is formed which can be lifted in one piece with a spoon, use 1 cup of sugar to each cup of juice in making jelly. If large flakes are formed, use 3/4 cup of sugar to each cup of juice. If small flakes are formed, boil the juice longer to concentrate the pectin. *Discard the tested jelly, as denatured alcohol is poisonous.*

Boil rapidly to the jelly stage. To test whether juice will jell, take up a spoonful of juice, cool a moment, and pour back into the pan from the side of the spoon. When the jelly is ready, drops of jelly will come together and "sheet" off the spoon. Begin testing after cooking 5 min-

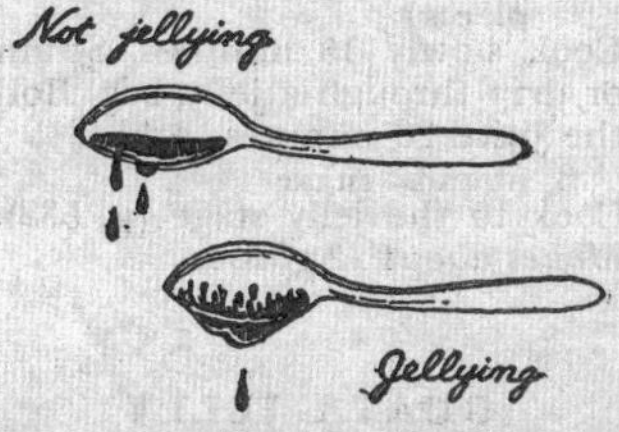

utes. The jelly stage as indicated on a jelly thermometer is 8 degrees above boiling (220°, except at high altitudes).

Skim the froth from the top of the jelly.

Fill the prepared (p. 532) glasses to within 1/4 inch of the rim or well above the curve if you are not using straight-sided glasses. Otherwise it may be difficult to remove the paraffin without crushing it into the jam or jelly.

Seal by covering with a thin layer of paraffin (melted in a small saucepan over hot water). Tilt the glass so that the paraffin will touch the edge all around. The jelly should be completely covered but the layer or paraffin should be no thicker than 1/8 inch. A thick layer will pull away from the edge. Do not reuse paraffin.

Label the glasses, stating the kind and the date.

Store in a cool dark place.

MAKING JELLY WITH ADDED PECTIN

Some fruits do not have enough acid or pectin if used alone but can be made into excellent jelly by combining with other fruits or by adding commercial pectin. Follow the manufacturer's instructions exactly.

Many like to add pectin even when making jelly of fruits naturally rich enough in pectin to jell because it increases the yield from the fruit and insures jellying. The flavor of jellies made with added pectin is fresh and appetizing but somewhat too sweet for some tastes.

APPLE JELLY

Wash tart red apples. Three pounds (with added water) yields about 4 cups of juice. Cut out any blemishes and the stem and blossom ends, but do not pare or remove the core. Cut in eighths. Follow the general directions for making jelly on page 532, adding 4 cups of water for each 3 pounds of apples. Tart apple juice is high in pectin and so can be combined successfully with other juices to make firm jelly.

Crabapple Jelly. Core, stem and cut in half.

Blueberry *or* **Raspberry Apple Jelly.** Use equal amounts of berry juice and apple juice. Add a tablespoon of lemon juice for each 2 cups of fruit juice.

Cherry *or* Pineapple Jelly. Use equal amounts of cherry or pineapple juice and apple juice.

Mint Jelly. Make in small quantities as the color is apt to fade. Use light-colored apples or crabapples or pare bright-colored apples before extracting the juice. Measure the juice and add chopped mint leaves and stems (1 cup to 4 cups of juice), or flavor to taste with spearmint extract when the jelly is ready to pour into glasses. Color delicately green with vegetable coloring while the jelly is boiling.

Rose Geranium Jelly. Place a rose geranium leaf in each glass and fill with apple jelly. Do not cover with paraffin until the jelly is almost firm, and lift the leaf so that it is suspended in the jelly.

Spiced Apple Jelly. For 3 pounds of apples, prepare a spice bag with 1 teaspoon whole cinnamon, 1 teaspoon whole allspice and ½ teaspoon whole cloves. Put in the pan with the apples, add ½ cup mild vinegar and 2½ cups of water, and extract the juice.

CURRANT JELLY

Remove bits of leaves but not the stems. Wash thoroughly. Follow the directions for making jelly on page 532.

Currant Raspberry Jelly. Use equal parts raspberry and currant juice.

Gooseberry Jelly. Remove stem and blossom ends.

GRAPE JELLY

Wash, drain and remove about half the stems. Extract the juice in a pressure cooker or crush in a flat-bottomed pan and cook slowly about 10 minutes or until the juice flows freely. Add a little water if necessary to keep the grapes from sticking to the pan. Store the juice in the refrigerator overnight so that the crystals which sometimes form will settle. Carefully pour off the juice. Follow the directions for making jelly on page 532.

WILD GRAPE JELLY

Wash, drain and remove the stems from

4 quarts wild grapes

Crush in a flat-bottomed pan. Add

1 pint mild cider vinegar
¼ cup whole cloves
¼ cup stick cinnamon (in pieces)

Cook slowly 15 minutes. Strain or drip through a jelly bag. Boil the juice 20 minutes. Add

3 pounds sugar

Cook to the jelly stage (p. 532). *Makes about 12 glasses.*

GUAVA JELLY

Wash and slice guavas. Follow the directions for making jelly on page 532 but cook the fruit 45 minutes or more to extract the juice, or extract it in a pressure cooker. For each 4 cups of guava juice, add the juice of 1 lime.

QUINCE JELLY

Wash firm ripe quinces and rub off the fuzz. Remove the stems, cores and seeds. Slice. Follow the directions for making jelly on page 532 but cook the fruit 45 minutes or more to extract the juice, or extract the juice in a pressure cooker. Equal parts of quince juice and apple juice make excellent jelly.

PARADISE JELLY

Cut in pieces, discarding the stem and blossom ends

12 tart apples

Wash, discarding bruised ones

1 pound cranberries

Quarter, core and chop fione

6 quinces

Combine the fruits, extract their juice and follow the directions for making jelly on page 532, using

1 cup sugar for each cup juice

Makes about 12 glasses.

MAKING JAM

Wash the fruit. Pare pineapples. Peel peaches and apricots. Remove pits, cores and stems. Crush berries and other small fruit in the pan. Cut other fruits in small pieces. One quart of fruit makes 2 or 3 pints of jam.

Measure the fruit into a flat-bottomed pan. Make only 4 cups at a time so that the fruit cooks quickly and keeps its fresh color and flavor. Cook until the fruit is tender and the juice begins to flow, adding just enough water to keep the fruit from burning.

Add the sugar (heated in the oven so that the hot fruit will not be cooled by it), using 3 cups for each 4 cups of fruit. Stir over the heat until the sugar dissolves.

Boil rapidly (to preserve color and flavor) until the syrup is thick and clear (8 to 20 minutes). Stir as needed to prevent sticking.

Fill prepared (p. 532) glasses or jars to within ½ inch of the tops. Seal, label and store. *Makes 2 pints.*

If there is a large amount of syrup in proportion to the fruit, let the jam stand until it is cool, and stir well to distribute the bits of fruit evenly before you fill the glasses.

MAKING JAM WITH ADDED PECTIN

Fruit low in natural pectin (fully ripe fruit) may be used for jam by adding prepared pectin. Follow the manufacturer's instructions exactly. The yield per pound of fruit is greater because the juice does not have to be reduced.

BLACK CURRANT JAM

Wash the currants and remove the stems. Put through a food chopper, then through a coarse sieve. Measure and add an equal amount of sugar. Bring rapidly to the boiling point, stirring well. Cook 20 minutes.

APRICOT PINEAPPLE JAM

Cover with cold water

1 pound dried apricots

Let stand overnight or several hours. Cook in the same water until soft. Drain, reserving the juice. Chop the fruit and add the drained juice. Add

1 large can crushed pineapple (with its juice)

Add

Sugar (⅔ the amount of juice or less, if liked less sweet)

Cook until thick. *Makes 4 pints.*

CHERRY JAM

Put in a flat-bottomed saucepan

¼ cup water
4 cups pitted cherries

Bring to the boiling point. Cover and simmer 15 minutes. Add

7 cups sugar

Bring to the boiling point. Boil rapidly 3 minutes, stirring constantly. Add

1 bottle commercial pectin
Stir 5 minutes and skim. Add
¼ teaspoon almond flavoring
Makes eleven 6-ounce glasses.

GOOSEBERRY JAM

Boil together for 5 minutes
3 pounds sugar
2 cups red currant juice
Add
4 pounds gooseberries
Boil 40 minutes, skimming occasionally. Set aside 24 hours. Drain off the syrup. Pack the berries in jars. Boil the syrup until as thick as honey and pour it over the berries. *Makes 6 pints.*

QUINCE JAM

After extracting the juice for Quince (p. 534) or Paradise Jelly (p. 535), rub the pulp through a fine sieve. Measure. Add an equal amount of sugar. Stir and cook to 222°.

RASPBERRY JAM

A jelly thermometer simplifies making this jam. Otherwise it may be overcooked.

Crush with a masher in a flat-bottomed saucepan
4 cups raspberries
Cook 15 minutes to reduce the liquid. Add
3 cups sugar (heated in oven)
Cook to 214°, stirring with a wooden spoon to keep the jam from sticking. Skim off the foam. Spread in a shallow dish and let stand until cool before putting in jars. *Makes 2 pints.*

Blackberry Jam. You may prefer to remove the seeds by putting the cooked berries through a coarse sieve or food mill before adding the sugar.

Raspberry Currant Jam. Use 3 cups raspberries and 1 cup currants.

SALLY'S STRAWBERRY *or* RASPBERRY JAM

Put in a flat-bottomed saucepan but do not crush
1 quart strawberries *or* raspberries
Add
1 cup sugar
Set over low heat, stir gently and bring to the boiling point. Boil 3 minutes. Add
1 cup sugar
Cook as before. Add
1 cup sugar
Cook as above. Skim off any foam and spread in a shallow dish to cool. Spoon into jars. *Makes 2 pints.*

STRAWBERRY PRESERVES

Cook together to 238° (soft ball stage)
3 cups sugar
1 cup water
Wash, hull and drain thoroughly
1 quart strawberries
Add to the syrup, cover and remove from the heat. Let stand 10 minutes. Skim if there is any foam on top. Remove the berries and set them aside. Cook the syrup to 238°, add the berries and let stand 15 minutes over very low heat. Skim, remove the berries and again cook the syrup to 238°. Add the berries and cook slowly until the syrup is thick. Let stand 24 hours before filling the jars. *Makes 2 pints.*

SUNSHINE STRAWBERRIES

Wash and hull perfect strawberries. Arrange in layers in a

deep kettle with an equal amount of sugar. Let stand ½ hour, then bring to the boiling point and cook 20 minutes. Spread on platters, cover with glass, and set in the sun several days or until the syrup is thick. Stir gently several times each day. Bring indoors after sunset.

Sunshine Cherries. Use sour cherries. Cook until just tender but still firm. Delicious with ice cream.

ORANGE MARMALADE

Select smooth unblemished oranges. Wash thoroughly. Slice as thin as possible and measure. To each quart of sliced fruit add 1½ quarts of water and let stand overnight. Cook slowly until the peel is tender (2 to 2½ hours). Measure and add two-thirds as much sugar. Cook rapidly to the jelly stage (p. 532) (30 to 60 minutes). *Makes about 5 pints.*

Ginger Marmalade. Add 2½ cups chopped ginger to each quart. For a sweeter marmalade, increase the sugar.

THREE-FRUIT MARMALADE

Select thin-skinned tart fruit.

Scrub thoroughly
- **1 grapefruit**
- **1 orange**
- **1 lemon**

Hold the fruit on a board and slice very thin, saving the juice. Discard all the seeds and the grapefruit core. Measure the fruit and the juice into a large saucepan. Add
- **Water (three times the quantity of fruit)**

Cover, simmer 2 hours, and let stand overnight. Measure. Add
- **Sugar (an equal amount)**
- **¼ teaspoon salt**

Divide into two or three pans. Cook to the jelly stage (p. 532), stirring frequently. Let stand 1 hour, stirring several times to distribute the peel evenly before putting in the glasses. *Makes about twelve 6-ounce glasses.*

RHUBARB FIG MARMALADE

Combine in a large saucepan
- **1 pound unpeeled rhubarb (cut fine)**
- **1 pound sugar**
- **¼ pound dried figs, cut small**
- **Juice ½ lemon**

Cover and let stand 24 hours. Cook rapidly to the jelly stage (p. 532). *Makes about six 6-ounce glasses.*

TOMATO MARMALADE

Cut in pieces
- **3 pounds tomatoes**

Cut in very thin slices, discarding the seeds
- **1 orange**
- **½ lemon**

Add to the tomatoes. Add
- **1½ pounds sugar**

Cook slowly 3 hours, stirring to prevent sticking. *Makes six 6-ounce glasses.*

Tomato Conserve. Cook ½ box seedless raisins with the marmalade. When ready to pour into glasses, stir in ¼ pound chopped walnuts.

CRANBERRY CONSERVE

Pick over and wash
- **4 cups cranberries**

Add
- **⅔ cup cold water**

Cook until the skins break. Force through a strainer or a food mill. Add
- **⅔ cup boiling water**
- **¼ pound seedless raisins**

1 orange, sliced, seeded and cut small
1½ pounds sugar
Bring to the boiling point. Simmer 20 minutes. Add
½ pound walnut meats, cut in pieces
Cook. *Makes about three 6-ounce glasses.*

GRAPE CONSERVE

Wash and remove the stems from
5 pounds Concord grapes
Separate the pulp from the skins. Heat the pulp gently to free the seeds, stirring so that it will not stick. Put through a sieve and discard the seeds. Cut into thin slivers
½ orange, preferably navel
Seed if necessary and add to the grape pulp and skins. Measure. Set out
Sugar (an equal amount)
Put half the fruit and half the sugar in each of two broad flat saucepans. Cook slowly until the conserve is thick (test by putting a spoonful on a cold plate). Add
½ cup walnut meats, in pieces
Makes about ten 6-ounce glasses.

PEAR HARLEQUIN

Wipe, stem and core
3 pounds pears (underripe)
Cut in small pieces. Add
1 small can pineapple, crushed *or* bits
1 orange, juice and grated rind
Measure. For each 4 cups add
3 cups sugar
Cover and let stand overnight. Simmer until thick (about 2 hours). Add (cutting the cherries in half)
1 4-ounce bottle maraschino cherries
Stir well. *Makes eight 6-ounce jars.*

PEAR GINGER

Wipe, stem and core
4 pounds pears (underripe)
Cut in small pieces. Add
2 pounds sugar
4 ounces (1 small jar) preserved ginger
Let stand overnight. Add
2 lemons, seeded and cut small
Cook slowly until thick (about 3 hours). *Makes about eight 6-ounce glasses.*

PLUM GUMBO

Wipe and remove the pits from
3 pounds plums
Cut in pieces. Chop
1 pound seeded raisins
Wipe, seed and cut in thin slices
2 oranges
Put the fruit in a deep kettle. Add
3 pounds sugar
Bring to the boiling point and simmer until as thick as marmalade. *Makes about eight 6-ounce jars.*

PEACH CONSERVE

Put in a kettle
1 quart cold water
1 pound dried skinned peaches
Let stand overnight. Add
1 cup seeded raisins, cut in pieces
Juice 1 lemon
Juice 1 orange
1 whole orange (cut in thin slices and seeded)
1 pound sugar
Bring to the boiling point. Boil rapidly until the syrup is thick and the fruit is clear, stirring occasionally to prevent sticking. Add
½ pound walnut meats, cut in pieces
Makes about eight 6-ounce jars.

RASPBERRY CURRANT PRESERVE

Wash and pick over
4 quarts raspberries

Extract the juice (p. 532) from

3 pounds currants

Add

3 pounds sugar

Heat to the boiling point and cook slowly 20 minutes. Add 1 quart of the raspberries. Bring the syrup to the boiling point, skim out the berries and put in a jar or jars. Repeat until all the berries are used. Fill the jars with syrup. *Makes about eight 6-ounce jars.*

RHUBARB CONSERVE

Wash, peel and cut in 1-inch pieces

4 pounds rhubarb

Put in a kettle. Add

5 pounds sugar
1 pound seeded raisins
2 oranges (grated rind and juice)
1 lemon (grated rind and juice)

Mix well. Cover and let stand ½ hour. Bring to the boiling point and simmer 45 minutes, stirring frequently. *Makes twelve 6-ounce glasses.*

PRESERVED KUMQUATS

Put in a saucepan

2 cups sugar
1 cup water

Boil 5 minutes. Add

1 quart fresh kumquats

Cook gently 45 minutes or until tender. *Makes six 6-ounce glasses.*

DAMSON PRESERVES

Wipe damson plums and prick them well with a darning needle. Weigh. For each pound of fruit, put in a saucepan 1½ cups sugar and ½ cup water. Bring to the boiling point and skim. Add the plums, a few at a time, so that the fruit will keep in shape during cooking. Cook until soft. To work faster, divide the syrup in two pans and work with both at once.

SPICED ORANGE SLICES

Cut in ¼-inch slices and seed

6 large oranges, unpeeled

Put in a saucepan. Cover with water, simmer ½ hour, and drain. Put in a saucepan

3½ cups sugar
1 cup mild vinegar
1 stick cinnamon
½ tablespoon whole cloves

Boil 5 minutes. Add some of the orange slices, having the syrup cover them completely. Cover and cook until the slices are clear (about ½ hour). Remove the slices and cook the remaining ones the same way. Cover with syrup and let stand overnight. Drain off the syrup and cook until it is thick. Add the orange slices and heat to the boiling point. *Makes about eight 6-ounce glasses.*

APPLE BUTTER

This is a general rule. Vary the spices to suit your taste. Make other fruit butters of fresh apricots, peaches, plums or the pulp left in the jelly bag after making jelly. Crush the fruit and add just enough water (not cider or vinegar) to keep it from sticking.

Cut into pieces (do not peel or core)

4 pounds tart apples

Cover with

2 cups cider, mild cider vinegar *or* water

Cook until soft. Put through a sieve. Measure. Add

½ cup sugar (for each cup of pulp)
Few grains salt
2 teaspoons cinnamon

1 teaspoon clove
½ teaspoon allspice
1 lemon (grated rind and juice)

Cover and cook over low heat until the sugar dissolves. Uncover and cook quickly until thick and smooth when you spoon a bit onto a cold plate. Stir with a wooden spoon during the cooking so that the apple butter will not stick and burn. *Makes about ten 6-ounce glasses.*

QUINCE HONEY

Pare and grate

3 large quinces (underripe)

Put in a saucepan

1 cup boiling water
5 cups sugar

Heat slowly, without boiling, until the sugar melts. Brush down the sides of the pan with a pastry brush dipped in cold water to remove any crystals. Add the quince pulp and cook 15 to 20 minutes. If the quinces are ripe, add, after the first 10 minutes of cooking

1 teaspoon lemon juice

This helps to prevent sugaring. *Makes about six 6-ounce jars.*

BRANDIED PEACHES

Dip perfect peaches quickly in hot water and peel. If the peaches have thin skins, you may prefer not to peel them—rub off the fuzz with a clean cloth and prick each peach twice with a fork.

For each 6 peaches, boil 3 cups water with 2 cups sugar 10 minutes. Cook the peaches in the syrup, a few at a time, until tender when tried with a toothpick (about 5 minutes). Pack into jars. Add 2 tablespoons brandy to each pint jar and fill the jars with syrup. Seal. Store a month before using.

Brandied Cherries. Wash firm cherries. Leave on the short stems and cook as above.

TUTTI-FRUTTI

Essential for success with this Victorian luxury are a big old-fashioned stone jar with a heavy cover and a cool storage place.

Put a pint of brandy in a large stone crock (at least 2-gallon size). Add strawberries, raspberries, cherries, apricots, peaches and chunks of pineapple as the fruits come into season. For each 2 cups fruit, add 2 cups sugar. Put on the cover, tying it on if necessary. Set in a cool place. Stir daily until all the fruit has been added. Cover tightly and store 3 months before using. The fruit will have produced its own liquor with the brandy as a starter. Seal in jars if more convenient.

Serve on ice cream or stir into soft ice cream and refreeze.

Pickles and Relishes

Even though excellent pickles are marketed, it is a satisfaction and an economy to prepare a stock of your own making. Pickles are easy to make and variations are innumerable. Develop your own specialties by adding different spices and vegetables to basic recipes.

INGREDIENTS

Vegetables and fruits should be slightly underripe so that the finished pickle will be crisp. Wash or wipe before cutting.

Vinegar should be mild. Read the label—the vinegar should contain no more than 5 per cent acid. White vinegar is often used for light-colored pickles, but it lacks the fruity flavor of cider vinegar.

Salt should be pure, not table salt, so that the liquid will not be cloudy.

Spices should be fresh. To keep the pickles from darkening, use whole spices and tie them loosely in a square of muslin. Remove them before packing the pickles in jars.

Sugar. Use granulated sugar unless the recipe calls for brown.

PICKLING PROBLEMS

Soft or slippery pickles are spoiled, due to inaccurate measurements or improper storage.

Shriveling comes from using too much vinegar, sugar or salt.

Darkening is caused by the minerals in hard water or by using ground spices. Do not cook pickles in copper or iron, which also causes change in color.

TO PACK PICKLES

Old-time cooks stored pickles in large jars or crocks in a cool cellar. Nowadays most families find it more convenient to store them in pint or half-pint jars. Prepare jars, fill to overflowing with hot pickles and seal immediately (p. 533) unless the recipe gives special directions.

BREAD AND BUTTER PICKLES

Young cucumbers (6-inch size) and tiny white onions make the best pickle.

Prepare
6 cups thin-sliced cucumbers, unpeeled
Peel and slice
1 pound onions
Seed and shred
1 green pepper
Mix well. Add
¼ cup salt
Cover and let stand 3 hours. Mix (omitting the turmeric if you prefer)
2 cups brown sugar
½ teaspoon turmeric
¼ teaspoon ground cloves
1 tablespoon mustard seed

½ teaspoon celery seed (or more)
2 cups mild cider vinegar

Bring slowly to the boiling point and boil 5 minutes. Drain the vegetables thoroughly in a colander, rinsing well with cold water. Add them to the hot syrup and heat slowly to just below the boiling point, stirring occasionally. *Makes 4 pints.*

SACCHARIN PICKLES

Particularly useful if you grow your own cucumbers. Add them a few at a time as they develop. If more convenient, pack the cucumbers in jars, fill to overflowing with the pickling syrup and seal at once. If you wish to omit the horseradish, increase the mustard to ½ cup.

Mix

1 gallon vinegar
1 teaspoon powdered saccharin
1 teaspoon powdered alum
½ cup salt
½ teaspoon powdered cloves
1 teaspoon powdered allspice
1 tablespoon powdered cinnamon
4 tablespoons dry mustard
1 cup grated horseradish

Pour into a large crock (2 gallons or larger). Add, as they grow to the proper size (1 to 2 inches)

Cucumbers, scrubbed

Add no more than will be covered by the liquid. Let stand at least two weeks before using.

CUCUMBER AND ONION PICKLE

Slice

12 young cucumbers
6 onions

Add

½ cup salt

Cover with water and let stand 2 hours. Drain. Add

2 cups mild cider vinegar
½ cup sugar
2 teaspoons mustard seed
2 teaspoons celery seed
2 teaspoons black pepper
1 teaspoon ginger
1 teaspoon turmeric

Bring to the boiling point. *Makes 4 pints.*

OLIVE OIL PICKLES

Slice paper-thin

1 dozen 6-inch cucumbers

Add

1 quart boiling water
½ cup salt

Let stand overnight. Drain thoroughly and pack in clean jars. Mix

½ cup olive oil
4 ounces white mustard seed
4 ounces black mustard seed
3 cups mild vinegar

Pour over the cucumbers. *Makes 3 pints.*

DILL PICKLES

Select small slim cucumbers 3 or 4 inches long.

Cover with cold water

Cucumbers (about 50)

Let stand overnight. Drain and pack in jars. Put in a saucepan

1 quart mild vinegar
¾ cup salt
2 quarts water

Bring to the boiling point. Pour over the cucumbers. Add to each jar

Dill, one or more sprigs
Garlic clove (if you like it)

If some of the liquid oozes out during the first week, open the jars, add enough more liquid (mixed in the same proportion) to cover the cucumbers completely, and reseal. *Makes 6 to 8 quarts.*

ICICLE PICKLES

Drain and serve well-chilled as a relish or hors d'oeuvre.

Peel and remove the seeds from
Large cucumbers
Cut in strips ½ inch wide. Cover with
Ice water
Let stand overnight. Drain and pack upright in sterilized jars. For each 3 or 4 jars, boil together for 3 minutes
3 cups white vinegar
1 cup water
3 cups sugar
Add
¼ cup salt
Pour over the cucumbers to fill the jars. Seal. Let stand 6 weeks before using.

RIPE CUCUMBER PICKLES

Pare and remove the seeds from
4 large ripe cucumbers
Cut into large chunks. Sprinkle with
Salt
Let stand 3 hours and drain. Mix in a saucepan
1½ cups vinegar
1½ cups sugar
1½ teaspoons mustard seed
1½ teaspoons celery seed
½ teaspoon turmeric
Add the cucumbers. Simmer until the cucumbers are easily pierced with a fork. Pack them in jars and cover with syrup. *Makes 2 pints.*

APPLE CHUTNEY

Put in a bowl
3 cups chopped green tomatoes
Sprinkle with
2 tablespoons salt
Let stand 12 hours and drain. Mix
1 quart mild cider vinegar
2 tablespoons salt
1 pound dark brown sugar
Chop
12 tart apples, cored
2 Spanish onions, sliced
Put all the ingredients in a saucepan. Add
1 pound raisins, seedless or sultanas
2 tablespoons ground ginger
⅔ cup finely cut mint leaves
Cook over low heat until the apples and onions are tender (about 30 minutes). Mix
2 tablespoons flour
¼ cup water
Stir it into the chutney. Simmer 5 minutes. *Makes about 4 pints.*

To vary, omit the ground ginger and use instead ½ pound chopped green ginger or 1 jar (6 ounces) preserved ginger, cut small. Use ripe tomatoes instead of green ones. Add 2 ounces chili peppers, if you like.

CELERY AND TOMATO RELISH

Put in a saucepan
2 cups sugar
2 tablespoons salt
1 teaspoon dry mustard
1 teaspoon powdered cloves
1 teaspoon allspice
1 teaspoon cinnamon
1 teaspoon celery seed
Mix thoroughly. Add
1½ cups vinegar
6 bunches celery, chopped (no leaves)
15 tomatoes, chopped
1 red pepper, chopped
Bring to the boiling point and simmer 1½ hours. *Makes about 4 pints.*

CHOWCHOW

Variations are endless. Change the proportions of vegetables or the seasoning as you like.

Cut in small pieces
1 quart small green tomatoes
6 small cucumbers
2 red *or* green peppers
1 small head of cauliflower
1 bunch celery
1 or 2 cups small onions
1 quart green beans (whole)
Cover with
2 quarts boiling water
¾ cup salt

Let stand 1 hour. Drain. Rinse with cold water. Heat to the boiling point

2 quarts vinegar
4 tablespoons mustard seed
1 ounce turmeric
1 tablespoon allspice
1 tablespoon pepper
1 tablespoon ground clove

Add the vegetables. Cook until tender, stirring frequently. *Makes about 10 pints.*

GOOSEBERRY RELISH

Put through a food chopper

5 cups gooseberries, washed and stemmed
1½ cups seeded raisins
1 onion, sliced

Add

1 cup brown sugar
3 tablespoons dry mustard
3 tablespoons ginger
3 tablespoons salt
¼ teaspoon cayenne
1 teaspoon turmeric (omit, if you prefer)
1 quart vinegar

Bring slowly to the boiling point and simmer 45 minutes. Strain through a coarse sieve. *Makes about 4 pints.*

CORN RELISH

Cut the corn from

1½ dozen ears corn

Remove and discard the leaves and roots from

1 bunch celery

Chop the rest fine. Put the corn and celery in a saucepan. Add

1 quart vinegar
1 small cabbage, chopped
4 onions, sliced thin
2 green peppers, chopped

Mix

2 cups sugar
1 cup flour
½ cup salt
½ teaspoon mustard
¼ teaspoon cayenne
½ teaspoon turmeric (for color)

Add

1 quart vinegar

Add to the vegetables and bring to the boiling point. Simmer 40 minutes. *Makes 4 to 6 pints.*

PEPPER RELISH

Remove the seeds from

24 peppers, green *or* red, *or* half of each

Peel and put through a chopper

12 onions

Put the vegetables in a saucepan. Cover with boiling water and drain. Cover with cold water, bring to the boiling point and drain. Add

1 quart mild vinegar
2 cups sugar
3 tablespoons salt
1 tablespoon mustard *or* celery seed

Cook 10 minutes. Taste and add more sugar or salt, if needed. *Makes 6 or 7 pints.*

Pepper Relish with Celery. Chop 6 stalks of celery and add with the vinegar.

RED PEPPER JELLY

This very hot sauce adds zest to cocktail sauces or sandwich and canapé spreads.

Seed and put through a chopper

6 large hot red peppers

Cover with cold water, bring to the boiling point, boil 5 minutes, and drain off the water thoroughly. Add

1 lemon, quartered and seeded
Vinegar (enough to cover)

Cook 30 minutes. Add

1½ cups sugar

Boil 10 minutes. Remove the lemon. *Makes four 6-ounce jars.*

RED CABBAGE PICKLE

Mix well and let stand overnight

2 teaspoons salt
2 small heads red cabbage, sliced thin (about 2 quarts)

Drain. Add

¼ teaspoon pepper
2 tablespoons mustard seed

Mix well. Mix

1 quart mild vinegar
½ cup sugar
2 tablespoons mixed pickling spices (in spice bag)

Bring slowly to the boiling point and pour, boiling hot, over the cabbage. *Makes 3 pints.*

PICCALILLI

Put through a chopper, using the coarse knife

5 green tomatoes
5 green peppers
2 sweet red peppers
5 onions, peeled
1 small cabbage, quartered

Sprinkle with

¼ cup salt

Cover and let stand overnight. Cover with cold water and drain. Add

3 cups brown sugar
1½ teaspoons celery seed
1 tablespoon mustard seed
1 tablespoon whole cloves
2-inch piece of stick cinnamon
1 tablespoon allspice berries
2 cups mild cider vinegar

Bring to the boiling point and cook slowly 15 minutes. *Makes 4 pints.*

GREEN TOMATO RELISH

Mix

2 quarts chopped green tomatoes
¾ cup salt

Cover, let stand 24 hours, and drain. Add

1 teaspoon pepper
1½ teaspoons mustard
1½ teaspoons cinnamon
½ teaspoon allspice
1½ teaspoons ground cloves
¼ cup white mustard seed
1 quart mild cider vinegar
2 red *or* green peppers, sliced
1 chopped onion

Bring to the boiling point and cook 15 minutes. *Makes 4 pints.*

SWEET TOMATO RELISH

Mix

2 quarts chopped green tomatoes
2 chopped green peppers
2 cups chopped onion
1 pint vinegar
¼ cup salt
3 cups sugar
½ cup mixed pickling spices (in bag)

Bring to the boiling point and cook slowly 30 minutes, stirring occasionally. Remove the spice bag. *Makes 4 pints.*

CHILI SAUCE

Increase the amount of spices if you like, but spices darken the sauce.

Put in a saucepan

8 cups peeled tomatoes, cut in pieces (about 12)

Cook slowly 1 hour. Put through a chopper

1 green pepper
1 onion

Add to the tomatoes. Cook 30 minutes. Add

½ cup sugar
1 tablespoon salt
½ teaspoon pepper
1 teaspoon cinnamon
1 teaspoon ground cloves
½ teaspoon allspice
1 teaspoon nutmeg
1 cup mild vinegar

Boil until thick (about 10 minutes). *Makes 3 pints.*

Sweet Chili Sauce. Chop 1 large tart apple with the pepper and onion. Increase the sugar to 1 cup.

TOMATO SOY

Mix

4 quarts sliced red tomatoes
2 onions, peeled and chopped
¼ cup salt

Let stand 24 hours and drain.

Add

¼ cup whole mixed spices (in a bag)
1 pint mild vinegar

Cook slowly 2 hours. Add

1 cup sugar
2 tablespoons white mustard seed

Cook 5 minutes. Remove the spice bag. *Makes 3 pints.*

RIPE TOMATO RELISH

Peel, chop and measure tomatoes to make

3 pints pulp

Add

1 cup chopped celery
4 tablespoons chopped red pepper
4 tablespoons chopped onion
4 tablespoons salt
6 tablespoons sugar
6 tablespoons mustard seed
1 tablespoon grated nutmeg
1 teaspoon cinnamon
½ teaspoon ground cloves
2 cups vinegar

Put in a stone jar and cover. Let stand at least 1 week before using. This uncooked mixture will keep 6 months. *Makes about 4 pints.*

TOMATO SAUCE

Put through a chopper

3 bunches celery (roots and leaves removed)
4 seeded green peppers
2 peeled onions

Add

12 large tomatoes, peeled and cut in pieces
2 tablespoons salt
2 tablespoons sugar
3 cups vinegar

Simmer until thick (about 1½ hours). *Makes 2 or 3 pints.*

TOMATO CATSUP

Peel and chop

10 pounds ripe tomatoes
3 onions
2 sweet red peppers, seeded

Add, if liked

½ clove garlic

Cook slowly until soft. Put through a fine sieve. Simmer until reduced one-half (about 30 minutes). Add, putting the whole spices in a spice bag

¾ cup brown sugar
2-inch stick cinnamon
1 teaspoon peppercorns
1 teaspoon whole cloves
1 teaspoon allspice berries
1 teaspoon celery seed
1 cup vinegar
1 tablespoon salt
2 teaspoons paprika
¼ teaspoon cayenne

Cook slowly until very thick. Stir frequently. Remove the spice bag. *Makes 3 or 4 pints.*

GRAPE CATSUP

Wash and crush in a saucepan

5 pounds ripe Concord grapes

Simmer until soft. Press through a sieve or vegetable mill, discarding skins and seeds. Add

3 pounds sugar
1 pint mild vinegar
1 tablespoon cinnamon
1 tablespoon allspice
1 tablespoon ground cloves
½ teaspoon salt
1 tablespoon pepper

Bring to the boiling point and simmer until as thick as liked (30 minutes or more). *Makes about 4 pints.*

To make in electric blender. Put the stemmed grapes in the blender and chop 30 seconds. Put through a sieve or vegetable mill to strain out the seeds. Continue as above.

PLUM CATSUP

Put in a saucepan

5 pounds plums
3 tart apples, quartered but not peeled or cored
2 cups vinegar

Cook until the fruit is tender. Put through a food mill. Add

4 cups brown sugar

3 tablespoons cinnamon
2 teaspoons powdered cloves
2 teaspoons salt
½ teaspoon mace
Cook until thick. *Makes 5 pints.*

MUSTARD PICKLE

Wash and prepare
1 quart small pickling cucumbers
1 quart cubed cucumbers (3 large)
1 quart green tomatoes, cut small
1 quart button onions, peeled
4 sweet green peppers, cut fine
1 large cauliflower, cut in small pieces
Mix
2 cups salt
4 quarts water
Pour over the vegetables. Let stand overnight. Bring to the boiling point and drain in a colander. Mix
1 cup flour
6 tablespoons dry mustard
1 tablespoon turmeric
Stir in
Enough vinegar to make a smooth paste
Add
2 cups sugar
Vinegar (2 quarts in all)
Boil until thick and smooth, stirring constantly. Add the vegetables and cook until they are just heated through. Overcooking makes them soft instead of crisp. Pour into jars and seal immediately. *Makes 8 pints.*

PICKLED FRUITS

Mix in a saucepan
1 cup vinegar
1 cup water
1 cup brown sugar
1 cup white sugar
1 tablespoon cloves
1 stick cinnamon, broken in pieces
Boil 5 minutes. Add the prepared fruit (see below), a little at a time, and simmer until tender. Lift out the fruit with a skimmer and pack into jars. Add hot syrup to within ¼ inch of the top, preparing more syrup if necessary.

Pickled Crabapples. Do not pare. Cut out the blossom end. Prick several times. *10 to 15 make a pint.*

Pickled Kumquats. Cover with salted water (1 tablespoon salt to each quart water). Let stand 24 hours. Rinse, cover with water, and boil 30 minutes. Drain, add fresh water, and cook until the kumquats are tender. Cook in the syrup until translucent.

Pickled Peaches. Dip in boiling water, then in cold, and slip off the skins. Cut freestone peaches in half and remove the pits. Leave clingstone peaches whole.

Pickled Pears. Use firm, slightly underripe fruit. Pare large fruit, cut in halves or quarters, and remove the cores. Remove the blossom end from Seckel pears, pare or not, and prick well. Use white vinegar to prevent darkening.

CHERRY OLIVES

Piquant with cocktails or salad.

Pack closely in two pint jars
1 quart sour cherries, washed but not stemmed
Add to each jar
1½ teaspoons salt
½ cup vinegar
Fill the jars with cold water. Seal and turn upside down. Let stand 2 weeks before using. *Makes 2 pints.*

Sweet Cherry Olives. Add 1½ teaspoons sugar to each jar. Large white cherries are especially delicious this way.

PICKLED CHERRIES

Pit firm sour cherries. Cover with vinegar. Let stand overnight. Drain and weigh. Put in a stone crock and add an equal weight of sugar. Cover. Stir daily until the sugar is entirely dissolved (7 or 8 days).

SPICED CURRANTS

Wash and drain
1½ pounds currants
Remove the stems. Add
1 pound brown sugar
½ cup mild cider vinegar
½-inch piece of stick cinnamon *or* 1 teaspoon cinnamon
1 teaspoon powdered cloves
1 teaspoon allspice (if liked)
Heat to the boiling point. Cook slowly 1 hour. Remove the cinnamon stick if used. *Makes about five 6-ounce glasses.*

Gooseberry Catsup. Use 2 pounds gooseberries in place of currants. Cook about 2 hours.

SPICED RHUBARB

Mix in a saucepan
2½ pounds young pink rhubarb in 1-inch pieces
2 pounds sugar
1 cup mild cider vinegar
1 teaspoon cinnamon
½ teaspoon ground cloves
Bring to the boiling point and simmer until as thick as marmalade. *Makes five or six 6-ounce glasses.*

WATERMELON PICKLE

Lime water makes crisper pickles than salt water. Buy lime (calcium oxide) at the drugstore.

Cut watermelon rind in 5- or 6-inch pieces. Cover with boiling water. Boil 5 minutes, drain and cool. Cut off the tough green skin and most of the pink pulp. Cut the rind in small squares or wedges or in fancy shapes with a tiny cooky cutter. Weigh or measure. Cover with salted water (½ cup to each quart of water) or lime water (2 tablespoons lime to each quart of water). Let stand 6 hours in salted water or 3 in lime water. Drain, rinse and cover with fresh water. Simmer until tender. Drain. Add to Pickling Syrup (below). Simmer until the rind is clear and the syrup thick, adding water if necessary. Remove the spice bag. Pack in jars and seal.

PICKLING SYRUP

For a spicier syrup, add 1 tablespoon allspice berries and/or a piece of gingerroot.

Put in a deep saucepan
1 quart vinegar
1 cup water
2 pounds sugar (or more)
Tie in a piece of cheesecloth
1 tablespoon whole cloves
1 stick cinnamon (1 ounce), broken in pieces
Add to the syrup. Simmer until the sugar dissolves. *Enough for about 2 pounds (or 1½ to 2 quarts) of fruit.*

PICKLED CANTALOUPE *or* CITRON MELON

Peel, cut in half and remove the seeds. Cut the flesh in cubes. Cook in Pickling Syrup (above) and pack in jars.

PICKLED BEETS

Cook until tender
4 bunches young beets
Plunge into cold water and slip off the skins. Leave tiny beets whole. Slice larger ones. Mix in a saucepan
1 quart vinegar
1½ cups sugar
½ teaspoon allspice berries
1 stick cinnamon
1 teaspoon whole cloves

Add the beets. Simmer 15 minutes. Pack the beets in clean hot jars. Fill the jars with the hot syrup. Seal. Process 20 minutes in a boiling water bath (p. 551).

PICKLED ONIONS

Peel small white onions. Cover with brine, allowing 1½ cups salt to 2 quarts boiling water. Let stand 2 days. Drain and cover with more brine. Let stand 2 days and again drain. Make more brine and heat to the boiling point. Put in the onions and boil 3 minutes. Put the onions in clean hot jars, mixing in bits of mace, white peppercorns, cloves, bits of bay leaf and slices of pimiento. Fill the jars to overflowing with vinegar heated with sugar (1 cup sugar to 1 gallon vinegar). Seal while hot.

To vary, add, for each gallon of vinegar, 1 ounce gingerroot or ¼ cup freshly grated horseradish. Other seasonings may be substituted for the combination suggested above, such as basil, nutmeg, celery seed, chili peppers, mustard seed, dill, chervil and rosemary.

HORSERADISH

Scrape horseradish roots and drop into cold water to prevent discoloration. Drain and put through a food chopper or crush in an electric blender. Fill clean, cold pint jars about two-thirds full. Add 1 teaspoon salt to each jar and fill with white vinegar. Seal.

Canning

Fashions in food preservation are changing rapidly. Markets offer a variety of fresh and frozen fruits and vegetables throughout the year. Modern apartments and houses often lack the cool, dry, dark cupboards needed for keeping home-canned foods in the best condition. Freezing is a simpler and safer process, and more and more families own freezers. Commercially canned foods are often better than homemade, unless you have a garden of your own or are near a source of freshly picked high-quality produce.

USING CANNED GOODS

Inspect commercial or home-canned foods carefully, and discard if there are indications of spoilage—"off" odor, color or texture, or cloudiness or sediment in the liquid. **Molds** are the result of incorrect processing, broken seal or contact of the food with equipment that is not completely sterilized (jars, tops, spoons, cloth, etc.). A light mold on fruits, tomatoes and rhubarb is not thought to affect the rest of the jar, but discard any food with a heavy mold.

Flat-sour may develop in products picked warm and canned on hot muggy days or stored too quickly where air cannot circulate around the jars. It may also result from canning too large a quantity at one time.

Do not throw away the liquid from the jar, since many vitamins are soluble in water. To serve it with the vegetable, pour off the liquid and boil it down until there is very little left, then add the vegetable and heat. If the liquid is not to be served with the vegetables or meat, store it in a jar and use it in soup or gravy.

PREPARING JARS FOR CANNING

Large-mouthed jars are easy to fill. Use jars with vacuum-seal metal covers (new covers for each canning) or with rubber rings and (1) solid metal screw tops, (2) glass tops and two bails or (3) glass tops and screw bands. Use new rubber rings each time.

Inspect the jars carefully and discard any with even a tiny nick. Run your finger around the edge to detect nicks or cracks. **Test rubber-ring jars** for leakage by half filling with hot water, sealing and inverting. **Test jar rubbers** by folding double and pressing firmly: a good rubber does not crack. Scrub thoroughly and rinse. **Wash** the jars thoroughly and rinse. Keep the jars, tops and rubbers in warm water until ready to fill.

FILLING THE JARS

Dip a tested rubber ring in hot water and fit it in place on the jar. Set a wide funnel on the jar. Pack to within ½ inch of the top. Pack vegetables loosely, especially corn, peas and shell beans. Press tomatoes down to squeeze out extra juice. Pack fruits as tightly as possible without crushing. If fruit has been precooked, lift it out of the syrup, pack in the jar and add the liquid to within ½ inch of the top. Tomatoes need only their own juice. Add ½ teaspoon salt for each pint of vegetables. Run a knife down into the jar to release any air bubbles. Wipe off the rim or rubbers.

To close. Dip the cover in hot water and set on the jar. If you are using a vacuum-seal cover, put on the screw band and screw gently but firmly into place, but do not force. Partially seal other jars: (1) Bail type. Put the upper bail in place, but leave the other one loose. (2) Screw top or band. Screw until resistance is felt, then turn back a quarter turn.

PROCESSING THE FILLED JARS

(Follow manufacturer's directions in using a pressure canner.)

Put the rack to hold the jars in a boiling water bath canner and fill with enough water so that it will be 1 inch deep above the tops of the jars. If you do not have a special canner, use a large covered kettle or a wash-boiler and put a rack or a pad of towels or paper in the bottom. If you use a pressure canner for this method, leave the petcock open.

Let the water heat to simmering while you prepare the fruit and fill the jars. As each jar is filled and closed, lower it carefully into the canner. Allow ½ inch between the jars for good circulation of water. When most of the jars are in place, increase the heat so that the water will boil quickly. After all the jars are added, bring the water to a full rolling boil and begin counting the processing time. Keep the water boiling steadily during the whole processing time.

REMOVING JARS FROM THE CANNER

Lift out the jars. Do not disturb the covers or bands on vacuum-seal jars. On all jars using rubbers, complete the seal by (1) lowering the other bail or (2) screwing the covers or bands tightly. Set on a wooden rack or a pad of towels or newspapers out of a draft. Do not invert. After 24 hours, check the seal on all jars. To check, remove the screw-bands or bails and lift by the lid; if the lid is loose, the seal is not firm. Reprocess or use the food immediately. Test zinc cover jars by inverting; if there is leakage, the seal is not tight.

Wipe the jars, label and store in a dark dry place, cool but not freezing.

SYRUP FOR CANNING AND FREEZING FRUIT

Cook the sugar and water together until the sugar dissolves. Add to the jar **boiling hot.** Syrup is added for flavor and to keep fruit firmer but fruit will keep perfectly canned in its own juice or in boiling water.

Thin syrup	1 cup sugar to 3 cups water
Medium syrup	1 cup sugar to 2 cups water
Heavy syrup	1 cup sugar to 1 cup water

CANNING FRUITS AND TOMATOES

Select clean, sound, fully ripe fruit. If it is to be canned whole or in halves, it should be uniform in size. Wash it thoroughly and prepare according to the directions below. Prepare only enough for one canner load at a time. Keep the rest in the refrigerator.

To keep apples, apricots and peaches from darkening, drop the pieces as you prepare them into water containing 1 tablespoon each of salt and vinegar to 2 quarts of water.

Pack the prepared fruit into jars, add syrup (p. 551), if used, adjust the lids and process the required time. For details, see page 551. Fruit and tomatoes contain enough acid so that they can be processed safely in a boiling water bath canner.

Apples (2½ to 3 pounds for a quart jar). Pare, core and cut in pieces. Boil 5 minutes in thin syrup or water. *Process pints 15 minutes, quarts 20.*

Applesauce. Prepare as usual. Heat to simmering and pack into jars within ¼ inch of the top. *Process 10 minutes.*

Apricots (2 or 3 pounds for a quart jar). Cut in half and remove pits. Simmer in syrup until tender. *Process pints 20 minutes, quarts 25.*

Blueberries (2 quarts for about 3 pint jars). Put in a square of cheesecloth. Gather up the corners of the cloth to form a bag and dip into a kettle of boiling water. After 15 seconds, remove from the water. If no spots of juice show on the cloth, dip again. Plunge into cold water, drain and pack tightly into jars. *Process pints 16 minutes.*

Cherries (2 to 2½ pounds for a quart jar if pits are removed). Stem and pit or not. Pack in jars and cover with syrup to within ½ inch of the top. *Process pints 20 minutes, quarts 25.* Or add ½ cup sugar to each quart of cherries (more for sour cherries) and heat slowly to the boiling point. *Process 10 minutes.*

Peaches (2 to 3 pounds for a quart jar). Dip in boiling water, then in cold, and remove the skins. Cut in half and remove the pits. Slice or not. Heat thoroughly in hot syrup. If the peaches are very juicy, heat with sugar instead of syrup until the sugar dissolves. *Process pints 20 minutes, quarts 25.*

Pears (2 to 3 pounds for a quart jar). Peel and core, cut in half or leave whole with the stems on. Heat thoroughly in hot syrup. *Process pints 20 minutes, quarts 25.*

Pineapple (2 pounds for a quart jar). Cut in ½-inch slices. Pare and cut out the core. Simmer in syrup until tender. *Process 20 minutes.*

Plums (1½ to 2½ pounds for a quart jar). Prick the skins if you are canning plums whole. Cut freestone plums in half and remove the pits. Heat to the boiling point in syrup or in sugar, if the plums are very juicy. *Process pints 20 minutes, quarts 25.*

Raspberries and Blackberries (1½ quarts for a quart jar). Remove caps and stems. Fill jars to within ½ inch of the top. Shake the berries down so that the jar will be full. Cover with boiling syrup to within ½ inch of the top. *Process pints 10 minutes, quarts 15.*

Rhubarb (1½ pounds for a pint jar). Cut in ½-inch pieces.

Measure and add ½ cup sugar for each quart. Let stand 30 minutes to draw out the juice and bring to the boiling point. *Process 10 minutes.*

Strawberries do not can successfully. Use them for jam.

Tomatoes (3 pounds for a quart jar; 1 bushel for 18 quarts). Dip in boiling water, then in cold to loosen the skins. Cut out the stem and the white core, if there is any. Peel and leave whole or cut in pieces. Press firmly into the jars. Add ½ teaspoon salt for each pint. Add no water. *Process pints 35 minutes, quarts 45. Or quarter peeled tomatoes, cook in their own juice to the boiling point, add salt and process 10 minutes.*

CANNING FRUIT JUICES

Canned juices are delicious as the basis for fruit drinks or sauces or as the liquid for jellied salads or dessert. Can juices without sugar to make up into fresh jellies during the winter as you need them.

Extract the juice as for jelly (p. 532) and sweeten or not. Fill jars to ¼ inch from the top, adjust the lids and process in a boiling water bath canner 5 minutes. Tighten the seal, label and store.

Spiced Blackberry Juice. Crush 2 quarts berries. Add 1 teaspoon each of allspice and whole cloves, 1 stick cinnamon and a whole nutmeg. Add ½ cup water and simmer 30 minutes, or put in a pressure saucepan, bring to 15 pounds pressure, remove from the heat, and let the pressure drop to normal. Strain. Add ½ cup sugar and bring to the boiling point. Put in jars and process. Use to add color and flavor to a summer punch or to hot mulled cider for a winter drink. *Makes about 1½ pints.*

Grape Juice. Wash and stem perfect grapes. Extract the juice (p. 532). Strain. Let stand in the refrigerator overnight. Carefully pour off the juice, discarding the dregs. Add ½ cup sugar for each quart of juice and boil 20 minutes.

Raspberry Juice. Crush raspberries and extract the juice (p. 532). Add sugar to taste and bring to the boiling point.

Rhubarb Juice. To extract the juice, see page 532.

TOMATO JUICE

Wash and drain firm, fresh ripe tomatoes. Cut out the stems, white cores and any soft spots. Cut small and simmer in small quantities until soft enough to put through a sieve or food mill. Add 1 teaspoon salt for each quart of juice. Reheat at once just to the boiling point. Fill jars to within ¼ inch of the top. Process pints or quarts in a boiling water bath 10 minutes (p. 551).

Vary by adding sugar and spices to taste.

SAVORY TOMATO JUICE

Delicious for tomato juice cocktail, tomato aspic or soup.

Cut in pieces into a saucepan

- **½ bushel tomatoes**
- **10 large carrots**
- **4 large green peppers**
- **4 large onions**
- **½ pound green beans**
- **3 kohlrabi**
- **1 bunch celery**
- **1 bunch parsley**

Cook until soft. Rub through a

food mill or a colander. Season to taste with

Salt, pepper and Worcestershire

Fill jars, process 5 minutes (p. 551), label and store. *Makes 12 quarts.*

CANNING VEGETABLES

Processing in a pressure canner is the only method approved for canning vegetables. If you use a pressure saucepan, add 20 minutes to the recommended processing time because a pressure saucepan cools quickly.

Select young tender vegetables of the same size and ripeness. Can as soon as possible after gathering, preferably within two hours.

Wash the vegetables thoroughly and prepare as directed below. Prepare only enough for one canner load at a time. Keep the rest in the refrigerator.

Cover with boiling water and boil 5 minutes. Drain and pack in hot jars. Add ½ teaspoon salt for each pint jar. Fill to within ½ inch of the top with boiling water.

Seal and process (p. 551).

Cool, label and store in a cool, dry, dark place.

The vegetables listed below are the ones most commonly canned. For canning other vegetables, see state or government bulletins or the booklets issued by the manufacturers of canning jars. **Broccoli, Brussels sprouts, cabbage, cauliflower, kohlrabi, onions and turnips** are apt to discolor when canned.

Asparagus (1½ pounds for a pint jar). Trim off the scales and tough ends. Leave whole or cut in 1-inch pieces. *Process pints 25 minutes, quarts 30.*

Beans, green or wax (¾ pound for a pint jar). Snip off the ends. Leave whole or cut in 1-inch pieces. *Process pints 20 minutes, quarts 23.*

Beets (1 to 1½ pounds for a pint jar). Cut off the tops, leaving 1-inch stems. Cook in boiling water 15 minutes. Dip in cold water and peel. Leave baby beets whole. Slice or dice larger beets. *Process pints 25 minutes, quarts 35.*

Corn (4 to 6 ears for a pint jar). Use only pint jars. Prepare only 2 or 3 dozen ears at a time and work quickly. Husk, remove silk and wash. For whole-kernel corn, cut off the kernels but do not scrape the cobs. For cream-style corn, use a corn scraper or cut off only the tips of the kernels and scrape the cob. Cover the soft pulp with boiling water (1 pint to 1 quart of corn) and bring to the boiling point. Pack whole-kernel corn to within 1 inch of the top and fill the jars with boiling water. Pack cream-style corn to within ½ inch of the top. Add ½ teaspoon salt to each jar. *Process whole-kernel corn 55 minutes, cream-style corn 85 minutes.*

Lima beans (2 pounds in the shell for a pint jar). Can only young limas. Shell. *Process pints 40 minutes, quarts 50.*

Peas (2 pounds in the shell for a pint jar). Shell. Can in pints only. *Process 40 minutes.*

GARDEN SPECIAL

A tasty basis for vegetable soup or to use in a meat stew, or a casserole dish with hamburg or chopped meat combined with cooked rice, spaghetti or potatoes, or as a sauce with fish. See also Jellied Garden Special (p. 293).

Put in a deep kettle

6 sweet peppers, green *or* red, cut in pieces and seeded
1 quart diced onions
1 quart diced celery, coarse stalks and leaves included
1 quart water *or* tomato juice

Cook 20 minutes. Add

4 quarts ripe tomatoes, peeled and quartered
3 tablespoons salt
2 tablespoons sugar
½ teaspoon pepper

Bring to a boil and put into hot jars. Process (p. 551) in boiling water 40 minutes for quarts, 30 minutes for pints. *Makes 10 to 12 pints.*

Freezing

Freezing is a simpler process than canning and it also preserves color, texture and flavor more successfully. As a result, more and more families own freezers, and even kitchenette cooks are finding many ways to use refrigerator freezer compartments. Freezers save shopping time and money by making it possible to take advantage of special bargains and quantity buying. Another big attraction is that much of the cooking for holiday and company meals can be out of the way days or even weeks in advance.

GENERAL DIRECTIONS

Select and prepare foods for freezing according to the special directions which follow.

Freeze as soon as possible after preparation. Speed is essential to success in freezing. Foods keep best if they are frozen quickly at 0° or below and stored at 0° or below as well. Higher temperatures may cause undesirable changes in flavor, texture and color. The temperature in the freezer compartment of a refrigerator usually fluctuates since the door is opened and closed frequently. For this reason a freezer compartment is principally useful for storing commercially frozen products and leftovers to be used within a short time.

If you use a community freezer locker, keep the food packed in ice until you take it to be frozen at the locker.

Bulletins from the United States Department of Agriculture as well as state publications and freezer booklets have many useful suggestions about freezing and give recommendations as to local varieties of fruits and vegetables which are especially suited to freezing.

Follow the manufacturer's directions for your freezer cabinet.

If you are freezing a large quantity of food at one time, set the freezer at −10°, so that the temperature will not rise too much when all the food is added. Have all packages touch the freezer walls during freezing, but leave some space around the packages for circulation of air. Foods must freeze quickly, so do not overload the freezer.

FREEZER CONTAINERS

Proper wrapping prolongs the storage life of hard-to-keep foods. Containers especially made for freezing are moistureproof and vaporproof. Select the size that will contain enough for only one meal for your family so that you will not have leftovers. Frozen food is never so delicious when reheated and should never be refrozen. Glass jars, designed especially for freezing, are excellent, especially for cooked foods. Round jars or packages take up more room than square ones.

Allow for expansion of food during freezing. Leave at least ½ inch head space in packages (1 to 1½ inches in glass). Packages which are too full will bulge and may open at the seams.

Label and date each package and use those with the earliest dates first.

FREEZING FRUIT

Freeze only fully ripe, freshly picked fruits in perfect condition. Berries, peaches and cherries keep their natural goodness especially well. Allow 1½ to 1⅔ cups of prepared fruit for a 1-pint carton.

Prepare syrup (p. 551) if the fruit requires it, and chill in the refrigerator.

Prepare the fruit for freezing (below).

Pack in containers, using sizes according to your plan for using the fruit—as for sauce, pie filling or ice cream topping, or for making jam or jelly. Add sugar or syrup, if used. Pack fruits mixed with sugar or syrup in leakproof containers. Leave ¾ inch headway, but fill the space with crumpled cellophane or wax paper to keep the fruit covered with syrup so that it will not lose its attractive color.

To keep the fresh color of peaches, apricots, cherries and plums, add to each cup of syrup ¼ teaspoon ascorbic acid crystals dissolved in 2 teaspoons cold water.

Label, giving contents and date.

Freeze at 0° or below. Put the packages into the freezer as soon as they are filled.

PREPARING FRUIT FOR FREEZING

Wash quickly but thoroughly. Discard imperfect berries and cut blemishes from large fruit.

Apples, baked: Chill. Pack in containers, separating from one another with cellophane.

Apples for pie: Peel, core, and slice directly into cold water enough apples for 1 pie. Drain, steam 2 minutes, and pack immediately into a plastic bag. To prevent darkening, sprinkle with ascorbic acid crystals or sugar (½ cup for 1 pint). Put immediately into the freezer. Repeat until all are used.

Applesauce: Cook as usual. Chill.

Apricots: Follow directions for peaches.

Blackberries, boysenberries, dewberries, loganberries: Freeze only fully ripe berries. **For dessert,** pack in *heavy syrup.* **For jam, pie or sauce,** mix 6 cups of fruit with 1 cup of sugar. Turn berries over and over until most of the sugar dissolves. Or pack without sugar. **For fruit purée,** crush berries, mix with 1 cup sugar to 8 cups berries, and stir until the sugar dissolves.

Blueberries, elderberries, huckleberries: Discard the stems. **For dessert,** crush slightly, pack in Medium Syrup (p. 551). **For pie, sauce, jelly or jam,** freeze without sugar, or use 1 cup sugar to 6 cups fruit, stirring until the sugar is dissolved.

Cherries sour: Stem and pit. **For dessert,** cover with Heavy Syrup (p. 551). **For pie and cooked desserts,** use 1 cup sugar to 1 quart cherries, stirring until the sugar is dissolved.

Cherries, sweet: Stem and pit, or leave whole. Work quickly so that the fruit will not darken. Cover with Heavy Syrup (p. 551) to which ascorbic acid crystals have been added (p. 557). A mixture of sour and sweet cherries is delicious.

Cranberries: Stem. Freeze whole without sugar.

Currants: Stem. Freeze whole, without sugar, or use 1 cup sugar to 1 quart currants, stirring until most of the sugar dissolves.

Gooseberries: Snip off both ends. For pie or preserves, freeze without sugar. Or crush slightly and mix with 1 cup sugar to 1 quart berries.

Grapefruit, lemons, oranges: Valencias are the best oranges for freezing. Peel. Divide into sections and remove all membranes and seeds. Pack in containers and cover with Heavy Syrup (p. 551) made with fruit juice instead of water, and with ascorbic acid crystals added (p. 557).

Peaches: Select perfect tree-ripened peaches. Keep at room temperature 2 or 3 days after picking. Peel one peach at a time and halve, quarter or slice directly into cartons. Cover completely with Medium or Heavy Syrup (p. 551). Freeze immediately and store at 0° or below, never higher.

Pears: Pears do not freeze well.

Pineapple: Pare and cube. Pack without added sugar, or with 1 part sugar to 4 fruit, or cover with Heavy Syrup (p. 551).

Plums, prunes: Cut in half and remove pits. Cover with Heavy Syrup containing ascorbic acid (p. 557).

Raspberries: If dusty, wash quickly in ice water. Cover with Medium or Heavy Syrup (p. 551). Or carefully mix 1 quart berries with 3/4 cup sugar. They may also be picked from the bushes directly into the freezing cartons and frozen without sugar.

Rhubarb: Early spring rhubarb freezes best. Cut into 1-inch lengths and make into sauce. Or pack and cover with Medium or Heavy Syrup (p. 551). Or freeze without cooking or adding sugar.

Strawberries: Wash in ice water and remove caps. Cut in half or slice into containers and cover with cold Medium or Heavy Syrup (p. 551). Or mix berries with sugar (3/4 cup to 1 quart berries). Stir to dissolve the sugar.

FREEZING VEGETABLES

Vegetables are at their best when young and tender, such as tiny green beans, sweet juicy peas, baby carrots and beets. Vegetables which do not freeze well are those usually served raw and ones with high water content like lettuce, cucumbers and fresh tomatoes.

The shorter the time from garden to freezer the better. If you cannot freeze vegetables immediately, keep them in the refrigerator until you are ready to prepare them.

Prepare for freezing according to the directions which follow.

Scald to retain fresh color and flavor, to save freezer space and to reduce the number of bacteria. Scald only small amounts at a time so that the water will return to the boiling point in no more than 1 minute after the vegetable is put in.

Have ready a large kettle of rapidly boiling water. Put the

prepared vegetable in a basket or a piece of cheesecloth. Lower into the water, lift up and down so that the vegetable is heated evenly. Scald the required time according to the table below, counting the time as soon as the vegetable is put into the kettle.

Chill. Remove the scalded vegetable from the kettle and chill immediately under running cold water or in ice water. Drain.

Pack in the freezer containers. Press down firmly to force out air, which tends to dry out the vegetable. Leave a little head space because packages that are too full tend to bulge. Too much head space may cause the food to dry out. No exact rule can be given for all vegetables—one must learn by trial and error.

Label, stating the date and the method of preparation, or keep a freezer record so that you can make changes the next time if you like.

Freeze at 0° or below. Put each package into the freezer as soon as it is filled.

PREPARING VEGETABLES

Wash thoroughly, removing every trace of garden grit or soil. Use a brush on solid vegetables, and wash spinach and other leafy or delicate vegetables in warm sudsy water, with all particles of soap or detergent completely dissolved. Rinse thoroughly in clear water. Cut off coarse stems and outer leaves.

Cut or sort the pieces so that they will be about the same size.

Artichokes: Pull off the outer leaves. Cut off ½ inch of the top. Trim the stem. Wash. *Scald 8 to 10 minutes in a solution of 3 teaspoons citric acid crystals to 2 quarts water.*

Asparagus: Do not freeze exceptionally thick or thin stalks. Discard tough ends. Remove scales. Cut stalks to fit package or cut in 1-inch pieces. *Scald 4 minutes.*

Beans, lima: Shell and sort, removing those that are too old. *Scald 3 minutes.*

Beans, snap: Sort, wash and snip off the stem end. Cut into short lengths or lengthwise, French style. *Scald 2 minutes.*

Beans, shell, green: Shell. *Scald 1 minute.*

Beans, green soy: Scald 4 minutes in the pod. Cool and remove the beans by squeezing the pods.

Beets: Freeze only young tender beets. *Scald baby beets 2½ minutes* but cook beets more than 2 inches in diameter until tender. Chill, peel, leave whole (if tiny), slice or cube.

Broccoli: Wash carefully. Let stand ½ hour in salt water. Drain and cut off woody sections. Separate into uniform pieces for packaging. *Scald 3 minutes.*

Brussels sprouts: Let stand ½ hour in salt water. Drain. *Scald 4 minutes.*

Carrots: Scrape young carrots. Leave baby carrots whole. Cut larger ones in pieces. *Scald 3 minutes.*

Cauliflower: Divide into flowerets. *Scald white cauliflower 3 minutes in 1 gallon of boiling water with 2 teaspoons of powdered citric acid added to it. Scald purple cauliflower 3 minutes in plain water.*

Celery: Cut in 1-inch pieces. *Scald 4 minutes.*

Corn on the cob: Husk, wash, and sort in even sizes. *Scald small ears (1¼ inches in diameter) for 6 minutes, me-*

dium ears for 8, and large ears (over 2 inches at the large end) for 10 minutes. Chill, wrap in aluminum foil or put into plastic bags and freeze.

Corn, whole-kernel: Scald the corn on the cob 4 minutes. Chill. Cut the whole kernels from the cob, being careful not to include any of the cob.

Corn, cream-style: Scald corn as above. Cut off the upper part of the kernels, scraping the cobs with the knife to remove the juice and heart of the kernel. Leave ½ inch head space in the containers.

Eggplant: Peel. Cut in ⅓-inch slices. *Scald 4 minutes in 1 gallon of boiling water to which 2 teaspoons of ascorbic acid have been added.*

Greens (Beet and turnip tops, kale, mustard, spinach, Swiss chard): Wash leaves carefully to remove all grit. Discard injured leaves and tough stems. *Scald 2 minutes,* using 3 gallons of boiling water for a small amount of vegetable.

Kohlrabi: Cut off tops and roots. Wash, peel and dice, or leave whole if small. *Scald 1 minute.*

Mushrooms: Trim and slice. Cook small amounts at a time in butter (about 5 minutes). Cool.

Okra: Leave whole. *Scald small and medium-size pods 3 minutes, large ones 4 to 5 minutes.* Package in amounts needed for soup or to serve as a vegetable.

Parsley: Scald 15 seconds, chill and drain. Put into small envelopes, seal and freeze. (To use, chop while still frozen.)

Parsnips: Trim and slice. *Scald 3 minutes.*

Peas: Shell. *Scald 1 minute.*

Peppers: Cut in halves or slices. Pack in small amounts convenient to use. *Scald 2 minutes.*

Pimientos: Roast 4 minutes in a 400° oven. Rinse in cold water to remove the charred skins.

Potatoes, French-fried: Fry as usual. Chill by setting in a pan over ice. Reheat by spreading in a shallow pan in a 350° oven.

Potatoes, mashed: Raw potatoes soften when frozen, but mashed potatoes freeze well. Cool quickly by setting the cooking pan in ice. When reheating, add a topping of crumbs or grated cheese.

Potatoes, sweet: Cook until almost tender. Cool, peel and cut in halves or slices, or mash. To prevent darkening, mix 2 tablespoons orange or lemon juice with each quart of mashed potatoes. Sliced or whole sweet potatoes may be covered with Heavy Syrup (p. 551).

Pumpkin: Cook until soft, mash and cool.

Squash, summer: Cut young tender squash in ½-inch slices. *Scald 3 minutes.*

Squash, winter: Cook until soft, mash and cool. Pack.

Succotash: Prepare corn and lima beans separately. (*See scalding time for corn and beans above.*) Mix and pack.

FREEZING JUICES

Frozen juices may be the basis for refreshing drinks, jellied salad or desserts, or may be made into jellies at any convenient time. Frozen fruit juices are especially delicious if you serve them while there are still a few ice crystals in them—thaw the sealed container in the refrigerator 6 hours or more. Mix juices well to blend evenly.

Prepare the juice, chill if necessary and pour quickly into glass jars, leaving 1-inch head space. Seal and freeze.

Orange (Valencias are best), Lemon and Grapefruit Juice. Chill, squeeze by hand with a glass juicer and strain.

Other fruit juices and tomato juice. Extract as described on page 532. Freeze without processing.

FREEZING MEAT AND LARGE GAME

Young healthy animals furnish the best meat. Have the meat prepared at a frozen food locker plant for storing in a home freezer, or follow the directions in the bulletins issued by the United States Department of Agriculture or by state extension services.

Age or ripen some meats to improve tenderness and flavor. Store the carcasses at 32° to 38° before cutting in pieces for freezing. This may be done at the freezer plant or in a cool, dark, airy place. Age lean young beef and game 5 days, heavy beef 5 to 10 days, mutton 2 to 3 days. Do not age lamb, veal or pork.

Cured and smoked meats may be stored in the freezer if there is no other convenient storage place. Hams and bacon keep in good condition longer in solid pieces rather than sliced.

Cut in sizes convenient for family meals. Bone to save space in the freezer. If any bones are left in the meat, be sure there are no rough edges which might punch holes in the wrapping. Trim off excess fat.

Package by wrapping snugly (to eliminate air pockets) in heavy aluminum foil or special freezer paper. If more than one piece is put in a package (steaks, chops or ground meat patties), put sheets of cellophane or freezer wrap between them. Seal completely with freezer tape. Stockinette outer covers are not essential for home freezers, where the packages are handled less than in freezer plants.

Label each package, giving contents and date.

Freeze immediately at 0° or below. Space the packages so that air will circulate around them until they are hard-frozen.

Store in the freezer no longer than the recommended time. Fat or salty meats do not keep their flavor as well as fresh lean meat. Use sausage and ground meat within 3 months, fresh pork 3 to 6, lamb and veal 6 to 9, and beef 6 to 12.

Thaw or not before cooking, as convenient. Solidly frozen meats cook less evenly than thawed meats unless they are cooked very slowly. Leave meats in the freezer wrapping while thawing to avoid defrosting. Thaw in the refrigerator or at room temperature. Thaw sliced meat such as chops and steaks at room temperature for 30 minutes.

FREEZING POULTRY AND GAME BIRDS

Freeze the various sizes of chicken and turkey at the time of year when they are the most plentiful and therefore at the lowest price (spring for broilers, summer for fryers, fall for larger birds).

Have the birds prepared for freezing at a freezer plant, or follow the directions for slaughtering, cleaning and dressing in the bulletins issued by the United States Department of Agriculture or by the state extension services.

Prepare the birds according to the way you plan to cook them.

Cut-up chickens take less freezer space than whole birds. (If the bird is to be roasted whole, remove most of the body fat, wrap the giblets and neck in freezer paper and place the package inside the bird.)

Do not stuff birds. Split broilers and pack with two pieces of freezer paper between the halves. Chill at least 12 hours before freezing.

Package, freeze, and store like meat (p. 561).

Thaw slowly to keep the flesh moist. Defrost in the refrigerator at room temperature (2½ hours for broilers and other small birds, 5½ hours for roasters, 8 hours for a 10-pound turkey). To shorten the time, place on the kitchen table in front of an electric fan.

FREEZING FISH

Fish should be frozen the day it is caught. For complete information, follow the directions in United States Government bulletins.

Prepare fish as if to cook immediately. Cut large fish in fillets or steaks.

Pack fatty fish (bonito, butterfish, herring, mackerel, salmon, shad, tuna and whitefish) immediately and freeze. Put all other fish in salt water (1 cup salt to 1 gallon of water) and let it stand 30 seconds. Drain and wrap in freezer paper.

Use within 3 months for best flavor and texture.

Thaw before cooking only enough to separate the pieces (about 45 minutes at room temperature or 3 to 4 hours in the refrigerator).

FREEZING SHELLFISH

To prepare, wash shucked oysters or clams in salt water (1½ tablespoons to 1 quart) and drain. Pick over cooked shrimp, lobster meat or crab meat, removing bits of shell.

Pack in freezer cartons.

Thaw slowly, for the best flavor, (6 hours in the refrigerator or 2 hours at room temperature).

Use cooked shellfish within a month—it toughens if stored too long.

FREEZING DAIRY PRODUCTS

Butter or margarine. Wrap in freezer paper or leave in store wrapper. Unsalted butter keeps longer than salted butter. Thaw in the refrigerator.

Cheese. Freeze in small packages, as cheese that has been frozen dries out rapidly after thawing.

Heavy cream. Freeze whipped or not.

FREEZING EGGS

Freeze only perfect fresh eggs. Do not freeze cracked eggs. Break the eggs and mix lightly with a fork or pack the whites and yolks separately. Put the amount in each carton which will be needed at one time. Yolks packed alone will coagulate unless mixed with salt, sugar, honey or corn syrup. For 6 yolks, add 1 teaspoon salt or 2 tablespoons sugar, honey or corn syrup. Whites need nothing added and are as satisfactory for making angel cakes as fresh whites.

FREEZING ICE CREAM AND SHERBETS

Freeze only smooth velvety ice cream made in a crank freezer.

French-type ice creams (p. 416) freeze well. Pack in freezer cartons and cover snugly with a piece of cellophane cut to fit to help prevent crystals. Close the carton.

Fruit sherbets made with gelatine (p. 414) keep well in a freezer. Commercial ice creams do not keep well more than 2 or 3 weeks in a home freezer.

FREEZING BREAD, CAKE, COOKIES AND PASTRY

Save fuel and time by baking more than enough for one meal and freezing the rest. Baked foods retain their full flavor, color and oven freshness from 4 to 12 months. Fruit cake, mince pies and fruit cookies will keep even longer.

Unbaked doughs and batters lose some of their leavening power after a few weeks. For the best results use within 1 month. Cooky and pie doughs keep several months.

Freeze packaged baked foods in their sealed wrappers if you plan to use them within a week. If they are to be kept longer, wrap them again in moistureproof and vaporproof paper.

Toast sliced frozen bread without thawing. Leave other foods at room temperature for a short time before using.

Bread and rolls made with yeast are more successful if they are baked and cooled before freezing. Baked bread thaws very quickly because it contains very little moisture. Without unwrapping, heat frozen baked rolls in a 400° oven 5 or 10 minutes. Reheating freshens rolls. See also the special recipe for Twice-baked Rolls (p. 345).

Quick breads, which are usually served cold, such as Date and Nut Bread, Honey Bread and Cranberry Bread. Heat gingerbread or cottage pudding if you are serving it with a sauce.

Waffles. Heat frozen waffles in an electric toaster.

Doughnuts. Reheat at 400° just long enough to thaw without drying.

Cakes. Freeze **angel, sponge and fruit cakes** after baking. Freeze **butter cakes** either baked or as batter. Cake batter made with egg yolks does not freeze successfully. Bake a cake for freezing in a pan with the bottom lined with greased wax paper or in a foil pan which can be wrapped and stored. Cool the cake thoroughly. Wrap in cellophane, seal and freeze at 0° or below. When the cake is frozen hard, put it in a box so that it will not be crushed. To freeze cake batter, spoon it into cartons or paper cups and freeze at 0° or below. Thaw before baking until the batter is just soft enough to put into pans. If the batter is thawed too long, the cake will be heavy.

Cookies. Freeze any stiff cooky dough in a roll or shaped into cookies. Defrost only enough to slice into cookies. Bake shaped cookies without defrosting. Bake delicate cookies before freezing and package carefully in a box so that they will not crush.

Fruit pies and mince pies freeze very well. Line aluminum foil freezer pans with pastry, put in the filling, and put on the top crust. Do not cut vents in the top crust. Freeze at 0°. Bake without thawing at 425° until the crust is golden-brown (about 1 hour). Cut the vents in the top crust after the pie has been in the oven about 5 minutes.

Deep-dish pies are very successful made with only a top crust.

Pie crust. Roll out in pie-size rounds or in smaller rounds for tarts. Stack with sheets of cellophane between the rounds and pack in boxes. Freeze.

FREEZING SANDWICHES

Spread both slices of bread with softened (not melted) butter. Fill and freeze. Use fillings made of meat, cheese or fish. Mix peanut butter with just enough jelly, applesauce or honey to spread well. Do not use fillings which contain raw vegetables or any material which would soak into the bread.

For lunchboxes and picnics. Frozen sandwiches thaw completely in about 4 hours and taste fresher (even though made days or weeks before) than sandwiches made the same day which have not been refrigerated. Freeze lunchbox sandwiches individually.

For parties. Wrap rolled, ribbon or checkerboard sandwiches firmly in freezer paper and seal. Arrange canapés and open-faced sandwiches on a tray, cooky sheet or cellophane-covered cardboard. Do not garnish. Wrap in cellophane and heat-seal. **To thaw,** remove thin canapés from the freezer 20 minutes before serving time. Thicker sandwiches or ones with shrimp topping will take longer. Thaw rolled, ribbon or checkerboard sandwiches and slice. Garnish the canapés or sandwiches as you like.

FREEZING PREPARED FOODS

Many cooked or ready-to-serve foods freeze successfully and are a great convenience in preparing emergency meals. Keep two or three complete meals in your freezer ready for unexpected guests or quick meals. Enjoy the extra carefree hours with your family or guests by preparing and freezing the dinner well in advance.

Freezing cooked foods is not always time-saving. Some foods take less time—and less heat—to prepare fresh than frozen. Best for freezing are seasonal foods, dishes that can be prepared in quantity almost as quickly as in small amounts, and foods that need only slight thawing. Cooked eggs do not freeze well—the whites toughen.

Casserole dishes and stews freeze best if they are made with enough sauce so that the meat balls or pieces of meat, fish or fowl are completely covered during freezing. For a fresh casserole topping when reheating, cover with buttered crumbs, wheat germ or grated cheese and set in a 400° oven to thaw and heat. Do not overcook casseroles when preparing them for freezing.

Cocktail tidbits. Freeze small cheese pastries, cooked shrimp, cocktail sausages or other small hors d'oeuvres. Pack cocktail spreads in small cartons.

Chicken and meat pies. Make individual deep-dish pies with pastry tops. Heat in a 450° oven without thawing.

Desserts. Freeze ice creams, sherbets, cakes, cookies, gingerbread and pies following directions on page 563. Freeze cut-up fruit for fruit cup (not fresh apples, grapes or nut meats) and serve while still partly frozen. Freeze individual or large puddings and reheat, frozen or thawed, in a steamer or in a pan of hot water in a 400° oven.

Roasts do not freeze as well cooked as raw. The outer slices may have a stale flavor. Roast chickens and turkeys take almost as long to thaw and heat as to roast fresh. Leftover roast meats may be frozen to use cold.

Salads. Do not freeze raw vegetables or salad greens. Aspics and other molded salads freeze especially well. Add the dressing at serving time. Freeze cooked meat and poultry ready to make into salad. Mixed fruit salad is successful, but do not include in the combination fresh apples or grapes or nut meats. Sprinkle fruit with lemon juice to help keep its bright color. Do not thaw salads completely before you serve them.

Sauces. Freeze barbecue and spaghetti sauces in cartons.

Soups. Soups which require long cooking can be made in quantity and frozen for later use. Sieve cooked vegetables to use as the basis for creamed soups. To drive out air, which destroys some food values, pack firmly in cartons. Thaw in a double boiler without stirring before you add the liquid.

Other foods which freeze well are baked beans, hash, Swiss steak, veal birds, chicken fricassee, stuffed papers, meat loaf, scrapple and puréed baby foods.

Leftovers. Chill quickly to prevent spoiling. Remove the bones from leftover meats. Leave in as large pieces as possible. Pack compactly. Reheat leftover gray, chill and pack.

Index

D

F

S

U

V

Y

Z